MENLO SCHOOL · MENLO COLLEGE

founded 1915

Gift of

The John W. Bowman Family

in memory of

TIMOTHY DILLON BOWMAN

THE MENTALLY RETARDED CHILD AND HIS FAMILY
A Multidisciplinary Handbook

The Mentally Retarded Child and His Family

A MULTIDISCIPLINARY HANDBOOK

Revised Edition

Edited by

RICHARD KOCH, M.D.

Manager, Community Services,
Department of Health, State of California

and

JAMES C. DOBSON, Ph.D.

Associate Clinical Professor of Pediatrics (Child Development),
School of Medicine, University of Southern California;
Director of Behavioral Research and Director of the
Collaborative Study of Children Treated for
Phenylketonuria in the Division of
Medical Genetics, Childrens
Hospital of Los Angeles

BRUNNER/MAZEL Publishers • New York

Library of Congress Cataloging in Publication Data

Koch, Richard, 1921—
    The mentally retarded child and his family.

    Includes biographies and indexes.
    1. Mentally handicapped children.   2. Mentally handicapped children—Family
relationships. I. Dobson, James C., 1936— joint author. II. Title. [DNLM: 1. Mental
retardation. 2. Parent-child relations. WS107 M551]
HV891.K58   1976   362.7'8'3   75-42133   ISBN 0-87630-121-9

Copyright © 1971, 1976 by Richard Koch and James C. Dobson

published by

BRUNNER/MAZEL, INC.
64 University Place
New York, N. Y. 10003

Library of Congress Catalog Card No. 76-122743
SBN 87630-121-9

MANUFACTURED IN THE UNITED STATES OF AMERICA

Contributors

Phyllis B. Acosta, Dr. P.H., is Associate Professor, Clinical Nutrition Program, School of Medicine, University of New Mexico, Albuquerque, New Mexico.

Ann Baerwald, A.C.S.W., is Chief Counselor, North Los Angeles Regional Center for the Developmentally Disabled, Van Nuys, Ca.

David A. Balla, Ph.D., is Research Associate, Department of Psychology and Child Study Center, Yale University; Consulting Editor, *American Journal of Mental Defficiency,* 1973-75.

William G. Bronston, M.D., is Special Consultant to the Division of Community Services, Department of Health, State of California, Sacramento, Ca.

Camille Legeay Cook, M.S., is Nursing Consultant in the Care of Mentally Retarded Children, Maternal and Child Health Services, Department of Health, Education and Welfare, Washington, D.C.

James C. Dobson, Ph.D., is Associate Clinical Professor of Pediatrics (Child Development), School of Medicine, University of Southern California, Los Angeles, Ca.; Director of Behavioral Research and Director of the Collaborative Study of Children Treated for PKU in the Division of Medical Genetics, Childrens Hospital of Los Angeles; Author of *Dare to Discipline* (Tyndale House, Wheaton, Ill.), *Hide or Seek* (Fleming H. Revell, Old Tappan, N.J.), and *What Wives Wish Their Husbands Knew about Women* (Tyndale House).

Karol Fishler, Ph.D., is Chief Clinical Psychologist, Division of Child Development, Childrens Hospital of Los Angeles; Associate Professor of Pediatrics (Psychology), School of Medicine, University of Southern California, Los Angeles, Ca.

Janet Forinash, R.P.T., is Physical Therapist, Regional Center for the Developmentally Disabled, Childrens Hospital of Los Angeles, Los Angeles, Ca.

Betty V. Graliker, M.S.W., is Chief Counselor, Regional Center for the Developmentally Disabled, Childrens Hospital of Los Angeles, Los Angeles, Ca.

Robert Henderson, Ed.D., is Professor of Special Education, Institute for Research on Exceptional Children; Chairman, Department of Special Education, University of Illinois, Urbana, Champaign, Ill.

Gene Hensley, Ph.D., is Associate Director of Elementary and Secondary Education, Education Commission of the States, Denver, Colorado

Richard Koch, M.D., is Manager, Community Services, Department of Health, State of California, Sacramento, Ca.; co-author of *Understanding the Mentally Retarded Child* (Random House, N.Y.).

Edward L. LaCrosse, Ed.D., is Coordinator of Extramural Projects and Resource Development, Boys Town Institute for Communication Disorders in Children; Children's Rehabilitation Institute, University of Nebraska School of Medicine, Omaha, Neb.

Donald L. MacMillan, Ed.D., is Professor of Education, School of Education, University of California at Riverside, Riverside, Ca.

John Melnyk, Ph.D., is Director, Department of Developmental Cytogenetics, City of Hope National Medical Center, Duarte, Ca.

Frank J. Menolascino, M.D., is Professor of Psychiatry and Pediatrics, Nebraska Psychiatric Institute, University of Nebraska Medical Center, Omaha, Neb.

Jane R. Mercer, Ph.D., is Professor of Sociology, Chairperson, Department of Sociology, University of California at Riverside, Riverside, Ca.

C. Edward Meyers, Ph.D., is Professor of Educational Psychology and Special Education, University of Southern California; Interim Research Psychologist, Neuropsychiatric Institute, Pacific State Hospital Research Group, University of California, Los Angeles, Ca.; Editor, Monographs of the American Association on Mental Deficiency; Consulting Editor, *Education and Training of the Mentally Retarded;* Consulting Editor, *Journal of School Psychology.*

Ivy Mooring, Ph.D., is Assistant Director, Center for Training in Community Psychiatry, Los Angeles, Ca.

Raymond M. Peterson, M.D., is Director, Child Development Division, Children's Health Center; Director, San Diego Regional Center for the Developmentally Disabled, Children's Hospital, San Diego, Ca.

Frederick Richardson, M.D., M.R.C.P., is Director, Mental Handicap and Child Mental Health, Health Commission of New South Wales, Sydney, Australia.

Herbert L. Rock, M. S. W. (Retired), is Field Work Instructor, University Affiliated Training Project, Division of Child Development, Childrens Hospital of Los Angeles, Los Angeles, Ca.

Sylvia Schild, D.S.W., is Professor, School of Social Work, California State University, Sacramento, Ca.; Assistant Clinical Professor, University of California School of Medicine, Davis, Ca.

Jack Share, Ph.D., is Associate Professor in Special Education, University of California, Los Angeles; Associate Professor in Psychology, Department of Psychology, California State University, Northridge, Ca.; Associate Professor in Guidance and Counseling, California State University, Los Angeles, Ca.

Elizabeth Wenz, M.S., is Nutritionist, Division of Child Development, Childrens Hospital of Los Angeles; Instructor, Department of Home Economics, Evening Division, Los Angeles City College, Los Angeles, Ca.

Harry T. Wright, Jr., M.D., M.P.H., is Professor of Pediatrics, School of Medicine, University of Southern California, Los Angeles, Ca.; Research Associate, Division of Virology, Attending Physician, Childrens Hospital of Los Angeles, Los Angeles, Ca.

Edward Zigler, Ph.D., is Professor of Psychology, Yale University; Director, Child Development Program, Yale University.

Table of Contents

vii

Section VI. COMMUNITY SERVICES FOR THE
MENTALLY RETARDED

Preface to the Revised Edition

The formation of the National Association for Retarded Citizens (NARC) in 1950 produced a strong surge of interest in providing new services for the mentally retarded. Since most states were already providing residential care for the retarded, this initial thrust by NARC resulted in the development of new community-based services. For example, many parent sponsored training classes were created for moderately retarded children in a community setting. Other factors were also influential in bringing increased attention to the needs of the retarded. With the election of John F. Kennedy to the Presidency in 1960 and his subsequent appointment of the President's Panel on Mental Retardation, inventive new programs were instituted which further stimulated the development of community facilities.

It was recognized from the beginning that the public schools had the primary responsibility to provide programs for the mildly retarded. The impressive ability of the educational profession to deal with these problems resulted in an immediate demand for additional services to individuals with more serious mental handicaps. Consequently, most states now provide classes for the educable and trainable retarded. Through these and related programs, public education has offered an entirely new system for delivering services to the mentally retarded, resulting in intensified professional interest in this field.

With these strong stimuli to the development of community services for the retarded, interdisciplinary groups in the professions of health and education have joined hands to teach a variety of relevant courses at the college and university level. *The Mentally Retarded Child and His Family* was written as a multidisciplinary handbook for use in such courses. It is hoped that the text will be useful to graduate and postgraduate students in education, medicine, nursing, nutrition, psychology, social work, speech and hearing therapy, community organization, rehabilitation, physical therapy, occupational therapy, law, architecture and recreation. In short, this text may be appropriate to any discipline which requires a broad understanding of the needs and problems of the mentally retarded. If the book fulfills this objective, then the authors will have accomplished their purpose.

This book was developed as a result of the editors' involvement in courses on mental retardation at the University of Southern California, California State University at Los Angeles, Arizona State University and Pasadena College. All of the contributing authors are professionals who have demonstrated a deep commitment to the welfare of the retarded and who have had extensive personal contact with handicapped individuals. Each participant was selected on the basis of his professional competence and demonstrated knowledge in this field. The talents of 26 authors were drawn upon, representing 14 different disciplines from 16 institutions of higher learning and one federal agency. None of the 30 chapters in the text has been published elsewhere.

The editors are pleased that the first edition of this book has been widely used as a text, and hope this new and revised version will enhance its usefulness. Many of the chapters have been updated to keep pace with the rapid advancements in the field of mental retardation, and two completely new chapters have been added—*Physical Therapy Services* by Janet Forinash, R.P.T. and *Normalization* by William Bronston, M.D.

During much of the career of the senior editor, he has received support from a variety of agencies, deserving commendation. He would particularly like to acknowledge support received from the Maternal and Child Health Service, Health Services and Mental Health Administration, and the Mental Retardation Division of the Social Rehabilitation Agency of the Department of Health, Education and Welfare, and from the California State Department of Health. And certainly, appreciation should be expressed to Childrens Hospital of Los Angeles. Without the administrative support of George Donnell, M.D., Chairman of the Department of Pediatrics, and Henry Dunlap, Executive Director of the hospital, this book would never have been written.

The editors also wish to acknowledge the influence of certain individuals on their professional lives, and on the philosophy of care which is expressed in this text. So many have contributed measurably, and we trust we will be forgiven if some names have been omitted. Rosemary and Gunnar Dybwad deserve special mention. Others worthy of recognition are William Bergren, Ph.D., Elizabeth Boggs, Ph.D., Merl Carson, M.D., Paul Culbertson, Ph.D., Robert W. Deisher, M.D., Edwin Harwood, Ph.D., Kenneth D. Hopkins, Ph.D., Rudolf Hormuth, M.S.W., Fred J. Krause, M.A., Robert B. Kugel, M.D., Allen R. Menefee, M.S.W., Theodore A. Montgomery, M.D., James Papai, M.A., Paul H. Pearson, M.D.,

Jack Share, Ph.D., Kenneth N. F. Shaw, Ph.D., Theodore D. Tjossem, Ph.D., and Malcolm L. Williamson, Ph.D.

The senior editor especially acknowledges the contribution of Dr. Arthur H. Parmalee, Sr., who was responsible for his having the opportunity to become involved in the field of mental retardation. It was through his tact, patience, understanding, sympathy and wisdom that the problems of parents of the mentally retarded were put into proper perspective.

Finally, the editors also extend their appreciation to the many parents who have contributed directly or indirectly to this volume by providing us with a base of experience from which to speak. To them, we express our most humble gratitude.

RICHARD KOCH, M.D.
JAMES C. DOBSON, PH.D.

Section I.

INTRODUCTION TO THE PROBLEM OF MENTAL RETARDATION

CHAPTER 1

The Origins of Intelligence

by JAMES C. DOBSON, Ph.D.

In 1914, Henry Goddard published a memorable book which was destined to mislead and confuse behavioral scientists for the next thirty years. In this text, titled *Feeble Mindedness—Its Causes and Consequences,* the author presented exhaustive "evidence" on the origins of human intelligence, from which he drew this conclusion: "That normal intelligence seems to be a unit character and transmitted in true Mendelian fashion is a conclusion that was forced upon us by the figures" (14:ix). With this statement, Goddard helped establish the pervasive belief in a "fixed intelligence"; that is, intellectual capacity is an innate dimension which unfolds automatically with anatomic maturation (25). Goddard was not the only authority to promote the heredity basis for intelligence, nor was he the first. Galton in the nineteenth century and Watson during the twentieth were also influential in the acceptance of this hypothesis.

The assumption that intelligence emerges totally from one's genetic endowment led to several unfortunate consequences: First, it reduced the apparent significance of early experience. If environment is of no importance in the development of cognitive ability, then it is unnecessary to train, encourage and cultivate intellectual growth during the first few years of life. The child's early years were viewed as a time to let nature have its way; stimulating intellectual experiences and mental discipline even represented threats to the developing psyche. Educational philosophy was another early casualty of the "heredity is everything" viewpoint. Quite obviously, the schools' traditional standards for intellectual excellence were not in keeping with this enlightened view of all-important heredity. Why should children be drilled and pushed to learn in school when maturation itself, if given time, would

3

contribute abilities that were desired? The major educational objective shifted radically from the teaching of factual content to the cultivation of "life adjustment," allowing basic nature to unfold (25).

Another consequence of the widely accepted genetic view of intelligence was seen in the understanding of mental retardation. All intellectually defective children were believed to have inherited an inferior quality of genes, or perhaps they were damaged during the prenatal period. The possibility that a bland preschool environment played a part in certain cases of mild retardation was given little credence. The mentally retarded were generally viewed as unfortunate have-nots, whom nature had slighted. The scientific community did not recognize the likelihood that children born with average mental potential might deteriorate from the moment of birth as a result of an unstimulating intellectual environment (4).

Gradually, however, the relationship and interaction between environment and intellectual functioning became more obvious. Evidence to this effect came from several sources, and the extreme concept of hereditary intelligence began to splinter. Several sources of dissonant evidence have been the subjects of considerable investigation in the twentieth century.

CO-TWIN STUDIES

The studies of identical twins reared apart provided data that were difficult to reconcile with the accepted concept of intelligence. Since identical twins apparently possess a duplicated genetic heritage, then differences in their mental capacities must be attributed to variations in their post-natal experiences. Newman, Freeman and Holzinger conducted a classic study of 19 pairs of identical twins who had been separated early in life. Substantial differences in intelligence tests results were found between twin pairs, varying by as much as 24 IQ points. The mean difference was only 8.2 points, although most of the separated twins lived in settings that were rather similar to those of their siblings. The authors concluded that the variability in intelligence between twin pairs was probably attributable to environmental influences, since the genetic pool was apparently held constant (32). In a more recent study by Gottesman and Shields, 38 pairs of identical twins were evaluated. They were reared in different environments, having been separated in infancy. The researchers found a mean IQ gap of 14 points, which is presumed to reflect experiential differences (19).

Not all of the co-twin studies have yielded consistent findings. In 1963, Johnson published a reanalysis of the data presented originally by Newman, Freeman and Holzinger, which disputes their conclusions. Johnson observed that the longer children were reared together, the less their eventual IQs tended to correlate. Despite this dissenting view, the preponderance would indicate that the intelligence of separated identical twins differs in proportion to the uniqueness of their environments. In the light of this conclusion, the "fixed" or "genetic" theory of intelligence appeared much less plausible (28).

EDUCATION AND TRAINING

The consequences of training represented another source of evidence which agitated against the hereditary view of intelligence. Wechsler defined intelligence as "the aggregate or global capacity of the individual to act purposefully, to think rationally, and to deal effectively with his environment" (41:7). Since a primary purpose of education is to better equip the student to think clearly and deal effectively with his environment, his heightened capability should be (and is) reflected in intelligence test results (41). Vincent and Martin have stated:

> For some people, development continues even to ages 65 to 70. Even more than the body, the mind responds to continued training, and goes on to a continuously higher peak of ability until middle adulthood. This does not mean that a low ability can be made into a higher one by training, but rather that whatever ability the individual has inherited can reach its greater actuality by training and usage (40:14).

Corroborating this view is the conclusion by English who believes that the growth of intelligence depends on the acquisition of the verbal tools of problem solving. He wrote, "Whatever may be the contribution of one's innate capacity, intelligence must be learned" (10:313). Thus, if intelligence is learned, then education and training are the logical vehicles for its advancement. Munn concurred, stating, ". . . we can certainly improve (an individual's) opportunities to acquire those skills which are necessary for intelligent behavior" (30:428).

GEOGRAPHICAL INFLUENCES

Children raised in isolated communities, such as inland mountain settings, have been shown to have intelligence quotients significantly below national averages. The differences are recognizable in the early years, but the IQ levels usually drop even lower as the children age. This phenomenon occurs because the intelligence test items for young children primarily assess sensorimotor and concrete kinds of skills; as the child matures, he is required to display an increasing sophistication with language and related faculties requiring higher mental processes. His deprived environment does not provide the training and instruction necessary for the child to keep pace with his peers in more advantageous areas, and the deficiency becomes more pronounced each succeeding year. If a child from an isolated, unstimulating setting is taken to an area offering greatly improved school conditions, his IQ is likely to reflect a marked rise on subsequent tests. Thus, it can be said that geography influences intelligence because certain areas provide a substandard milieu for intellectual development, while others are superior (30). If heredity contributed a "fixed" level of intelligence, geographical influences would be inconsequential to a child's cognitive capabilities.

Evidence continued to mount in opposition to the theory that environment plays no significant part in a child's intellectual development. The origins of cognitive ability have been subjected to extensive research efforts in the past twenty years, and most findings have been solidly contradictory to the "fixed intelligence" viewpoint. Intelligence is now widely believed to emanate from an inseparable interaction between heredity and environment. Hunt has summarized the role of environment in this way:

> . . . the belief that the wherewithal to solve problems comes automatically with the maturation of somatic tissues, especially with the maturation of the neural tissues of the cerebrum, is being shown to be palpably false. Even the development of such relatively static skills as the human infant's abilities to sit alone, to stand, and to walk, for instance, depend on his getting varied stimulation from the environment and opportunities for appropriate interaction with it (25:6).

Conversely, one must recognize the fact that heredity does have an important role to play in intellectual development. Simply because we acknowledge the contributions of the environment does not detract from the importance of heredity. Hunt described the genetic involvement in this manner:

> It is obviously true, for instance, that one cannot get apple trees by planting radish seeds, nor can he get chimpanzees by breeding rats. Moreover, no one has ever taught a chimpanzee to solve problems with the calculus, or even to speak. Neither has anyone ever

got, nor will get, a chimpanzee interested in abstract art or in the principles and methods of behavioral science. Neither is it argued that one can get every human being to learn to use the calculus or to get interested in the principles and methods of behavioral science. It is obvious that the genes operate both to prescribe certain basic directions in organismic development and to set irrevocable limits on the range of capacities that can be developed within an organism. Moreover, they undoubtedly prescribed these directions and set these limits much more finely than these illustrations, purposely posed broadly to make the general point obvious, would imply (25:16).

PRESENT UNDERSTANDING

Although the nature-nurture controversy will probably remain unsettled for many years, there is growing evidence to indicate the combined importance of environment and heredity. Recently, Jensen has received wide publicity from his stated belief that 70 to 80 percent of the variance in IQ's (in our population) is determined by genetic factors alone (27). The social implication that there are intellectually "inferior" races is exceedingly inflammatory at this stage in American history, and this fact has resulted in the rapid dissemination of Jensen's view. It is the belief of the author, however, that Jensen has not produced sufficient evidence to warrant this degree of excitement. Rather, it appears that he has merely restated, albeit eloquently, the old "fixed intelligence" viewpoint from decades past.

The "present understanding" by the majority of experts seems to be as follows. Two critical ingredients are necessary if intelligent behavior is to be manifest: First, one's neurological apparatus must be of sufficient quality to permit a sophisticated level of electrochemical processes. In other words, the brain must be capable of performing its assigned function and profiting from the sensory input it receives. This organic matter is produced and modified by heredity, prenatal variables, nutrition, and other physical influences. Secondly, intelligent behavior depends on the programming of the intrinsic portion of the cerebrum for learning and problem solving. That programming must be accomplished by rich, profitable kinds of experience.

It is naive and simplistic to minimize either of these necessary components of human intelligence; their true relationship is one of interlocking influences. As Munn states, "each . . . would be ineffective without the other. It is thus meaningless to ask whether an individual's intelligence is of heredity or environmental origin" (30:419).

Recent studies of human development have unveiled a further requirement upon which the acquisition of intellectual behavior seems to depend. It now appears evident that a critical period for the realization of intellectual potential begins shortly after birth, yet is diminished if the child is unable to seize this opportunity during his first few years of life. At least three reasons have been proposed to explain the crucial importance of the child's initial environment. The first relates to the very rapid growth of intellectual faculties during the early years. Environmental variations shape these faculties during their most vulnerable and active periods of formation. Secondly, human development seems to be pyramidal and sequential in nature. Each characteristic is built on a foundation of some developmental phase which preceded it. Thus, the early years provide the understructure which supports all subsequent intellectual activity. Thirdly, it is much easier to learn some new concept than it is to blot out erroneous ideas and replace them with new learning. The cognition possible in the early years is accomplished with a relatively clean slate, and the importance of forming correct concepts at that stage is obvious (4).

Animal experiments have yielded consistent evidence attesting to the importance of early learning. Travers reports the following examples:

> In all of the cases we have studied up to this point in which there has been a deprivation of early learning experiences, the result has been a certain stupidity of behavior which is not easily overcome. Prolonged learning is necessary if this deficiency is to be removed; and this fact suggests that the slowness at which the very young child learns may reflect the slowness with which early learning takes place. The term "early learning" refers to the learning of the fundamental ability to discriminate and identify stimuli, and the evidence indicates that these learnings must precede more complex learnings. We do not know at this time whether deficiences in early learning can ever be entirely made up in later life. This is a matter which requires systematic investigation. A few pieces of evidence suggest that some of the deficiencies produced by lack of early learning may be rather permanent (39:232).

Hebb reported several experiments which indicate that animals subjected to a "rich experience" during their early years score significantly higher on performance tests than their unstimulated littermates. He also observed that rats exposed to early learning experience were better able than their littermate controls to profit from new experience at maturity (22). He conducted a similar study with dogs, as described below:

> Laboratory animals that are deprived of learning experiences early in life commonly demonstrate extraordinarily stupid behavior. The behavior is sometimes unbelievably stupid. Hebb (21) describes the case of a dog that was raised in an environment in which it did not have opportunities for learning to avoid some of the common hazards of life. When this same dog was later let loose in the laboratory, it showed a striking inability to avoid bumping its head against a low pipe. While other dogs that had been raised in a typical dog environment were able to avoid this pipe almost at once, the dog brought up in the restricted environment bumped its head a score or more times and without any indication that it had benefited at all from its experience. Presumably this dog was engaged in a process of early learning, which here again involved a very simple function (39:231).

Hymovitch (26) conducted a comparative study with two groups of infant rats. One group was raised in a tight cage which permitted very restricted activity and limited perceptual stimulation. The second group of rats, genetically comparable to the first group, was raised in an atmosphere of stimulation and perceptual enrichment. Their cages included corridors and places to be explored, and generally offered a "free environment." When tests of learning ability were administered during maturity, the restricted environment group scored almost twice as many errors as the enriched group (233 compared with 132). It was concluded from this and similar studies that a cause and effect relationship probably exists between the impoverishment or enrichment of early environment and the relative sophistication of later cognitive abilities (26).

Since a reduction of early cognitive stimulation has been shown to correlate with later intellectual inefficiencies, then there must be a biochemical or physiological basis for the cerebral deficit. Intelligence tests measure a secondary, behavioral manifestation of brain function. By contrast, the direct evaluation of neurophysiology and the chemistry of learning provides some of the most fascinating findings now coming to light. Kretch et al. conducted a series of investigations which are worthy of considerable note at this point. Specifically, they sought to determine the effects of memory storage on the chemistry and anatomy of the brain. They theorized that animals which have been required to undergo extensive learning and remembering should acquire brains enzymatically different from those animals experiencing a less stimulating environment; this should be especially true of the enzymes which facilitate the neural firing of electrochemical signals across the synapse (between cells). They further hoped to learn whether or not the early neural activity produced morphological differences in the brains of animals raised in stimulating environments when compared to their unstimulated counterparts.

To test their hypotheses, Kretch and associates randomly divided dozens of twin male rats into two groups. The first group was foreordained to experience a superior educational environment. They lived in a well lighted, noisy and busy cage, which was equipped with ladders, running wheels, and other "creative" rat toys. They were allowed to explore outside their cages for one-half hour each day, and sugar was used as primary reinforcement during learning exercises. Group two rats endured an almost totally bland environment. They lived in solitary confinement in a dimly lit and quiet cage. They were neither trained nor handled by the examiners, nor were they allowed contact with other rats. Despite the environmental contrasts between groups one and two, both samples were allowed unlimited access to the same standard food throughout the experiment. When the rats reached 105 days of age, they were sacrificed and their brains were analyzed morphologically and chemically. The findings from this experiment, repeated dozens of times, are startling.

The enriched environment groups showed vast cerebral advantages over their deprived counterparts. In the first place, the cortex was larger, deeper and heavier, accounted for in part by an increase in the number of glia cells. (Glia cells are important in the nutrition of neurones and possibly in memory, itself.) Secondly, the neural cell bodies and their nuclei were larger, as were the diameters of the blood vessels supplying the cortex. Thirdly, the high-stimulation group had more efficient enzyme systems in the brain, especially the trans-synaptic enzyme called acetylcholinesterase. In short, the brains of the "early stimulation" group were better equipped physically and biochemically to do their work. Kretch has since shown these superior neural characteristics to be evident in rats bred to display heightened intellectual ability.

What does this mean? Kretch answered the question:

> It means that the effects of the psychological and educational environment are not restricted to something called "mental" realm. Permitting the young rat to grow up in an educationally and experimentally inadequate and unstimulating environment created an animal with a relatively deteriorated brain—a brain with a thin

and light cortex, lowered blood supply, diminished enzymatic activities, smaller neuronal cell bodies, and fewer glia cells. A lack of adequate educational fare for the young animal—no matter how large the food supply or how good the family—and a lack of adequate psychological enrichment result in palpable, measurable, deteriorative changes in the brain's chemistry and anatomy (29:68).

THE ENVIRONMENTAL ORIGINS OF MENTAL RETARDATION

If it can be accepted that optimal environmental conditions during early childhood contribute to later intelligent behavior, then the converse must also be recognized. Destructive or unprofitable experiences during the first few years of life should be carefully explored in examining the etiology of mental retardation. That exploration could well begin with an evaluation of the milieu which inflicts cultural and maternal deprivation on the children who are trapped in its web. Such children often fail to receive the necessary sensory stimulation for intellectual growth, and as a consequence, are much more likely than their middle class counterparts to become borderline mentally retarded. The following sections deal with these overlapping problems of cultural, maternal and sensory deprivation.

CULTURAL DEPRIVATION

Poverty may be a leading cause of mental retardation. It is estimated that only one-quarter of the cases of diminished intellectual capacity can be traced to faulty genes, virus infections, accidents and diseases causing brain damage before birth or in early infancy. Many mentally retarded individuals with unknown etiology may be victims of urban and rural slums, having been subjected to social and cultural deprivation. Studies which have measured the cognitive abilities of children from severely limited environments have consistently shown these youngsters to be functioning at a lower level than those from less deprived homes (24). Many reports have documented the findings of Eisenberg, who studied 300 children and obtained a mean *Wechsler* IQ of 90 for "low" class children, compared with 111 for those in a "middle" class (9). Follow-up studies seem to indicate that the ability levels decline over a period of time (24). Other investigators have indicated that a vast proportion of educable mentally retarded children in public schools come from families of poor schooling and lower socio-economic status. Most of these children in the "borderline" classification of mental retardation suffer no clinically discernible neurological defects, and may owe their handicap to environmental factors (13). Stedman states that four and one-half million Americans are victims of nutritional, social and cultural deprivation (1).

The President's Committee on Mental Retardation listed these startling statistics in its 1968 report titled "The Edge of Change": (1) Three-fourths of the nation's mentally retarded are to be found in the isolated and impoverished urban slums. (2) Conservative estimates of the incidence of mental retardation in the inner city neighborhoods begin at seven percent. (3) A child in a low-income rural or urban family is 15 times more likely to be diagnosed as retarded than is a child from a higher income family. (4) Twenty-five percent of all women having babies in public hospitals have had no prenatal care. Avoidable complications of pregnancy, which are often the harbingers of crippling conditions, soar in this group. (5) Incidence of premature births (among whom neurological and physical disorders are 75 percent more frequent than in full-term babies) is almost three times as great among low income women as among other groups of women. (6) The mortality rate of infants born to low income mothers is nearly double that of infants born to mothers in other income brackets. (7) The children of low income families often arrive at school age with neither the experience nor the skills necessary for systematic learning. Many are found functionally retarded in language and in the ability to do the abstract thinking required to read, write and count. An appalling number of these children fall further behind with the passing of each school year. (8) Students in the public schools of inner city low income areas have been found in numerous studies to be from six months to three years behind the national norm of achievement for their age and grade. About three times as many low income as higher income children fail in school. The child whose father is an urban laborer has only one chance in 3,581,370 of being named a National Merit Scholar; but the child whose father has a professional or technical position has one chance in 12,672. (9) The rate of Selective Service System rejections for intellectual underachievement is 23 percent nationally and soars to 60 percent and more among groups whose members are largely from low income areas (32:19).

Whitney Young, Executive Director of the National Urban League, translated these disturbing figures into graphic human terms at the 1967 Annual Meeting of the National Association for Retarded Children. In describing the cycle of futility which faces residents of urban and rural ghettos, he said the poverty world of the Negro, Mexican laborer, American Indian, Puerto Rican immigrant and poor white is "the breeding ground of as much as half of our mentally retarded people, the dull-eyed children, the juvenile delinquents, the dropouts and socially unadaptable youngsters, who drive teachers, lawmakers and governments to despair" (42).

The nature and extent of the interaction between adults and children are perhaps the most important differentiations between abundant and deprived environments. Language development can hardly flourish in a setting where adults are either too busy or too disinterested to guide the child's early verbal attempts (4).

Stedman states that the critical period for establishing eventual limits on the child's intellectual ability may be between his twelfth and thirtieth months of life. That eighteen-month period is the time during which children develop lifetime intellectual habits and skills, including the rudiments of language usage. It is also a time of maximum parental influence. A child from a repressed environment often has severely limited exposure to proper parental models with which he can identify during this critical phase. He is also less likely to receive encouragement or reinforcement for use of rational processes; rather he is taught to respond primarily to physical stimuli (1). One team of researchers examined the cognitive skills that were present (and absent) in a large group of children living on the edge of a slum area in New York. They found decreased abilities in concept formation, auditory and visual discrimination, language acquisition, and IQ. They concluded that all these factors are dependent to some degree on the quality of the social and physical stimulation to which children have been exposed. In a middle or upper class home the major source of that stimulation is usually derived from the child's parents; conversely, the child from a depressed environment is often subjected to minimal training and guidance from his mother and father (13).

Children born in poverty often grow up in homes where there is no known father. Since the mothers have to work, the children may be left alone all day in a kind of solitary confinement to a crib. They may hear some noises, but they are exposed to little adult conversation. The words they do hear are often exasperated, tired, despairing or profane. Not only are the mothers unable to provide intellectual stimulation, but they often have no resource from which to offer "tender loving care." For a mother who has been harassed and defeated by life, the loving maternal role may have long-since faded into lethargy and depression. In such a home, the mother may not react to the symptoms of retardation in the child, even if she is able to recognize them. Or if she does observe the child's failure to develop mentally, she may consider this to be God's punishment for some sin. Such parents are usually so involved in their struggle to exist that they are unable to provide their children with any of the intellectual or cultural stimuli which are available to children of more affluent parents. Many simply cannot afford books or paints or records or toys. If they can afford a television set, it may become the child's intellectual parent (13).

It is not possible at this time to measure the amount of influence a particular environment can have on one's IQ, although a conservative estimate of the effect of extreme environments has been judged by Bloom to be 20 IQ points. As he stated:

> This could mean the difference between a life in an institution for the feebleminded or a productive life in society. It could mean the difference between a professional career and an occupation which is at the semiskilled or unskilled level. A society which places great emphasis on verbal learning and rational problem solving and which greatly needs highly skilled and well trained individuals to carry on political-social-economic functions in an increasingly complex world cannot ignore the enormous consequences of deprivation as it affects the development of general intelligence. Increased research is needed to determine the precise consequences of the environment for general intelligence. However, even with the relatively crude data already available, the implications for public education and social policy are fairly clear. Where significantly lower intelligence can be clearly attributed to the effects of environmental deprivation, steps must be taken to ameliorate these conditions as early in the individual's development as education and other social forces can be utilized (4:89).

MATERNAL DEPRIVATION

Studies by Spitz (37) and others emphasize the importance of the mother-child relationship during the first two years of life. Proper intellectual and emotional development depends, according to Spitz, on frequent and consistent mothering throughout this critical period. Even if a child is given first-rate physical care, he can be permanently damaged by a deprival of this intimate contact with one adult (who need not be his actual mother or even a female). Spitz described the symptoms of maternal deprivation, calling the syndrome "anaclitic depression." Children for whom the mother relationship has been broken (or never established) usually cry for long periods of time. After this weeping stage has passed, they sink into a moodiness which seems to reflect hopeless and silent grief. About a month later, a dull and persistent apathy permeates their being. As they grow, their behavior gradually assumes the characteristics of the adult psychotic, becoming progressively more bizarre and ineffectual each month. According to Spitz, the infant usually shows an amazingly rapid recovery if the mother should return during the first three months or so after the separation. If that anticipated reunion does not occur within a few months, however, the infant's total development is depressed. Walking, talking, and all aspects of socialization are affected. A two year old may remain helpless in his crib. Mental retardation becomes increasingly apparent as language skills and concept formation fail to develop, and the consequences seem to be irreversible. Finally, in the severe cases, death occurs from causes which could normally be cured (37).

Institutions for orphaned or homeless children offer the most readily available sample of children who have been "maternally deprived." Goldfarb conducted extensive studies of orphaned children who were institutionalized at this early age. They were found to be inferior to foster children with whom they were matched in age and sex, on all tests of intelligence. They scored lowest in tests measuring concept formation, abstract reasoning and thinking. Their retarded mental growth was clearly measurable during adolescence and later, and Goldfarb concluded that the effects were largely irreversible (15-16).

The specific defects occurring in conjunction with early institutionalization have been the subjects of considerable research in the past twenty-five years. Language proficiency has been found to be the most likely casualty of such restricted early life. Fischer noted that language may suffer because of the absence of reinforcement of the infant's vocalizations; consequently, the child experiences a reduced opportunity to acquire the signal and expressive functions of communication (11).

Other physical and intellectual consequences of group living have also been observed, which include serious defects in time and spatial concepts (17); disturbances in abstract thinking (2); and to a lesser extent, malfunctions in motor development (11). The findings of deviant motor patterns and the data on defects in conceptual thinking suggest the possibility of permanent central nervous system deterioration as a result of institutionalization.

Mussen, Conger and Kagan summarized the emotional consequences of early institutionalization in this way:

> The behavior of the institution-reared children differed from the foster home children in three major ways. The former were notice-

ably more aggressive (temper tantrums, lying, stealing, destruction of property, kicking and hitting other children), more dependent on adults (demand attention, ask for unnecessary help), and more distractible and hyperactive. Personality tests revealed that long after they had been placed with families, institution children were less self-controlled. Case records showed that children reared in institutions did not develop strong or affectionate personal attachments, but remained emotionally cold and isolated, capable of only the most superficial interpersonal reationships. According to the author, these social and emotional difficulties, which persisted into adolescence, were related to the severe deprivations experienced in infancy when "strong anchors to specific adults were not established." The impersonal care, coldness, and isolation of the institutional program apparently left permanent marks on the children (31:169).

There can be little doubt that institutionalized children are more likely to be handicapped, emotionally as well as intellectually, than their peers from good homes. However, the etiology of those deficits is not quite so apparent. Whereas, Spitz, Goldfarb, and others attribute the problems to an absence or rupture of the emotional bond between the child and a key adult figure, this concept is difficult to align with the findings from cultural environments where infants develop normally despite the absence of a deep emotional attachment to one adult. Such a setting is seen in the Israeli Kibbutz, an agricultural commune. Spiro described the intermittent mothering that occurs in the Kibbutz. A few days after birth, the mother places the child in an infant's dormitory with about 15 other infants ranging in age from four days to approximately one year. He is cared for by a head nurse and two full-time assistant nurses who are also Kibbutz members; these women provide for most of the physical needs and many of the emotional needs of their charges. The mother does breast feed the child and spend a few extra minutes each day with him. On Saturdays and Sundays, the front lawn and the porch of the nursery are crowded with mothers and fathers who have come to visit their offspring. At six months of age, the child may be taken to his parents' room for an hour each day. At about one year of age he is moved to the toddlers' dormitory where he must get acquainted with new nurses and different age mates. It is in this setting that he is toilet trained and taught how to feed himself. Such is the pattern that follows for the first six or more years of life; a battery of nurses and attendants provide the services from which the mother-child relationship usually grows. It is meaningful to examine the consequences of such multiple mothering, since Goldfarb and Spitz have stated that the child is damaged by changes in his relationship with key adults. By contrast, Spiro believes that the combination of institutional care and multiple-mothering, as reported from the Kibbutz, can be a satisfactory form of child rearing. He found no evidence of emotional damage or reduced cognitive ability as a result of Kibbutz life (36).

SENSORY DEPRIVATION

As a possible resolution to the contradictory evidence cited above, it has been hypothesized that the specific ill effects of early institutionalization do not actually result from maternal deprivation, per se. Neither can poverty nor cultural deprivation be directly responsible for instances of mental retardation. Rather, evidence is accumulating that the symptoms may represent the consequences of infant perceptual and sensory deprival, perhaps resulting in an atrophying brain in the absence of sensory input (8). The sharing of adult attention in a crowded nursery is likely to result in long hours of isolated crib experience with nothing more stimulating than the surrounding walls on which to focus. Neurological development might well depend on the frequent activation of the infant's cerebral equipment, and the absence of such stimulation could account for a wide variety of intellectual and psychological defects (8).

In attempting to understand the child's need for active stimulation, it should be remembered that the adult neurological apparatus also requires constant stimulation. For centuries it has been recognized that long periods of total isolation bring marked changes in behavior; sailors who were thrown in the hold of a ship for punishment were soon observed to exhibit bizarre responses including deterioration in their ability to think and reason, perceptual distortion, hallucinations and delusions. These and related observations have led to the conclusion that most higher organisms require a steady influx of variable sensory stimulation to maintain the operation of their central nervous systems, and they apparently seek to avoid a monotonous environment. A rat in a maze will use different routes to food if they are available, rather than follow the same one all the time. Even if every known physical drive has been satisfied, the rat will continue to explore and examine his cage, usually choosing to avoid areas in which he has spent considerable time in the past (39). A bored ecclesiastical congregation obediently endures a monotonous sermon, although the "listeners" will yawningly investigate any available distraction which might prove stimulating. Matters which would ordinarily be ignored are given the closest attention: a crawling fly on the pew in front; the entering or egress of another person; or the characteristics of one's fingernails or hand callouses. It would appear that their levels of sensory input have fallen below a critical minimum, and a search is underway for a remedy.

Boredom can not only make one uncomfortable, but it can also prove to be disruptive and deadening. Persons assigned to perform lengthy, repetitive tasks often report themselves to be unhappy with work; their efficiency and accuracy are also adversely affected by boredom. During World War II, the Royal Air Force conducted a study to determine why radar operators occasionally failed to detect submarines which were represented on their radar screens. The investigation observed that the operators sat in solitary cubicles, watching radar screens for long hours without interruption. In subsequent laboratory experiments, subjects were required to function in a similar setting. They were instructed to watch a screen and press a button whenever a pointer made a double jump. Within one-half hour, their efficiency and accuracy began to deteriorate. The findings from this and similar studies resulted in a shortening of work periods for radar operators (23).

The effects of sensory deprivation have been studied most extensively by D. O. Hebb in a series of investigations sponsored by the Canadian Government since 1949. Hebb examined the cognitive responses of volunteers who agreed to having their sensory apparatus temporarily shielded from stimuli. In one such study, repeated numerous times, male college students were paid to lie 24 hours a day on a comfortable bed in a lighted, semi-soundproof cubicle, which had an observation window. Throughout the experiment, the students wore translucent goggles which admitted diffused light but prevented pattern vision. Except when eating or at the toilet, they wore cotton gloves and cardboard cuffs, which extended below the elbow to beyond the fingertips in order to limit tactual perception. A U-shaped foam rubber pillow, the walls of the cubicle, and the masking of noise by a thermostatically regulated air conditioner and other equipment severely limited auditory perception. A two-way speaker system allowed communication between subject and experimenter. The subjects were asked to stay as long as they could (usually two to three days) and during this period they were prevented, as far as possible, from finding out the time. An experimenter was always in attendance, and the subjects were told that if they needed anything, they had only to call for it. They were fed and went to the toilet on request. Meals were eaten from a tray beside the bed, and a toilet was in an adjacent room. A total of 29 subjects volunteered for the experimental group, although only 18 stayed in isolation long enough to be given the complete testing schedule. Twenty-seven control subjects were used.

Most of the subjects participating in the investigation reported some form of hallucinatory activity, occurring as early as 20 minutes (or as late as 70 hours) after the start of isolation. Some participants saw abstract designs and patterns. Others observed integrated scenes, such as "prehistoric animals walking about in a jungle." The visual halluci-nations appeared to be in front of the subjects instead of seeming to be somewhere between their ears. If they wanted to examine part of a scene more closely, they found that they could do so easily by moving their eyes in direction as if they were looking at a picture. They had little control over the content of the hallucinations (one subject, for instance, could see nothing but eyeglasses, however hard he tried), nor were they able to start or stop them. The images were often so vivid as to prevent the subject from sleeping. One individual withdrew from the experiment situation because he was upset by what he saw. There was considerable movement of the hallucinatory patterns. Scenes or isolated objects would drift across the visual field, causing the subjects to com-plain that their eyes became tired from attempting to fixate and focus. This type of movement was also disturbing to some of the subjects, who said that it made them nauseated. A battery of psychometric tests was administered to measure the intellectual and emotional reactions to sensory deprival. It was concluded that prolonged exposure to a mono-tonous environment has measurable deleterious effects. In addition to the visual disturbances described above, the subjects' thinking ability was impared, and their emotional responses were characteristically childish. Their electroencephalographic examinations revealed changes in brain wave patterns.

It was concluded from this investigation that the normal functioning of the brain seems to require constant sensory bombardment through exposure to varying external stimuli. Monotonous stimuli rapidly lose their power to activate the brain in this way, resulting in an abnormal neural mechanism (23).

These and related studies demonstrate the dynamic characteristics of the human brain. The cortex is not like a computer that can remain unused for a year and then be made to respond to the touch of a button. As Heron states, "A changing sensory environment seems essential for human beings; without it, the brain ceases to function in an adequate way, and abnormalities of behavior develop" (23:73). If this statement is accurate in its description of the need for constant neural stimulation, then the significance of consistent childhood learning is evident. Since the brain will not continue to perform properly for more than a few days under sensory isolation, it is logical to believe that prolonged periods of uninteresting, unchallenging, monotonous existence in the formative days of childhood may account for the mental retardation that has been grossly attributed to maternal and cultural deprivation.

CONCLUSION

The necessity of providing rich, edifying experiences for young children has never been so apparent as it is today. This critical importance of stimulating young minds during their most vulnerable periods of awakening has been emphasized by the research presented in this chapter, particularly that related to the neurophysiological consequences of early learning. The concept of early learning is being shown to have profound implications for academic performance during the school years. If learning is to proceed systematically in the classroom, the child must not only have inherited adequate cognitive apparatus, but he must also have been subjected to favorable learning experiences during early childhood which predispose him to further learning. If, for example, the child has not had sufficient opportunities to learn shape and form discrimination during his preschool days, he might be expected to experience difficulty in learning to read. It is likely that many children are educationally handicapped by such inexperience very early in life. It must now become the responsibility of the school to provide remedial approaches to deficiencies in early learning which block educational advancement. Attempts should be made to organize compensatory learning programs that extend down to infancy, because the opportunities that are available there may never present themselves again.

Lessons in human development can be extrapolated from the consistent finding that animals subjected to early training were more easily taught throughout their lives. Is not the human infant better equipped to profit from his experience than any other creature? And if he has so much to gain from an optimal environment, does he not likewise have much more to lose by exposure to bland and unstimulating circumstances? The answer can be found in every ghetto and slum; it is evident by examining the background of students placed in classes for the borderline mentally retarded. With the advent of this cognitive understanding, society has now been charged with a new and awesome responsibility of eliminating this unnecessary blight on the reservoir of human potential. Disasters which have no remedy are unfortunate. But preventable human tragedies that recur in the full light of scientific solution are doubly intolerable. Psychologists and other behavioral scientists have long recognized the importance of early experience in the shaping of the human personality; new appreciation must now be given to the parallel significance of early environment on intellectual and educational development.

BIBLIOGRAPHY

1. Anonymous, "Roche Report," Frontiers of Hospital Psychiatry, V, June 15, 1968.
2. Bender, L., and H. Yarnell, "An Observation Nursery: A Study of 250 Children in the Psychiatric Division of Bellevue Hospital," *Amer. J. Psychiatry,* 97: 1158, 1941.
3. Bexton, W., W. Heron, and T. Scott, "Effect of Decreased Variations in the Sensory Environment," *Canadian J. of Psychology,* 8:70, 1954.
4. Bloom, B. S., *Stability and Change in Human Characteristics,* New York: John Wiley & Sons, Inc., 1965.
5. Bowlby, J., *Maternal Care and Mental Health,* New York: Schocken Books, 1951.
6. Brown, F., "Depression and Childhood Bereavement." *J. of Ment. Sc.,* 107:754, 1961.
7. Bruner, J. S., "The Cognitive Consequences of Early Sensory Deprivation," in *The Disadvantaged Child: Issues and Innovations,* J. Frost and G. Hawkes (Eds.), Boston: Houghton Mifflin Co., 1966.
8. Casler, L., "Maternal Deprivation: A Critical Review of the Literature," *Monographs of the Society for Research in Child Development,* Vol. 26 #2, Serial #80, 1961.
9. Eisenberg, L., "Social Class and Individual Development," in *Prospectives in Psychiatry and Psychoanalysis,* R. Gibson (Ed.), Philadelphia: J. B. Lippincott, 1967.
10. English, H., *Child Psychology,* New York: Holt, Rinehart & Winston, Inc., 1951.
11. Fischer, L., "Psychological Appraisal of the Unattached Preschool Child," *Amer. J. of Orthopsychiatry,* 23:803, 1953.
12. Forgays, D., and J. Forgays, "The Nature of the Effect of Free Environmental Experience in the Rat," *Journal of Comp. Physio. Psychol.,* 45:322, 1952.
13. Frost, J., and G. Hawkes, *The Disadvantaged Child: Issues and Innovations,* Boston: Houghton Mifflin Co., 1966.
14. Goddard, H., *Feeble Mindedness—Its Causes and Consequences,* New York: MacMillan Co., 1914.
15. Goldfarb, W., "Effects of Psychological Deprivation in Infancy and Subsequent Stimulation," *Amer. J. of Psychiatry,* 102:18, 1945.
16. Goldfarb, W., "Emotional and Intellectual Consequences of Psychologic Deprivation in Infancy: a Re-evaluation," in *Psychopathology of Childhood,* P. Hoch and J. Zubin (Eds.), New York: Grune and Stratton, 1955.
17. Goldfarb, W., "Variations in Adolescent Adjustment of Institutionally Reared Children," *Amer. J. of Orthopsychiatry,* 17:449, 1947.

18. Gordon, M., "The Influence of Background Factors Upon the Prediction of Success in Air Force Training Schools," *USAF Personnel Training,* Res. Pub. AFPTRC-IN-55-4, V, 1955.

19. Gottesman, I., "Biogenetics of Race and Class," in *Social Class, Race and Psychological Development,* M. Deutsch, I. Katz and A. Jensen (Eds.), New York: Holt, Rinehart and Winston, 1968.

20. Haywood, C. H., "Experimental Factors in Intellectual Development: The Concept of Dynamic Intelligence," in *Psychopathology of Mental Development,* New York: Grune & Stratton, Inc., 1967.

21. Hebb, D. O., *Introduction to Psychology,* Philadelphia: W. B. Saunders Co., 1958.

22. Hebb, D. O., *The Organization of Behavior,* New York: John Wiley & Sons, Inc., 1949.

23. Heron, W., "The Pathology of Boredom," *Scientific American,* 94:52, 1957.

24. Hoffman, M., and L. Hoffman, *Review of Child Development Research,* Vol. 1, New York: Russell Sage Foundation, 1964.

25. Hunt, J., *Intelligence and Experience,* New York: Ronald Press Co., 1961.

26. Hymovitch, F., "The Effects of Experimental Variations in Early Experience on Problem Solving in the Rat," *J. of Comp. Physiol. Psychol.,* 45:313, 1952.

27. Jensen, A., "How Much Can We Boost IQ and Scholastic Achievement?" *Harvard Educational Review,* 39:1, 1969.

28. Johnson, R., "Similarity in IQ of Separated Identical Twins As Related to Length of Time Spent in the Same Environment." *Child Development,* 34:745, 1963.

29. Kretch, D., "The Chemistry of Learning," *Saturday Review,* Jan. 20, 1968.

30. Munn, N., *The Evolution and Growth of Human Behavior,* Edition II, Boston: Houghton Mifflin Co., 1965.

31. Mussen, P., J. Conger, and J. Kagan, *Child Development and Personality,* Second Ed., New York: Harper and Row, 1963.

32. Newman, H., F. Freeman, and K. Holzinger, *Twins: A Study of Heredity and Environment,* Chicago: University of Chicago Press, 1937.

33. President's Committee on Mental Retardation, *MR 68, The Edge of Change—A Report to the President on Mental Retardation Programs, Trends, and Innovations, with Recommendations of Residential Care, Man Power and Deprivations,* Washington, D.C.: U.S. Govt. Printing Office, 1968.

34. Skeels, H. M., "Effects of Adoption on Children From Institutions," *Children,* 12:33, 1965.

35. Sontag, L., C. Baker, and V. Nelson, "Mental Growth and Personality Development," *Monographs of Soc. Res. Child. Dev.,* Vol. 23, #2, 1958.

36. Spiro, M. E., "Education in a Communal Village in Israel," *Amer. J. of Orthopsychiatry,* 25:283, 1955.

37. Spitz, R., "Anaclitic Depression," *Psychoanalytic Study of the Child,* 2:313, 1946.

38. Stone, L., and J. Church, *Childhood and Adolescence: A Psychology of the Growing Person,* New York: Random House, 1966.

39. Travers, R., *Essentials of Learning,* New York: MacMillan Co., 1963.

40. Vincent, E., and P. C. Martin, *Human Psychological Development,* New York: Ronald Press Co., 1961.

41. Wechsler, D., *The Measurement and Appraisal of Adult Intelligence,* Fourth Ed., Baltimore: William & Wilkins Co., 1958.

42. Young, W., (Executive Director of the National Urban League), Address delivered to the *National Association for Retarded Children,* Annual Meeting, 1967.

CHAPTER 2

The Meaning of Mental Retardation

by JANE R. MERCER, Ph.D.

Definitions of Mental Deficiency have an extra-scientific interest . . .
they decide the fate of thousands of human beings every year and
are intimately related to social welfare in general.

Kuhlman, 1924

What does it mean to be mentally retarded? We have recently completed a study of mental retardates in a southern California community with a population of 130,000. As part of that study, we developed a case register of all those persons who were identified as mentally retarded by one or more community agencies. When we analyzed the characteristics of those nominated by agencies which employ professional diagnosticians to evaluate mental retardates, we found that the persons referred as retarded had the following characteristics: persons five through twenty-four years of age were overrepresented and those under five and over twenty-four were underrepresented; persons from the poorest sections of the community were overrepresented and those from wealthier neighborhoods were underrepresented; when socioeconomic status was held constant, persons of Mexican-American heritage were overrepresented, Negroes appeared in proportionate numbers, and Caucasians from English-speaking homes were underrepresented (5).*

What is the meaning of these differences? The answer to this question depends upon one's viewpoint. The traditional clinical viewpoint regards mental retardation as a handicapping condition which exists

* This investigation was supported by Public Health Service Research Grant No. MH-08667 from the National Institute of Mental Health, Department of Health, Education, and Welfare and Public Health Service General Research Support Grant No. 1-SO1-FR-05632, from the Department of Health, Education and Welfare. Computing assistance was obtained from the Health Sciences Computing Facility, UCLA, sponsored by NIH Grant FR-3.

in individual persons. From this vantage point, these group differences would be explained primarily as the result of medical-etiological factors which weigh more heavily upon the young, the poor, and ethnic minorities.

The sociologist defines mental retardation as an acquired social status to which individuals are assigned by social systems such as the public school, diagnostic clinics, and welfare agencies. Because their standards and procedures vary, the meaning of mental retardation in one system will differ somewhat from that in another. While the sociological perspective agrees that a disadvantaged social position may result in medical, nutritional, and hygienic conditions which could lead to biological damage and clinical symptoms of mental retardation, such factors alone are not believed sufficient to explain differential rates such as those cited above. To understand the nature of mental retardation in the community, one must also comprehend the social processes which select out certain persons for labeling while passing over others who may be equally eligible (7). This discussion will use data on elementary school children to illustrate the meaning of mental retardation from a social system perspective.

A *Wechsler Intelligence Scale for Children* was administered to 1,298 public school children attending regular classes and 40 minority children attending classes for the educable mentally retarded. A team of qualified psychometrists, who received special training to assure that their testing and scoring procedures would be standardized, did the testing.*

Of the 1,298 children in regular classrooms, the 509 children of Mexican-American heritage and the 289 Negro children were from the three segregated elementary schools in the district while the 500 Caucasian children from English-speaking homes were a randomly selected sample from eleven predominantly middle class schools. Henceforth, we

* The cost of testing these children was supported by the Public Health Service Contract #PH-4367-756. Collection of other measures on these children was supported by funds from the California State Department of Education, Bureau of Intergroup Relations, McAteer Grant M8-14. Data analysis was supported by the Socio-Behavioral Study Center for Mental Retardation, Pacific State Hospital, Pomona, California, Grant No. MH-08667.

We wish to thank the Board of Education of the Riverside Unified School District, Riverside, California, headed by President Arthur L. Littleworth, for granting permission for the Study and to Superintendent Bruce Miller; Associate Superintendent E. Raymond Berry; Director of Research, Dr. Mabel Purl; Director of Psychological Services, Dr. Albert D. Marley; and Director of Intergroup Relations, Mr. Jesse Wall for facilitating the complex logistical arrangements which made it possible for these children to be tested during school hours in testing trailers moved to each campus for this purpose.

TABLE 1

DISTRIBUTION OF FULL SCALE IQs FOR 1,298 PUBLIC SCHOOL
CHILDREN IN REGULAR CLASSES

Ages Eight through Fourteen

IQ	Anglo		Mex.-American		Negro	
	N	%	N	%	N	%
80 and above	494	98.8	429	84.3	253	87.5
75-79	3	0.6	47	9.2	21	7.3
70-74	1	0.2	22	4.3	10	3.5
65-69	0	0.0	7	1.4	5	1.7
60-64	1	0.2	2	0.4	0	0.0
55-59	1	0.2	2	0.4	0	0.0
Total below 80	6	1.2	80	15.7	36	12.5
Total	500	100.0	509	100.0	289	100.0
Mean IQ	107.00		90.88		91 14	

will refer to the latter group as Anglo children. These schools had been designated as "receiving" schools in a desegregation program which bused all minority children to integrated educational settings. The WISC tests were administered shortly after the desegregation program was launched.

One hundred and twenty-two of the children were found to have a Full Scale IQ of 79 or below. Table 1 shows that there were marked differences in Full Scale IQs by ethnic group for the children who were holding the status of "normal" students in the regular classrooms. The mean IQ score was 107.0 for Anglo children, 90.9 for Mexican-American children, and 91.1 for Negro children. All children who scored below 80 were legally eligible for placement in classes for the educable mentally retarded. While we found only six Anglo children (1.2%) still in regular classrooms who had IQs below 80, there were 80 Mexican-American children (15.7%) and 36 Negro children (12.5%) in this category.

From our data, we cannot determine whether the low percentage of Anglo children with IQs below 80 in regular classrooms results from having relatively fewer Anglo children who score low on IQ tests or results from more stringent screening of Anglo children by the teacher. Some combination of the two factors was probably operating. In any case, there were 116 children from minority backgrounds who were legally eligible for classes for the educable mentally retarded who had never been placed in that status.

Are these children "mentally retarded" or are they "normal?" There are two possible answers to this question, depending upon whether one assumes a medical-psychological perspective or a sociological perspective.

The medical-psychological viewpoint uses a combined pathological and statistical model to define mental retardation (8). We have called this perspective the "clinical perspective" because it is designed to serve the needs of the helping professions, such as medicine, psychology, and education. Over the years, clinicians have developed a relatively high level of consensus on the definition of mental retardation and the clinical symptoms which are accepted as evidence of its presence. In the United States, the definition of the American Association on Mental Deficiency is probably the most universally accepted. This definition states that "mental retardation refers to subaverage general intellectual functioning which originates during the developmental period and is associated with impairment in adaptive behavior." "Subaverage" is defined as scoring more than one standard deviation below the mean of the general population on a standardized test (4). Other definitions have been proposed which incorporate additional requirements. For example, the Group for the Advancement of Psychiatry defines mental retardation as a chronic condition, while some earlier definitions explicitly state that mental retardation has a biological base.*

Although the American Association for Mental Deficiency definition requires that a person be subnormal in both intelligence and adaptive behavior before being defined as mentally retarded, the only normal measures of adaptive behavior in general use are applicable primarily to young children or to the severely and profoundly retarded.* Conse-

---

* According to the Group for the Advancement of Psychiatry, "Mental retardation is a chronic condition present from birth or early childhood and characterized by impaired intellectual functioning as measured by standardized tests. It manifests itself in impaired adaptation to the daily demands of the individual's own social environment. Commonly these patients show a slow rate of maturation, physical and/or psychological, together with impaired learning capacity." Group for the Advancement of Psychiatry, *Basic Consideration in Mental Retardation: A Preliminary Report*, Report No. 43, p. 7.

An early definition by Doll specified six criteria. "We observe that six criteria by statement or implication have been generally considered essential to an adequate definition and concept. These are: (1) social incompetence (2) due to mental subnormality (3) which has been developmentally arrested (4) which obtains at maturity, (5) is of constitutional origin and (6) is essentially incurable." E. A. Doll, "The Essentials of an Inclusive Concept of Mental Deficiency," *American Journal of Mental Deficiency*, 1941, vol. 46, p. 215.

* Scales frequently used are: E. A. Doll, *Vineland Social Maturity Scale*, American Guidance Service, Incorporated, Minneapolis, Minnesota 1965; A. L. Gesell, *The*

quently, the practicing clinician, such as the school psychologist, must lean heavily on standardized measures of intelligence in making evaluations. Assessments of adaptive behavior are, necessarily, less formal and more unsystematic than those of intelligence. Persons who show no evidence of organic damage and, hence, cannot be diagnosed medically, tend to be identified as mentally retarded primarily on the basis of intelligence testing.

The meaning of mental retardation from the clinical perspective is the pattern of symptoms which characterize the condition and the operations which are used to determine whether these symptoms are present in an individual case. The diagnostician begins with the definition and moves to the empirical world to identify cases.**

In clinical practice, a person *is* mentally retarded *if* he has the symptoms of mental retardation in much the same sense as a person *is* tubercular if he has the symptoms of active tuberculosis. Mental retardation is perceived as a characteristic of the individual which exists apart from its diagnosis. A person may be retarded even if he has not been diagnosed and no one in his social milieu is aware he has the symptoms. There is a decided tendency for most mental retardation to be perceived as a condition that is biologically determined, chronic, and essentially incurable. From a clinical perspective, most, if not all of the children in Table 1 with IQs below 80 would be regarded as moderate, mild, or borderline retardates, depending on the level of their IQs scores. The fact that they are still in regular classes would be interpreted as a school-system error in identification and placement.

A second approach to the meaning of mental retardation is essentially sociological. It proceeds from the concept of the social system (6-7). Sociologists conceptualize society as composed of a network of interlocking social systems. Among the most important social systems

---

First Five Years of Life, Harper and Bros., N. Y. 1948; A. L. Gesell, *Youth: The Years From Ten to Sixteen,* Harper and Bros., N. Y. 1956; Leo F. Cain, Samuel Levine, Freeman F. Elzey, *Cain-Levine Social Competency Scale,* Consulting Psychologists Press, Palo Alto, Calif. 1963. A comprehensive Adaptive Behavior Scale is currently being developed at Parsons State Hospital and Training Center, Parsons, Kansas under the auspices of NIMH Grant No. 5-R11 14901.

** We recognize that, historically, the currently accepted symtomatology for mental retardation was evolved inductively by observing many cases of persons regarded as mentally retarded and then abstracting from their individual characteristics the elements which they had in common and which came to be regarded as symptoms of the condition. However, in clinical practice, the definition is taken as a given and the clinician uses it as a conceptual tool to categorize persons in the empirical world.

in the life of the child are the family, the neighborhood and the public school. Each social system consists of a group of statuses which are the positions that a person may occupy in that system. The usual statuses in the nuclear family are mother, father, son and daughter. In the public school, the usual statuses are teacher, student in the regular classroom, principal, school secretary, custodian and so forth. Some statuses, such as son and daughter, are ascribed at birth but other statuses must be acquired—statuses such as husband, wife, mother, father or teacher.

For each status there is a set of prescribed behaviors which make up the role that persons occupying that status are expected to play. If a person fulfills role expectations, he may be rewarded in many ways by other system members. One of the most desirable rewards in most systems is to be assigned to a more valued status, that is, to be promoted. If a person fails to meet role expectations, he may be punished in many ways. One of the more drastic punishments is to be assigned to a less valued status. For example, a child may be retained when other children are promoted to the next grade or he may be removed from the regular classroom and placed in the status of mental retardate.

Sociologically, a person is a mental retardate when he acquires the status of mental retardate and plays the role of mental retardate. He is not a mental retardate by virtue of having certain personal attributes, although these may play a part in his acquiring the status. Admittedly, persons who are assigned to the status of mental retardate do have many characteristics in common because they are sorted out and categorized by teachers, psychologists, medical doctors and other persons who have been trained in the clinical tradition and who share a common set of norms by which they evaluate behavior and assign persons to statuses. This type of regularity occurs in the characteristics of occupants of any social status. Indeed, we cannot even conceive of the notion of a social status at all except as an abstraction defined by the regularities and commonalities which characterize persons who hold the status.

Let us return to the issue of the children in Table 1. "Are they retarded?" Looking at the social system of the school, we see that these children are playing the role of normal students in the regular classroom. They have not been assigned the status of a mental retardate nor are they playing the role of a mental retardate. From a social system perspective they are not mental retardates. The fact that they are "discreditable" because their status as regular students would be jeopardized *if* the stigma of their low IQ were known is irrelevant (3). They are playing normal roles; they are perceived by teachers, peers, and parents as normal; they have not been assigned to the status of mental retardate.

Although an IQ below 80 may be necessary before one can acquire the status of mental retardate, low IQ alone is not sufficient. Sociologically, we can think of these children with IQs below 80 as "the population at risk" of becoming mental retardates. An example from demography will illustrate what is meant by "the population at risk." Females between puberty and the menopause are the population exposed to the risk of becoming pregnant, bearing a child, and acquiring the status of "biological mother." Males are not part of the population exposed to the risk of acquiring the status of "biological mother" nor are pre-pubescent or post-menopausal females. However, until a woman actually bears a child, she does not hold the status of "biological mother"; nor does she play the role of "biological mother." She simply remains in "the population at risk," the pool of eligibles. The meaning of the status "biological mother" can be described by specifying what a person must do to achieve that status, e.g., bear a child. Similarly, the children with IQs below 80 in the public schools are the population at risk of becoming mental retardates but they do not become mentally retarded, sociologically, until they have actually achieved the status and are playing the role of a mental retardate. Until then, they remain in the field of eligibles.

The meaning of mental retardation from the social system perspective then is described by delineating what a person in the field of eligibles must do to acquire the status of mental retardate. The situation provided by the data on children with low IQs still in regular class gives us the opportunity to try to establish, empirically, the sociological meaning of mental retardation in the public schools.

For Anglo children in the sample, the field of eligibles and the group of persons who are actually holding the status of mental retardate coincide very closely. Consequently, Anglo children do not provide a propitious sample for studying the selective factors which operate to determine which children in the field of eligibles actually acquire the status of mental retardate. It appears that most Anglo children in the population at risk do acquire the status of mental retardate in the public schools. However, there is a large number of eligible minority children who do not hold the status of mental retardate. For this group, it is possible to pose the question, "What differentiates minority children who move from the field of eligibles into the status of mental retardate from those who are not assigned the status of retardate?"

We examined three types of variables in seeking factors which might differentiate minority children in classes for the educable retarded from minority children in the group of eligibles: (1) the characteristics of the child as revealed in individual testing and evaluation sessions conducted by the research staff; (2) characteristics of the child's family; (3) characteristics of the school system. Each set of factors will be examined in turn.

CHARACTERISTICS OF THE CHILD

The 40 minority children in classes for the educable retarded and the 116 minority children who were eligible but not placed had all attended the same three segregated schools until shortly before the study. Children in both groups had been evaluated by the same staff of teachers during the critical primary grades. Three individual testing and interviewing sessions, spread over a three week period, were held with each child for purposes of the study. In one session, each child received the WISC. In the other two sessions, he responded to various attitudinal and social-psychological measurements.

Differences in Intellectual Profiles

The first characteristic investigated was performance on the WISC. Although all children had Full Scale IQs qualifying them for the status of mental retardate, we wished to investigate possible qualitative differences in the performance of the two groups. Therefore, we compared the WISC subtest scores of the 12 Negro mental retardates with the 36 Negro eligibles and the 28 Mexican-American retardates with the 80 Mexican-American eligibles. Table 2 presents the average Full Scale IQ, Verbal IQ, and Performance IQ for each group as well as the scaled scores on each of the eleven subtests which were administered.

When the two ethnic groups were analyzed separately, there were no significant differences in Full Scale IQs, Performance IQs or Verbal IQs comparing children in special education with those in regular class. However, when the ethnic groups were combined and all mental retardates were compared with all eligibles, a significant difference in Verbal IQ emerged ($t=2.4$ $p<.02$). The mental retardates performed less well on the verbal portions of the test than the eligibles. However, there were no differences in performance on the *Peabody Picture Vocabulary Test,* either within ethnic group or when the groups were combined (2).

TABLE 2

Intellectual Performance of Children Holding Status of Mental Retardate Compared to Children in the Field of Eligibles

	NEGRO			MEXICAN-AMERICAN			BOTH		
	MR (N=12)	Eligibles (N=36)	t value	MR (N=28)	Eligibles (N=80)	t value	MR (N=40)	Eligibles (N=116)	t value
WISC Full Scale IQ	70.6	74.1	1.5	72.3	73.8	.7	71.8	73.9	2.4*
WISC Verbal IQ	71.3	75.2	1.7	68.7	71.7	1.8	69.4	72.8	1.3
WISC Performance IQ	75.5	77.9	.7	81.4	81.0	.1	79.7	80.0	.1
WISC Scaled Scores:									
Verbal Tests									
Information	4.5	5.8	2.8*	5.1	5.0	.3	4.9	5.2	1.1
Comprehension	5.9	6.2	.5	5.3	5.9	1.0	5.5	6.0	1.2
Arithmetic	4.3	6.1	3.2**	5.0	6.3	3.3**	4.8	6.3	4.3**
Similarities	5.9	6.4	.8	4.9	5.3	.8	5.2	5.6	1.1
Vocabulary	5.2	5.4	.3	4.2	4.4	.4	4.5	4.7	.6
Digit Span	5.6	6.4	1.1	5.6	6.0	.9	5.6	6.1	1.4
Performance Tests									
Picture Completion	6.8	7.0	.2	7.4	7.4	.1	7.2	7.2	.0
Picture Arrangement	7.1	6.2	1.1	6.9	7.0	.1	6.9	6.7	.4
Block Design	5.6	6.5	1.1	6.6	6.6	.1	6.3	6.5	.5
Object Assembly	6.5	6.4	.2	8.1	7.6	.7	7.6	7.2	.8
Digit Symbol	6.3	8.1	2.1*	7.6	8.9	2.2**	7.2	8.7	2.8**
Peabody IQ	79.2	78.9	.1	65.1	68.1	.8	69.1	71.5	.8

* Significant at p $<$ .05
** Significant at p $<$ .01

An analysis of the mean scores for the individual subtests reveals the pattern of the major differences between the groups. In general, the eligibles scored slightly higher than the mental retardates on all the verbal tests (Information, Comprehension, Arithmetic, Similarities, Vocabulary, Digit Span). The Arithmetic sub-test was differentiating. The average scaled score for the mentally retarded group was 4.8 compared to 6.3 for the eligibles (t=4.3, p<.01). Differences on the Information subtest reached significance for Negro children (t=2.8, p<.02) but a small reversal for the Mexican-American children prevented this subject from being significant when the groups were combined. Wechsler has noted that both the Arithmetic and Information subtests are highly predictive of academic achievement.

> It appeared that children who do poorly in arithmetical reasoning often have difficulty with other subjects. A number of examiners reported they were sometimes able to diagnose educational abilities on the basis of scores obtained on this test, especially when supplemented by scores obtained on the general information test. The combined scores of these two tests frequently furnish an accurate estimate of the subject's scholastic achievement (12).

Scaled scores on the performance tests (Picture Completion, Picture Arrangement, Block Design, Object Assembly, Digit Symbol) were essentially equal for the two groups. On Picture Arrangement and Object Assembly, the mentally retarded did slightly better than the eligibles. However, the eligibles were distinctly superior to the retardates on the Digit Symbol test (t=2.8, p<.01). The average scaled score for the eligibles (8.1) was higher on this subtest than on any other subtest of the WISC. The Digit Symbol test requires a child to associate certain symbols with certain other symbols. The speed and accuracy with which he performs this task are the measure of his ability. Performance on this test requires visual acuity, motor coordination, and speed. It is also a measure of the extent to which a child is able to concentrate and apply himself with persistent effort for any length of time.

We conclude that the eligible children showed superior ability in arithmetic and in coding the digit symbols. In addition, Negro eligibles were better informed than their peers in special education. The tendency for eligibles to do slightly better on all verbal tests resulted in a cumulative effect which produced a significantly higher Verbal IQ when both ethnic groups were combined.

Differences in Social-Psychological Profiles

Numerous social-psychological measures were secured during the individual interviews with each child. There were no differences in the children's expressed attitudes toward school or their feelings of involvement in school activities as revealed in responses made to pictures of children participating in classroom and playground groups. Similarly, there were no differences between the mentally retarded and the eligibles in their level of "school anxiety," as revealed in a series of questions adapted from Sarason's work. A general anxiety scale, also containing selected items from Sarason, found no differences between the groups (10). There were no differences in the children's expressed educational aspirations or their occupational expectations.

One series of questions explored each child's self-concept and another similar series measured his perception of the attitude of others toward himself. Both groups of children achieved equally positive scores. Thus, the mental retardates and the eligibles proved indistinguishable on all the attitudinal scales and other measures which were analyzed.

CHARACTERISTICS OF THE CHILD'S FAMILY

Both parents of each of the children in the study were individually interviewed and asked questions intended to measure the socioeconomic status of the family, the extent to which the family participates in school activities, the educational and occupational aspirations of the parents for the children, and other aspects of the value climate of the home.

Although the socioeconomic index score of families with retarded children was slightly lower than that for families of the eligibles, these differences were not statistically significant (1). There were no differences in the extent to which the mothers participated in child oriented groups, such as the PTA, nor the amount of interaction the mother had with the child's teachers and the school. The mothers and fathers of all the children expected them to complete approximately 13 years of formal education. Parental occupation aspirations for the mental retardates were slightly higher than for the eligibles. Indeed, Mexican-American mothers had significantly higher occupational expectations for the children in classes for the mentally retarded ($t=2.69$, $p<.01$). However, this was the only statistically significant difference in thirty-eight comparisons and could easily have occurred by chance.

The interview included several scales designed to measure parental attitudes and values on dimensions likely to be related to a child's academic performance. None of these measures differentiated the parents of the two groups of children. Mothers had equally positive perceptions of the opportunities available for their children in American society, had equivalent desires for upward mobility themselves, and had experienced an equal amount of social mobility in their own lives. Similarly, there were no differences in the fathers' perceptions of the opportunity structure for their children. Mothers in both groups expressed equal willingness for children to become independent of the family. The mothers of eligibles placed no greater value on active mastery nor did they show greater adherence to middle class values (11). However, Negro parents placed greater emphasis on both of these values than the Mexican-American parents.

CHARACTERISTICS OF THE SCHOOL AS A SOCIAL SYSTEM

We next turned to an analysis of the social processes of the school system to determine if the two groups could be differentiated within the context of the school. We focused on the most critical juncture in acquiring the status of mental retardate, the initial referral by the classroom teacher (5).

In an earlier analysis of the same school system, we studied all the children referred for any reason to the central pupil personnel office during a one year period. Of the 1,234 referrals, two-thirds were initiated by teacher-principal teams. Approximately 8.3% of the children referred were subsequently placed in classes for the educable mentally retarded. Of these children, over 90% were initially referred as suspected of mental retardation by the elementary classroom teacher. Such referrals usually came during the primary grades. Very few children were referred or placed in special education after the sixth grade (9).

If the elementary teacher does not initiate a referral, the child is not likely to be individually tested by the school psychologist. If he is not certified mentally subnormal by the school psychologist, he cannot acquire the status of mental retardate. The school district has seven school psychologists on its staff and a well developed program for the educable mentally retarded. What factors operate to select out those minority children who are referred for mental retardation? Two alternatives were explored: the standard test information available in a child's file and the teacher's subjective evaluation of the child's attributes.

Standardized Test Information Available

The school district has had a regular policy of administering group tests of ability and achievement to all children at specified grade levels.

This policy antedates the mandated testing program of the state and extends back into the 1940's.* Consequently, each child who grows up in the system will probably have received a *Metropolitan Readiness Test* in kindergarten, may have received a *Metropolitan Achievement Test* in second or third grade, and may possibly have received a *California Test of Mental Maturity* by the time he reached fourth grade. These scores are recorded in the student's cumulative record folder and are available to elementary teachers. A teacher's decision to refer a particular child could be sparked by her knowledge that he has performed poorly on standardized group tests.

We have no way of knowing whether teachers systematically read the test information in the cumulative folders of their students. However, if there is no test information in the folder or if the information available is essentially the same for both groups of children, we would have to conclude that the availability of standard test information could not have influenced the teacher's decision.

Therefore, we examined the cumulative record folders for all of the children in the sample and recorded the type of test information which was available to the classroom teacher in the file at the time she made her decision to refer the child for psychological evaluation. When we examined the cumulative records for each of the 40 children holding the status of mental retardate, we found 12 cases for whom no standard test information was available to the teacher at the time of referral. *Metropolitan Readiness Test* scores, secured in kindergarten, were available for 20 of the children; *Metropolitan Readiness* and *Metropolitan Achievement Test* scores were available for three cases; *Metropolitan Achievement Test* scores were available for three cases. There were other combinations of tests available for the two remaining cases. There were no differences in the amount of information available when the eligibles and the children in special education were compared.

Because the scores available to the reader at the time of referral were mainly from the *Metropolitan Readiness Test,* we compared the average score made on this test by children selected for referral as mentally retarded (36.7) with the average earned by the eligible children not referred (38.6). The difference between these two means could be accounted for by chance ($t = .3$, $p > .05$). Results were similar for the *Metropolitan Achievement Test.*

---

* As part of the mandated testing program of the State of California, children are now administered Stanford Achievement Tests and Lorge-Thorndike Ability Tests. However, these data were not available in children's files at the time referrals were made by the teachers and could not have influenced their decisions.

Therefore, we conclude that teachers either referred children as possible mental retardates without any test information whatsoever or with essentially the same information for those they referred as for those they did not refer. In fact, one teacher was not deterred by the knowledge that a child she was referring had an IQ of 93 on the *California Test of Mental Maturity*. We cannot cite differences in performance on primary grade standardized test scores as a selective factor. What does a child do to acquire the status of mental retardate? The differentiating behaviors must, somehow, rest with teachers' subjective evaluations.

Teachers' Subjective Evaluations

Because of the key position played by the classroom teacher in nominating children for the status of mental retardate, we decided to focus our search for the meaning of mental retardation on the selection processes operating in the elementary classroom. Why were the 40 children selected and not the 116?

A child is not eligible for placement in a class for the mentally retarded in California until he is eight years of age. Therefore, few children are referred for testing in kindergarten but many are referred in first, second, and third grades. This pattern is exemplified by the mentally retarded children in our sample. Only four children were referred and tested in kindergarten, 14 were tested in first grade, nine were tested in second grade, seven in third grade, five in fourth grade, and one in fifth grade.

Although the official referral for testing may not take place until the second or third grade, all earlier teachers are likely to participate in formulating the collective definition of the child as mentally retarded. They grade him, write verbal evaluations of him and discuss him with their colleagues. Their opinions are likely to influence the teacher who makes the actual referral.

However, direct questioning of the teachers involved was precluded at the outset. We did not wish to reveal the identity of the eligible children to the teachers because we did not want to jeopardize the normal statuses which the children were occupying in the classroom. In addition, we reasoned that a teacher who has committed herself to a decision, such as referring a child as suspected of mental retardation, will develop post factum explanations to rationalize and justify her earlier action. We wished to secure data on teachers' perceptions prior to the decision to refer the child, data which would reflect perceptions at that time undistorted by selective, retrospective recall. For this reason, we decided to conduct a content analysis of teachers' comments recorded in the permanent school records for both groups of low IQ children and to compare them with a random sample of teacher comments about minority children in the regular classes of the same schools.

Every spring, each classroom teacher is expected to write a brief, verbal description of each child in her class. These descriptions are permanently recorded in the child's cumulative record folder and thus become part of the collective definition of the child from the viewpoint of the school, a definition which follows the child throughout his school career. These evaluations are confidential and are intended to assist subsequent teachers in assessing and understanding the child.

Although the school system provides each new teacher with a general guide containing a list of areas which she may wish to cover in her comments, she is free to record any observations she believes are germane and she is in no way bound by the guide. Therefore, these teacher evaluations of children are relatively spontaneous expressions coming after teaching the child for a year.

For the mentally retarded, only the verbal descriptions of the regular classroom teachers who had had them prior to placement were analyzed. We were concerned with the teachers' perceptions of the child while he was still in the regular classroom because these are the cumulative definitions which would influence his referral. The content of these descriptions was compared to those made by the regular classroom teachers of the eligible children. In addition, a randomly selected sample of 59 children in the regular classrooms (43 Mexican-American children and 16 Negro children) was also analyzed to provide a comparative group of evaluations made on children representing the full range of IQs found in the regular classroom.

Each verbal description was first divided into meaning units and each unit was coded independently. Every time a new idea was introduced or a new behavior described, that adjective or phrase, as the case might be, was coded as a separate meaning unit. The average number of meaning units per teacher for the mentally retarded was 4.3; for the eligibles was 4.1; and for the random sample was 4.2. Thus, approximately the same amount of descriptive material was available, per teacher, on the children in the three groups.

The fifty categories used to classify the meaning units were developed in an earlier study which involved the analysis of over 500 cumulative records from the same school district.* Categories describe not only the nature of the behavior but the positive or negative direction of the evaluation. For example, there are separate categories for comments about low mental ability and high mental ability; high perseverance and low perseverance; good adjustment and poor adjustment, and so forth. Because of these mutually exclusive categories, the rank orders shown in Table 3 present several instances in which descriptions of behaviors on opposite poles of the same dimension appear at different locations in the ranking.

Three coders read the files, divided each record into meaning units, and classified each unit. In a reliability check of the coding of 1500 randomly selected meaning units, there was complete coder agreement on 84.2% of the classifications and agreement by two out of the three coders on 14.3% of the additional cases. Therefore, it was concluded that the coding was sufficiently reliable to warrant analysis.

Because there was great variability in the total number of comments appearing in the records of different children, the comments in each child's record were weighted so that equal weight would be given to the comments about each child. The results for each group were then combined and ranged by the frequency with which a particular category was used in describing the children in that group. The nineteen most used categories were included in the analysis. A rank of 1 indicates the attribute having the highest number of mentions in that group, a rank of 2 is for the attribute with the next higher frequency, and so forth.

Table 3 shows the rank ordering of the attributes as perceived and reported by the regular classroom teachers for the three groups of children.** A Spearman rank order correlation indicates that the rank-

---

* Mental Retardation in the Community. NIMH Grant No. MH 5687.

** Following are illustrations of the types of adjectives and phrases which were coded into each of the nineteen categories shown in Table 3.

Cooperative—Friendly, kind, helpful, thoughtful, courteous, sweet, volunteers for activities, outgoing.

High perseverance and/or commitment—Finishes his work, tries hard, industrious, likes to work, good work habits, does job thoroughly.

Withdrawn, shy—Reserved, retiring, isolated, plays by self, unresponsive, easily hurt, lacks self confidence.

Positive emotional tone—Buoyant, happy, smiling, enthusiastic, tries new things, enjoys school, alert, good loser, interested in school.

Low perseverance and/or commitment—Does not finish work, poor work habits, does not complete tasks, makes no effort, will not try, short attention span.

Low mental ability—Slow learner, retarded, limited ability, immature intellectually, below average intellectually, should be placed in special education, promoted only because of age.

ings of the behavioral descriptions of the children in the random sample and the group of eligibles are significantly correlated ($r_s = .62$, $p < .01$). It also indicates that ranked behaviors of the eligibles compared to the mental retardates are statistically similar ($r_s = .73$, $p < .01$). This means that the eligibles cannot be clearly differentiated from the children in the general classroom, nor can they be clearly differentiated from the labeled mental retardates. However, the correlation between the children in the random sample and the children who were in special education ($r_s = .32$) is not statistically significant, indicating that the mental retardates can be differentiated from children in the general classroom by the attributes which teachers use to describe them. It appears that the eligibles, those children who have low IQs but have not been placed in the status of mental retardate, fall *between* the general classroom and mental retardates in the perceptions which teachers have of their

---

High mental ability—Bright, learns easily, quick, good student, fast learner, above average ability.

Quiet, little noise—Seldom talks, will not speak up, is very quiet.

High academic competence—Good at reading, writing, arithmetic, any comment indicating good academic work, above grade level, good comprehension in general.

Good adjustment—Well adjusted, good social adjustment, stable, normal adjustment, includes all statements using the word adjustment which do not refer to intellectual or academic matters.

High demand on teacher—Needs constant supervision, has to be watched, always needs attention, needs a lot of individual help, shows off, distracts other children, does not work independently, high demand on teacher time, attention and energy.

Negative emotional tone—Sullen, sulky, cannot take defeat, poor loser, thinks he is being picked on, does not smile, depressed, moody, cries easily, dislikes school, discouraged.

Difficult to manage or control—Disobedient, always breaks the rules, no self discipline, does not listen when reprimanded, difficult to control, does not respect authority, sassy, talks back.

Low academic competence—Poor reader, has trouble with arithmetic, poor handwriting, needs to improve his reading.

Low competence in language, speech or English usage—Difficulty with English, cannot speak well, low in language skills, low mastery of English, does not understand English.

Average academic competence—Normal understanding, at grade level in reading, arithmetic or other academic subjects.

Easy to manage or control—Obeys rules, follows directions, does what he is told, tries to please teacher, good self discipline, responds to praise, wants to please, respectful.

Poor adjustment—Low adjustment, poorly adjusted, poor social adjustment, cannot adjust to school, will not settle down, unspecified immaturity.

Poor home situation—Low parental concern, little parental involvement in school, no cooperation from home, parents are not interested, parents uncooperative, child neglected, child unsupervised, child does not get help at home.

TABLE 3

COMPARISON OF TEACHERS' PERCEPTIONS OF A RANDOM SAMPLE
OF ELEMENTARY SCHOOL CHILDREN WITH THE ELIGIBLES AND
THE MENTALLY RETARDED

Perceived Attributes	Random Sample[a] (N=59) Ranks	Eligibles (N=116) Ranks	Mentally Retarded (N=40) Ranks
Cooperative	1	3	4
High Perseverance	2	1	5
Withdrawn, Shy	3	2	2
Positive Emotional Tone	4	5	10
Low Perseverance	5	4	7.5
Low Mental Ability	6	6	1
High Mental Ability	7	18	19
Quiet, Little Noise	8	14	16
High Academic Competence	9	19	18
Good Adjustment	10	9	11
Makes High Demand on Teacher	11	7	6
Negative Emotional Tone	12	13	9
Difficult to Manage, Control	13.5	15	14
Low Academic Competence	13.5	8	17
Low Competence in English	15.5	10	7.5
Average Academic Competence	15.5	16	15
Easy to Manage, Control	17	11	13
Poor Adjustment	18	12	3
Poor Home Condition	19	17	12

Random Sample vs Eligibles	$r_s = .62$	$t = 3.3$ $p<.01$
Eligibles vs Mentally Retarded	$r_s = .73$	$t = 4.43$ $p<.01$
Random Sample vs Mentally Retarded	$r_s = .32$	$t = 1.4$ NS

a All children are Mexican-American and Negro children in the same elementary schools.

behavior. The eligibles cannot be clearly differentiated from either adjoining group although the labeled mental retardates can be clearly differentiated from children in the general classroom.

It is illuminating to examine the attributes showing the largest discrepancies in rank order between groups. By looking at differences of five or more ranks, we can identify the salient characteristics of each group which serve to differentiate it from the others in the comments of the teachers. We will first compare children in the random sample with those in special education. "High mental ability" ranks seventh in frequency of mentions for the random sample but is ranked nineteenth, e.g., twelve ranks lower, for the special education group. For the mental retardates, positive comments about mental ability were non-existent. Children in the regular classroom are nine ranks higher in "academic competence," eight ranks higher in "quiet, makes little noise," and six ranks higher in "positive emotional tone." On the other hand, children in classes for the mentally retarded are fifteen ranks higher than the random sample on "poor adjustment," eight ranks higher on "low competence in English," and five ranks higher on "low mental ability" and on "making high demands on the teacher." Random sample children rank high on positive characteristics while special education children rank high on negative characteristics. The differences in verbal competence found in the WISC scores are confirmed by the relatively high number of teacher comments about the low level language skills of children subsequently placed in special education.

When eligibles are compared to the random sample, the pattern is almost identical to that differentiating the random sample from the mental retardates but the discrepancies in rank order are much smaller. Random sample children rate eleven ranks higher on "high ability"; ten ranks higher on "high academic competence"; and six ranks higher on "quiet, makes little noise." Unlike the mental retardates, the eligibles are perceived as having the same level of "positive emotional tone" as the random sample. Like the mental retardates, the eligibles are rated high on "low academic competence," "low competence in English," and "poor adjustment," but, again, the differences between them and the random sample are smaller than those between mental retardates and the random sample. They are *not* ranked higher on "low mental ability" than the children in the random sample. Low mental ability ranks sixth for the random sample, sixth for the eligibles but first in frequency for the mental retardates. While teachers more frequently describe the eligible children as having "low mental ability" than other children in the classroom, they mention this characteristic relatively more often in the records of the children subsequently assigned the status of mental retardates.

Table 4 clarifies and tests the statistical significance of these differences. It reports the percentage of cases for each group of students in which a particular attribute was mentioned one or more times. The six attributes differentiating the groups at the .05 level of significance or beyond are reported.

"Poor adjustment" is the most differentiating characteristic ($p < .001$). The percentage of children described as poorly adjusted declines from 55% of the labeled mental retardates to 34% of the eligibles and 15%

of the random sample. All differences are significant. The eligibles fall between the random sample and the mental retardates.

There are few positive comments about the academic competence of either eligibles or retardates (p<.001). While 32% of the random sample children were described as academically able, only 14% of the eligibles and 2% of the retardates received such commendations. Similarly, not one of the regular classroom teachers remarked about "high mental ability" in any of the children later placed in the status of retardate. However, 11% of the eligibles and 41% of the random sample children received favorable comments on this score. On both these characteristics, comments about eligibles are more like those about labeled mental retardates than like the general classroom (p<.001).

However, on comments about "low mental ability," eligibles are more like the random sample. While 70% of the mental retardates are spontaneously described as having "low mental ability," only 48% of the eligibles and 36% of the random sample are so characterized (p<.01). The difference between mental retardates and eligibles is statistically significant but not that between eligibles and the random sample.

These differences in teachers' perceptions of children's mental abilities appear to be at the crux of the labeling process. Very few teachers are likely to describe a child with a low IQ as academically competent or intelligent. On the other hand, there are many minority children with low IQs who are not described as dull or mentally retarded. Certain other behaviors influence which of these children are seen as intellectually subnormal and which are seen as academic problems but not mentally deficient.

Competence in English is one behavioral area which differentiates the mental retardates from the general classroom. Over twice as many mental retardates as regular classroom children are "incompetent in the use of English" (p<.05). The eligibles again fall between. The eligibles are more often perceived as "easy to manage" than those in the random sample.

One final attribute, which ranked too low to appear on Table 3, differentiated mental retardates from eligibles, "being liked by peers." More eligibles were described as being liked by the other children in the class (p<.05).

The Meaning of Mental Retardation in the Public Schools

What is the meaning of mental retardation? From a clinical perspective, a mental retardate is one who has the symptoms of mental

TABLE 4

ATTRIBUTES MENTIONED ONE OR MORE TIMES COMPARING ELIGIBLES, MENTAL RETARDATES AND THE RANDOM SAMPLE

	% Attribute Mentioned One or More Times			Mental Retardates vs Random Sample		Mental Retardates vs Eligibles		Eligibles vs Random Sample	
	Mental Retardate (N=40)	Eligibles (N=116)	Random Sample (N=59)	x^2	p	x^2	p	x^2	p
Poor Adjustment	55%	34%	15%	15.7	<.001	4.3	<.05	5.7	<.02
Low Ability	70%	48%	36%	9.9	<.01	4.8	<.05	2.1	NS
High Ability	0	11%	41%	19.3	<.001	3.5	NS	18.6	<.001
Academic Competence	2%	14%	32%	11.3	<.001	2.8	NS	7.2	<.01
Low Competence in English	37%	25%	15%	5.3	<.02	1.7	NS	1.6	NS
Easy to Manage	32%	37%	19%	1.8	NS	.1	NS	5.4	<.05
Liked by Peers	10%	29%	22%	1.7	NS	5.0	<.05	.7	NS

retardation: subnormal intellectual ability and subnormal adaptive be-havior. Clinically, most of the 156 children with low IQs would be rated as retarded. From the social system perspective, a mental retardate is one who holds the status of mental retardate and plays the role of retardate. The meaning of the status "mental retardate" can be described by specifying what a person must do to achieve that status. As we have seen in our analysis of the social system of the public school, not all chil-dren who have low IQs are occupying the status of mental retardate. The discrepancy between those who are "eligible" and those who are "actual" retardates is quite large for Mexican-American and Negro children but negligible for Anglo children. Therefore, we conclude that acquired roles and clinical definitions correspond closely for Anglo children and most of the clinically eligible are actually playing the role of retardate. It does not matter which perspective we adopt. The results are almost identical from either viewpoint.

However, among children from ethnically different backgrounds, a low IQ was necessary but not sufficient to place the child in the status of mental retardate. There were almost three times more children with IQs below 80 playing "normal" roles as there were children playing "retarded" roles. That is, only 25% of "the eligibles" were "actuals" in the sociological sense.

Therefore, mental retardation for ethnic minorities in the school sys-tem means having a low IQ *plus* other attributes which are unspeci-fied and, hence, largely unknown and unrecognized. The only clinical characteristic that differentiated "eligibles" from "actuals" was verbal performance on the WISC, especially the Arithmetic and Information subtests, and lower performance on the Digit Symbol subtest. There were no differences in educational or occupational aspirations, self-con-cepts, emotional adjustment, attitudes towards school, or any of the social psychological variables measured. Likewise, family characteristics did not distinguish the groups. It was only when the analysis focused on the normative structure of the elementary classroom and the percep-tions of elementary teachers as revealed in their spontaneous descriptions of children that the sociological meaning of mental retardation in the public schools became clear.

The children who were placed and the children who were eligible but not placed had three characteristics in common which differentiated them from other children in the classroom: They were less often described as having high mental ability, less often described as academically com-petent, and more often described as poorly adjusted. However, on every variable the eligibles received more favorable comments and fewer unfavorable comments than the children who were placed.

Mental retardates in special education received significantly more comments about their poor adjustment and their low mental ability and fewer comments about being liked by peers than the eligibles. In addition, the children assigned the status of mental retardate were more often described as incompetent in the use of English. Those with low IQ who were not placed were more frequently described as easy to manage. Thus, we learned that a child must *do* to acquire the status of retardate.

Low academic competence + poor adjustment + low competence in English + few friends = perceived low mental ability = mental retardation.

However, if a child has low academic competence and poor adjustment but is relatively competent in English, easy to manage and liked by his peers, he will probably not be perceived as having low mental ability and will not be referred as suspected of retardation.

Low academic competence + poor adjustment + relative competence in English + being easy to manage + being liked by peers + perceived low mental ability does not equal mental retardation.

Clinical symptoms alone cannot describe mental retardation. While low IQ is a necessary attribute in acquiring the social status of retardate, it alone is not sufficient for selection from the school population. We assume that similar processes operate in other social systems and in the community in general. Some comprehension of these processes is essential if we are to understand the meaning of mental retardation in the community.

BIBLIOGRAPHY

1. Duncan, D. D., in Reiss, A. J., *Occupations and Social Status,* The Free Press of Glencoe, Inc., 1961.
2. Dunn, L. M., *Peabody Picture Vocabulary Test,* American Guidance Service, Inc., Minneapolis, Minn., 1965.
3. Goffman, E., *Stigma: Notes on the Management of Spoiled Identity,* Prentice-Hall, Inc., New Jersey, 1964.
4. Heber, R., *A Manual on Terminology and Classification in Mental Retardation.* A Monograph Supplement to the *American Journal of Mental Deficiency.* Second Edition, 1961.
5. Mercer, J. R., *Labeling the Mentally Retarded: Clinical and Social System Perspectives on Mental Retardation,* Berkeley: University of California Press, 1973.
6. Mercer, R., "Sociological Perspectives on Mild Mental Retardation." In *Socio-cultural Aspects of Mental Retardation: Proceedings of the Peabody-NIMH Conference,* C. Hayward (Ed.), New York: Appleton-Century-Crofts, 1970.

7. Mercer, J. R., "Social System Perspective and Clinical Perspective: Frames of Reference for Understanding Career Patterns of Persons Labelled as Mentally Retarded," *Social Problems,* 1965, 13, 18-34.
8. Mercer, J. R., "Who Is Normal? Two Perspectives on Mild Mental Retardation," in *Patients, Physicians and Illness,* 2nd Edition. E. G. Jaco (Ed.), New York: The Free Press of Glencoe, 1972, pp. 66-85.
9. Robins, R. C., Mercer, J. R., and Myers, C. E., "The School as a Selecting-Labelling System," *Journal of School Psychology, Summer,* 1967, vol. V No. 4, pp. 270-279.
10. Sarason, S., Davidson, S., Lighthall, F., Waite, R., and Ruebush, K., *Anxiety in Elementary School Children,* Wiley, New York, 1960.
11. Turner, R., *The Social Context of Ambition: A Study of High School Seniors in Los Angeles,* Chandler Publishers, San Francisco, 1964.
12. Wechsler, D., *The Measurement and Appraisal of Adult Intelligence,* Fourth edition, Baltimore: Williams and Wilkins Co., 1958.

Section II.

BIOLOGICAL FACTORS AND CAUSATION OF MENTAL RETARDATION

CHAPTER 3

Genetic Factors in Causation

by JOHN MELNYK, Ph.D. and
RICHARD KOCH, M.D.

The relative importance of the roles of genetic and environmental factors in the development of mentally retarded children has been in some dispute for years. During the period of time when intelligence was thought of as a fixed, inherent quality of the human organism, genetic factors were considered all important. The lack of knowledge concerning the importance of environmental variables on intelligence increased the effort to apply genetic concepts in the care of the mentally retarded. In fact, for several decades sterilization was practiced widely in institutions for the retarded in certain states. Finally, however, the medical community recognized the likelihood that intellectual ability is a product of the interaction between environmental and genetic components; such important programs as Head Start developed from this newer understanding. The recent developments in cytogenetics (3:6-7, 20) and inborn errors of metabolism (2:4) have re-emphasized the importance of genetics. Although we are more aware of an increasing variety of specific genetic diseases, the exact contribution of the environmental and genetic factors is still in dispute.

Genetic processes are not capricious or accidental. They are the result of complicated sets of instructions for the manufacture of the myriad of enzymes and other proteins that constitute the basis of life. The sets of instructions can duplicate and distribute themselves during mitosis so that each cell of the body has the same set of directions. During mitosis the sets can also sort out their components in the repro-

49

ductive cells that unite with similar cells produced by individuals of the opposite sex, resulting in the production of a new individual. Thus, each human cell contains sets of instructions derived equally from both contributing parents and representing unique combinations of various genes. The science of genetics is the study of the function of these genes and the manner in which they pass from one generation to the next by reproduction.

Genes reproduce themselves generation after generation; therefore, the daughter cells carry the same instructions as were present in their progenitors. Occasionally, errors do occur in the reproduction of genes. These errors may result either in the failure of production of some enzymes or in the formation of an enzyme or protein somewhat different from the usual or original one. The errors (which are as heritable as were the original instructions) are called *mutations*. The individuals with characteristics somewhat different from the usual types because of these mutations are called *mutants*. When mutation produces an enzyme similar to the original gene's product, the effect may not be noticeable. Occasionally, the new product is better than the old. But sometimes the result of a mutation is a protein so incompatible with the whole system that the organism is unable to live; such mutations are called *lethal*. In between the extremes there are mutations that seriously disturb normal development of functioning of the individual and are thus deleterious but do not result in death. Phenylketonuria is an example of a non-lethal, yet serious, consequence of a mutation. Genes and their mutations which affect the central nervous system either directly or indirectly may result in mental retardation. These genes fall into two ill-defined classes. In one category are the numerous common genes and their mutations with small individual effects whose cumulative consequences combine later with environmental variables to produce the normal range of intelligence from retarded to gifted. These genes distribute themselves in families in such a way that the children tend to have levels of intelligence near or between those of the parents. Sometimes extreme variants may result from unusual chance combinations. Other mutations so seriously interfere with some essential metabolic process as to result by themselves in a severe mental defect, even when all the other genes present might lead to normal or even superior intelligence.

The distribution of genes from one cell to another is accurate and relatively simple, resulting partially from the fact that the genes are located on microscopic intra-cellular (nuclear) bodies called chromosomes. In most higher organisms, such as vertebrates, the chromosomes present in each body cell consist of two sets: one derived from the sperm of the male and the other from the egg of the female, united at conception. Each set (haploid) of chromosomes, whether from male or female, is like every other set found in the particular species. Each chromosome within one set is, with a fair degree of accuracy, distinguishable from each of the other chromosomes by its total length and the possession of certain markers. Each contains its own special group of genes. The number of chromosomes in each species is characteristic of that species. When two haploid sets are united by fertilization, the diploid set of chromosomes now consists of pairs of chromosomes, and each gene is present in two "doses"—one on each member of its particular pair of chromosomes.

The cells in man contain a haploid set of 23 chromosomes and a diploid set of 46. Twenty-two of these pairs of chromosomes (called autosomes) are not concerned with the determination of sex; the members of each pair are (normally) alike in gene constitution, size and shape. The twenty-third pair is comprised of chromosomes that are important in determining the sex of the individual. In females, these two chromosomes are similar and are of medium size. They are called X-chromosomes. In males, the sex determining pair consists of one X-chromosome and one small chromosome called the Y-chromosome. Males produce two kinds of sperm cells: half with one each of the 22 autosomal pairs plus an X, and half with one each of the other 22 autosomes plus a Y. All ova contain one X-chromosome along with one of the members of each of the 22 pairs of autosomes. It is the fertilization of X-bearing eggs by X-bearing sperm that results in daughters and by Y-bearing sperm that results in sons.

Under usual circumstances there are no difficulties in the distribution and inheritance of the chromosomes and the genes they carry. Sometimes, however, errors occur in cell division processes that result in chromosomal aberrations. Some of these aberrations consist of changes in the number of chromosomes from the normal. Some individuals' cells might have fewer than the usual number of chromosomes, and others one or more extra. These are usually called aneuploid changes. Other aberrations consist of the loss of a part of a chromosome (deletion), the presence of a part of a chromosome in excess of its usual quantity (duplication) or the exchange of parts of chromosomes that belong to different pairs (translocation). Occasionally the results may be very complex. In general, the loss of any considerable quantity of chromosomal material (deletion) has a lethal effect; and the addition of any detectable quantity usually has a deleterious, if not lethal, effect that may include mental retardation.

SIMPLE GENE EFFECTS

Mutation in a gene produces a form of that gene which results in the production of a modified enzyme (or other protein) that in turn may affect cellular metabolism. Each gene at the same locus in different individuals may exist in different forms which are called alleles. Since (for autosomal genes) an individual normally has two "doses" of each gene, it is evident that they may both be of the same allele (homozygous) or of different alleles (heterozygous). In the heterozygote, we can distinguish three modes of gene interaction. If the normal gene is expressed in this state (that is, it is revealed in the physical or chemical characteristics of the individual) while the mutant is hidden or without visible effect, we call the mutant recessive (and the normal allele dominant). On the other hand, the mutant might be expressed in the heterozygous state and the normal not expressed; in this case the mutant would be called dominant. In some cases the heterozygous state is characterized by some intermediate effect. This is variously known as lack of dominance, co-dominance, incomplete dominance, or incomplete recessivity. A recessive allele is expressed when it is homozygous (present in two doses). Usually, the heterozygous state (carrier) cannot be detected clinically but in some diseases such as galactosemia, the carrier can be identified by special enzyme studies.

The most common examples of single gene mutants leading to mental retardation are recessively inherited.

Since recessive inheritance requires that the allele in question be present in the homozygous state in order to be expressed, and since an individual inherits one dose of each gene from each parent, it is clear that both must be carriers of the recessive allele in order to produce a defective offspring. Usually the parents are heterozygous for the gene and are not affected. When each parent carries one recessive and one dominant allele, the chance of producing an affected child with each pregnancy is one in four. Well-known examples of recessively inherited

TABLE 1

PARTIAL LIST OF DISEASES DUE TO ENZYME DEFECTS

Disease	Enzyme	Source of Enzyme
Acatalasia	Catalase	Blood, liver, muscle, bone marrow
Adrenal hyperplasia	1. 21-Hydroxylase	Adrenal
	2. 11-Hydroxylase	Adrenal
	3. 3β-Hydroxy steroid dehydrogenase	Adrenal
Albinism	Tyrosinase	Skin
Alkaptonuria	Homogentisic oxidase	Liver, kidney
Argininosuccinic aciduria	Argininosuccinase	Liver
Congenital nonsphero-cytic hemolytic anemia	1. Glucose-6-phosphate dehydrogenase	Erythrocytes
	2. Pyruvate kinase	Erythrocytes
	3. Glutathione reductase	Erythrocytes
	4. Triosephosphate isomerase	Erythrocytes
	5. 2,3-diphosphoglycerate mutase	Erythrocytes
Crigler-Najjar syndrome	Glucuronyl transferase	Liver
Familial nonhemolytic jaundice	Glucuronyl transferase	Liver
Familial cretinism with goiter	Iodotyrosine deiodinase	Thyroid
Galactosemia	Gal-1-P-uridyl transferase	Erythrocytes
Glucose-6-phosphate dehydrogenase deficiency	Glucose-6-phosphate dehydrogenase	Erythrocytes
Glycogen storage diseases:		
Type I (von Gierke's)	Glucose-6-phosphatase	Liver
Type II (Pompe's')	a (1→4)-glucosidase	Erythrocytes
Type III (debrancher deficiency)	Amylo-1,6-glucosidase	Liver, leukocytes
	Amylo- (1,4→1,6)-transgluco-sidase	Liver
Type IV		
Type V	Myophosphorylase	Muscle
Type VI	Hepatophosphorylase	Liver, leukocytes
Type VII	Glycogen synthetase	Liver
Hereditary disaccharide intolerance	Invertase Maltase, Isomaltase	Intestine

TABLE 1 *(continued)*

Disease	Enzyme	Source of Enzyme
Hereditary fructose intolerance	Aldolase	Liver
Hereditary methemo- globinemia	NADH diaphorase	Erythrocytes
Histidinemia	Histidase	Skin
Homocystinuria	Cystathionine synthetase	Liver
Hypophosphatasia	Alkaline phosphatase	Serum, leukocytes, renal tubules
Lactose intolerance	Lactase	Intestine
Maple syrup urine disease	Decarboxylase for a-keto acids from leucine, isoleucine, and valine	Leukocytes, skin
Oroticaciduria	Orotidylic pyrophosphorylase Orotidylic decarboxylase	Saliva Erythrocytes
Phenylketonuria	Phenylalanine hydroxylase	Liver
6-Phosphogluconic dehydrogenase deficiency	6-Phosphogluconic dehydrogenase	Erythrocytes
Tyrosinosis	p-hydroxyphenylpyruvate oxidase	Liver

defects are galactosemia (5) and phenylketonuria (9). Recessive alleles in phenylketonuria result in a failure of transformation of the amino acid, phenylalanine, into another, tyrosine. As a consequence of this failure, phenylalanine accumulates in the body and is transformed by other pathways into products that have deleterious effects on the development of the central nervous system. The result is usually severe mental retardation. Fortunately, this entity can be recognized soon after birth. By removing nearly all the phenylalanine from the diet of the affected child, the deleterious effects of this disease can be minimized significantly with early diagnosis and treatment (2).

Phenylketonuria (PKU) occurs at a frequency of about one in every 10,000 to 15,000 live births. The rarity of PKU results in part from the fact that defective individuals do not ordinarily reproduce (at least to the present time), so that the genes they carry are effectively lost from the population. On the other hand, statistical considerations indicate that ten to twelve persons in every thousand are carriers of this allele. Phenylketonuria would ultimately be eliminated from the population if defective genes producing the disorder were not being replaced by new mutations. These new mutations are usually carried along in the heterozygous state until one carrier chances to mate with another. Once a phenylketonuric child is born to a couple, it is clear that both pareners are heterozygotes (carriers), and the risk of bearing additional phenyl-ketonuric children is one chance in four for each successive pregnancy.

As is commonly the case in recessive inheritance, the parents of phenylketonuric children are more frequently consanguinous than would be expected by chance. For persons not related by blood, the probability that two carriers will mate by chance alone is approximately 15 in 100,000. This risk is not great but it is obvious that such matings do occur among the many millions in our society. For relatives, however, the risks of mating are greater. If one of their common grandparents had been a carrier of the recessive allele for phenylketonuria, the chance that two first-cousins will both carry the defective allele is one in 16. If the gene was present but undetected in a family, the chance that first-cousins on mating would have an affected child is one in 64. Considering the probability that the gene might be present in the family, the risk that first cousin matings will produce a phenylketonuric child is about five times greater than it is for matings between unrelated persons.

With early diagnosis and treatment, we are now able to minimize the damaging effects of the homozygous condition in phenylketonuria. Therefore, persons who formerly would never have reproduced might now be expected to do so. If they marry unrelated individuals homozygous for the normal allele, every one of their children will be carriers of the defect but none could be phenylketonuric. If, by chance, their mates should be carriers, half of the children would be affected; of course, if they were to marry another PKU person, then all children would be affected. It is possible to identify carriers in certain recessive conditions, such as galactosemia, with some confidence through bio-chemical techniques; this is still not possible with phenylketonuria. Tay Sachs Disease (1) and Hurler's Disease (gargoylism) (10) are examples of two metabolic diseases for which no therapy is yet available.

The other mode of inheritance of mental defect is X-linked (Fig. 1). In this case, the genes concerned are on the X-chromosome, rather than on one of the autosomes. Since females carry two X-chromosomes, they may be heterozygous or homozygous for any given trait. Males on the other hand have only one X-Chromosome and thus may be called hemizygous. Whereas in females a defective allele on the X-chromosome may behave in a recessive fashion there is no compensating normal gene in the male because only one X-chromosome is present. The short

FIGURE 1

- SCHEMATIC PRESENTATION OF A SEX LINKED PATTERN OF INHERITANCE

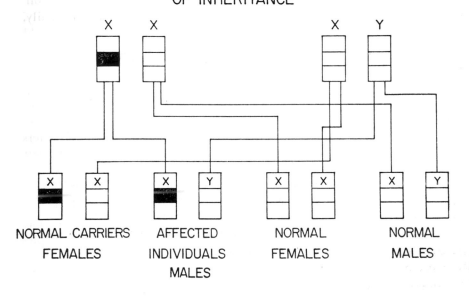

Y-chromosome is paired with the X-chromosome in males. In this combination, recessive genes on the X-chromosome have no dominant counterparts to mask their effects. For this reason we observe more defective males than females when a gene is X-linked. Oculo-cerebro-renal syndrome is an example of an X-linked disease causing mental deficiency associated with defects of the brain, eye, muscles, skeletal system, genitalia, and kidneys (12). The probability is that half of the offspring of carrier mothers will be affected and half will be completely normal (See Diagram below). Half of the daughters of such carrier mothers are themselves expected to be carriers and half normal. A defective female can be produced only if a carrier mother mates with an affected male. In this syndrome, affected males are incapable of reproduction, so no affected females are expected. The same is true for kinky hair syndrome (13). On the other hand, it is not unusual to find females with benign recessive conditions, such as red-green color blindness.

TABLE 2

Inherited Metabolic Disorders that Have Been Diagnosed Prenatally

Adrenogenital syndrome
Cystic fibrosis
Fabry's disease
Galactosemia
Lysosomal acid phosphatase deficiency
Marfan's syndrome
Metachromatic leucodystrophy
Methylmalonic aciduria
Mucopolysaccharidosis
Niemann-Pick disease
Pompe's disease
Tay-Sachs disease
X-linked uric aciduria

Mental defects may aslo be produced by mutations that are dominant. If the defect is so severe as to prevent reproduction of carriers, then the defect can be expressed only as a result of a new mutation in a subsequent generation. If the inherited condition permits reproduction, about half the children of an affected individual will usually exhibit the same defect.

ANTENATAL DIAGNOSIS OF GENETIC DEFECTS

In 1953 Bevis (4) reported studies on the content of bile pigments in the fluid cases of erythroblastosis fetalis due to Rh-isoimmunization of the mother. Subsequently Riis and Fuchs (19) studied the sex-chromatin of fetal cells and were able to prevent some hereditary diseases which were known to be X-linked. In 1966 Steele and Breg (21) reported successful karyotype analysis from amniotic specimens. These pioneering studies formed the basis for development of one of the most powerful tools in reducing the incidence of mental retardation in the newborn population. The use of cultured amniotic fluid cells for either biochemical or cytogenetic testing has become an established diagnostic procedure (14). Large scale screening projects have been initiated in several states and in two, Tennessee and Nebraska, an effort to reduce the number of births with Down's syndrome through an offer of free amniocentesis and cell culture for women over 35 years is underway (18). Various aspects of prenatal testing including scientific and ethical concerns have been discussed thoroughly (23).

Some of the conditions that can be detected in utero are listed in Table 2. This is only a partial listing as new laboratory techniques of characterizing enzymes are adding to the list rapidly.

CHROMOSOME EFFECTS

It was only in 1956 that we learned that the chromosome number in man (long thought to be 48) is, in fact, 46. This was reported first by Tjio and Levan in cells of a normal child (22). These cells were cultured in artificial media according to new techniques. The normal chromosome complement in man is usually described by international agreement according to the "Denver System," developed by leading workers in the field. In this system, the individual chromosomes are identified by their total length, relative to the others in a particular cell being studied, and by the position of a constriction or point of junction of the two halves of a chromosome, called the centromere. Following these criteria, the 23 pairs are easily separated into seven groups. The identification of the individual members within each group is reliably accomplished. The seven groups are arranged in order of decreasing length and are identified briefly as follows:

GROUP A: Contains the longest three pairs, numbered 1, 2, and 3, and are metacentric (the centromere constriction is near the middle of the chromosome). These are readily identified.

GROUP B: Consists of two pairs, numbered 4 and 5, of submetacentrics (centromeres are somewhat higher than the middle). The chromosomes are shorter than those in Group A.

GROUP C: Includes seven pairs of still shorter submetacentric chromosomes, numbered 6 to 12, including the X-chromosomes. In females this group consists of 16 chromosomes (2 X-chromosomes) but in males only 15 (one X-chromosome).

GROUP D: Has three somewhat shorter acrocentric chromosomes (13-15) with almost terminal centromeres.

GROUP E: Consists of three pairs of shorter submetacentrics (16-18). These three pairs can be distinguished from each other by the position of the centromere.

GROUP F: Includes two pairs of small metacentric chromosomes (19 and 20).

GROUP G: Includes two pairs of small acrocentric chromosomes (21 and 22) as well as the Y-chromosomes. In females this group has four chromosomes and in males five, due to the presence of the Y chromosome.

The simplest kinds of genetic aberrations result from variations in the number of chromosomes present. In 1959, LeJeune demonstrated that Down's Syndrome (mongolism) results from the presence in triplicate of one of the G chromosomes (11). Trisomy, as this condition is termed, is the most commonly described aberration occurring among the autosomes, and is a consequence of an error in cell division called non-disjunction. In this anomaly, three of one type of chromosome are found rather than the usual two; thus the total number in each cell is 47. Numerous studies have since shown that several other syndromes, most of which are more severe in their effects than Down's Syndrome, also result from the duplication of particular chromosomes or from other cytogenetic aberrations.

In cell division that produces the sex cells (meiosis) the members of each pair of chromosomes called homologs first locate each other and become very closely associated. In a later stage in the division the homologs separate (disjoint) from each other and migrate to opposite sides of the cell. This results in the production of sex cells that have one member of each pair of chromosomes and half the total number that is found in the normal somatic cell. On occasion one pair of chromosomes fails to disjoin, producing one daughter cell that has both members of that pair and another daughter cell that has neither member of the pair. When such cells are fertilized the results are: 1) trisomic cells with one extra chromosome, and 2) monosomic cells with one less. This latter type is usually lethal. Further details regarding meiotic and mitotic non-disjunction are presented in the chapter on Down's Syndrome.

Three kinds of autosomal trisomics are found rather commonly in man. One of these involves the presence in triplicate of a member of chromosome Group D, often called trisomy 13-15; another is a trisomic for a member of Group E (chromosome 18), and the third variety involves a trisomic for a member of Group G, usually called trisomy 21 (Down's Syndrome). Each of these trisomics is associated with a rather specific and complex syndrome of physical abnormalities. They are now well known and can be identified clinically. Patients with trisomics are usually severely retarded. The least severely affected of the trisomics is Down's Syndrome. Perhaps the latter individuals survive because chromosome number 21 is small and thus contains fewer genes. It is postulated that trisomics for the other autosomes occur but it seems likely that they are so defective that they do not survive.

While it is usual to consider trisomy as the result of non-disjunction in meiosis, it is also possible for it to occur in mitosis, the division process by which somatic cells are produced. In this case, both the chromatids of a dividing chromosome would go to one of the daughter cells, rendering it trisomic, and neither to the other daughter cell, leaving it monosomic. The monosomic cell is probably not viable. This produces a mosaic pattern whereby individuals display varying proportion of normal and trisomic cells, depending on how soon the abnormal cell division occurred following fertilization. Experience suggests that Down's Syndrome mosaics are less affected mentally and physically than those with classical trisomy 21.

The best known and most common chromosome abnormalities are those associated with sex chromosomes. It is thought that every cell must have at least one X-chromosome to survive, but cells tolerate the absence of or the addition of an extra sex chromosome better than they do an autosome. That is to say, these individuals are less abnormal than those with trisomy 21. X-chromosomes in excess of one in a cell are condensed and are inactive, so that one functional X-chromosome is normal for all cells (Lyon Hypothesis). The additional X's appear in many cells as deeply staining chromatin masses called Barr Bodies, or sex chromatin bodies, and the numbers of these are useful in diagnosing some of the numerical anomalies of the X-chromosomes. However, it is too simple to state that the additional X-chromosomes are totally inactive since abnormal distributions are associated with definite clinical manifestations including mental deficiency.

A sex chromosome abnormality characterized by a single X-chromosome (XO) is associated with female gonadal dysgenesis (Turner's Syndrome). Those with the constitution XXY are usually associated with seminiferous tubuler dysgenesis (Kleinfelter's Syndrome). Both types are sterile and there may be some degree of mental retardation present. Other known types occur more rarely, such as, XXX, XYY, XXXY, XXYY, XXXYY, etc. Many mosaics have also been found with combinations of cell lines as XO/XY, XO/XYY, and XO/XX/XXX.

Other chromosomal anomalies are the result of structural changes in single chromosomes. The loss of a portion of a chromosome leaves the individual effectively deficient for those genes (deletions). If the deleted part is large the loss of genes is likely to prove lethal; however, small deficiencies are tolerated and this fact is well documented. In one case, the loss of part of a Group B chromosome (number 5) is associated with the syndrome called "cri du chat," in which the affected individuals have a peculiar appearance, cry like a cat and are severely retarded. Another deficient chromosome, possibly part of number 21 in the G Group, is called the "Philadelphia Ph' Chromosome" and is frequently identified in a chronic myelogenous leukemia.

Still another kind of structural chromosomal anomaly is called a translocation, in which parts of non-homologous chromosomes are exchanged. One of the results of such an event is a reduction in fertility associated with the way in which the chromosomes pair and disjoin in meiosis. The translocation itself is not associated with physical or mental aberrations because there is no loss of genetic material. It is merely rearranged. On the other hand, the abnormal divisions may result in gametes lacking or carrying extra amounts of certain genes and may result in abnormal offspring (see chapter 9 on Down's Syndrome).

HEREDITY AND ENVIRONMENT

There is general agreement that certain types of mental retardation have a genetic origin, although the number of genes involved or the mode of transmission is not fully known. Most workers feel that the majority of such individuals are but mildly affected. At the other extreme, however, are the families in which one or more children are severely retarded. In the latter case, the inheritance pattern may be due to specific gene inheritance. The problem involves the interlocking influences of heredity and environment. Intelligence seems likely to be the result of multiple gene inheritance interacting with environment.

The difficulties which have faced the geneticist in his search for scientific answers in the area of mental retardation are well known to those who have worked in this field, but should be discussed at this point. At the present time, one must conclude that the interpretations drawn from much of the work done in previous years are unacceptable in view of modern knowledge. Mental retardation is a symptom of more than 100 different disease processes, only a few of which would lend themselves to analyses by such genetic methods as additive gene hypothesis and other approaches. Unfortunately, most of the studies reported in the literature reflect this methodological difficulty. This does not mean that all previous studies of this kind are invalid, of course, but it does mean we must temper the application of our conclusions to social action. As was stated earlier, the eugenicists led a strong movement in the early 20th Century to sterilize retarded persons in the United States, "for the benefit of society." This laid the groundwork, unwittingly, for public acceptance of the right of society to impose its will on an individual's right to procreate. This acceptance by society reached its zenith in Nazi Germany with extinction of millions of Jewish people.

It could be hypothesized that, at the time of conception, most fertilized ova have the potential for producing an individual with superior intelligence just as they have the potential for producing a child with two hands, two eyes, etc. If this were true, then society should seek to provide the best of every requirement for the expectant mother in the way of nutrition, obstetrical facilities, etc., in order to enable each product of conception to achieve its maximum potential.

At the present time, the two most useful predictors of intelligence in infants are the social status of their parents and the average of the parents' I.Q.'s (6). Neither index is perfectly valid, but they do provide some indication of what the child's intelligence will be. Another rough index can be derived from the anticipated regression of intelligence toward the population mean (15, 16). That is, the children of superiorly endowed parents are more likely to have intelligence quotients closer to the population mean than their parents. On the other hand, the intelligence of children of dull or feebleminded parents will frequently move higher toward the population mean of I.Q. 100. There are frequent exceptions to this principle, obviously, else all I.Q.'s would soon cluster around a mean of 100.

In summary, the familiar discussion of the importance of heredity and environment in procreation is far from settled (16, 17). The reader is reminded that this subject was reviewed in greater detail in the previous chapter by Dobson, titled "The Origins of Intelligence." Suffice to say that a middle ground is comfortable for most investigators. Since we can apparently influence environment more easily than heredity, we should concentrate our efforts to improve this aspect of the problem as much as possible.

BIBLIOGRAPHY

1. Abt, I. A., "Amaurotic Family Idiocy," *Amer. J. Dis. Child.*, 1:59, 1911.
2. Anderson, J. A., and K. F. Swaiman (Ed.), *Phenylketonuria and Allied Metabolic Diseases*, Washington, D.C.: U.S. Government Printing Office, 1966.
3. Bartalos, M., and T. A. Baramki, *Medical Cytogenetics*, Baltimore, Maryland: Williams and Wilkins, 1966.
4. Bevis, D. C. A., "Composition of Liquor Amnii in Hemolytic Disease of Newborns." *J. Obstet. Gynaec. Brit. Comm.*, 60:244, 1953.
5. Donnell, G. N., W. R. Bergren, and R. S. Cleland, "Galactosemia," *Pediatric Clinics of North America*, 7:315, 1960.
6. Doll, E. A., "The Inheritance of Social Competence." *J. Heredity*, 28:153, 1937.
7. Hamerton, J. L., *Chromosomes in Medicine*, London: William Heineman Medical Books, 1965.
8. Knudson, A., *Genetics and Disease*, New York: McGraw-Hill Book Co., 1965.
9. Kretchmer, N., and D. D. Etzwiler, "Disorders Associated with the Metabolism of Phenylalanine and Tyrosine." *Pediatrics*, 21:445, 1958.
10. Lahey, M. E., R. D. Lomas, and T. C. Worth, "Gargoylism." *J. Pediatr.*, 31:220, 1947.
11. Lejeune, J., M. Gautier, and R. Turpin, "Etudes des chromosomes somatiques de neuf enfants mongoliens." *Compt. Rend.*, 284-1721, 1959.
12. Lowe, C. H., M. Terrey, and E. A. MacLachlan, "Organic Aciduria, Decreased Renal Ammonia Production, Hydrophthalmus and Mental Retardation." *A.M.A.J. Dis. Child.*, 83:164, 1952.
13. Menkes, J. H., M. Alter, G. K. Steigleder, D. R. Weakley, and J. H. Sung, "A Sex-linked Recessive Disorder with Retardation of Growth, Peculiar Hair, and Focal Cerebral and Cerebellar Degeneration." *Pediatrics*, 29:764, 1962.
14. Nadler, H. L., and C. A. Ryan, "Amniotic Cell Culture. In *Human Chromosome Methodology*, 2nd Ed., J. J. Yunis (Ed.), New York: Acad. Press Inc., 1974, 375 pp.
15. Penrose, L. S., *The Biology of Mental Defect*, New York: Grune and Stratton, InIc. 1963.

16. Pevsner, M. S., *Oligophrenia, Mental Deficiency in Children,* New York: Consultants Bureau, 1961.
17. Reed, E. W., and S. C. Reed, *Mental Retardation: A Family Study,* Philadelphia: W. B. Saunders, Co., 1965.
18. Reilly, P., "Current State-supported Neonatal Screening Programs." *Am. J. Hum. Genet.,* 27;5:691-692, 1975.
19. Riis, P., and F. Fuchs, "Antenatal Determination of Faetal Sex in Prevention of Hereditary Disease." Lancet, 2:180, 1960.
20. Stearn, D., *Principles of Human Genetics,* 2nd Ed., San Francisco: Witt, Freeman and Co., 1960.
21. Steele, M. W., and W. R. Breg, "Chromosome Analyses of Human Amniotic Fluid Cells." *Lancet,* 1:383, 1966.
22. Tjio, J. H., and A. Levan, "The Chromosome Number of Man." *Hereditas,* 42:1, 1956.
23. Harris, Maureen (Ed.), "Early Diagnosis of Human Genetic Defects." *Fogarty International Center Proceedings,* No. 6, Bethesda, Maryland: National Institutes of Health, 1970.

CHAPTER 4

Prenatal Factors in Causation (General)

by RICHARD KOCH, M.D.

Contrary to what would be expected, little is known about the prenatal influences that precipitate mental retardation in a developing embryo (3:11). The study of human reproduction has lagged far behind other areas of medical research, possibly resulting from cultural and religious biases. This resistance is reflected in the fact that one of the last divisions of the National Institute of Health to be organized in 1963 was that of Child Health and Human Development. The establishment of this Institute has already stimulated a great deal of research in this vital area of concern. The current understanding of the non-viral prenatal influences on mental retardation is presented in this chapter. The effects of maternal rubella, cytomegalovirus and other viral diseases will be discussed in a subsequent chapter.

SOURCES OF PRENATAL DAMAGE

As early as the eighteenth day of pregnancy, the cells of the embryo are being arranged in three germinal layers, called ectoderm, mesoderm and endoderm. The new organism is highly vulnerable to adverse conditions during this early stage of development; infection, maternal malnutrition or illness, maternal drug ingestion, radiation, trauma, and anoxia can each be devastating to the embryo. Later in pregnancy, it can also be damaged by premature delivery, toxemia of pregnancy or blood incompatibility. It has been suggested that maternal emotional instability can interfere with embryonic or fetal development, although evidence in support of this position is scanty. In essence, any factor causing maternal ill health may adversely affect the unborn child; the most common prenatal influences which are linked to mental retardation are discussed below.

65

Maternal Infection

Historically, our information concerning the role of maternal infection is better known than any other factors affecting the fetus. Before the advent of antibiotics, syphilis was a common form of congenital disease, causing prematurity, keratitis, rhagades, snuffles, mental defect and bony changes (2). The mental defect results from spirochetal invasion of the nervous system. Fortunately, with compulsory premarital and prenatal tests for syphilis, and adequate penicillin therapy, this form of mental defect is rare today. Toxoplasmosis, a protozoan disease, is usually undiagnosed in the general population; yet nearly one-third of the population carries antibodies to this organism. When a mother contracts the disease early in pregnancy, congenital anomalies involving the central nervous system may occur in her developing embryo. The manner of infection is not definitely known, but raw meat (mutton) is known to be a vector. Presumably, there are other important avenues of spreading toxoplasmosis, as demonstrated by its widespread dissemination around of the world. An infant infected by toxoplasma may exhibit serious anomalies of the choroid and central nervous system. Skull roentgenogram may reveal intracranial calcification. Mental defect and convulsions usually occur (7). Unfortunately, there is no therapy of proven value as yet. This condition may account for one-half percent of the mentally retarded. The clinical diagnosis can be confirmed by antibody studies on the mother and a positive skin test on the affected child. See Chapter 5 on viral disease for further details.

Hormonal Imbalance

The role of maternal hormonal imbalance is still somewhat unclear, but may be significant. The lack of iodine in the diet in some parts of the world still causes maternal goiters, which in turn may be associated with endemic cretinism in the offspring. The serious mental and physical retardation in such infants is due to an inability of the thyroid gland to produce thyroxine. Serious diseases associated with hormonal dysfunction are usually associated with sterility; however, with improved medical technology, it must be anticipated that such women will conceive and deliver viable infants. The experience with diabetes mellitus suggests that increased fetal and neonatal mortality and morbidity will occur in such cases.

Chronic Maternal Illness

Any chronic maternal illness, such as hypertension, renal disease, diabetes, etc., increases the risk to the unborn child. One such example is maternal phenylketonuria (10). In this disease, the serum phenylalanine is elevated in the mother, causing *in utero* damage to the infant's developing brain. In the same manner, it could be postulated that the fetus of a galactosemic mother might sustain brain damage if the mother did not observe dietary restriction of galactose during her pregnancy. To date, this situation has not been described (5). Mental retardation has been seen in children of mothers who develop and were not treated for pernicious anemia during pregnancy. It is possible that a deficiency of vitamin B-12 *in utero* is damaging to the central nervous system. Studies in experimental animals have shown increased occurrences of anomalies with various maternal vitamin deficiencies (12). The evidence that maternal malnutrition causes mental defect in offspring is suggestive (1).

Drug Ingestion

Various kinds of drug ingestion have been shown to cause a variety of malformations. Damage from the drug, Thalidomide, is the most recent example of the danger of maternal ingestion of drugs during pregnancy. Thalidomide taken during the first trimester causes limb malformations of severe degree. Various antimetabolic drugs, such as folic acid antagonist, mercaptopurine, etc., induce miscarriage. Antidiabetic drugs may be dangerous. In experimental animals, cortisone has been shown to increase the rate of congenital defects. Excessive maternal cigarette smoking has been associated with an increased rate of prematurity (11). Quinine taken to induce abortion may cause deafness in the newborn in unsuccessful attempts. Chronic alcoholism is now known to be an adverse factor as well.

Radiation

Radiation of the fetus when less than three months of age is harmful. This was discovered in the 1930's when irradiation of cancer of the uterus in pregnant mothers caused microcephaly and other anomalies in their offspring. Dilatation and curettage of the womb is now performed prior to initiation of radiation therapy for cancer of the uterus. Other evidence supporting the conclusion that radiation exposure of the pregnant mother is harmful was obtained in studies of Japanese mothers who survived the atomic bombings of Hiroshima and Nagasaki. A high incidence of microcephaly was observed in the offspring of women who were in the early period of pregnancy and located close to the bomb's epicenter. Similar evidence has been gathered by study of experimental animals exposed to radiation during pregnancy and examination of their offspring.

Maternal Anoxia

Maternal anoxia resulting from near drowning, accidental suffocation, or carbon monoxide poisoning can affect the unborn child. It is of historical importance that Julius Caesar was born by caesarean section as his mother lay dying. While history shows that he was a man of many unusual abilities, he did suffer from a convulsive disorder, perhaps caused by neonatal anoxia occurring in conjunction with his mother's death.

Maternal Trauma

The evidence that maternal trauma can cause damage to the unborn baby is unclear, but logic dictates that it is a reasonable assumption that trauma of any kind to the abdomen might cause premature separation of the placenta and thus secondary anoxia and premature delivery. Attempted abortion by introduction of foreign objects into the uterus can, of course, cause injury to the fetus.

Emotional Stress

The role of emotional stress during pregnancy is unclear, but again it is reasonable to assume that any severe stress, whether mental or physical, can affect the unborn child. It is difficult to gather scientific data on this problem. Suffice to say that the healthier the pregnancy from all aspects, the better the chance there is for the newborn baby to be normal (11).

Prematurity

Prematurity is a major contributor to mental retardation (6). This condition alone accounts for 24.5 percent of all neonatal deaths (8). It is associated with 15 to 20 percent of all cases of mental retardation. An infant is classified as premature if his birth weight is less than 2500 grams (5 pounds and 8 ounces). In some South American countries where maternal nutrition is inadequate, this empirical figure is estimated to range between 2200-2300 grams. Mortality and morbidity are directly related to birth weight. Survival chances are excellent for infants weighing more than 2000 grams; the probability of survival drops markedly when the neonate is less than 1000 grams in weight. This relationship of mortality to birth weight is not completely understood. It is thought that the more premature the fetus, the greater the chance the mortality will be related to the immaturity of certain body tissues, such as the lungs, liver, etc. This conclusion is probably accurate, but remembering the unhappy consequences from over-zealous administration of oxygen in the infants with retrolental fibroplasia,* one cannot be sure. It is worth emphasizing again that iatrogenic factors may be playing a role in the high mortality and morbidity in very small babies.

CEREBRAL DAMAGE IN THE PREMATURE INFANT

Several factors account for the high prevalence of cerebral damage in the premature baby, including those discussed below (11):

Fetal Position

Fetal position is important due to the premature infant's small size which predisposes him to abnormal position within the womb. The occurrence of breech, transverse, or other abnormal presentation is higher in the premature. Since increased mortality and morbidity are associated with abnormal presentation, it is understandable that the premature infant is at greater risk (4).

Immaturity of Organs

The immaturity of certain organ systems is an obvious factor in the increased risk of cerebral damage in the premature infant. He is a delicate "unfinished" creature. Neonatal atelectasis** is more common in the premature. The problem of hyaline membrane† disease is peculiarly related to premature birth. Liver immaturity is a serious prob-

---

* Retrolental fibroplasia is a condition wherein the retina of the eye is damaged by administration of excessive oxygen, resulting in visual difficulties.
** Neonatal atelectasis refers to a condition in which the lungs of a newborn fail to expand with inspired air.
† Hyaline membrane disease is a respiratory disorder of the newborn, occurring chiefly in the premature. Etiology is still unclear.

lem. The liver may be unable to handle the many metabolic tasks which it must in order to carry on extrauterine existence. Hyperbilirubinemia is common in the newborn. It is related to deficient transferase activity in the liver which results in the baby being unable to properly metabolize bilirubin, a bile pigment. The retained pigment accumulates in the blood stream causing the infant to become jaundiced (yellow). When the level of bilirubin exceeds 20 mgm. percent, resultant damage may be manifested by deafness, athetosis, and mental retardation. The kidneys are also known to be immature. Accordingly, formulae requiring less renal function are usually prescribed for the premature baby.

Twinning (3)

Twinning often causes prematurity. It is not as yet clear why this is true. The second twin born is at greater risk, resulting from longer labor, premature separation of the placenta, anoxia, and occasionally from the failure of the physician to recognize the twin birth.

Maternal Illness (2)

Premature births are at greater risk because they are more often associated with significant maternal illness, such as Rh incompatibility, toxemia of pregnancy, maternal diabetes, etc. Frequent pregnancy is a contributing factor in some cases.

Maternal Toxemia

Maternal toxemia is a severe condition of pregnancy which can usually be prevented by good prenatal care. The cause of toxemia is as yet unknown. It almost always occurs in the third trimester of pregnancy and manifests itself by hypertension, headache, edema, and albuminuria. If untreated, convulsions, coma, and death may result. It accounts for one-third of maternal deaths! Treatment consists of salt restriction, rest, and sedation. The condition is easily identified by blood pressure determination and frequent urinalysis for albumin. There is some suggestion that infants born of mothers with unrecognized toxemia are at greater risk. This is certainly true in severe cases of convulsion and coma. If toxemia results in premature delivery, then morbidity is also related to the degree of prematurity. A longitudinal study of babies born to toxemic mothers is urgently needed.

INTRAUTERINE GROWTH RETARDATION

Another condition which is poorly understood is intrauterine growth retardation. Some refer to this condition as Warkany's Syndrome, named for the clinician who most forcibly brought this condition to clinical prominence. The placenta is often small and the infant is invariably of low birth weight, despite the normal gestational period. The appearance of affected infants is similar; they have been described as "bird-headed dwarfs." The head is small, the nose prominent, and the lower jaw hypoplastic. Small stature and mental retardation are usually present. As yet, the etiology of the syndrome is unclear.

SUMMARY

In summary, many prenatal factors are of grave importance to the eventual intellectual development of the child. It may be that adverse maternal factors are the most important causes of mental retardation. Many of the related variables have been discussed in this chapter, although one additional matter should be mentioned. There is a curious relationship between maternal age and several types of congenital abnormalities, such as Down's Syndrome. Very young and older mothers run greater risk in both neonatal mortality and morbidity. The significant increase of these problems in the unwed mother also calls for greater study. The author believes that we are just beginning to give the proper degree of attention to this very important period of fetal life (9). It is anticipated that the maternal-infant care projects of the Department of Health, Education and Welfare and the Collaborative Cerebral Palsy Project of the National Institute of Neurological Diseases and Blindness will do much to shed light on this much-neglected period of life.

BIBLIOGRAPHY

1. Antonov, A. N., "Children Born During the Siege of Leningrad in 1942," *J. Pediat.*, 30:250, 1947.
2. Benda, C. E., "Congenital Syphilis in Mental Deficiency," *Amer. J. Ment. Defic.*, 45:42, 1942.
3. Bowman, P. W. and H. V. Mautner, *Mental Retardation: Proceedings of the First International Medical Conference at Portland, Maine,* New York: Grune & Stratton, 1960.
4. Crothers, B. and R. S. Paine, *The Natural History of Cerebral Palsy,* Cambridge, Mass.: Harvard University Press, 1959.
5. Donnell, G. N., M. Collado and R. Koch, "Growth and Development of Children with Galactosemia," *J. Pediat.*, 58:836, 1961.

6. Drillien, C. M., *The Growth and Development of the Prematurely Born Infant,* Baltimore: Williams and Wilkins Co., 1964.
7. Feldman, H. A. and L. T. Miller, "Congenital Human Toxoplasmosis," *Amer. New York Acad. Sc.,* 64:180, 1956.
8. Gold, E. M., "A Broad View of Maternity Care," *Children,* 52, 1962.
9. Lesser, A. J., "Accent on Prevention Through Improved Service," *Children,* 13, 1964.
10. Mabry, C. C., J. C. Denniston and J. G. Caldwell, "Mental Retardation in Children of Phenylketonuric Mothers," *New Eng. J. Med.,* 275:1331, 1966.
11. Montagu, M. F., *Prenatal Influences,* Springfield, Ill.: Charles C Thomas, 1962.
12. Warkany, J., "Etiology of Congenital Malformations," *Ad. Pediat.,* 2:1, 1947.

CHAPTER 5

Prenatal Factors in Causation (Viral)

by HARRY T. WRIGHT, Jr., M.D., M.P.H.

INTRODUCTION

Viral infections during pregnancy may be associated with fetal mortality, intrauterine infections and perinatal disease, or congenital malformations including mental retardation and cerebral palsy (1, 13). The mechanism of pathogenesis for fetal damage due to congenital viral infections, where known, involves direct infection of the fetal tissues.

In many cases, the infection results in no apparent damage to the fetus. It has been suggested that greater susceptibility of embryonic tissue and relative immaturity of immunological responses of the developing fetus may play significant roles in the observed chronicity of some congenital infections (21).

The portals of entry through which viruses gain access to the fetus from the pregnant host are poorly understood; however, they most likely include transplacental spread (viremia) and direct spread of virus from the exterior by the birth canal.

Experiments in which pregnant guinea pigs were inoculated with certain viruses indicate that the placenta usually acts as an effective barrier against viral agents and the transfer of such agents may be due to placental damage (15). Infection of fetuses with viruses, such as herpes simplex, Coxsackieviruses Group B (Cox B), rubella, and cytomegalovirus (CMV), suggests that some viral infections in the mother are capable of crossing the placental barrier. Some infections, such as Coxsackievirus Group B and CMV, cause little or no illness in the maternal host, but do cause severe or fatal disease in the fetus.

It would appear that there are at least three factors involved in whether or not the fetus will be affected by maternal infection. The severity of the infection in the mother (virulence of the infecting organ-

73

ism) probably influences the severity of the infection in the fetus or newborn. The type of maternal infection is another important factor, since certain viral infections seem to cause a more severe problem in the fetus than they do in the mother. Finally, the gestational age at the time of infection is an important factor. In general, the earlier the infection, the more numerous are the defects; the later the infection, the more limited are the defects (13). However, infection with some viruses might create a problem regardless of when the mother becomes infected. Fetal death may be the most frequent result of viral infection and, therefore, only fetuses with relatively avirulent viral infections would be compatible with survival.

Infectious diseases in the mother may be accompanied by a marked febrile response, by profound system toxemia, and by a reduction in the arterial oxygen saturation if pulmonary or cardiac function is compromised. Maternal illness of this sort may result in fetal death or injury even in the absence of overt fetal infection (8).

More than a dozen viral diseases occurring during pregnancy have been tentatively associated with untoward effects on the fetus or newborn. However, only two, rubella and CMV infection, have been associated definitely with an increased risk of anomalies in infants. Other observed anomalies in infants following maternal viral disease could be coincidental occurrences. The observed effects on the fetus following these diseases in the mother are briefly described.

RUBELLA (GERMAN MEASLES)

Gregg in 1941 (7) first reported the relationship between rubella in the pregnant woman and the occurrence of congenital malformations in her offspring. The frequency and type of abnormality in the child differ with the time of the maternal infection. The overall frequency of recognized congenital anomalies approaches 50 percent when rubella occurs in the first month of pregnancy, 22 percent in the second month and 6 percent in the third month (21). If exposure occurs during the second or third trimester, there is much less risk of the rubella syndrome resulting; however, the infant may be infected and shed rubella virus for many months after birth.

In 1962 the cultivation of rubella virus in tissue culture by Weller and Neva (28) and Parkman and associates (19) made it possible for virus isolation and serological studies of patients with typical, atypical and subclinical types of rubella. Studies of the nation-wide epidemic

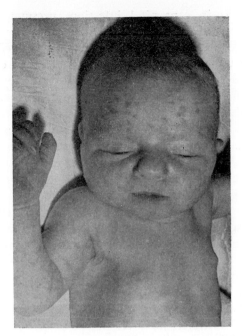

FIG. 1—A six-day-old female infant who had
a cataract and congenital heart disease as
well as the purpuric rash on her face characteristic of the rubella syndrome.

of rubella in 1964 clarified our understanding of the pathogenesis of
congenital rubella.

Clinical manifestations of the expanded rubella syndrome include:
(1) low birth weight, (2) eye lesions, i.e., cataract, glaucoma, retinitis,
(3) deafness, (4) brain lesions associated with microcephaly, meningoencephalitis, hydrocephalus and mental retardation, (5) cardiac defects,
i.e., patent ductus arteriosus, ventricular septal defect, (6) thrombocy-
topenic purpura, (7) hepatosplenomegaly, (8) pneumonitis, (9) jaundice, i.e., hepatitis, and (10) bone lesions. Infants with congenital rubella infection excrete virus from the pharynx and urine for many
months after birth and may spread the disease (19). By one year of
age, fewer than 10 percent of children have detectable virus in the
nasopharynx; however, virus has been recovered from cataract in a
child who underwent surgery at three years of age (16). The prolonged

persistence of virus in congenital infections presumably indicates an impairment of mechanisms concerned with recovery from viral infection.

In 1958, studies by Krugman and Ward (14) showed that neutralizing antibody to the virus of rubella was present in ordinary gamma globulin; they suggested the relative efficacy of these preparations in the prevention of clinical manifestations of the disease. Recent studies have indicated that human gamma globulin may suppress the clinical manifestations of rubella in the mother without preventing the occurrence of viremia. An answer to the important questions—does gamma globulin reduce the risk of the occurrence of congenital malformations, stillbirths, or abortions—must await controlled trials with hyperimmune serum or gamma globulin of known potency (9).

Recently, the significance of the occurrence of elevated IgM antibodies in cord sera or sera from newborn infants has been reported. Such an elevation has been found in the rubella syndrome and cytomegalic inclusion disease as well as in certain non-viral infections (21).

Today, susceptibility to rubella can be determined with considerable accuracy by tests for the presence or absence of neutralizing or hemagglutination inhibiting antibody. In the fetus, infection with rubella virus causes impairment of the development of certain tissues, resulting in growth retardation including microcephaly (21). It would appear that clinical findings, at least partially, are associated with an actual reduction in the number of cells present in affected tissues (17). To speculate, perhaps mental retardation occurs in infants suffering from the rubella syndrome when rubella virus infects cells of the brain, causing cell death and slow cell growth (failure of mitosis), which ultimately results in a small organ (brain) incapable of functioning optimally.

CYTOMEGALIC INCLUSION DISEASE

Cytomegalic inclusion disease has become a more familiar problem within the past decade since exfoliative cytologic studies (inclusion-bearing cells in the urine) and techniques for isolation of the human cytomegalovirus have resulted in the recognition of cases during life. Human cytomegalovirus appears to produce no demonstrable illness in the mother, yet may give rise to severe, frequently fatal disease in the fetus and newborn (26). In retrospect, a stillborn with inclusion-bearing cells in the liver, lung, and kidney, reported by Jesionek in 1904, probably represents the first example of generalized cytomegalic inclusion disease (10).

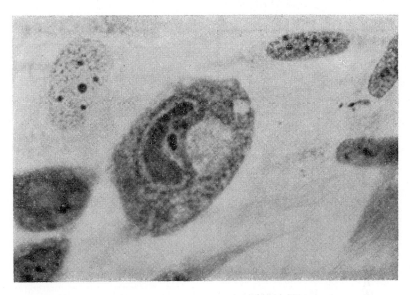

Fig. 2—Tissue culture of human embryo fibroblasts infected with human cytomegalovirus showing a cell with intranuclear and intracytoplasmic lesions. (Reprinted from McAllister, R. M., H. T. Wright, Jr., and W. M. Tasem: "Cytomegalic Inclusion Disease in Newborn Twins," *J. Pediat.* 64: 278-281, 1964.)

The distinctive morphologic feature of sytomegalic inclusion disease is the large inclusion-bearing cell, which may appear in almost any organ. The large intranuclear inclusion is surrounded by a clear halo, which separates it from a distinct nuclear membrane. A cytoplasmic or perinuclear inclusion may be found frequently in infected cells.

In 1953, Fetterman (5) detected the inclusion-bearing cells in urinary sediment, thereby introducing exfoliative cytology as a diagnostic procedure. Finally, in 1956, Smith (23), Rowe (20), and Weller (27) isolated the virus from the urine, salivary gland, adenoids and liver of infected infants, thereby introducing viral isolation techniques for diagnosis.

The clinical manifestations regularly observed in patients with this disease include jaundice, hepatosplenomegaly, petechiae, and microcephaly, as well as radiographic findings of paraventricular intracerebral calcifications and laboratory findings of anemia, hyperbilirubinemia, thrombocytopenia, inclusion-bearing cells in the urine, and the presence of virus in the urine and throat swabbings.

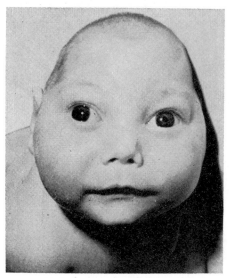

Fig. 3—A 7½-month-old male infant with cytomegalic inclusion disease of infancy showing remarkable microcephaly.

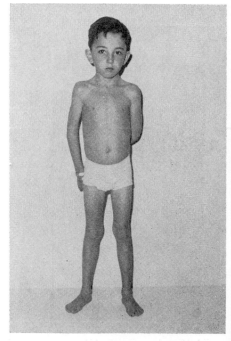

Fig. 4—A 5½-year-old boy who had cytomegalic inclusion disease of infancy with no significant sequelae.

The sequelae of such infections may range from recovery to varying degrees of neurologic involvement, including hydrocephalus, microcephaly, and cerebral calcifications, usually in association with motor impairment and mental retardation (26). The persistence of hepato-splenomegaly and the variety of tissues in which inclusions have been found suggest that the sequelae of this disease may not necessarily be limited to the central nervous system.

A preliminary report of unusual findings in a long-term evaluation of the physical and mental development of patients with cytomegalic inclusion disease of infancy includes: severe retardation, abnormal electro-encephalograms associated with convulsive disorders, eye defects including cataracts, microphthalmia, and chorioretinitis, unusual dermato-glyphics, pneumonitis, and deafness (30).

OTHER VIRAL DISEASES POSSIBLY ASSOCIATED WITH
CONGENITAL ANOMALIES

Herpes Simplex

Infection with herpes simplex virus is extremely common in older children and adults and is usually unapparent or associated with a vesicular infection of the skin or mucous membranes. However, if newborn infants become infected with this agent, a severe disseminated disease characterized by extensive infection of many organs (primarily the liver, lungs, and adrenals) occurs within the first week of life, usually resulting in death (31).

Infants with this disease have fever, profound weakness, skin vesicles, jaundice, hepatosplenomegaly, ulceration of the esophagus, dyspnea, cyanosis and bleeding tendencies associated with intravascular coagulation (22, 31).

Recent studies suggest that two main types of herpes simplex viruses exist: the "nongenital" (type I) has been generally isolated from the upper parts of the body, mucous membranes and central nervous system of older children and adults; and the "genital" (type II) has been most frequently recovered from the genital area and from children with congenital infection (21). Pathologically, affected organs are riddled with pale yellow, firm necrotic nodules measuring a few millimeters in diameter. Characteristic inclusion-bearing cells (Cowdry Type A) may be seen microscopically in the infected organs.

Transmission of infection from the mother to the infant most frequently occurs during passage through the birth canal or by contact after birth; however, transplacental infection is known to occur (31).

The generalized disease in the newborn infant due to herpes simplex virus is so rarely encountered and has such a wide spectrum of clinical manifestations that this diagnosis is usually not considered, even in infants with severe disease. The infants who recover have a poor prognosis. Chorioretinitis and blindness, as well as severe mental and psychomotor retardation, are the rule and not the exception in surviving infants with this disease.

Coxsackievirus Group B Infections

Coxsackieviruses Group B types 1 to 5 have been established as etiologic agents of severe, often fatal, illness in newborn infants in whom there is encephalitis and extensive focal myocarditis (32). The liver, pancreas, adrenals, and other abdominal organs may also be affected. Usually the mother has experienced a pleurodynia-like illness late in pregnancy and this, together with early signs of clinical illness in the infant, suggests intrauterine infection.

The clinical manifestations include a biphasic course, feeding difficulty, respiratory distress, lethargy, cyanosis, hepatomegaly, and jaundice. Collapse and death may occur within a few days, or apparent recovery may occur over the succeeding few weeks. Myocarditis has been the most constant pathologic finding; however, meningoencephalitis and hepatic necrosis are also frequently encountered at the post-mortem examination (6).

Known cases of this disease in newborns may be divided into two groups. Infants may have extremely severe and generalized disease associated primarily with myocarditis, encephalitis, vascular collapse and death, or they may have minor illness, i.e., aseptic meningitis, and recover. The data on long-term follow-up of such patients are scanty, and it is possible that certain cases of chronic myocarditis or mental retardation appearing in later life may represent sequelae of early infection with Group B Coxsackievirus (13).

Rubeola (Regular Measles)

Apparently, the virus of measles can cross the placental barrier at any stage of gestation. There are several well-documented cases in which maternal measles has been followed by the birth of defective children. The observed malformations have included mental retardation as well as congenital heart disease, deafness, cleft lip, talipes equinovarus and genu valgum (18).

Varicella and Herpes Zoster

Although varicella is frequently transferred from a mother with the disease to the fetus *in utero,* no case of congenital anomaly or mental retardation in the infant has been reported. However, maternal infection with herpes zoster virus within the first trimester of pregnancy has been associated with congenital cataracts as well as mental retardation, microphthalmus, and talipes equinovarus (3).

Hepatitis

Stokes and associates (24) were among the first to present evidence that neonatal hepatitis could be associated with transmission of virus across the placenta. In some cases, consideration of the incubation period pointed to intrauterine infection, and in one case, the presence of virus was demonstrated by the inoculation of mother's and infant's blood into human volunteers with resulting disease. The relatively low incidence of infectious hepatitis in pregnancy has made it difficult to obtain accurate data concerning the effect of these agents upon the fetus. In 1951 Kass (11) described a markedly hydrocephalic and microphthalmic infant whose mother suffered from epidemic hepatitis in the second and third months of pregnancy, and Blattner (1) reported on an infant followed by Hellbrügge born to a mother who had hepatitis during her fifth week of pregnancy; the infant showed signs of physical and mental retardation at 3 months of age, as well as eye disease involving the iris, choroid and optic nerve.

In one report, the incidence of infectious hepatitis was found to be closely related to the incidence of births of infants with Down's Syndrome (mongolism) nine months later. Both conditions varied periodically, with a seven-year interval between epidemic peaks (25). A relationship remains to be confirmed.

Influenza

Influenza is often a severe disease in the pregnant woman and the incidence of abortion, stillbirth and premature birth has been considered high during some epidemic periods. Evidence available appears very suggestive, but not conclusive, of an adverse effect of influenzal infection during the first trimester of pregnancy. Kaye and associates

(12) reviewed congenital anomalies over a five-year period in Chicago. Three infants with multiple defects and mental retardation were born to mothers who experienced an illness in their first trimester described as severe influenza, due to "Virus-X," with high fever. A more recent study prompted by the appearance of Asian influenza in California indicates no significant difference with respect to anomalies in infants born to mothers who had been infected during pregnancy when compared with infants born to mothers who were not infected during pregnancy (29). Two infants were anencephalic in the former group, however.

Arthropod-borne Encephalitides

Eichenwald and Shinefield (4) pointed out that of the arthropod-borne (Arboviruses) encephalitides, western equine encephalomyelitis (WEE) and eastern equine encephalomyelitis (EEE) are the only two virus types causing infections of clinical importance during the newborn period in the Northern Hemisphere. Infection with viruses causing St. Louis encephalitis and Japanese B encephalitis is virtually nonexistent during the neonatal period. Newborn infants may be infected by the bite of infected mosquitoes or may acquire WEE by the transplacental transmission of this agent. Many of the manifestations of CNS damage caused by this virus, such as seizures, motor impairment and mental retardation, may not become clinically apparent until some months after the initial infection.

Poliomyelitis

Abortion, stillbirth, premature delivery and congenital infection have been the more common results of poliomyelitis during pregnancy. However, Bowers and Danforth (2) followed the course of 24 full-term infants whose mothers had poliomyelitis during pregnancy, and presented data indicating that these babies showed a significant retardation in general development and birth weight.

SUMMARY

The possible effects of transplacental viral infections are several. Fetal loss may occur by means of abortion or stillbirth. There may be infection of the fetus with clinical manifestations, such as rash, or without clinical manifestations. The infant may be born with congenital defects; these may include such deformities as cataracts, cardiac defects, mental retardation or cerebral palsy.

Although a number of maternal viral diseases have been incriminated in the etiology of congenital defects, only two—rubella and cytomegalovirus infection—are definitely associated with anomalies or retardation in infants.

BIBLIOGRAPHY

1. Blattner, R. J., and F. M. Heys, "Role of Viruses in the Etiology of Congenital Malformations," *Progress in Medical Virology,* Vol. 3, Basel/New York: Karger, 1961.
2. Bowers, V. H., Jr., and D. N. Danforth, "The Significance of Poliomyelitis During Pregnancy," *Am. J. Obst. Gyn.,* 65:34, 1953.
3. Duehr, P. A., "Herpes Zoster as a Cause of Congenital Cataract," *Am. J. Ophthal.,* 39:157, 1955.
4. Eichenwald, H. F., and H. R. Shinefield, "Viral Infections of the Fetus, Premature and Newborn Infant," *Advances in Pediatrics,* 12:249, 1962.
5. Fetterman, G. H., "A New Laboratory Aid in the Clinical Diagnosis of Inclusion Disease of Infancy," *Am. J. Clin. Path.,* 22:424, 1952.
6. Gear, J. H. S., "Coxsackievirus Infections of the Newborn," *Progress in Medical Virology,* Vol. 1, Basel/New York: Karger, 1958.
7. Gregg, N. M., "Congenital Cataract Following German Measles in the Mother," *Tr. Ophth. Soc. Australia,* 3:35, 1941. Quoted by R. J. Blattner in (1).
8. Hardy, J. B., "Viral Infection in Pregnancy: A Review," *Am. J. Obst. Gyn.,* 93: 1052, 1965.
9. Horstmann, D. M., "Rubella and the Rubella Syndrome: Problems and Progress," *Med. Clin. No. Am.,* 51:587, 1967.
10. Jesionek and Kiolemenoglou, "Ubereinen Befund von Protozoenartigen Gebilden in den Organen Eines Feten," *Münch. Med. Wschr.,* 51:1905, 104.
11. Kass, A., "Congenital Hydrocephalus in a Newborn Infant: Epidemic Hepatitis in the Mother in the 2nd and 3rd Month of Pregnancy," *Acta. Paed.,* 40:239, 1951.
12. Kaye, B. M., D. G. Rosner, and I. F. Stein, "Viral Diseases in Pregnancy and Their Effect Upon the Embryo and Fetus," *Am. J. Obst. Gyn.,* 65:109, 1953.
13. Kibrick, S., "Viral Infections of the Fetus and Newborn," in *Perspectives in Virology,* Vol. II, M. Pollard, Ed. Minneapolis: Burgess Publishing Company, 1961.
14. Krugman, S., and R. Ward, "Rubella: Demonstration of Neutralizing Antibody in Gamma Globulin and Re-evaluation of the Rubella Problem," *New Eng. J. Med.,* 259:16, 1958.
15. Markham, F. S., and N. P. Hudson, "Susceptibility of the Guinea Pig Fetus to the Submaxillary Gland Virus of Guinea Pigs," *Am. J. Path.,* 12:175, 1936.
16. Menser, M. A., J. D. Harley, R. Hertzberg, D. C. Dorman, and A. M. Murphy, "Persistence of Virus in Lens for Three Years After Prenatal Rubella," *Lancet,* 2:387, 1967.
17. Naeye, R. L., and W. Blanc, "Pathogenesis of Congenital Rubella," *J.A.M.A.,* 194:1277, 1965.
18. Packer, A. D., "The Influence of Maternal Measles on the Unborn Child," *Med. J. Aust.,* 1:835, 1950.
19. Parkman, P. D., E. L. Buescher, and M. S. Artenstein, "Recovery of Rubella Virus from Army Recruits," *Proc. Soc. Exper. Biol. Med.,* 111:225, 1962.

20. Rowe, W. P., J. W. Hartley, S. Waterman, H. C. Turner, and R. J. Huebner, "Cytopathogenic Agent Resembling Human Salivary Gland Virus Recovered from Tissue Cultures of Human Adenoids," *Proc. Soc. Exper. Biol. Med.*, 92:418, 1956.
21. Sever, J., and L. R. White, "Intrauterine Viral Infections," *Ann. Rev. Med.*, 19:471, 1968.
22. Shershow, L. W., H. Ekert, V. L. Swanson, H. T. Wright, Jr., and G. S. Gilchrist, "Intravascular Coagulation in Generalized Herpes Simplex Infection of the Newborn," *Acta Paed. Scand.*, 58:535, 1969.
23. Smith, M. G., "Propagation in Tissue Cultures of Cytopathogenic Virus from Human Salivary Gland Virus (SGV) Disease," *Proc. Soc. Exper. Biol. Med.*, 92:424, 1956.
24. Stokes, J., Jr., "Viral Hepatitis in the Newborn: Clinical Features, Epidemiology and Pathology," *Am. J. Dis. Child.*, 82:213, 1951.
25. Stoller, A., and R. D. Collmann, "Incidence of Infective Hepatitis Followed by Down's Syndrome Nine Months Later," *Lancet*, 2:1221, 1965.
26. Weller, T. H., and J. B. Hanshaw, "Virological and Clinical Observations on Cytomegalic Inclusion Disease," *New Eng. J. Med.*, 266:1233, 1962.
27. Weller, T. H., J. C. Macaulay, J. M. Craig, and P. Wirth, "Isolation of Intranuclear Inclusion Producing Agents from Infants with Illness Resembling Cytomegalic Inclusion Disease," *Proc. Soc. Exper. Biol. Med.*, 94:4, 1957.
28. Weller, T. H., and F. A. Neva, "Propagation in Tissue Culture of Cytopathic Agents from Patients with Rubella-like Illness," *Proc. Soc. Exper. Biol. Med.*, 111:215, 1962.
29. Wilson, M. G., H. L. Heins, D. T. Imagawa, and J. L. Adams, "Teratogenic Effects of Asian Influenza," *J.A.M.A.*, 171:638, 1959.
30. Wright, H. T., Jr., and R. M. McAllister. Unpublished data.
31. Wright, H. T., Jr., and A. Miller, "Fatal Infection in a Newborn Infant Due to Herpes Simplex Virus," *J. Pediat.*, 67:130, 1965.
32. Wright, H. T., Jr., K. Okuyama, and R. M. McAllister, "An Infant Fatality Associated with Coxsackie B Virus," *J. Pedit.*, 63:428, 1963.

CHAPTER 6

Intrapartum and Neonatal Factors in Causation

by RICHARD KOCH, M.D. and
JAMES C. DOBSON, Ph.D.

Three important variables are critical to the future of the developing neonate: his mother's health, the process of labor and delivery, and his physical condition at birth. Since the first matter, maternal health, was reviewed in the previous chapters on prenatal influences, the emphasis for this discussion will be on the other two sets of circumstances.

LABOR AND DELIVERY
Three Stages of Labor

The process of labor is as yet incompletely understood, especially in regard to the factors which initiate its onset or govern its pace. Medical scientists arbitrarily divide labor into three stages: amniotic fluid escape, cervical dilation and delivery of the placenta. Uterine contractions and rupture of the "bag of waters" (amniotic fluid escape) usually represent onset of the first stage of active labor. The speed with which labor proceeds from that point is itself important to the health of the child (5). A woman who is delivering her first child (a primipara) is more likely to have longer and harder labor than that of the mother who is delivering her third or fourth baby (a multipara). The length of labor for a primiparous woman is normally about 18 hours. Labor may proceed too rapidly and result in a precipitate delivery, which may occur in a matter of several minutes. This is undesirable because the fetal head molds quickly and then re-expands too rapidly following delivery, predisposing to rupture of capillary vessels and resulting in intracranial hemorrhage. On the other hand, prolonged labor, which may result from a variety of factors, may be harmful too. Uterine inertia, contracted pelvis, excessive head size, an exceedingly large

85

baby, and an abnormal position of the baby *in utero* are the common causes of prolonged labor and can result in maternal exhaustion or neonatal anoxia. Decrease in fetal heart rate or elimination of meconium into the amniotic fluid by the fetus are the usual signs of fetal distress.

The second stage of labor begins with completion of cervical dilation and is completed with delivery of the baby. Usually this stage is the most uncomfortable for the mother, and the physician is likely to prescribe analgesia (pain-killing agent) and/or anaesthesia. Morphine and ether anaesthesia are seldom used today. Chloroform usage has been abandoned for many years in the United States. The administration of nitrous oxide (laughing gas) and oxygen, spinal anaesthesia, saddleblock, and caudal anaesthesia are the procedures now in vogue. Natural delivery without medication is practiced widely in Russia and is now not uncommon in America.

The third stage of labor begins with completion of delivery of the child and ends with delivery of the placenta. Inspection of the placenta may reveal valuable information related to intrauterine development of the fetus, particularly with respect to disturbances in fetal-placental circulation.

FETAL POSITION

The position of the baby *in utero* influences the course of labor. The cephalic delivery (head first) is more easily delivered than a breech birth (buttocks first). A transverse position, where an infant may present with an arm or shoulder, is the most serious. Delivery is impossible for the normal-sized neonate in a transverse position. Before the day of modern obstetrics, such infants usually resulted in arrested labor and maternal death. Today, an emergency caesarian section or an actual turning of the baby can be performed. About three percent of babies are born from a breech or transverse position. It is believed that brain damage occurs more frequently in deliveries occurring from these positions. Presentation of the baby is defined by the position of the occiput of the head with reference to the pelvis. The most common is the left occiput anterior (LOA). Face presentations are more difficult to deliver, but usually pose no problem to a skilled obstetrician.

UTERINE ANOMALIES

The birth process is occasionally complicated by anomalies of the uterus. These are rare, but the possibility of rupture of the uterus resulting from prior surgical procedures must always be considered. The location of placental implantation is important. The placenta is nearly always located in the fundus (upper part) of the uterus. On occasion, though, it may implant over the cervical opening. This condition, called placenta previa, is dangerous to both mother and child because the infant cannot be delivered without removal of the placenta first. When this happens, neonatal anoxia may result from interference with the baby's oxygen supply from the maternal circulation. When this condition is recognized, caesarian section may be performed.

In rare cases, the placenta separates prematurely from the wall of the uterus. This condition, known as "placenta abruptio," is dangerous because intrauterine bleeding may occur without detection. In such cases, the baby often succumbs; if the bleeding is not discovered, the mother may be endangered by shock and loss of blood.

UMBILICAL CORD HAZARDS

The umbilical cord (the vessels leading from the placenta to the baby) may be too short or too long. When it is too short, rupture may occur with hemorrhage; when too long, the cord may prolapse and present at the cervical opening before the head is delivered. This, of course, causes compression of the cord between the head and pelvis, resulting in anoxia. Fortunately, this disaster is unusual.

PELVIC ABNORMALITY

In the past, maternal rickets caused significant pelvic deformity. Accompanying the reduction of this threat, however, came another with the same consequence: Automobile accidents now result in a high rate of pelvic injury. Any such injury and deformity should be evaluated by a skilled obstetrician to prevent interference with normal labor. The use of safety belts while driving would reduce this problem.

THE NEWBORN PERIOD

Neonatal Health

Immediately after birth (within 60 seconds) each baby should be carefully examined. By experience it has been shown that systematized observations of the baby's appearance, pulse rate, type of cry, activity, and respirations are valuable indicators. These observations were first organized as a method of scoring infants by Virginia Apgar. In her honor, this sytem is called an Apgar score (2).

Sixty seconds after birth, a delivery room nurse, anesthesiologist or pediatrician rates the baby on these 5 measures using a scale of 0 to 2. If the newborn is completely pink, a value of 2 is assigned. If the body is pink but the extremities bluish, a value of 1 is assigned. If the baby is generally cyanotic, the baby is rated zero. A newborn whose pulse is greater than 100 is rated 2, if less than 100, one, and if pulse is absent, zero. A newborn with a vigorous cry is rated 2, one with a weak cry, one, and one with no response to stimulation, zero. A newborn with normal active movements would be rated 2, one with decreased muscle tone but able to move his extremities would be rated one, and a limp unresponsive baby would be rated zero. Normal vigorous respirations would be rated 2, slow irregular breathing, one, and absent respirations, zero.

Normal babies usually score from 7 to 10. In other words, they are pink, with good activity, muscle tone, regular, strong pulse, and normal respirations. Conversely, babies with scores of 4 or less need expert emergency care. They are usually limp with poor color, irregular respirations, absent cry and weak pulse. In such cases, the airway must be cleared and the lungs inflated as soon as possible. Oxygen is administered and artificial respiration provided until the baby can breathe on its own. The Apgar score is then repeated 5 minutes after birth and again recorded. It is important to write these values on the chart because of their predictive value. A low score would indicate a "high risk" baby that should be carefully followed. It is important to remember that the parent-child relationship must be nurtured rather than interfered with by such scoring techniques. The parent should be encouraged to handle the baby as normally as possible and reassured by home visits by professionals skilled in providing parental support, but at the same time observing the baby for signs of neurological impairment. Early intervention in the case of seizures, cerebral palsy and mental handicaps leads to optimal improvement, whereas delay in diagnosis decreases the baby's opportunity to respond to different treatment modalities.

The child may be affected by congenital anomalies of the brain, convulsions, metabolic disorders or respiratory depression. If the baby has a developmental abnormality of the brain, he may be apneic or lethargic, with poor sucking and cough reflexes. Convulsions during the newborn period are not an uncommon problem, and may result from a variety of causes; it is thought that intracranial hemorrhage is the most common etiology. Tetany of the newborn results from a disorder of calcium and phosphorous metabolism caused by immature kidneys. The convulsions due to tetany rarely cause brain damage; however, those associated with intracranial hemorrhage are often related to various degrees of brain injury. Some convulsions are associated with infections of the brain, in which cases the rate of mortality is high. Hypoglycemia (low blood sugar content) is another cause of convulsions and brain damage. Treatment consists of the administration of intravenous glucose solutions.

Rh Blood Incompatibility

The problem of Rh incompatibility must be recognized and treated appropriately during the newborn period (1). Eighty-five per cent of the population has blood that is Rh positive, meaning that the Rhesus factor is present. Rh negative (absence of Rhesus factor) causes difficulty only if the mother is Rh negative and the father is Rh positive. Since Rh positive is dominant in such a mating, only Rh positive offspring usually occur. Thus, the Rh negative mother carries an Rh positive fetus. The Rh positive fetus immunizes the mother slowly during pregnancy or during delivery. This occurs when traces of fetal blood enter the maternal circulation. The Rh negative mother then begins to build antibody defenses against the Rh positive factor. Small amounts of the antibody enter the fetal circulation which then cause an antigen-antibody reaction which in turn destroys the fetal red blood cells (the location of the Rh factor). Fortunately, there is a test known as the Coombs Test that can be performed before or at the time of birth to determine whether maternal antibodies have been produced against the Rh factor in suspected cases. If the Coombs Test is positive, an exchange transfusion may be indicated. Recently fluorescent lights have been shown to lessen bilirubin levels, too. If untreated, the breakdown products of red cell destruction (bilirubin) can cause damage by toxic effects upon nerve tissue. For this reason, exchange transfusion may need to be done once, twice, or three times to remove recurring quantities of bilirubin. This substance can be measured chemically in the baby's blood and level of over 20 mgm. per cent is considered unsafe. Newer techniques utilizing anti-Rh immunizing procedures are now receiving clinical trial and may make exchange transfusion unnecessary in the near future. Other blood problems, such as major blood group incompatibility (AB-O) can cause neonatal difficulty too, but fortunately are less common. It seems obvious that routine Rh testing of all mothers during their first pregnancy should be indicated.

Birth injury with intracranial hemorrhage or neonatal anoxia was formerly known to be a common cause of mental retardation. Advances in modern obstetrics, however, have reduced the probability of intellectual damage from birth trauma (9). Nowadays only five percent of the retarded children evaluated in the Mental Retardation Clinic at Childrens Hospital of Los Angeles have conditions related to birth injury (6).

It should be noted that many children who show abnormal neurological symptoms at birth do not necessarily have lasting indications or trouble in later life (3); therefore, it is not wise to predict dire consequences from such manifestations during the neonatal period. A recent study indicates that even an abnormal electroencephalogram obtained during the newborn period has little prognostic value (8). When neurological damage is suspected, the best treatment should be provided and the child carefully checked over a period of time for signs of brain damage during routine pediatric examinations (1).

Forceps deliveries were once thought to be the cause of many birth injuries resulting in neurological disturbances in the newborn. It is now felt that more probable causative factors are associated with the effects of either too prolonged or too precipitate a delivery. Low forceps delivery actually minimizes the chance of birth injury. High or mid-forceps delivery should be performed only when medically necessary.

The care of the premature baby has been the subject of many investigations. Adequate care requires special equipment and considerable training and skill of attendants. Temperature regulation, oxygen administration, moisture content, feeding routines with varying caloric and protein content and different methods of fluid administration have all been studied extensively. Much is still to be learned in this important field (7).

NEONATAL MORTALITY

Forty-six per cent of neonatal deaths are related in one way or another to premature birth. Only 15 per cent of neonatal deaths are related to birth injury and 12 per cent to congenital anomalies. While it is well documented that neonatal mortality has been dropping progressively from 44 per 1,000 in 1915, 28 per 1,000 in 1941, 23 per 1,000 in 1967, and 14 per 1,000 in 1974, comparable data for morbidity are unknown. Improved obstetrical services and nursery care account for much of the reduction in neonatal mortality (4). Maternal toxemia occasionally manifests itself during the process of labor by onset of convulsions. This can, of course, complicate delivery, and is accompanied by increased infant and maternal mortality. More study is needed to validate the clinical impression that maternal toxemia itself is a causative factor in mental retardation. It can be stated, in summary, that most of the causes of neonatal death are closely related to the occurrence of mental retardation in those infants who survive. If applied, modern technology could do much to minimize both maternal and neonatal mortality and morbidity.

BIBLIOGRAPHY

1. *Mental Retardation: A Handbook for the Primary Physician, American Medical Association Report of the Conference on Mental Retardation,* Chicago, second edition, 1975.
2. Apgar, V. and J. Beck, *Is My Baby All Right?* New York: Pocket Book Edition, 1974.
3. Beintema, D. J., *A Neurological Study of Newborn Infants,* Clinics in Developmental Medicine, No. 28, Spastics International Medical Publications in Association with William Heinemann Medical Books, 1968.
4. Children's Bureau. Data from the United States Bureau of the Census, 1960.
5. Grinker, R. R., *Trauma of the Central Nervous System in Neurology,* 3rd Edition, Springfield: Charles C Thomas, 1946.
6. Koch, R., "Mental Retardation: An Important Public Health Program," *J. Amer. Phy. Therapy Assn.,* 46:745, 1966.
7. Masland, R., S. B. Sarason, and T. Gladwin, *Mental Subnormality,* New York: Basic Books, Inc., 1958.
8. Torres, F., and M. E. Blaw, "Longitudinal EEG—Clinical Correlations in Children from Birth to 4 Years-of-Age," *Pediatrics,* 41:945, 1968.
9. U.S. Government, *Infant Care,* Washington, D.C.: Universal Publishing and Distributing Corporation, 1968.

CHAPTER 7

Postnatal Factors in Causation

by RICHARD KOCH, M.D.

Brain damage that produces mental retardation may be traceable to a variety of postnatal causes which are often difficult to identify. The diagnostic task with neurological disorders is complicated by the fact that several types of physical handicaps, emotional problems, and cultural and maternal deprivation may cause a child with average intellectual potential to function at a retarded level (5:11). The causes most easily and frequently recognized are infections of the central nervous system, traumas, poisons, anoxia and endocrine disorders; less common contributors are neoplasms, uncontrolled convulsive disorders and allergic reactions (16). This chapter is devoted to a brief examination of these postnatal factors which are thought to precipitate mental retardation.

NUTRITIONAL DEPRIVATION AND INFECTION

Whether severe nutritional deprivation in itself causes mental retardation is not as yet clear (9), although Cravioto has expressed the view that nutritional depletion during infancy causes intellectual deterioration (6). Evidence has accumulated that older children seem to be able to withstand caloric deprivation without sustaining mental retardation (7), but certain vitamin deficiencies are known to cause mental defects. Pellagra is a common disease resulting from a vitamin deficiency, and it develops from an insufficient intake of nicotinamide (B-5). Deficiency of Vitamin B-6 (pyridoxine) causes convulsions in infancy, but it is not known whether mental retardation ensues. Lack of iodine in the diet has been known for many years to cause goiter, secondary hypothyroidism and mental retardation. This condition was very common at one time in the Great Lakes region of the United States and in the Alps in Europe. The use of iodized salt has eliminated the problem in many countries, but it is a remarkable fact that several South American countries still do not utilize this simple preventable method. Iron deficiency does not itself affect intellectual growth. However, secondary anemia caused by iron deficiency certainly inhibits development and predisposes infants to infection which may, in turn, reduce learning potential. The addition of fluoride to drinking water would do much to improve the dental health of retarded individuals.

Infections of the central nervous system may represent an invasion of either viruses, rickettsiae, bacteria, protozoans, fungi or other parasites. The term encephalitis is applied to viral infections of the brain. The viruses responsible for such illnesses have been difficult to identify, and progress in their eradication has been slow. The Eastern Equine, Western Equine, and Japanese B viruses are all known to cause encephalitis (16). Occasionally, even the poliomyelitis virus can cause polioencephalitis. Other viruses, such as echo, coxsackie, measles, varicella and mumps also may invade the central nervous system; they do not ordinarily cause brain damage.

Infection of the meninges which cover the brain due to bacteria is termed purulent meningitis (12). Any of the common bacterial agents can cause meningitis. The most common organisms causing meningitis in children are Hemophilus influenzae, Type B, pneumococcus, and the meningococcus. Children with meningitis are acutely and seriously ill and are always considered medical emergencies. Fever, headache, a stiff neck and back are common early symptoms. Convulsions occurring during meningitis are serious. Fortunately, most children can survive with adequate therapy, although 10 to 20 percent may exhibit residual brain damage resulting in mental retardation, convulsions, behavior disorders or deafness. Fortunately, rickettsiae, protozoan and fungal infections are relatively rare in the United States. Nor is tuberculosis a serious cause of mental retardation in our country. The organism responsible for tuberculosis may invade the central nervous system in children, however, and can cause serious damage. Tuberculous meningitis is invariably secondary to a primary pulmonary infection which is generally contracted from a family member. When infection of the brain occurs, fever, headache, vomiting and convulsions develop. Prompt diagnosis by examination of the cerebrospinal fluid can be made by finding lymphocytic cells and staining the fluid for the acid-fast bacilli. Treatment consists of isoniazide, streptomycin and para-aminosalycyclic acid. Recovery is dependent on the extent of tuberculous invasion present at the time of initiation of therapy. Early diagnosis favors recovery. The pediatrician can play an important role in society by encouraging widespread skin testing for tuberculosis so as to identify tuberculosis in its early stages and institute therapy. Treatment of the asymptomatic case is remarkably efficacious in reducing the spread of the organism to the central nervous system.

INJURY

Trauma (injury) is an increasing problem in our country as a result of the high rate of automobile accidents (18). Any serious injury to the skull can cause brain damage of consequence. Trauma to the brain is often accompanied by unconsciousness; in addition, nausea, vomiting and incoherency are usually present. In a minor injury, with or without skull fracture, recovery is rapid and complete within a week or two. In cases of serious cerebral injury, the patient may remain unconscious for weeks and still recover. Where actual destruction of brain tissue occurs, as in the case of a depressed skull fracture, recovery is determined by the extent of injury. If persistent vomiting follows cerebral injury, subdural hematoma should be suspected. These can be acute or chronic. In acute subdural hematoma, an artery of the brain has usually been damaged and is releasing blood into the subdural space (between the dura and the brain). The accumulation of blood compresses the brain and must be treated promptly by surgery to release the pressure. The child with chronic subdural hematoma is usually an infant who presents with a history of vomiting, enlarging head, failing vision and convulsions. Treatment consists of surgical removal of the blood clots over the brain. The "battered child" syndrome is suspected clinically in an infant with a skull fracture or subdural hematoma in which a history of injury is not volunteered by the parent. The author has seen several such children who are mentally retarded due to repetitive cerebral injury.

POISONING

Various poisons can cause brain damage. Lead poisoning is the worst offender in the Eastern States (3). If lead ingestion is chronic, deposits in various tissues occur and there is interference with brain cell metabolism. The retardation is generally severe. The common sources of lead intoxication are ingestion of old paint and inhalation of battery fumes. The physician should be aware of the nearest poison information center from which he can obtain information on all kinds of accidental poisoning.

SUFFOCATION

Anoxia can occur secondarily to any suffocating episode, including the common occurrence of accidental drowning. Cardiac arrest during the crisis may produce severe brain damage because of lack of oxygenated blood circulating through the brain. Accidental suffocation in plastic bags or by cord strangulation imposes oxygen deprivation resulting ultimately in death. Another example of oxygen deprivation occurs in carbon monoxide poisoning, which causes anoxia by preventing hemoglobin from carrying oxygen to the brain.

HYPOTHYROIDISM

A major endocrine disease associated with mental retardation is hypothyroidism. The condition results in mental retardation because of defective thyroid hormone function which is necessary for proper brain cell metabolism. The early symptoms are lethargy, weight gain in spite of poor appetite, personality changes, stunted growth, pudgy and coarse facial features, sparse hair, dry skin, constipation, anemia, and mental retardation. The experienced physician will easily recognize hypothyroidism from these symptoms. The disease is verified by finding elevated blood cholesterol levels, reduced circulating protein-bound iodine in the blood and by measuring skeletal growth by x-rays of the wrist. The protein-bound iodine test is usually below 4.8 micrograms and the skeletal age is retarded to a significant degree. Early diagnosis is paramount for optimal therapeutic results. Treatment is effective and consists of prescribing thyroid extract (15). There are no other major endocrine causes of mental retardation known at this time. Newborn screening may be available soon.

METABOLIC DISEASES

Metabolic diseases account for an estimated 5 percent of all retardation (13). These are usually genetically determined diseases which make their presence known only after birth. For instance, the phenylketonuric child is usually not recognized clinically until 3 to 12 months of age when retardation becomes apparent (25). Hypoglycemia is another metabolic disease causing mental retardation (1). Hypoglycemia is characterized by a low uncontrollable blood sugar level. It is thought that since the brain depends upon glucose for energy that low blood glucose level causes low tissue levels of glucose and thus deprives the brain of energy. The low blood sugar level induces convulsions, which ordinarily permit the physician to make the proper diagnosis. Steroid drugs and dietary measures are used for treatment. See Chapter 8 for further details. Undoubtedly newborn screening programs for early detection and treatment are the best approach.

OTHER CAUSES

While severe and uncontrolled convulsive disorders can also cause mental retardation, these are uncommon, as are cerebrovascular accidents in childhood (16). Neoplasms of the brain (cancer and tumors) can cause retardation because of the progressive expansion of the diseased portion. Fortunately, this is not a common problem, and with improved surgical techniques there are means of combating these unusual causes. The degenerative diseases of the central nervous system are not well classified as yet and they are even less well understood. Schilder's Disease is an example of a degenerative disorder. Allergic reactions are sometimes responsible for brain damage. Examples of such reactions or auto-immune reactions are the post-vaccinal encephalitis cases after smallpox or rabies post-immunization reactions (16).

PSYCHIATRIC FACTORS

Psychiatric factors have been studied extensively (2, 21, 22, 24, 26 and 28). It is not uncommon for a severely disturbed child with presumably normal intelligence to be referred to a mental retardation clinic (10). Five percent of the children seen in the Child Development Clinic at Childrens Hospital of Los Angeles are variously diagnosed as autistic, schizophrenic or atypical. They are typically males, aged 3 to 6 years, whose parents described them as having been "different" from early infancy. They tend to twirl and play with spinning objects. Toe walking is sometimes seen. These children are often mute, play for long periods alone and are seldom affectionate. Whether or not this condition results from purely environmental causes has been hotly disputed. Opinion presently suggests this is a state which can be precipitated by both physical and environmental factors, operating together or alone (19). Regardless of etiology, prognosis is poor even with treatment. Behavior disorders accompanying mental retardation are also common (27).

Occasionally, a normal child with a speech or hearing defect is mistakenly thought to be retarded (8, 11). Familial-cultural factors may further confuse the issue (4). Sometimes a clear-cut diagnosis cannot be made until the child has been seen several times over a period of several months or even years. For further discussion of the broad aspects of environmental deprivation, the reader is referred to a recent book by Lichter et al. (14).

CRANIOSYNOSTOSIS

A skull x-ray of the normal newborn reveals open coronal, saggital, lamboid, metopic, and temporal sutures. These sutures, or joints, are available for expansion. They are open similar to a joint between boards. In the newborn the cranial bones can be separated very easily, and as the brain grows the skull stretches. In the adult skull, the sutures are solid and the two parts of the skull are fused securely. The term "craniosynostosis" refers to the early fusion of the various cranial bones. The most common form of craniosynostosis ts the saggital, referring to the central suture which extends down the crown of the head from front to back. Saggital synostosis accounted for 63 percent of the cases of craniosynostosis seen at the Childrens Hospital of Los Angeles. This suture should remain open for several years so that the brain can grow; in babies with craniosynostosis, however, it is fused at birth. The head of such a child is called doliochocephalic because it cannot broaden. It assumes a shape that is long in proportion to its breadth and remains narrow on this account. In babies with coronal synostosis, the shape of the head is broad and high, but short. Occasionally only one side of the coronal suture is fused early. In such cases, asymmetry of the skull results. Left coronal fusion results in the left parietal-frontal cranial bones being smaller than those of the right. There is elevation of the right eyebrow, some recession of the left eye and a flattening of the left forehead on the one side only. If the metopic suture is fused at birth, the head becomes rather triangular in anterior appearance. It maintains a fetal or prenatal appearance on this account. This is called trigonocephaly. In rare cases, all the joints in the skull are fused prematurely. This is a serious problem and is usually associated with brain anomaly. Operative procedures have been devised to deal with these problems (17).

HYDROCEPHALUS

The term hydrocephalus refers to children with disproportionately large heads. The head may be large for a considerable number of reasons. Some people just have unusually large heads (macrocephaly) which may be familial and normal. However, subdural hematoma and brain tumor may also cause enlargement of the skull.

In pathological hydrocephalus, the cerebrospinal fluid is obstructed in its normal flow in the ventricles of the brain, or the fluid is not properly absorbed back into the blood stream. The former type is called an obstructive hydrocephalus whereas the latter is termed a communicating type. The cause is usually congenital but can follow meningitis, brain tumor and subdural hematoma. In hydrocephalus, the ventricles become enlarged from the retained fluid which causes pressure atrophy of the cortex. Early operation is mandatory for satisfactory results. The excess fluid is usually drained from the ventricle by a small tube via the superior vena cava into the heart (23).

Another cause of hydrocephalus is congenital deformity of the spine. The so-called spina bifida or myeleomeningocele is accompanied by distortion or derangement of the spinal cord, cerebellum, and base of the brain. When these occur, the head may enlarge, but the spinal deformity is the major problem. Interruption of spinal nerve pathways occur and spastic diplegia, loss of bladder and rectal control, and loss of sensation of the lower extremities are common. When hydrocephalus complicates the problem, neurological intervention may not be feasible. The prognosis is poor in such cases (23).

SUMMARY

In summary, the postnatal causes of mental retardation are so numerous and varied that it is difficult to categorize them adequately. Many of these problems are controllable, but society has not yet demanded the constructive action that is now possible (20). There are hopeful signs, however, that the prevention of mental retardation is finally receiving the increasing attention it deserves. It is hoped that this interest will be strengthened by an enlightened citizenry.

BIBLIOGRAPHY

1. Blattner, R. J., "Central Nervous System Damage and Hypoglycemia," *J. Pediat.,* 72:905, 1968.
2. Bowlby, J., *Maternal Care and Mental Health,* New York: Schocken Books, p. 11-14, 1952.
3. Cohen, G. S., and W. E. Ahrens, "Chronic Lead Poisoning," *Pediatrics,* 54:271, 1959.
4. Coleman, R. W., and S. Provence, "Environmental Retardation in Infants Living in Families," *Pediatrics,* 19:285, 1957.

5. Conot, R., *Rivers of Blood, Years of Darkness,* New York: Bantam Books, Inc., 1967.
6. Cravioto, J., DeLicardie, E. R., and Birch, H. G., "Nutrition, Growth and Neuro-integrative Development: An Experimental and Ecologic Study," *Pediatrics,* 38: 319-372, 1966.
7. Dobbing, J., "Vulnerable Periods in Developing Brain in Applied Neurochemistry," A.N. Davison and J. Dobbing, Ed., Oxford, 1968.
8. Dunn, S., *Exceptional Children in School.* Chapter 2, "Trainable Mentally Retarded Children." New York: Holt, Rinehart and Winston, Inc., 1966.
9. Editorial, "Nutrition and the Developing Brain," *Brit. Med. J.,* 1:333, 1968.
10. Kaplan, G. (ed.), *Prevention of Mental Handicaps in Children,* New York: Basic Books, Inc., 1961.
11. Koch, R., B. G. Graliker, W. Bronston, and K. Fishler, "Mental Retardation in Early Childhood," *A. J. Dis. Child.,* 109:243, 1965.
12. Koch, R., M. Kogut, and L. Asay, "Management of Bacterial Meningitis in Children," *Ped. Clinics North America,* 8:1177, 1961.
13. Koch, R., B. Graliker, K. Fishler, and A. H. Parmelee, "Mental Retardation in Early Childhood," *Post. Grad. Med.,* 31:169, 1962.
14. Lichter, S. O., E. B. Rapier, F. M. Serbort, and M. A. Sklansky, *The Drop Outs,* New York: Free Press, 1968.
15. Man, E. B., A. E. Mermann, and R. E. Cooke, "The Development of Children with Congenital Hypothyroidism," *J. Pediat.,* 63:926, 1963.
16. Masland, R. L., S. B. Sarason, and T. Gladwin, *Mental Subnormality.* Chapter VI, "Post-Natal Causes of Mental Subnormality," New York: Basic Books, Inc., 1958.
17. McLaurin, R. L., and D. D. Matson, "Importance of Early Surgical Treatment of Craniostenosis," *Pediatrics,* 10:637, 1952.
18. *Mental Retardation: A Handbook for the Primary Physician.* Report of the American Medical Association Conference on Mental Retardation, Chicago, Illinois, April 9-11, 1964, second edition, 1975.
19. Ornitz, E. M. and E. R. Ritvo, "Perceptual Inconstancy in Early Infantile Autism," *Arch. Gen. Psychiatry,* 18:76, 1968.
20. Poole, B. D., "Mental Retardation and Maternal and Child Health Programs," *A.J.P.H.,* 55:27, 1965.
21. Provence, S., Some Determinants of Relevance of Stimuli in Infant Development, in *Exceptional Infant* Vol. 1: *The Normal Infant,* edited by J. Hellmuth, New York: Brunner/Mazel, Inc., 1967.
22. Rainwater, L., and W. L. Yancy, *The Moynihan Report and the Politics of Controversy.* Cambridge, Mass.: The M. I. T. Press, 1967.
23. *Research into Hydrocephalus and Spina Bifida.* Published by Spastics Society Medical Education, Heinemann Medical Books, Ltd., 1967.
24. Skeels, H. M., and E. A. Fillmore, "The Mental Development of Children from Underprivileged Homes," *J. Genet. Psychol.,* 50:427, 1937.
25. Slack, J., K. Simpson, and D. H. Hsia, "Hereditary Metabolic Disorders Involving the Nervous System," *Ped. Clinics of North America,* 7:627, 1960.
26. Spitz, R. A.: "The Role of Ecological Factors in Emotional Development in Infancy," *Child Development,* 20:145, 1949.
27. Tarjan, G., S. W. Wright, H. F. Dingman, and G. Sabagh, "The Natural History of Mental Deficiency in a State Hospital," *A.M.A.J. Dis. Child.,* 98:370, 1959.
28. U.S. Riot Commission Report. *Report of the National Advisory Commission on Civic Disorders,* New York: Bantam Books, Inc., 1968.

CHAPTER 8

Two Metabolic Factors in Causation

by RICHARD KOCH, M.D., PHYLLIS B. ACOSTA, Dr.P.H. and JAMES C. DOBSON, Ph.D.

INTRODUCTION

Rapid development in knowledge about various metabolic disorders has occurred during the last two decades. While there are now many well described metabolic diseases associated with developmental deviations, only two are known to date which can be easily identified and treated, and which respond to therapy when diagnosis is established in early infancy. These are galactosemia and phenylketonuria. Medical progress is being made in several others, although experience is too scant to have yielded firm conclusions. There have been attempts made to utilize dietary methods of treatment for children with maple syrup urine disease, homocystinuria, hyperglycinemia, tyrosinosis, and histidinemia. However, in view of the very limited experiences with these diseases, they will not be discussed in this chapter; rather, the reader is referred to the excellent text of Stanbury, Wyngaarden, and Fredrickson, entitled *The Metabolic Basis of Inherited Disease,* published by Mc-Graw-Hill in 1972. Thus, this chapter is devoted to a review of galactosemia and phenylketonuria.

GALACTOSEMIA

Galactosemia has been known as a clinical entity since 1908 (25, 61). Untreated infants usually die during the newborn period or become mentally retarded if they survive. The specific metabolic defect has been localized in galactose-l-phosphate uridyl transferase (transferase),

The work in galactosemia has been supported by a special grant (2 RO1 AM 04837—14 from the National Institute for Arthritis and Metabolic Diseases, Department of Health, Education and Welfare, Washington, D.C.

an enzyme which is active in converting galactose into glucose (41). The other steps in the galactose pathway have been demonstrated to be intact in this disease (38). For some years it has been postulated that an accumulation of galactose or galactose-1-phosphate in various body tissues, resulting from the enzyme deficiency, accounts for the clinical symptoms seen during the neonatal period (56). Also, recent observations suggest that galactitol, a sugar alcohol derived from galactose, may have a role, especially in cataract formation (24, 30, 63).

It has been established that a galactose restricted diet is effective in halting the progression of hepatic, ophthalmologic, renal and central nervous system manifestations of the disease. Early cataracts show improvement on such a diet (64), as do hepatic and renal manifestations. Intellectual ability seems protected by dietary therapy; however, this is obscured by a variety of factors which researchers have not been able to control fully. Questions also remain unanswered concerning such factors as incidence of the disease (15), the degree of prenatal damage to the affected individual (54), the occurrence of asymptomatic galactosemia (5), the desirable rigidity of dietary control (21), and required duration of dietary restriction of galactose (45).

Our present purpose is to discuss the background of galactosemia, the clinical problems presented, and an approach to management of the disease. The guidelines recommended for dietary treatment have been developed through a multidisciplinary approach to the child and family by a team consisting of a pediatrician, biochemist, nutritionist, nurse, social worker, and psychologist (26).

Genetic Aspects

It has been established that galactosemia is transmitted as an autosomal, recessive trait. Both parents of an affected individual exhibit decreased transferase activity consistent with heterozygosity (20, 37, 43). The occurrence of galactosemia in consanguineous marriages, the presence of the disease in siblings, the equal distribution by sex, and the absence of disease in the parents are additional factors consistent with the concept of a recessively transmitted autosomal pattern of inheritance. Incidence has been estimated to be from 1 in 40,000 to 1 in 70,000 births (14, 57).

The possibility of genetic variation has been suggested by Segal, Mellman and others (51, 55). Beutler has described the "Duarte Variant," in which quantitative differences in transferase activity have been shown (10) and for which a qualitative difference in electrophoretic mobility of the transferase has been demonstrated (49).

Clinical Findings

Our experience with galactosemia at Childrens Hospital, Los Angeles, encompasses 54 cases in 33 families.* Of the 54 patients, 41 are now living. In only 2 out of the 13 who died during infancy was the diagnosis made prior to death; in the remaining 11, the diagnosis was made retrospectively on the basis of history, autopsy information and the presence in the family of a known galactosemic sibling. Twenty-seven were male and 27 female. All but two were Caucasian. Consanguinity was present in one family.

Typically, clinical manifestations occur following lactose-containing milk feedings. Hepatic, ophthalmologic and gastrointestinal signs and symptoms predominate. Jaundice usually develops within two to three days after beginning milk feedings and usually persists in varying degrees until institution of a galactose restricted diet. Hepatomegaly is a common clinical finding. Weight loss resulting from vomiting is also frequent.

Cataracts are noted in some patients as early as a few days of age and were detected in 16 of the affected children. However, this figure may be a minimal one, in view of the difficulties in detecting small lenticular opacities in the young infant. The cataracts are more dense in children with late diagnosis. The central nervous system sequelae are usually late manifestations.

Treatment

The treatment for galactosemia is directed toward avoiding accumulation of galactose metabolites in body tissues. This is accomplished by the exclusion of galactose from the diet. While a "galactose-restricted" diet is the major treatment, occasional supplementary means may be required to correct hypoglycemia, hyperbilirubinemia, hypoprothrombinemia and anemia. The successful treatment of infection if present in affected infants is dependent upon concomitant dietary therapy, as well as the use of appropriate anti-bacterial agents.

The basis for a "galactose-restricted" diet is a milk substitute formula substantially free of galactose. In our clinic, a casein hydrolysate

---

* Special thanks are due Dr. George N. Donnell for his assistance in serving the galactosemic children described herein.

(Nutramigen*) is employed. Soyabean milk has been utilized in the treatment of galactosemia. Gitzelmann and Auricchio (29) have shown that the oligosaccharides which contain galactose are not hydrolyzed to simple sugars by the intestinal enzymes and thus they presumably are harmless to patients with galactosemia.

The wide variety of products in which lactose may be used points to the need for careful scrutiny of labels. Manufacturers should be contacted if there is doubt concerning ingredients in any product.

Meat, poultry, fish and eggs are excellent protein sources, but it is advisable to avoid eating galactose-storing organs, such as liver, pancreas and brain. Labels on cold cuts and similar meats commonly containing fillers should be examined to make sure that no milk or milk products have been included. Likewise, creamed and breaded meats should be excluded from the diet.

Most vegetables and fruits may be included in the diet. Legumes and sugar beets generally have been excluded because of their content of galactose-containing oligosaccharides. Presumably, these foods can be considered in the same category as soyabeans, but experimental evidence is incomplete. It has been shown that peas, for example, do contain some free galactose (58).

Most oils, shortening and lard on the market may be used freely. However, labels on margarine must be scrutinized to insure that milk in the form of whey, casein, dry milk solids or lactose is not included. It is thought that some form of dietary restriction of galactose may be necessary for life.

Genetic Counseling

Counseling is important in the management of any hereditary disorder. In galactosemia, the defect is transmitted as a simple autosomal recessive character. This knowledge facilitates explaining to parents the known factors and risks involved in future pregnancies. One point which must be emphasized is the need for prompt examination at birth of further children born in known galactosemic families. If facilities for evaluation of such an infant are not immediately available, the newborn sibling should be treated at once as galactosemic and the treatment continued until the child is proven otherwise by appropriate biochemical studies.

It is now well known that exclusion of galactose-containing com-

---

* Nutramigen is produced by Mead Johnson and Co., Evansville, Indiana.

pounds will usually reverse the major clinical manifestations of the disease when started in early infancy. Long-term studies have shown that treatment results in normal patterns of physical development (22). Only two youngsters in our group are moderately retarded in growth due to poor dietary control.

Intellectual Progress

Variation in adherence to the galactose-restricted diet may affect mental development. Usually, individuals with excellent dietary control demonstrate better intellectual achievement than those with poor dietary management. A total of 41 galactosemic patients (21 boys and 20 girls) have been evaluated over a period of years in the Childrens Hospital Clinic. Assessment of adherence to dietary galactose restriction was made on the basis of dietary history, physical progress and various blood measurements.

Results of Intelligence Testing. Thirty-eight patients were diagnosed from birth to a few months of age, while two were identified as late as 14 and 17 months respectively. One other patient, whose diagnosis was established at 11 years of age is now 18 years old and is in institution for the retarded.

The results of the latest intelligence test on all of our galactosemic patients indicate that among the 41 subjects, 29 fall within the dull-normal or above range (IQ: 85-128), six are within the borderline range (IQ: 70-84), four are mildly retarded (IQ: 55-69) and two are severely retarded. The two severely retarded patients essentially have been untreated (Cases 2 and 9). The mean DQ/IQ score for 21 galactosemic males was 93 and that for 20 galactosemic females was 91 (26). One must conclude from this data that a newborn screening program for galactosemia is an important advance which we must actively advocate and start as soon as possible.

Summary

Galactosemia is a genetic disease associated with high infant mortality when delay in diagnosis and treatment occurs. It has been established that activity of a specific enzyme (galactose-1-phosphate uridyl transferase) is deficient in affected individuals. Clinical manifestations are variable, although the most frequent early symptoms are jaundice, failure to thrive, hepatomegaly and cataracts. If the untreated child survives the early period, cataracts, liver disease and mental retardation usually develop. Many of the clinical manifestations can be reversed by dietary treatment. Our experience indicates that early treatment is effective in most cases in preventing mental retardation. A newborn screening program is a mandatory part of our future services to assist us in diagnosis before clinical symptoms occur. The technology is available to do this.

PHENYLKETONURIA

Phenylketonuria (PKU) was described over 30 years ago (27, 40, 53, 67) although treatment aimed at prevention of the neurological sequelae of the disease is relatively recent (4, 8, 11-12, 34-36, 65). The possibility of actually preventing the development of mental retardation by early diagnosis and institution of a low-phenylalanine diet has evoked intense scientific as well as lay interest (6, 13, 17, 44, 47). Mass screening programs became practical following development of the Guthrie Inhibition Assay for phenylalanine (19, 28, 31-32), and legislation establishing mandatory testing of the newborn soon followed in many states. One consequence of mass screening was the detection of more patients with elevated serum phenylalanine levels (hyperphenylalanemia) than expected on the basis of earlier statistics concerning incidence of phenylketonuria. Recognition that an elevated blood level of phenylalanine might be associated with conditions other than phenylketonuria was not general (9, 16, 23, 42, 48). This feature, combined with the urgency to prevent development of mental retardation, resulted in unnecessary treatment for some patients. This confusion of diagnosis and treatment of non-phenylketonuric infants led to pointed criticism of mandated screening programs initially. Now, however, they are accepted as a routine part of newborn care.

The purpose of this section is to describe the results of treatment of 140 patients in the PKU Clinic at Childrens Hospital of Los Angeles.* The phenylalanine restricted diet is being administered to 104 patients, to some for as long as 15 years. A pediatrician, nutritionist, nurse, psychologist, social worker, and biochemist work as a collaborative group in providing services to phenylketonuric patients and their families.

* Grateful acknowledgment for assistance in caring for the children reported is due to Drs. Milan Blaskovics, Charles E. Parker and Karol Fishler. Special thanks are due to Elizabeth Wenz and Kenneth Shaw, Ph.D. for their nutritional and biochemical assistance respectively. The work performed in this report was partially supported by Contract No. 466 from the Maternal and Child Health Service of the Department of Health, Education and Welfare, Washington, D.C. and the Department of Health of the State of California, Sacramento, California.

Diagnosis

The diagnosis of phenylketonuria is suspected in any mentally retarded child with blond hair and blue eyes. Until recently, the diagnosis was thought to be confirmed on the basis of a positive test for phenylpyruvic acid in urine (7, 23, 27, 40, 53, 67). With the advent of blood screening techniques (19, 28, 31-32, 48, 59), it was quickly demonstrated that some individuals had intermediate levels of serum phenylalanine (6 to 20 mg%), but the usual urinary metabolites associated with phenylketonuria were absent or diminished. Present findings suggest that several clinical conditions may be associated with elevated neonatal serum phenylalanine levels (2). With the passage of time and increased experience, diagnosis has become easier to make accurately (45a).

Present Method of Treatment at Childrens Hospital of Los Angeles

At the time of referral,* the infant is hospitalized and maintained on adequate protein intake. Serum phenylalanine and tyrosine,** urine amino acid chromatography, blood count, and routine urinalysis are obtained in addition to the history and physical examination. Particular attention is focused on the family history. Diagnosis of PKU is confirmed by a persistently elevated serum phenylalanine (above 20 mgm. percent), normal serum tyrosine, and presence of phenylpyruvic and orthohydroxyphenylacetic acids in excessive amounts in the urine. When the diagnosis is confirmed, infants are started on the low phenylalanine diet with an intake of 70 to 90 milligrams of phenylalanine per kilogram of body weight per day, allowing for adequate vitamin, protein and caloric intake. Serum phenylalanine levels are determined daily until levels of 1.0 to 10.0 mgm. percent are achieved. Serum levels are also obtained from all siblings, both parents, and any available relatives. The nutritionist teaches the parents the essentials of the phenylalanine-restricted diet based on the use of Lofenalac,® a low phenylalanine product manufactured by Mead-Johnson Company. The social worker evaluates the family structure; developmental or psychological assessment is performed by the psychologist; and arrangements are made for the public health nurse to visit the home one week following the discharge

---

* Many physicians deserve acknowledgment for assisting us in obtaining follow-up data. Drs. Thomas Nelson and Stanley Wright were particularly helpful.

** Phenylalanine is determined spectrophotometrically by the method of McCaman and Robins (50) and tyrosine by the method of Waalkes and Udenfriend (62).

from the hospital. The public health nurse advises the parents on health practices, reinforces the physician's instructions, assists with management problems and demonstrates to the parents how to collect blood needed for monitoring the infant's serum phenylalanine. The samples are mailed to the clinical laboratory, along with a record of food intake for the preceding three days. After one year of age, the frequency of biochemical monitoring is decreased from one week to twice monthly. The infant continues to receive well-baby care from the family physician who is kept informed of dietary changes and serum phenylalanine levels. Literature on phenylketonuria is also furnished to the family physician and the parents (1). The infant is seen in the PKU Clinic monthly at first, then bi-monthly and later at three to four month intervals until he reaches five years of age. After that, he is seen every six months, provided dietary control is good. An attempt is made to treat nearly all newly discovered patients regardless of age or intellectual ability. Some less retarded older children have been treated (i.e., kept on the phenyl-alanine-restricted diet) because they showed improvement in attention span and learning ability, as well as greater ease of management. Close maintenance of dietary control is not always possible in the older child, because of the distaste of Lofenalac® and the severe limitation in desirable foods, but it is surprising how well some patients have accepted dietary restriction. Some of the older children starve themselves for several days before accepting this formula. Parents need reassurance that this is not harmful. Serum phenylalanine levels remain elevated during this period even though oral intake of protein is at a minimum. This elevation results from some breakdown and release of phenyl-alanine from tissue protein.

Case Material

One hundred and forty phenylketonuric patients have been studied; of these, 67 were female and 73 male; 126 had classical PKU and 14 were hyperphenylalaninemic variants. The latter were not treated with the low phenylalanine diet. Ages of diagnoses ranged from the newborn period to 29 years. Two patients exhibited other apparently unrelated diseases; one had scleroderma and the other cystathioninuria. The ethnic backgrounds were predominantly Irish, English, Scottish, Italian and German. One was part Jewish and another part Japanese. There were two Negroes, one Lebanese and one Armenian.

Mental retardation was the presenting symptom in 79 of our 126 cases of classical PKU. The others were identified through various PKU screening programs: 31 through newborn screening programs, seven through testing of newborn siblings of known PKU children, and nine were found by sibling screening. Twelve of the hyperphenylalaninemic patients were identified by the newborn screening program. Of the remaining two, one was discovered because he was psychotic and one because he exhibited mental retardation.

Psychological Data Related to Method of Ascertainment of Diagnosis

In the newborn group,* the mean age of diagnosis was 27 days. Following 15 months of dietary therapy, a mean developmental quotient of 102 (range 74-160) was obtained. The newborn siblings of known PKU children were diagnosed at a mean age of 14 days. At a mean age of 52 months, these children now have a mean IQ of 97 (range 80-118). The children identified by screening PKU siblings presented at a mean age of 49 months with a mean IQ of 64 (range 10-100). Some of these children were not treated. After an average of 64 months of follow-up, the present mean IQ is 77 (range 10-99).

The largest group of children (79) were determined to have PKU at a mean age of 53 months. The mean IQ in this group was 44 (range from non-measurable to 84). Again, some children in this group were not treated. After a mean of 51 months of follow-up, this group exhibits a mean IQ of 65 (the range was from non-measurable to 107).

Psychological Data When Related to Quality of Dietary Control

When results of psychological testing were investigated in relation to degree of dietary control, 34 children were found with excellent dietary control,** 45 with good control, and 21 with poor control. The mean age of diagnosis in children under excellent control was one year nine months. Their initial mean DQ was 71 (range of 29-100). When their mean age reached four years 2 months, the IQ was 81 (range 45-125).

---

* The unreliability of early developmental testing in terms of intellectual predictability is well known. Therefore, some of the data will undoubtedly change as our population of patients matures. *Gesell Developmental Scales* were utilized for this study of all children less than 3 years of age. A DQ of 100 was arbitrarily assigned to all infants tested at less than one month of age if the baby appeared normal in all respects.

** Dietary control was judged *excellent* when serum phenylalanines were 2-6 mgm. percent at least seventy-five percent of the time; *good* when serum phenylalanines were 2-12 mgm. percent seventy-five percent of the time; *poor* when serum phenylalanines were more than 12 mgm. percent at least seventy-five percent of the time.

The mean age of diagnosis in children under good dietary control was 1 year 3 months. Their initial DQ was 67 (range non-measurable to 104). Following 3 years 7 months of treatment, mean IQ was 83 (range 25-160).

Twenty-one children were categorized as having poor dietary control. They were diagnosed at a mean age of one year 11 months, at which time their mean DQ was 61. At seven years one month of age, their mean IQ was 67.

Twenty-two children were untreated as a result of late diagnosis associated with profound mental retardation. This group presented at a mean age of 11 years, 8 months. The mean IQ was 36 (range non-measurable to 96). No follow-up data on intelligence are available for this group: 12 are in residential care, one has expired, and nine others are in a variety of community programs.

When age of diagnosis and dietary control were considered, children diagnosed prior to three months of age in the "excellent" or "good" dietary control groups were found to maintain normal development.

The children diagnosed between 4 and 12 months of age who maintained excellent dietary control exhibited a mean IQ of 75 after a mean period of 1 year, 9 months of treatment. At a mean age of five years and ten months, ten children diagnosed at a mean age of 9 months and maintained under "good" dietary control showed a mean IQ of 82. Three children with poorly controlled diets revealed an IQ of 70 after six years, seven months of treatment.

Thirty-three children were diagnosed between one and three years of age. Nine of these children were maintained in "excellent" control. These children exhibited an IQ of 79 while the 14 children in "good" control showed an IQ of 74 at a mean age of seven years, six months. The ten children with poorly controlled diets showed little change.

Twelve children were placed on the low phenylalanine diet between 3 and 6 years of age. Six with excellent control increased by a mean of 5 points in IQ. Three children under good control increased 4 points and three who were poorly controlled increased 18 points.*

Five children diagnosed after 6 years of age were placed on diet. Control was excellent for two, good for two, and poor for one. Psychological data on this group are incomplete and unimpressive.

---

* One case showed marked improvement in IQ from 10 to 63 while under good dietary control for three years; subsequently, dietary control was poor. IQ showed no further change.

Present Status of PKU Children

Of the 126 PKU patients known at this time, 104 are at home. Fifty-one are old enough to attend school, although only 18 attend regular classes. The others are in special classes for the mentally retarded. Only twelve are in institutions for the mentally retarded and one has expired.

Children with Hyperphenylalaninemia

Fourteen children were classified as hyperphenylalaninemic variants based on initial serum phenylalanine levels and follow-up loading tests. Age of diagnosis ranged from 3 days to 1 year and 6 months. It is of interest that IQs of these children ranged from a low of 65 to a high of 122. One child who scored at a borderline level is psychotic. Long-term follow-up of this group of children is indicated before conclusions or recommendations concerning treatment can be made. The occurrence of both mental retardation and psychosis suggests that hyperphenylala-ninemia may not be a benign condition.

Discussion

Most of the large surveys of PKU children reported in the literature are based on institutionalized populations (31, 36, 39). The most frequent signs and symptoms mentioned in previous reports are mental deficiency, blond hair, blue eyes and seizures; however, these signs are not common in infancy. Early clinical signs in infants, such as vomiting, eczema and urine odor, have been emphasized by Partington (52).

The untreated PKU child is usually hyperactive and exhibits unpredictable, erratic behavior. Excessive rocking movements, grinding of teeth, arm-waving and overall aimless behavior occasionally are misdiagnosed as early childhood schizophrenia. Six of our patients were considered autistic until the identifying urine test for phenylpyruvic acid revealed the true basis for their behavior. Only 7 patients manifested seizures: 3 myoclonic, 3 petit mal, and one psychomotor. Thirteen of our patients exhibited severe eczema unresponsive to usual therapy until a diagnosis of PKU was established and phenylalanine intake was restricted. In each, the onset of eczema preceded the development of mental retardation. In our experience, obesity has been frequent in the older untreated PKU child and has sometimes led to a mistaken diagnosis of hypothyroidism because of mental retardation. Three had been treated with thyroid in spite of a normal blood protein-bound iodine value. The marked contrast in the signs and symptoms observed in these patients and those reported in the literature is undoubtedly due to the younger age of most of our patients at the time of diagnosis. This emphasizes the value of continuing routine testing for PKU in high risk populations seen in various clinics, such as neurology, seizure, dermatology, cerebral palsy, metabolic, child guidance and others.

It has been our practice to ascertain serum phenylalanine and tyrosine levels on newborn siblings of known PKU patients as obtained from cord blood and from the infant at three or four days of age. If the serum phenylalanine is normal, milk intake is continued. Serum phenylalanine levels are rechecked at two months of age to confirm normalcy. On the other hand, if the serum phenylalanine level rises rapidly and the tyrosine level remains normal, the infant is considered possibly phenylketonuric, and further confirmation of the diagnosis is sought by paper chromatography of urine and serial serum phenylalanine and tyrosine determinations.

It has been our practice to reconfirm the diagnosis by "challenging" all PKU infants at six to twelve months of age. This is accomplished by the addition of a calculated amount of evaporated milk to the Lofenalac formula. Two patients who were thought to be phenylketonuric were found to be normal by virtue of this procedure.

It is sometimes difficult to decide whether or not to treat an older PKU child. General agreement exists among physicians that patients less than 3 years of age should be treated. Centerwall (18) points out, however, that improvement in older children may become apparent only after months to years of careful treatment. Our experience substantiates his observations. Whether to treat PKU children with normal intelligence is another difficult problem (3, 16, 33, 66).

Every effort should be made to maintain the serum phenylalanine level within the prescribed limits after treatment has been initiated. In our experience, maintenance of a level from one to three mgm. percent as recommended by Bickel (13) and Kretchmer (46) has been difficult with older children. When too many restrictions are placed on their diets, the older children generally do not cooperate readily and may obtain forbidden food from neighbors, schoolmates and the family refrigerator.

A well-rounded treatment program for phenylketonuria requires the skills of various disciplines including a physician, a nutritionist, biochemist, public health nurse, social worker and psychologist (6, 60). California has established nine diagnostic and evaluation centers to facilitate the care of PKU children by such an interdisciplinary team.

SUMMARY

In summary, comprehensive reviews of phenylketonuria and galactosemia have been presented. The beneficial results of treatment with phenylketonuria and galactosemia are sufficiently rewarding to warrant routine screening for both diseases during the neonatal period.

REFERENCES

1. Acosta, P. B., E. Wenz, G. Schaeffler, and R. Koch. *Phenylketonuria. A Diet Guide,* Evansville: Mead Johnson Laboratories, 1969.
2. Anderson, J. A., and K. F. Swaiman. "Phenylketonuria and Allied Metabolic Diseases," U.S. Department of Health, Education and Welfare, Social and Rehabilitation Service, Children's Bureau, 1967.
3. Armstrong, M. D., and N. L. Low. "Studies on Phenylketonuria VIII. Relation Between Age, Serum Phenylalanine Level and Phenylpyruvic Acid Secretion," *Pro. Soc. Exp. Biol. Med.,* 94:142, 1957.
4. Armstrong, M. D., and F. H. Tyler. "Studies on Phenylketonuria. Restricted Phenylalanine Intake in Phenylketonuria," *J. Clin. Invest.,* 34:565, 1955.
5. Baker, L., W. J. Mellman, T. A. Tedesco, and S. Segal. "Galactosemia: Symtomatic and Asymptomatic Homozygotes in One Negro Sibship," *J. Pediat.,* 68:551, 1966.
6. Berman, P. W., F. K. Graham, P. Eichman, and H. A. Waisman. "Psychologic and Neurologic Status of Diet-Treated Phenylketonuric Children and Their Siblings," *Pediatrics,* 28:924, 1961.
7. Berry, H. K., B. Sutherland, and G. M. Guest. "Simple Method for Detection of Phenylketonuria," *J.A.M.A.,* 167:2189, 1958.
8. Berry, H. K., B. S. Sutherland, G. M. Guest, and B. Umbarger. "Chemical and Clinical Observations During Treatment of Children with Phenylketonuria," *Pediatrics,* 21:929, 1958.
9. Berry, H. K., B. S. Sutherland, and B. Umbarger. "Diagnosis and Treatment: Interpretation of Results of Blood Screening Studies for Detection of Phenylketonuria," *Pediatrics,* 37:102, 1966.
10. Beutler, E., M. C. Baluda, P. Sturgeon, and R. Day. "A New Genetic Abnormality Resulting in Galactose-1-Phosphate Uridyltransferase Deficiency," *Lancet,* I:353, 1965.
11. Bickel, H. "Influence of Phenylalanine Intake on Phenylketonuria," *Lancet,* 2: 812, 1953.
12. Bickel, H., J. Gerrard, and E. M. Hickmaus. "The Influence of Phenylalanine Intake on the Chemistry and Behavior of a Phenylketonuric Child," *Acta. Paediat.,* 46:64, 1954.
13. Bickel, H., and W. P. Gruter. "Prophylaxe und Behandlung der Phenylketonuria," (Prophylaxis and Treatment of Phenylketonuria. A Preliminary Report), *Deutsch Med. Wachr.,* 86:39, 1961.
14. Brandt, N. J. "Frequency of Heterozygotes for Hereditary Galactosemia in a Normal Population," *Acta Genet. Basel,* 17:289, 1967.
15. Brandt, N. J. 'Galaktose-1-Fosfat-Uridyl-Transferase," Doctoral thesis, Munksgaard, Copenhagen, 1966.
16. Caudle, H. V. "Phenylketonuria Without Mental Retardation," (Letters to the Editor), *Pediatrics,* 26:502, 1960.
17. Centerwall, W. R., S. A. Centerwall, P. Acosta, and R. F. Chinnock, "Phenylketonuria. Dietary Management of Infants and Young Children," *J. Pediat.,* 59:93, 1961.

18. Centerwall, W. R., S. A. Centerall, V. Armon, and L. B. Mann. "Phenylketonuria. Results of Treatment of Infants and Young Children: A Report of 10 Cases," *J. Pediat.,* 59:102, 1961.
19. Centerwall, W. R., R. F. Chinnock, and A. Pusavat. "Phenylketonuria: Screening Programs and Testing Methods," *Amer. J. Public Health,* 50:1667, 1960.
20. Donnell, G. N., W. R. Bergren, R. K. Bretthauer, and R. G. Hansen. "The Enzymatic Expression of Heterozygosity in Families of Children with Galactosemia," *Pediatrics,* 25:572, 1960.
21. Donnell, G. N., W. R. Bergren, G. Perry, and R. Koch. "Galactose-1-Phosphate in Galactosemia," *Pediatrics,* 31:802, 1963.
22. Donnell, G. N., M. Collado, and R. Koch. "Growth and Development of Children with Galactosemia," *J. Pediat.,* 58:836, 1961.
23. Efron, M. "Aminoaciduria," *New Eng. J. Med.,* 272:1058, 1965.
24. Egan, T. J., W. W. Wells, H. J. Wells, and T. A. Pittman. "The Metabolism of Galactose in Galactosemia," *J. Pediat.,* 67:710, 1965.
25. Fanconi, G. "Hochgradige Galaktose-Intoleranz (Galactose-Diabetes) bei einem Kinde mit Neurofibromatosis Recklinghausen," *Jb. Kinderhalkunde,* 138:1, 1933.
26. Fishler, K., R. Koch, G. N. Donnell, and B. V. Graliker. "Psychological Correlates in Galactosemia," *Am. J. Ment. Def.,* 71:116, 1966.
27. Folling, A. "Ueber Ausscheidung von Phenylbrenztraubensaure in den Harn als Staffwechselanomalie in Verbindung mit Imbezilitaet," (Excretion of Urinary Phenylpyruvic Acid as a Metabolic Anomaly in Connection with Imbecility), *Hoppe Seyler Z. Physiol. Chem.,* 227:169, 1934.
28. Gibbs, N. K., and L. I. Woolf. "Tests for Phenylketonuria: Results of a One-Year Programme for its Detection in Infancy Among Mental Defectives," *Brit. Med. J.,* 2:532, 1959.
29. Gitzelmann, R., and S. Auricchio. "The Handling of Soya Alpha-Galactosides by a Normal and a Galactosemic Child," *Pediatrics,* 36:231, 1965.
30. Gitzelmann, R., H. C. Curtius, and I. Schneller, "Galactitol and Galactose-1-phosphate in the Lens of a Galactosemic Infant," *Exper. Eye Res.,* 6:1, 1967.
31. Guthrie, R. "Blood Screening for Phenylketonuria," (Letters to the Journal), *J.A.M.A.,* 178:863, 1961.
32. Guthrie, R., and A. Susi. "A Simple Phenylalanine Method for Detecting Phenylketonuria in Large Populations of Newborn Infants," *Pediatrics,* 32:338, 1963.
33. Horner, F. A., *et al.* "Termination of Dietary Treatment of Phenylketonuria," *New Eng. J. Med.,* 266:79, 1962.
34. Horner, F. A., and C. W. Streamer, "Effect of a Phenylalanine-Restricted Diet on Patients with Phenylketonuria; Clinical Observations in Three Cases," *J.A.M.A.,* 161:1628, 1956.
35. Horner, F. A., C. W. Streamer, D. E. Clader, L. L. Hassell, E. L. Binkley, and K. W. Dumars. "Effect of Phenylalanine Restricted Diet in Phenylketonuria," *A.M.A. J. Dis. Child.,* 93:615, 1957.
36. Hsia, D. Y-Y., W. E. Knox, K. V. Quinn, and R. S. Paine. "A One-Year Controlled Study of the Effect of Low Phenylalanine Diet on Phenylketonuria," *Pediatrics,* 21:178, 1958.
37. Huang, I., K. Hugh-Jones, and D. Y. Hsia. "Studies on the Heterozygous Carrier in Galactosemia," *J. Lab. Clin. Med.,* 54:585, 1959.
38. Isselbacher, K. J. "A Mammalian Uridinediphosphate Galactose Pyrophosphorylase," *J. Biol. Chem.,* 232:429, 1958.
39. Jervis, G. A. "Phenylpyruvic Oligophrenia. Introductory Study of 50 Cases of Mental Deficiency Associated with Excretion of Phenylpyruvic Acid," *Arch. Neurol.,* (Chicago), 38:944, 1937.

40. Jervis, G. A. "The Genetics of Phenylpyruvic Oligophrenia" (A Contribution to the study of the Influence of Heredity on Mental Defect), *J. Ment. Sc.,* (London), 85:719, 1939.

41. Kalcker, H. M., E. P. Anderson, and K. J. Isselbacher. "Galactosemia, A Congenital Defect in A Nucleotide Transferase: A Preliminary Report," *Proc. Nat. Acad., Sci.,* 42:49, 1956.

42. Kang, E., T. Kennedy, L. Cates, I. Burwash, and A. McKinnon. "Clinical Observations in PKU," *Pediatrics,* 35:932, 1965.

43. Kirkman, H. N. and E. Bynum. "Enzymatic Evidence of a Galactosemia Trait in Parents of Galactosemic Children," *Ann. Human Genet.,* 23:117, 1959.

44. Knox, W. E. "An Evaluation of the Treatment of Phenylketonuria with Diets Low in Phenylalanine," *Pediatrics,* 26:1, 1961.

45. Koch, R., P. Acosta, G. Donnell, and E. Lieberman. "Nutritional Therapy of Galactosemia." *Clinical Pediatrics,* 4:10, 1965.

45a. Koch, R. *et al.* "Phenylalaninemia and Phenylketonuria." In Nyhan, W., ed., *Heritable Disorders of Amino Acid Metabolism,* New York: Wiley, 1974.

46. Kretchmer, N., and D. D. Etzwiler. "Disorders Associated with Metabolism of Phenylalanine and Tyrosine," *Pediatrics,* 21:445, 1958.

47. LaDu, B. N. "The Importance of Early Diagnosis and Treatment of Phenylketonuria," (Editorial), *Ann. Intern. Med.,* 51:1427, 1959.

48. MacCready, R. A., and M. G. Hussey. "Newborn Phenylketonuria Program in Massachusetts—A Progress Report," *A.J.P.H.,* 54:2075, 1964.

49. Mathai, C. K., and E. Beutler. "Electrophoretic Variation of Galactose-1-Phosphate Uridyltransferase," *Science,* 154:1179, 1966.

50. McCaman, M. W., and E. Robins. "Fluorimetric Method for the Determination of Phenylalanine in Serum," *J. Lab. and Clin. Med.,* 59:885, 1962.

51. Mellman, W. J., T. A. Tedesco, and L. Baker. "A New Genetic Abnormality," *Lancet,* I:1395, 1965.

52. Partington, M. W. "The Early Symptoms of Phenylketonuria," *Pediatrics,* 27: 465, 1961.

53. Penrose, L. S. "Inheritance of Phenylpyruvic Amentia," *Lancet,* 2:192, 1935.

54. Segal, S., and H. Berstein. "Observations on Cataract Formation in the Newborn Offspring of Rats Fed a High-galactose Diet," *J. Pediat.,* 62:363, 1963.

55. Segal, S., A. Blair, and H. Roth. "The Metabolism of Galactose by Patients with Congenital Galactosemia," *Am. J. Med.,* 38:62, 1965.

56. Schwarz, V. "Metabolic Disturbances in Galactosemia." In *Modern Problems in Pediatrics,* Vol. 4, p. 402. New York: Edited by A. Hottinger, H. Berger, and S. Karger, 1959.

57. Schwarz, V., A. R. Wells, A. Holzel, and G. M. Komrower. "A Study of the Genetics of Galactosemia," *Ann. Human Genet.,* 25:179, 1961.

58. Shallenberger, R. S., and J. C. Moyer. "Relation between Changes in Glucose, Fructose, Galactose, Sucrose and Stachyose and the Formation of Starch in Peas," *Agricultural and Food Chemistry,* 9:137, 1961.

59. Stewart, J. M., and C. G. Ashley. "Phenylketonuria: Report of the Oregon Detection and Evaluation Program," *Lancet,* 87:162, 1967.

60. Umbarger, B. J. "Phenylketonuria. Treating the Disease and Feeding the Child," *Amer. J. Dis. Child.,* 100:908, 1960.

61. Von Reuss, A. "Zuckerausscheidung im Sauglingsalter," *Wein Med. Wchnschr.,* 58:799, 1908.

62. Waalkes, T. P., and S. Udenfriend. "A Fluorometric Method for Estimation of Tyrosine in Plasma and Tissues," *J. Lab. and Clin. Med.,* 50:733, 1957.

63. Wells, W. W., T. A. Pittman, H. J. Wells, and T. J. Egan. "The Isolation and

Identification of Galactitol from the Brains of Galactosemia Patients," *J. Biol. Chem.*, 240:1002, 1965.

64. Wilson, W. A., and G. N. Donnell. "Cataracts in Galactosemia," *A.M.A. Arch. Ophthalmol.*, 660:215, 1958.

65. Woolf, L. I., R. Griffiths, and A. Moncrieff. "Treatment of Phenylketonuria with a Diet Low in Phenylalanine," *Brit. Med. J.*, 1:57, 1955.

66. Woolf, L. I., C. Ounsted, D. Lee, M. Humphrey, and G. R. Steed. "Atypical Phenylketonuria in Sisters with Normal Offspring," *Lancet*, 2:464, 1961.

67. Wright, S. W. "Phenylketonuria," *J.A.M.A.*, 165:2079, 1957.

CHAPTER 9

Chromosomal Anomalies in Causation: Down's Syndrome

by RICHARD KOCH, M.D.,
KAROL FISHLER, Ph.D.,
and JOHN MELNYK, Ph.D.

PART I

DIAGNOSIS, CYTOGENETIC FINDINGS, AND EVALUATION

The term "mongolism" is a familiar term to most people, but few laymen understand the implications of this disorder. Mongolism, more appropriately termed Down's Syndrome (D.S.), is characterized by a number of physical and mental peculiarities which contribute to a clinical diagnosis. The accumulated data gathered on patients seen at Childrens Hospital of Los Angeles and other recent research findings concerning D.S. provide the basis for this discussion. It is hoped that the material gathered here will help the reader with the management and future planning for these children and their families.

INCIDENCE

The incidence of Down's Syndrome in the United States is approximately one case in every 700 births (24). It is estimated that 65,000 patients live in this country. The significance of D.S. lies in the fact that this condition produces the largest single, easily identifiable group of mentally retarded individuals. Many members of this group ultimately require closely supervised care, comprising about 10 percent of all retarded persons receiving residential care out of their home.

116

CLINICAL SIGNS

D.S. was first clearly described as early as 1866 by Langdon Down (8), a British physician who coined the term "mongolism" to describe those individuals who suffered from a marked arrest in physical and mental development, and whose slanting eyes and flat nose gave them an appearance resembling members of the Mongolian race. Even though some other names have been suggested from time to time—such as congenital acromicria, fetalism or peristatic amentia—these names have not become popular.

Because of certain distinguishing characteristics (1), the diagnosis can be made on clinical grounds in 90 to 95 percent of cases. The most important clinical findings are mental retardation, facial appearance, lack of muscular tone and dermatologlyphic findings. Other typical stigmata or signs include the following:

1. Small round head
2. Upward and outward slanting of the eyes
3. Epicanthal folds
4. White speckled iris (Brushfield spots)
5. Frequent eye complications (strabismus, myopia, cataracts, etc.)
6. "Saddle," low bridge nose
7. Brachycephaly of head (broad, short skull)
8. Low set, misshapen ear lobes
9. Small mouth with drooping corners
10. Protruding tongue
11. Highly arched palate
12. Excess of loose skin at the nape of the neck
13. Broad and short hand with stubby fingers
14. Short, incurved fifth finger (small)
15. Palmar crease (simian line) across one or both palms
16. Distally located palmar triradius
17. Broad and stubby feet
18. Widely spaced great toe
19. Deep longitudinal plantar crease
20. Weak and floppy Moro reflex
21. Hypermobility of the joints
22. Small external genitals (both sexes)
23. Lack of breast engorgement at birth
24. High incidence of congenital heart and bowel defects
25. High incidence of respiratory ailments with chronic T & A

Only the more common stigmata of this condition are listed here. Actually, some 50 known characteristics are associated with D.S. Only a few of these peculiarities may be noted in any one case, but unfortunately, retarded mental development is usually found. Rarely is there a well documented exception to this statement. Of all these symptoms, the intellectual deficit is the most difficult aspect for parents to accept and manage. Gibson and Gibbons (12) demonstrated a positive relationship between the number of physical stigmata of D.S. and intellectual ability. According to their findings, the more "mongoloid" the subject appears (per the selected diagnostic signs), the more intelligence he manifests on psychological examination. Conversely, those whose appearance is less obviously mongoloid are more likely to be more retarded; there are, of course, many exceptions to this observation. Recent research does not support this viewpoint.

RELIABILITY OF DIAGNOSIS

The diagnosis of D.S. is usually made on the basis of certain signs which can be identified by a physician shortly after the baby's birth. In a few atypical cases, the characteristic signs may be so minimal that even the most experienced physician may have difficulty in making a correct diagnosis. Such "borderline" cases can only be diagnosed accurately by careful cytogenetic study.

It was pointed out earlier that one of the most reliable characteristics in diagnosis is mental retardation. Since the child's development follows a fairly uniform pattern, it is possible to assess his progress with fair accuracy by comparing his actual performance with the norms derived from large samples of children at various age levels. As part of our routine procedure, all children referred for medical evaluation are given a developmental or psychometric examination by the clinical psychologist to estimate their mental age on the basis of performance. For example, if a 12-month-old baby exhibits certain behavior that is more typical of a six-month-old baby (such as rolling to the prone instead of walking, using a primitive palmar grasp rather than a neat pincer grasp, grunting or babbling instead of beginning formation of a few words like "mama" or "dada"), this baby would essentially be functioning, developmentally, at one-half the rate expected for his chronological age. By administering Gesell Developmental Schedules, it is possible to arrive at a developmental quotient (DQ) for the examined child which indicates his developmental progress in motor, adaptive, language and personal-social areas. Furthermore, by repeating such measurements biennially, a fairly good estimate of the child's rate of development may be obtained; this, in turn, will provide useful informa-

TABLE I

A COMPARISON OF MALE AND FEMALE DOWN'S SYNDROME CHILDREN ON SOME DEVELOPMENTAL DIMENSIONS

Developmental Dimensions	MALE			FEMALE		
	Mean Age in Months	Range in Months	Number of Patients	Mean Age in Months	Range in Months	Number of Patients
1. ROLLING OVER	5.80	2-10	26	6.41	3-12	17
2. SITTING UNSUPPORTED	12.00	7-30	28	11.47	7-18	17
3. CRAWLING	14.38	7-28	16	13.08	7-24	13
4. CREEPING	18.50	8-34	14	16.17	9-20	12
5. STANDING WITH SUPPORT	16.88	11-30	17	18.67	12-30	9
6. STANDING UNSUPPORTED	21.55	14-44	11	22.09	15-33	11
7. WALKING WITH SUPPORT	22.30	12-44	20	22.92	17-33	12
8. WALKING UNSUPPORTED	28.27	15-50	15	26.77	16-52	13
9. WORDS	27.83	15-42	18	21.92	12-33	12
10. WORD COMBINATIONS	40.50	30-56	6	31.80	21-44	5
11. SMILING	2.61	1-5	31	2.80	1-4	20
12. SOLIDS (takes well)	11.67	9-18	18	9.00	5-15	8
13. FEEDS SELF IN PART (finger feeds beyond cookie-cracker)	26.74	17-38	19	27.92	16-52	13
14. DRINKS FROM CUP UNASSISTED	37:17	24-48	12	35.00	21-76	9
15. FEEDS SELF "FULLY" (cup-glass utensil)	35.67	31-40	3	42.45	24-76	8
16. DRESSES SELF PARTIALLY (pulls on at least a simple garment)	44.43	30-65	7	46.60	30-76	5
17. URINE CONTROL (only occasional lapses)	42.78	36-56	9	36.63	24-52	8
18. BOWEL CONTROL (only occasional lapses)	33.44	14-50	16	35.73	24-52	11

tion about his present level of functioning and his expected progress. Our data show that the rate of development decelerates as the infant grows older (26). Mongoloid children usually test higher during the first year of life, but by the time they reach the third year their mental achievement drops considerably and moderate retardation becomes apparent. The initial progress probably explains why many parents of relatively asymptomatic children are reluctant to accept the diagnosis and prefer to "shop around" from one clinic to another, in the hope that the diagnosis may be shown to be wrong. (Table I lists the ages at which various developmental tasks are typically accomplished by D.S. children.)

While there are variations in the degree of defective development among D.S. infants, most of them follow a general pattern of development. This permits one to predict the child's ultimate mental status. While many reach a mental status ranging from three to seven years, their rate of progress is significantly slower than that of normal children. Thus, it is not unusual to see some three-year-olds who are barely beginning to walk, or who still have no speech at four or even five years. However, most of these children eventually learn to walk and talk, even though their speech may be significantly limited. Rarely are they able to go into the regular classes of the public school system, although a good many are able to qualify for enrollment in the special classes designed for trainable mentally retarded children.

CYTOGENETICS OF THE DOWN'S SYNDROME COMPLEX

The underlying defect in Down's Syndrome (D.S.) is still considered by many parents to result from faulty intra-uterine conditions and it is with some surprise that they receive the news that this condition is associated with a chromosomal abnormality. Several years have elapsed since Lejeune, Gautier and Turpin (20) found that an extra chromosome was present in all of the cells studied in patients with D.S. Since that time, a large number of other studies have confirmed this fact, and have revealed that there are at least fourteen types of chromosome abnormalities in the complex. Table II lists most of the chromosomal abnormalities in the Down's Syndrome complex, together with the chromosome number and phenotype associated with each. These are not all of the possible combinations but are representative of those which occur most frequently, or of those which are considered to occur but are not as yet identified. Translocations between chromosome 21 and any chromosome in the complement are hypothetically possible, but not seen clinically.

Before considering some of these classes in detail, it may be helpful to describe the karyotypes of a D.S. patient. In the chromosomes of a female D.S. patient, there is a total of 47 chromosomes, with three chromosomes in the 21st position, instead of the normal two. There is still some uncertainty as to whether the extra chromosome in this syndrome is 21 or 22. It is often referred to as G_1 trisomy, indicating that the extra chromosome is in the G group. However, for the sake of illustration and explanation, the term trisomy 21 will be used when referring to D.S.

TABLE II

Chromosome Abnormalities in Down's Syndrome Complex

	Karyotype	Number of Chromosomes	Phenotype
1.	Trisomy 21	47	Down's
2.	Normal/trisomy 21 mosaic	46/47	Down's or apparently normal
3.	Balanced 15-21 translocation	45	Normal
4.	Balanced 15-21 translocation/normal mosaic	45/46	Normal
5.	Unbalanced 15-21 translocation	46	Down's
6.	Unbalanced 15-21 translocation/normal mosaic	46	Down's**
7.	Balanced 21-22 translocation	45	Normal
8.	Balanced 21-22 translocation/normal mosaic	45/46	Normal
9.	Unbalanced 21-22 translocation	46	Down's
10.	Unbalanced 21-22 translocation/normal mosaic	46	Down's**
11.*	Balanced 21-21 translocation	45	Normal
12.	Balanced 21-21 translocation/normal mosaic	45/46	Down's**
13.	Unbalanced 21-21 translocation	46	Down's
14.	Unbalanced 21-21 translocation/normal mosaic	46	Down's**

* From 11 to 14, isochromosome 21 may be substituted because it is undistinguishable from a 21-21 translocation in effect.
** Cases with this characteristic are theoretically possible, but have not yet been identified.

The following four major classes of chromosome abnormalities in D.S. patients will be discussed:

1. Trisomy 21, in which all cells have 47 chromosomes with an extra chromosome in the G group. These cells are called trisomic.
2. Trisomy 21/normal mosaicism, in which a variable proportion of the cells are trisomic, the others being normal.
3. Translocation D.S., in which chromosome 21 is fused with another chromosome. This is the class which is frequently involved in the inherited type of D.S., and contains several sub-classes.
4. Translocation mosaicism: There are two kinds of translocation mosaicism:
   (a) 45/46 mosaicism, in which a phenotypically normal parent has a normal population of cells and another population with a balanced translocation.
   (b) A D.S. patient who has 46 chromosomes in all cells but in which there are two population of cells in terms of the karyotypes.

Because each of these classes carries different implications in parent counseling, it is important to analyze each of them critically and, where

TABLE III

Risk of a Mongoloid Infant According to Maternal Age*

Age of Mother (years)	Approximate Risk per Pregnancy
Less than 29	1 in 3,000
30 to 34	1 in 600
35 to 39	1 in 280
40 to 44	1 in 70
45 to 49	1 in 40
All mothers in the population	1 in 665

* From Motulsky, Arno G., and Hecht, Frederick: Genetic prognosis and counseling, *Amer. J. Obstet. Gynec.* 90:1227-1241, 1964; based on data of Carter, C., and McCarthy, D.: *Brit. J. Prev. Soc. Med.* 5:83, 1951.

possible, to consider some of the available empiric or calculated risk figures for future pregnancies.

1. *Trisomy 21*

All of the cells in patients with trisomy 21 have 47 chromosomes and have an extra chromosome in the G group. This is the non-inherited or sporadic type of D.S. It occurs in the general population with a frequency of 1 in 700 births and has a variable empiric risk figure which is dependent upon the age of the mother. In Table III, the risk of giving birth to an affected child is presented according to maternal age. It is clear that as the mother grows older, her chances of having a D.S. child are increased considerably.

The birth of a D.S. child raises the question of bearing another affected child. If the parents are over 37 years of age, however, it is a general practice to discourage further pregnancies or to suggest amniocentesis for chromosome analysis.

The maternal age effect has been reviewed extensively (6, 21, 22, 24, 27). The cells which are destined to form ova are already present in the fetus as öocytes which have completed the early stages of meiosis. They remain in a dormant state until puberty, at which time they complete meiosis and form mature ova which are released at monthly intervals from the follicles. Therefore, before fertilization, the ovum has been exposed to many years of environmental insults such as irradiation, viruses and certain chemicals which are now known to have a deleterious effect on chromosomes. The longer this exposure, the greater the possibility of chromosome damage and misdivision. In addition to this, there is an "aging effect" on the ova which may be related to changes in the mother's metabolism (24). Consequently, a mother over 40 years of age has a much greater risk of producing an ovum with an extra chromosome than has a mother under 20 years. Studies have failed to show any similar age effect for fathers of D.S. children.

Penrose suggests that there is a slight added risk for the mother who has already had one D.S. child, because of the possibility of localized ovarian mosaicism or genetic predisposition to non-disjunction (24). For this reason amniocentesis is usually recommended for all mothers who have had one D.S. child already in any subsequent pregnancy.

2. *Normal/Trisomy 21 Mosaicism*

In this group of patients, generally referred to as Down's mosaics, there are two populations of cells, one normal and the other with an extra chromosome in the G group. This form of D.S. arises from a chromosomal misdivision in an embryonic cell after a number of normal divisions have taken place. Such a misdivision, which is called non-disjunction in this case, results in two cells, one with 47 chromosomes and one with 45. It is postulated that the cells with 45 chromosomes fail to survive because of the loss of so many genes, although the remaining cells with 46 and those with 47 chromosomes continue to divide normally and eventually form the fetus and the newborn baby.

The presence of D.S. stigmata in mosaics is variable and is dependent upon the relative proportion of normal to trisomic cells; this ratio, in turn, is dependent upon the stage of embryogenesis at which misdivision occurred. Thus, early misdivision will likely produce nearly equal numbers of normal and trisomic cells and a marked D.S. phenotype. A late misdivision will probably result in a decreased number of trisomic cells and the patient may have minimal signs of D.S., or, in the rare case, no obvious stigmata at all.

Since the chromosomal disorder results from an event following fertilization, this form of D.S. is non-hereditary; therefore, parental reassurance can be given. Child-bearing should be discouraged in the case of mosaic individuals because the chance of having a Down's Syndrome offspring is usually high (30).

3. *Translocation D.S.*

(a) *14-21 Translocation*—A fusion or translocation between chromosome 21 and any chromosome in the cell may be possible but it usually takes place with a satellited chromosome from either the D or G group. The most common translocation is with one from the D group (15) which has now been demonstrated to involve chromosome number 14 (18). Another type is 21-22 translocation, which involves another small chromosome in the G group. An example of these translocations will provide some understanding of the importance of such abnormalities in the inherited form of D.S.

Chromosomes in the nucleus are very long and intertwined as compared with those at metaphase. If a 14 and a 21 chromosome overlap and they break at the point of contact, reunion of the broken ends restoring the original chromosomes does not always occur. Occasionally, reunion takes place between the 14 and 21 ends, resulting in a translocation chromosome which reduces the total number of chromosomes by one (to 45) and provides a new chromosome to the cell during subsequent divisions (Figure 1). This is called a *balanced* translocation because none of the genes is thought to be lost. If such a translocation is present in the ovum or sperm, fertilization will result in a child with 45 chromosomes in each cell. Often these individuals are called translocation carriers.

FIGURE 1

SCHEMATIC DIAGRAM OF A 14-21 TRANSLOCATION

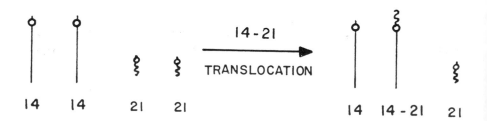

FIGURE 2

14 - 21 TRANSLOCATION SEGREGATION OF CHROMOSOMES

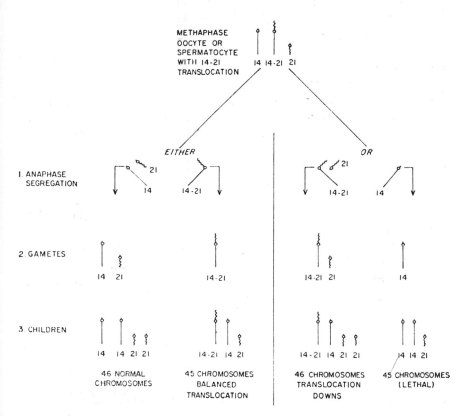

Such an individual with 45 chromosomes and a balanced 14-21 translocation is not affected physically or mentally as determined by present methods of testing. Although only their peripheral blood and occasionally skin fibroblasts have been examined, it is believed that all of their cells, including the germinal cells, have 45 chromosomes.

Either parent can be a carrier of a balanced translocation and can produce affected children, although this defect has been more commonly reported in the female. The diagram in Figure 2 shows how the normal 14 and 21 and the 14-21 translocation chromosomes segregate during meiosis, the four kinds of sperm or ova (gametes) which are formed, and the chromosome constitution of the four products of fertilization which are possible.

As seen in the first row, the normal chromosome 21 can move together with either the translocation chromosome or the normal 14 during anaphase separation. This results in the four types of gametes shown in the second row. Upon fertilization by a normal sperm, the four possible combinations are shown in the third row.

The four combinations result in only three types of children. The first is a normal child with 46 chromosomes. The second is a child with 45 chromosomes including a 14-21 translocation chromosome in a balanced state like the affected parent. The third type also has 46 chromosomes but, because the translocation chromosome carries an attached 21, there are three of chromosome 21 in all, resulting in an individual with translocation Down's Syndrome. The fourth type, having only one chromosome 21, has not been found; therefore, either this combination is lethal or gametes which lack a chromosome 21 fail to develop. The outcome, on the average, of a number of pregnancies for a female 14-21 translocation carrier is that one-third of the children will be translocation carriers and one-third will be Down's Syndrome with 46 chromosomes. In view of these high risks future pregnancies should be discouraged or monitored by amniotic chromosome analysis.

(b) *21-22 Translocation*—The 21-22 type of translocation occurs in much the same manner as the 14-21. An end-to-end fusion of the two small chromosomes results in a chromosome which appears in size and shape like one of the chromosomes in the F group (Figure 3). A parent who is a carrier of such a balanced translocation will produce sperm or ova with similar results as those shown for a 14-21 translocation (Figure 2). This translocation generally occurs sporadically (*de novo*) and thus the parents exhibit normal chromosomes. In situations with normal parental chromosomal patterns, the recurrence rate is very low and reassurance can be given to the parents. Obviously, in situations in which one of the parents is a balanced carrier of a translocation, future pregnancies should be monitored by amniotic chromosome analysis.

(c) *21-21 Translocation*—This type of translocation in which fusion occurs between both of the chromosomes involved in mongolism is cytologically indistinguishable from the 21-22 type. As shown in Figure 4, a translocation between both of chromosomes 21 results in a balanced 21-21 translocation. If such a translocation is present in a parent during meiosis, the translocation chromosome will go to the same cell

FIGURE 3

SCHEMATIC DIAGRAM OF A 21-22 TRANSLOCATION

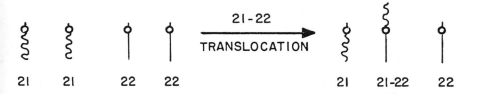

FIGURE 4

SCHEMATIC DIAGRAM OF A 21-21 TRANSLOCATION

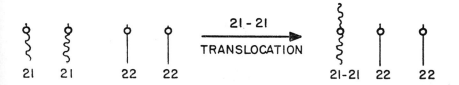

with chromosome 22 during anaphase and the other cell receives only a chromosome 22, as is seen in Figure 5. The kinds of gametes that are formed are shown in the second row. The products of fertilization are shown in the third row. Only two possible combinations are seen in this instance. In the first combination, the child is a translocation 21-21 Down's Syndrome and in the second, where a chromosome is missing, the condition is thought to be lethal, since no such cases have been recorded. Therefore, all of the children born to a parent with a 21-21 balanced translocation will have Down's Syndrome. However, there have been only rare instances of this abnormality (7, 10). As before, future pregnancy should be discouraged in such situations or should be analyzed cytogenetically.

4. *Translocation Mosaicism*

(a) *Parental 45/46 Mosaicism*—In this type of translocation mosaicism, fertilization results from fusion of normal gametes and a number of normal mitotic divisions take place during embryogenesis before the translocation occurs. Thus, a normal population of cells exists in the early embryo at the time when two chromosomes break in a single cell and rejoin to form a translocation chromosome. Subsequent divisions of this cell form the second population of cells with 45 chromosomes. As in the 14-21 or 21-22 translocation described earlier, presumably no genes are lost because such a translocation mosaic is apparently normal insofar as our methods of testing can determine (Figure 6). If the translocation occurs early during embryogenesis, perhaps 50 percent of the cells may have a translocation chromosome. However, if it occurs late, only a small proportion of cells may be affected. It is possible for only a single organ to develop mosaicism if the translocation event occurs during organogeneses.

G/G (21-22) translocation/normal mosaicism has been described by Waxman and Arakaki (29). The mother showed a normal chromosome count in her leukocytes but a mosaicism of normal and 21-22 translocation cells in her skin. She had three D.S. children. Fraccaro, Kaijser and Lindsten (11), and Hamerton, Briggs, Giannelli and Carter (16) also reported similar translocation mosaicism. In our own studies, two translocation mosaics were found, one involving 14-21 and the other 21-22 translocations.

(b) *Down's Syndrome with Translocation Mosaicism*—No D.S. individual with translocation mosaicism has been reported, to the best

FIGURE 5

METAPHASE
ÖOCYTE OR
SPERMATOCYTE
TRANSLOCATION

21-21   22   22

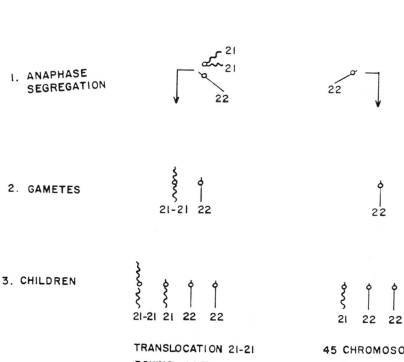

1. ANAPHASE
   SEGREGATION

2. GAMETES

3. CHILDREN

TRANSLOCATION 21-21
DOWNS WITH
46 CHROMOSOMES

45 CHROMOSOMES
(LETHAL)

FIGURE 6

TRANSLOCATION MOSAICISM

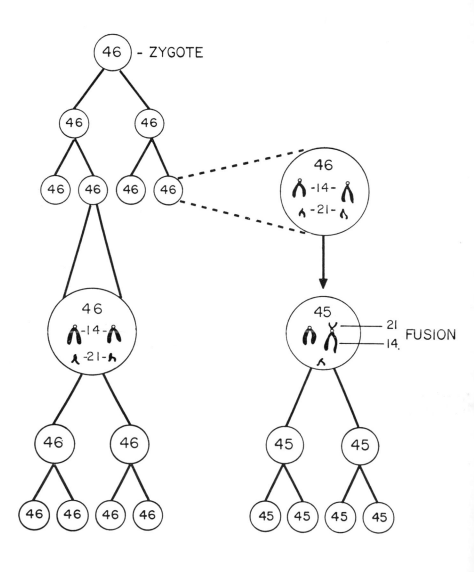

of our knowledge, but one will most likely be discovered before long. Two cases of apparent D_1 trisomy with 46 chromosomes in which two populations of cells (one normal and the other with an unbalanced translocation) have been described.

The mechanism producing such an abnormality, in which all cells have 46 chromosomes but in which there are two populations, is based on a translocation event which occurs during the two-strand stage. In other words, the chromosomes have replicated and they consist of two chromatids which are still united by the centromere. After normal fertilization and after several normal divisions, and overlap of a chromatid from each of a 14 and 21 chromosome occurs. A break at the point of the overlap and a rejoining involving the broken ends of the 14 and 21 chromatids results in asymmetrical chromosomes. During anaphase the normal chromatid 21 goes to the same pole as the one carrying the translocated sister chromatid. The other chromosome 21, which was not involved in the translocation, also divides at anaphase and provides the third chromatid 21. The ensuing cell, therefore, is genetically trisomy 21. The karyotype will show one member of the D group missing, but an additional chromosome in the G group which is the 14-21 translocation chromosome.

CYTOGENETIC COUNSELING

Parents who seek counseling after the birth of a D.S. child are understandably anxious about their chances of having another child who is similarly affected. Before such information can be given it is necessary to determine the category of Down's Syndrome in which the child belongs. This can only be done by means of a chromosome analysis in which the peripheral blood of the child is cultured. During the first visit it is advisable to explain some of the categories of Down's Syndrome and to explain the recurrence risk figures associated with each. This will establish the basis for counseling the parents on the second visit when the results of the chromosome analysis are available. Experience shows that the parents do not absorb or retain all of the information which is given on the first visit; therefore, it is helpful to repeat this information to assist them in understanding the problem.

1. *Trisomy 21*

At least 10 cells, and preferable 20 cells, should be analyzed to evaluate the possibility of mosaicism in the child. Ideally, both parents should also be analyzed in order to evaluate the possibility of parental mosaicism.

Having established the fact that the patient has trisomy 21 and that the parents have normal chromosomes, a table of the incidence of D.S. births according to the age of the mother at the time of birth may be used. This probability figure then becomes the empiric risk figure. For example, the mother in the age group 22-24 who has had a D.S. child would have one chance in 1,600 of having another Down's Syndrome child, according to Penrose (24). It must be emphasized that these are approximate figures involving factors which are difficult to evaluate and which may increase this risk. For instance, if one of the parents has localized mosaicism in the ovaries or testes which cannot be detected by a study of the chromosomes in peripheral blood, the risk may be much greater. Another factor is the possible presence of a gene which increases non-disjunction in either mother or father. These factors should be considered and allowance should be made for a slightly greater risk for each age group.

There is considerable disagreement regarding the empiric risk figure for mothers who have had one D.S. child. Hamerton (16) suggests that the risk of recurrence after the birth of one child with trisomy 21 whose parents have normal chromosomes is six times greater if the mother is under 35 years of age, but that there is no apparent increase in risk if she is over 35. Carter and Evans (4) suggest that, in the absence of chromosome studies, parents who have had one D.S. child and have no familial history of the condition, have a risk of one to two percent, irrespective of maternal age.

If one of the parents is mosaic for trisomy 21, the counseling situation becomes more difficult. Mosaic mothers have been reported with little or no stigmata of Down's Syndrome (28, 30), whereas others have marked signs of the condition. Therefore, the exact risk depends on the proportion of cells in the ovaries which carry the extra chromosome, and one-half of this value would be the risk figure. For example, if one-third of the ovarian cells are trisomy 21, the risk of Down's Syndrome would be one-sixth. A rough estimate of this proportion may be determined from fibroblast or leucocyte cultures; the risk figure arrived at can then be added to the ordinary risk for the mother's age group (24).

2. *Translocation 14-21*

If both parents have normal chromosomes, the risks of having another D.S. child of the sporadic type are similar to those described for trisomy

TABLE IV

SUMMARY OF CHROMOSOMAL FINDINGS WITH DOWN'S SYNDROME*

Maternal Age (years)	No. of Patients	Trisomy 21 and Mosaics	Sporadic		Translocations Inherited		Unknown		Total		%
			G/G	D/G	G/G	D/G	G/G	D/G	G/G	D/G	
<30	722	658	23	16	2	11	6	6	31	33	8.9
>30	660	646	6	5	0	2	1	0	7	7	2.1
Total:	1,382	1,304	29	21	2	13	7	6	38	40	

* Summary of data from Wright et al. (31). The data are from series reported by a large number of researchers whose original studies are listed in Wright et al. (31).

21. Again, allowance should be made for the possibility of mosaicism for a translocation in parental reproductive organs.

If one of the parents is a carrier of a balanced 14-21 translocation the cytogenetic prognosis is poor. If the mother is the carrier, approximately 20 percent of the children will be translocation Down's Syndrome, 40 percent will be balanced carriers and 40 percent will be entirely normal. If the father is a translocation carrier the risk is probably less than one in twenty (17). Such fathers produce normal children and translocation carriers in nearly equal frequencies (17).

3. 21-22 Translocation

This type of translocation is less frequent than the 14-21 type. It is usually sporadic, and the counseling situation is optimistic. If both parents have normal karyotypes, the risk is much the same as for parents in the general population, although there is some suggestion that advancing paternal age may increase the risk somewhat (23).

In a recent review, Wright *et al.* (31) showed that out of a total of 1,382 D.S. patients, 38 had a 21-22 translocation, 29 of whom were sporadic. Only two of those that were sporadic were inherited, and the origin of the translocation could not be determined in seven. Table IV (based on these results) shows that translocations are more frequent at younger maternal ages. Approximately nine percent of the D.S. patients born to mothers under 30 years of age have a translocation, as compared to approximately two percent in the older age group. The number of 14-21 translocations and 21-22 translocations were approximately equal in both groups. In the younger age group, about 40 percent of the 14-21 translocations were inherited and 60 percent were sporadic. There is a marked difference, however, in the 21-22 translocation patients: Here only 8 percent were inherited whereas 92 percent were sporadic.

4. 21-21 Translocation

As indicated earlier, the 21-21 type of translocation is very rare. The families reported by Forssman and Lehmann (10) and Dallaire *et al.* (7) had 13 children, all of whom had Down's Syndrome. It is now possible to distinguish a 21-22 from 21-21 translocation by chromosome studies. Counseling such a parent is difficult. Adoption is probably the best approach in this situation.

5. Amniocentesis

Amniocentesis is a technique devised to obtain amniotic fluid from the pregnant uterus by needle aspiration. It is a simple test and can be performed safely by the average obstetrician or surgeon. Usually it is performed 10-14 weeks after conception. There are several reasons for selecting 10-14 weeks as the appropriate time for performing amniocentesis. By this period, enough amniotic fluid has accumulated in the uterus so that an adequate sample can be obtained. In addition, the small size of the fetus at this time during pregnancy makes injury to the fetus unlikely. Lastly, if therapeutic abortion is chosen as a course of action by the parents, it can be safely performed up to the 20th week of gestation. Amniocentesis is now an accepted procedure, and is readily available. It has been recommended that every pregnant woman over the age of 35 years have the test as a matter of routine and that all pregnant women who have had a child with a chromosome disorder such as Down's syndrome have the test routinely in all subsequent pregnancies. The aspirated amniotic fluid contains cells that can be grown on artificial media and then tested for chromosomal abnormality. In addition, the fluid can be tested for viruses, certain amino acid disorders and for alpha-fetoprotein. The last test can detect such conditions as spina bifida and anencephaly *in utero*. If the cells do show a chromosome disorder such as trisomy 21 or if some other serious defect is disclosed, the parents will have to make the difficult choice of therapeutic abortion and trying again to conceive a normal fetus, or of carrying an abnormal fetus to term and having another handicapped child in the family. To date, the author's experience has been that parents have chosen to have a therapeutic abortion and to try another time to have a normal child. This has been true of parents of all religious faiths. Forgiveness is a part of all religions and under these circumstances, it certainly is indicated. After all, families have an obligation to raise healthy, normal children for the benefit of society as a whole whenever possible.

PART II

MANAGEMENT

WHAT ADVICE CAN THE PHYSICIAN PROVIDE?

Once the diagnosis is made, it is the responsibility of the physician to decide how to handle the difficult situation of informing the parents about the problem. This demands a great deal of tact, wisdom and kindly understanding. No matter how experienced a doctor may be, the situation is not easy because of the impact on the parents of the diagnosis and the associated mental retardation (9).

It is our practice to perform cytogenetic studies on all Down's Syndrome children and their parents.

In confirmed cases, it has been our practice to follow a philosophy of truthfulness and openness. There are several reasons why it is thought that withholding such important information from the parents would likely do more harm than good. For one thing, the parents are entitled to share the knowledge of their baby's condition as soon as the diagnosis is established. The sooner parents gain the necessary information concerning this problem, the better are their chances of acceptance and adjustment, both in terms of their responsibilities to the infant and of working out a long-term satisfactory solution. Although the initial explanation need not be too exhaustive, the physician has to be prepared to answer many questions that parents will ask. Periodic conferences with the parents, and sometimes with other relatives, are often imperative.

The conference should be conducted by an experienced pediatrician. He should offer suggestions and general advice but should not insist on any particular method of handling the problem. No matter how experienced the medical staff, only the parents should make the final decision as to what is best for them and the baby. The course of action that is best for one family may not be satisfactory for another. Each case requires careful consideration because of differences in cultural, educational or religious background; in the total family picture; in the emotional maturity of the parents; and in their attitude toward other children in the family. The physician should provide continued medical care of the child, as well as moral support and guidance. It is chiefly through a close working relationship with the physician that parents gradually accept the fact that they have a D.S. infant through no fault of their own. They gain from the physician the reassurance and the strength they need to assume their responsibility to the child. This acceptance is often impossible without the support of their physician.

Early Decisions

The question asked most frequently by parents of a newborn D.S. baby concerns the choice of home care or placement outside of the home. While parents feel that their baby should stay at home, some physicians indiscriminately advocate immediate placement away from home, either in a foster home or in an institution for retarded children. Some parents have such strong feelings of guilt or shame that they prefer to conceal the fact of the baby's defect by surrendering him soon after birth. On the other hand, the socio-cultural background of the parents may be such that they are unable to accept placement outside the home (9). Whatever solution is decided upon by the parents, it requires the careful consideration and support of the professional personnel caring for the child.

As a general rule, home care for the D.S. child is advantageous for several reasons. Many D.S. children have such physical defects as abnormalities of the eye, heart, bowel, respiratory system or other handicaps which are best cared for in pediatric centers rather than in an institution which may have limited medical resources. It is generally agreed that even the best of institutional care cannot substitute for parental care. This is clearly evident when one reviews prior statistics of the life expectancy with reference to the causes of death (3). Of live-born D.S. infants, 30 percent die before the age of one month, about 53 percent in one year, and 60 percent by the age of ten years. This study was done in the forties and fifties and indicated that only two-thirds of those alive at six months were still alive at ten years. With modern medical care, survival has been considerably increased. The implication is that if the infant can survive the first months of his life, he has a good chance of living for many years. In our experience, this is more easily accomplished by home care than in a hospital or institutional setting where younger children are prone to develop communicable diseases which decrease their chances of survival. Other evidence in favor of home care in the early years comes from studies by Centerwall (5), Kugel (19), and Schipper (25).

Centerwall (5) compared the physical and mental development of D.S. children who were put into placement very soon after birth with similar children who were reared in their homes until two and one-half years of age or older. Those who were cared for at home showed significantly better nutrition and growth, and walked at a much earlier age. The average IQ of the home group was 43 as compared with an average of 34 for the foster-home group. It was the author's impression that the children who were placed in an institution early in infancy functioned within the severely retarded range, whereas those kept at home were within the moderately retarded or trainable range. Another important consideration in favor of early home care comes from the knowledge that these children are usually happy, playful and relatively easy to manage in their early years. They have certain potentialities which will develop under optimal home conditions. They can learn to care for themselves and perform other useful functions. Judging from our own observations, the attitudes of normal siblings toward their D.S. siblings did not reveal a detrimental effect on the happiness and welfare of the whole family structure when parents were given proper guidance and professional support (13). Furthermore, our findings suggest that normal siblings not only closely reflect their own parents' attitudes toward the affected child, but they often consider him as a special problem and have no qualms in acknowledging this among their own peers. Perhaps the most crucial consideration against early placement is the parental doubt which follows such a decision. Parents should observe, judge and decide on the basis of facts and experience, rather than accepting a professional opinion alone, regardless of the expertness of that opinion. It is our belief that hasty placement is a greater psychological hazard to parental stability than dealing with the problem firsthand in the home. The small chance of error in diagnosis is another cogent reason for advising against early placement (14). In addition, mosaic Down's children may have near normal intelligence, and early placement would be harmful.

A word might be said about the child who has been, or should be, placed in an institution because of the particular circumstances of the case at hand. Sometimes placement away from home may be the only possible solution for both child and family. For example, at times a child may need treatment or help that cannot be provided at home or in his own community. The same may hold true when the family is not able to care for him because of marital discord, separation or divorce. Sometimes the mother may not be physically able to give him the kind of care he requires, and sometimes one or both of the parents are so disturbed that they are unable to provide proper care. Oftentimes, when there are many other young, normal children in the family, the addition of a D.S. child may precipitate such a great burden on the mother that it may prevent her from giving adequate attention to her other children. Usually, however, such problems do not become obvious until the child reaches preschool age. Since most D.S. children realize that they are unable to compete with normal children by adolescence, they may become frustrated and unhappy and may become more difficult to manage. It is possible that they will be happier in later life through association with others more nearly their own mental age. Usually by that time, each child can be fitted into some type of special educational setting which will be of benefit.

What Can Be Done for the Child at Home?

Much to the surprise of many uninformed parents, a D.S. child usually does not present a problem in his early years. His care does not differ significantly from the care given to a normal child. A mentally retarded baby, like all babies, requires personal attention and love, as well as good physical care. He needs to know that he belongs to the family and that he is loved and wanted. Mentally retarded children have the same feelings as other children. Even though they are limited mentally, they are sensitive to a wide range of normal feelings and are quite capable of expressing their own emotions of love, fear or anger. Actually, D.S. infants are usually quite affectionate in both giving and accepting the love of those around them. Consequently, if they are treated in a warm and accepting manner by their parents, they readily reciprocate these feelings.

Thus, it is important that they be treated as normally as possible in a home setting. They may require more attentive care for a longer time than most babies. The parents will not be able to hide from their other children the fact that this child is different. The children should not deny the fact in front of their friends. Fortunately, we are now witnessing a pronounced change in the attitude of society which is evidenced by greater understanding of the retarded child in the community. There is an increasing number of community facilities and educational settings where parents can plan cooperatively for the training and education of these children. The present attitude of acceptance capitalizes on the assets of the mentally handicapped child and engenders in him the feeling that he can help himself and probably help others. Some of these children can learn to contribute useful services in the home, and in a sheltered working environment.

In the early years of development, home management of any retarded child can be enhanced greatly by adhering to a consistent training program. The three R's, which should be followed by all parents of a retarded child, are: Routine, Relaxation and Repetition. Since retarded children are obviously slower to learn things, establishing *routines* in their basic training is of tremendous help. This is particularly true in the areas of feeding, toilet training or dressing ability. Furthermore, when the parent is *relaxed* with the child, that is, does not show his impatience, the child will respond much better to a new learning situation, and he will more likely master the task at hand. Finally, because the child is slower mentally, it will be necessary for the parent to go over and over certain routines; hence, *repetition* is an important contribution to success.

The question often raised by parents involves how to explain to siblings the fact that a D.S. child is "different." Again, truthfulness is probably the most sensible and simplest way of avoiding further difficulties in this respect. Sometimes a simple explanation will help normal brothers and sisters to understand that Johnny is "slower," but he is just as much a part of the family as anyone else. Such an attitude not only gives the normal siblings a better understanding of the family situation, but will help them explain to their friends why their brother is different. As was indicated earlier, it is the parental attitude toward the retarded child at home that will affect the attitudes of normal siblings toward acceptance or rejection of their handicapped brother or sister.

Parents often become harassed, particularly if they lack experience. Many mothers become distraught and feel somewhat helpless in meeting various problems. In such instances, they may obtain considerable help through the services of a public health nurse who can visit the household and offer useful advice regarding home management. Such service can be requested for the parents by a family physician or be obtained through a local health department. The experience of the public health nurse in such problems as feeding management, discipline, toilet training, and dressing is of inestimable value to the overburdened mother. In many communities at the present time, infant stimulation programs are available at minimal cost. Usually a phone call to the local Association for Retarded Citizens will help new parents find such resources.

COUNSELING

Certainly, the presence of a D.S. child in a home environment may precipitate some physical, psychological or financial stress upon the family at one time or other. Few parents are capable of carrying such a burden entirely on their own shoulders, and they are most assuredly entitled to professional guidance. This they can obtain from their own family doctor, or they may take advantage of special services, such as clinics, nursery groups or parent groups for retarded children. On the other hand, the responsibility for careful planning, apart from purely medical aspects, places an undue burden upon the family doctor who may not always know the answers to the questions posed by parents.

It has been our experience that a multidisciplinary approach to this problem is the most effective way of helping parents to plan intelligently to utilize the maximum potential of their child. By employing a team of experts from various professions, effective planning is most easily accomplished. Thus, by having a medical social worker obtain a comprehensive family history, a better understanding of the family situation is available. Parents' feelings toward the child are revealed, and these need to be considered before further planning can be undertaken. The participation of a clinical psychologist provides an accurate estimate of a child's mental potential and his emotional adjustment, allowing the pediatrician to concentrate on the medical evaluation of the child. The contribution of a public health nurse in home evaluation is especially valuable.

The essential value of the multidisciplinary approach is best realized in the parental counseling situation, when all representatives of the various professions participate in the staff conference with the parents. This not only allows the parents to ask specific questions of different team members, but benefits them through the integrated findings of the team, so that the best possible planning for the child may occur. Those who may object to this type of counseling, done as it is in front of a "group," may feel reassured to learn that following this interview a "face-to-face" counseling session is given routinely to the parents by the social worker. Such an intimate situation is also more conducive to the free expression of their feelings than is possible in the presence of several team members.

A question which many parents undoubtedly ask themselves is, "What does the future hold for my child?" Fortunately, during the last decades, medical science, through extensive research programs, has made amazing gains. The use of antibiotics and improved medical care have reduced the mortality rate greatly so that the child can be expected to live for many years. With increasing community awareness of the need for better care of the mentally handicapped, we have witnessed continuous expansion of educational facilities for these children. Special classes for educable and trainable children have been established in many of the public schools. This means that most will likely find a suitable placement in a public school, depending, of course, on the child's mental capacity. The growing use of mentally handicapped individuals in industry through sheltered workshop programs is another sign that some of these youngsters can become useful citizens, maintaining their self-respect and contributing in a limited way to their own livelihood. Unfortunately, most D.S. patients are retarded with IQs of less than 50. A few, however, have IQs from 50 to 70 and an occasional one may have a normal IQ, although this is rare.

With the ongoing research activities of hundreds of doctors and research scientists, it seems likely that some day we will be able to pinpoint the causes and prevention of this condition. But until such a time, it is good for parents to know that they are not alone in their plight. Physicians and other specialists in mental retardation are becoming more skillful in serving the patients and their families.

During recent years, the development of parent groups for retarded children has made amazing progress. The National Association for Retarded Citizens has a membership of over 1,000 parent groups. Individual parents can gain much by joining such a group. This affords them the opportunity of seeing other parents with similar problems and expands their social outlets. The political influence of such groups* is impressive and much can and still needs to be done for retarded individuals.

A comment should be offered regarding medical therapy. No treatment, thus far, has proven effective. Many approaches have been tried —special diets, vitamins, hormones and other forms are constantly being advocated. Parents need to recognize that various types of therapy may be tried, but they should accept their physician's guidance in protecting the child's health from possible ill effects of exploratory treatment.

---

* A Down's Syndrome Congress has been organized and annual meetings are held in conjunction with those of the National Association for Retarded Citizens. Two newsletters are also available by writing to 1) George Johnson, 1800 Rhodesia St., Friendly, Md. 20022, and 2) Sharon Shimizu, c/o Down's Syndrome Congress, 628 Ashland Ave., River Forest, Ill. 60305.

A recent study by Bazelon reported physical improvement with 5 hydroxy-tryptophan therapy. This, however, awaits more extensive trial and confirmation (2). Our own experience suggests that it is the placebo effect that accounts for improvement.

SUMMARY

Lastly, it should be emphasized that parents have certain respon-sibilities to any child that they bear, regardless of the level of its intel-ligence. Recent court decisions make it clear that parents must provide protection and support to a new baby. They may not withhold per-mission for life-giving surgical procedures such as in the case of a new-born with intestinal obstruction, etc. Even if the parents cannot accept a retarded infant in their home, they cannot purposefully let it die. Sometimes parents, in their confusion, make decisions they would not make at another time. Such parents need firm guidance and support. In later years, they will be grateful for this.

From the preceding, it is apparent that cytogenetics in Down's Syn-drome has become considerably more complicated in the last few years. It is no longer advisable to analyze only the affected child and to counsel the parents on the basis of empiric risk figures related to parental age. Ideally, the counselor should have a thorough understanding of the basic principles of cytogenetics and a reasonable period of training in a genetic clinic before he attempts to undertake such a task.

BIBLIOGRAPHY

1. Benda, C. E., *The Child with Mongolism,* New York: Grune and Stratton, 1960, pp. 9-22.
2. Bazelon, M., R. S. Paine, V. A. Cowie, P. Hunt, J. C. Honck, and D. Mahanand, "Reversal of Hypotonia in Infants with Down's Syndrome by Administration of 5-Hydroxytryptophan," *Lancet,* 1:1130, 1967.
3. Carter, C. O., "A Life Table for Mongols with the Causes of Death," *J. Ment. Defic. Research,* 2:64, 1958.
4. Carter, C. O. and K. A. Evans, "Risks of Parents Who Had One Child with Down's Syndrome Having Another Child Similarly Affected," *Lancet,* 2:785, 1961.
5. Centerwall, S. A. and W. R. Centerwall, "A Study of Children with Mongolism Reared in the Home Compared with Those Reared Away from Home," *Pediatrics,* 25:678, 1960.
6. Collmann, R. D. and A. A. Stoller, "Survey of Mongoloid Births in Victoria, Aus-tralia, 1942-57," *Amer. J. Pub. Health,* 52:813, 1962.
7. Dallaire, L. L., F. C. Fraser, and J. W. Boges, "Translocations Causing Malforma-tion in Man," *Abstr. Mtg. Amer. Soc. Human Genetics,* 1962.
8. Down, J. L., "Observations on Ethnic Classification of Idiots," *London Hospital Report,* 3:259, 1866.
9. Evans, D., *Angel Unaware,* Westwood, N. J.: Revell, 1953.

10. Forssman, H. and O. Lehmann, "Chromosome Studies in 11 Families with Mongolism in More Than One Member," *Acta Pediatrica*, 51:180, 1962.
11. Fraccaro, M., K. Kaijser, and J. Lindsten, "Chromosomal Abnormalities in Father and Mongol Child," *Lancet*, 1:724, 1960.
12. Gibson, D. and R. J. Gibbons, "The Relation of Mongolian Stigmata to Intellectual Status," *Amer. J. Ment. Def.*, 63:345, 1958.
13. Graliker, B. V., K. Fishler, and R. Koch, "Attitude Study of Parents of Mentally Retarded Children: Teenage Reaction to a Retarded Sibling," *Amer. J. Ment. Defic.*, 66:838, 1962.
14. Gustavson, K. H., *Down's Syndrome: A Clinical and Cytogenetical Investigation*. The Institute for Medical Genetics of the University of Uppsala, Sweden. Uppsala, Sweden: Almquist and Wiksells, 1964, 115.
15. Hamerton, J. L., *Chromosomes in Medicine*, London: The National Spastic's Society Medical Education and Information Unit, with William Heinemann Books, Ltd., 1965, 168.
16. Hamerton, J. L., S. M. Briggs, F. Giannelli, and C. O. Carter, "Chromosome Studies in Detection of Parents with High Risk of Second Child with Down's Syndrome," *Lancet*, 2:788, 1961.
17. Hamerton, J. L., V. Cowie, F. Giannelli, P. E. Polani, and S. M. Briggs, "Differential Transmission of Down's Syndrome Through Male and Female Translocation Carriers," *Lancet*, 2:956, 1961.
18. Hecht, F., M. P. Case, E. W. Loorien, J. V. Higgins, H. C. Thuline, and J. Melnyk, "Nonrandomness of Translocations in Man: Preferential Entry of Chromosomes into 13-15/21 Translocations," *Science*, 161:371, 1968.
19. Kugel, R. and D. Reque, "Development of Mongoloid Children Reared at Home," *J.A.M.A.*, 175:959, 1961.
20. Lejeune, J., M. Gautier, and R. Turpin, "Etudes des chromosomes somatiques de neuf enfants mongoliens," *C. R. Acad. Sci.*, 248:1721, 1959.
21. Motulsky, A. G. and F. Hecht, "Genetic Prognosis and Counseling," *Amer. J. Obst. and Gynec.*, 90:1227, 1964.
22. Oster, F., "The Causes of Mongolism," *Danish Med. Bulletin*, 3:158, 1956.
23. Penrose, L. S., "Paternal Age in Mongolism," *Lancet*, 1:1101, 1962.
24. Penrose, L. S. and G. F. Smith, *Down's Anomaly*, Boston, Massachusetts: Little Brown & Company, 1966, 150.
25. Schipper, M. T., "The Child with Mongolism in the Home," *Pediatrics*, 24:132, 1959.
26. Share, J., A. Webb, and R. Koch, "A Preliminary Investigation of the Early Developmental Levels of Mongoloid Infants," *Amer. J. Ment. Def.*, 66:238, 1961.
27. Sigler, A. T., A. M. Lilienfeld, B. H. Cohen, and J. E. Westlake, "Parental Age in Down's Syndrome," *J. Pediatrics*, 67:631, 1965.
28. Verresen, H., H. Van Den Berghe, and J. Creemers, "Mosaic Trisomy in Phenotypically Normal Mother of Mongol," *Lancet*, 1:526, 1964.
29. Waxman, S. H. and D. T. Arakaki, "Familial Mongolism by a G/G Mosaic Carrier," *J. Pediatrics*, 69:274, 1966.
30. Weinstein, E. D. and J. Warkany, "Maternal Mosaicism and Down's Syndrome," *J. Pediat.*, 63:599, 1963.
31. Wright, S. W., R. W. Day, and H. Muller, "The Frequency of Trisomy and Translocation in Down's Syndrome," *J. Pediatrics*, 70, 420, 1967.

CHAPTER 10

Neurological Factors in Causation

by RAYMOND M. PETERSON, M.D.

In dealing with the retarded child we are often exposed to the so-called "neurologically handicapped" individual. Many of these children are unable to function in the usual school-room situation and may be called retarded. Frequently they are seen by the professional with a request from the teacher or parent for help in understanding the child's problem. Included in this group is the physically handicapped child in whom intelligence is not easily assessed because his handicap renders him unable to perform the tasks requested of him. Those children with motor problems, such as cerebral palsy, congenital abnormalities, or defective vision or hearing, are often considered "untestable." The category of neurological handicaps also includes those children with specific learning defects and so-called minimal brain dysfunction. In this group are children who, for one reason or another, cannot learn specific skills. Their intelligence is often average or better, although the individual cannot succeed in academic pursuits.

Classification and terminology relating to these neurological problems are often very confusing and many diagnostic descriptions have been used for the same clinical findings. Although there is much overlap, this chapter will be divided, for purposes of discussion, according to the following disturbances of cerebral function: (1) minimal brain dysfunction; (2) specific disorders of communication; (3) visual or hearing deficits; (4) cerebral palsy; (5) convulsive disorders, and (6) primary emotional disturbances.

MINIMAL BRAIN DYSFUNCTION

The term minimal brain dysfunction (also called minor cerebral palsy, hyperkinetic syndrome, minimal brain damage) (7, 28, 37, 38, 43) has been used to describe a syndrome in children characterized by hyperkinesis, emotional instability, short attention span, perseveration and various minor perceptual disturbances. The lack of definite motor deficits distinguishes this syndrome from cerebral palsy, although it most likely is a continuance of the same process. An organic basis is considered by many to be present (4). Poor school performance is usually seen related to the inability to concentrate and the visual and auditory perceptual deficits. Incidence figures are not available, but it has been estimated to be present in as many as five percent of school age children, with boys being affected more commonly than girls in a ratio of approximately 4:1.

Diagnosis is made by careful history, with special emphasis on the child's relationships to his home, his school and his environment. Past medical history may reveal an etiology of the problem but in most cases this is not true. These children as infants are described as being inquisitive, very active, "all boy," mischievious, "always on the go," and high strung. It is rare that a diagnosis is made until the child is confined in the classroom situation, where he is required to display periods of quiet and attentiveness. Usual teacher complaints reflect his hyperactivity, impulsivenes, aggressiveness, immaturity, poor peer relationship and low frustration tolerance.

Physical examination usually is considered normal and neurological evaluation rarely reveals any abnormalities other than so-called "soft neurologic signs." Some of these are: unsustained ankle clonus, hyperactive deep tendon reflexes, dysdiadochokinesia (inability to perform symmetrical alternating movements), motor awkwardness, directionality confusion (inability to differentiate right from left), inability to stand or hop on one foot and poor fine coordination with tremors or slight choreo-athetosis.

Psychological testing is essential in defining these problems and should be performed by someone who is very familiar with the administration of test materials. A standard comprehensive individual intelligence test (either *Wechsler Intelligence Scale for Children,* or *Stanford Binet Intelligence Scale*), a measure of visual-motor perception (*Bender-Gestalt* and *Frostig*) and a simple projective test (*Draw-A-Person, Draw-A-Family*) present a basis from which other studies may be instituted. Special tests, such as the *Illinois Test of Psycholinguistic Abilities* (**ITPA**) may elicit specific language deficits. Emotional problems, which are often found in children with minimal brain dysfunction, can be further defined by more specific tests.

Laboratory tests are rarely of much assistance in the diagnosis of these problems. The electroencephalogram (EEG) has long been noted as a useful tool in the diagnosis of "brain damage," and reports have frequently lauded it as a valuable diagnostic instrument in minimal cerebral dysfunction (42). Although an EEG is recommended in many cases, especially in those with a questionable seizure history, it has been found that this procedure is usually unrewarding; many persons with no signs of minimal brain dysfunction have nonspecific abnormal EEG's, while approximately fifty percent of those with the hyperactive syndrome have normal tracings (6).

Although drugs may be very helpful in the management of the neurologically handicapped individual, it is felt that the primary treatment requires parent and teacher understanding of the problem, proper school placement and counseling of patient and his family as needed. Surgical management of the hyperactive child is described but this is not recommended (47).

Hyperactivity and poor attention span can often be alleviated by the use of drugs. Although no one drug nor single combination seems to especially control their behavior, many children will respond to administration of those drugs used primarily as stimulants in the adult patient—namely, amphetamines (Dexedrine), methylphenidate (Ritalin), and pemolite (Cylert). Tranquilizers, such as chlorpromazine (Thorazine), thioridazine (Mellaril), hydroxyzine (Atarax), chlordiazepoxide (Librium), and others are effective in some of these individuals. In the small number where neither stimulants nor tranquilizers have been effective, a trial of an anticonvulsant, such as diphenylhydantoin (Dilantin), is worthwhile, especially if the electroencephalogram is abnormal (15, 17, 18, 34).

Although there are many reports as to the efficacy of the above-mentioned drugs, other reports are contradictory and the placebo effect may be very important. With experience, a choice of effective drugs can be made but it is impossible to determine prior to instituting therapy which drug will be beneficial to a particular child. There are preliminary reports of mild improvement in visual motor perception by the use of central nervous system stimulants, but long-term effects are not known (29, 35).

The prognosis for the hyperkinetic child can be considered to be fairly good, since restlessness usually disappears in the early teens. It is rare to have a child on medication (stimulants) after the age of fourteen. A 25 year follow-up on 18 patients diagnosed as being hyperkinetic with minimal brain dysfunction showed that only eight of these were self-supporting; however, more recent studies show a better prognosis (33). Certainly, success is related to intellectual ability. As we become more aware of the problems involved and learn better how to handle the educational needs of these persons, our prognosis will continue to improve (32).

SPECIFIC DISORDERS OF COMMUNICATION

Many authors consider the communication disorders to be another manifestation of minimal brain dysfunction. Although this viewpoint is probably correct, these categories have been separated in this chapter for ease in classification and discussion. As with all types of learning problems (8, 9, 10, 11, 45), a complete history, physical and neurological examination and psychological study are essential to establish the diagnosis (22, 41).

When the child enters school, he is expected to be able to communicate in an effective manner. As with the child with minimal brain dysfunction, identification of the child with specific communication difficulties is usually not made until entrance into the classroom. Two exceptions to this rule are the aphasic child and the child who stutters.

Treatment of the child with communicative disorders must be a coordinated, multidisciplinary program. After a diagnosis is confirmed by evaluation of the history, physical and neurological findings, and appropriate psychological tests and laboratory studies, the family must be counseled as to diagnosis, management and prognosis. Educational plans must be formulated so that those involved with the child can understand what his deficits and problems may be. Great educational advancements have been made with the recognition by professionals of special needs of these youngsters. In many school districts, there are classes for the educationally handicapped where individualized programs are available, taught by teachers who are specially trained to work with these problem students through the use of special education methods.

The aphasic child is often diagnosed before the age of three years because of parental concern. True aphasia may be defined as a defective ability to comprehend and use language (16). Gesell has noted that the first word usually occurs within a month or two of the end of the first year (19). The use of jargon is present until approximately 18 months of age, at which time verbal expression rapidly increases. It is not unusual, however, to see children with normal motor development who have slow speech development using no words until eighteen months or later and no phrases until three years of age. Although there is an increased incidence of "minimal neurological signs," many children progress normally in their language development after the use of these single words (40). In order to make the diagnosis of aphasia, other impairments must be ruled out, such as hearing loss, emotional disturbance, structural or motor defects and intellectual defects. Aphasia may be acquired by a localized insult to the appropriate language area of the brain, and although this is a permanent condition in the adult, it generally disappears in the young child because of the plasticity of brain function. Rarely, a child will have an inability to acquire language skill from birth. This type of defect is called "congenital aphasia" (developmental aphasia, congenital word deafness, specific language disability, or delayed language development), and may be receptive or expressive. The child with congenital receptive aphasia responds in infancy to his parents and the babble stage is usually normal. He is able to express himself by gestures, but speech development is markedly delayed. He may understand frequently used words and some gestures, but does not understand the significance of spoken words. Children with expressive aphasia have an adequate, but often incomplete understanding of what is said to them. These children often communicate by pantomiming and pointing, because speech is difficult and usually limited. This speech delay is caused by focal brain lesions usually located in the parietal lobe of the brain. Therapy is concentrated on strengthening those areas in which the individual has satisfactory function (1). Prognosis in general will be good if the disability is not too severe and other brain functions are intact.

Speech disorders in children such as dysphonia (loss or impairment of the tone and volume of the voice), dysarthria (defective articulation due to anatomical or physiological abnormalities of the lips, tongue or palate) and speech dysrhythmia (abnormal respiratory coordination during speech), are common problems encountered by the professional working with the retarded child (2, 5, 24). Laryngoscopy is helpful in determining the etiology of the dysphonia, with treatment and prognosis related to the causative factors. Physical abnormalities, such as cleft lip and palate or hypoplasia of the mandible, and neurologic disease, such as muscular dystrophy, myasthenia gravis, and damage to the cranial nerves, may all precipitate dysarthria. Specific medical treatment and coordinated speech therapy are necessary to give maximum benefit to the individual. Prognosis is related to etiology, early initiation of treatment, availability of therapy, and related disabilities. Speech dysrhythmia may be manifest by hesitations, repetition and undue prolongation of word sounds or stuttering. It has been estimated to be present in as much as four percent of children, with persistence in less than one percent of the school age population. It is increased in difficult environmental situations, especially when the child is experiencing academic problems in school and pressures are placed on him at home. Therapy must be coordinated with parental counseling and speech training. Prognosis is very good if proper management is instituted early.

VISUAL OR HEARING DEFICITS

It is imperative to evaluate vision and hearing in the child who has slow developmental patterns or in the child who is failing in school. Although it is difficult to obtain exact evaluations in the very young or severely handicapped child, observations are noted and gross testing can be performed. Advances are being made in the evaluation of these functions in the very young through various electronic devices.

Visually handicapped children are arbitrarily defined as those whose binocular vision or whose vision with the better eye is in the range from 20/70 to 20/200. Blind children may be defined as those whose binocular vision is poorer than 20/200. The prevalence of visually handicapped children in the United States has been estimated to be one in 1000 to 1500 and blindness has been estimated to be one in 3000 to 4000. Approximately fifty percent of the ocular abnormalities are found to be due to refractive errors, twenty percent due to developmental defects, such as cataracts, twenty percent due to other miscellaneous diseases and defects. Therapy is determined by the type of defect present. Educational plans are determined by the degree of correction possible and by the presence or absence of other handicaps (44).

Although the visually handicapped child is usually accepted by society, the child with defective hearing may be considered to be only inattentive or disinterested. A child may be congenitally hard of hearing or acquire this problem prior to his developing speech patterns, with the result that speech is markedly altered or delayed. With this in mind, it can be seen how important early identification is. Children have been placed into institutions for the retarded, only to be discovered later to have normal intelligence but total deafness. Hearing loss may be either conductive or sensorineural. Conductive hearing loss results from an obstruction of the sound being transmitted from its source to the inner ear, where the nerve structures are located. This type of deafness can generally be completely cured or at least considerably improved. The sensorineural hearing loss is usually due to obstruction or abnormal development of the essential nerve structures of the inner ear and is generally irreversible. Rehabilitation is centered on definitive corrective measures, if available, with a well integrated program of speech and hearing therapy geared to the individual needs (46).

CEREBRAL PALSY

The term cerebral palsy refers to a number of disorders with many etiological factors and is by no means a single disease entity. The definition given by the American Academy of Cerebral Palsy is as follows: "Cerebral Palsy is a persistent, but not unchanging, disorder of movement and posture appearing in the early years of life and due to traumatic or inflammatory brain damage or, again to a nonprogressive disorder of the brain, the result of interference during development." The incidence of this crippling disorder in the United States has been estimated to be seven per 100,000 births each year, of which one-third has such severe intellectual impairment that effective training is difficult, and one-sixth has such mild disability that little in the way of special training programs is needed. Approximately fifty percent of children with cerebral palsy have eye problems such as strabismus and refractory errors. Another fifty percent have defects in their speech and thirty to forty percent have seizures, a majority of which are grand mal. With these multi-handicaps, it is obvious that each patient must be evaluated individually as to the extent and range of his handicap in order to determine the proper therapeutic approach (12, 14, 23, 36).

CONVULSIVE DISORDERS

The child with seizures (epilepsy, convulsions) may have serious school problems related either to his basic brain pathology or to the emotional turmoil related to his condition (13). Seizures may have an infinite variety of manifestations varying from a grand mal attack, in which the individual falls to the floor unconscious with gross movement of all portions of his body, to the petit mal attack, which may be of such brief duration that although the individual has a lapse of consciousness, neither the casual observer nor the individual himself is aware of the attack. It is imperative that the professional be aware that seizures may be present in the retarded child or in the child who is having school difficulties, and that he look for their presence.

Convulsions are clinical symptoms and it follows, therefore, that the cause, severity and treatment of the child with these symptoms vary with the underlying pathology. Diagnosis is made by a careful and complete history with the physical and neurological examination, electroencephalogram and various other laboratory studies helping to delineate a cause of the seizure. Often the cause is obscure, despite extensive evaluations. Medications are available for the treatment of the various types of seizures, although their effectiveness must be weighed against their side effects. Most physicians who have experience in the medical management of seizures will agree on basic management principles; however, the medical management of seizures is an inexact art and drug therapy must be individualized. With appropriate medical treatment it is estimated that fifty percent of children with seizures will become seizure-free and twenty-five percent may have excellent control so that the individual may function well in society (30, 31). Surgical treatment of seizures has been used in some cases of intractable seizures, but this is not a common procedure.

PRIMARY EMOTIONAL DISTURBANCE

Children frequently are referred for evaluation because of school failure in which the primary problem is related to emotional disturbances. This may result from difficulty in the classroom situation, problems in his outside environment or primary psychiatric disease. It must be remembered that all children who have failed in school will have some degree of emotional turmoil, including anxiety, feelings of inadequacy and poor self-concept. This is especially true in the individual who has above average intelligence, but fails because he cannot perceive or understand materials that are presented to him. School phobia is a definite diagnostic entity in which the child resists going to school because of an irrational dread of the school situation (20). Many of these children are in a state of acute anxiety or even panic, with symptoms of anorexia, nausea, vomiting, loose stools, abnormal pain and headaches. These symptoms may be seen in any child who is anxious regarding his home or social situation. Symptoms promptly disappear as the child is able to resolve his fears and is settled in school.

Primary emotional disturbances, as seen in the schizophrenic or autistic child, may usually be diagnosed by the history and physical examination. The childhood schizophrenic characteristically presents with withdrawal of interest from the realities of everyday living, bizarre mannerisms and periods of hypoactivity, alternated with hyperactivity and altered emotional responsiveness (3, 21).

Infantile autism, as originally described by Kanner, has been defined as an inability to relate to people and situations from the beginning of life (25, 26, 39). In both of these severe psychoses, there is little closeness between parent and child and these children tend to relate better to things than to people. Causes of these problems are unknown, although there have been many theories as to etiology. Despite the various new therapies, the prognosis in either childhood schizophrenia or autism is guarded (27). The emotional disturbances related to situational problems in the young child usually do not stand in the way of academic progress if handled properly.

SUMMARY

In summary, it must be remembered that neurological impairments may contribute to school failure and give an erroneous diagnosis of mental retardation. These impairments may also complicate management programs for the retarded child. Thorough evaluation must be made and treatment must be individualized to fit the needs of each afflicted child.

BIBLIOGRAPHY

1. Arganowitz, A., and M. R. McKeown, *Aphasic Handbook for Adults and Children,* Springfield: Charles C Thomas, 1964.
2. Bakwin, H., and R. M. Bakwin, *Behavior Disorders in Children,* Philadelphia: W. B. Saunders, 1972.
3. Bender, L., "Childhood Schizophrenia." *Psychiatry Quart.,* 21:1, 1953.
4. Birch, H. G. (Ed.), *Brain Damage in Children,* Baltimore: Williams and Wilkins, 1964.
5. Burgi, E. J., and J. Mathews, "Disorders of Speech," *J. Pediatr.,* 62:15, 1963.
6. Capute, A. J., F. L. Niedermeyer and R. Richardson, "The Electroencephalogram in Children with Minimal Cerebral Dysfunction." *Pediatrics,* 41:1104, 1968.
7. Clements, S. D., "Minimal Brain Dysfunction in Children." NINDB Monograph No. 3, Washington, D.C., U.S. Department of Health, Education and Welfare, 1966.
8. Cohn, R., "Developmental Dyscalculia." *Pediatr. Clin. N. Amer.,* 15:651, 1968.
9. Critchley, M., "Developmental Dyslexia." *Pediatr. Clin. N. Amer.,* 15:669, 1968.
10. Critchley, M., *The Dyslexic Child,* Second Edition. Springfield: Charles C Thomas, 1975.
11. Critchley, M., "Dysgraphia and Other Anomalies of Written Speech." *Pediatr. Clin. N. Amer.,* 15:639, 1968.

12. Crothers, B., and R. S. Paine, *The Natural History of Cerebral Palsy*. Cambridge: Harvard University Press, 1959.
13. Crowther, D. L., "Psychosocial Aspects of Epilepsy." *Pediatr. Clin. N. Amer.*, 14: 921, 1967.
14. Denhoff, E., *Cerebral Palsy—The Preschool Years*. Springfield: Charles C Thomas, 1967.
15. Eisenberg, L., "Symposium: Behavior Modification by Drugs; III. The Clinical Use of Stimulant Drugs in Children." *Pediatrics*, 49:709, 1972.
16. Eisenson, J., "Disorders of Language in Children." *J. Pediatr.*, 62:20, 1963.
17. Erenberg, G., "Drug Therapy in Minimal Brain Dysfunction: A Commentary." *J. Pediatr.*, 81:359, 1972.
18. Freeman, R. D., "Prognosis for the Drug Treatment of Learning Disorders: Continuing Confusion." *J. Pediatr.*, 81:112, 1972.
19. Gesell, A., et al., *The First Five Years of Life: A Guide to the Study of the Preschool Child*. New York: Harper and Row, 1940.
20. Glasee, K., "Problems in School Attendance: School Phobia and Related Conditions. *Pediatrics*, 23:371, 1959.
21. Goldfarb, W., *Childhood Schizophrenia*. Cambridge: Harvard University Press, 1961.
22. Grossman, H. J. (Ed.), "Learning Disorders." *Pediatr. Clin. N. Amer.*, 20:3, 1973.
23. Illingworth, R. S., *Development of the Infant and Young Child, Normal and Abnormal*, Fifth Edition. Edinburgh: E. and S. Livingstone, 1972.
24. Ingram, T. S., "Speech Disorders in Childhood." *Pediatr. Clin. N. Amer.*, 15:611, 1968.
25. Kanner, L., "Early Infantile Autism." *J. Pediatr.*, 25:211, 1944.
26. Kanner, L., *Child Psychiatry*, Third Edition. Springfield: Charles C Thomas, 1957.
27. Knobloch, H., and B. Pasamanick, "Some Etiologic and Prognostic Factors in Early Infantile Autism and Psychosis." *Pediatrics*, 55:182, 1975.
28. Knobloch, H., and B. Pasamanick, "Syndrome of Minimal Brain Damage in Infancy." *J.A.M.A.*, 170:1384, 1959.
29. Laufer, M. W., "Long-term Management and Some Follow-up Findings on the Use of Drugs with Minimal Cerebral Syndromes." *J. Learn. Disabil.*, 4:518, 1971.
30. Livingston, S., *Comprehensive Management of Epilepsy in Infancy, Childhood, and Adolescence*. Springfield: Charles C Thomas, 1972.
31. Livingston, S., *Living with Epileptic Seizures*. Springfield: Charles C Thomas, 1963.
32. Mendelson, W., N. Johnson, and M. Stewart, "Hyperactive Children as Teenagers: A Follow-up Study." *J. Nerv. Ment. Dis.*, 153:273, 1971.
33. Menkes, M. M., J. S. Rowe, and J. H. Menkes, "A Twenty-Five Year Follow-up Study on the Hyperkinetic Child with Minimal Brain Dysfunction." *Pediatrics*, 39:393, 1967.
34. Millichap, J. G., "Drugs in Management of Hyperkinetic and Perceptually Handicapped Children." *J.A.M.A.*, 206:1527, 1968.
35. Millichap, J. G., F. Aymat, L. H. Sturgis, K. W. Larsen, and R. A. Egan, "Hyperkinetic Behavior and Learning Disorders: Battery of Neuropsychological Tests in Controlled Trial of Methylphenidate. *Amer. J. Dis. Child.*, 116:235, 1968.
36 Minear, W. L., "A Classification of Cerebral Palsy." *Pediatrics*, 18:841, 1956.
37. Paine, R. S., "Minimal Chronic Brain Syndromes in Children." *Dev. Med. Child. Neurol.*, 4:21, 1962.
38. Paine, R. S., "Syndromes of Minimal Cerebral Damage." *Pediatr. Clin. N. Amer.*, 15:779, 1968.
39. Rimland, B., *Infantile Autism*. New York: Appleton-Century-Crofts, Inc., 1964.

40. Roberts, A. C., *The Aphasic Child. A Neurological Basis for His Education and Rehabilitation*. Springfield: Charles C Thomas, 1966.
41. Shain, R. J., *Neurology of Childhood Learning Disorders*. Baltimore: Williams and Wilkins, 1972.
42. Stevens, J. R., K. Sachdeo, and V. Milstein, "Behavior Disorders of Childhood and the Electroencephalogram." *Arch. Neurol.,* 18:160, 1968.
43. Stewart, M., "Hyperactive Child Syndrome Recognized 100 Years Ago." *J.A.M.A.,* 202:28, 1967.
44. "The Visually Handicapped Child." Washington, D.C., U.S. Department of Health, Education, and Welfare, 1963.
45. Thompson, J. L., *Reading Disability*. Springfield: Charles C Thomas, 1966.
46. Whetnall, E., and D. B. Fry, *The Deaf Child*. London: William Heinemann Medical Books, Ltd., 1964.
47. Wood, M. W., and J. P. Rowland, "Bilateral Anterior Thalamotomy for the Hyperactive Child." *Southern Med. J.,* 61:36, 1968.

Section III.

THE MULTIDISCIPLINARY APPROACH
TO MENTAL RETARDATION

CHAPTER 11

The Multidisciplinary Team:
A Comprehensive Program for
Diagnosis and Treatment
of the Retarded

by RICHARD KOCH, M.D. and
JAMES C. DOBSON, Ph.D.

INTRODUCTION

The family physician is usually the first professional to examine and evaluate a young mentally retarded child (3, 5). If his tentative diagnosis indicates the presence of a mental handicap, he should, and often does, seek pediatric consultation. It then becomes the responsibility of the pediatrician to inform the parents of the intellectual deficit and any concomitant physical disorders that exist. The pediatrician's explanation is of critical importance and affects the future of both parent and child; unfortunately, however, this first contact is often unsatisfying and frustrating for parents. Too frequently, the physician is unable to diagnose a positive cause for the mental retardation, and even if the etiology is ascertainable, he may have no adequate therapy to recommend. He may also lack the techniques which will help him predict the child's future intellectual potential. Consequently, it is not uncommon for such parents to "shop" for additional medical opinions; they are dissatisfied with their physician's initial appraisal and they hope for miracle solutions (6).

Perhaps the frustration experienced by parents is related to the fact that their pediatricians have attempted to apply an impossible "one man" approach to meeting their needs. As the only professional resource, the pediatrician is forced to provide the intellectual assessment of a psychologist, the understanding and guidance of a social worker, the additional medical support of a nurse, and the auditory and linguistic evaluation of a speech and hearing consultant. Even if time permitted the physician to become a universal expert in these related professions, he could not hope to provide all needed services. Therefore, it is becoming more common for the pediatrician to call upon other disciplines to assist in formulating the diagnosis, prescription and care of the retarded child. Certainly, the importance of the pediatrician has not diminished in this changing role; in fact, recent advances in specific areas of metabolism, enzymology and genetics have expanded the extent to which he can effectively care for the retarded. This multidisciplinary team approach is proving to be much more effective than the service available through the efforts of the pediatrician alone.

THE TEAM

Diagnosis is not an end in itself. It is the beginning of realistic planning by a professional staff in cooperation with the parents of the retarded child. The "core" team needed for proper evaluation of a preschool child is typically composed of the pediatrician, psychologist, social worker, speech and hearing consultant and public health nurse. These professionals should take an active part in all aspects of the problem, including the task of helping parents find integrated help in the community. Although most types of mental retardation are permanent in nature, a few preventable forms are known that respond to medical measures if instituted early in infancy (2). The complete multidisciplinary team is more likely to recognize the many facets of such disorders and subsequently direct the parents to the proper community resource than is a less well-rounded staff. A brief description of each team member's role is presented below; the broader responsibilities of each discipline are discussed in succeeding chapter of this text.

The Clinical or Educational Psychologist

The psychologist should assume a large responsibility for the child's initial evaluation. His usual role is to assess the mental capacity of the child by means of appropriate psychological tests, and to appraise the personality factors which are so crucial in planning for a future rehabilitative program. He may be called upon to help the parents understand the principles of discipline and emotional development, and other aspects of the parent-child relationship. The psychologist can also be of great service in the development of a prescriptive learning and remedial education program.

The Social Worker

The social worker's role in the multidisciplinary team is a delicate one. He must help parents find ways of coping with the awesome realization that their child is, and will probably always be, mentally retarded. Parental acceptance of the child's condition is often difficult to achieve; patience, sustained interest and skill are required in bringing them to a position of greater insight and understanding. Early in the diagnostic process, the social worker should contribute an important assessment of the family's social structure, economic status and ability to carry out the recommendations of the team. In short, the social worker is charged with the responsibility of extending a warm, understanding and guiding hand to families which are probably experiencing their hours of greatest need.

Public Health Nurse

The home visits of the public health nurse are valuable to the family's morale. These contacts with the parents are also important in encouraging the best possible care and management at home. She also brings to the team an assessment of the child's home management and assists the parents in implementing team recommendations.

Speech and Hearing Clinician

Too frequently in the past, deaf children and those with defective hearing have been mistakenly diagnosed as mentally retarded. The child who does not respond to his mother's voice might not hear it, which is a distinctly different problem from the child with good hearing who lacks the capability to respond. On the other hand, a mentally retarded child might *also* be deaf or hard of hearing; rubella and other diseases are known to precipitate intellectual and sensory difficulties. Therefore, the assessment of the speech and hearing clinician is a most important aspect of the team evaluation. No estimate of intellectual potential is complete until it is known to what degree the child will be handicapped, if at all, by inadequate hearing.

Laboratory Personnel

Although the biochemist does not usually become an active member of the multidisciplinary team, he and his technicians provide essential information regarding the child's health. As medical knowledge has become more sophisticated, there has been a dramatic increase in the number of laboratory tests which can be useful in understanding the retarded child. Certain laboratory procedures are now essential. In most clinics, a routine blood count, serum phenylalanine determination, tuberculin skin test, urinalysis (including an assessment for the presence of phenylpyruvic acid), electroencephalogram and skull x-rays are performed. It is the practice at Childrens Hospital of Los Angeles to perform urine amino-acid chromatography in all undiagnosed retardates. When hypothyroidism is suspected, an x-ray of the wrist for skeletal age determination is performed. If the skeletal age is retarded, a blood protein bound iodine or other measure of thyroid function is frequently performed to rule out the presence of hypothyroidism. When clinically indicated, buccal smear and chromosomal analyses are done. Further diagnostic studies, such as spinal puncture, pneumoencephalogram or ventriculogram, are occasionally required. A toxoplasmosis dye test and a urine for cytomegalic inclusion virus culture are advisable in young infants with multiple congenital defects. While the routine use of laboratory studies is decried by some, they are essential to a complete evaluation.

Other Team Members

Additional disciplines are represented in some multidisciplinary teams, depending on the nature of the clinic and the types of mental retardation being evaluated. The nutritionist is essential, for example, when a child with phenylketonuria or galactosemia is being examined. Educational consultants, occupational and physical therapists and related medical specialists contribute to the team on various occasions.

SUMMARY

In summary, it can be stated that the problem experienced by the mentally retarded child and his family is not solely a medical matter. It also involves psychological, social, educational and related parameters. Therefore, the accurate diagnosis and effective course of action can best be formulated by a group of professionals with the specific skills required to evaluate the whole child and his family (1). Although parents must be encouraged to accept the level of responsibility which they are capable of shouldering, their mentally retarded child is more likely to reach his full potential when a team of professionals works cooperatively to furnish integrated support.

The chapter in the foregoing section of this text deal with the pediatric and medical aspects of mental retardation. The chapters following in this section are devoted to an examination of the other disciplines which contribute to the diagnosis and treatment of mental retardation.

BIBLIOGRAPHY

1. Buck, P., *The Child Who Never Grew*, New York: The John Day Company, 1950.
2. Hsia, D., *Inborn Errors of Metabolism*, Chicago: Year Book Publishers, Inc., pp. 107-112, 132-137, 1959.
3. Illingworth, R. S., *The Development of the Infant and Young Child, Normal and Abnormal*, London: E. & S. Livingstone, Ltd., 1960.
4. Kirk, S. A., M. D. Karnes, and W. D. Kirk, *You and Your Retarded Child*, Fifth Edition. New York: Macmillan Company, 1958.
5. Levinson, A., and J. A. Bigler, *Mental Retardation in Infants and Children*, Chicago: The Year Book Publishers, Inc., 1960.
6. Sigurdson, W. E., and M. S. Evangelakis, "A Five Year Report on the Services of the Child Study Unit of the Kansas Neurological Institute," *M.R.*, 6:22, 1968.

CHAPTER 12

Psychological Assessment Services

by KAROL FISHLER, Ph.D.

INTRODUCTION

The vast field of mental retardation has attracted great interest from mental health workers in the United States during the past decade, undoubtedly sparked by the very personal involvement of the family of the late President John F. Kennedy. Availability of federal, state and private funds has made possible the establishment of new services concerned with the diagnosis, evaluation and treatment aspects of mentally retarded individuals. One outcome of these efforts has been the concept that these services can best be effectuated by means of a multidisciplinary clinical team of professional individuals. If one accepts the definition of mental retardation as a syndrome, or group of symptoms, resulting from a wide variety of conditions affecting the physical, psychological and social well-being of the retarded individual, it follows that a reliable diagnosis of mental retardation must include a comprehensive evaluation in these varied spheres.

The question of the normality or abnormality of the child is traditionally asked of the pediatrician, and his answer is relatively straightforward when limited to such purely physical aspects as weight, height, head-circumference, etc. However, the question becomes much more complex when it concerns mental and emotional aspects of the child. Many parents ask their child's pediatrician to answer a multitude of questions concerning developmental landmarks, toilet training, behavioral patterns and other matters related to psychological development. The physician may find that these issues go beyond the scope of his medical training, resulting in his need to call upon the services of a variety of child-care practitioners. One such specialist, the psychologist, is uniquely qualified to render assistance in such matters. Traditionally, a psychologist has been viewed as a "behavioral scientist" who can provide the overall evaluation of a child's achievements in intellectual, emotional-social and adaptive areas. He can contribute to educational and vocational planning by interpreting his findings with regard to proper school planning. Furthermore, because of his knowledge of human dynamics, the psychologist can assist the entire family through guidance or counseling to resolve the intra-family problems, including those associated with the "atypical" child. Although it is true that the psychologist is best qualified to evaluate the behavioral aspects associated with mental retardation, there are other specialists on a multidisciplinary clinical team who focus on other aspects of the problem. The psychologist's chief contribution to the team often involves the use of psychometric and psychological tests in the assessment of the child's strengths and liabilities. This information he obtains is then combined with the findings of other professionals. The assimilated data are then utilized to formulate rehabilitative plans for the child, and may be crucial in recommending one type of a school program over another, or in maintaining the child in his community rather than in his placement in a residential facility.

THE PURPOSES OF PSYCHOLOGICAL TESTING

Most laymen visualize a psychological test as being composed of a series of questions requiring written or oral answers. Although such general understanding is correct, psychological tests are not limited to this description. They are extremely varied, and it would take many different criteria to include them all. Perhaps the best definition was offered by Cronbach: "A test is a systematic procedure for comparing the behavior of two or more persons" (11). This definition requires that tests be standardized—which implies that the procedure and scoring have been agreed upon and accepted, so that the same test will produce similar results, even when given at different times and places by different examiners. Tests for which tables of norms are available, stating what scores are usually earned by representative subjects, are also called "standardized tests." Tests may differ in their degree of objectivity. Full objectivity is achieved when every judge or observer of the test performance arrives at precisely the same results. The degree of objectivity, thus, is a product of the degree of agreement obtained by two or more independent judges. Although psychometric testing traditionally yields numerical estimates of single aspects of performance, other tests allow the psychologist to formulate a comprehensive, more descriptive type of assessment of the individual's performance. This more subjective evaluation is often referred to as "impressionistic." Within this approach, the examiner pays close attention to the emotional tone the subject uses in giving his answers. Obviously, each approach has its advantages and limitations. However, it is the skill of the examiner in the use of a particular test through adherence to the standardized procedure, as well as his sensitivity in interpretation of his findings, that helps him formulate a more objective picture of a child's abilities. Although many examiners seek to obtain a well-rounded evaluation of their subject, the use of psychological tests is not the only technique on which they rely. Some may look for meaning beyond the responses, and may prefer to rely on their own clinical skills.

Thus, in applying a psychological test, a psychologist hopes to obtain a "sample" of the subject's behavior under standardized circumstances which should enable him to make both quantitative and qualitative observations. He must be able to assemble enough information from the clues obtained in the psychological evaluation to support his generalizations concerning "real life" situations. This attempt is designed to obtain some conclusion concerning the subject's present level of functioning, as well as his predicted capability—i.e., a measure of probable future academic success or failure, based on intelligence testing.

There may also be an attempt to assess the subject's personality characteristics, using a more *descriptive* approach. In this respect, projective techniques serve as a means of identifying the nature and depth of possible conflict areas. Naturally, there is much overlap between predictive and descriptive aspects of psychologic tests, even though psychologists prefer to rely on the more concrete evidence of the standardized psychometric tests. However, a skillful clinician also utilizes all the circumstantial evidence of impressionistic testing to help him arrive at the total picture of the individual.

The remaining portion of this present chapter explains the role of the psychologist as a member of the multidisciplinary team, and also outlines some of the techniques he uses in working with the mentally handicapped youngster.

INFANT DEVELOPMENTAL TESTING

Obviously, the development of the child begins long before birth. When an individual is born he is already a highly organized biological unit. The structural and functional growth of the central nervous system

(CNS) starts in intrauterine life and continues through early infancy and childhood. By the eighteenth day of fetal life, the cells of the embryo are found to be arranged in three germinal layers: ectoderm, mesoderm and entoderm. Since the ectoderm is the structural basis of the CNS, the foundation is laid quite early. Initially, the CNS functions by reflex; therefore, the pediatrician usually considers the examination of a neonate's reflexes to be an important area of concern.

At birth, only gross differentiation of the CNS is present, since the cortex in the newborn lacks the myelin sheath, this white lipid (fatty) protective structure. This covering insulates the neurons and nerve fibers which are responsible for transmitting electrical impulses to various muscles. In the absence of myelin the newborn is quite helpless in his motor functions. The same is true of the spinal and nerve tracts which are not yet developed. There is very little integration of parts of the brain and cord, and this is why, for example, sitting up cannot be accomplished much before the sixth or seventh month of life following development of the myelin sheath. It is not surprising, therefore, that a human being is considered the most helpless creature of all living beings at birth, and could not survive if left to his resources. Nowhere in the animal kingdom is there a more dramatic illustration of the prolongation of the helpless period of infancy and the long delay of maturation of the CNS than in man.

Early Reflex Patterns

Until the baby is born, his breathing, eating and eliminating have been performed for him through his mother's bloodstream. At birth he is suddenly forced to perform these functions for himself. The birth cry is usually thought to result in the inflating of his lungs, which initiates them to the task of breathing. One can observe an infant's sucking reflex by touching his lips lightly. Even though the child performs these basic functions without instruction, he is still dependent upon others for his food supply and for the satisfaction of all his other physical needs.

The early diagnostic evaluation of newborn infants and those in the first few months of life depends greatly upon the presence or absence of reflexes which are ordinarily manifested by all normal babies at birth. Thus, a normal newborn is well-equipped with many of the neurological reflex-movements commonly found in human beings at any age. He can hiccup, sneeze, cough, blink, yawn or stretch. He can swallow, though at times imperfectly, but needs a little time before he can swallow his saliva well.

The following reflexes are usually present at birth or soon thereafter and provide the basis of early pediatric examination.

Sucking and taste reflexes. These are present soon after birth.

Lip reflex. In the "rooting" or "search" reflex, the baby turns his head to the side which is stroked next to the lip. It is somewhat similar to the lip reflex, but is not concerned with sucking. It enables him to find the nipple without being directed to it.

Tonic neck reflex. Usually seen in the first two months, this reflex is better known as the asymmetrical reflex. When the child is in supine position and his head is turned quickly to one side, he extends his arm and leg on the side to which the head is facing and simultaneously flexes the extremities on the opposite side. It bears some resemblance to the popular "on guard" stance in fencing. The reflex normally disappears by the age of two or three months.

Grasp reflex. The tendency of the hand to close tightly upon stimulation of the palm actually consists of two parts: the grip reflex, and the response to traction. The grip reflex is easily elicited by introducing a finger, pencil or other suitable object into the palm from the ulnar side; in response to this stimulus, the child will flex his fingers and grip the object. This reflex weakens noticeably by the end of 2 months as the child matures, and disappears in most normal babies by the end of the third month when more advanced hand skills are learned.

Moro reflex. This is one of the infant's most important reflexes. Named after the man who described it first in 1918, the baby is placed supine with the back of the head supported on the palm of the hand or crib. Rapid release of the head's support when raised about an inch above the firm surface will initiate the characteristic abduction and extension of the arms. The infant spreads his arms apart and then brings them together again in a bow, while the legs make a similar movement. Similar reaction can be obtained by tapping on the abdomen, or by creating a loud noise or other startling stimulus. The reflex is somewhat difficult to obtain in premature babies, but is always present in normal infants, ordinarily disappearing at about three months of age.

Plantar reflex. The withdrawal reaction of the foot is best accomplished by a noxious stimulus, such as a pin prick, to the sole of the foot. It usually occurs when the infant's foot is held perpendicular to the ground while the anterior part of the sole is stimulated. This stimulus should cause the movement of the limb away from the stimulus and the movement of the contralateral limb toward it. There may be a downward movement of the toes. It is normally obtained after the first month and disappears by the age of 8 months. It depends on the maturing of nerve centers, the result of myelination of the pyramidal tracts.

Babinski response. In this reaction, a typical fanning of the toes downward with the upward extension of the big toe is elicited when the sole of the foot is stimulated. If it is evoked beyond the age of 24 months and persists at later age levels, the Babinski "sign" is indicative of some neuropathology.

Summary. Motor accomplishments follow a fairly set pattern in normal infants and children. Within the framework of individual differences of maturity rate, the development in control of the body usually proceeds from the control of the head through the trunk to the legs, then from the control of the trunk at the center of the body, outward through the arms and legs. Deviations from these norms become important diagnostic clues as to the normal or delayed development of the infant.

Infant Developmental Tests

The history of developmental testing begins with the original work of Binet, who attempted to identify children of school age who were unable to benefit from regular school instruction. However, it was not until 1925 that Arnold Gesell of Yale University set out to study the normal infant in search of early signs of mental deficiency. Gesell's rationale utilized the notion that by obtaining detailed observations of the course of development in a large number of babies and maintaining careful records of the age at which various skills were achieved, it should be possible to document the relationship between such records and subsequent progress through childhood. Gesell advocated follow-up evaluations at intervals in order to assess the rate of developmental progress. Even though he was not able to denote clearly what is "normal," he was quite successful in defining the "average." Consequently, the observer can now determine the sequence and rate of growth in the average child, and to note the frequency of deviations from the normal growth patterns. Thus, taking into account the child's own rate of development and the effects of his environment, it should be possible to venture a reasonable prediction of his future progress. Gesell and his staff at the Yale Clinic of Child Development conducted studies for more than 40 years and by 1930 had examined more than 10,000 infants on a longitudinal basis (21). He actually followed one group of 30 infants through their adolescence. The work of Gesell is reported in a series of books of which perhaps most valuable are *Developmental Diagnosis, Normal and Abnormal Child Development* (22), *The First Five Years of Life* (23), and *Biographies of Child Development* (24). It should be pointed out that Gesell's standardization procedure has raised many criticisms, particularly among the psychologists. For this reason, many examiners prefer the use of other infant tests. Charlote Buhler (8), one of the original explorers of infant testing, attempted to cover aspects of development other than sensori-motor skills. However, she has been criticized (particularly by physicians) for attributing too little importance to the child's history and environment. The *Cattell Infant Intelligence Scale* is weak in the same characteristic. Cattell (9) modified and utilized most of the Gesell tests, and provided a concise description and instruction for the application of tests and the reporting of results in terms of IQ scores. Griffiths (27) whose developmental scales are still much in use in England, also modified Gesell's tests, and was among the first to pay some attention to the historical and environmental circumstances. In contrast is the work of Haeusserman (29), whose chief interest was a developmental assessment of handicapped children, taking full account of background information in the interpretation of the results. More recently, *Bayley's Scales of Infant Development* (5) have been developed on an experimental basis in selected research projects, but the test is now available for commercial distribution. Bayley's scales provide the evaluation of a child's developmental status from two months of age up to two and one half years and consist of three parts of assessment: (1) The Mental Scale, designed to assess sensory-perceptual acuities, discrimination and the ability to respond to these; (2) The Motor Scale, designed to measure the degree of body control, coordination of large muscles and fine manipulatory skills of the hands and fingers; (3) The Infant Behavior Record, which helps the clinician to assess the child's social and objective orientations toward his environment. This part of the test is completed after the Mental and Motor Scales have been administered.

It is still too early to assess the usefulness of the *Bayley Scales of Infant Development,* even though the test has been developed in a most scientific manner. However, one of the more serious limitations is the time required for administration of the Scales, which for the Mental and Motor Scales alone takes from 45 to 75 minutes, with the additional

FIGURE 1

GESELL DEVELOPMENTAL SCHEDULES and some of the test items utilized during the examination.

time spent by the examiner, after the child has left, in computing the scores and filling out the infant Behavior Record.

Gesell Developmental Schedules. Gesell's systematic observations of developmental progress in normal infants led to establishment of developmental norms which identify crucial landmarks of child growth. Gesell's scales (see figure 1) have been used successfully by pediatricians and psychologists as a diagnostic tool in determining child developmental levels at any point in time by comparing the child's achievements with those typically expected in a normal population of children. Obviously, this approach is easily adapted when dealing with infants who manifest some "delay" or "deficiency," and ultimately mental retardation.

The technique developed by Gesell calls for assessment of the child's progress in the following four areas of development: motor, adaptive, language and personal-social. The examination can be given to infants from the age of 4 weeks through 5 years of age, and is particularly useful at the younger age levels. The findings yield a numerical score expressed as Developmental Quotient (DQ), which is based on the averaged scores obtained in the four main areas of development listed above. Thus, a 12-month old baby who is only able to roll over, just begins to sit up alone, transfers objects or simply performs more like a six-month-old in terms of his developmental age (DA), would have an approximate DQ of 50. Thus DQ is an index of the rate of development and represents a ratio of developmental progress to age at the time the child is tested.

According to Gesell's developmental levels, a normal infant will show the following patterns:

1 Month:	Begins to have some regard of his surroundings.
2 Months:	Begins to smile and vocalizes by cooing.
3 Months:	Has head control and turns in direction of sound.
4 Months:	Reaches to grasp objects with both hands.
5 Months:	Rolls over.
6 Months:	Begins to transfer objects from hand to hand.
7 Months:	Sits alone.
8 Months:	Creeps.
9 Months:	Pulls up and begins to use forefinger-thumb apposition.
10 Months:	Stands holding on.
12 Months:	Stands alone and begins to use single words.
12-15 Months:	Walks alone and creeps upstairs.
15-18 Months:	Walks and rarely falls; begins to throw a ball.
18-24 Months:	Runs, climbs, jumps, walks upstairs, kicks a ball; points to various parts of the body; puts two words together.

Controversy regarding developmental testing. A deviation of two or three months from the norms listed above may not necessarily be considered abnormal. Some infants are simply slow developers and catch up, while others, viewed as fast, reach their developmental landmarks earlier. These minor variations in timing are not necessarily predictive of future capabilities. The Gesell test relies heavily on the motor and physical achievements of the child and does not attempt to evaluate intellectual development. These sensory and neuro-muscular functions have little to do with "intelligence," which is the term reserved for a variety of mental functions involving reasoning ability, abstraction, utilization of numerical concepts, adaptability, etc. These more cognitive functions can best be assessed after the onset of verbal communication, which is a prerequisite for the application of most standardized intelligence tests. Since children younger than two years old are not mature enough to manifest such skills, it follows that estimates of early infant abilities are more appropriately reported in terms of developmental quotients rather than intelligence quotients. It is appropriate to keep in mind that DQ and IQ measures are not synonymous, although they are often confused.

Not all investigators agree that the developmental tests are of no predictive value. Gesell and Amatruda, some 20 years after creating the scales, discussed the question of predictive validity. They recognized that the schedules "in no sense are a formal examination, but a selective, screening device which will serve to indicate those cases which do need a formal developmental examination and watchful oversight" (22). Nevertheless, Gesell, while cautious, was optimistic about the predictive possibilities of early developmental scores. Studies by pediatricians have been generally more supportive in the use of developmental tests as predictive instruments, notably investigations by Drillien (13), Ausubel (1), Knobloch and Pasamanick (36) and Illingworth (32). By contrast, studies conducted by psychologists, such as Terman (45), Honzik (31), Eysenck (16), Escalona (15), and Bayley (3-4), have reported low correlations between DQs and subsequent IQs.

Our longitudinal studies conducted at Childrens Hospital, Los Angeles, of infants in various diagnostic groupings suggest that DQ scores in the first year of life are not good predictors of a child's later mental potential. However, if such measurements are obtained at regular intervals over a period of time between ages two and one-half and four years, they tend to correlate more closely with subsequent IQ scores (37). This observation has been well documented in a longitudinal study of children with Down's Syndrome (17, 47), as well as in such other diagnostic entities as cerebral palsy, congenital cerebral anomaly, "pseudo-retardation," and hypothyroidism (18).

Conclusion. The value of developmental tests in infancy and early childhood has undergone a long history of controversy. Many investigators point to the limitations in using tests for predictive purposes. Others cite evidence in support of their usefulness. Although it is generally agreed that mental superiority cannot be detected in infancy, the use of such infant tests as the Gesell scales does permit one to make systematic observations of infant achievements, and to record infant developmental progress. It permits the examiner to investigate the presence or absence of physical and sensory handicaps, even though it is obvious that environmental factors, including illness, may affect his subsequent development and performance. In conclusion, developmental tests in infancy are of considerable value, not only for the reasons cited below, but also in assessing the child's neurological apparatus.

INTELLIGENCE TESTING

Some cases of mental deficiency can be easily recognized soon after birth by a pediatrician without the aid of intelligence tests because they are associated with visible abnormalities of the skull, face, spine or other physical deformities. In this group associated with mental retardation fall such diagnostic categories as Down's Syndrome, microcephaly and other congenital anomalies. However, in approximately 75 percent there are no obvious medical signs present, and for the most part, the laboratory analyses of biochemical samples also fail to detect abnormalities. The only evident symptom is intellectual retardation, and the only diagnostic tool available is the psychological test, namely the intelligence test.

THE NATURE OF INTELLIGENCE

Intelligence was once defined, with tongue in cheek, as "that which an intelligence test measures." This definition, although operationally correct, hardly adds meaning to the concept. Psychologists of an earlier day were inclined to assess a relatively small number of abilities. Beginning with Thorndike, however, they began to recognize various "kinds" of intelligence. Thorndike (47) pioneered the idea that intelligence could be categorized into three main types: (1) abstract or verbal intelligence, involving the use of symbols; (2) practical intelligence, involving applied knowledge as required in manipulating objects; and (3) social intelligence involving ability to deal with human beings. The significant contribution of this classification was Thorndike's awareness not only of what the child could do, but also of *how* he could do it. Thus, he perceived that the measurement of intelligence must take into account both quantitative and qualitative evaluation of mental abilities.

Nearly 50 years ago, Spearman (43) attempted to demonstrate through rigorous mathematical approaches that all intellectual abilities could be expressed as a function of two factors—one a general or intellectual factor, (a "g" factor) common to every ability; and the other a specific factor, characteristic of a particular skill. However, what a "g" factor is, psychologically, and to what extent it may be identified with general intelligence, is still a matter of speculation.

Other, non-intellectual factors in general intelligence were recognized by Alexander, who proposed what he termed a *unique traits theory* (20). According to this theory, intelligence involves several abilities or factors, each *independent* of one another. Guilford has since hypothesized the existence of 120 or more uncorrelated factors which he has arranged in a model called the "Structure of Intellect." According to this understanding, then, intelligence is not a single, global ability; rather, the human intellect is represented by numerous cognitive skills which appear in varying proficiency (28). Alexander was probably the first to recognize that in all actual measures of intelligence, such important variables as the child's interest in performing the set tasks, his persistence in attacking them, or his desire to succeed exert a great influence on his overall output, and must enter into the evaluation. These are the aspects which, more appropriately, should be referred to as personality factors.

Among the more widely-accepted definitions of intelligence is one offered by Wechsler, who views intelligence as "the aggregate or global capacity of the individual to act purposefully, to think rationally, and to deal effectively with his environment (48)." It is global because it characterizes the individual's behavior as a whole; it is aggregate because it is composed of elements of abilities which, though not entirely independent, are qualitatively differentiable.

Psychologists have developed instruments which purport to measure certain forms of intelligence in a child; these tests place the child in new problem situations which allow the examiner to observe how quickly and accurately the child resolves them; a comparison is then made between his performance and that of other children in his age group. These problem situations are scaled in difficulty according to the child's age level, and are known as *intelligence tests*.

THE DEVELOPMENT OF INTELLIGENCE TESTS

Alfred Binet, a Parisian psychologist, is usually credited with being the originator of modern intelligence testing. His development of a series of tests arose out of the practical necessity of having to decide which school children should be sent to institutions for the mentally defective. Specifically, the problem of how to teach feeble-minded children in the public schools was posed by the Ministry of Public Instruction in France, in 1904. Binet, who for some years had been engaged in research on the intelligence of adults, was asked to serve on a commission to select the children who should be permanently institutionalized. He felt that, in all fairness to the children who were to be examined, the method of selection should be one which would distinguish between children who were bright and teachable, and those who were too dull to benefit from regular class instruction. He was also faced with the need to develop a method that could be used by different examiners at different times and that would yield consistent and objective results. His first test of intelligence, tried out in 1905, contained problem situations which were carefully selected and which could be accurately scored. The required tasks were varied in nature, were little influenced by the child's environment, and emphasized judgment and reasoning rather than mere rote. For example, Binet would expect a normal child at:

Age 2 To place a circle, square and triangle in a formboard; to identify at least three parts of the body; and to build a tower of four or more blocks.

Age 3 To string at least four beads in two minutes; to copy a circle; to repeat three digits; and to give his family name.

Age 4 To name objects from memory; to identify objects from a picture card; and to discriminate simple geometric forms.

Concepts of Mental Age and Intelligence Quotient

Binet reported the scores earned by the mentally retarded children in terms of the ages at which normal children could make equivalent scores. For example, if the score earned by a particular mentally deficient child could be earned by an average child of five years, the individual being tested was said to have a *mental age* (M.A.) of five years, regardless of his chronological age. This method of defining the unit of intelligence was so convenient that Binet later administered his tests to a large sample of children of various age levels. He was then able to determine what to expect of normal children of different ages. Thus, he established for French children what we now refer to as "norms."

When intelligence tests were first used, the results were somewhat unwieldy because they were expressed in terms of acceleration or retardation. This classification made it difficult to interpret the results; for example, a four-year-old child with a mental age of three, although retarded only one year, was actually significantly more retarded than a 12-year-old child whose MA was 11. To solve this difficulty, an intelligence quotient (IQ) was devised, which was simply a ratio of mental age of the subject (as obtained on an intelligence test) to his chronological age, and multiplied by one hundred according to the following formula:

$$IQ = \frac{MA}{CA} \times 100$$

The multiplication eliminates fractions and decimals, making IQ scores expressible as whole numbers. In this way, the IQ had a similar meaning at all age levels and did away with the problem of expressing intellectual development in terms of acceleration or retardation.

As intelligence tests were given to children at successive ages over a number of years, and as the results became better available for study by psychologists, it was found that the peak in the growth of intelligence seemed to be reached at approximately 16 to 17 years. This was true for all groups of children, normal, sub-normal, and gifted. These findings, when plotted as mean scores against the age variable, yielded a characteristic curve of mental growth that exhibited a tendency to flatten out upon reaching the age of 16. Further tests given to persons over 16 years of age showed that the relationship between the age and test performance slowly but gradually declined. The curve of mental growth follows very closely the physiological counterpart of the human brain's growth, which usually reaches completion by the age of 16 or 17 years. This may also explain why many creators of IQ tests accepted the chronological age of 16 as the equivalent of adult maturity, as far as mental development of intellectual abilities is concerned. A more recent refinement has occurred with most intelligence tests, where a deviation IQ is achieved. Instead of using a ratio of mental age to chronological age, a representative distribution is obtained from the general population for each age level. The standard deviation of intelligence scores earned by the sample at each age level is held constant (usually being 15 or 16 IQ points), so that a particular IQ will represent the same percentile at all age levels. For example, an IQ of 132 on the *Stanford Binet* is two standard deviations above the mean (97.5th percentile), regardless of whether it is earned by a four, six, ten or twenty year old. Use of the deviation IQ also avoids the problems associated with adult mental age, discussed above.

The distribution of intelligence. Psychologists, as well as physicians, teachers and other professionally trained persons dealing with problem cases, have associated certain IQ values with certain general pictures of adaptive behavior. For a lay person who has not had this training and practical experience, the numbers mean little. Even if he is told that the person's IQ is 75, for example, he probably has no clear picture of what such an individual can and cannot do.

The intelligence quotient (IQ) as measured by an intelligence test is an estimation of a person's "general intelligence," more typically in terms of one's ability to make appropriate or adaptive responses to a variety of situations occurring in everyday life. In order to facilitate the understanding of this concept, it is helpful to view general intelligence as if it were a non-interrupted continuum. One level of intelligence merges into the next, just as colors do when seen through a refracting prism. Levels of behavior which present certain patterns are called defective; still others dull-normal and so on until the other end of the scale is reached, at which point they are labeled as "very superior" or "genius." In the general population this spread of intelligence follows what is usually referred to as a normal distribution curve. In practice, it is customary to classify intelligence according to the following IQ indices:

140 and above	Near-genius
130-139	Very superior intelligence
120-129	Superior intelligence
110-119	Bright, normal intelligence
90-109	Normal, average intelligence
80-89	Dull, normal intelligence
70-79	Borderline retardation
Below 70	Definite retardation

Thus, children with IQ's below 70 are classified as mentally retarded. Experience has shown that below this level most children cannot function on their own in society. Nevertheless, they certainly can benefit through special educational programs, and as many as 80 percent of those considered to be "mildly" mentally retarded will eventually merge into the total population as adults.

It is of historical interest that for many years, most of the early textbooks listed the following three classifications of mental retardation:

1. Morons (range of IQ from 51 to 70), usually able to learn to read and write and are capable of performing certain routine tasks, such as factory work in adulthood.
2. Imbeciles (range of IQ from 26 to 50) could learn simple verbal communication, and could be trained to do simple menial work (floor-mopping, ditch-digging) under supervision.
3. Idiots (range of IQ from zero to 25), those most severely handicapped, who often fail to develop control over bodily functions and ability to speak. These individuals cannot develop their mental achievements much beyond a 2-year-old level, and will be dependent all of their lives.

Fortunately, much progress has been made during recent years in the acceptance of a more differentiated terminology and classification of mental retardation as has been suggested by the American Association on Mental Deficiency (AAMD). According to the Manual proposed by the AAMD (30), the psychologist is responsible for the assessment of the mentally retarded child in three aspects of behavior: (1) an assessment of "measured intelligence"; (2) an evaluation of "adaptive behavior"; and (3) an account of the nature of emotional and other personality factors.

(1) *Measured intelligence.* As described before, intelligence is expressed in terms of deviation from the normative mean. The statistical concept of a standard deviation is a useful measure of variability, which refers simply to the manner in which the scores are distributed around their mean. Thus, if we view the IQ of 100 as the population mean IQ, falling at the center of the normal distribution curve, then the individuals with IQs up to 115 (on most tests) are within one standard deviation above the mean, while those with IQs from 85 to 100 are also within one standard deviation below the mean. Since the Greek letter sigma represents the standard deviation, another way of describing the relative positions of the two groups described above would be $+1$ or -1 from the mean. According to the AAMD classification the following are the levels of measured intelligence, accepting a standard deviation of 15 IQ points:

IQ Range	Classification
85-115	Normality
70-84	Borderline
55-69	Mild
40-54	Moderate
26-39	Severe
9-25	Profound

(2) *Adaptive behavior.* Adaptive behavior is also expressed as a score representing deviation from the mean. According to the Manual, the mean and the first standard deviation below are considered as "no retardation in adaptive behavior." However, the statistical width of each category is larger (1¼ standard deviation) for the adaptive behavior than for the IQ range. Accordingly there are only levels of adaptive behavior, and these are described as follows:

Deviations of Adaptive Behavior
None (or borderline)
Mild   —I
Moderate —II
Severe   —III
Profound —IV

The main source of information about the child's adaptive behavior is measured by use of the *Vineland Social Maturity Scale,* which yields a social quotient (SQ). The SQ is described in greater detail at a later point in this chapter.

(3) *Emotional, social and personality traits.* Finally, the psychologist, in his evaluation of a mentally retarded individual, reports on the "personal-social," "emotional-social" or "sensory-motor" characteristics of the subject being tested. There is no formal scaling defined under these headings, and the traits which are to be described are only tentatively defined. The amount and quality of reported material will obviously depend on the clinical skills and competence of the examiner.

TESTS OF INTELLIGENCE

Listed below are some of the more widely used verbal tests used to evaluate intellectual functions in children two years of age and older.

Stanford-Binet Scale

Because the Binet tests were practical and more easily adapted to other settings than other available methods, their use quickly spread throughout the world. In the United States, credit for adapting the Binet test goes to Lewis M. Terman of Stanford University (45). In 1916, Terman re-standardized the test on a large sample of American children, and the new test was retitled the "Stanford-Binet." It still enjoys widespread use for young children of preschool and school age. In 1937, the test was revised and again restandardized by Terman and

FIGURE 2

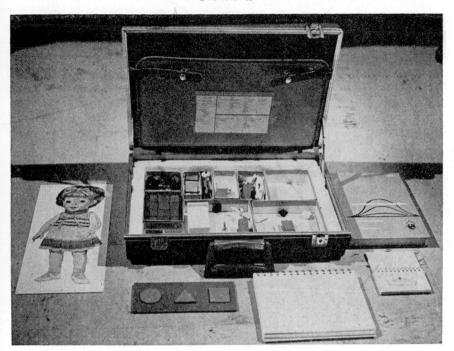

STANFORD-BINET SCALE TEST KIT

Lewis (46) in two alternate forms: L & M. Again in 1960, the test was revised and "streamlined" to reflect the progress of modern times. It is now used in a combined form L-M (Figure 2). The Stanford-Binet Scale is one of the most widely used tests with young children, since it allows assessment of the mental ability and correlates significantly with grades in school; hence, it is of great value for predicting a child's academic progress. However, it is predominantly a test of verbal intelligence. Thus, with a deaf child or one handicapped in the development of speech, the *Stanford-Binet Scale* may not give a fair indication of intelligence. On the other hand, the test has been adapted for use with the blind. The age range of the *Stanford-Binet* extends to a lower limit of two years through age 14, besides three levels of adult achievements; Average Adult, Superior Adult I, and Superior Adult II. Each age level consists of six subtests that tap the various aspects of verbal abilities, such as vocabulary, comprehension, abstraction and handling of numerical concepts as well as some of the non-verbal abilities involving the use of hands. For children from age two through four-and-one-half years, the test advances in half-yearly steps; thereafter, it increases in annual increments. The standardized procedure requires that the subject establish a "basal age" level—the level at which all six subtests can be passed. Additional credits are given at each subsequent age level until the subject fails all six subtests. At this point, he is considered as having reached his "ceiling age," and further testing is terminated. The mental age is calculated by adding to his basal age all the credits earned to his ceiling age; the IQ score is then read from normative tables provided at the back of the manual.

In more recent years, notably in the beginning of the 70's, the test was often criticized for yielding somewhat "biased" scores when applied to children coming from lower sociocultural and minority groups. The original norms established in 1930's were derived exclusively from the white population of the United States and of English-speaking background. With this in mind, the norms of the Stanford-Binet Intelligence Scale underwent a third revision and were published as 1972 Norms Tables (48). A more representative sample with regard to race, language and community background was used with a substantial proportion of black and Spanish-surnamed individuals.

The procedures for obtaining MA's remain the same as they were for the 1960 revision, but they reflect the continuity between the earlier and the present norms. The changes in the level of performance of children, particularly at the preschool level, do not necessarily conform to the traditional relationship between the MA, CA and IQ. For example, a 5 year old whose MA is 5-0 receives now an IQ of 91 rather than 100, while a 10 year old with MA 10-0 receives now an IQ of 96 instead of 97 on the 1960 norms. In general, the shifts are greater for average and above average ability subjects, with MA's above their CA's and smaller for those with below average potential. Basically, then, the "new" norms tend to reflect a better sampling of contemporary children in the 70's than those tested in the 30's.

Administering the scale requires skill, and the examiner must exercise great care in securing clear answers from his subject so as to avoid confusion or uncertainty in scoring. Depending upon the child's age, the testing procedure may take a minimum of less than 20 minutes (for a young child) to more than an hour (with an older subject or adult).

Wechsler Intelligence Scale for Children (WISC)

The WISC (Figure 3) is one of the best standardized and most easily administered IQ tests for school-age children from ages five through fifteen (49). It has one marked advantage over the Binet test, in that test items are arranged in two parts—verbal and performance. The test yields IQ estimates in both areas, as well as the combined IQ score based on the full scale. Wechsler utilized eleven subtests, grouped according to Verbal or Performance scales. The Verbal scale includes subtests titled Information, Comprehension, Arithmetic, Similarities (between words and concepts), Vocabulary, and Digit Span. The Performance Scale includes such non-verbal tasks as Picture Completion, Picture Arrangement, Block Design, Object Assembly, and Digit Symbol subtests.

Values of the test lie in its ability to distinguish a child's achievements on verbal versus performance tasks, as well as in denoting the intra-test "scatter" within each area. The verbal subtests tap not only the level of acquisition of knowledge, as in the Information subtest, but also considers the experience of words, objects and facts through integrated relationship. The memory and concept formation aspects of thought functioning, the use of social judgment, the ability to concentrate, and the general level of attention can be easily assessed. In contrast, the performance subtests are helpful in evaluating visual-perceptual and motor functions. These include specific abilities of visual organization, the processes of reconstruction needed in analyzing and synthesizing block designs, and visual-motor coordination as in Digit Symbol and Object Assembly tests.

It is found that children with some cerebral damage, from whatever cause (whether anoxia at birth, infection, seizures or trauma), tend to score lower in performance. In this respect, the WISC in the hands of a qualified clinical psychologist becomes a valuable tool in differential diagnosis, providing clues to possible brain damage versus personality or emotional factors in the child's functioning.

It should be pointed out that the test was originally designed to measure the intelligence of adults, and was known as the *Wechsler Adult Intelligence Scale* (WAIS) which covered the age range from 16 to 74 years of age. The test was later adapted for use with children (WISC) after norms and standardization had been derived from a large child population between the ages of five and fifteen. Figures 4, 5 and 6 depict examples of "correct" and "failure" solutions on Picture Arrangement, Block Designs, and Object Assembly subtests.

FIGURE 3

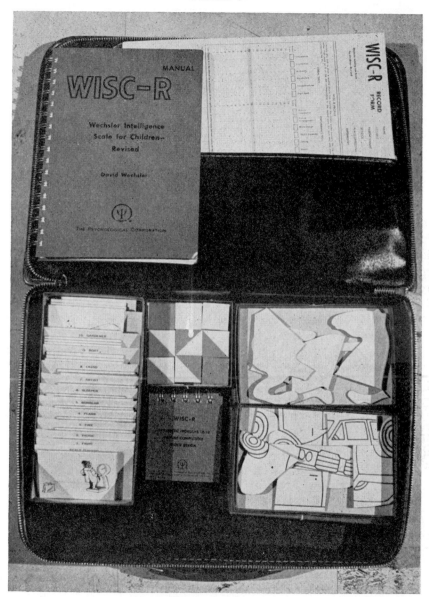

WECHSLER INTELLIGENCE SCALE FOR CHILDREN
(WISCR) Test Kit

FIGURE 4

standardized random presentation

correct card arrangement

standardized random presentation

incorrect card arrangement

WISC PICTURE ARRANGEMENT SUBTEST

The WISC was re-standardized in the 1970's on a sample of 2200 children representing four major geographic regions specified in the Census reports: Northeast, North Central, South and West of the United States. The cases were selected to reflect proper racial representation in each region, and include whites and non-whites—notably blacks, American Indians, Orientals, Puerto Ricans and Mexican-Americans. The same subtests on the Verbal and Performance portions of the tests were retained, but the age range now covers the levels from 6 years through

FIGURE 5

WISC Block Design Subtest
Correct block patterns on the left side; incorrect block patterns as perceived by a "brain damaged" child on the right side.

FIGURE 6

WISC OBJECT ASSEMBLY SUBTEST
Upper sequence — correct solution of "horse";
lower sequence — incorrect solution of "face."

16 years. The revised version of the test is known as Wechsler Intelligence Scale for Children-Revised (WISC-R) (52).

Wechsler Preschool and Primary Scale of Intelligence (WPPSI)

This is one of the newer individual intelligence tests for ages four to six-and-one-half, representing a downward extension of the WISC for children. It is not a simple test and requires special training to administer; it also awaits further investigating and wider clinical use before its value as a screening instrument can be accurately determined (51).

Slosson Intelligence Test (SIT)

The *Slosson* test is a short, individual intelligence test which can be used with children and adults. At its lower age range, it is based on Gesell Scales and Stanford-Binet, and is strictly a "verbal" test of a question-and-answer type. It takes from 10 to 20 minutes to administer and yields an IQ score. The test was designed as a quick screening device which teachers, principals, guidance counselors, nurses, social workers and physicians could use with children and adults. Although the author claims an amazing correlation with the Binet Scale (.93), the test has not been thoroughly validated by other investigators. Obviously, this may not be the test of choice with a suspected mentally retarded child whose verbal abilities may be more limited (42). While intelligence tests such as the *Stanford-Binet Scale* and *Wechsler Intelligence Scales for Children and Adults* are in very wide use, there are many other techniques used by various examiners. These include some of the "group" intelligence tests, particularly popular with school systems because they can be administered in a classroom situation by a teacher. Perhaps the most comprehensive reference material on psychological tests can be obtained from the *Mental Measurements Yearbooks,* edited by Oscar Krisen Buros. This regularly updated volume includes considerable information on specific tests, authors of the tests, critical reviews, excerpts, books and references.

PERFORMANCE AND NON-VERBAL TESTS

The mental status of non-verbal children can often be established by means of non-verbal tests, which are often the only means of assessing the capabilities of the mentally retarded, deaf or mute and those from foreign cultures. Most of these non-verbal tests substitute hand reactions for verbal reactions, although the subject is still required to demonstrate his ability for abstract thinking, reasoning, analyzing and synthesizing and discrimination of numerical concepts. Non-verbal tests include such devices as the following:

Leiter International Performance Scale

This instrument is useful with children who are deaf, aphasic, have a speech problem, or face a barrier of foreign language in communicating. The test requires placement of one inch cubes of various colors and designs into a wooden frame which can be fitted with interchangeable strips of comparable design and increasing difficulty (see Figure 7). The tasks require perceptual matching, making analogies, demonstrating memory and other abilities, many of which depend upon thought processes similar to those involved in verbal tests. The test is given with very simple instructions that may be administered orally or through pantomime. The items do not require any language functions. The test is well suited to handicapped children and covers the age range from two to eighteen years. The test becomes quite complex at the upper limit. It yields an IQ score, although intelligence estimates at the preschool level are of a somewhat questionable accuracy. This test is enjoyed by young children who take pleasure in manipulating the blocks in a game-like situation (38).

Merrill-Palmer Scale

The *Merrill-Palmer* non-verbal instrument employs a variety of performance tasks that increase in difficulty involving such activities as completing two, three, five and multiple-piece puzzles and pictures, as is shown on Figure 8. The subtests permit evaluation, beginning at age 18 months and continuing to the 69 months level. The scales appear to be best suited for testing preschool children. Language questions are simple tests of comprehension, as, for example: "What cries." Some tests involve manual dexterity, as in cutting with scissors. In others, a record is kept of the time required for completion and the number of errors committed. These are compared with the available norms from which the mental age of the child is derived. Obviously, a careful examiner is able to take advantage of many other clinical clues when observing the child's performance by noting the attitude toward the task at hand, the ability to tolerate frustration, and the actual quality of the performance (44).

FIGURE 7

INTERNATIONAL PERFORMANCE SCALE

BY DR. RUSSELL GRAYDON LEITER

LEITER INTERNATIONAL PERFORMANCE SCALE TEST KIT

MERRILL-PALMER SCALE SUBTESTS

"Manikin"—upper left; "Mare and Foal Picture Completion Test"—upper right; "Seguin Formboard"—lower center.

Peabody Picture Vocabulary Test

The *Peabody* is a more recent individual test of intelligence for children ages two to eighteen years. The test is particularly useful for children with speech problems or cerebral palsy, or those who are withdrawn, distractible, mentally retarded or in need of remedial reading. The test is an easily administered, wide-range picture vocabulary test utilizing a carefully graduated series of 150 plates, each containing four pictures. To administer the scale, the examiner provides a stimulus word orally, as "Where is . . ." or "Show me cat." The subject points to, or in some other way indicates the answer on the plate which best illustrates the stimulus word (see Figure 9). The pictures are arranged in ascending order of difficulty and the scale is administered only over the critical range for the particular subject being tested. It takes only 10 to 15 minutes to administer. Raw scores can then be converted into mental ages, standard score IQs and percentiles. The test tends to yield scores approximately 10 IQ points higher than the Binet scale (14).

Columbia Mental Maturity Scale

This non-verbal scale was designed to be used in testing children between the ages of three and twelve years with physical handicaps and limited verbal communication. Each item consists of three or more drawings, printed on a large card. No verbal response is required and only a minimum of motor ability must be manifest. The child is asked to point out "one which does not belong with others." The mental age and IQ scores are based on normal, non-handicapped children. The test seems to be more popular with school personnel and is reported to correlate about .75 with the Stanford-Binet scale (10).

PENCIL AND PAPER TESTS

A typical battery of psychological tests, whether of a verbal or non-verbal type, should include at least one drawing task. The child's ability or difficulty in handling paper and pencil is often invaluable in denoting problems in visual-perceptual functions or eye-hand motor coordination. Paper and pencil tests also offer a simple, and, in most instances, accurate way of estimating mental age. They are generally easy to administer to children of all ages, since most children are familiar with crayons, paints and pencils.

With a young child, the use of paper and pencil can be improvised

FIGURE 9

PEABODY PICTURE VOCABULARY TEST
Actual administration

by any professional person, simply by copying or drawing geometric forms. Knowing the child's chronological age from his maturational level of motor achievement, it is possible to select the tasks he should be expected to reproduce from the following geometric forms: circle (2½ years), cross (4 years), square (5 years), triangle (6 years), and star or diamond (7 years). His ability or failure to draw these forms at the expected age level may provide helpful clinical clues, especially if one suspects some neurological handicap or other motor limitation.

Bender-Visual-Motor-Gestalt Test

The "Bender," as it is called, is a test of spatial perception and neuromuscular coordination and is perhaps among the most sensitive instruments in which a child's or adult's reproduction of specific forms lends itself to both formal scoring and clinical interpretation. Figures with different patterns of organization are shown to the subject on individual cards, and he is asked to copy the figures on a separate sheet of paper. The examiner takes note of many variables which affect the arrangement

FIGURE 10

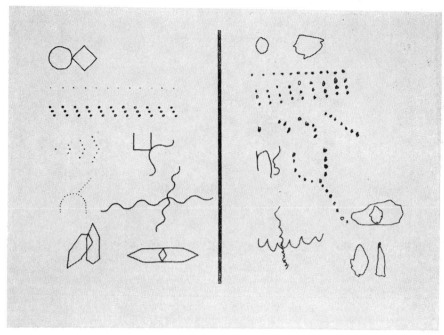

On right, reproduction of Bender figures by an eight year old child with normal IQ, but visual-perceptual handicap.

of the drawings, such as order, cohesion and margin, modification of size, and actual modification of the "gestalt" quality. The type and degree of deviation in drawings of *Bender* figures often reveal a possible "brain damage" pattern, and so are helpful in making the diagnosis. Among the more typical distortions are simplification, fragmentation, integration, collision, rotation, incorrect number of units, perseveration, poor line quality and distortions of dashes and commas. Figure 10 illustrates a significant visual-perceptual handicap in an 8 year old child of otherwise normal intelligence who had a distinct reading disability and difficulty in handling numerical concepts. Besides being a test of visual-motor maturation, the *Bender-Gestalt* test is also sensitive to distortions caused by the presence of significant emotional factors and schizophrenia. The accurate evaluation of this type of clinical material requires considerable experience and skill of the examiner, although scoring rules have been developed by Pascal and Suttell in 1951 and by Koppitz in 1964 (7).

Other techniques similar to the *Bender-Gestalt* can also be used in the diagnosis of brain damage in children, notably, the *Graham-Kendall-Memory-for-Designs-Test* and the *Ellis Visual Designs Test.*

These types of tests may also be included in a discussion of special techniques (see p. 196), although specifically, the *Bender-Gestalt Test* is appropriate in any discussion of projective techniques.

Draw-A-Person Test

This is a valuable, quickly-administered, fairly accurate intelligence test which can be given by others than a psychologist to children of all ages. However, standardized norms are available only for children from two to ten years of age. Most young children like to draw or paint and, in most instances, they respond readily when given paper and pencils and asked to "draw a man." The task of drawing a "person" is a creative experience, and both motor and expressive aspects are regarded as the formal and structural characteristics of the drawing. Scoring takes into account the basic structure of the drawing, the amount of details of head, other body parts, clothing and the quality of the child's production. The scoring rules were carefully prepared by Goodenough (25) and can be translated into IQ scores. Although the D-A-P can be applied in all cultures, performance does depend on cultural influences and the child's own life experiences. The child's drawings may have a diagnostic value since, in organic brain disease, the drawn figure may appear "disorganized," revealing significant distortion in the awareness of the basic body structure. By the same token, the analysis of the child's drawing often renders valuable insight into his personality dynamics and level of emotional adjustment. In this respect, the examiner may choose not to follow the Goodenough scoring system as an intelligence test, but may prefer to use the D-A-P as a projective technique.

PROJECTIVE TECHNIQUES

The use of projective techniques offers one of the most valuable diagnostic tools in personality appraisal with both children and adults. The basic rationale of a projective test assumes that, when an individual is presented with a vague, semi-structured or even fairly well structured set of stimuli or problem situations, (e.g. tell a story; complete a sentence; respond to an ink blot, etc.), he will tend to react in a manner which is unique to him. This subjective attempt to organize the material allows the examiner to assess the way a person "projects" himself and at the same time permits the identification of his personality dynamics. In these projections, the individual has no place to "hide" his personality characteristics, for there is no right or wrong answer to what he wishes to reveal. The mosaic of many responses, when pieced together, combines to form a personality profile of one's emotional strengths and weaknesses and helps to pinpoint major conflict areas. It has been well known that individuals often project their attitudes onto the ambiguous stimuli, whereas they are often guarded at a conscious level. The main advantage of the projective tests is primarily seen in uncovering some of these unconscious psychodynamics. Some of the more widely used projective techniques are mentioned in this section.

Draw-A-Person Test

A *Draw-A-Person test,* or any variety of comparable tests such as *Draw-Your Family,* or *House-Tree-Person,* can be used as a projective tool. Here, the psychologist uses such clues as the sex and age of the drawn figure as compared with the child's own sex and age level. In our experience, some eighty to ninety percent of young children will identify with their own sex and age when asked to "draw-a-person." Only those who are dominated by persons of the opposite sex (e.g. older sibling, mother or father, teacher or other relative) or those who have developed specific interest in members of the opposite sex are likely to deviate from this general rule. The size of the figure and other salient details, such as facial expression, use of clothing and possible verbal comments about the drawing, are noted and used in the interpretation.

Sentence Completion Test

The *Sentence-Completion* method is one of the simplest methods of obtaining information on conflicts and subconscious motivation of the subject. The test comes in various versions and can be geared toward children and adults or toward the sex of the subject. The individual merely completes a sentence, such as "I often wish I could . . . ," or "My mother. . . ." Although responses can be consciously controlled, children generally tend to "blurt out" their first response, often revealing material of clinical significance, rather than carefully screening their responses.

Thematic-Apperception-Test (T-A-T)

The T-A-T developed by Murray and his co-workers (1938) requires the subject to interpret a picture by telling a story following the general outline of "What is happening, what led up to the scene, and what will be the outcome?" The T-A-T consists of twenty pictures, different pictures being used for men and for women, the assumption being that their responses will be dictated by their experiences, constructs, conflicts and wishes projected into the scenes they view. The subject often believes that his imagination is being tested, whereas the examiner pays more attention to the themes behind the plots, general mood and attitude of given stories and general style, as when using the whole picture rather than piecemeal descriptions of details. In this respect, a skillful clinician may wish to conduct an additional inquiry regarding "Who is the hero? How does he feel? What happened to him? Who did what to whom?" It has been our experience that the test is usually more valuable with adolescent and adult subjects.

Children's-Apperception-Test

The C-A-T is essentially an adaptation of the T-A-T type of instrument to a younger age group. Since children identify more readily with animals than with adults, Bellak (6) developed the C-A-T for ages three to ten years, utilizing ten pictures of animals engaged in a variety of activities more suitable for this age group. Pictures of animals often used in nursery stories (chickens, rabbits, bears or lions) are designed to elicit information on feeding conflicts, sibling rivalry and other problems of early childhood. This technique is more effective with young children who are more willing to talk about the problem of the animal "in the picture" than to talk about themselves in connection with other human figures.

Rorschach Ink Blot Test

This test, devised by a Swiss psychiatrist, Hermann Rorschach (40), consists of ten inkblots, each printed on a white background and mounted on a 7 x 9½ inch cardboard. Five of the blots are grayish black, two are black and red, and three are multicolored. The blots are numbered from one to ten, and are presented in numerical order. The subject is asked to tell what he sees in each inkblot or what these irregular forms "remind him of." The blots are calculated to arouse emotional responses because of their color or achromatic impact, as well as forms suggestive of nursery animals, overpowering giants, and sex organs. While the task is intellectual, it also reveals emotional patterns. The scoring and interpretation of the Rorschach responses are quite complex, because each answer is analyzed in terms of such variables as movement, use of color or avoidance, use of shading, proper perception of the form of the blot, use of human or animal concepts, or use of the total blot as compared with certain parts (35). Although the Rorschach test is used very extensively in clinical psychology, the real value of this test depends largely on the skill and clinical acumen of the examiner.

Other projective techniques are also used by some examiners: Word Association Test, Mosaic Test, the Szondi Test, Make-a-Picture-Story Test, Rosenzweig Picture Frustration Test and Blacky Pictures. The last two are used mostly with children.

Most of the projective techniques rely heavily on creative aspects of the individual and require either adequate verbal communication or the ability to write. They place a retarded child at a distinct disadvantage. It has been our experience that most of the projective tests have been of little value with the young mentally retarded children because of their limited intellectual potential and the usual limitations mentioned above.

SPECIAL TECHNIQUES

In addition to the psychological tests described on the preceding pages, some examiners use a variety of supplemental tools for specific purposes. The following techniques warrant special mention.

Illinois Test of Psycholinguistic Abilities

The ITPA was developed by Kirk and associates (33) at the Institute for Research on Exceptional Children at the University of Illinois. The test has been used experimentally for several years and offers a new approach in evaluating a child's abilities, the emphasis being on organization, on psycholinguistic processes, and on channels of communication. It attempts to assess nine psycholinguistic abilities at two crucial levels: (1) The Representational Level, measuring ability to deal meaningfully with symbols; and (2) The Automatic-Sequential Level, dealing with the non-meaningful use of symbols. The ultimate goal of this method of diagnostic assessment of a child's abilities and deficiencies in various aspects of language development was to provide a psycholinguistic profile. This, in turn, could lead to a program of remediation or treatment which would utilize the child's assets to develop his deficiencies.

This tool was constructed to yield a Language Age rather than an IQ estimate and can be administered to children between two-and-one-half and nine-and-one-half years of age. However, the test is rather cumbersome to administer, requiring a minimum of 30-45 minutes, even when given by an experienced examiner.

The ITPA was revised in 1968 (34) with improvements over the earlier experimental edition described above. The theoretical model postulates three dimensions of cognitive abilities: (1) Channels of Communication; (2) Psycholinguistic Processes; and (3) Levels of Organization. The twelve subtests of the revised ITPA are given in the order presented on the Record Form:

1. Auditory Reception
2. Visual Reception
3. Visual Sequential Memory
4. Auditory Association
5. Auditory Sequential Memory
6. Visual Association
7. Visual Closure
8. Verbal Expression
9. Grammatic Closure
10. Manual Expression
11. Auditory Closure
12. Sound Blending

The last two subtests are supplementary; hence, they are placed at the end of the test and need not be administered to all children. Their chief clinical use is to show potential or actual problems in reading and/or spelling, and obviously are more useful with older children. The ceiling age of the test has been raised on most subtests to provide norms extending to ten years of age; the new version also offers some improvement over the earlier experimental edition in clarity and durability of test components. This new instrument appears promising, although the final judgment of its usefulness awaits further clinical assessment.

Raven's Progressive Matrices Test

This test was developed in England and has been used as the principal screening test for military classification during World War II, somewhat as a general intelligence test (39). It has been used in the United States as a measure of organic brain damage. In this non-verbal test, a child is presented a series of colored designs. A section has been omitted from each design. Beneath the main design are six design sections. Each of the designs fits the shape of the missing section of the main design but only one of them contains the correct pattern (see Figure 11).

FIGURE 11
AB 7

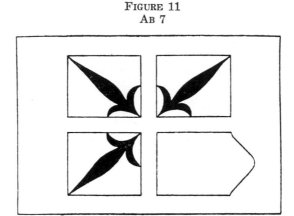

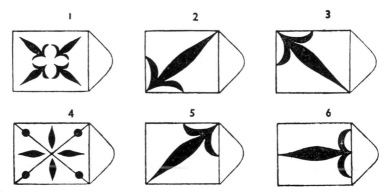

RAVEN PROGRESSIVE MATRICES TEST
There is only one correct solution (#3) for completing the pattern

The child is told to select one of the six pieces which would complete the design if placed in the missing section. Since the task requires, first, a correct perceptual discrimination of properties which the missing part should contain, and second, transporting bits of information to reconstruct the total design, the measurement of these processes provides a sensitive measure of organic brain damage or other cerebral dysfunction. The test covers the age range from four-and-one-half to eleven-and-one-half years, and consists of 36 colored designs presented in three sections of 12 each. Administration and scoring take from 10-15 minutes

Vineland Social Maturity Scale

The *Vineland* provides an individual measure of successive stages of social competence, or social judgment, from infancy to 25 years of age. It is a checklist for assessing self-help, self-direction, occupation, communication, locomotion and socialization in a child. The information is obtained by means of an interview, usually with the parent or person who is familiar with the child's background. Most items on this scale reveal the child's degree of socialization and his maturation toward goals of self-help and independence. Items are arranged in the order of average age norms, and the score is expressed as social age (SA), which is converted into a social quotient (SQ) (12). Testing takes from 10 to 15 minutes and can be administered by any professional person. Since the test furnishes an estimate of the child's social maturity as seen through parents' eyes, it also serves as a useful indicator of parental awareness of the child's achievements. It has been our experience that the SQ score on the Vineland Scale usually correlates within 10 points with the IQ score on an objective test of intelligence; thus, it provides a realistic appraisal of the child's functioning level as viewed by his parents. When the SQ score is excessively high, it usually suggests a parental tendency to deny the problem; when the SQ score is unduly low, it frequently reflects the parents' high level of expectation.

Occasionally, a physician, nurse or social worker may be confronted with the results of psychological tests with which they are not familiar. These less well-known tests include the *Frostig Developmental Test of Visual Perception, Moss Test of Basic Information, Ozer Tests of Neurological Maturity, Rogers Test of Personality Adjustment,* or the *Attitude-Interest Analysis Test.* Of these, the *Frostig Developmental Test of Visual Perception* (19) warrants special recognition as a useful screening test for neurologically handicapped children between the ages of three and nine years. It permits the assessment of the perceptual difficulties and the level of perceptual maturation regardless of etiology, whether it is caused by brain injury, developmental lag or emotional disturbance. Specifically, the *Frostig* test purports to measure the following perceptual functions: (1) Eye-Motor Coordination, (2) Figure-Ground, (3) Form Constancy, (4) Position in Space, and (5) Spatial Relations. It also yields a score in terms of a Perceptual Quotient (PQ). The findings often provide the basis for the proper remedial educational therapy. For children who manifest some motor limitations, uncoordination, aphasia and other neurological signs, the *Ayres Space Test* (2) can be useful. It

consists of tests of spatial ability, perceptual speed, directionality or position in space and visualization, with the normative data for ages three
to ten years. This technique seems to be favored more by occupational
therapists than by psychologists, since the results serve as guidelines to
physical rehabilitation of the child's handicap rather than as a basis for
his educational planning. The tests discussed above may be used in
screening pupils for special education placement, and should not be
confused with tests of mental ability.

TO TEST OR NOT TO TEST?

Discussion of the use of mental tests by a psychologist would not be
complete without recognizing some of the major controversial issues
related to their use. The reliance on results of standardized tests raises
questions regarding the validity of the tests used, the possible effects on
those to whom they are administered, and the value to the society that
uses them to differentiate among individuals. Criticisms of the validity
of tests proposed by Goslin (26) suggest that tests may be unfair to
certain groups and individuals, especially to the extremely gifted, the
culturally disadvantaged, and those who lack experience in taking tests.
On the other hand, it is well recognized by psychologists that tests are
not perfect predictors of subsequent performance. Test results should not
be applied in a rigid manner; also it should be recognized that there are
inherent qualities of individuals that are not amenable to test measurement. Other criticisms include the effects of tests on thinking patterns of
those tested frequently, their impact on school curricula, self-image and
motivation, and an individual's basic need for privacy, to mention only
a few. The question regarding a potential invasion of privacy need not
be viewed as detrimental when testing young children. The school clearly
does have a responsibility to require pupils to demonstrate their proficiency in school subjects before promoting or rewarding their learning
achievements. It is exactly along these lines that judicious use of psychological tests can be of great assistance. The tests can help to identify a
child's best assets; it can pinpoint his greatest deficiencies. On the basis
of this rationale, those who are charged with his care and training are
enabled to provide for his most suitable educational planning. The
variety of standardized tests available for measuring many kinds of
performance enables the examiner to assess the child's verbal ability, his
manual dexterity and his discrimination of form and spatial orientation.

Any of these abilities may be impaired in a mentally retarded child resulting from a variety of causes.

The psychologist's role as a member of the multidisciplinary clinical team is to unravel, by means of his diagnostic tools, some of the deficiencies of the retarded child, and bring them to the attention of other team members. When a suspicion of mental retardation is confirmed, the psychologist is then in a position to provide the physician and the rest of his team with information concerning the child's intellectual ability, emotional maturity and parent-child interaction. Children less than three years of age are usually tested in the presence of at least one parent to avoid separation anxiety and to ensure better rapport with the child during the session. This affords the examiner excellent opportunity to observe the child's response under the stress of a new environment, and to assess parental reaction toward the child. The role of a psychologist in the clinical assessment of the child's performance becomes even more significant when he can translate his findings meaningfully to other team members, and provide the parents with guidelines for proper stimulation or rehabilitation of the child. He can help the family by pointing out the relationship between the child's mental age and signs of readiness to accomplish certain tasks of learning. With children who are already of school age or in need of appropriate school placement, the psychologist may work with school authorities in implementing educational planning for the child.

Finally, the psychologist can be of assistance in cases of acute stress or a crisis situation in the child's family. Parents are less likely to challenge the physician's opinion, when it is unfavorable or difficult for them to accept, when that opinion is supported by that of other experts. The psychologist is uniquely equipped to assist with this type of problem. He may be called to assume direct guidance in developmental or situational conflicts when other professional personnel are not available.

SUMMARY

The psychologist's role in clinical assessment of mental retardation was described from the point of view of his contribution to the diagnostic process. Starting with a discussion of the broad concepts that underlie psychological testing, a review was given of infant testing from early reflex patterns through developmental testing of infants. Special attention was given to the *Gesell Developmental Scales*. The discussion of mental testing was preceded by a general consideration of the nature of intelligence, the development of intelligence tests, and the relationship between the concept of mental age and that of the intelligence quotient. Some of the more important psychological tests of intellectual function that utilize verbal, performance and non-verbal abilities were reviewed with special emphasis on paper-and-pencil tests, projective techniques and other specialized instruments. A final portion of the chapter was devoted to consideration of some philosophical questions which have aroused controversy as to the value of psychological tes's. Their value was seen to be significant in providing the tools needed for diagnosis and rehabilitation, especially in cases involving mental retardation.

BIBLIOGRAPHY

1. Ausubel, D. P., *Theory and Problems of Child Development*. New York: Grune and Stratton, 1968.
2. Ayres, A. J., *The Ayres Space Test*. Manual. Western Psychol. Services, Box 775, Beverly Hills, Calif., 1962.
3. Bayley, N., "Mental Growth During the First Three Years," *Genet. Psychol. Monogr.*, 14:1, 1933.
4. Bayley, N., "Value and Limitation on Infant Testing," *Children*, 6:129, 1958.
5. Bayley, N., *Manual for the Bayley Scales of Infant Development*. New York: The Psychological Corporation, 1969.
6. Bellak, L., and S. Bellak, "Introductory Note on Children's Apperception Test (CAT)," *J. Project. Techniques*, 14:173, 1950.
7. Bender, L., *A Visual Motor Gestalt Test and Its Clinical Use*. Research Monograph No. 3, New York: Publ. by the Amer. Orthopsychiatric Association, 1938.
8. Buhler, C., *From Birth to Maturity*. London: Kegan Paul, 1935.
9. Cattell, P., *The Measurement of Intelligence of Infants and Young Children*. New York: The Psychological Corporation, 1947.
10. Columbia Mental Maturity Scale, Rev. ed., New York: Psychol. Corporation, 1959.
11. Cronbach, L. J., *Essentials of Psychological Testing*. 2nd Ed., New York: Harper and Row, 1960.
12. Doll, E. A., *The Measurement of Social Competence: A Manual for the Vineland Social Maturity Scale*. Minneapolis: Educational Publishers, 1953.
13. Drillien, C. M., "A Longitudinal Study of the Growth and Development of Prematurely and Maturely Born Children," *Arch. Dis. Child.*, 36:233, 1961.
14. Dunn, L., *Peabody Picture Vocabulary Test*. Minneapolis: Amer. Guidance Service, Inc., 1959.
15. Escalona, S., *The Use of Infant Tests for Predictive Purposes*. New York: Basic Books, Inc., 1950.
16. Eysenck, H. J., *Uses and Abuses of Psychology*. London: Pelican, 1952.
17. Fishler, K., J. Share, and R. Koch, "Adaptation of Gesell Developmental Scales for Evaluation of Development in Children with Down's Syndrome (Mongolism)," *Am. J. Ment. Defic.*, 68:5, 1964.
18. Fishler, K., B. Graliker, and R. Koch, "The Predictability of Intelligence with Gesell Developmental Scales in Mentally Retarded Infants and Young Children," *Am. J. Ment. Defic.*, 66:4, 1965.

19. Frostig, M., *Developmental Test of Visual Perception. Manual.* Consulting Psychologists Press, Palo Alto, Calif., 1964.
20. Garrison, K. C., *The Psychology of Exceptional Children.* New York: The Ronald Press Company, 1950.
21. Gesell, A., and H. Thompson, *The Psychology of Early Growth.* New York: Macmillan, 1938.
22. Gesell, A. and C. S. Amatruda, *Developmental Diagnosis, Normal and Abnormal Child Development; Clinical Methods and Practical Applications.* 2nd Ed., New York: Paul B. Hoeber, Inc., 1947.
23. Gesell, A., *The First Five Years of Life.* New York: Harper and Brothers, 1940.
24. Gesell, A., C. S. Amatruda, B. M. Castner, and H. Thompson, *Biographies of Child Development.* New York: Paul B. Hoeber, 1939.
25. Goodenough, F. L., "Studies in the Psychology of Children's Drawings," *Psych. Bull.,* 25:272, 1928.
26. Goslin, D. A., "Standardized Ability Tests and Testing," *Science,* 159:851, 1968.
27. Griffiths, R., *The Abilities of Babies.* London: University of London Press, 1954.
28. Guilford, J. P., "A Revised Structure of Intellect," *Rep. Psychol. Lab.,* No. 19, Los Angeles: University of Southern California, 1957.
29. Haeusserman, E., *Developmental Potential of Preschool Children.* London: Grune and Stratton, 1958.
30. Heber, R., *A Manual on Terminology and Classification in Mental Retardation.* Amer. Assoc. on Mental Defic. Special Public Series, No. 2, 1973.
31. Honzik, M. P., "The Constancy of Mental Test Performance During the Preschool Period," *J. Genet. Psychol.,* 52:285, 1938.
32. Illingworth, R. S., *The Development of the Infant and Young Child Normal and Abnormal.* 3rd Ed., Edinburgh and London: E. & S. Livingstone Ltd., 1967.
33. Kirk, S. and J. McCarthy, *Illinois Test of Psycholinguistic Abilities.* Urbana, Illinois: Institute for Research on Exceptional Children, 1961.
34. Kirk, S., J. McCarthy, and W. D. Kirk, *Examiner's Manual Illinois Test of Psycholinguistic Abilities,* Urbana, Illinois: University of Illinois, 1968.
35. Klopfer, B., and D. Kelly, *The Rorschach Technique.* Yonkers: World Book Company, 1942.
36. Knobloch, H., and B. Pasamanick, "Predicting Intellectual Potential in Infancy," *Amer. J. Dis. Child.,* 106:43, 1963.
37. Koch, R., B. Graliker, K. Fishler, and A. H. Parmalee, "Mental Retardation Early Childhood. A Study of 143 Infants." *Postgrad. Medic.,* 66:238, 1961.
38. Leiter, R. G., "Manual for the 1948 Revision of the Leiter International Performance Scale." *Psychol. Serv. Center J.,* 11:4, 1950.
39. Raven, J. C., *Coloured Progressive Matrices.* Publ. H. K. Lewis & Co. Ltd. London, W. C. 1, available through Western Psychol. Services, Box 775, Beverly Hills, Calif., 1960.
40. Rorschach, H., *Psychodiagnostics* (English translation), New York: Grune and Stratton, Inc., 1945.
41. Share, J., A. Webb, and R. Koch, "A Preliminary Investigation of the Early Developmental Levels of Mongoloid Infants." *Am. J. Ment. Defic.,* 55:238, 1961.
42. Slosson, R. L., *Slosson Intelligence Test (SIT) for Children and Adults.* East Aurora, New York: Slosson Educ. Publ., 1963.
43. Spearman, C., *The Abilities of Man.* New York: Macmillan, 1927.
44. Stutsman, R., *Guide for Administering the Merrill-Palmer Scale of Mental Tests.* A reprint of part three of Mental Measurement of Preschool Children in Measurement and Adjustment Series, ed. by L. Terman, World Book Co., 1948.
45. Terman, L. M. *The Intelligence of School Children,* New York: Houghton Mifflin Co., 1919.

46. Terman, L. M., and M. A. Merrill, *Measuring Intelligence.* Boston: Houghton Mifflin Co., 1937.
47. Thorndike, E. L., "Intelligence and Its Measurement," *J. Educ. Psychol.*, 12:123, 1921.
48. Thorndike, R. L., *Stanford-Binet Intelligence Scale, 1972 Norms Tables.* Boston: Houghton Mifflin Co., 1973.
49. Wechsler, D., *The Measurement of Adult Intelligence.* The Williams & Wilkins Co., 1944.
50. Wechsler, D., *Wechsler Intelligence Scales.* New York: Psychol. Corpor., 1955.
51. Wechsler, D., *Manual for the Wechsler Preschool and Primary Scale of Intelligence.* Psychol. Corpor., 1967.
52. Wechsler, D., *Manual for the Wechsler Intelligence Scale for Children-Revised.* New York: Psychol. Corpor., 1974.

CHAPTER 13

Social Work Services

by SYLVIA SCHILD, D.S.W.

INTRODUCTION

Diagnosis and treatment of the mentally retarded necessitates differential assessment of their social needs and the services required to satisfy these needs. Otherwise, it is not possible to provide the affected individual with the kind of help which enables him to achieve optimal performance and utilization of his abilities. The milieu in which the retarded person lives, the people in his environment and the demands made upon him by the world that surrounds him are significant social pressures which impinge upon him. He invariably needs assistance if he is to cope adequately with these pressures. Furthermore, effective care of the retarded person involves his family in the diagnostic and treatment processes. Social assessment of the family situation and functioning is pertinent not only to facilitate maximum care for the retardate but also to provide amelioration and support to stressed family members.

The social worker is especially well-suited for making valuable contributions to the team management of the mentally retarded. Historically, social workers have long experience in working with family units, which permits skillful diagnoses and treatment of social problems. Social workers have traditionally worked with the impact of crisis situations on individuals and families. They have studied ways of helping clients

The author, having reviewed this chapter for the revised text, believes the role description of the social worker on the mental retardation multidisciplinary team and the framework of referral for social work practice in the field of mental retardation described remain basically sound and need no elaboration here. For a more comprehensive understanding of the relationship of social work and mental retardation, the reader is referred to the following publications: Margaret Adams, *Mental Retardation and Its Social Dimensions,* Columbia University Press, 1971; Meyer Schreiber, (ed.) *Social Work and Mental Retardation,* John Day Co., 1970.

to draw upon their own strengths and the external resources available to them to permit resolution of crisis situations in the best possible problem-solving way. Furthermore, social workers have traditionally been concerned with the appropriate use of community resources on behalf of their clients. They have participated on teams in mental health settings, as well as in work with the ill and handicapped in medical institutions.

Prior to the development of community-based services for the care and treatment of the mentally retarded, social workers in mental retardation generally worked in institutions, helping with out-of-home placements and maintaining the links between institution, family and patient. With the development of community diagnostic and evaluation clinics patterned on the multi-disciplinary model, the role of the social worker in mental retardation expanded to include a variety of functions in addition to the usual child welfare and placement services. A high degree of variability, flexibility, and creativity are essential characteristics of the role, resulting from the complex nature of the condition of mental retardation. For this reason, the role of a social worker on a mental retardation multi-disciplinary team is extremely challenging; it is one in which important and unique contributions to the team effectiveness can be made.

The following sections present a frame of reference for guiding social work services in the field of mental retardation; further, they describe social work functions and contributions of the social worker to the objectives of the multi-disciplinary team.

FRAMEWORK FOR SOCIAL WORK SERVICES IN MENTAL RETARDATION

The current trend in the profession of social work is moving rapidly toward a broader, yet differentiated, conceptualization of its responsibilities in social welfare. This new concept recognizes that the complexities of societal systems are equally as important as the psychodynamic conflicts of the individual and his difficulties in interpersonal relationships. It is this kind of perspective which opens the door for successful and gratifying social work practice in mental retardation. In the field of mental retardation, the social worker must understand the individual's relation to society, its institutions and the forces for social change. He needs to know this content because of the intricate nature of mental retardation which precipitates new crises, creates conflicts with existing psycho-social functioning, or reactivates latent problems in individuals or family units.

Several cardinal features characterize the problem of mental retardation and are now well known and generally accepted. They implicitly identify the wide scope amenable to social work interventions as well as providing the rationale for social work engagement in the field:

1). More often than not, the social problems precipitated by mental retardation are more stressful and critical than the pathology. The disruption of established role relationships, the burden on the mother for physical care of the handicapped individual, the anxieties of siblings, concerns about future childbearing . . . these are some of the problems which may be more stressful for family unity than the disorder itself.

2). Mental retardation is a symptom which results from a wide variety of conditions in the physical, psychological, and social spheres. Social forces may, in some instances, be the causative factors for the mental limitation.

3). Mental retardation is a chronic, handicapping condition. The retardate requires a continuum of services across his life span, particularly at times of crisis related to the natural course of his growth and development.

4). The multi-dimensional aspects of etiology, diagnosis, treatment, prevention and protective care make imperative the provision of services by many professional disciplines and community groups.

5). The multi-disciplinary approach, whether by collaborating agencies or by formally structured staff teams in an agency, needs to be a continuous process of shared responsibility rather than co-ordinated operations of an essentially discrete nature in order to provide service with maximum benefit.

6). The array of services required to meet the special needs of the retardate and his family, and the need for collaborative efforts of professionals and agencies, dictate a need for built-in machinery for coordination of services to avoid gaps and duplications, and to plan for the availability of appropriate new services.

7). Most mentally retarded persons are more like normal individuals than they are unalike. Wherever possible, their normal needs should be met in the same manner as the rest of the population.

8). Mental retardation is first and foremost a *family problem*. The question of how much responsibility society will need to assume for the retardate (how well the retardate may be maintained in the community) depends largely on the adaptation of the family to the deviant member and to the effectiveness of the family's coping strategies in dealing with the problem.

9). Retarded children become retarded adults. Their own rights as well as those of their parents must be respected. There needs to be appropriate societal expectations for the continued maintenance of the retardate within his family unit. This is necessary to insure adequate community services for the adult retardate as well as for the mentally retarded child.

These features of mental retardation help to shape the form of social work engagement in the field, coupled with basic social work principles, concepts, and practical knowledge. Some basic assumptions underlying the generic practice of social work are particularly pertinent to work with the mentally retarded.

A primary premise holds that the needs of the retarded are both generic and specific; that is, retardates and their families have the same common needs as other human beings which must be met at the same time that special needs related to the mental deficiency or retardation must be met. The basic needs of families in disadvantaged societal groups are often so pressing that they take precedence over other needs; this means that the mildly retarded children among the 15 to 20 million children living in deprived poverty-stricken environments are not provided with the necessary means to enrich their mental abilities. On the other hand, the basic needs of families with retarded members may be overlooked when the concern is focused on the special needs of the retardate. Decisions about which needs should be met and in which order can be made upon reference to the desired objectives. Three basic goals guide social work activity with the retarded and their families: to support the integrity of the family which is placed under unusual stress as a result of the presence of a mentally retarded member; to provide the opportunities for the maximum personality, physical, and mental growth and development of the retardate; and, to help the retardate reach his full potentiality in becoming an autonomous, contributing and participating citizen.

A second principle, a correlate to the previous premise, is that the human rights of retardates and their families need to be safeguarded and respected. This involves the dual recognition by the social worker of seeing that parents have the right to make their own decisions about their children and family life and that the retardate has the rightful claim to parental protection and life with his family. These rights sometimes conflict, such as when parents wish to place their child out of the home although objective observers and counselors may feel the child is deriving benefits from the family environment which cannot be provided in the placement situation. Value judgments need to be withheld and solutions sought objectively to solve such conflicts. With rights come responsibilities! This understanding often brings about the accommodation between competing rights. Parents seek to discharge their responsibilities as much for the purpose of maintaining their own sense of integrity as for the child's benefit. And, where possible, the retardate should be expected and required to take as much self-responsibility for his behavior as is compatible with his abilities and limitations.

A third principle holds that the nurturance of the retardate is generally provided best in the family unit. Like other children, the basis of the retardate's adult behaviors and successful social adaptations depends in large measure on how he has been reared. In some instances, the nature of the individual's upbringing may determine if he will be characterized as retarded in adulthood. It is important for the social worker to bear in mind that the presence of the retarded member has a significant and lasting effect on the lives of other family members. Therefore, the social worker must individualize each case and consider the needs, rights and problems of all the family members as they are related to the presence of the mentally retarded member. Thus, although a general philosophy is supported, wherever possible, that the retardate should be cared for in his home, vital acknowledgment should be given to the fact that people vary in their psychological and physical capabilities to deal with the problem of mental retardation.

The nature of mental retardation is such that the family unit generally requires the support of community services and resources to carry out its nurturing and socializing functions and cope with the special stresses of the retardate. However, the kind of nurturance and special services required by the retardate is dictated in part by the degree and nature of his mental handicap, and partly by the abilities and capacities of his caretakers to give the requisite care and training. Consequently, the social work approach taken must at all times be oriented to the facts of reality; it must be empathetically supportive and understanding, yet simultaneously oriented within a practical and feasible framework.

FUNCTIONS OF THE TEAM SOCIAL WORKER

The functions of the social worker on the mental retardation team are the traditional tasks of providing direct and indirect social services to the clients with this problem. Depending upon the setting, the social worker may have added responsibilities for research, teaching and community activities.

The direct services entail participation in diagnosis and treatment planning with other team professionals. Based upon the team assessment, the social worker may provide direct casework services to the retardate or to members of his family to help with the psycho-social problems deriving from the mental retardation. This may involve helping clients to understand their feelings, attitudes, and emotional reactions; helping families reestablish role relationships; aiding family members in the management and training of the retardate; or, consulting with and enlisting the help of other significant persons on behalf of the retardate and his family. It may include interpretation and clarification of diagnostic information, team recommendations, agency procedures, and community resources. In traditional fashion, referrals to other community sources are carried out to assist the retardate and his family to obtain needed services.

Another way the social worker may engage in direct services is through provision of group-work. Groups for parents and retardates having similar needs and problems have been found therapeutically beneficial. Groups are an effective medium for educational or orientation purposes; in some settings, experimental use of groups for intake processing has been highly effective.

Indirect services on behalf of clientele are as vital as direct services. Indirectly, the social worker has responsibility to improve the agency's program to more effectively meet the needs of the retarded and their families. On the community level, the social worker may need to work through social welfare planning bodies and citizen groups, particularly parent associations for retarded children, to identify unmet needs and to develop programs of services. The interdependency of various areas of treatment for the retarded makes community cooperation imperative. No one agency and no one person can cope with or treat the multiplicity of interrelated needs of the retardate. As a result of this interrelatedness and dependency upon a wide array of srevices, the social worker in mental retardation generally is assigned multiple functions, often "covering the waterfront," carrying a combination of direct and indirect responsibilities. The social worker for the mentally retarded learns to transpose readily from direct client services to assuming group leadership to engaging in community activity. Not infrequently, teaching, training, research and administrative tasks are added to the assignment. All of this stems from the need to have an integrative approach in dealing with mental retardation and because there are social needs to be met at every level of care.

The basic assumption underlying the multi-disciplinary team approach is that the collaborative understandings and knowledge of the multi-professional disciplines will result in the best possible diagnosis and treatment plan to foster the growth and development of the retarded child. The personality development and social adjustment of the retardate is greatly influenced by the people with whom he interacts and upon whom he is dependent. Therefore, much of the success of the team plan depends in large measure upon the support, understanding, and cooperation given by the family members with whom the retardate lives. One of the major contributions made by the social worker to the team is the objective assessment of the family situation, including relevant family history and facts about the current family situation. An important area is the capacity of the family to cope with the problems precipitated by the retardate; this involves identification of the strengths of family members, the problems in the home environment which need to be resolved or hurdled to make achievement of team goals possible, and the environmental supports available to assist the family in carrying out team recommendations. As previously indicated, the social worker has the specialized knowledge of community resources which can be brought into play to provide necessary services. Where environmental manipulation is desirable, the social worker can bring the benefit of knowledge and expertise in effecting such changes so as to provide a growth-producing, enriching, dynamic experience for the retarded child, his family and community.

A main task of the social worker is to provide the team with an individualized, objective assessment of the particular case, so that management, treatment, and rehabilitation plans can be formulated. Assessment of the family situation can help the other team members understand the effect their decisions might have on family functioning. In the light of the social worker's assessment of family and individual psycho-social dynamics, the team will be more adequately equipped to determine priorities of treatment needs and appropriateness of team recommendations. The relationship is reciprocal; the social worker has as much need of the other team members in performing social work services in the best possible way. The social worker will need to have accurate information about the nature of the intellectual deficit, the level of intellectual functioning, physical and medical facts, psychiatric data, etc., to be able to help the parents and the retardates with their concerns.

The social worker's service to the family is achieved through a variety of approaches: counseling, casework and group services. The retardate and his family can be helped to accept the handicap and to live with his problem without disabling defenses. Parents who are fearful, confused, or unclear about the retardate's condition are not in a position to help him live comfortably or positively with the defect. Most of these parents have feelings about the burden of having a handicapped child and about the condition of mental retardation *per se,* which need to be considered and resolved if they are to be freed to assist their child with his own anxieties and feelings.

The focus of social work intervention is on the strengthening of family ties and relationships and on enlisting the maximum support of the family to carry out the team recommendations for the retardate. By enhancing family relationships, the way is paved for the redirection of their energies to other concerns and interests, thereby improving family life for all members, including the retardate.

SUMMARY

As a representative of the social work profession, the social worker on the multi-disciplinary mental retardation team applies specialized training and knowledge about helping people with their psycho-social problems. Since mental retardation is a complex problem, the ability of the retarded person to make successful social adaptations will largely determine whether or not he can remain in the wider community. The successfulness of making adequate adjustments in social living also depends upon the effectiveness with which the family is able to master and cope with his problems. Finally, success will hinge upon the availability of necessary services in the community.

As a team member, the social worker contributes the professional assessment of the psycho-social dynamics and factors in the family situation. This information contributes to the formulation of a collaborative diagnosis and treatment plan by the multi-disciplinary team. The social worker's contributions need to be coordinated with the findings of other team members so as to permit arrival at an integrated plan which avoids duplication and overlapping of services. The social worker, secure in his professional competence, asks for consultation from team members and supports the team decisions regardless of differing judgment.

By functioning in the manner described herein, the social worker can, through direct and indirect services, provide valuable assistance to the retarded child, his family and community.

BIBLIOGRAPHY

1. Beck, H., "Casework with Parents of Mentally Retarded Children," *Amer. J. of Ortho.*, Oct., 870, 1962.
2. Begab, J., *The Mentally Retarded Child. A Guide to Services of Social Agencies,* Health, Education and Welfare, U.S. Children's Bureau Publication No. 404, 1963.
3. Cohen, P., "The Impact of the Handicapped Child on the Family," *Social Casework,* 14:137, 1962.
4. Drayer, C., and E. A. Schlesinger, "The Informing Interview," *Amer. J. Ment. Def.*, 65, 1960.
5. Dye, E. A., "A Social Work Approach to the Mentally Retarded and Their Families," *Amer. J. Ment. Def.*, 63:534, 1958.
6. Hersh, A., "Casework with Parents of Retarded Children," *Social Work,* 6:61, 1961.
7. Goodman, L., "The Social Worker's Role in Clinics for the Retarded," *Child Welf.*, April, 1965.
8. Goodman, L., and R. Rothman, "The Development of a Group Counselling Program in a Clinic for Retarded Children," *Amer. J. Ment. Def.*, May, 1961.
9. Kozier, A., "Casework with Parents of Children Born with Severe Brain Defects," *Soc. Casework,* 38, April, 1957.
10. Kelman, H., "Some Problems in Casework with Parents of Mentally Retarded Children," *Amer. J. Ment. Def.*, 61:595, 1957.
11. Mednick, M. F., "Casework Service to the Mentally Retarded Child and His Parents," *Casework Papers.* New York: Family Service Association of America, 1957.
12. Milligan, G. E., "Counseling Parents of the Mentally Retarded," *Mental Retardation Abstracts*, Nat'l. Clearinghouse for Mental Health Information, II, No. 3, July-Sept., 1965.
13. Perlman, H., "Social Diagnosis Leading to Social Treatment," *Social Work in Child Health Projects for Mentally Retarded Children,* Selected Papers, District of Columbia, Dept. of Public Health, 1963.
14. Schild, S., "Counseling with Parents of Retarded Children Living at Home," *Social Work,* 9:866, 1964.
15. Schild, S., "Parents of PKU Children," *Children,* May-June, 1964.
16. Schild, S., "The Challenging Opportunity for Social Workers in Genetics," *Social Work,* 11:22, 1966.
17. Schotland, L., "Social Work Approach to the Chronically Handicapped," *Social Work,* 9:68, 1964.

CHAPTER 14

Nursing Services

by CAMILLE LEGEAY COOK, M.S.

Nursing, the largest of the health professions, has over 800,000 registered nurses in the United States in active practice today. This represents the largest potential health resource available to care for intellectually impaired children with associated developmental problems.

Nurses of varying levels of professional preparation work with pediatric patients in both normal newborn and intensive care nurseries; in inpatient units of hospitals; in community agencies, such as public health departments or schools; in state schools and institutions for the retarded; in outpatient departments; and in offices of private physicians. Few of these nurses work exclusively with mentally retarded and multiply handicapped children. Most care for groups of patients which include mentally retarded children.

The amount of help a nurse is able to give a child and his family depends on the function of the agency as well as on the nurse's education and clinical experience. The job title does not necessarily indicate level of professional education or particular skills in working with children and their families. While the majority of nurses have only a basic education in nursing, an increasing number, through graduate training in pediatric nursing and mental retardation, may practice in any of the variety of settings listed above, often serving as consultants to nurses with more generalized responsibility.

Some schools of ursing, particularly in universities with both baccalaureate and graduate programs, have faculty members qualified as clinical nursing specialists who teach nursing students the knowledge and skills they need to care for infants and children who are considered high risk because of developmental problems or who may become at risk because such problems seem likely to occur.

214

Each state has at least one child development clinic which has a multidisciplinary group of professional health practitioners specializing in the care of infants and children suspected of being mentally retarded. A nurse is customarily a member of the team.

About 75 pediatric clinical nurse specialists are currently associated with university-affiliated facilities training programs in mental retardation supported by federal maternal and child health funds. These nurses provide direct services to infants and children, teach graduate students of all disciplines, and participate in research.

Nursing functions in mental retardation can conveniently be classified into three broad categories: prevention, casefinding, and treatment or intervention. These functions frequently overlap. Some nurses have responsibilities in all three; others concentrate in one or two. For example, a nurse in a state residential facility may be concerned primarily with treatment, whereas a public health nurse working in the community would be likely to perform all three functions. These areas of responsibility are described in greater detail in the remaining sections of this chapter.

PREVENTION

The prevention of mental retardation through health programs and practices is receiving increasing attention. In 1962, the President's Committee on Mental Retardation reported that women of low income, who receive inadequate prenatal care (or none), not only give birth to infants that are more apt to die in the first year of life, but also have a higher proportion of premature or low-birth-weight babies with a subsequent high incidence of brain damage and retardation. The report helped the nation focus on this segment of the population and its need for many services.

Some of the problems frequently associated with low-income families are: inadequate maternal nutrition, chronic illness in women of childbearing age, pregnancy in girls younger than 16 years or women over 35 years of age, and intervals between pregnancies of less than 12 months. These problems are related to the twin complexities of prematurity and an excessive infant death rate.

A recommendation made by the Panel of the President's Committee resulted in enactment of the Maternal and Child Health and Mental Retardation Planning Amendments of 1963, which authorized federal assistance to provide quality care to such high-risk maternity patients and their infants in the communities where they live.

The thrust of this program was toward the reduction of the incidence of mental retardation and other handicapping conditions caused by complications associated with childbearing and toward helping to reduce infant and maternal mortality. Infant mortality has always been considered a useful index of health status, since it is affected by economic and demographic factors, as well as by availability of medical and health resources.

In the Maternity and Infant Care program, a multidisciplinary team (usually including an obstetrician, pediatrician, nurse, nutritionist and social worker) developed projects using a variety of innovative measures to increase the accessibility and quality of care in areas of high infant mortality and low family income.

Some of these projects were in urban areas in the inner cities; some were in rural areas which were medically underserved. Each project provided for medical services at a site and at times convenient to the women, arranged transportation when necessary, and provided community workers for outreach. The clinical services included prenatal, hospital delivery, postpartum, interconceptional and infant care through the first year of the child's life.

In the decade 1956-65, infant mortality in the United States decreased by only 5 percent. Since 1964, when the first project was funded, the rate decreased from 24.8 per 1,000 live births to 17.6 in 1973, slightly more than a 28 percent drop. By 1973, 55 projects were in operation.

Major factors which are believed to have contributed to this dramatic decrease include the Maternity and Infant Care program, neonatal intensive care units and increased family planning services. Since 1970, liberalized abortion laws may also have contributed to the reduction.

The social and medical risk to the mother is directly related to the incidence of prematurity or low-birth-weight infants, as well as infant mortality. For vulnerable women at risk who receive inadequate care, the prematurity rate may be twice or more that of no-risk women. Another factor, indicated by both Kessner et al. (13) and Bronstein (6), is that family planning as a part of comprehensive maternal and infant care programs is effective in reducing prematurity rates.

The nursing profession has the largest number of practitioners in maternal, infant and child health programs. In the prevention of mental retardation, here are some ways the nurse can use technical knowledge and skills:

Providing care to women: Bringing them under medical supervision within the first trimester, counseling them about the availability of community social service resources, providing nutrition and dietary information, arranging for hospital delivery, providing care during labor, delivery and the postpartum period and helping them with family planning, with emphasis on the importance of child-spacing to improve the health of mothers and their infants.

Providing care to infants: Care to the newborn both immediately after delivery and in the hospital nursery, well-baby care during the first year of life, immunizations, referral for correction of sensory and potentially handicapping defects, anticipatory guidance in accident prevention and early attention to childhood infections.

Lead poisoning is still an important cause of mental retardation. Public health nurses are aware of the dangers to young children associated with flaking paint and broken plaster found in poor and dilapidated housing in the slums of old cities. If these potentially harmful conditions cannot be corrected, the nurse may offer the family assistance in finding safe housing.

There are also implications for nursing in current studies about the role of early stimulation in the development of the infant. Neal (22) investigated the effects of vestibular stimulation in the neurosensory development of infants who were premature by gestational age. Study findings indicated that a program of motion stimulation may favorably influence the development of a baby born prematurely.

Barnard (3), too, is concerned with the prematurely born infant, particularly one who is placed in an incubator for an extended period of time in order to survive. She suggests a systematic plan of stimulation with special attention to low frequency repetitive sounds and visual and tactile stimuli.

Barnard (4) further suggests that the nurse responsible for the care of the infant in the intensive care unit should initiate a plan that encourages positive relationships of parents with the infant. It would be directed toward facilitating frequent visiting of the infant by the parents and promoting parent-infant interactions. As soon as possible, these should include such activities as bathing, feeding, rocking, and handling. In addition to customary nursing referral for continuity of care after discharge from the nursery, Barnard utilizes a network of parents who have had premature babies to help new parents through hospitalization and the transition to the home.

LeLouis (18) has studied the effects on the motor development of normal infants 12 to 16 weeks of age of a program of exercise and positioning. Findings in this small sample indicate that a program of motor stimulation may encourage development and therefore be appropriate to use with infants who are at risk because of social, education and economic factors. There are implications for nursing intervention to promote growth of other babies, such as those born with Down's Syndrome, cerebral palsy or drug addiction. The role of the nurse should be expanded as there is further study in the use of stimulation in both sensory and motor development.

The prevention or amelioration of secondary problems in both the child and his family when a diagnosis of mental retardation is made also requires specialized nursing services. The need for such services may occur as early as birth, since diagnosis sometimes can be made at that time. Nurses should be prepared to help the distressed parents cope with their feelings of grief and with the reality of their infant's potential for development.

When an infant is born with Down's Syndrome, for example, it is important for a nurse in the maternity unit to understand the meaning of the diagnosis, both as it relates to the baby's development and to the parents' feelings. A well prepared nurse, who understands the grieving process, is in a key position to help parents begin to cope constructively with a stressful situation. The nurse who has a realistic but sensitive understanding about mental retardation and handicapping conditions is not likely to withdraw her availability to the mother. Such a nurse ministers to the mother's physical comfort and provides her opportunities to talk about her feelings of anger, resentment and disappointment. The nurse can help parents recognize the realities of the baby's needs and their competency to provide for these needs.

When the mother and infant are discharged, a nursing referral to the community's resources for follow-up services is appropriate. Only when continuity of care is effected and families are given ongoing help can we expect to avoid the problems so frequently encountered when families continue to deny the existence of retardation in their child. When the infant's lesser potentialities are understood by all family members and when the infant is provided with appropriate learning opportunities, difficulties in family relationships may be averted.

CASEFINDING

Casefinding includes the elements of assessment and referral, since both are prerequisite to a comprehensive evaluation. Wherever nurses work with infants and children, they need to know about normal growth and behavior as well as about mental retardation. They should understand the common causes of mental retardation, which will help them detect early signs of developmental delay.

The developmental assessment tool is an aid to their active search for manifestations of retardation. As the practice of medicine shifted from its almost exclusive treatment of the sick child to the broader aspects of health maintenance, physicians became interested in assessment of the child's growth and development. In the 1930's, Gesell studied a number of infants and young children and devised his set of developmental schedules, the first such tool to receive wide recognition. Although his work has been criticized by psychologists and others in the field of child development for its limitations, sub-sections from this instrument are included, with refinement, in many of the tests that are in use today.

Even though some of the developmental assessment tests may have little predictive value for future intellectual functioning in the infant or very young child, they do allow an appraisal of the child's behavior in a number of areas and, therefore, can be valuable to nurses.

Probably the developmental assessment tool used most widely by pediatric and public health nurses is the Denver Developmental Screening Test (10). It is suggested in the *Medicaid Guidelines* (20) as an appropriate screening test to be used in the Early and Periodic Screening Diagnosis and Treatment (EPSDT) Program. Another tool, although not designed specifically for screening, is the Washington Guide to Promoting Development in the Young Child (5) which offers the nurse a frame of reference about growth and development in a systematic way. The Washington Guide also includes suggestions for activities that the parents or caretaker might initiate when the child is developmentally behind his age group.

Nurses have traditionally been concerned with children's feeding and sleeping patterns, their diet, their toileting and other aspects of daily care. Developmental assessment tools have helped them to record and to utilize their observations in a more structured fashion for the purpose of detecting early signs of lag in any area of growth development.

Frequently, a public health nurse is the only member of the health professions to see an infant consistently during his early life; she is in a position to detect any developmental deviation and to refer the child for medical evaluation. Nurses working in well-baby and well-child clinics also have opportunities to observe many infants and children. In addition, they may have routine access to birth records, hospital discharge notices and other information which may indicate a baby at risk, such as one born with a physical anomaly, a premature baby or a baby born to a family with several retarded children. When a child is suspected of being mentally retarded, he is referred for a medical evaluation to his private physician, an outpatient department, or a specialized clinic. He is often referred to a multidisciplinary child development clinic which specializes in the care of children with some impairment of performance. Most of these community clinics offer a comprehensive program which provides a long-range health and educational regimen for each child. Recent advances in early identification, etiology, prevention and treatment of mental retardation emphasize the need for these programs. The multidisciplinary team approach has evolved as a result of the complexities of the problems of the mentally retarded child. A "team" implies the coordination of the efforts of a variety of professional workers representing several health disciplines. A nurse with special preparation in the care of children with mental retardation and other handicapping conditions should be a member of the team. Other disciplines regularly represented include medicine (pediatrics), social work, psychology, speech pathology, audiology, physical therapy, occupational therapy and nutrition.

An assessment of the child and his family by a nurse is customarily a part of the clinic's comprehensive evaluation. Usually, however, this assessment is made in the child's home, as the nurse is a member of a profession that regularly carries out part of its function in the home.

The home observation of the child's performance and behavior is basic to an assessment of the child's level of performance. The nurse also evaluates the family's behavior and attitudes, as well as those of relatives who live with the family or who are frequently in the home. Often, such an assessment is more meaningful than one obtained in a clinic where all family members may not be present or where the family, away from its familiar surroundings, may be ill at ease.

Included in the nursing evaluation is a summary of the child's special needs, an appraisal of the family's (particularly the mother's) ability to meet these needs, and recommendations and suggestions for the treatment plan.

TREATMENT OR INTERVENTION

A program of intervention or treatment and follow-up services is essential to the optimal development of an infant or child who is diagnosed is being retarded. Evaluation and diagnosis have no meaning for a family unless a program is developed which the parents can implement with the resources available to them in their community. Whether the child is to be followed for medical or other services in the clinic or is to be referred back to his own private physician, nursing services are frequently recommended in the plan for treatment. Specific recommendations may be: to counsel the family which has recently become aware of their child's diagnosis; to interpret and reinforce the medical treatment; to help the mother teach the child self-care skills, such as feeding and dressing; to help the mother with behavior and discipline problems or guide her in selection of toys and play activities that promote motor skills and socialization. The mother usually needs to be shown how to give the child auditory, visual and tactile stimulation.

As the retarded child grows older, parents frequently need help and guidance in areas of psychosocial behavior including that of learning about sex and sexuality. A few nurses have developed special skills in counseling about sexuality and sex education for the mentally retarded or developmentally handicapped.

Clinical nurse specialists utilize behavior modification techniques derived from operant learning theory in working with retarded children (33). These techniques involve a restructuring of the child's environment and the reinforcement of appropriate behavior in order to help him learn the tasks necessary for everyday living. The child who feeds himself, tends to his toilet needs and acquires other socially valued skills is more apt to develop self-esteem and to win approval and acceptance from parents and siblings than is an overly dependent, ill-mannered child. Behavior modification techniques, when used in conjunction with the nurse's other knowledge and skills, facilitate the promotion of independence and growth in the child. Nurses have also found these techniques effective in working with groups of children in institutions.

Generally, when the clinic team recommends nursing intervention, the child is returned to the community agency for this service. However, the team nurse keeps a small caseload of children to maintain skills and to provide a role model. If the public health nurse needs help with the team's recommendations for the child and his family, consultation may be provided by the clinic nurse or by therapists of other disciplines as indicated. Consultation is often available also through the state or local health agencies. The public health nurse frequently knows the family and may be of help at times of crises affecting the mentally retarded child, such as during an illness of the mother or birth of a new baby.

Although a medical evaluation is imperative, not all infants and children with developmental lag need be referred to a child development clinic. A private physician may decide that distance or other problems makes such all referral impractical for some families and that the needs of other families do not require the attention of the whole gamut of professional services from a health-oriented multidisciplinary team. The problems and manifestations of mental retardation are manifold, however, and when this diagnosis is suspected most families could benefit from nursing services. Parents of retarded infants and children who are under private medical care frequently need assistance in problems of day-to-day care at home, understanding of the diagnosis, interpretation to neighbors and relatives, and long-term planning. A nurse can offer parents some practical approaches to child-rearing problems complicated by mental retardation.

In addition to helping parents cope with the stresses common to all families with a retarded youngster, a nurse can collaborate with the physician in specific aspects of medical treatment, such as in drug therapy for hyperactivity and seizure control or in diet management in children with disorders such as phenylketonuria and galactosemia. Another equally important function of the nurse is to help parents accept realistic goals for their child's physical and intellectual development once they realize that the hoped for medical or surgical cure is not possible. Through sustained contacts, the nurse can report on developments within the family which may indicate a change in a plan of treatment.

A public health nurse can be of much help to the private physician and the family because of knowledge of community resources for children who have special needs, such as day-care centers, schools and recreational programs. Maintaining continuity of health care for the child among the various community agencies is also a nursing function.

Keeping a child in his own home or in a foster home as long as his family or the community can provide adequate programs is the current philosophy of care for children who perform at lower levels of competency. Actually, only about 4 percent of children who are mentally retarded enter institutions today; the majority remain in the home and community. If a family wishes to place a child in an institution, however, a nurse can assist them.

Another challenge to nursing today is to make its services a part of a broad health and education program for children with familial retardation, which has many causes and requires a multifaceted program. Such a program must include adequate nutrition, optimal maternal and child health, improved education and the alleviation of poverty and its social disadvantages. The success of Head Start and many other programs for the disadvantaged preschool child is an example of coordination of the community's health, education and social resources. Research into the nature of motivation and of the learning process will no doubt furnish additional insights for the nursing role.

One of the first attempts in which team members of a child development clinic tried to change the life course of families with members diagnosed as familially retarded was undertaken by Kugel (15) in Iowa City. A nurse was an active participant in the study, which demonstrated that constructive change is possible when intensive work along several channels is carried out with the family. The families in the study improved their housing, secured stable employment, advanced the health of all members and upgraded their children's educational experiences.

Nurses play an important role, also, in regard to abused and neglected children. Some multiproblem families react to stresses of disturbed marital relationships and emotional or financial problems by overtly neglecting babies; others respond by inflicting severe physical mistreatment on them. Occasionally, a nurse of a pediatric inpatient unit or a public health nurse visiting in the home becomes suspicious of the possibility of this kind of family problem. The infant may evidence anything from minor neglect to gross neglect or assault, and if hospitalized, may have such diagnoses as failure to thrive or severe trauma.

Growing evidence indicates that a substantial number of children suffer from physical mistreatment in their homes. The trauma may be in the form of cigarette or hot water burns, multiple fractures from being hit against a wall or struck with an implement, or any of a variety of other injuries. A follow-up study (8) of children hospitalized between two months and ten years of age for repeated multiple bone injuries shows the seriousness of the complex child abuse problem. The incidence of death, institutionalization, mental retardation, physical defects, speech and personality problems that occurred in the study group is distressing. Frequently, the child abuse occurred to a premature baby or one born out of wedlock, or when the family was under excessive tension associated with having several small children with birth spacings of less than one year. When a nurse has evidence of child abuse, a referral should be made to the agency in the community responsible for legal and social action in such instances. Nurses with special preparation may be involved also in the treatmen program for the parents, particularly in helping them with child-rearing practices.

Babies who fail to thrive physically in the absence of organic disease may be suffering from overt neglect. These babies frequently display associated developmental lag believed to result from lack of maternal stimulation. Because of disturbed interpersonal relationships observed within families of infants hospitalized for failure to thrive, an exploratory study (19) was undertaken of the social histories from a number of these infants and their families. A nurse participated in the study (28), gathering data about the infants since birth and recording her observations of the infants' behavior in the hospital. When this information was evaluated, along with that contributed by other study participants, a plan for intervention was begun. The purpose of the plan was to help the mothers establish a mutually satisfying relationship with their babies. An integral part of the nursing care that evolved included teaching the mother to provide the infants with the sensory stimulation that they had been lacking.

Durand's (7) study of a 5-year-old child living at home diagnosed as Down's Syndrome and severe failure to thrive demonstrated the effectiveness of a 17-day program of developmental nursing care. Findings supported the assumptions that there would be an increase in height, weight, amount of sleep, active mobility, awareness of the environment and prelanguage vocalizations and a decrease in self-stimulation. The child had no increase however in either caloric intake or play activity with toys. This study supported Legeay's (17) recommendations to use nursing care in infants and children identified as failure to thrive in the absence of demonstrable organic disease.

Nurses who provide health supervision in homes have many opportunities to recognize potential crises in families and to initiate a preventive program designed to help the parents cope with the day-by-day problems in managing their small children before such serious consequences as abuse and neglect occur. Children of migrant workers and other severely deprived families particularly need such supervision.

NURSING EDUCATION

Educators in basic nursing programs are now making changes in their curricula, in recognition of the potential offered by nurses in the prevention and amelioration of mental retardation. Increased emphasis is being placed on the physical and biological sciences, as well as on courses in child growth and development. Students learn more about the major etiological factors influencing growth and how to maximize the development of each child as a member of his family. They are also becoming familiar with the contributions other disciplines can make. Improvement in teaching certain skills basic to all nursing—observation, interviewing and communication—benefits nurses who will work with the mentally retarded. It is important for the students to learn about their own feelings about mental retardation and handicapping conditions in children. In some schools (31), faculty members recognize this need and plan experiences appropriate to the students' abilities. Opportunities are provided for the students to discuss their feelings with their peers and faculty.

Continuing education programs offer practicing nurses an opportunity to learn new concepts, upgrade their factual knowledge and acquire new skills. State and local maternal and child health nursing consultants, state mental retardation nursing consultants and other nurses in leadership positions have asked for the development of short-term programs dealing with the variety of aspects of mental retardation concerned in the areas of prevention, early identification, treatment or intervention. Continuing education departments of schools of nursing and, when possible, the nursing departments of university-affiliated facilities have responded to these requests. It is through this mechanism that new information from research and practice reaches most registered nurses.

Many graduate programs in pediatric nursing offer students an opportunity to specialize in an area such as mental retardation or intensive care of the high-risk newborn. Courses include both theory and clinical experience in the care of infant and children at risk for developmental, genetic, social or other causes. An increasing number of students are learning to perform physical examinations as well as developmental assessments; to work cooperatively with other members of the team; and to become expert practitioners, teachers or supervisors.

Nurses who elect the clinical specialist role and choose a program associated with a university affiliated facility have a unique opportunity to work and study in an interdisciplinary setting. All students attend what has come to be called a "core curriculum" and participate in faculty and student team evaluations of children, individualized treatment or intervention programs, and research. They learn the roles and functions of other team members and how to work collaboratively to provide optimal care to children and their families within the community.

SUMMARY

Many nurses with differing levels of professional preparation contribute to prevention, casefinding and treatment of mental retardation in a variety of health settings. Nurses in generalized maternal and child health programs, particularly public health nurses, are intimately involved in the total area of mental retardation. They provide health care to women throughout their childbearing years and to infants and children in their homes and in a variety of health agencies. Increasing numbers of nurses working with pediatric patients are utilizing developmental screening tests to help them in planning an individualized health program for children, as well as in detecting deviations that may suggest the need for referral to a team of specialists for a comprehensive evaluation.

As part of such an evaluation, a nurse makes an assessment of the child's level of performance in the home. The written report includes impressions of the child's special needs, the effect of the handicapped child on his parents and siblings, the family's ability to meet his needs and the nurse's recommendations for the total plan of treatment.

When a diagnosis of retardation is made—particularly in an infant or preschool child—a nurse has something positive to offer the family, especially with the day-to-day problems faced by parents in managing the care of such a child. Through a sustained relationship with the family, the nurse is in a position to offer them guidance in the complexities of the problem of mental retardation.

Nurses who have graduate preparation and experience in pediatric nursing and mental retardation can offer specialized care to children suspected of being mentally retarded. Since early intervention can often do much to reduce the degree of the child's handicap, they are in a position to anticipate the emotional and social stresses that may occur and help the family respond realistically in order to promote maximum self-care and independence. They teach parents to modify the child's behavior by manipulating his environment and using positive reinforcement techniques helpful in promoting acceptable behavior. Such nurses, as team members in community child development clinics and university-affiliated facilities, offer and participate in a practical plan of action that is feasible to carry out. Using a family-centered approach to the problem, they often coordinate the child's recommended program of treatment and follow-up care. They provide for continuity of patient care through their relationships with their nursing counterparts in hospitals, schools, and public health agencies to whom they offer consultation. These clinical nurse specialists with advanced preparation also work in pediatric hospital units, serve as consultants in state and local health departments and teach in schools of nursing. Where some of their activities can be combined with related studies and research, additional dividends may ensue.

BIBLIOGRAPHY

1. Anderson, E., "Nursing Education in the University Affiliated Center for the Mentally Retarded," *Nursing in Mental Retardation Programs. Proceedings of the Fourth Annual Workshop for Nurses in Mental Retardation*, Miami: University of Miami Press, April, 1967.
2. Barnard, K., "Teaching the Retarded Child is a Family Affair," *Amer. J. of Nurs.* 68:305, 1968.
3. Barnard, K., "The Effect of Stimulation on the Duration and Amount of Sleep and Wakefulness in the Premature Infant," unpublished doctoral dissertation. University of Washington, Seattle, 1972. University Microfilms, Ann Arbor, Michigan, #72-28, 573.
4. Barnard, K., "State of the Art. Nursing: High Risk Infants," *Intervention Strategies for High Risk Infants and Young Children*. Tjessem, T. D. (Ed.), University Park Press, Baltimore, Md. 1975 (publication pending).
5. Barnard, K. and M. Powell, *Teaching the Mentally Retarded Child, a Family Care Approach*, St. Louis: C. V. Mosby Company, 1972.
6. Bronstein, E. S., "Factors in the Reduction of Infant Mortality in a Maternity and Infant Care Project," *Journal of the Medical Association of Georgia*, Nov. 1974, Vol. 63 425-429.
7. Durand, B., "Failure to Thrive in a Child with Down's Syndrome: A Clinical Nursing Study." *Nursing Research*, 24:272, 1975.
8. Elmer, E., *Children in Jeopardy*, Pittsburgh: University of Pittsburgh Press, 1967.
9. Erickson, M. P., "Talking with Fathers of Young Children with Down's Syndrome," *Children Today*, Vol. 3, No. 6:22, 1974.
10. Frankenberg, W. K. and J. B. Dodds: *Denver Developmental Screening Test Kit*, Denver: Ladoca Project and Publishing Foundation, 1957.
11. Haynes, U., *A Developmental Approach to Case Finding*, U.S. Department of Health, Education and Welfare, Public Health Service, Bureau of Community Health Services (HSA) 75-5403 (formerly PHS Pub. 2017—1969), U.S. Government Printing Office.
12. Keogh, B., and C. Legeay, "Recoil from the Diagnosis of Mental Retardation," *Amer. J. of Nursing*, 66:778, 1966.
13. Kessner, D. M., et al. *Infant Death: An Analysis by Maternal Risk and Health Care*, Institute of Medicine, National Academy of Sciences, Washington, D.C. 1973.
14. Koch, R., A. Baerwald, J. McDonald, K. Fishler, and D. Boyle, "The Child Development Traveling Clinic Project in Southern California," *Ped.*, 42:505, 1968.
15. Kugel, R., and M. Parsons, *Children of Deprivation*, U.S. Department of Health, Education and Welfare, Social & Rehabilitation Service. Children's Bureau Publication 440. Washington, D.C., U.S. Government Printing Office, 1967.

16. Legeay, C. and B. Keogh, "Impact of Mental Retardation on Family Life," *Amer. J. of Nursing,* 66:1062, 1966.
17. Legeay, C., "Failure to Thrive: A Nursing Problem," *Nursing Forum,* Vol. IV No. 1, 1965.
18. LeLouis, M., "An Experimental Program to Increase Sitting-Up Behavior in Normal and Deviant Infants," *Nursing in Mental Retardation Programs. Proceedings of the Fourth Annual Workshop for Nurses in Mental Retardation, University of Miami,* Miami: University of Miami Press, April, 1967.
19. Leonard, M., J. P. Rhymes and A. J. Solnit, "Failure to Thrive in Infants," *Amer. J. Dis. Child.,* 3:600, 1966.
20. *MEDICAID: Early and Periodic Screening Diagnosis Treatment for Individuals Under 21, Guidelines,* U.S. Department of Health, Education and Welfare, (SRS) 73-24921, U.S. Government Printing Office, Washington, D.C., 1972.
21. Murray, B., and K. Barnard, "The Nursing Specialist in Mental Retardation," *Nurs. Clinics of N. Amer.,* Philadelphia: W. B. Saunders Company, 1:631, 1966.
22. Neal, M. V., "Vestibular Stimulation and Developmental Behavior of the Small Premature Infant," *Nurs. Res. Rep.,* 3:1-4, (March), 1968.
23. Norris, G. J., "Detecting Early Developmental Delays Using the Denver Developmental Screening Test," *Nursing in Mental Retardation Programs. Proceedings of the Fourth Annual Workshop for Nurses in Mental Retardation, University of Miami,* Miami: University of Miami Press, April, 1967.
24. Pesek, S., "Developmental Assessment Tools for Nurses," *Nursing in Mental Retardation Programs. Proceedings of the Fourth Annual Workshop for Nurses in Mental Retardation,* Miami: University of Miami Press, April, 1967.
25. Peterson, L. W., "Operant Approach to Observation and Recording," *Nurs. Outlook,* 15:28, 1967.
26. Powell, M., "An Interpretation of Effective Management and Discipline of the Mentally Retarded Child," *Nurs. Clinics of N. Amer.,* Philadelphia: W. B. Saunders Company, 1:689, 1966.
27. Reaser, G. P., "Identification of Infants and Young Children with High Risk for Mental Retardation and Some Approaches to Early Intervention," *Nursing in Mental Retardation Programs. Proceedings of the Fourth Annual Workshop for Nurses in Mental Retardation,* Miami: University of Miami Press, April, 1967.
28. Rhymes, J. P., "Working with Mothers and Babies Who Fail to Thrive," *Amer. J. of Nurs.,* 66:1972, 1966.
29. Teague, B. E., "Implementing Changes in the Traditional Institutional Environment of the Mentally Retarded," *Nurs. Clinics of N. Amer.,* Philadelphia: W. B. Saunders Company, 1:651, 1966.
30. Triplett, J. L., "A Women's Club for Deprived Mothers," *Nurs. Outlook,* 13:33, 1967.
31. Vevang, B., P. Leonard and L. Pierson, "Experience in Mental Retardation for Basic Nursing Students," *Nursing Forum,* 6:183, 1967.
32. Whitney, L. R., "Behavioral Approaches to the Nursing of the Mentally Retarded," *Nurs. Clinics of N. Amer.,* Philadelphia: W. B. Saunders, 1:6641, 1966.
33. Whitney, L. R., "Operant Learning Theory, A Framework Deserving Nursing Investigation," *Nurs. Res.,* 15:299, 1966.

CHAPTER 15

Speech and Language Services

by FREDERICK RICHARDSON, M.D., M.R.C.P.

"He gave man speech, and speech created thought,
which is the measure of the universe . . ."

Prometheus Unbound. P. B. SHELLEY (1792-1822)

The relationship between intelligence and speech is well recognized and severe mental retardation has a profound effect on speech development, both in its receptive and expressive aspects. The effect of less severe degrees of mental retardation upon language and speech is more varied and changes with each stage of the child's development, particularly in the first decade of life. Although it is generally accepted that mentally retarded children are slow to speak, considerable confusion remains about the range of disability that may exist and the predictability of what can be expected in an individual child. The vast majority of mentally retarded children have some impairment or limitation of language and vocabulary development, and there is usually a delay in the onset of speech. The use of single words occurs at a later age and Morley (38) and others have observed that this stage of speech development may persist with minimal growth of vocabulary for several years; often little or no spontaneous use of simple sentences or phrases occurs during this time. This limitation of language development depends upon many factors which include the degree or severity of the retardation, the nature of the environment and stimulation to which the child has been exposed, the age of the child, the presence of associated defects of hearing, learning disabilities, emotional disturbance or brain damage affecting speech and language.

After a lifetime of clinical otolaryngological experience, Bordley (6) lists the most common causes of communicative difficulty in the preschool child as: (1) hearing loss, (2) retarded mental development, (3) severe emotional disturbances and (4) aphasia. However, it is probable that retarded mental development outranks hearing loss as a cause of delayed speech in the total population of preschool children.

The presence of mental retardation of mild or severe degree does not preclude the possibility of associated specific hearing, speech, or language disorders. Nor does it preclude concurrent emotional disturbance. However, most commonly, the language delay and associated speech delay in retarded children are not due to hearing loss, emotional disturbance, or specific brain damage. To some extent, the language and speech development can be associated directly with the level of intellectual development which affects the appreciation of the meaning of word sequences. Kirk (30) has stated that in the retarded there is a high correlation between mental age and speech and language development. Where there is relative poverty of thought there may be little to communicate. Alternatively, speech may reflect an elementary thought content.

A natural and physiologic lag in speech development is seen in children of normal intelligence if their expressive speech is contrasted with their comprehension or understanding of language or the spoken word. An intelligent one-year-old infant can understad at least parts of a simple command such as, "Give the ball to Daddy," and can select the ball from several objects and execute this demand. However, it is not until the child is aged 24 to 30 months that he can express such a complex sentence himself, perhaps as, "Daddy give ball," where the basic concepts are good but experience with the mechanics of language is limited. Later, when the floodgates of speech are opened to the normal child, there is still a considerable difference between the quantity of language comprehended and the amount used in everyday situations. Templin (59) has demonstrated that children aged six years with normal hearing and speech have a mean basic vocabulary of approximately 8,000 words and there are estimates of a total vocabulary with variations of 13,000 words or more. However, the same six-year-olds may use only 155 words in everyday play with their peers. In some ways, this simple difference between what has been called passive vocabulary and the active vocabulary used in everyday speech points out the difference between language and speech. It is possible for an intelligent one-year-old child to have a developing language and "vocabulary" of several hundred meaningful *words and sounds,* although he may speak only five or six words such as, "Mommy, Daddy, bye-bye," or words of similar caliber

In a similar way it is possible for a retarded child to have an understanding of many words, sentences and phrases, often through repetition which is the basis for much of learning, and yet be able to say only a few single words and be unable to structure a sentence effectively.

The natural developmental difference that exists between the levels of inner language and expressive speech development can be regarded as physiologic in the preschool developmental years of life of the normal child. If, however, there is a disparity of more than two or three years between the level of intellectual development (mental age) and the measured level of speech and vocabulary development on standardized intelligence tests, there may be a more complex disorder of language present. Marked disparity between speech and mental age may occur in the retarded child. It is important to keep in mind the possibility that the intellectual defect is not necessarily the sole cause of the delayed language and speech development.

The physiologic lag between the passive vocabulary of words comprehended and the use of spontaneous speech in the intelligent child is usually *increased* in the *preschool* child who is mentally retarded. Leaving aside for the moment the questions of brain damage, short attention span, deafness, emotional disturbance or other factors that might complicate learning, let us consider the effects of impaired intelligence on speech and language development in a retarded child with normal hearing. Just as the normal infant exhibits a delay between comprehension and vocalization, so the retarded child exhibits a similar phenomenon. However, this natural delay is exaggerated as a result of the intellectual impairment. Thus, a five-year-old child of average intelligence is expected to have speech and language development of an average five-year-old, provided the hearing and supporting auditory system are normal. In theory, a preschool mentally retarded child might be expected to have developed speech and language abilities which are consistent with his mental age level. This is not usually the case in the preschool child; a mentally retarded five-year-old with a mental age of $2\frac{1}{2}$ years (or IQ 50) does not usually have the language or speech development of a $2\frac{1}{2}$-year-old. The mental retardation is associated with a secondary delay in speech and langugage development.

It is as if the remarkable and complex human faculty of speech and language development takes the mentally retarded child longer to learn. In practice, it is common to find that a five-year-old with a mental age of 2½ years (IQ 50) has a speech language development of a 12-to-18-month-old child. In most children, this secondary delay is an understandable accompaniment of the mental retardation and it spontaneously improves in many children over a period of a few years. The speech and language development usually catches up with the mental age level. If the child used in the example above is examined at ten years when he has the mental age of five years (IQ 50), it is quite common to find that the speech development at that time is compatible with the mental age of five years. Thus, there is a spontaneous improvement in speech and language which catches up with and parallels the mental age of the patient over a period of years (30). Speech and language stimulation and training have been advocated in an attempt to accelerate this improvement in retarded children; this may well be beneficial in some cases, for although many well-stimulated retarded children exhibit spontaneous improvement in their home and special schools if their intellectual development is not too grossly impaired, there is good evidence that most retarded children, particularly in the lower socio-economic groupings, receive inadequate stimulation.

Many standardized intelligence tests have well-defined language and speech test items appropriate to a child's mental age. Although there is little or no standardized test material suitable for the speech and language development of retarded children, it is nevertheless possible to evaluate language abilities and their potential for speech development by careful examination of the child's ability to comprehend information, presented by auditory or visual means, even if he is not able to talk.

FACTORS WHICH AFFECT THE PREDICTABILITY OF
SPEECH DEVELOPMENT IN THE RETARDED CHILD

Once parents suspect or are told that they have a retarded or slow-to-develop child, they usually become prey to innumerable questions about the child and his future progress. As delay in speech development is not uncommon, it raises the classic spectre of the severe retardate or even imbecile-like child who is totally unable to communicate. For this reason, it can be anticipated that the parents who are concerned that they might have a mentally retarded child will ask, "Will my child talk, doctor?" In response to this question, it would be wise to review briefly some of the important factors which influence the answer to their question.

A great deal of time and perhaps unnecessary invesstigation can be saved by a careful and complete history with special emphasis on the child's development. Specific inquiry should be directed to the pregnancy, with special emphasis given to toxemia, threatened miscarriages and possible prenatal infections such as rubella; the delivery and possible complications should be reviewed, as well as the child's birth weight, condition at birth and health during the neonatal period when respiratory difficulty, cyanosis, poor sucking or jaundice may be indicative of birth trauma, infection or hemolytic disease of the newborn. The developmental milestones are of particular importance when mental retardation is a possibility or if speech and language development is in question. Although motor development cannot always be correlated directly with intellectual development, delayed acquisition of motor skills may be the first sign of mental retardation, such as delay in reaching for objects, lack of alert interest in surroundings, delay in sitting, standing or walking (1, 24-25). There should be little or no delay in most motor performances in a child with uncomplicated congenital deafness or a communication disorder.

Careful inquiry into the family history may reveal a significant incidence of mental retardation, congenital deafness or other problems occurring in relatives. However, vague hearsay evidence that near or distant relatives were deaf or retarded is not sufficiently reliable without further careful corroboration of the information. A history of unexplained fevers, infections, infection accompanied by severe dehydration, or cerebral involvement may be of great significance, particularly if followed by arrest or regression in any aspect of motor, intellectual, speech or social development. A detailed documentation of behavior as it relates to hearing, comprehension, language or speech development is a critical part of the developmental history affecting the differential diagnosis of deafness, mental retardation or emotional disturbance.

It is self-evident that in a preschool child the presence of meaningful speech, comprehension of simple sentences and commands, and the ability to give meaningful answers to simple questions (unaccompanied by visual cue or gesture), suggests a level of speech and language development that excludes severe bilateral deafness or a severe communication disorder. Apparent failure to take notice of sounds or speech accompanied by lack of meaningful vocalizations means that a more detailed inquiry into hearing and speech is indicated. Simple questions which may give some clue as to the level of the disorder are listed below, but caution must be observed in placing too much weight on any single observation:

At what age (if ever) did the infant startle to loud sounds?

Does he only startle to sounds that are accompanied by vibration, such as a bang on his crib?

Did he ever imitate or parrot maternal or other sounds made to him?

Did the infant ever turn his head to any sound, such as the telephone bell, a knock at the door, the dog barking, the human voice, his name?

Does he enjoy music or imitate sounds from the environment?

Has there ever been any rhythmic response to music on the radio or television?

At what age did he first make consistent vocalization with communicative intent? (As long as the word used is consistent it does not have to be a recognizable word.)

At what age did he first vocalize a simple sentence joining two separate word concepts, such as "mummy bye-bye?"

Hearing loss may occasionally simulate mental retardation because of the child's failure to take notice of important signals or communication in the environment. Impaired intelligence may also be confused with deafness because of the lack of interest in environmental sounds or voices. Whetnall (63) has suggested that even normal children will often pay no attention to speech that occurs in situations that do not interest them and that an important part of the maternal child relationship in the first months and years of life is the constant speech accompaniment to events which interest the child. Mowrer (39) has suggested that words are reproduced if and only if they are made to sound good in the context of affectionate care and attention. Hardy *et al.* (22) describe an unwanted, severely neglected infant from a deprived home who failed repeated audiologic examinations at five months of age. Following improved care and verbal stimulation in a foster home situation, he performed normally in the Hearing and Speech Center at nine and twelve months.

The picture becomes even more complicated when both mental retardation and deafness co-exist, as may occur in a child damaged by rubella. A child with severe deafness or dysfunction of the auditory system may become withdrawn, emotionally disturbed, or even psychotic, posing a complicated diagnostic problem even to those who have expertise in this area of child development (62). This would suggest that mothers of apparently less responsive, retarded or deaf children must be encouraged to persevere with the constant speech accompaniment and stimulation for even longer than usual.

How, then, is it possible to differentiate between these conditions or to evaluate the severity of each if the patient has a multiple problem? A great deal is known about hearing and language development in the developing child, and failure of certain patterns of behavior to emerge may clarify the situation. If the nature of the child's difficulty is still undetermined, then this basic information, taken in conjunction with pediatric, psychologic, neurologic, otolaryngologic, audiologic, psychiatric and special tests, can clarify the diagnostic problem and indicate the type of therapy most likely to help the child.

A brief review of the usual patterns of hearing, language and speech development in normal children will help to identify the deviations or aberrations that may occur when the child's development is unusual or abnormal.

DEVELOPMENT OF HEARING, LANGUAGE AND SPEECH

Valuable information can be gained from careful questioning of parents or other observers concerning their observations of the child in his natural environment. Many of their viewpoints can be substantiated, questioned or refuted by careful pediatric evaluation of the child's behavior in certain situations. Many pediatricians have missed much of the excitement of observing normal or unusual responses by not fully exercising their diagnostic skill in this area of child development, which begins even before the child is born.

Fetal Hearing in Utero

From the sixth month of pregnancy onward, an unborn child will respond with violent movements in response to a loud sound, even if the mother's hearing is completely obscured or blocked by a continual broad frequency of noise. Such a reaction has also been obtained from the unborn children of totally deaf and mute mothers (16, 56). It has been demonstrated that this response is not due to tactile sense or vibration, and there is no question that the hearing of the six- or seven-month fetus can readily be activated or stimulated consistently by sound (46).

The Newborn Infant

At the time of birth, the central auditory pathways are only partially mature, as is most of the brain. This permits the development of the brain and the process of learning and storage of information to occur simultaneously and is probably critical to optimal human learning as we know it. The newborn child, whose auditory nerve is mature but whose supportive auditory pathways are still developing, will turn his head or eyes to the source of sound (6, 40). Some observers have suggested that after repeated breastfeedings and exposure to the mother's voice, the child in the newborn nursery will recognize the mother's voice and cease crying while other infants continue to cry (57). Sucking movements of young infants cease on sound stimuli (10). O'Doherty (44) found that infants from birth up to the age of six weeks would cease crying in response to an auditory stimulus of intensity or loudness comparable to the crying. Walden (61) found that both normal and retarded brain damaged children, aged one month to three years, will respond consistently in the quiet state. The results of experimental study by Birns *et al.* (4) suggest that the response to the stimulus depends upon the state of arousal of the baby—the quiet baby being alerted and the aroused infant being quieted by a stimulus of comparable intensity. There is no question that in the first weeks of life a hungry baby will stop crying when it hears the "clink" of the bottle in the container where it is being heated or the sounds of food preparation. If food is not rapidly forthcoming, increased crying reinforced by anger results (56). Murphy observed that infants only a few hours old will turn their head toward a sound and avert their head from a loud sound. Gesell and Amatruda (18) observed that infants of six to seven weeks cease to be disturbed by loud sounds; rather, they accept them and attempt to listen to specific sounds. The alerting response to sound can be seen as a blink (auro-palpebral response), a startle reflex, interruption or cessation of onging activities. At twelve weeks, the head may be turned rapidly toward the sound, which illustrates the so-called orienting reflex (45,52). If different loud sounds are introduced into the environment, the child's head will turn consistently to the source of each new sound until fatigue develops. It must be stressed that the transient or apparent absence of these responses or reflexes does not permit a diagnosis of deafness. If, however, repeated attempts to elicit a satisfactory response fail, under good conditions, the possibility of dysfunction must be considered (12).

The child of 24 weeks locates sound accurately and becomes quite adept at this task (18). Ewing and Ewing (15) note that the child between 12 and 24 weeks responds consistently and specifically to the mother's voice and ignores other sounds even if they are intense. From 24 to 36 weeks, familiar household sounds are observed and result in the production of proper responses. On the other hand, loud sounds are are frequently ignored.

Confusion about the presence or absence of useful hearing will not arise if great care is taken to exclude the child's response to other environmental stimuli, particularly visual cues. The majority of parents believe that they do not point or gesture toward objects when they talk to their child. By simply asking them to demonstrate how they give the child a simple command, one can observe that almost inevitably the order will be accompanied by gesture or pointing, thus giving visual cues to the child which supplement purely auditory information.

In summary, during the first weeks and months of life, we have evidence that a highly developed, selective auditory system is grown rapidly which is capable of recognizing sounds, voices, words, and animal noises. This is of course to be expected, for we can no longer judge the memory storage capacities or other functions of the nervous system or its pathways by its anatomic structure, degree of myelination or gross state of development (20).

Warming Up of the Vocal Apparatus as a Preliminary to Speech

In the development of normal vocalization and speech, Murphy (41) differentiates three stages which are at times overlapping and may occur simultaneously. First, the cry predominates and then is followed at about three to five weeks (in a normal infant) by the coo of pleasure which matures quickly to the social coo and smile. This social response then develops into a chuckle and soft guttural noises. Soon, harder gutturals appear, following by lalling, shrieks, laughter, labials, the early dental sounds, and by eight months of age, an inflected babble consistent with imperfectly reproduced patterns of speech that lack verbal structure. Stage one of early noisemaking is followed by stage two of early articulation, including jargon (18), and stage three of speech.

Babbling contains sounds which never appear in later language and which may not exist in the language of the people around the child. Later, the child may find it difficult to relearn the sounds he has previously uttered, apparently without difficulty, in the babble period. "Fixation in memory is not at all simply dependent upon repetition and only those repeated events which are embedded in meaningful relation to the total organism are kept in memory. The first utterances of the infant are not kept in memory because they do not possess such relation" (19).

Deaf infants will make baby noises through all stages up to babble, but without auditory support, such children will begin to lose vocal quality by the age of nine months. Murphy (41) has pointed out that children of normal hearing born of deaf and dumb parents do not normally suffer the same speech retardation as institutionalized infants and he suggests that, at least in the early months of life, social stimulation is a more potent stimulant of articulation than is heard speech. If there is a clinical probability of deafness, it is essential that the child be examined by an otolaryngologist familiar with these problems and that the audiologic examination be made. The risk of deafness is increased if the child is of low birth weight, or was exposed to kernicterus, maternal rubella or infection such as meningitis (7, 9).

SPEECH AND LANGUAGE DEVELOPMENT IN THE RETARDED CHILD

In the normal child of average intelligence, it is fairly safe to predict that verbal comprehension will be followed by speech, provided there is no hearing defect or other disturbance. If an intelligent one-year-old understands many sentences by hearing alone, such as, "Give the ball to Daddy," or the question, "Where is the doggie?" it is usually safe to predict that this child will talk in time, even though there is a physiologic lag. It may be another twelve months before the child says the equivalent sentence spontaneously. The speech of the two- or three-year-old may lack clarity, but as Gesell has pointed out, provided that the speech context is meaningful and the "words" used consistently, clarity of speech will usually follow.

How is it possible to predict speech development in an individual retarded child? Do we have enough information in either general or specific terms which would suggest that the child is likely or unlikely to develop useful speech? Even though we are lacking norms for speech and language development in the retarded child, we can make certain predictions by extrapolating, albeit cautiously, from the normal child's speech and language development to that of the retarded child. However, there are many degrees and types of mental retardation which in turn may be affected by factors which, although not as obvious or direct in their effects on speech and language as severe deafness, may be devastating in the early developmental months and years of life.

In the earlier example it was suggested that a normal two-year-old needs a mental age of two years before he can speak simple sentences like a child aged two years. If a two-year-old has a mental age of one year, he is going to speak a few words like a one-year-old. Or more probably, he will exhibit the additional developmental language lag usually seen in a retarded child, having unspoken or inner language development of a few months younger than his mental age, in this instance, perhaps that of a six-month-old baby. As it is uncommon for six-month-old babies to speak words, it is not to be expected that a two-year-old mentally retarded child will talk if he has a mental age of one year and developmental language delay at the six-month level. We cannot expect consistent vocalizations or use of word symbols until the mental age and language development are at the one-year level or more.

The extremes that may exist between speech and language development even within a well-defined category of retardation can be seen in Down's Syndrome (mongolism). There is a wide variation in the development of intelligence of D.S. children, and leaving aside for the moment the reasons for the variations in intellectual development, there is likely to be a parallel variation in speech and other abilities in these children. In an examination of the developmental pattern of fifty children with Down's Syndrome, Levinson *et al.* (33) found that language development was very variable. Some D.S. children were reported to have used words at twelve months* whereas others delayed until six years and progress in speech was very slow when compared to normal child development. However, of 30 D.S. children who at the time of examination were still unable to use sentences, twenty percent ranged in age from six to seventeen years. Strazzulla (58) found that D.S. children with I.Q. ratings between 40 and 70 begin using words at an average age of 33.4 months; they use phrases at a mean age of 48 months and sentences at 60.8 months. Engler (15) found that in institutionalized D.S. children, only forty-nine percent had begun to speak by the age of three years, sixty-two percent by the age of four years, and eighty-one percent by the age of five years. A study of noninstitutionalized D.S. children has suggested that stages of language development are more significantly related to chronological age and the appearance of motor milestones than to traditional intelligence quotients (32).

The wide variation in speech and language development in children with Down's Syndrome illustrates two important points. First, even if a child fits into a particular mental retardation category, it does not

---

* I have not seen a child with Down's Syndrome who used words meaningfully at twelve months. The sounds "ma-ma-ma" and "da-da-da," which are made by most infants are often misinterpreted as being meaningful speech. These sounds may be made as a "warming up" of the vocal apparatus and without meaning. Only if they are purposefully and consistently used to label a person, object or toy can they be considered to represent language and speech development.

permit one to make accurate predictions based on a specific disease or syndrome. Second, a child with intellectual impairment may show considerable variation and be susceptible to environmental and other influences which affect the level of intellectual attainment regardless of the basic disease entity present. With this wide variation in performance, is it then possible to predict speech in a particular mentally retarded child? What information might suggest that the child, although retarded, is likely or unlikely to develop spontaneous speech that is adequate or useful for communication? Normal hearing is of prime importance. If the child has never given evidence of making expected responses to sound, such as being able to comprehend speech or respond to his name, this suggests that deafness or other conditions might be present in addition to mental retardation. By normal hearing we understand that hearing response which is adequate for the reception of sounds of everyday life, and for speech (38). Absence of or inconsistency in the usual alerting or orienting responses does not typically result from middle ear disease unless unusually severe. More likely causes of a child's absent or inconsistent responses to sound are: (1) deafness resulting from inner ear disease, (2) neural or brain disease (including auditory agnosia), (3) a combination of 1 and 2, and (4) some cases of severe mental disturbance (childhood schizophrenia).

Neural or Brain Disease (including congenital auditory imperfection, auditory agnosia, receptive expressive aphasia).

The presence of alerting and orienting responses are so basic to the function of the auditory system in a child with measurable intelligence that their total absence must be construed not as a sign of peripheral deafness but of central auditory dysfunction. Unless a bilateral hearing loss is absolute, a high intensity sound will elicit a response. There is suggestive evidence that children with severe auditory dysfunction may inhibit their response to environmental sounds or words if they are meaningless, just as people with normal hearing constantly shut out many of the everyday environmental sounds by which their hearing is constantly assailed. However, people with normal hearing have the ability to "tune in" at will to any sound in the environment if there is reason to do so.

Many children with central auditory dysfunction are characterized by *inconsistent* responses to sound. The responses in an individual child may vary considerably from no response to a very high intensity sound (such as an iron skillet struck hard with a hammer approximately one foot behind the subject's head) to an immediate response to a soft click made between the fingernails a few seconds later.

When this occurs, the response can rarely be elicited again within a period of hours or days. It is almost as if the system has learned to inhibit yet one more response to a meaningless stimulus. None of these patients recognize the meaning of environmental sounds or words, but in a test situation, they may be able to tell that two sounds are different and may have measurable peripheral hearing on an audiogram. However, in patients who fit the category of auditory agnosia, it is questionable if the hearing is normal, as defined by Morley. It is also doubtful if the majority of children who fail to alert or orient to sound have useful auditory function. Such children may fail to respond to intensive training. Central auditory dysfunction can co-exist in the presence of mental retardation of all degrees (50, 51).

Some varieties of childhood schizophrenia are difficult to distinguish from mental retardation, in that such children may score poorly on standardized intelligence tests, with intelligence quotients in the severely retarded range. Although the social and adaptive behavior of the schizophrenic child is severely retarded, the gait, dexterity, apparent responses to inner stimuli (which may exist only in the mind of the observer) and their physiognomy may all suggest that the child is severely mentally deranged or disturbed rather than basically mentally retarded. The prognosis for the severely disturbed or psychotic preschool child is usually poor and the practical differences between severe disturbance and severe mental retardation may be academic.

THE EFFECTS OF DEAFNESS AND MENTAL RETARDATION
ON SPEECH AND LANGUAGE DEVELOPMENT

Deafness and mental retardation occur together quite commonly. The epidemic of rubella in 1963 and 1964 damaged many children, among them many who are now mentally retarded with disproportionately small heads, pigmented stippling of the retina and unusual dermatoglyphic patterns. Other stigmata of intrauterine rubella, such as deafness, have been noted (8, 28).

A mentally retarded child may also have a central communication disorder—that is to say, a disorder of communication not attributable to a peripheral hearing loss or dysfunction nor to a dysarthria or motor speech problem. While it is apparent that severe mental retardation can cause a marked breakdown in communicative function, it is equally obvious that many retarded children even in the trainable range of intelligence can speak and communicate adequately for their needs. A communication disorder should be suspected when there is a continued and considerable disparity between the level of measured performance abilities representing intelligence and those items representing verbal or language comprehension skills. In any child suspected of a central communication disorder, it is essential to ascertain that the peripheral end organ of hearing and basic auditory abilities are intact before it is possible to state categorically that the problem lies within the brain. Provided that mental retardation is not too severe, normal hearing will permit the storage in the brain of a repertoire or vocabulary of meaningful sounds and words which, over a period of years, are built into language. This language is then integrated with other important information received through other sense modalities, such as vision and touch. Presence of partial or severe deafness in a retarded child takes away an important channel for information and may deprive the child of speech and useful communication. As Whetnall and Fry (63) pointed out, "The child makes a big step forward when he realizes that a certain sound will control the activities of another person." Renfrew (48) has emphasized that "many young retarded children . . . have not yet become aware of the extent to which the environment can be manipulated by the use of words." Self-expression is also necessary for personality development because through it we learn who we are, what we are thinking and feeling, what we hope to do and gradually learn what we can do (21). There is little doubt that these concepts are accurate and any additional handicap to the retarded child such as hearing, speech or communication disorder may well make the difference between institutionalization or habilitation into society.

Special tests, such as the audiogram, may be hard to administer to retarded children. They are difficult to interpret without the special skills, background and knowledge acquired from seeing many children with complex disorders in the area of communication (23). Even if the audiogram suggests the presence of a somewhat specific hearing loss, such as a loss in the high frequencies (high tone loss), there is no guarantee that the dysfunction can be improved by the use of a hearing aid, although an intensive and prolonged trial and training are indicated.

It would be a mistake to believe that it is always possible to estimate the ability to understand speech from assessment of thresholds of hearing for pure tone. Cawthorne and Harvey (11) point out that while there is a fairly constant relationship between speech and loss of hearing for pure tones, perceptive deafness often behaves quite differently and a test for the hearing capacity for speech is essential. This is done routinely as part of the audiologic examination conducted in special centers (17). It can be readily recognized that the presence of mental retardation will only compound the problems already facing the audiologist and those assessing these difficulties. Many speech pathologists, including Eisenson (13), believe that speech defective children with related language and articulatory defects are defective in auditory memory abilities. Several authors have suggested that there is a higher incidence of hearing loss in mental defectives than in the general population (3, 27, 31, 53). Schlanger (55) later cast some doubt on the higher prevalence figures; after training mentally retarded children to take hearing tests, he found a decrease from thirty-three to nine percent. Even so, it is possible that there is a higher prevalence of hearing loss in the mentally retarded. Luria (35) feels that children who are admitted to schools for the retarded with a twenty to twenty-five decibel loss of hearing early in development may suffer some degree of mental retardation from this defect of hearing alone.

It is this writer's simple rule of thumb that a communication disorder is likely to exist when a child's speech and language development lags persistently behind the mental age by two or more years. Thus, a ten-year-old child with a mental age of five years (IQ 50) and normal hearing who has a speech and language development approximating that of a two-year-old would be likely to have a central communication disorder of some severity. However, such disorders in communication may range in severity from mild difficulties with the use of language through complete failure to respond to sound in spite of normal peripheral auditory function. Even with severe bilateral deafness, a child can be expected to respond to high intensity sounds by an alerting or orienting response. Alerting can be seen as a startle reflex, interruption of on-going activities, commencement of crying, cessation of crying— a response which can be elicited consistently provided that there is sufficient physiologic recovery time between each stimulus. It has been suggested that failure to make "expected response" to sound and total absence of speech or vocalizations with communicative intent are pathognomonic of congenital central communication disorders in children (36). The presence of mental retardation also makes the absence of speech a distinct possibility and for this reason the absence of expected responses to sound is important in the retarded child when attempting to determine presence or absence of hearing. Similarly, the ability of the child to respond to a meaningful sound, such as a sound accompanying a food stimulus, will also establish whether or not the auditory system is functioning adequately for sound recognition.

LOSS OF SPEECH AND LANGUAGE

If a child becomes retarded as the result of meningitis, encephalitis or brain damage, there may be complete loss or severe regression in speech and language function, with gradual recovery of these functions over a period of weeks, months or years. The recovery is often commensurate with recovery of mental ability. Loss of hearing alone, where intelligence is unaffected, is usually easy to detect and should be suspected after an individual has undergone one of the illnesses listed above (42). However, it must be kept in mind that meningitis, severe dehydration and vomiting, or febrile encephalitic-like illnesses (with or without convulsions) may occasionally damage central auditory pathways, giving the confusing picture of a child who may have normal intelligence, normal peripheral hearing, no comprehension of speech and a gradual loss of his own speech and communicative skills during the months following the illness (64). This may be followed by a secondary withdrawal of the child from the adults and world around him as a consequence of emotional distress at his inability to communicate. Early recognition of this problem can diminish much of the confusion that might otherwise arise and permit treatment and planning for the child, based on trial and error until the extent of the dysfunctional damage can be determined.

The language concepts, background, vocabulary and language skills in a child who has lost hearing at the age of two, three or four years are vastly superior (other things being equal) to a child who has been impaired in this area of function since birth.

THE CEREBRAL PALSIED CHILD

The majority of spastic children with evidence of extensive upper motor neuron damage are intellectually impaired, the degree ranging in severity from mild learning disability to severe mental retardation. The majority of spastic children do not have severe or complex hearing dysfunction but may have considerable difficulty in speaking, resulting from both the dysarthria of motor impairment and the associated intellectual deficit if this is also present. An exception occurs when the spasticity is due to intrauterine rubella, which may in itself cause associated deafness. In the athetoid child, with variable rigidity and involuntary movements occurring as a result of extrapyramidal disease, there may also be severe dysarthria and motor impairment affecting speech. However, the intelligence is more likely to be preserved; there is a higher risk of deafness based on the common etiology of athetosis, such as kernicterus or jaundice of the newborn. When talking with an athetoid child, it is important not to confuse a delay in the child's vocal response with failure to hear the question, since an athetoid may exhibit a delay of many seconds before he is able to coordinate the necessary skills to turn his head in the right direction or verbalize his reply. A good basic rule is to have all cerebral palsied children—whatever their etiology—examined at a center where expert and skillful professionals can exclude or define problems in the hearing, speech and language areas.

TREATMENT OF SPEECH AND LANGUAGE DISORDERS
(ASSISTING SPEECH AND LANGUAGE DEVELOPMENT)

As described earlier, the poorer responses of retarded children make it difficult for parents to continue to provide the needed stimulation. We would like to know how far vocalization is reduced in mentally handicapped babies. Gulliford (21) feels, from seeing retarded babies and their parents, that the delayed emergence of speech in such children might well result in poorer parental stimulation of speech. It is easy to respond to the vocalization of a 12-month baby, but it is not so easy to respond to a two- or three-year-old child who is still in an early stage of speech development. Gulliford suggests that parents of retarded children are often emotionally upset and that we do not know how adequately they provide their retarded children with appropriate play materials and situations, or how well they help them to learn to play. Play, of course, should be accompanied by verbal experience to all events of potential interest to the child.

Kirk (29) examined an experimental group of retarded children with I.Q.'s between 40 and 70 and age four to six years who were given a nursery school experience. Small but significant gains were found in verbal intelligence tests, whereas the control group remained at the same level or even decreased in their rate of development. As might be expected, the preponderance of evidence points to institutionalization as a debilitative and depressive influence on vocalization, language structure, intelligibility of speech, and vocabulary (37, 43). A comparison of the verbal output of two groups of mentally retarded children revealed differences in favor of the non-institutionalized group in mean sentence length and the number of words per minute (54).

Since it is the pediatrician who, as a rule, sees the intellectually handicapped child before he ever reaches the teacher or therapist, the pediatrician should be the first to encourage the parents to take an interest in developing the child's understanding of speech and the use of language (47). In this way, not only can an early learning be advanced, but also consistent and realistic demands can be made of the growing child at home and at school. Although he may have low intelligence, the mentally retarded child should be encouraged to express himself verbally as well as in other expressive media such as dancing, music and other recreational and constructive activities.

Many young retarded children need encouragement and practice in order that they can manipulate their own environment and the people in it by the use of words, in addition to gaining confidence in expression of their own ideas. The linguistic inadequacies of retarded children may well be increased because of their feelings of inferiority (2), and as they grow older, they may have found that withdrawal or silence is the safest way to avoid appearing foolishly wrong.

Where the basic condition is such that spoken and written language is delayed considerably, whatever the etiology, there is likely to be inadequate use of spoken and written language throughout life. It must be re-emphasized that children will often pay no attention to speech that does not occur in situations that interest them. Mothers of retarded children must be encouraged to give continued stimulation which is appropriate for the speech and language stimulation used. A good psychological examination with estimation of language ability will set the sights for the mother's program and define the immediate goal when she experiments with the suggested stimulation. However, there may be considerable difficulty in involving the mother or family in such stimulation; many mentally handicapped children come from a poor language environment and a social class which is woefully deficient in speech models from which the mentally handicapped child can learn (26, 34).

Valletutti (60) has pointed out the deficiencies that exist in the language and speech of the adolescent retardate, and his study showed that not only did the retarded have less to say, but they said it at a slower rate, suggesting the importance of increased rate and quality of speech production. If the retarded did not sound retarded, one would suspect that they would fare better vocationally and socially. Valletutti suggests that there may have been too much emphasis on literature and reading skills with neglect of the more important skills of listening and speaking. The speech abilities of a retarded child should be explored in depth and the search for causes and their treatment must reach beyond the obvious symptoms of retardation.

BIBLIOGRAPHY

1. André-Thomas, Y. Chesni, and S. Saint-Anne Dargassies, "The Neurological Examination of the Infant. Little Club Clinics in Developmental Medicine No. 1," *Medical Advisory Committee of the National Spastics Society,* London, 1960.
2. Berry, M. F., and J. Eisenson, *Speech Disorders: Principles and Practices of Therapy,* New York: Appleton-Century-Crofts, Inc., 1956.
3. Birch, J. V., and J. Matthews, "The Hearing of Mental Defectives: Its Measurement and Characteristics," *Am. J. Ment. Defic.,* 55:384, 1951.
4. Birns, B., M. Blank, W. H. Bridger, and S. K. Escalona, "Behavioral Inhibition in Neonates Produced by Auditory Stimuli," *Child Develop.,* 36:639, 1965.
5. Blanton, M. G., "The Behavior of the Human Infant During the First Thirty Days of Life," *Psychol. Rev. (Am.),* 24:456, 1917.
6. Bordley, J. E., "Deafness in Young Children," *Minn. Med.,* 50:827, 1967.
7. Bordley, J. E., "Office Detection of Hearing Defects in Children," *Pediatrics,* 23: 980, 1959.
8. Bordley, J. E., P. E. Brookhouser, J. Hardy, and W. G. Hardy, "Prenatal Rubella," *Acta Oto-Laryngologica,* 66:1, 1968.
9. Bordley, J., and W. G. Hardy, *The Biologic Basis of Pediatric Practice,* Ed. R. E. Cooke, New York: McGraw-Hill Book Co., 1968.
10. Bronschtein, A. J., and J. P. Petrova, "Pavlov's Zschr. höh. Nerventät," *Dtsch.,* 2:441, 1952.
11. Cawthorne, T., and R. M. Harvey, "A Comparison Between Hearing for Pure Tones and for Speech," *J. Laryngol.,* 667:233, 1953.
12. DiCarlo, L., and W. Bradley, "A Simplified Auditory Test for Infants and Young Children," *Laryngoscope,* 71:628, 1961.
13. Eisenson, J., "The Nature of Defective Speech," from *Psychology of Exceptional Children and Youth,* New Jersey: Prentice-Hall, Inc., 1963.
14. Engler, M., *Mongolism (Peristatic Amentia),* Baltimore: Williams & Wilkins, 1949.
15. Ewing, I. R., and A. W. G. Ewing, "The Ascertainment of Deafness in Infancy and Early Childhood," *J. Laryngol.,* 59:309, 1944.
16. Forbes, H. S., and H. B. Forbes, "Fetal Sense Reaction: Hearing," *J. Comp. Psychol.,* 7:353, 1927.
17. Frisina, D., "Measurement of Hearing in Children," from *Modern Developments in Audiology,* Ed. J. Jerger, New York: Academic Press, 1963.
18. Gesell, A., and C. S. Amatruda, *Developmental Diagnosis: Normal and Abnormal Child Development,* New York: Paul B. Hoeber, Inc., 1947.
19. Goldstein, K., *Language and Language Disturbances: Aphasic Symptom Complexes and Their Significance for Medicine and Theory of Language,* New York: Grune & Stratton, 1948.
20. Grafstein, B., "Postnatal Development of the Transcallosal Evoked Response in the Cerebral Cortex of the Cat," *J. Neurophysiol.,* 26:79, 1963.
21. Gulliford, R., "The Effect of Language Deficit in Intellectual Handicap," from, *The Child Who Does Not Talk, Clinics in Developmental Medicine* No. 13, Ed.

C. Renfrew and K. Murphy. Spastics International Med. Public., New York: William Heinemann Medical Books, Ltd., 1964.

22. Hardy, J. B., A. Dougherty, and W. G. Hardy, "Hearing Responses and Audiologic Screening in Infants," *J. Pediat.*, 55:382, 1959.
23. Hardy, W. G., "Auditory Deficits of the Kernicterus Child," from *Kernicterus and Its Importance in Cerebral Palsy*, Springfield: Charles C Thomas, 1961.
24. Illingworth, R. S., "An Introduction to Developmental Assessment in the First Year," *Little Club Clinics in Developmental Medicine* No. 3, London: Medical Advisory Committee of the National Spastics Society, 1962.
25. Illingworth, R. S., *The Development of the Infant and Young Child: Normal and Abnormal*, Baltimore: Williams & Wilkins Co., 1966.
26. Johnson, G. O., "The Education of Mentally Handicapped Children," from *Education of Exceptional Children and Youth*, New Jersey: Prentice-Hall Inc., 1961.
27. Johnston, P., and M. Farrell, "Auditory Impairments Among Resident School Children at the Walter E. Fernald State School," *Am. J. Ment. Defic.*, 58:640, 1954.
28. Karzon, D. T., *The Biologic Basis of Pediatric Practice*, Ed. R. E. Cooke, New York: McGraw-Hill Book Co., 1968.
29. Kirk, S. A., *The Early Education of the Mentally Retarded: An Experimental Study*, Urbana: University of Illinois Press, 1959.
30. Kirk, S. A., *Educating Exceptional Children*, Boston: Houghton-Mifflin Co., 1962.
31. Kodman, F., "The Incidence of Hearing Loss in Mentally Retarded Children," *Am. J. Ment. Defic.*, 62:675, 1958.
32. Lenneberg, E. H., A. Nicholls, and F. Rosenberger, "Primitive Stages of Language Development in Mongolism," *Proc. of the Assoc. for Research in Nervous & Mental Disease*, Baltimore: Williams & Wilkins Co., 1962.
33. Levinson, A. A. Friedman, and F. Stamps, "Variability of Mongolism," *Pediatrics* 16:43, 1955.
34. Luria, A. R., *The Role of Speech in the Regulation of Normal and Abnormal Behavior*, New York: Liveright Publishing Corp., 1961.
35. Luria, A. R., "Psychological Studies of Mental Deficiency in the Soviet Union," from *Handbook on Mental Deficiency*. New York: McGraw-Hill Book Co., 1963.
36. Mark, H. J., "Two Symptoms Pathognomonic for Congenital Central Communication Disorders in Children," *J. Pediat.*, 55:391, 1959.
37. McCarthy, D., *Language Development in Children. Manual of Child Psychology*, New York: John Wiley & Sons, 1954.
38. Morley, M. E., *The Development and Disorders of Speech in Childhood*, London: E. & S. Livingstone Ltd., 1957.
39. Mowrer, O. H., "Hearing and Speaking: An Analysis of Language Learning," *J. Speech Hearing Dis.*, 23:143, 1958.
40. Murphy, K., Personal communication, 1955.
41. Murphy, Kevin, "Development of Normal Vocalization and Speech," from *The Child Who Does Not Talk, Clinics in Developmental Medicine*, No. 13, Ed. C. Renfrew and K. Murphy. Spastics International Medical Pub., New York: William Heinemann Medical Books Ltd., 1964.
42. Nyhan, W. L., and F. Richardson, "Complications of Meningitis," *Annual Review of Medicine*, 14:243, 1963.
43. O'Conner, N., and B. Hermelin, *Speech and Thought in Severe Subnormality: An Experimental Study*, New York: Macmillan Co., 1963.
44. O'Doherty, N., "A Hearing Test Applicable to the Crying Newborn Infant," *Develop. Med. Child Neurol.*, 10:380, 1968.
45. Pavlov, I. P., *Lectures on Conditioned Reflexes*, Vol. I, Ed. W. Horsley Gantt, New York: International Publishers, 1928.

46. Peiper, A., *Cerebral Function in Infancy and Childhood,* New York: Consultants Bureau, 1963.
47. Renfrew, C. E., "Speech Problems of Backward Children," *Speech Path. Ther.,* 3:34, 1959.
48. Renfrew, C. E., "Spoken Language in Intellectually Handicapped Children," from *The Child Who Does Not Talk, Clinics in Developmental Medicine* No. 13, Ed. C. Renfrew and K. Murphy. Spastics International Medical Pub., New York: William Heinemann Medical Books Ltd., 1964.
49. Richardson, F., Unpublished observation, 1956.
50. Richardson, F., "Complexities of Diagnosis of Central Auditory Problems Interfering with Speech in Childhood," Lisbon: Proc. Xth Int. Congress Pediatrics, 1962.
51. Richardson, F., "Developmental Auditory Impairment and Associated Disorders of Speech," from *The Child Who Does Not Talk, Clinics in Developmental Medicine,* No. 13, Ed. C. Renfrew and K. Murphy. Spastics International Med. Public., New York: William Heinemann Medical Books Ltd., 1964.
52. Robinson, J., and W. H. Gantt, "The Orienting Reflex (Questioning Reaction): Cardiac, Respiratory, Salivary and Motor Components," *Bull. Johns Hopkins Hosp.,* 80:231, 1947.
53. Schlanger, B. B., "Speech Examination of a Group of Institutionalized Mentally Handicapped Children," *J. Speech Hearing Dis.,* 18:339, 1953.
54. Schlanger, B. B., "Environmental Influences on the Verbal Output of Mentally Retarded Children," *J. Speech Hearing Dis.,* 19:339, 1954.
55. Schlanger, B. B., "Effects of Listening Training on Auditory Thresholds of Mentally Retarded Children," *A.S.H.A.,* 4:273, 1962.
56. Sontag, L. W., and R. F. Wallace, "The Movement Response of the Human Fetus to Sound Stimuli," *Child Develop.,* 6:253, 1935.
57. Stirnimann, F., "Das Kind und seine früheste Umwelt (The Child and His Earliest Environment)," Psychol. Praxis., Basel, from Peiper, 1947.
58. Strazzulla, M., "Speech Problems of the Mongoloid Child. Mongolism, a Symposium," *Quart. Rev. Pediat.,* 8:268, 1953.
59. Templin, M. C., *Certain Language Skills in Children: Their Development and Interrelationships,* Minneapolis: The Univ. of Minnesota Press, 1957.
60. Valletutti, P. J., *I.Q. and Social Class as Determinants of Speech,* Unpublished Thesis for Ed. D., Teachers College, Columbia University, 1966.
61. Walden, E. F., "The Baby-Cry Test (BCT): A New Audiometric Technique for Testing Very Young Children," *Report of the Proceedings of the International Congress on Education of the Deaf, 88th Congress, 2nd Session,* Document No. 106, U.S. Government Printing Office, Washington, D.C. 1964.
62. Wergeland, H., "Autistic Children" from *The Child Who Does Not Talk, Clinics in Developmental Medicine,* No. 13, Ed. C. Renfrew and K. Murphy. Spastics International Med. Public., New York: William Heinemann Medical Books, Ltd., 1964.
63. Whetnall, E., and D. B. Fry, *The Deaf Child,* Springfield: Charles C Thomas, 1964.
64. Worster-Drought, C., "An Unusual Form of Acquired Aphasia in Children," *Folia Phoniat.* 16:223, 1964.

CHAPTER 16

Educational Services

by JACK SHARE, Ph.D.

INTRODUCTION

There is a growing trend in the United States, as can be seen in the state of California, to bring together various disciplines and services for the mentally retarded. In California, the Regional Centers for the Developmentally Disabled (1) provide a multidisciplinary team setting for the evaluation, prescription, and follow-through of clients, as well as assuming a strong advocacy role.

Evaluation and counseling centers have been developed throughout the state. These are community-based focal points where mentally retarded individuals and their families can obtain essential services, beginning with comprehensive diagnosis and, subsequently, providing counseling on a continuing, lifetime basis. The importance of the educational consultant, as part of the Regional Center clinic team, has now been well established. The educator on such a team not only provides educational assessments, but is also able to work with preschools, private and public schools, and post-school programs. Consultation services are offered, on request, to private as well as public schools. Techniques and research results in the management, training, and education of children and adults are provided to parents, as well as guidelines in such areas as behavior-shaping and readiness programs.

SPECIAL EDUCATION AND THE LAW

The need for changes in the law surrounding special education has been recognized by the courts and state legislative bodies. Recent court decisions and legislative actions are setting the direction for the future of special education. The direction is focused on two important thrusts, both stressing equal educational opportunity for the handicapped. The first of these directions stems from the October, 1971 landmark case, *Pennsylvania Association for Retarded Children* v. *Commonwealth of Pennsylvania* (2). This made mandatory, rather than permissive, a program of free public education for every retarded child by no later than September 1, 1972. In addition, the state, with the help of local school districts, was given 90 days to identify every retarded child who was not receiving education and/or training at that time.

The second apparent trend in the future of special education is seen in the court decision in *Diana* v. *State Board of Education* (3), which, unlike the Pennsylvania court decision, did not deal with the issue of exclusion from schooling. Rather, its aim was to keep exceptional individuals from being misplaced in inappropriate programs. The focus was on issues of identification, classification, and placement standards and procedures. Another case, *Covarrubias* v. *San Diego Unified School System* (4), filed as a class action suit on behalf of a group of Black and Mexican-American students who had been mislabeled as educable mentally retarded (EMR), cited inappropriate evaluations and placement procedures (5).

The Pennsylvania decision and some of the California cases have served as a foundation for numerous other court actions. Such cases indicate that schools, in the very near future, will need to make provisions to provide public school programs for severely and profoundly handicapped individuals who are of school age. Furthermore, schools must be prepared to serve a greater age range.

Early education of retarded children should be mandated, and extended downward to whatever point such education for these children and/or their parents can result in significant gains, or to where it can be shown to prevent more serious disabilities. These progarms must also extend beyond the usual school-leaving age for those people who need additional time. Programs for a differentiated education must be organized to minimize the chance of inappropriate placement and unnecessary segregation. It was with such a background that the California Master Plan for Special Education was formulated.

CALIFORNIA MASTER PLAN FOR SPECIAL EDUCATION

In California, the State Board of Education has adopted the California Master Plan for Special Education (6), which is based on the principle that education is for *all* children, regardless of differences in abilities. It is also based on the principle that no child shall be denied educational opportunity commensurate with his ability. Special education is seen as including both direct and indirect services to individuals with special needs, as well as to their teachers and parents. Direct services may either supplement the pupil's regular program, such as individual or small-group tutoring, or provide an alternate program, such as full-time special class. Special education of an indirect nature consists of services, such as special consultation provided to the teacher and parents of the students.

Such educational services attempt to provide individually tailored programs which are designed to not only lessen or eliminate those problems which handicap the individual, wherever possible, but also to provide the best learning environment for each student. The variety and types of experiences planned for these students will vary greatly depending on the particular pupil. The Master Plan also provides for a smooth transition for students as they are prepared for the complexities of the regular classroom. If these transitions are to work, special education personnel must consult with and train regular teachers, and equip them to deal with those exceptional individuals who can be integrated into regular programs. Mildly handicapped students will generally be better served through the modification of the regular program instead of creating additional special education categories. The special educator in the Regional Center is seen as a consultant to the schools in implementing such a program.

Under the Master Plan, school districts are expected to come up with comprehensive plans. A comprehensive plan describes a program which will be provided by the schools to meet the educational needs of eligible exceptional individuals living within the geographic boundaries covered by the plan. Educational agencies have three options in developing comprehensive plans to provide educational services to the handicapped. They are: 1) a school district may develop its own comprehensive plan; 2) a combination of school districts may join with the Office of the County Superintendent of Schools to develop a joint comprehensive plan; 3) contiguous districts may join together to develop a joint comprehensive plan.

The Master Plan includes the following classification system: 1) communicatively handicapped, which includes programs for the deaf, deaf-blind, severely hard of hearing, severely language handicapped (including aphasic), and language and speech; 2) physically handicapped, including blind, partially seeing, orthopedically handicapped, and other health-impaired minors, including drug dependent and pregnant minors; 3) learning handicapped including programs for learning disabilities, behavior disorders, and educationally retarded (EMR); 4) severely handicapped, including programs for the developmentally handicapped, trainable mentally retarded, autistic, and seriously emotionally disturbed.

This subclassification system regroups current categories in the four areas in order to maintain a structure for data collection purposes. Through the classification of programs, pupil enrollments can be reported on the basis of program rather than by a label attached to the child. While it is possible that the label could be attached to the pupil, the legal provisions proposed for implementing the Master Plan do not dictate this process, as under the current law. A specific classification may be needed for reporting requirements of the U.S. Office of Education.

The Master Plan includes a program specialist. This individual provides consultation, coordination, planning, curricular resources, and evaluation of the programs for the handicapped. He participates in in-service training, research development, and innovation of special methods and approaches.

A resource specialist program provides instructional planning, special instruction, tutorial assistance, and other services to the handicapped in special programs or in regular classes. The program is coordinated by the resource specialist who is a special education teacher with advanced training in the education of individuals with exceptional needs. A particular pupil's participation is determined by his needs, as specified in an individual pupil plan written by the school appraisal team. The resource specialist program coordinates designated instruction and services for the pupils assigned to regular classroom teachers for the majority of the day. The resource specialist further coordinates interpretation and implementation of educational and psychological findings. He may also coordinate educational guidance for children with special problems and for their parents. Resource material, including professional literature related to special education and services to regular staff members, parents, and others, is further provided.

The intent of the Master Plan is to insure that the child is regarded not as a passive recipient of the instructional resources offered in the educational systems administered, but as a unique individual whose curiosity and potential deserve to be the focus of all our professional energies. The Master Plan seeks to equalize opportunities for all children in need of special education services. Instead of labeling children by categories, the Master Plan proposes a single designation—"individuals with exceptional needs"—for all children receiving special services. This change should correct two long-standing problems: 1) stigmatization by label; and 2) rigid categorical programming and funding which imply that children must be grouped by handicap, rather than by educational need.

EDUCATOR'S ROLE IN THE REGIONAL CENTER

The educator serves as a coordinator of educational services, providing practical application of the diagnostic process in the community. He may function as a diagnostician, but more frequently he is used as a resource in identifying and locating the most appropriate educational facility for the child, interpreting clinic findings to schools and educators who will be working with the youngster, and functioning as an advocate for the retarded individual in areas of training and education.

A wide variety of programs has been established by educators in attempts to serve the needs of the handicapped—infant stimulation programs, nursery schools for the retarded, normalization for those who can tolerate or manage in a normal type of setting, workshops, activity centers, etc. The educational consultant assists families in their initial contacts with the professionals in special education programs. Facilitation of initial school contact can provide a smooth enrollment, accompanied by positive attitudes. Without it, a child may sit idly at home with little, if any, training or help until he reaches mandatory school age or comes to the attention of the professional because of growing management problems.

The information sent to the schools by the consultant is a synthesis of all the educationally pertinent material gathered through the diagnostic process. These reports serve two functions: (1) as a guideline to the public school in making an accurate class placement and (2) equally, if not more important, as a guide used by the teacher in designing a tailor-made program for the individual child. A realistic educational program using the best teaching methods will provide most retarded individuals with the skills needed for self-fulfillment. The full utilization of potential requires an accurate assessment and a well defined plan to help the individual develop that potential.

The following cases demonstrate how educational assessments may assist when recommendations are understood and followed (7). One case illustrating this success is that of K.M., (BD:9-20-57), an 11-year-old boy who had been treated on a regular basis for a metabolic disorder. He seemed to be developing normally except for some minor symptoms of emotional tension, such as thumb sucking and bed wetting. No academic problems were noted until the second grade when his teacher's comments began to indicate that "he has difficulty retaining words over an extended period of time," "his work span seems limited," "written work consists of one sentence," etc. He was retained in the third grade because of difficulty in reading, handwriting and spelling; he also developed a facial tic. The psychological evaluation at that time revealed definite visual perceptual problems, and it was at that point that the educational consultant became involved with the case.

Mrs. M., his mother, was distraught at the thought of her son's needing special education. However, after the consultant explained K's problems from the child's and the teacher's point of view, and was further able to point out specific remedial steps possible within the framework of special education, the idea became more palatable; indeed she came to view special education as imperative for K's academic and emotional progress. He was enrolled in a public school class for the educationally handicapped and made one and a half years of progress in reading and spelling abilities during one school year, as measured by an achievement test. Handwriting was still difficult, although he could, at the end of the year, write a story of several paragraphs in length. The facial tic disappeared and his attention span was increased. Two years later the psychologist wrote, "This responsive, almost ten-year-old boy maintains his normal intellectual progress and reveals marked improvement in (the) visual-perceptual area."

Mistakes occasionally are made in assessment and placement. One mildly retarded patient, C.H. (BD: 6-29-61), a seven-year-old girl who was thought to have hypercalcemia, was placed in a private school for the retarded where the curriculum was based on the Montessori method. C's psychological profile revealed severe visual-motor coordination difficulties. However, she was much more adept verbally. It was thought that in a Montessori class, consisting of eight children, the discrepancy between C's verbal ability and motor inabilities would be minimized through the use of sensory-motor materials presented on a developmental basis. Each child was allowed to proceed at his own rate. In theory, this was an appropriate placement; however, with the freedom offered by this Montessori class, C was allowed to repeat the same errors; her mistakes were not corrected, and she did not have the judgment to choose a task or the appropriate materials where she could succeed. Her attention was diverted constantly because of the movement of students and the teacher in the room. It now appears that C's retardation is more global than was suspected. Now that she is of public school age, she has been placed in a class for the trainable mentally retarded where the activities are more directed and the short work periods more structured than those in the Montessori class. After one year in the TMR class, C progressed from being a shy child who constantly needed reassurance to one who could complete a three-part task independently. At the beginning of the year she had trouble walking up and down steps; in June of that school year she was able to enjoy playing on the playground slide.

Another patient presenting with the same problem was D.S. (BD: 4-27-61), a seven-year-old girl who was also diagnosed as having hypercalcemia. Her verbal facility and reasoning abilities were superior to those of C.H. However, D's motor problems were more severe. At age six, she was still very unsteady on her feet, could not ride a tricycle and her eye-hand coordination was exceptionally poor. She could hardly hold a pencil. She was accepted in a public school primary class for the orthopedically handicapped, where she was able to receive physical therapy for her hypertonia. She has now been in this setting for a year; her gross coordination has noticeably improved and her fine motor coordination has developed so markedly that she can now color with a crayon.

The inclusion of an educational consultant as a member of a diagnostic team in a medical facility has provided an important resource for families with retarded children. In some cases, the educator is the only team member to maintain contact with the family once the diagnostic evaluation has been completed. Even though a child may be placed in school, the consultant may visit and observe the child, then spend time in interpreting the program, the child's behavior or future educational goals to the parents. Before an educator was included as a member of the diagnostic team at Childrens Hospital of Los Angeles, the psychologist or the social worker was relied upon to make an educational referral. However, none of the clinic professionals previously dealing with the retarded had backgrounds in special education. To make accurate and meaningful referrals, one should know the local (or preferred) procedures, the local and state requirements for special education, as well as curriculum contents on various special educational levels. It has been noted that schools are less likely to exclude a child if they know that the clinic will maintain its interest and support. In this way, the consultant provides hospital-school-family liaison. It is helpful for the families to hear a consistent viewpoint in regard to their child's achievement. Often the schools and the diagnostic facility give the family differing opinions. When families know that the two agencies are working in harmony and partnership, the results have been gratifying.

The educational consultant should have a Master's degree in special education. Direct experience with children in a teaching capacity is of great preparatory value as it allows him to more readily appreciate the likelihood of a child's success in various educational placements, as well as the role of the teacher. Should the educator have a degree in educational psychology, it would be a definite asset.

In summary, the educator's role should encompass the following:

1. Discuss client's educational and/or behavioral problems with counseling staff and with client's parents.
2. Train parents of clients in behavior modification techniques where applicable.
3. Visit schools to observe and assess client's needs and formulate remedial plans with school personnel.
4. Evaluate clients who are ready for discharge from state hospitals and survey possible school and/or training placements in the community.
5. Make follow-up visits to schools and residential facilities and help plan appropriate programs.
6. Participate in pre-admission conferences and post-hospital conferences whenever preschool and school-age clients are discussed.
7. Serve as an advocate for the child at admission and discharge committee meetings held by school districts.
8. Visit and evaluate private day and residential schools, camps, convalescent hospitals and sheltered workshops to determine their effectiveness for the client, and their compliance with established standards.
9. Provide in-service training to public and private schools, convalescent hospitals, camp personnel, and to Regional Center staff in subjects related to the educational needs of clients.
10. Be knowledgeable on job opportunities, student projects, educational careers.
11. Be available to community agencies to present updated information in special education, keeping them well-informed.
12. Be knowledgeable of educational legal rights and provisions.
13. Provide educational assessments of clients and/or be able to communicate to parents and schools results of diagnostic center findings in relevant educational terms.

BIBLIOGRAPHY

1. Lanterman Mental Retardation Services Act, *Liason,* Sacramento, California, March 1973, Vol. II No. 2.
2. *Pennsylvania Association for Retarded Children* v. *Commonwealth of Pennsylvania,* 343 F. Supp. L79, E.D. Pa., 1972.
3. *Diana et al.* v. *State Board of Education et al.,* Case No. C-7037RFP, United States District Court, Northern District of California, 1970.
4. *Covarrubias et al.* v. *San Diego Unified School System et al.,* ase No. 70-394-S, Calif., 1972.
5. Share, J. "Los estudiantes Mexicano Norteamericanos y el retraso mental leve: Un Problema Socio-Económico y Cultural (Mexican-American Students and Mild Mental Retardation: A Socio-economic and Cultural Problem)." *Revista de la Clínica de la Conducta,* 4 (8), 38-48, Mexico, D.F., Feb., 1971.
6. California Master Plan for Special Education, Calif. State Dept. of Educ., Sacramento, Jan. 1974.
7. Baldwin, F. B. Special education teacher and coordinator of Occupational Education, Pasadena City College. Special recognition and thanks for providing the educational cases.

CHAPTER 17

Nutritional Services

by PHYLLIS B. ACOSTA, Dr.P.H. and
ELIZABETH WENZ, M.S.

The role of nutrition and the nutritionist is vital in the prevention and treatment of mental retardation (22) since nutrition is intimately involved with the physiological and biochemical processes of each cell. The science of nutrition and the study of human development are closely interrelated; thus the physiological, psychological and sociological implications of nutrition, foods and eating in the lives of children should not be overlooked (22).

NUTRITION IN PREVENTION OF MENTAL RETARDATION

Prenatal Nutrition. Hille and Reeves (10) have pointed out that in order to reduce mental retardation, the accent must be on prevention, that is, elimination of the physical conditions in mothers and infants that lead to mental retardation. The President's Committee on Mental Retardation (18) indicated that the prevalence of mental retardation was higher in population groups having inadequate prenatal care. The rate of premature births is also highest among these groups, and the incidence of mental retardation is substantially higher among premature infants than among full-term infants (17).

The mother's diet before and during pregnancy is of prime importance to the outcome of pregnancy (20). The percentage of mothers delivering prematurely has been shown to be more than twice as high in groups with the poorest dietary habits as in those with better nutrition (2, 3, 8, 11). Thus, efforts to reduce mental retardation caused by premature birth and complications associated with child bearing must include programs aimed at improving the nutritional state of all women of child bearing age, especially during early pregnancy (10).

Present programs involve dietitians and nutritionists in well baby clinics, adolescent clinics, prenatal and maternal and infant care clinics. In projects concerned with maternity and infant care, the nutritionist has an opportunity to reach a group whose diet may be poor. Although her concern is with the nutritional status of the expectant mother and infants born with handicapping conditions, she strives to improve family food practices that carry over to future pregnancies and benefit the health of the family (10). Hille has outlined the manner in which dietitians and nutritionists should function on the maternity and infant care team as follows (10):

> ... Securing adequate information and evaluating the food habits of the expectant mother and her family.
>
> ... Providing both initial and continuing instruction so that the mother can maintain or improve her own diet during the following pregnancy, as well as that of her family.
>
> ... Knowing resources and making appropriate referrals to community agencies.
>
> ... Counseling the mother in regard to finances and home management practices.
>
> ... Determining the need for easily available nourishing food.
>
> ... Providing adequate, nourishing food during hospitalization.

In addition the dietitian or nutritionist may also assist the clinic staff in preparing diet histories and evaluation forms, or counseling with members of the team on individual dietary or management problems, preparing educational material and exhibits, and participating in in-service education for the staff. She may also be asked to give assistance to other agencies concerned with services to mothers and infants, such as welfare agencies and homemaker service agencies, and to administrators and staff members of group care facilities.

Early Childhood Nutrition. While many studies have been carried out to define the effects of nutritional deprivation on growth, very little is known about the completeness of recovery from severe malnutrition. Even less is known about the mental development of children after a period of undernutrition. The effects of nutritional deprivation on central nervous system function may be classified into three different groups. First, the retardation may be noted in children with inborn errors of metabolism. These disorders affect the central nervous system and may produce serious defects in the brain. A second group of central nervous system disorders has been caused by a wide variety of specific vitamin deficiencies. Most of the cases in this category have been described as responding to therapy. The third category is made up of individuals who have been subjected to undernutrition for prolonged periods of time during their infancy and childhood. These children may exhibit persistence of minimal deficiencies of performance with scoring in the IQ range of 75 to 90 (5).

The brain develops rapidly during intrauterine life. After birth, the brain grows much faster than the rest of the body. By one year of age, the child's brain is about 70 per cent of the adult size; by the age of four, brain growth is almost complete. The anatomy, biochemistry and physiology of the brain become more complex as it increases in size. These changes are reflected in the infant's capacities for neuromuscular activity, socialization and intellectual performance. During the first years of life, timing of the acquisition of each new specific brain function and the integration of the process into the total pattern of performance are of critical importance. If there is disruption of this normal sequence, the individual may have limited capacity for certain abilities. For optimal development of the brain, the required nutrients must be available at the critical period of maturation, very early in life (15). What is this critical period? Experimentally, it would appear to be in the nursing period. It has been suggested that variations in the environment have greatest quantitative effect on a characteristic at its most rapid period of change and the least effect during the least rapid period of change (24).

In a review by Smith (19) on the phenomena of retarded growth, the results from uncontrolled observations lead to the conclusion that a malnourished child is likely to be dull and lethargic. On the other hand, a number of investigators have indicated that the brighter children in school were, on the average, taller and heavier than the less bright, even though their chronological ages were the same (1).

Kugelmass, *et al.* (14) studied the effects of nutritional improvement on child mentality in 182 children from two to nine years of age. Group 1 included 41 mentally retarded children and 50 normal children malnourished at the time of the first mental test and well-nourished at the time of the second. Group 2 included 41 retarded and 50 normal children, well nourished at the time of the first test and still well-nourished at the time of the second test. Table I outlines results obtained in this study. The data revealed an average rise of 10 IQ points for retarded and 18 points for normal children in Group 1 in contrast with an average

TABLE I

Effect of Nutrition on Mentality

	41 Retarded		50 Normal	
	Range in Age	Mean	Range in Age	Mean
Malnourished Groups (Group 1)				
Age	2-8 yr.	3 yr. 10 mo.	2-10 yr.	4 yr. 8 mo.
IQ	20-90	45	95-145	110
Interval	1-7 yr.	3 yr. 6 mo.	1-3 yr. 6 mo.	2 yr.
IQ change	—8 to +44	·+10	—12 to +55	+18
Well-Nourished Groups (Group 2)				
Age	2-8 yr.	4 yr. 10 mo.	2-10 yr.	5 yr.
IQ	20-90	52	95-140	110
Interval	1-8 yr.	3 yr. 6 mo.	1-3 yr.	2 yr.
IQ change	—20 to +11	—0.3	—25 to +20	—0.9

of no change in the retarded and a mean of 1 point decline for the normal in Group 2.

There was a significant correlation in this study between the age at the time of dietary improvement and subsequent IQ rise. The younger the malnourished child when nutritional therapy was instituted, the greater was the chance of improvement in mental function. The IQ rise after four years of age was insignificant.

In an attempt to answer the question, "Does undernutrition during infancy inhibit brain growth and subsequent intellectual development?", Stoch and Smythe (21) studied 42 Cape Colored children. Eighteen children in each of two groups were between ten months and two years of age, the remaining three of each group between two and three years. The main difference between the two groups was in their state of nutrition. The undernourished group consisted of eleven girls and ten boys. The children in the control group were matched with the undernourished children on the basis of age and sex. The children were evaluated for periods of from two to seven years. At all ages the mean IQ of the undernourished group was well below the control group. Initially the undernourished group exhibited a mean IQ of 65 while the control group had a mean IQ of 90. At the final testing the mean IQ of the undernourished group (70) differed from that of the control group (93) by 23 points.

Cabak and Najdanvic (4, 15) reported a follow-up study of Serbian children who had been hospitalized for malnutrition. At the time of hospitalization their ages were between four and twenty-four months; most were less than twelve months old. They were all 27 per cent or more below the appropriate weight for their age. At the time of the follow-up assessment when the children were between seven and fourteen years old, they had achieved the heights and weights of healthy children. However, results of intelligence tests showed that only half (18 out of 36) were within the normal IQ limits (91-110), 12 were between 71 and 90, and the remaining 6 were below 70. None showed an IQ greater than 110.

Clinicians have often remarked about the extreme apathy and peevishness of babies with kwashiorkor, a condition characterized by growth failure, edema, hepatomegaly and anemia caused by severely restricted protein intake of poor quality. In children with severe protein malnutrition in Mexico, the aspects of mental development explored by the Gesell techniques were found to be well below average. In general, psychomotor responses were least affected while the greatest deficit was in the area of language (23).

Cravioto (6) points out that if data for somatic growth are plotted against the mental scores, the direct association between the deficits in height and weight and the developmental scores becomes apparent. In five Mexican communities, high correlations between deficits in height and weight and developmental scores were found. Weight and IQ were positively related, so that as the child's weight increased at a given age, the mental performance also reflected gains. Children admitted to the Hospital Infantil of Mexico because of severe protein-calorie malnutrition earned very low developmental scores. Results of retesting at two-week intervals during successful treatment revealed that as recovery took place, the difference between chronological age and mental age decreased, except in those children whose chronological age was less than six months at the time of their hospital admission. These younger infants did not improve their performance, suggesting the possibility that nutritional rehabilitation is less effective in producing mental recovery in the younger individuals (6).

Cravioto *et al.* (7) conducted a cross-sectional retrospective study of intersensory functioning in the total population of Guatemalan primary school children in whom extreme differences in height at school age were used as an index of preschool nutritional adequacy. The visual, touch, and sensory modalities were explored for geometric form recognition to evaluate intersensory equivalencies. Each of the pairs of intersensory relations improved with age, the visual-touch integration being significantly more organized at every age than were the other sensory interactions tested. Differences in the development of these parameters were evident in isolated groups (rural less than urban) and educational level of the mother. It was also demonstrated that, in general, taller children, because they were better nourished, exhibited superior intersensory development than did the children in the shorter quartile. The authors suggested that malnutrition before six months of age results in permanent damage to intersensory development which could not be fully corrected regardless of the subsequent state of nutrition.

Egan (9) has summarized legislation which provides a basis for projects that can be utilized to prevent malnutrition in children, which reads:

> The 1965 Amendments to the Social Security Act included amendment to Title V, providing for a new five-year program of special project grants for comprehensive health care and services for school and preschool children, particularly in areas of low-income families. These "Projects for Comprehensive Health Services for Children and Youth" will provide screening, diagnosis, and preventive services for all children in the project area; treatment, correction of defects, and after-care are limited to children in low-income families. The purposes of the projects are to increase the availability and to improve the quality of health care services, including nutrition.
>
> In addition to these Projects, other resources were strengthened and extended by recent legislation which provides for an evaluation of a child's nutritional status or diagnosis and treatment of a nutrition problem. The provisions include:
>
> (a) The regular maternal and child health services, such as well child conferences, pediatric clinics, and school health examinations, as well as the crippled children's services. The same 1965 Amendments to the Social Security Act increased the authorizations for money to support these programs and required that each state satisfactorily show a progressive extension of the availability of such services to children in all parts of the state by July 1, 1975.
>
> (b) The clinical programs in mental retardation were strengthened and expanded under amendments to Title V of the Social Security Act in 1963, as well as 1965. Many of these clinics are known as child development clinics. In more than one hundred mental retardation clinics, complete medical histories are taken, recommendations for treatment made, and follow-up services provided.
>
> (c) The health services of community Action Programs, Project Headstart child development centers, pilot follow-through programs, and Parent and Child Centers provided under the Economic Opportunity Act of 1964 and its Amendments of 1965. Health appraisals given in these programs usually include a nutrition component.

The 1963 and 1965 Amendments to the Social Security Act and the Economic Opportunity Act of 1964 and its amendments not only made possible new resources for evaluation of nutritional status and diagnosis and treatment of nutritional problems, but strengthened and extended some resources already in existence.

NUTRITION IN TREATMENT OF MENTAL RETARDATION

The retarded child has the basic nutritional requirements of the normal child, although he may be unable to eat as well, or he may require more nutrients because of hyperactivity or a physical anomaly. Physically handicapped children, especially those with cerebral palsy, are likely to suffer from multiple problems as a result of inadequate dietary intake. Children with cerebral palsy may be poorly nourished because their intake is restricted by feeding difficulties related to tongue thrust, inability to swallow properly and dental disorders.

Nutrition Problems of the Retarded. Malnutrition may be defined as an insufficient intake of nutrients, or a nutritional imbalance, which can result in a poor rate of growth or illness; it may also be caused by improper or inadequate absorption.

Some of the problems of a retarded child may be:

a. Inadequacy of calories, protein, vitamins or minerals
b. Overnutrition in terms of calories, leading to obesity
c. Constipation
d. Metabolic disorders which interfere with utilization, even though food intake is adequate
e. Iron deficiency anemia.

Inadequacy of calories, protein, vitamins or minerals may result from a number of causes:

a. The child may be unable to chew and swallow adequate amounts of food or he may be unable to self feed
b. Parents may be unaware of the child's nutritional requirements and thus feed him insufficient quantities
c. Parental neglect
d. Excessive expenditure of energy resulting from hyperactivity

Overnutrition leading to obesity may result from:

a. Inadequate or inconsistent physical activity
b. Lack of proper variety of food being offered, with an excess of concentrated carbohydrate foods
c. Parents' guilt feelings, prompting them to give their child oral gratification in the form of excess food

Constipation may result from several causes. The most frequent are:

a. Hypotonia
b. Lack of sufficient fluids
c. Lack of sufficient bulk-containing foods, such as whole grain cereals, fruits and vegetables

A number of metabolic disorders are known which are amenable to dietary therapy.

Assessment and Treatment. In order to assess nutrition problems, it is helpful to obtain information about the child's diet. A valuable tool in assessing intake is the dietary history and three-day diet record. The history includes a report of early feeding, current eating practices and developmental milestones. In addition to the nutrient content of food, the texture of foods eaten and food preferences can be obtained from the diet record. Information concerning the child's ability to drink from a cup and his handling of eating utensils is important in counseling the parents in ways of correcting problems which may be present. Whenever possible, an observation of the child in his own home should be made; in this way, the child demonstrates his ability to eat and drink, and provides invaluable information regarding the child's eating habits and degree of development. The history should give the parents' observations, but the child may prove to be more or less proficient than the parent indicates.

After the assessment of dietary intake and feeding ability, a realistic plan for the child can be established based on clinical observations. A suggested outline of this plan would include immediate and future goals, and a step-by-step procedure for achieving these goals. Reassessment should take place at regular intervals. The reward or merit system can be used for reinforcement of accomplishments; the use of a meal or a specific food as a symbol of approval is often effective. However, unless food contributes to the nutritional needs of the child, the learning experience defeats part of the established goals. The parents and the nutritionist should develop the plan together. The nutritionist can sometimes be more objective and is probably trained to teach nutrition, but the parents can be more effective if motivated and will benefit from achieving the goals. If there are siblings close in age to the retarded child, it is good to involve them. Sometimes they can communicate better with the child or they seem to recall how they learned a feeding skill.

If the dietary history reveals a deficient intake of specific nutrients, the child's typical meal pattern and food preferences should be the bases for recommendations. Cultural food habits and financial ability of the family should also guide the nutritionist. Modification of recommended foods to conform to the child's meals will be more successful than recommending a standard pattern.

The retarded child may have difficulty in chewing and swallowing because his physical development may be slow. The child who is retarded learns more slowly, forgets more easily, and is usually unable to learn at the same age as the normal child. It is important that the retarded child be given solid foods; a diet can be made nutritionally adequate in liquid form, but development of facial and throat muscles cannot occur without chewing. Although parents may continue to feed the child only liquids or pureed foods over prolonged periods, it is important to offer more advanced forms of food. Gradually, foods of more coarse textures can be eaten, and should be offered periodically, at a time when the child is hungry and more willing to attempt a new texture of food. Solids should be offered on the tip of a spoon, just at the lips, so the child removes food with his lips and then uses his tongue to aid in swallowing. If only liquids or strained foods are offered, over prolonged periods, the child may resist any foods with texture.

Self-feeding and drinking from a cup (or any intermediate step toward these skills) will often bring a feeling of accomplishment for the parent as well as the child. When to begin depends on the readiness of the individual child. When the child shows an interest in feeding himself, even if he is messy, it is time to begin and then progress toward self-feeding. This is usually possible when he begins to put toys or cookies in his mouth. Occasionally, the child needs to be given a demonstration by dipping his fingers in a dish of food and then raising his hand to his mouth. A spoon can be placed in the child's hand, and the parent's hand closed over it. The child's hand is guided from the food to his mouth throughout the meal. Gradually, the parents can give less help, and the child becomes better able to feed himself.

Sociability at meals is important. Whenever possible, the child should be fed or allowed to eat while others are eating. The example of other children eating will reinforce the self-feeding experience. It also gives the child a sense of belonging and accomplishment when he is able to eat at the table with others. Appropriate mealtime behavior should be encouraged and taught to the child. Setting a reasonable time limit at meals discourages dawdling.

Giving the child experiences in food preparation or tasks related to eating can be a pleasant way of teaching him to follow instructions;

these experiences can also provide practice in arithmetic skills. Setting the table, preparing fruits and vegetables, cooking or following simple recipes can be more pleasurable than exercises unrelated to the family's experiences. It also gives the child a sense of contributing to the meal and the family's duties.

The retarded child may not be able to eat as well as the normal child because of a physical anomaly, or he may tire easily from eating a meal. Smaller meals served more frequently, at regular intervals, may be more appropriate. The caloric content of foods can be made more concentrated, so that the volume is decreased. The nutritive value of the food, particularly protein and vitamins, should be mantained. Foods which provide only calories, such as soft drinks, candy, or potato chips, satisfy the appetite and the child is less willing to eat other needed foods.

The hyperactive child may require more calories than he is able to ingest. The atonic child may not require as many calories to maintain his physical structure as the normally active child. The National Research Council Recommended Dietary Allowances can offer guidance in prescribing caloric requirements for a child, but the child's appearance, body structure, and physical activity are more reliable indications of caloric need.

The retarded child may be overweight because of an excess of calories and/or lack of physical activity. Food is one tangible way parents can communicate concern and affection for the child. It may be difficult for parents to withhold food from the child, although they should be reminded that the physical limitation is likely to be more pronounced if the child becomes overweight. If a child is unable to walk and is overweight, the excess weight is thought to limit his ability to learn to walk. A modification of the present diet with substitution of lower calorie foods and limits on concentrated sweets and fats is a more successful approach to a reducing diet than a standard low calorie diet. An increase of activity will increase the effectiveness of the limited calorie diet. Again, as in deficiency, the child's typical meal pattern and food preferences should be the bases for recommendations. Cultural food habits and financial ability of the family should be considered in developing the diet pattern.

Iron deficiency anemia is most frequently caused by excess intake of milk, which results in exclusion of iron-containing foods from the diet. Many retarded children have difficulty accepting and swallowing solids. When the child rejects solids, the mother may substitute milk for the rejected foods, assuming that milk will be nutritionally adequate. The child is usually satisfied with milk and is not hungry at the next meal, so milk is again substituted. A dietary intake record probably reveals that the child is ingesting 40 or more ounces of milk and very little solid food. The child may be content with milk, the mother finds feeding the child less of a chore, and the child maintains his weight. He will probably be anemic, however, and he is not developing chewing and swallowing mechanisms appropriate to his ability. The parent needs to be reassured that the child will not become depleted if he eats less food for several days. The intake of milk should be decreased and solids should be introduced at each meal. The child may resist the introduction of textured foods, but should be able to accept solids more readily because he is hungry.

Dental disorders, such as malocclusion and gum disorders due to certain medications, are common in the mentally retarded child. Dental problems may also be compounded by poor food habits, for example too many sweets, or an inability to chew. Failure to rinse or brush food particles away after meals may accelerate tooth decay. On recommendation of the dentist or physician, fluoride may be prescribed which helps harden tooth enamel and prevents decay. Again, as in deficiency, the child's typical meal pattern and food preferences should be the bases for recommendations. Cultural food habits and financial ability of the family should be considered in developing the diet pattern.

A metabolic disorder or a malabsorption of food should be suspected if a reliable diet record indicates that the food intake appears adequate but the child does not tolerate food properly or is failing to grow and develop. Treatment of metabolic disorders is most successful when the efforts of the physician, nutritionist, biochemist and nurse are combined (13). See Chapter 8 for a discussion of phenylketonuria and galactosemia.

While dietary treatment of phenylketonuria is well established, treatment of other disorders of amino acid metabolism must still be considered experimental. Treatment of disorders of carbohydrate metabolism, such as in galactosemia, is less difficult since the other sugars can replace the substance which cannot be utilized by the patient (12).

NUTRITION SERVICES TO THE MENTALLY RETARDED

The services of a nutritionist are available to most health, education and welfare agencies which offer programs and services for the mentally retarded (16). The nutritionist's participation may depend upon such factors as: her training and experience, readiness of the project or program director and staff to include her as a consultant and/or team member, and the amount of time she can make available.

Since programs vary, the nutritionist may be used in different ways, depending upon the objectives and focus of the specifific program. Program areas to which a nutritionist can contribute include:

A. Program Planning
B. Diagnosis and Evaluation of a Child's Problem
C. Treatment and Follow-up
D. Training of Professional Staff
E. Research

Each of these program areas is considered below, and specific ways in which a nutritionist can contribute include:

A. *Program Planning.* The nutritionist can contribute to program planning by:

1. Surveying needs and resources to outline the job to be done.
2. Recruiting and training personnel to provide nutrition services.
3. Planning with administrators and program directors for ways to implement the nutrition component of services for the mentally retarded.
4. Determining priorities. Nutritionists can help the staff decide upon the services in which there is most immediate need for calling attention to the nutrition component.
5. Evaluating the nutrition component.

B. *Diagnosis and Evaluation of a Child's Problem.* The nutritionist can contribute to diagnostic and evaluative services and tools in some of the following ways:

1. Case history and records, by:
   a. Assisting in the development of the nutrition component of records and reports.
   b. Advising and/or assisting the staff on methods for securing and recording dietary data.
   c. Reviewing and summarizing pertinent nutrition information in records. Work with the staff members on the interpretation and use of such data.

2. Other diagnostic and evaluative tools, such as:
   a. Acquainting the staff with the opportunities which the feeding situation affords for observation of problems and related useful information.

    b. Arranging for the parent to feed the child in a clinic observation room where it might be possible for the team to observe. In other instances, this might be done in the home.

3. Evaluation conferences—The nutritionist can:
    a. Evaluate diet and food habit history, interpret findings to staff, and suggest how the family could be helped with planning a diet to insure nutritional adequacy for the retarded child.
    b. Interpret the role of a nutritionist in relation to continuing work with the family.
    c. Suggest a local resource person who could assist with the follow-up on the dietary aspects of the case.

4. Interpretation of findings to parents:
    a. The nutritionist might, if it seems indicated, participate in this area of service.

C. *Treatment and Follow-up.* The nutritionist can participate by:

1. Helping staff members plan practical ways of assisting the patient and family in carrying out the dietary aspects of the medical recommendations and of home training in the activities of daily living.
2. Providing guidance and consultation to the staff members of the agency or special project on food and nutrition problems related to special medical conditions.
3. Determining the need to consider cost of therapeutic dietary regimens and the possible need for financial support.
4. Working with administrators and staff members of agencies and institutions concerned with group care to improve nutrition and food service standards and practices.
5. Meeting with parent clubs and other community organizations to interpret the nutritional needs of mentally retarded children and way of handling their feeding problems.

D. *Training of Professional Staff.* The nutritionist can contribute in many ways to a variety of training programs, including: (1) basic training. Nutritionists can work with persons responsible for the basic professional preparation of the various disciplines such as physicians, dentists, nurses, social workers, dietitians, nutritionists and teachers. (2) Pre-service and in-service training. The nutritionist can contribute to these types of training in some of the following ways:

1. Related to special projects, by:
    a. Participating in evaluation conferences.

b. Giving guidance to project staff on the need for meeting normal nutritional needs of children as well as needs due to special condition.
c. Demonstrating ways of dealing with specific problems, such as methods of feeding and the use of equipment which might be useful; discussing meal planning and food preparation for the phenylketonuric child.
d. Interpreting nutrition components of projects to groups or individuals in communities.
e. Preparing teaching materials related to nutrition, including pamphlets, posters and charts.

2. Related to overall in-service training program within agency, by:
   a. Participating in workshops or institutes.
   b. Planning and participating in training programs for food service personnel in schools, and other group care facilities.
   c. Keeping agency and project staff aware of current literature and developments in other projects as related to nutrition.

3. Related to training programs of other groups and agencies such as welfare and education departments concerned with services to mentally retarded children.

E. *Research.* The nutritionist might function in planning, collecting and analyzing data:

1. As an actual member of research staff.
2. In an advisory capacity to a study group.

SUMMARY

The role of nutrition and the nutritionist in the prevention and treatment of mental retardation are outlined. The function of nutrition in the prevention of prematurity and the frequent attendant mental retardation are discussed. Specific methods and techniques of improving feeding abilities and the nutrition of the retarded child are given. Specific duties of a dietitian or nutritionist as a member of the maternity and infant care team are included.

BIBLIOGRAPHY

1. "Accelerated Growth of Rats," *Nutr. Rev.,* 19:247, 1961.
2. Burke, B., V. A. Beal, S. B. Kirkwood and H. C. Stuart, "The Influence of Nutrition During Pregnancy upon the Condition of the Infant at Birth," *J. Nutr.,* 26:569, 1943.

3. Burke, M., S. S. Stevenson, J. Worcester and H. C. Stuart, "Nutrition Studies During Pregnancy. V. Relation of Maternal Nutrition to Condition of Infant at Birth: Study of Siblings," *J. Nutr.*, 38:453, 1949.

4. Cabak, V. and R. Najdanvic, "Effect of Undernutrition in Early Life on Physical and Mental Development," *Arch. Dis. Childh.*, 40:532, 1965.

5. Coursin, D., "Undernutrition and Brain Function," *Borden's Rev. Nutr. Res.*, 26:1, 1965.

6. Cravioto, J., "Application of Newer Knowledge of Nutrition on Physical and Mental Growth and Development," *Amer. J. Pub. Health*, 53:1803, 1963.

7. Cravioto, J., E. R. DeLicardie and H. G. Birch, "Nutrition, Growth and Neurointegrative Development: An Experimental and Ecologic Study," *Pediatrics* (Suppl.), 38:319, 1966.

8. Ebbs, J., F. Tisdall and W. Scott, "The Influence of Prenatal Diet on the Mother and Child.," *J. Nutr.*, 22:515, 1941.

9. Egan, M., "Recent Legislation Affecting Child Nutrition," *J. Amer. Diet. Assn.*, 52:377, 1968.

10. Hille, H. and M. Reeves, "The Battle Against Mental Retardation: the Dietitian's Share," *Hospitals*, 38:101, November 16, 1964.

11. Jeans, P., M. Smith and G. Stearns, "Incidence of Prematurity in Relation to Maternal Nutrition," *J. Amer. Diet. Assn.*, 31:576, 1955.

12. Koch, R., P. Acosta, G. Donnell and E. Lieberman, "Nutritional Therapy of Galactosemia," *Clin. Pediat.*, 4:571, 1965.

13. Koch, R., K. Shaw and P. Acosta, *Diagnosis and Treatment of Phenylketonuria*. Brussels: International League of Societies for the Mentally Handicapped, 1968.

14. Kugelmass, I., L. E. Poull and E. L. Samuel, "Nutritional Improvement of Child Mentality," *Amer. J. Med. Sci.*, 208:631, 1944.

15. "Nutrition and Mental Development," *Dairy Council Digest*, 37:25, 1966.

16. Nutrition Section, Division of Health Services. *Guide for Nutrition Services for Mentally Retarded Children*. U.S. Department of Health, Education, and Welfare, Welfare Administration, Children's Bureau. Washington, D.C.: U.S. Government Printing Office, 1962.

17. Pasamanick, B. and A. Lilienfeld, "Association of Maternal and Fetal Factors with Development of Mental Deficiency. I. Abnormalities in the Prenatal and Perinatal Periods," *J. Amer. Med. Assn.*, 159:153, 1955.

18. The President's Committee on Mental Retardation. *Report to the President. A Proposed Program for National Action to Combat Mental Retardation*. Washington, D.C.: U.S. Government Printing Office, 1962.

19. Smith, A., "Phenomena of Retarded Growth," *J. Nutr.*, 4:427, 1931.

20. Stearns, G., "Nutritional State of the Mother Prior to Conception," *J. Amer. Med. Assn.*, 168:1655, 1958.

21. Stoch, M. and P. Smythe, "Does Undernutrition During Infancy Inhibit Brain Growth and Subsequent Intellectual Development?" *Arch. Dis. Childh.*, 38:546, 1963.

22. Umbarger, B., "Role of the Nutritionist or Dietitian in Clinic Services for the Mentally Retarded," *Mental Retard.*, 3:25, 1965.

23. Waterlow, T., J. Cravioto and J. Stephen, "Protein Malnutrition in Man," *Advan. Protein Chem.*, 15:131, 1960.

24. Woodruff, C., "Nutritional Aspects of Metabolism on Growth and Development," *J. Amer. Med. Assn.*, 196:124, 1966.

CHAPTER 18

Counseling Services

by SYLVIA SCHILD, D.S.W.

INTRODUCTION

Professionals diagnosing and treating mentally retarded persons face the ever-present problem of how best to counsel the patient and his family, just as they do with other disorders. However, in mental retardation, more likely than not, the professional is confronted with more than the usual number of *unfavorable* factors. Frequently, there are disappointingly few, if any, positive elements in the situation. Zwerling's comment, made in 1954, still aptly characterizes the usual situation facing the physician and others who counsel the mentally retarded: "Here the prognosis is almost uniformly poor, the etiology only infrequently ascertainable, the parents frequently anxious, and the physician seldom confident of a therapeutic regimen" (32:49). And, despite the mushrooming of multi-disciplinary diagnostic, evaluation and treatment clinics for retarded children throughout the country, the follow-up medical management of these children (and those never seen in these clinics) generally remains in their home communities. Oberman (19) pointed out that the family physician or pediatrician should be one of the major counselors and advisors to the parents of a mentally retarded child. However, many other professionals also participate in this process, and the prospect of being the primary counselor to the retarded and their families need not necessarily be viewed as a dismal one because the professional is better prepared today than ever before to offer positive and prudent guidance to this group of handicapped patients.

In addition to new scientific knowledge and clinical experience, the professional now has available to him the understanding derived from the accrued experience of many who have counseled in mental retardation. Wolfensberger (31), in his review of the literature, found that while there was scant mention of parents in the early writings in mental retardation, there has been "almost a flood of such papers" since the mid 1950's. The societal climate has become more favorable during the same period of time; this has allowed far better acceptance by communities of the mentally retarded and their families. The enlightenment about mental retardation has served, also, to facilitate the physician's efforts on behalf of his retarded patients. Except in remote or rural areas, most communities have enhanced their resources to one degree or other; consequently, they are better able to provide specialized services to meet the needs of the retarded. Skillful and sensitive counseling can do much to ease the problems of families as well as to promote opportunities for maximizing the potential of retardates for productive, satisfying lives. The intent of this chapter is to present some current perspectives in counseling in mental retardation. As an overview, no attempt was made to be comprehensive or to deal with all aspects of counseling in depth due to the wide scope of the subject matter. It is hoped that the material presented will provide a salient framework of reference for counseling in mental retardation.

THE ROLE OF THE COUNSELOR

The chronicity of the lifelong handicapping condition of mental retardation has implications for the professional's role in counseling which are closely linked with his responsibilities across the life span of the client. The physician is most often the first professional source to which parents turn when puzzled, suspicious or concerned about their child's developmental progress. Parental anxieties require the empathetic, considered attention of the physician, not only with relevance to the immediate management of the child's problem, but also as an important precursor to the effective long-range planning needed to insure continuous care and enable the retardate to achieve his maximum potential. As the first person consulted, the physician often has a unique opportunity to establish a continuous professional relationship with the child and his family; more likely than not, the physician may be the only professional person mantaining a relationship with the family over the lifetime of the retarded individual (2). Consequently, he will be called upon for guidance at differing points in time when new problems arise in relation to the developing, shifting needs of the retardate at varying maturational levels and chronological ages.

When the physician serves as a counselor, he may find that the management of the retarded person can be a source of repeated strain and stress. The complexities of the problems presented can be overwhelming and frustrating. He may begin to feel he is called upon to be all things to all men. Realistically, the diverse needs of the retarded cannot be dealt with by one individual, one discipline, no matter how well meaning are the intentions. Families need to be counseled within a framework of feasibility. For this reason, the physician, mindful of his limitations, should engage in resourceful collaboration with other professionals. In most communities, the enterprising physician can find competent persons to help him, such as the local public health nurse, school teacher or minister. In large, urban areas, the service of other disciplines— social work, psychology, psychiatry—can assist in the diagnosis and treatment of the emotional and psycho-social problems taxing the family's capacity to cope with the burdens of mental retardation. One important task of the physician in his counseling is to help families understand and accept the services of other disciplines; this involves actively supporting the therapeutic efforts of the other professionals and viewing these not as competitive or independent, but as integral activities comprising part of the total medical management and treatment plan.

Regardless of which discipline the counselor represents, he is likely to face many intense emotional situations in dealing with families which are in crises precipitated by the presence of mental retardation. It is not uncommon to feel great pressure to help solve the family's unsolvable problems (12). The birth of a defective child, the decision about home versus residential care, genetic risks, etc., typify the emotionally laden problems brought to the counselor for guidance. His dilemma may be compounded by his own reactions and attitudes toward the family, the child, and the disorder itself. He may be unable to deal with the difficulties associated with mental retardation; unwittingly, his inability to understand and manage the problems may influence the ultimate outcome for the child who is retarded. However, as pointed out by the Group for the Advancement of Psychiatry (12), if the problem is approached as a complex and challenging one (for which there is no single answer or formula), and early use is made of consultant and diagnostic services, the rewards of successful management will more than outweigh the additional effort that may be required.

In general, there are many more generic than specific aspects in counseling with the retarded. Expertise in dealing with other chronic disorders is transferable to the care and management in mental retardation. Retarded children in pre-school years pass through the same stages of development as do normal children, albeit at a slower rate. Retarded children eventually become adults and most go through similar stages in personality and physiological maturation as normal people. The counselor can bring his training and knowledge of normal growth and development to bear most satisfactorily on the management of his retarded client. Oberman (19) believes that the counselor should use his knowledge and experience to provide "anticipatory guidance" to parents. The child's developmental needs should be interpreted and his parents need guidance regarding the next steps to take in training the child. Above all, the overall counseling goal is no different than in counseling other parents. The major objective is to help parents to treat their child in such a way as to promote the best physical care and healthy personality development.

MENTAL RETARDATION: A FAMILY PROBLEM

The current approach of community-based care of the retarded has placed considerable importance on the family unit. Begab emphasizes that "how efficiently the family can adapt to and handle the problem determines to a large extent how much responsibility society will need to assume in the care, management and treatment of the retarded individual" (5:35). The vulnerability of the family to disruption and stress is increased by the burden placed on it by the social stresses stemming from the presence of a retarded member. Stevens has pointed out the fact that multiple factors determine how well a family can cope with the problem:

> "The presence of a retarded child in a home presents a variety of complex problems involving all facets of family life and all family members. The nature and level of mental retardation of the child, the emotional climate the parents create in the home, as well as the community tolerance for the mentally retarded, all affect the manner in which the parents plan to meet the needs of their retarded child." (28:6)

Mental retardation, thus, should be viewed as a family problem with counseling directed towards the needs and concerns of the total family unit.

It is general knowledge that the level of well-being and integration of the family exerts influence on the functioning of its members. In most instances, the family influence is even greater on a retarded member, due to his extended dependency on the family group for care, training and protection. His special needs aside, the retardate requires the same basic nurturance as normal individuals. Much of this nurture is best provided by the family unit; however, the family needs support from the community to carry out its nurturing responsibilities in an effective manner. How much and what kind of care the retardate needs is dictated partially by the degree of his mental limitation. In greater part, the determination is made by the abilities and capacities of his caretakers to provide the essential ingredients of affection, responsive interaction, care and training. The nature of the environment in which the retardate grows and develops is shaped by the emotional reactions of his family to his problem. One can see, thus, the logical evolution which has occurred of placing primary emphasis on the counseling of parents of the retarded.

Consistent with the trend in other fields, those counseling in mental retardation have increasingly recognized the importance of working with the total family unit. The circular interaction of parents and children can flow in a positive or negative direction. Intervention into the family interaction can utilize positive family dynamics to help troubled individuals achieve more effective functioning. Individual help can be sabotaged if the close members in the patient's family are not helped as well.

The impact of a retarded child on his parents and sibling cannot avoid being traumatic to one degree or another. The family itself is immediately differentiated by virtue of having a "special," "different" or "exceptional" child. The family roles, structurally and dynamically, are affected by the interactional relationship with the retarded member. The attitudes and adjustment of the siblings will depend on parental reactions and attitudes toward the retarded member. How well the family can comfortably accept the deviance will have a bearing on the quality of home care provided to the retardate.

Evidence indicates that families of the retarded in general have more problems in individual and marital adjustment, child-rearing practices and sibling relationships. They are significantly affected socially, economically and psychologically by mental retardation. Holt (13) concluded in his study of British families that they often gained better spiritual and ethical values. Farber and colleagues (9-10) have contributed important findings on the impact of a retarded child on family life. Their research suffers from shortcomings, notably in that their sample consisted primarily of white, upper socio-economic class parents of severely retarded children. Their findings do tend to support the clinical impression that the nature of family adjustment to retardation is associated with the nature of the marital integration of the parents, sex of the retarded child, social class status, and family interactional patterns (31).

The stressful impact of mental retardation is felt by all members of the family unit—this is reason enough to be concerned with the counseling needs of the total group. Adams (1:3) has emphasized that the problems of the siblings of the retarded can be seen as a normal response to a highly stressful situation and merit professional help to prevent their becoming worse. Adams underscores the important point that mental retardation has to be viewed as a . . .

> ". . . total family handicap because of its adverse social consequences. A family with such a burden is ipso facto a family at social and psychological risk and if the pressures of caring for the handicapped child overwhelm the normal needs of the other children, there is real danger that their vital developmental years become blighted by emotional neglect, distorted family relationship and roles, and curtailed opportunity for social contacts. As a result the siblings may grow up as warped in their capacity for self-fulfillment as, in another way or for another reason, the retarded child is." (1:3)

The notable point is that having a retarded sibling does cause problems for normal children which require special understanding. Evidence shows that counseling can help normal siblings to deal constructively with these problems (21, 26).

PARENTAL REACTIONS TO MENTAL RETARDATION

Most knowledge about parental reactions has been gleaned from clinical practice. Wolfensberger (31:329) points out that "observations can occasionally be as valid as, and more profound than, information collected by controlled and empirical methods, and scarcity of experimental work does not ipso facto mean that we do not possess valuable information." One limitation is that present practice knowledge has been derived primarily from experience with white, middle and upper-class parents of young, lower functioning children seen in outpatient diagnostic clinics for the retarded. The resulting bias may be likened to that which prevailed when knowledge was circumscribed to institutionalized retardates. Another limitation is the overreliance which has been given to maternal information, with insignificant attention paid to fathers and other family members.

There is general agreement that parental reactions to the diagnosis of retardation in their child is highly individualistic (5, 8, 25, 31). The intensity of response and manifestation of reaction vary widely within and between people, depending on a variety of dynamic factors: individual personality, nature of the marital relationship, parental aspirations, feelings about deviancy, parental roles, socio-cultural-economic status, etc.

Despite the wide range of reactions described in the literature, some are noted to be more prevalent than others. *Guilt* is a commonly reported response to the diagnosis. A number of causal factors have been suggested, such as that the parents feel destructive, hostile and rejecting toward the defective child. Parents often resort to self-blame in reviewing the circumstances and their own behavior prior to the child's birth. For certain religious parents, the child may be viewed as a punishment for past sins. Kramm (14) found that 12 percent of parents of Down's Syndrome children believed it was a direct act of God that caused the mongolism. Despite the lack of evidence, there is sufficient clinical experience to conclude that most parents suffer guilt reactions to the diagnosis. The feelings of guilt (real or fantasied) are often very intense and may create emotional conflicts which precipitate a need for parent counseling. In the course of counseling, guilt must be dealt with in terms of its dynamic significance for the individual involved and with the goal of utilizing the guilt, assistance should be given to help promote constructive and effective adaptation to the problem.

Ambivalence is another reaction to the diagnosis frequently experienced by parents. In such a stressful situation, both positive and negative forces come into play. Parents have mixed feelings about the affected child, their own adequacies to cope with the problem, and in their attitudes towards professionals they are encountering. Anger, disappointment, grief, and frustration are some of the negative feelings which are experienced. On the other hand, normal impulses to love, nurture and cope effectively are positive tugs. Ambivalence is stirred by each new crisis and may never be completely resolved. The ambivalence is often sustained by the fact that no rational way can be found to project blame on the child (25). Overprotection, according to Roos (24), may be viewed as a manifestation of the parental ambivalence.

The concept of ambivalence has important relevance for counselors. Much of the problem-solving process in counseling can be focused on helping parents find comfortable resolutions to their ambivalent conflicts. In supporting the positive feelings of parents, counselors enable parents to cope more effectively with their negative emotions. Resolution of the ambivalence helps parents to utilize their energies more productively in tackling other responsibilities and problems related to the retarded child.

Disappointment, frustration, anger, shame, and sorrow are other parental reactions to the diagnosis. Graliker, Parmalee and Koch (11) showed that 48 percent of the families they studied expressed guilt, shame, embarrassment and frank rejection of the diagnosis. The concept that the intense and often chronic emotionality of parents is related to grief and sorrow is widely accepted and well described in the literature (4, 8, 10, 20, 27, 30). Olshansky (20), in his concept of chronic sorrow, asserts that parents find it culturally unacceptable to express their pervasive grief. The parental denial of the chronic sorrow is often reinforced by the counselor's tendency to view it as a neurotic manifestation rather than as an appropriate response to a tragic reality situation.

It is important when counseling to understand the sorrow empathetically: the fact of retardation is a reality which evokes normal responses such as bereavement. Counselors must constantly keep in mind that pathology in and of itself wakes responses and problems that are normal consequences of the deviant situation (25). If reactions and problems are not adequately dealt with by parents, maladaptive coping may result and be integrated into the parents' armamentarium of coping strategies. The danger lies in the perpetuation and rigidity of maladaptive coping to other life situations as well as to the problem of the retarded child.

COUNSELING THE RETARDATE

Equally important to parent and family guidance is counseling with the retardate about his personal concerns and desires. Less emphasis has been placed, historically, on counseling with retardates. This is related partly to societal attitudes which hold little promise or hope for retarded individuals. The fact that mildly retarded individuals tend to blend into the general population on leaving formal schooling has somewhat obscured the relatedness between their mental handicaps and their difficulties in coping with life problems. Many mildly retarded persons are able to make adequate social adjustments in which they are accepted as workers, marital partners and community members, etc. Thus, by definition, they are no longer categorized as mentally retarded. Nonetheless, many do encounter difficulties in coping with their life situations. Added to their existing mental limitations, further handicaps are created for retardates by the lack of adequate training and guidance for dealing with work, marriage, family and community relationships.

The lack of attention to retardate counseling has also resulted from misconceptions held about the retarded. One such assumption is that the retardate is always child-like and doomed to utter and complete dependence. The retardate has been rarely viewed as capable of achieving sufficient maturity for self-direction. Boggs believes that the 1957 Amendments to the Social Security Act were seemingly predicated on this assumption:

> "That the retarded person should be regarded as an eternal child who is required to continue indefinitely at the level of entitlement to parental support and protection which he enjoys in childhood and youth." (6:B66-42)

Another misconception is that the retardates are unable to change their behavior on the basis of personal therapy or counseling. In contradiction, another fallacy holds that retardates, because of unusual suggestibility, can be led by their noses—all that is needed is firm direction for change to occur. Neither assumption is fully valid. Many retardates can benefit from counseling although there are qualitative differences in the nature of their participation and progress in the process.

It is vital to see the retardate as a member of the total family system with equal need for establishing a satisfying role and communication in his interaction with other family members. Obviously, this presumes at least minimal capacity for affective and intellectual behavior. Brown (7) postulates a creative approach to working with the retardate by viewing him individually in his significant social systems—that is, the pattern of relationships established among people where there are expectations of behavior to guide the interaction. The retardate frequently needs help in forming relationships with others and in learning appropriate role behavior. The retardate suffers frequently from limited social contacts and development. Often, he is further handicapped by the social rejection or negative attributes expressed toward him by other persons.

Retarded individuals may have personality problems which are not necessarily unique to retardation. However, the stresses of their mental handicaps make them more vulnerable to behavioral and personality disorders. Nitzberg (18), who has had extensive clinical experience, finds that personality problems are quite prevalent among this group. In addition to vocational counseling, Nitzberg's clients express need for help with problems of sex, marriage, sibling conflicts and with their feelings about being retarded.

Counseling retardates acquires specific characteristics related to the nature of their handicaps. Counselors find their patience is heavily taxed by the need for constant repetition, restatement and recalling. The counselor is forced to be more directive and active than usual as the retardate learns his role in the counseling process step by step. Heavy reliance is placed frequently on an educational approach in the counseling. To quote Nitzberg:

> "The worker needs to teach 'him' to be a client, to relate to feelings, to seek them out, to scrutinize thinking and behavior, to regard his emotional as well as behavioral life as areas in which change may occur." (18:9)

Counseling with retardates has been proven productive where clients have some capacity to feel troubled and to articulate their problems. Nitzberg quotes from an 18-year-old girl with a tested IQ of 53:

> "Retardation is not good to have. A lot of people don't understand what it means. You go around feeling that parents don't want you around because you are retarded. But sometimes we have to face it. We have to live with it all our lives." (18:11)

Counseling with retardates may well demand unusual flexibility and imagination to meet their special needs. This in no way negates the valuable need which can be rendered to this group, although it places more responsibility on the helping professions to re-examine their own misconceptions, as well as on selecting the targets for their counseling services.

A CRISIS FRAMEWORK FOR COUNSELING

Counseling, in this writer's viewpoint, is best understood within the framework of crisis theory. The problems in mental retardation characteristically precipitate crises for the persons involved. It is a priori reasonable to assume that if the diagnosis of mental defect poses no threat or stress to the parent or family, there will be no problematic emotional reactions. As a chronic disorder, repeated crises occur over the space of the patient's life and their families are subjected to chronic stresses. Thurston (29) has shown that parents often have intense and unresolved feelings and reactions over time, and may experience fears following the initial diagnosis. It appears that for most parents the presence of mental handicap in a family member is stressful to their emotional well-being.

Various typologies of crisis reactions have been offered by professionals in the field. Farber (10) views the "tragic crisis" as a typical mourning for destroyed hopes and the "role organizational crisis" as the inability of parents to cope with the child over an extended period of time. A prerequisite to strategic crisis intervention is the understanding of the particular crises to be "intervened in." To talk with vague generality of the "crises of mental retardation" skirts around the task of identifying the nature of the traumatic event which precipitates or eventuates in the potential for crises, and of the psychological tasks requiring mastery for successful outcome.

Mental retardation as a heterogeneous condition poses difficulty in construction of a useful generic crisis framework. The number of etiologic factors, the variations in degree of mental limitation, individual differences, and the multiplicity of environmental factors complicate a generic ordering into classes. The individualization of cases is an understood imperative. Nevertheless, assuming a base knowledge for mental retardation and acknowledging the limitations imposed by the existence of innumerable variations, the writer proposes that the crises of retardation can be categorized into two broad classes to provide a useful framework of reference for counseling.

The first class is the *Deviancy Crisis* which occurs either from the stresses resulting from (1) the identification or diagnosis of the condition or (2) the stresses related to the specific nature of the diagnosed disorder including etiologic factors. The second class of crises, the *Chronic-Strain Crisis* occurs as a result of built up stresses and recurrent crises due to the chronicity of the problem and to insufficient or inadequate coping efforts or environmental supports.

The Deviancy Crisis

The *Deviancy crisis* related to diagnosis has been discussed in terms of the parental reactions to the initial impact of retardation in a family. In addition to coping with their emotional reactions, parents are faced with immediate problem-solving in relation to such matters as medical treatment, the question of whether to provide home care or arrange residential care for the child, appropriate schooling and training, etc. As suggested by Wolfensberger (31), value conflicts may come into play at this time. Parents are confronted with the need to absorb new knowledge and information; they also must seek out proper guidance, a task often complicated by dilemmas in determining whose advice to seek and accept. Many times it is impossible to make definitive diagnoses due to the nature of the disorder. Parents are required to cope with the attitudes and feelings of relatives, friends, and community even before, sometimes, they understand and have come to grips with their own.

The psychological tasks parents need to master are to: (1) cope with their emotional responses, (2) accept the reality of the situation sufficiently to engage in needed problem-solving activity on behalf of the child or the family, and (3) understand and alter, if need be, attitudes about mental retardation. These tasks may be subsumed under one task: the requirement for parents to learn and take on a new parental role as "Parent-of-a-mentally-retarded-child."

The pathology of the specific condition of the child produces certain consequences which become stressful in themselves. For example, in certain metabolic disorders stresses placed on family and child may include frequent clinic visits, repeated laboratory work, rigid dietary regimens, etc. Children born with anomalies may be unattractive physically and require special nursing care—a double strain on already harassed parents. In many cases, the insult resulting in mental dysfunction has affected other central nervous and physical systems; hence, many parents have children with associated handicaps, ranging from physical defect to behavioral and psychiatric symptomatology. The associated disabilities may be as much an harassment to parents as, if not more than, the mental retardation. Thus, many deviancy crises are prone to occur in relation to the associated handicaps of the retardation.

Psychologically, parents need to gain mastery of their feelings about the pathology in terms of what it has meant to be the producers of mental defect in extensions of themselves. The meaning that family members attach to the pathology is crucial to the ability to tolerate the unusual tensions stemming from its presence (25). Concurrently, parents are required to make adaptations in daily routines to meet special needs arising out of the pathology, i.e., medical visits, nursing tasks, dietary management, etc.

Another important psychological task may confront parents when the etiologic basis is clear and certain, particularly in the case of generic and hereditary disorders. The parent generally needs to evaluate the situation as it influences or affects family planning wishes (25). Counseling which is geared not only to help parents understand genetic risks but also to the emotional responses to those risks can best help parents to achieve the intellectual and emotional clarity essential for their person decision-making.

The Chronic-strain Crisis

The ability to cope with *chronic-strain crises* is in large measure dependent on the nature of the outcome to the *deviancy crisis*. In part, however, the potential for stressful outcome is contingent upon the availability of appropriate external supports to the family and the retardate. There are some periods when there may be less need for supports outside the immediate family, such as in early infancy when infant care may be usually and normally gratifying. There are also stretches of quiescence between various crisis points when the family may function well in relation to outside helps, in so far as environmental provisions are concerned. Some families are not as quiescent as they may appear; smoldering just under the surface may be mounting anxieties, unsettled ambivalences and increasing fear of the uncertain future.

A *chronic-strain crisis* may result from the incompatibility of the special needs of the retardate and the normal development pattern of the family. The unusual dependency of the retardate places strain on parental capacity for extended child-rearing. Over time, constraints may be put on various aspects of family life such as social activities, work, travel, etc. The lifetime feature of the mental handicap may precipitate crisis in terms of the psychological reaction to the chronic burden in which the parent can no longer maintain individual integrity and still meet the needs of the maturing retardate. As the parent copes through time with the child's problems, each adjustment may be made at a considerable psychological expense. A diminishing gratification may ensue with each coping effort until the parent finds the relationship with the child intolerable.

While the *crisis of deviancy* precipitates problems related to the taking on of new or unaccepted roles, the *chronicity-crisis* problems relate to the disorganization or reorganization of role systems and the allocation of role tasks within the family. Siblings may be pressed into assuming parental roles with the retarded member. Husbands may take on mothering tasks of nursing, supervising or feeding. Perlman (23) suggests that "parents and the total family may be caught up in crises of conflict and turmoil because deviance disrupts usual taken-for-granted role relationships and often requires consciously managed modes of behavior." A psychological task of the *chronic-strain crisis* is for the parent to identify in what ways his usual parental role needs to be altered to meet the special needs of the retardate. Family members need to clarify in what ways the presence of the retardate is influencing and changing intra-familial relationships. Another psychological task requires the parent to recognize, regardless of his self-perception in this area, that he must be dependent on external support to help with the long-term pull of meeting reality needs of the retardate for special schooling, job training, protective care, and the like. Parents may also need to be dependent to a greater degree on environmental resources to meet their own personal need than before they had to rear a retarded child.

Chronic-strain crises may occur in relation to other important persons in the situation: immediate family members, friends and neighbors. Reality problems occurring as a result of gaps and unavailability of community services may hamper a family's ability to manage the problem, and consequently, add to the chronic stresses. Although much effort has recently gone into expanding pre-school and early school age services, a marked lag in services for the post-school age retardate exists. Families maintaining their child in the home in early years are thrust into crises when they are unable to find resources for employment or job-training after schooling terminates. In this area of environmental supports, parents are confronted with unaccustomed psychological tasks: to communicate needs to strangers, to cope with frustrations and unfriendly attitudes, to master techniques, to cope with agencies and professionals, and to accept the dependent role of client.

Institutionalization

The question of institutionalization may precipitate a *deviancy* or *chronic-strain crisis* and, therefore, was not considered as a separate class of crisis in this paper. For whatever reason the parents decide to place their child, the situation generally takes on the characteristics of crisis. The consequences of child placement and separation dynamics are so well known they need no elaboration here. Institutionalization precipitated by some sudden stress or event, such as diagnosis of retardation or deviance at birth, creates a crisis situation for the parent. Logically, too, institutionalization may result from long-term stresses and deliberate decision. Regardless of how long a family contemplates placement before acting, the placement situation critically upsets the established equilibrium in the family and new or revised coping strategies are required.

Implications for Counselors

Utilization of this crisis framework suggests important clues to the counselor regarding his engagement with the client in the problem-solving process. The framework helps to pinpoint key areas to be explored by placing the crisis in a context which is diagnostic in itself. The *deviancy crisis* puts the diagnostic importance on the present and on the precipitating stress. The *chronic-strain crisis* points to the value of history-taking of both past and present. In both classes of crisis, consideration of family diagnosis and treatment is indicated.

Treatment goals can be predicated on the knowledge of the psychological tasks to be mastered, meshed with the diagnostic case evaluation. The utilization of the opportunity for growth and change in crisis suggests the application of an ego-supportive approach; the emphasis is on the here and now and on the healthy aspects of client functioning.

VARIATIONS IN COUNSELING APPROACHES

Modalities in counseling tend to vary, depending on the goals, counselor expertise and the environmental setting in which the guidance is offered. Historically, counseling of parents tended to be confined to a one-shot interview, subsequent to diagnostic work-up of the child (31). Although most counseling still occurs around the evaluation process, there has been increasing recognition that successful guidance necessitates repeated contacts which allow for adequate feed-back and reinforcement. This ongoing relationship allows the client to "work through" the emotional problems precipitated by the diagnosis. Clients need time to work out their solutions step by step and need help not only at points of crisis but in relation to practical reality problems arising in daily living. These latter contacts need to be on a continuing basis in which an educational focus is taken to help clients learn how to deal with daily living demands (25).

The vastly increased number of clinic services for the retarded, notably those in the specialized mental retardation clinics supported by the United States Children's Bureau, has influenced the modalities through which counseling is provided. The use of multi-disciplinary teams has led to a variety of approaches to informing and counseling. In many clinics, the physician alone carries out the counseling. In others, counseling is jointly done by the team; in still others, counseling responsibilities are parceled out among team members in relation to the nature of the problem requiring solution. Depending upon the individual preferences and biases of the professional staff, clinics have developed counseling services for parents, siblings, or retardates beyond the initial evaluation, interpretation and counseling session.

Most interviewing has tended to be conducted with individual parents; however, there is a marked trend toward seeing parents jointly. The latter approach is more favorably viewed by some writers (15, 25) because it leads to more productive parental understanding and communication. Placing the burden of responsibility and decision-making on one parent (usually the mother) may lead to unrealistic perceptions and may precipitate or add to friction between marital partners. The joint interview provides the opportunity to enhance communication between parents and support them in their collaborative problem-solving efforts.

Some clinics have established group services ranging from therapeutic groups at one end of the spectrum to information and parent education groups on the other. The number of sessions has varied as has the nature of the goals. The group process is a very effective means for counseling peer and family groups; however, the skills and expertise of the counselor in the group method are crucial to success.

Hazards in Advice-Giving

Milligan (16) describes the role of the counselor as helping the individual identify his problem, activate a plan, and place his plan into action to alleviate the anxiety, discomfort and imbalance caused by the problem. The help is achieved through the medium of the relationship established with the client. The counseling relationship evolves out of the motivation of client to be helped and counselor to help, out of trust and respect in and for one another and out of meaningful communication between the parties involved. Underlying the effectiveness of the relationship is the knowledge and expertise of the professional which is brought to bear with discriminating individualism on the problems of the specific client. Advice giving which fails to focus the therapeutic efforts on the conceptual understanding of the nature of the client's problem or the dynamics of the individuals involved usually proves to be highly ineffectual, according to Mosher (17).

Professionals in mental retardation have too often been prone to give advice freely to parents of the retarded on how to rear their retarded children. The psycho-social locus of the parental concern often conflicts with the professional interest in the retardation problem. Stresses and anxieties propel parents to seek easy, simple solutions to their problems. This eagerness of over-anxious parents often seduces counselors to masquerade as a universal "expert," offering wide range recommendations and advice. In so doing, the counselor usurps the client role; it is the client's responsibility in the counseling process to reach his own solutions, with the counselor's knowledge used as a means of stimulating the problem-solving process.

Time in counseling is an important variable. Impatience or lack of follow-up contact leads to oversimplified, stereotyped advising. The tendency to flood parents with detailed information and numerous directives gives them little opportunity to assimilate the knowledge and guidance wisely.

SUMMARY

The social and emotional stresses which stem from mental retardation generate considerable need for competent and empathic counseling services. The literature abounds with illustrations from clinical experience which amply document the needs of families for professional guidance. The intense impact on parents has resulted in heavy emphasis on parent counseling, with relatively little attention turned to the potential effectiveness of counseling with siblings and retardates. There has, however, been increasing recognition accorded to the need for counseling the family unit as a whole.

There has been little empirical research to test clinical impressions and theoretical rationales underlying counseling practices in retardation. Still, experience has demonstrated that successful counseling depends upon specialized training and positive attitudes towards retardation as well as all handicapping conditions. It also requires a sound knowledge base of retardation, behavior and personality functioning and sociological factors relevant to the problem.

A critical event like the diagnosis of retardation brings reality problems in its wake which are the normal complement of the pathology. Instead of perceiving parents as disturbed individuals, their behavior should be construed in the context of the crisis situation. As a result of the chronic nature of the condition, retardates and their families are particularly vulnerable to recurrent crises and to dissipation of their coping energies. When these crises occur, reality-oriented intervention can help the retarded and their families to resolve problems most constructively and lessen the burdens imposed on them by the mental retardation.

The physician, usually the first to see the patient and the most likely professional to have a long-time relationship with the family, is in a key position to provide strategic, skillful guidance. The physician dealing with the retarded should develop collaborative working relationships with related disciplines which can assist in devising and implementing plans to meet the long-range needs of the retarded.

BIBLIOGRAPHY

1. Adams, M., "Siblings of the Retarded and Their Problems and Treatment," paper presented at 90th Annual Conference, *AAMD*, 1966.
2. Ama, A. B., "Group Education for Parents of the Handicapped," *Children*, 8:135, 1961.
3. Beck, H. L., "Counseling Parents of Retarded Children," *Children*, 8:135, 1961.
4. Beddie, A., and H. Osmond, "Mothers, Mongols and Mores," *Canad. Med. Ass. J.*, 73:167, 1955.
5. Begab, M., *The Mentally Retarded Child . . . A Guide to Services of Social Agencies*, Children's Bureau Publication, No. 404, 1963.
6. Boggs, E., "Some Issues Related to Long Term Disability," in *Source Book on Mental Retardation for School of Social Work*, Eds. Meyer Schreiber and Stephanie Burnhardt, *Selected Academic Readings*, New York, 1967.
7. Brown, L. N., "Social Work with Retardates in Their Social Systems," Paper presented at the 90th Annual Conference, *AAMD* (Chicago), 1966.
8. Cohen, C., "The Impact of the Handicapped Child on the Family," *Social Casework*, 42:137, 1962.
10. Farber, B., W. Jenne, and R. Toigo, "Family Crisis and the Decision to Institutionalize the Retarded Child," *Cec. Res. Mong.*, No. 1, 1960.
9. Downey, K. J., "Parental Interest in the Institutionalized Severely Mentally Retarded Child., *Soc. Prob.*, 11:186, 1963.
11. Graliker, B. V., A. H. Parmalee, and R. Koch, "Attitude Study of Parents of Mentally Retarded Children: Initial Reactions and Concerns of Parents to a Diagnosis of Mental Retardation," *Ped.*, 24:819, 1959.
12. Group for the Advancement of Psychiatry.
13. Holt, K. S., "Home Care for Severely Retarded Children," *Ped.*, 22:744, 1958.
14. Kramm, E. R., *Families of Mongoloid Children*, Washington, D.C.: Government Printing Office, 1963.
15. McDonald, E. T., *Understanding Those Feelings*, Pittsburgh: Stanwix House, 1962.
16. Milligan, G. E., "Counseling Parents of the Mentally Retarded," *Mental Retardation Abstracts*, 2 (3), (July-September), 1965.
17. Mosher, L., "On Advising Parents to Set Limits for Their Children," *Social Casework*, 56 (2), (February), 1965.
18. Nitzberg, J., "The Role of Social Service in a Sheltered Workshop and Vocational Training Center for Mentally Retarded Adults, paper presented at 90th Annual Conference," *AAMD*, 1966.
19. Oberman, J., "The Physician and Parents of the Retarded Child," *Children* May-June, 1963.
20. Olshansky, S., "Chronic Sorrow: A Response to Having a Mentally Defective Child," *Social Casework*, 43:191, 1962.
21. O'Neill, J., "Siblings of the Retarded: II. Individual Counseling," *Children*, 12:226.
22. Parad, H. J., "Common Maturational and Situational Crises," in *Crisis Intervention: Selected Readings*, Ed. H. J. Parad, Family Service Association of America, New York, 1965.
23. Perlman, H. H., "Social Diagnosis Leading to Social Treatment," in *Selected*

Papers: Social Work in Child Health Projects for Mentally Retarded Children, D. C. Department of Public Health, 1963.

24. Roos, P., "Psychological Counseling with Parents of Retarded Children," *Ment. Retard.,* 1:345, 1963.

25. Schild, S., "Counseling with Parents of Retarded Children Living at Home," *Social Work,* 9:86, 1964.

26. Schreiber, M., and M. Feeley, "Siblings of the Retarded: I. A Guided Experience," *Children,* 12:221, 1965.

27. Solnit, A. J., and M. H. Stark, "Mourning and the Birth of a Defective Child," in *Psychoanalytic Study of the Child,* 16:523, 1961.

28. Stevens, H. A., "Overview," in *Mental Retardation: A Review of Research,* Eds. Harvey Stevens and Rick Heber, Chicago: University of Chicago Press, 1964.

29. Thurston, J. R., "Attitudes and Emotional Reactions of Parents of Institutionalized Cerebral Palsied Retarded Patients," *Amer. J. Ment. Def.,* 65:227, 1960.

30. Tizza, V. B., "Management of the Parents of the Chronically Ill Child," *Amer. J. Orthopsychiatry,* 32:53, 1962.

31. Wolfensberger, W., "Counseling the Parents of the Retarded," in *Mental Retardation,* Ed. Alfred A. Baumeister, Chicago: Aldine Publishing Co., 1967.

32. Zwerling, I., "Initial Counseling of Parents with Mentally Retarded Children," *J. of Ped.,* 44:469, 1952.

CHAPTER 19

Physical Therapy Services

by JANET FORINASH, R.P.T.

INTRODUCTION

Previous reading has well defined the retarded person and the problems he and his family face. This chapter will endeavor to relate the physical therapist's relationship to the mentally retarded child and his parents as well as to the retarded adult.

The frequent use of the word "normal" in writings on physical therapy for the retarded child is not by accident. It is to denote the constant goal: "as normal as is reasonably possible for a given patient." "Handling" refers to the "normal" care of, and play with, an infant or child by his parent (s).

ROLE OF THE PHYSICAL THERAPIST

The therapist developmentally assesses a patient and gives appropriate guidance for the parents in normal handling of the child in order to obtain a more normal sensory input which is valuable for the patient's future. Normal is determined by *where the patient is* on the developmental sequence scale vs. *where he should be* according to a chronological developmental scale (i.e. Gesell, Denver, et al.). At this point a treatment judgment must be made by the therapist (often with the parents' input) as to what is normal for that patient in his growing experience.

Functions of Physical Therapy

1. *Assess* levels of reflexes, sensory responses and physical skills of subjects noting differences in *static skills* (i.e. being placed sitting) vs. *dynamic skills* (transition from all fours to sitting position, etc.). Transi-

tions between prone and all fours, all fours and sitting, etc., are necessary to note.

2. *Teach* parents on a one-to-one basis how to handle their child better to make sure he uses his present maximum potential for a "more normal" life experience. Teaching or consulting is often done in the community on a follow-up basis as requested. Some minimally to moderately involved children with Down's Syndrome do well in community infant stimulation programs with frequent therapy consultation for each patient.

It is suggested that the therapist initially devote three sessions to getting to know the subject and to determining how and to what the patient (0-2) years) responds. There are three highly important aspects to consider in the parent/child relationship as it applies to the home therapy program: a) *How* the parent and child are able to interact, b) how able the patient is to accomplish the home program with the child, and c) how the mother and child can be helped to experience as "normal" an interaction as possible. The underlying principle is the importance of the child's responding to the mother, and the mother's "feeling" this response as being related to her very person.

Three to six sessions are needed for the following purposes: 1) giving good home guidance in handling the child for normal sensory experiences; 2) maintaining range of motion and improving muscle tone and strength; and 3) guiding and encouraging parents to investigate one or two community programs suggested so they can become more active decision makers concerning future programs for the patient (i.e. to decide on infant programs, preschool or school, developmental center, with or without therapy, etc.). If the parents decide to place their child, support them in their decision. It is important to have the parents make appropriate facility inquiries and visits, depending on their present emotional crisis level. In a team approach, it is quite likely that placement suggestons have been made by a social worker and/or physician and the physical therapist should function appropriately for the given time and situation.

3. Long-range follow-up *referrals* may be made as appropriate. Follow-up may mean physical therapy visits several times a week, once every few weeks, or on a consultative basis only. Referrals may be made to infant stimulation programs, preschool or school programs, ophthalmologist, pediatrician, orthopedist, etc.

Be supportive to the parents. They usually know the patient's problems better than we professionals do, since they daily experience the child's "slowness" or "inefficiencies." It is impossible to relate all the considerations. Sometimes parents report the child's irritating them (e.g. up all night, cries at anything, etc.). They may be bothered by his "inability to get what he wants" while other parents may indicate their child is no problem at all. Very important are the parents' comments and point of view, and from this perspective and the actual developmental assessment the therapist interprets the problem and begins a therapy program with the parent and child. Subjects are often evaluated several times, and the parent may be more of an observer than a participant. This may make the assessment incomplete. The physical therapist must get to know the kind of parent he's dealing with so that the parent's ability to teach the child can be assessed. With parental participation a more accurate assessment of the patient's will and motivation can be made.

4. On a broader scope, the therapist may be called upon for a surgery opinion, equipment suggestions (i.e. bracing, wheelchair, etc.) to aid in posturing a patient, or to make recommendations in a community facility and/or help to instigate a program for the severely disabled in institutions. In these facilities the therapist can provide input but relies on other dedicated workers to do follow-up programs.

It is well-established that parents of young (0-3 year) infants who are diagnosed as retarded (CP, autistic, MR, seizure) are not receiving the depth of home instruction and emotional support they need. Of course, there are many parents who do not desire this, but those that do need the chance to work personally and intensively with their child, for a period of time. This should occur prior to relinquishing the child to an agency such as a preschool or school program which would do most of the therapy. This is also a time (0-3 years) when a child can potentially reap the greatest benefit from home instruction.

It is well known in therapy that the 30-60-minute, once or twice a week sessions (or even less often), during which the therapist works with a patient, have little carry-over value at home unless the parent is taught to do the therapy at home in regular activities of daily living. For the infant this refers to routine home activities. For the preschool, developmental center and school-age child this refers more to classroom activities, and therefore involves teaching the child's educators.

In infant work, the therapist relies heavily on the parents to follow up on the home therapy program. As the child gets older (i.e. 3 years), the therapist often decreases home instruction and consults with the patient's educators in getting therapeutic postures and activities to help a child in his normal classroom day.

The therapist must assess the functional level of the patient specifically for range of motion, strength, *extension endurance* and developmental abilities and disabilities, and note the child's functional social responses, his self-motivation and disposition. In addition, he must try to see the problems the parents face wth the patient's inabilities. It requires one to three sessions to complete a fair beginning for treatment. However, actual therapy is, in part, begun with the first session. For example, one thing—either a sensory or motor mode—is selected and taught to begin at home. This enables the therapist to evaluate how the patient tolerates or responds to the chosen items, and also to communicate better with the parent.

In treatment my technical guide is a developmental sequence scale criteria (Gesell's standards plus my own work experiences) and the normal siblings' development. The therapist designs a program for the patient that is unique, individual and changing. In teaching the parents how to play and work with their child therapeutically, it has been my experience that they often become better "therapists" with *their* child than a professional could be. They are the familiar nurturing and disciplining figures in the home and can add more of the "what's normal for their family" to that child. I admire the parents of the developmentally disabled child who are willing to impart a living experience to their child by working so hard. This motivates me to help them help their child help himself. All of this is in context with being more normal.

Evaluation for quality care, especially for severely retarded children, is a heavy responsibility for the therapist. A therapy evaluation, unlike vision evaluations, changes at more frequent intervals as the patient changes. Even the smallest improvement should be recorded. This improvement should approximate the normal growth and development sequence (i.e. gross skills of prone, rolling, sitting, standing and the subtle changes of extension endurance, etc.). If the evaluation does not change, one must assume the patient is *not* progressing. The total program then needs re-evaluation. One must take a closer and more specific look at the patient; review therapy goals; review neurological, physiological and mechanical principles of therapy; and review the present program to see if it is too difficult or too easy. In good therapy, re-evaluation (i.e. seeing and feeling changes in the patient) and teaching are a must. Teaching is the guiding of the parent in the *art of handling* the child to get the maximum benefit of handling stimulation before he literally gets too big.

A diagnosis of mental retardation leads one to a spectrum of images in terms of physical therapy—a patient with floppy muscle tone, good tone, or stiffness as a little one; the image of being either ambulatory or non-ambulatory as an older child or an adult, or being a totally dependent person in an institution. A child with slow development and questionable muscle tone and parents anxious about slow progress are reasons for physical therapy referral.

Mechanically speaking, physical therapy is concerned with minimizing joint contractures and aiming for a functional level of development (i.e. rolling, sitting, creeping, walking and running) and decreasing the patient's dependence on others as much as possible. The therapist needs the knowledge of normal cerebral development as it relates to normal growth and development, and experience in facilitating normal growth and development in minimally and moderately involved individuals. Thus, he will gain insight and greater success in facilitating progress in severely disabled infants. I would like to see more dedicated therapists with a background experience in dealing with the severely retarded child. These therapists must be willing to adopt the philosophy that 90 percent of the responsibility lies in the teaching, and a readiness to learn from the parents.

Many times young children with a diagnosis of minimal to moderate retardation can, with early remediation referral, progress to a functional level of ambulation. If the patient is evaluated developmentally and found to be well within normal play and motor milestones, the therapist can recommend other appropriate community resources such as infant stimulation programs. Then it is the therapist's responsibility to continue one- to three-month evaluations and therapy until the child progresses to functional ambulation and no longer needs physical therapy. Two to three such evaluations are suggested in the first 12 to 18 months of life.

The therapist is concerned with the overall balance of the patient's nervous system (i.e. Does he tolerate "normal" parent handling? How does he react to that handling? Is his strength, range of motion, muscle tone and growth and development normal for his age? What are his vision and hearing responses? What are his speech sounds? Are there eating problems? Does the parent desire guidance in the physical aspects of the child's growing?).

A *young infant* retarded in his sensory responses and/or motor development may have a diagnosis of mental retardation, floppy baby (diagnosis unknown), delayed development, or other label. It is important for the physician to decide whether the patient needs a physical therapy evaluation or follow-up. This author feels that the parents will reveal clues to their physician of needing help on handling their child. With some patients, the physician *knows* that *later on* the child will need physical therapy to help him crawl or walk.

A physician recently asked concerning a four-month-old infant with a diagnosis of mental retardation, "Is it really that important to start therapy so young (before 18 months)? All he needs is to be pushed." This is a valid question. Here are two possible viewpoints:

a. Yes, the child really is too young. If no therapy evaluation or follow-up is begun, at 18 months, when it is more than obvious that the child and parent need help, the home situation may be such that the child's behavior is "running" the mother's life. At this point, early placement may be desired by the family. The child will often have missed out on much stimulating experience because the parents have picked up negative attitudes from medical professionals and they have given up on their retarded child. The child and parent may have missed out on some of the early joys of handling that therapy can bring.

b. Yes, it really is important to begin therapy early (at four months). Infant and mother, quite normally, are not completely separate individuals at this time. In handling her baby, mother often desires and needs guidance in giving her young infant as normal a sensory experience in being handled as possible. By 18 months, this mildly to moderately physically involved infant will, most likely, have increased in strength, endurance and motor development to a near normal level of function because of the special handling helps taught to the mother by the therapist. If the baby is severely retarded but has still had the previously mentioned therapy, he may be enjoyable to the mother and be showing extremely slow *but noticeable* progress so that she will have a more satisfying relationship with her little helpless one than would have been possible without the therapy guidance.

Early intervention with therapy is extremely important in order to teach mother to handle and play with her baby in order to build strength and endurance in ways similar to that of a normal baby who, being self-motivated, moves and increases his endurance quite naturally on his own. Early intervention gives support and encouragement to the parents and helps them to *see* their baby and to reach more realistic self-expectations for him.

Early remediation makes for a more positive future outlook and can decrease cost to the state government.* Consider a hypothetical case. A very retarded child who, without therapy, would not walk until eight or nine years of age, could, with therapy, be ambulatory by age three to five years. Ambulation has meaning for this child in terms of independently getting what he wants and enhances his desire for some level of self-sufficiency. Independent ambulation will have proportionate ramifications socially, psychologically, etc. If this child has not walked until nine years of age and has been assisted or waited upon, he has probably learned to fuss, point, or perform some other kind of attention getting behavior to get what he wants. Even after he has learned to walk he often retains this passive, yet demanding, behavior with which the parent or caretaker must deal. Walking is not as meaningful to him as it should be. Often, with this independence, he receives less attention (which was previously required in his daily care). One can easily see how this problem becomes magnified proportionately in the case of a non-ambulatory or partially ambulatory 35-year-old retarded person who still lives at home. Therapy can help to bring the adult, patient to a more functional level of physical performance but changing attitudes (desire for independence) and habits is not always possible. "Being assisted" in ambulation has had much meaning to the patient in terms of love and attention. Without this assistance, the patient will often have a fear of space and adjusting to upright posture. Therapy is important and can help but is less successful with older clients. Therefore my strong emphasis is on early intervention for the infant.

At this point it seems appropriate to recognize the good work that is being done in community programs for the developmentally disabled. More stimulating programs are available to the ambulatory MR client who reaches adult age. Practically speaking, it behooves the physician to become aware of possible referrals for therapy for his very young developmentally delayed, mentally retarded and cerebral palsied infants as well.

In summary, the therapist's role with children and adult clients is to prevent or reduce deformity and increase the client's physical functioning level to its maximum. In work with infants, the therapist's role

---

* R. Koch, M.D., 1975, reports $5-6,000 per year increased cost for each institutionalized, non-ambulatory patient. *Crippled Children Services* may be found in each state by contacting the local Department of Health and asking for available services, brochures, etc. These should be helpful to a new therapist or physician building resources for assistance and referrals.

also includes the preventative goals that enable the parent to deal more effectively with their child. But improving the patient's performance to his maximum potential more specifically means increasing extension endurance and facilitating sensory-motor development, which will help the parent to better handle and cope with the infant.

Physical therapy is a useful and important adjunct in the treatment of an infant who is behind the norms in development. It is good to begin therapy in the first few months of life if the pediatrician finds the baby with stable vital signs and in good health.

In conclusion, *knowledge* of growth and development tells us what to do. *Experience* tells us to observe patient responses or lack thereof. The *art* of physical therapy enables us to integrate both of the above into an approach to handling the infant.

BIBLIOGRAPHY

1. Bobath, B., "Very Early Therapy of Cerebral Palsy," *Developmental Medicine and Child Neurology*, Vol. 9 No. 4, 1967.
2. Fiorenteno, M., *Reflex Testing Methods for Evaluating Central Nervous System Development*, Springfield, Illinois: Charles C Thomas, 1973.
3. Gesell, A. and C. S. Amatruda, *Developmental Diagnosis*, New York: Harper and Row, 1947.
4. McGraw, M. *The Neuromuscular Maturation of the Human Infant*, New York: Columbia University Press, 1943.
5. Peiper, A., *Cerebral Function in Infancy to Childhood*, New York: Consultants Bureau, 1963. (See: Sections on "Institutionalization," pp. 628-631, and "The Mother and Her Child," p. 600).
6. Finnie, N. *Handling the Cerebrally Palsied Child at Home*, New York: E. P. Dutton, 1970.
7. Cliff, S., J. Gray and C. Nyman, *Parents Can Help: A Therapist's Guide*, El Paso, Texas: El Paso Rehabilitation Center, 1974.
8. Roberts, R. and B. Roberts, *David*, Richmond, Va.: John Knox Press, 1964.

Section IV.

EDUCATION AND TRAINING OF THE MENTALLY RETARDED

CHAPTER 20

The Contribution of Education

by GENE HENSLEY, Ph.D.

INTRODUCTION

For more than two decades, programs for the education and rehabilitation of mentally retarded children and adults have been expanded and refined. Of the approximate five and one-half million retarded persons in the United States, the large majority can be classified as moderately or mildly retarded and are responsive to programs of education and habilitation. Parents, educators, and organized community groups have increasingly become aware of this fact and have continued to provide impetus for more and better services from education and rehabilitation personnel. Although there remain large numbers of retarded persons in our society who are not now receiving services from education and rehabilitation, there are services now available to the mentally retarded which were previously non-existent or at best were only token programs.

The number of mentally retarded children enrolled in public school special education classes has more than doubled in the past ten years and there are federal and state supported programs to provide more appropriate educational experiences for retarded children who remain in the regular classrooms. In addition, there is a growing concern among educators regarding the relation of poverty to mental retardation and the effects of poor nutrition, bad housing, inadequate sensory stimulation and countless environmental factors which can influence the total development of children, particularly the very young.

Fellowships and traineeships are now available from the Federal Government for training teachers and administrators to serve the retarded. In the field of rehabilitation, there is greater emphasis on coordinating community resources to serve the retarded; focus is also placed on the training and placement of persons in these jobs. Further, the importance of cooperative services between special education and vocational rehabilitation agencies and among related social service programs is now recognized and the concept of total rehabilitation may in time become a reality.

SPECIAL EDUCATION-REHABILITATION AND THE MENTALLY RETARDED

The stmulation of large-scale interest of public and private groups in educating and rehabilitating the mentally retarded may be viewed as a comparatively recent phenomenon, although there have been fractionated attempts at providing these and related services to the handicapped in our society for more than a century. Historically, the manner in which various societies have dealt with their disabled has varied. Some cultures have destroyed them; others have cared for them; and a few have worshipped them. The desire to educate or habilitate the mentally retarded has been an outgrowth of our concern for our fellow man, and in this respect, concern for the mentally retarded has varied from one culture to another and from one century to another. But concern is not action, and it was not until the 17th Century that we began to build institutions for them (27). It was much later that anything resembling education was provided for them. Most writers who have dealt with the history of special education have set the beginning of educational services for the retarded at about 1800 when Jean Marc Itard, a physician, initiated a form of sensory traning and socialization with a "wild" boy, about 12 years of age, who had been captured in the forest of Aveyron, France. At the end of five years, his dedicated effort to educate the "Wild Boy of Aveyron" ended in defeat. Although this experiment in learning was considered a failure, later accounts of the instructional process and the publication of Itard's book, *Wild Boy of Aveyron,* signaled the beginning of a series of educational programs on behalf of the retarded.

It was Itard's student, Edward Seguin, who spearheaded the programs of training and treatment for the mentally retarded in the United States.

His first book, *The Moral Treatment, Hygiene and Education of Idiots, and Other Backward Children,* was published in 1846 while he was still in France. For this contribution he was crowned by the French Academy and commended by Pope Pius IX. However, it was his second book, published in 1866, which set forth his "physiological method"

(48). Seguin believed that mental defect could be divided into two types—the superficial and the profound. Accordingly, the superficial was the type in which the peripheral nervous system was damaged and the profound type was thought to be produced by defects in the central nervous system. In both cases, however, the treatment was essentially the same, consisting of a form of muscle and sensory training. In addition to his emphasis on muscular training and the education of the senses, he became well known for his focus on the "whole child" and for emphasizing the importance of individualized instruction, and the feelings and desires of children.

Another important early educator of the mentally retarded was Maria Montessori (41). Her early conclusion that mental deficiency was an educational problem—her stress on sense and muscular training, self training, and on practical activities—and the fact that her original work in Rome was with tenement children give her a position of importance in the history of the education of the mentally retarded. The impact of her work continues to be felt in this country, particularly in the area of preschool education for both normal and retarded children.

Other workers, such as Decroly, Descoeudres, and Binet, contributed greatly to the educational literature. Decroly, a physician, developed a number of educational games which were designed to improve attention span and improve sensory discrimination. Descoeudres (10) published one of the first comprehensive educational programs for the retarded. Binet is probably best known for his contributions to the testing of intelligence and for the diagnosis of retarded children in the schools. Unlike his predecessors, his work was with identification and diagnosis, and not with educational methodology or instruction.

In more recent times, the history of the education of the mentally retarded has become increasingly identified with the expansion of different philosophies, administrative practices and comprehensive educational programs, i.e., "progressive education," special classes, preschools, and adult education. Although there were educational efforts on behalf of the mentally retarded prior to the 20th century, there were few special education teachers of any type before that time, i.e., teachers with specialized preparation or experience in a given disability area. In fact, teachers with special training prior to 1920 were mostly instructors of the blind or deaf (46).

Until recently, almost all special education programs for the mentally retarded were in the form of special classes and from about 1915 to 1930 the number of public school classes of this type increased. However, as in many other specializations, interest in promoting these special classes slowed in the '30's, probably because of inadequate planning and economic factors of that era. It was not until the end of World War II when many new educational programs were emerging that special classes again became popular. In the ten-year-period, 1950-1960, the number of exceptional children enrolled in special programs of all kinds more than doubled. The number of mentally retarded children enrolled in special classes increased from 87,000 in 1948 (Office of Education, 1954) to more than 213,000 in 1960 (39).

Since this time, the implementation of special day classes for the mentally retarded has increased markedly. Recently, the Office of Education reported that there are currently 32,000 teachers of the mentally retarded employed in local schools, and that special teachers as a group constitute over one-third of all special educators in the nation (1967-1968).

WHY SPECIAL EDUCATION HAS GROWN

There are many reasons why special education services for the retarded have become so popular in recent years. For one, it is well known that societies seek to solve their general education problems first, i.e., providing minimal elementary and secondary education opportunities for those with relatively uncomplicated learning needs, or in other terms, to raise the average literacy level of its citizenry to some arbitrary point. Once general education programs are underway which are consistent with the desired social and economic expectations of the culture, then increased attention may be given to refining and modifying existing programs, and implementing specialized instruction for those with complicated learning needs.

Another factor is the growing awareness in this nation that handicapped persons can become contributing and independent members of society. Educational literature attests to the fact that large numbers of mildly retarded persons can, and do, become socially and economically successful, and that given the appropriate training and instruction even larger numbers of mildly and moderately retarded persons will succeed.

Other factors have contributed to the rapid growth of educational programs for the retarded: the enactment of compulsory attendance laws; the establishing of divisions of special education with the state departments of public instruction; increased legislation in support of special education; the assistance of the Office of Education and other federal agencies; the growth of university programs of professional preparation; and the ever-widening target population of our educational enterprise.

But, in the writer's opinion, the single most powerful impetus to the development of special services, particularly the establishment of special classes, was the parent movement. Legislators, teachers, and administrators have felt the effects of parents and friends of the retarded who continue to demand that all children receive the educational opportunities to which they are entitled. While no one can predict the exact pattern of growth of future educational opportunities for the retarded, there is every reason to believe that this growth will continue.

TERMINOLOGY

Perhaps the number one task in coming to grips with education and habilitation of the mentally retarded is the need for understanding the term "mental retardation." Educators and others use this term rather freely in discussing the implications for teaching and learning. Terms like mental deficiency, slow learning, subnormal, or mentally handicapped continue to be used interchangeably in the educational literature despite acceptance by many disciplines of the American Association on Mental Deficiency System of Classification (20). The AAMD definition refers to mental retardation as "subaverage general intellectual functioning which originates during the developmental period and is associated with impairments in adaptive behavior." In terms of this definition, the following would constitute generally accepted classifications for mental retardation based on measured intelligence (standardized tests which yield an intelligence quotient):

Profound	IQ less than 20
Severe	IQ 20-35
Moderate	IQ 36-51
Mild	IQ 52-67
Borderline	IQ 68-83

In terms of adaptive behavior, it is assumed that profoundly retarded persons would require virtually constant care and supervision and would have major physical and sensory impairment. Severely retarded persons would manifest retarded speech, language, and motor development. Those classified as moderately retarded would be rated as slow or retarded in general development, and in adulthood would require supervision and a sheltered environment. Mildly retarded persons are considered educable within limits and as adults could be placed in competitive employment, although their general development would be expected to be slower than normal.

For purposes of educational planning, most identified retarded children have, in the past, been classified as educable (IQ 50-75) or trainable (IQ 30-50). Notable exceptions would include young retarded children who are enrolled in preschools within our communities, and have not yet been classified according to IQ or some other criterion, slow learning children (IQ 75-85), and severely or profoundly retarded children. Educationally speaking, mentally retarded children are classified as trainable (IQ 30-50) when they have demonstrated potential capabilities in self-care, sociability, and verbal communication. They are not ordinarily expected to become literate. Children assigned to the educable classifications are generally presumed capable of acquiring limited skills and consequent literacy.

SPECIAL EDUCATION PROGRAMS AND THE ROLE OF THE EDUCATOR

Education is one of several community systems involved in providing total care for the retarded. Teachers, administrators and other educational personnel are now providing instruction and training for persons with varying degrees of retardation from preschool levels to adulthood. Further, there are many new arenas for education and training located in day schools, residential institutions, centers, and hospitals. The educator's increased involvement in the total care and planning for retarded persons outside the traditional school framework has significantly increased in the last decade. However, there are more retarded children enrolled in the regular classrooms of public day schools than in any other type of educational facility. Teachers spend more time with children than do other professional persons and probably have a greater opportunity to influence their behavior. In this respect, the educator's role is somewhat unique in comparison with workers in related disciplines who have less routine contact with retarded children.

In our society, most school-age children go to school whether retarded or not. While this has not always been the case, our school laws are now fairly explicit on this point. In most states, the schools now accept children at an appropriate school age and are required by law to provide some type of educational service for them. Exceptions would include the severely retarded and certain children with multiple handicapping conditions, although increased numbers of retarded children with severe and complicating crippling conditions are now being served in private and in public schools (5).

Probably the oldest administrative arrangement for the care of retarded children and adults is the residential school. Historically, residential programs were organized to provide simple custodial care. Educational programs within these institutions received little attention, although for many years, this plan provided virtually the only organized educational programs specifically available for retarded children. In recent years, the trend has been away from institutional or residential care for most exceptional children, including the mentally retarded, with new admissions to institutions limited to the more severely handicapped. An exception to this trend would be the "community centers" operating in conjunction with state institutions for the mentally retarded and designed to provide total care with emphasis on habilitation and education of older retardates.

Special school programs within public school districts wherein all who are enrolled are mentally retarded have decreased in popularity, although a few are still in operation. Recently, there have been some renewed efforts to utilize the special school concept through a variety of unique and locally relevant administrative arrangements. While it is difficult to evaluate the relative effectiveness of various administrative arrangements, the decreasing popularity of special school and residential programs is in part due to education's resistance to programs which totally isolate retarded children from their peers and from the mainstream of school activities. Comparatively, the special school has been viewed as more educationally advantageous for educable and trainable retarded children than is the residential-type program, but both have declined for reasons associated with peer-group and family isolation, transportation problems and program limitations.

The most common educational arrangement continues to be the special class located in one or more regular schools in a local district. Particular administrative procedures vary with local school policies and perceived needs, but it is not uncommon to find several special classes integrated with regular classes in one school. The expressed purpose of this arrangement is to facilitate grouping practices as well as to foster economies in operation, but related considerations are proximity of the class to the child's home, and availability of supportive school services. Most classes of this type have been for educable retarded children, although for several years, classes for the trainable retarded have been slowly introduced in the public school programs. There is little question that this type of educational arrangement will continue to provide the major framework for special education services for some time to come since financial support for educational services in most states is based on the "special-class concept" and since a majority of special education personnel appear to support the philosophical principles on which placement in special classes is established.

However, the best administrative framework for providing special education services is a matter of debate. Research in special education does not provide overwhelming support for any single administrative procedure. In fact, there is a notable lack of experimental evidence to support the efficacy of special class placement at all. On the other hand, there is a considerable body of older data which suggests that educable retarded children are rejected by their non-handicapped peers in regular classes (3, 22, 27), and that there may be particular benefits of special class placement which are extremely difficult to assess. Teachers who are responsible for the education of the mentally retarded have generally supported the idea that curriculum planning and instruction are efficient when the class size is reduced (classes for retarded children are typically smaller when children are placed in special classes at an early age), and when they are grouped homogeneously according to chronological age and mental age. No single arrangement has been completely satisfactory, including the regular classroom. One of the problems is that special classes are not all alike; curricula, teaching procedures, quality of instruction and administrative acceptance of the special education program differ. Further, it is difficult to evaluate the success of a particular special education program against nuclear standards of achievement. Criteria of these types are difficult to establish and well-controlled longitudinal studies of mentally retarded children in different school environments are rare. Despite some obvious shortcomings, both teachers and administrators who have had experience with special class placement, particularly for educable mentally retarded children, have in the past reacted positively to this type of arrangement and have felt that a more functional curriculum can be provided under these conditions.

Then, too, it is sometimes expressed that retarded children in special classes need to be sheltered from any of the pressures which occur in the regular classroom. It has also been stressed that special education teachers are able to give retarded children more attention in the special class than would otherwise be possible, particularly in instances where more able students are also making demands or where individual differences in achievement among students are greatest. School programs for educable retarded children have typically stressed competence, personal adequacy and ultimate occupational skills. Academic subjects are taught with the assumption that all adults in a modern society need minimal academic skills.

Special classes are frequently grouped so that they correspond roughly with the regular school classes. In rural areas, however, it is not unusual to find special classes containing both educable and trainable youngsters with wide variation in chronological age. In some cases, the chronological ages of children range from seven through fourteen or fifteen. In urban areas, mentally retarded children will have access to a larger number of school services available at preschool, elementary (primary and intermediate) and secondary levels.

PRESCHOOL PROGRAMS

Mentally retarded children in preschool programs range typically from three to six years of chronological age (similar to ordinary nursery and kindergarten classes) with mental ages of two to four years. These classes are designed to provide enriched experiences for retarded youngsters. Frequently, they are offered as private preparatory programs for children who will ultimately spend some time in educable or trainable classes in public schools. They sometimes function as part of larger community or institutional sponsored programs. Communities are not now providing large numbers of classes at this level, and it is probable that most children who are ultimately introduced to educable or trainable classes in the public schools have not been enrolled in preschool classes. Those who were enrolled probably were in regular preschool classes or short-term programs operated during the summer months for the benefit of specific groups of children within the community, e.g., Head Start Program. Children from middle and upper class families often attend public or private nurseries and kindergartens whether or not they are mentally retarded. Unfortunately, children from the lower socioeconomic families who might profit most from early childhood education programs find few of them available.

ELEMENTARY PROGRAMS

Elementary classes for educable children are designed for children with chronological ages from six to thirteen years. Children enrolled in classes at the primary level range from six to nine years chronological age and three to six years mental age. Ordinarily, these children are not expected to function effectively in most regular class programs;

at least, they are not academically ready for them when they reach school age. It is assumed that within the framework of the primary class, retarded youngsters can develop better vocabularies, improved habits of health and safety and can be stimulated greatly by experiences that would not otherwise be available to them.

The intermediate classes are for children from approximately nine to thirteen years chronological age and who have correspondingly lower mental ages. These are the most common classes for educable retardates to be found in the public schools. It is paradoxical that we stress the importance of early childhood education, yet continue to wait so long to develop services for the mentally retarded. This peculiar situation stems from the fact that children are referred for special services and special class placement *only* when they become serious educational problems. By the time the retarded child has spent several years in school, he may have become a significant problem for his teachers. Perhaps he has failed in his academic subjects, or has consistently demonstrated his inability to understand or tolerate the behavior of other children or meet the demanding social requirements of his peers.

To be sure, the mentally retarded child of a given age is not the only child who has personal problems, but the fact that he has not functioned efficiently with regular classes places greater pressure on the public schools to provide some type of special program for him. Consequently, the intermediate special class is often the first to materialize in a public school, followed at a later date by some type of primary and secondary class arrangements. Hopefully, children who are admitted to the intermediate classes are ready for instruction in tool subjects, e.g., reading, writing, and mathematics. Some will have sufficient background to profit from some type of social studies program and will be in a position for the teacher to concentrate on helping them understand their own goals and desires. Others will require an extended readiness program for an unspecified length of time. But the best instructional program will be individualized and geared to the capabilities of the child—a basic principle of special education.

SECONDARY PROGRAMS

Educable and slow-learning children at more advanced levels may also profit from specialized programs. Certainly, advanced programs are becoming more prevalent as school districts and communities realize that it is meaningless to develop programs at primary and intermediate levels unless there is continuity extending through secondary programs for the child. Secondary school classes continue the instructional pattern in various tool subjects, but increasingly emphasize the practical and functional relationships between what is studied in school and the practical tasks of living and working as young adults, e.g., reading the newspaper, following instructions and getting along with fellow workers on the job.

Programs of this type at the secondary level generally reflect the idea that adolescent students will require assistance in relating school experiences to the demands of the home, community, and working adult world. Modern programs for adolescent retardates are designed to provide for this transition through the establishment of work-study programs, with the ultimate goal of providing appropriate vocational placement for the young retarded person. Most programs of this type have developed logically and sequentially from school services offered at elementary levels.

Guidelines for program development and execution have been drawn from the philosophies of both special education and vocational rehabilitation, emphasizing the importance of education and work to the student's personal fulfillment. Work-study programs, therefore, attempt to bridge the gap between school experiences and the realities and responsibilities inherent in most work situations. Work experiences are generally incorporated logically into the curriculum, although the organizational structure of the school will determine the complexity of the program. Programs of this type generally follow a sequence which includes supervised work experiences in class, pre-vocational evaluation, work experiences within the immediate school environment, supervised work outside the school in conjunction with related school instruction, and ultimately full-time employment.

The emphasis in work-study programs is on general skills training as opposed to instruction in specific skills, but assistance toward the acquisition of specific skills is available through arrangements with state vocational rehabilitation personnel. Work-study programs of necessity reflect the socio-economic conditions of the community. Programs are usually community-centered and are heavily influenced by labor conditions, including job availability and future local and regional employment prospects. Because of variability in community needs and resources, guidelines for the development of successful work-study programs must take into account numerous factors relating to school conditions, available agencies, and community services. There is little doubt that successful programs are the result of careful fact-finding and curriculum-planning by administrators, teachers, and supportive personnel. Of major importance is the degree to which the community is prepared to receive and provide for students in training and graduates of the programs.

In most work-study programs, detailed planning aimed at gaining the confidence and cooperation of community leaders and representatives of various agencies has been essential. Another factor is planned program flexibility, including provisions for continuous program evaluation. Curriculum content at this level and procedures in the field of mental retardation must always be tentative, since economic conditions are constantly creating changes in working conditions and opportunities.

Other important conditions include the careful and systematic selection and placement of students who are eligible for the program and well-defined professional roles for teachers, administrators, and counselors.

SCHOOL PROGRAMS FOR THE SEVERELY RETARDED

Several years ago, special educators were actively debating the efficacy of public school programs for trainable mentally retarded children (14, 29). While the nature of these programs may change as both special and general education become more effective in dealing with problems of exceptional children, the number of programs specifically designed for trainable children continues to increase. School services for the severely retarded have emerged since World War II, partly as a result of the influence of well-educated and economically secure parents becoming actively involved in community programs for retarded children, and perhaps as a result of the increase in birth rate (15).

The trend toward increasing the number of these public school programs is not without support from educational researchers. In recent years, several studies have provided data which have been useful in backing up this trend. A number of investigations have followed up children who have been admitted to special classes for the trainable mentally retarded. Cited in Farber (15) are numerous studies: Lorenz (1953), Delp and Lorenz (1953), Saenger (1957), and Tisdell (1960). Cited in Dunn (14), are the following: Reynolds and Kiland (1953), Goldstein (1956), Guenther (1956), Hottel (1958), Johnson and Capobianco (1957) and Cain and Levine (1961). Although several of these studies may have had certain methodological limitations, e.g., weaknesses relating to an absence of control group, inadequate measuring devices, small sample sizes, etc., they do suggest that moderately and severely retarded persons may, under certain conditions, become well integrated into their societies. The Delp and Lorenz study followed 75 adults who had attended classes in a special program in Minnesota. At the time of the follow-up, 25 persons in this group were in institutions and nine had died. Of the 41 living in the community, 27 were making a reasonable adjustment; five had regular full-time or part-time jobs and five were performing odd jobs. An additional 25 of those living at home did worthwhile tasks around the house.

Saenger (1957) was concerned with the adjustment of 520 severely retarded adults who had been randomly selected from more than 2,600 former pupils of public classes for trainable retarded between 1929-1955. It was found that two-thirds of all former pupils in this group were living in the community at the time they were studied; 26 percent were institutionalized and eight percent had died. Saenger's findings could be interpreted as providing evidence that many severely handicapped persons can lead satisfying and useful lives (46). Although the community adjustment is not necessarily the same as school adjustment and while not all moderate to severely retarded individuals can effect successful adjustments, these and other studies do support the notion that institutionalization is not necessarily the best or the only solution for the care and habilitation of severely retarded persons. The fact is that the number of educational programs for the trainable mentally retarded have increased, and public schools continue to assume greater responsibility for children with all degrees of mental retardation (5).

Special educators continue to call for greater attention by researchers to long term studies (14), and curriculum evaluation (29), and careful study of the organization and goals of these school programs. In recent years, educators have suggested that training programs for the more severely retarded should begin early (29); that year-round programs should be expanded as should programs to span the gap between public school experience and adulthood (29).

Of major importance is the fact that programs for the more severely retarded at all chronological ages are becoming a significant part of public school education. It is an unwarranted assumption to hold that a given child is too retarded to profit from educational services.

FUTURE PROGRAMS

Change is in the air. Progress in the education of exceptional children and modifications in educational practices applicable to those with mental retardation are apparent. Some trends which have implications for the educator's approach to mental retardation are as follows:

1. New systems of classification. There appears to be a trend toward more educationally relevant classifications which emphasize individual problems of learning and which have implications for teaching and training. Among many educators, fewer references are now made to the traditional categories, e.g., mentally retarded, physically handicapped, behaviorally disordered. Better educational opportunities for children with unusual combinations of handicaps and attempts to deal specifically with the child's learning problems may be forthcoming.

2. There are new efforts to establish functional relationships between theory and practice in special education. These efforts are aimed at narrowing the gulf between the educational researcher and the practitioner. New models for research and for program development in special education, particularly in the field of mental retardation, are emerging, with attention given to factors such as urban and rural differences, poverty, sparsity, language development, and personality. Furthermore, methods, procedures, and teaching of educators in special education are undergoing reassessment.

3. There are changes in administration and placement procedures. For many years, it was a generally accepted idea that mentally retarded children "belonged" in institutions or in "state schools." Educational opportunities which were available were required to conform to the general purposes of the institutions. This meant that special education services were decidedly limited in certain programs but better in others. As the demand for community facilities developed and public schools began to provide for increasingly larger number of retarded children, administrative problems increased.

At least two important factors confront administrators who are seeking to provide for increased numbers of retarded persons within the local schools: first, children who are mentally retarded may have other potentially handicapping conditions which can affect learning and which must be considered whenever specialized personnel, supportive services or specialized administrative services are requested; second, no single plan for extending services can effectively provide for all types and levels of mental retardation. For example, middle-class children who have mental retardation and are "brain injured" may require different plans, as compared to mentally retarded children who are known to also be bilingual, and who come from homes characterized by poverty and a general lack of enthusiasm for what is taught in the local school.

Lord (31) has described administrative practices for exceptional children in terms of two major plans: 1) those which provide for services to teachers or to children; and 2) those arrangements which require that the child be transported to special programs of various types, e.g., special classes, short-term instructional sessions or clinics, or special arrangements in schools for tutoring, evaluation or enrichment. While these broad administrative practices are utilized in serving all types of exceptional children, they have definite implications for the mentally retarded. A single procedure may be utilized or several may be implemented concurrently to provide for children with complicated handicapping conditions, e.g., the multiple-handicapped child who has mental retardation. Of importance, however, is the fact that many schools are not sufficiently large to support elaborate and extensive services, and specific programs may find that factors like transportation, classroom space, or the availability of teachers are highly significant in determining desired outcomes, even if programs are well-financed and are generally supported by the community.

4. Curricular changes are taking place. The extent and precise direction of change in curriculum for the mentally retarded are difficult to evaluate and modifications in programs for particular groups of retarded children may not be indicative of trends, e.g., programs for "brain injured" children. There does, however, appear to be greater inter-disciplinary management of mentally retarded children; increased application of techniques of instruction in language arts, quantitative skills, and social studies; emphasis on the sensory capabilities of children; and in general, a more systematic approach to instruction. Newer approaches appear to be more enlightened and positively oriented, emphasizing the value of manual skills *and* experiences in verbal learning with a concern for both similarities and differences among children. Negative philosophies which gave impetus to programs for "getting rid" of the child or simply keeping him occupied for a period of years are rapidly being replaced by programs which have, as their goal, to provide for extending the retarded person into a role in society which will be of benefit to him and to his culture. Cooperative rehabilitation-special education relationships have done a great deal to extend the curricula of educational programs well beyond formal school experiences.

5. There have been attempts to investigate changes in behavior (achievement) of mentally retarded children under various conditions of school learning. There appears to be a growing interest among edu-

cators to test the "value" of various administrative arrangements for providing educational services to exceptional children, especially grouping practices or special classes. At the present time, educators are finding that they must solve certain administrative and procedural issues if positive effects of special education are to be continued. Foremost among issues are those relating to the efficacy of special class placement, problems of systematic instruction, and the relation of educational services to the needs of trainable retarded children.

In the minds of most educators, conclusions as to the relative success or failure of special classes for mentally retarded children are not possible at this time. Additional carefully controlled longitudinal studies plus continued study of the variabilities in special class placement are clearly indicated (26). Questions concerning the superiority of one teaching method over another, particularly where academic skills are concerned, are still unresolved. Additional information is needed regarding the relative effects of curriculum, methods, and teacher characteristics on the achievement and the total school adjustment of the retarded child, along with comparative data on administrative and teaching arrangements in the public schools. Comparisons of various programs are difficult and information of this type is hard to obtain (17). The question of how beneficial classes or other educational arrangements have been to trainable retarded children continues to merit serious attention of educators. Financial consideration, manpower (teachers and other specialists) and the possible alternatives to public school services for severely retarded, multiple handicapped, and other deserving children are practical considerations whenever an extension of educational services is under consideration.

6. There have been some attempts to evaluate teaching competencies, establish professional standards, refine teacher education programs, and deal directly with manpower problems in special education. In recent years, programs for the preparation of teachers to work with mentally retarded have been greatly stimulated by program development grants from the U.S. Office of Education and by additional support from various educational foundations, and community agencies. Recent developments include the following:

A. Systematic attempts to evaluate teacher education programs in terms of established goals, program effectiveness, curricular content, and supply and demand for professional personnel.

B. Increased numbers of programs particularly at undergraduate levels for preparing teachers of the mentally retarded.

C. In-service program development aimed at increasing the sophistication of regular elementary and secondary teachers in the field of mental retardation.

D. Exploring of "pre-professional" programs for those working in educational settings serving the mentally retarded, or the use of "teacher aides" in extending the available manpower supply.

E. Development of minimum standards for teacher certification in mental retardation and in related areas of specialization.

F. Increased standards of admission and retention for teachers in preparation who enter advanced programs of specialized preparation.

REHABILITATION AND THE ROLE OF THE COUNSELOR

Vocational rehabilitation is a relatively new specialized service for the handicapped, yet it is one of the older Federal grant-in-aid programs (7). It began as a service to disabled veterans after World War I and has grown steadily as a helping service to millions of handicapped persons. The enactment of the Vocational Rehabilitation Amendments of 1943 broadened the original law of 1920 with the following definition: "The term 'vocational rehabilitation' and the term 'rehabilitation services' mean any service necessary to render a disabled individual fit to engage in a remunerative occupation. . . ." DiMichael (12) has pointed out that it was this concept which made vocational rehabilitation services available to the mentally retarded. Since that time there has been an ever increasing number of mentally retarded persons who have been assisted through organized rehabilitation programs. Between 1945-1950, there were 2,091 mentally retarded persons who received these services and, in 1957, state rehabilitation agencies placed almost 1,100 retarded adults in jobs (13). In 1962 alone, there were 3,562 retarded persons who received rehabilitation services through state agency programs, and in 1966, an estimated 13,700 mentally retarded persons were rehabilitated (50).

Until after World War II, rehabilitation services, like special education services, were not widely available to the mentally retarded. Again about 1950, through the efforts of parents and with the cooperation of organizations like the National Association for Retarded Children, vocational rehabilitation services for the retarded were given increased attention. It was then that DiMichael's book, *Vocational Rehabilitation of the Mentally Retarded,* was published and widely distributed. This document stimulated a great deal of interest in mental retardation on the part of vocational rehabilitation personnel and it was not long until organized groups (i.e., the National Association for Retarded Children, The American Association on Mental Deficiency, and various educators, physicians, counselors, and legislators) were combining forces to bring rehabilitation services to the mentally retarded. Special educators have worked cooperatively with state vocational rehabilitation agencies for many years. The development of work-study programs in the public schools as a type of vocational preparation for retarded adolescents and young adults provided the meeting ground for increased cooperation between education and rehabilitation, and cooperative arrangements between vocational rehabilitation agencies and the schools have provided services to the mentally retarded for more than ten years.

The realignment of programs of the Department of Health, Education and Welfare into the Social and Rehabilitation Service (SRS) in 1967 may yet have important positive effects on the total services to the mentally retarded. The Division of Mental Retardation, now part of the new Social and Rehabilitation Service, is in a position to provide continuity of cooperative programming involving the specializations of health, education, rehabilitation, and various other social agencies in habilitating the mentally retarded. Cooperation among state services for the mentally retarded should be greatly increased by this new concept of total rehabilitation.

The most recent estimates of the Vocational Rehabilitation Administration reveal a minimum of 3.7 million disabled persons in need of rehabilitation and as many as 536,000 additional persons who will require these services annually. The real impact of rehabilitation can best be understood when one looks at the rapid growth of rehabilitation services and at a cross section of those who apply for them. DiMichael (11) estimates that upon examining 100 typical rehabilitants, one would find 37 with skeletal impairments, 10 mentally ill, 6 with visual impairments, 6 with speech and hearing disorders, 4 blind, 5 cardiac cases, 5 with tuberculosis, 2 deaf, 6 mentally retarded, and 19 with a variety of other disabilities. In addition, 95 of these 100 cases would come from families with an annual income of less than $3,000 and virtually all would be classifiable as poor. In view of our broadening concepts of mental retardation and our interest in the relation of poverty, income level, nutrition, and health to mental retardation, the importance of rehabilitation as a concept of total assistance to the mentally retarded cannot be overestimated.

REHABILITATION PROGRAMS

Describing the status of rehabilitation for the mentally retarded, William A. Fraenkel (16) points to four types of rehabilitation programs identified by the National Association for Retarded Children as required for retarded adults: employment programs, sheltered employment programs, community activities, and home care programs.

Employment Programs

An increasingly larger number of retarded adults are being assisted into competitive work situations. To a large degree, placement in gainful employment is being accomplished through work experience or work-study programs in which educable mentally retarded students in secondary school programs are combining classwork and part-time employment in actual work situations within the community. The effectiveness of specific work experience programs in which rehabilitation and education cooperate to provide employment for retarded adolescents and adults is yet to be fully evaluated. However, a number of studies of community adjustment and employment success which support the continuation and expansion of these programs have been conducted. Studies conducted in the 1950's have been reported by Tizard (51); Charles (6) has summarized a number of follow-up investigations of adjustment. These and other studies suggest that mildly retarded adults can succeed in community life. Kidd, Cross, and Higginbotham (25) studied retarded persons who had completed school programs in the St. Louis Special School District. They found that a majority (81%) of the group studied were employed. A study by Neuhaus (42) in which adult retardates were compared with nonretarded physically disabled workers reports that the retarded persons experienced success in semi-skilled and clerical tasks.

Many retarded adolescents and adults will require the direct services of counselors and other rehabilitation personnel in state rehabilitation agencies and schools. These services often include the assessment of interests and aptitudes, work evaluations, personal counseling and a variety of follow-up services. In addition, a number of physical restoration services may be provided if needed. Speech therapy, the fitting of prosthetic devices, glasses, and hearing aids, as well as medical referral are all services which can be coordinated by rehabilitation personnel and which may be essential to the rehabilitant's success on the job.

Sheltered Workshops

For several years, sheltered workshops have provided employment opportunities for large numbers of retarded persons. Because of limitations or neglect, many retarded adults have not had the skills essential for competitive employment. Some have multiple handicaps, unrealistic aspirations, poor educational backgrounds, or more limited abilities. These persons are often assisted through sheltered programs. These facilities are typically work-oriented rehabilitation programs which provide opportunities for training and work as well as a number of helping services such as work evaluations, counseling, and supervision. Occupational centers are similar to sheltered workships but differ in the degree of sheltered employment and long-term supervision. In most instances, the goal of the occupational center is to prepare the client for eventual outside employment.

By contrast, the sheltered workshop is designed to prepare the client for sheltered work. Recently there has been emphasis on developing sheltered work projects which extend beyond the facility itself. There are many productive opportunities for sheltered work outside the traditional facility—included are: domestic work, gardening, agricultural positions, and a variety of public and private maintenance opportunities. Sheltered work programs of this type appear to be on the increase.

Other Workshops and Activities

Wolfensberger (52) suggests that at least three types of workshops can be differentiated. They are 1) the habilitation workshop in which training is aimed at preparing the person for competitive employment, 2) the terminal workshop which is the sheltered workshop, and 3) the occupational workshop which functions as a day care center for the adult retarded but which does provide opportunities for light and simple work.

Some retarded persons are so disabled that, instead of employment objectives, community programs should focus services which will assist the clients to become more self-efficient, primarily through the development of social skills. The objectives of these programs are to provide social and recreation opportunities and some opportunities for limited work. Activity programs of this type have been initiated in many cities throughout the nation. In most cases, counseling programs, particularly for parents, are operated in conjunction with the activity center. Although many retarded persons who are enrolled in activity programs may not initially be considered candidates for employment programs or sheltered workshops, eventual placement in work-oriented or vocational programs may become a possibility for some.

Home Care

Home care programs, which can be provided for the mentally retarded who require extensive supervision, are highly individualized programs which are designed to develop minimal skills useful to that person within the family setting. Emphasis may be on becoming ambulatory, learning to care for personal needs or on communications. In all cases, home care programs are planned, executed, and based on the known capabilities and limitations of the person.

Role of the Counselor

The occupational role of the rehabilitation counselor is yet to be established. There are major differences of opinion among counselors or rehabilitation workers as to what their role is, or should be. McGowan (33), Lofquist (30) and others have provided definitions of rehabilitation counseling.

McGowan has stated:

> For me, personally, the vocational rehabilitation counselor's unique contribution to handicapped clients consists of intrinsic interest, special training, and supervised experience, which have prepared him to combine medical data from the physician, psychological data based on his own special training in testing and counseling, and finally information about the world of work obtained from the employment service and other sources, and, to transmit these data through the counseling process to the client in such a way that they are able to arrive at a vocational plan which is acceptable to both the client and the counselor, and which promises the client the best possible chance of achieving job satisfaction and vocational success. (33).

Lofquist provided the following operational definition:

> Vocational counseling is a continuous learning process involving interaction in a nonauthoritarian fashion, between two individuals whose problem solving efforts are oriented toward vocational planning. The professional vocational counselor and the counselee with a problem are concerned not only with the solution of the immediate problem, but also with planning new techniques for meeting future

problems. While the counselee has need for anxiety reduction concerning his vocational problem or set of problems, psychopathology is not involved and the counselee is capable of learning new attitudes and appraising vocational realities with reference to his unique assets and liabilities, without first requiring a major restructuring of his personality. Psychotherapy may result in some measure; but vocational planning, not psychotherapy, is the primary orientation of the process. The vocational counselor serves in this learning process as the reinforcing agency, facilitator of counselee activity, resource person, and expert on the techniques for discovering additional data relevant to the vocational planning. A counselor also learns continuously in the process, but keeps his need-satisfaction demands at a level subservient to those of the counselee. (30)

In a manual written for rehabilitation counselors published by the Department of Health, Education and Welfare, McGowan and Porter have described the functions of the vocational rehabilitation counselor as follows:

> The major functions of the counselor require assuming responsibility for the evaluation of the client, planning with the individual from the initial counseling interview and diagnostic services to the establishment of eligibility, planning and arranging for supervision of services, and being responsible for final job adjustment. Also included in his job is the responsibility for effective management of his caseload, case records, correspondence, reports, and workflow.
>
> An essential characteristic which differentiates the work of the vocational rehabilitation counselor from that of other counseling specialists is the fact that the rehabilitation counselor's final aim is to bring about the vocational rehabilitation of the handicapped individual. (33)

Models of the Counselor Role

At least two models of the counselor role are discernible in current rehabilitation literature. They are the "coordinator" model and the "counselor" model. Detailed discussions of the counselor's role in terms of these models are found in articles by Patterson (43), Cottle (9), Hamilton (19), Johnson (24), Hall and Warren (18), and Miller, Garrett and Stewart (40). Proponents of the "coordinator" model view the counselor's function as that of an interdisciplinary worker who coordinates services for the client. Under this model the counselor's duties involve the coordination of a variety of services, i.e., interviewing, evaluating, maintaining relationships with a number of agencies, assessing resources, arranging for medical services, providing for placement of any number of additional services which might be required in order to complete successful rehabilitation of the client. Those who hold to the "counselor" model see the counselor's role as primarily that of counseling, and they stress the importance of personal and vocational counseling, providing information and maintaining a warm personal relationship in assisting the client to become self-directing and economically self-sustaining.

It is clear that what the counselor actually does on the job will vary from one setting to another, i.e., state agency, school, hospital, or rehabilitation center. McLaughlin discussed the changing roles of the rehabilitation counselor in terms of the many new settings in which the counselors are employed:

> In some of these settings it is expected that the counselor will operate more as a therapist, helping in a therapeutic way through development and interpretation of the necessary information. It is expected that the counselor will spend consdierable time and effort in working through the information that has been secured with the client. The vocational aspect of the rehabilitation process may be submerged in such a case for a long period of time.
>
> In still another setting we find that the rehabilitation counselor is working in a medical setting and is supported by many services available to him from other staff members—the social worker, psychologist, occupational therapist, and vocational evaluator. In a situation like this it may be well that the counselor spends a considerable amount of time in coordinating the services that are required for an individual. Here he may be thought of not so much as a vocational counselor developing the building of a plan for the individual, but more as a person who approves the plan and sees that the services are available when needed. (34).

COORDINATING REHABILITATION AND SPECIAL EDUCATION SERVICES

Effective programming for the mentally retarded has presented special problems for both education and rehabilitation personnel (50). Teachers and rehabilitation counselors have long been confronted with critical issues in mental retardation, whether dealing with children or adults in public schools, institutions, or community programs. In schools where special classes were not available, the regular classroom teacher often felt unqualified to deal with the mentally retarded or felt that the curriculum was inappropriate. Where special classes or special schools have been available, there have been issues raised concerning relevance of the curriculum to the learning problems of an individual child or the practicality of grouping children in such a way that they might be restricted from many school activities. Other problems which cut across different educational settings and program levels have been: 1) bridging the gap between programs in institutions and public school programs, 2) developing sequential and uninterrupted programs which extend from early school years through secondary levels in the public schools, 3) preparing sufficient numbers of teachers who are competent to work with a wide range of ability levels, particularly where special classes are not available, i.e., sparsely populated areas and rural communities, and 4) effecting and maintaining relationships with community or state agencies which can provide supportive services. Rehabilitation counselors have faced similar problems. In fact, the above issues in education and in training the mentally retarded are shared by both education and rehabilitation since the continuum of service which extends from preschool levels through adulthood involves the skills of both education and rehabilitation personnel.

The role of special education in the habilitation of the mentally retarded has been discussed by Shane (49). He suggests that the heart of modern philosophies of educating the mentally retarded is occupational education and that the curriculum for the retarded must be planned by special education teachers at all levels—primary, intermediate, and secondary; that educational programs for the retarded must be coordinated at all levels if children and adolescents are to develop the skills, and attitudes they will need as adults. He emphasizes the need to direct all public school preparation toward post school activities and points out that the instructional program cannot accomplish this end unless attention is given to factors such as: 1) making the child feel successful, 2) providing guidance toward realistic goals, 3) comprehensively studying each individual child, 4) emphasizing communication skills, and 5) providing concrete experiences aimed toward building an understanding of the community.

Allen and Cross (1) have stressed the importance of work-study for the retarded at elementary school levels and have suggested that, even at primary levels, educable mentally retarded chidren, through good instructional planning, can become acquainted with the work of their parents and others in the neighborhoods in which they live. At more advanced levels, i.e., intermediate programs, they can become aware of the varieties of work opportunities which are potentially available to them. Certainly, work-study programs at the secondary level, where special education and rehabilitation personnel are most actively involved in cooperative planning, could be greatly enhanced if children from the elementary levels had already begun to differentiate areas of interest in community activities and become acquainted with the "world of work." Other important factors in job success, such as good attitudes, favorable personality, and appearance, and acceptable social behavior relate to the goals of both education and rehabilitation in serving the retarded. McColl (32) has cited classroom routine and social behavior as having implications for vocational training and suggests that it is important to "model" these experiences as closely as possible to real jobs in which the adult might be involved.

Cooperative arrangements involving special education and vocational rehabilitation services are most clearly visible in work-study programs at the secondary level. In discussing various aspects of work-experience programs, Kokaska (28) has noted that cooperative arrangements appear to have benefited all parties concerned because of the program innovations and improved attitudes resulting from the interaction of special education, rehabilitation, and business personnel.

Another successful type of cooperative program consists of special rehabilitation units operating in conjunction with public schools or communities. The purpose of such units is to obtain samples of the student's work prior to the initiation of actual skills training or placement in the community for employment experience. In schools, students may be referred to the units for assessment when they are ready to leave school or in some cases when they are not functioning effectively in the school program. These units frequently focus on the sampling of mechanical, manipulative, service or clerical skills, and are staffed by persons with rehabilitation and education experience.

In some locales, special education personnel have been assigned to work in community rehabilitation units which serve adolescents and adults. In others, vocational rehabilitation counselors are assigned full-time to work with large special education programs. Both types of arrangements have been successful.

The late Mary Switzer expressed the optimism of educators and rehabilitation specialists alike when she stated:

> No matter what the format of these cooperative programs may be —whether they rely on workshops or on-the-job training—their great value has been proven. Necessary services can now be provided before the disabled teenager becomes discouraged and drops out of school unprepared to cope effectively with life's demands. The fact that a continuum of educational and rehabilitation services

may now be provided to the school age retarded means new hope and new promise for the retarded adults of the future (50).

BIBLIOGRAPHY

1. Allen, A. A., and J. L. Cross, "Work Study for the Retarded—the Elementary School Years," *Education and Training of the Mentally Retarded,* 2:7, 1967.
2. Ashlock, P., and A. Stevens, *Education Therapy in the Elementary Schools,* Springfield: Charles C Thomas, 1966.
3. Baldwin, W. K., "The Educable Mentally Retarded Child in the Regular Grades," *Exceptional Children,* 25:106, 1958.
4. Cain, L., "Special Education Moves Ahead: A Comment on the Education of Teachers," *Exceptional Children,* 30:211, 1964.
5. California State Department of Education, *California's Development Center for Handicapped Minors Program,* June, 1968.
6. Charles, D. C., "Longitudinal Follow-up Studies of Community Adjustment," *New Vocational Pathways for the Mentally Retarded,* Washington, D.C.: American Personnel and Guidance Association, 1966.
7. Cohen, J. S., R. J. Gregory, and J. W. Pelosi, *Vocational Rehabilitation and the Socially Disabled,* Syracuse: Syracuse University Press, 1966.
8. Connors, F., "Excellence in Special Education," *Exceptional Children,* 30:206, 1964.
9. Cottle, W. C., "Personal Characteristics of Counselors: Review of the Literature," *Pers. Guid. J.,* 31:445, 1953.
10. Descoeudres, A., *The Education of Mentally Defective Children,* trans. from the Second French Edition by Ernest F. Row, Boston: D. C. Heath and Company, 1928.
11. DiMichael, S., "The Current Scene," *Vocational Rehabilitation of the Disabled,* by David Malikin and Herbert Rusalem, New York: New York University Press, 1969.
12. DiMichael, S. G., "Historical Development of Rehabilitation for the Mentally Retarded," *J. of Rehab.,* November-December, 1962.
13. DiMichael, S. G., *Preparation of Mentally Retarded Youth for Gainful Employment,* Department of Health, Education and Welfare, Bulletin, 1959, No. 28, (Washington, D.C.: Government Printing Office, 1959).
14. Dunn, L. M., *Exceptional Children in the Schools,* New York: Holt, Rinehart, and Winston, Inc., 1963.
15. Farber, B., *Mental Retardation: Its Social Context and Social Consequences,* New York: Houghton Mifflin Company, 1968.
16. Fraenkel, W. A., "Present Status of Rehabilitation for the Mentally Retarded," *J. of Rehab.,* November-December, 1962.
17. Goldstein, H., "Methodological Problems in Research in the Educational Programs for the Treatment and Habilitation of the Mentally Retarded," *Amer. J. of Ment. Def.,* 64:341, 1959.
18. Hall, J. H., and S. H. Warren, *Rehabilitation Counselor Preparation,* Washington, D.C.: National Rehabilitation Association, National Vocational Guidance Association, 1956.
19. Hamilton, K. W., *Counseling the Handicapped in the Rehabilitation Process,* New York: Ronald Press, 1950.
20. Heber, R. F., "A Manual on Terminology and Classification in Mental Retardation," *Amer. J. of Ment. Def.,* 64, Monogr. Suppl., 1959, (Rev. ed., 1961).
21. Hensley, G., "Therapeutic Teachers of Exceptional Children," *Educ. Therapy,* Editors Bernie Straub and Jerome Hellmuth, Special Child Publications, 1966.
22. Johnson, G. O., "A Study of Social Position of Mentally Handicapped Children in the Regular Grades," *Amer. J. of Ment. Def.,* 55:60, 1950.

23. Johnson, G. O., and M. J. Steigman, "Forum: Paradox in Special Education, A Reply," G. O. Johnson, *Except. Child,* 31:67, 1964.
24. Johnson, L. T., "The Counselor as Others See Him," in C. H. Patterson (Ed.), *Readings in Rehabilitation Counseling,* Champaign, Illinois: Stikes Publishing Company, 1960.
25. Kidd, J. W., T. J. Cross, and J. L. Higginbotham, "The World of Work for the Educable Mentally Retarded," *Except. Child,* 33:648, 1967.
26. Kirk, S. A., "Research in Education," *Ment. Retard.* Editors II. A. Stevens and R. Heber, Chicago: University of Chicago Press, 1964.
27. Kirk, S. A. and G. Johnson, *Educating the Retarded Child,* New York: Houghton Mifflin Company, 1951.
28. Kokaska, C. J., "Secondary Education for the Retarded: A Brief Historical Review," *Education and Training of the Mentally Retarded,* 3:17, 1968.
29. Lance, W., "School Programs for the Trainable Mentally Retarded," *Education and Training of the Mentally Retarded,* 3:3, 1968.
30. Lofquist, L. H., "An Operational Definition of Rehabilitation Counseling," *J. of Rehab.,* 25:7, 1959.
31. Lord, F. E. and R. M. Isenberg, *Cooperative Programs in Special Education,* Council for Exceptional Children and Department of Rural Education, National Education Association, 1964.
32. McColl, D., "Vocation Preparation of the Mentally Retarded at the Primary Class Level," *Education and Training of the Mentally Retarded,* 2:56, 1967.
33. McGowan, J. F., and T. L. Porter, *An Introduction to the Vocational Rehabilitation Process, A Training Manual,* U.S. Government Printing Office, July, 1967.
34. McLaughlin, P., "The New Roles of the Rehabilitation Counselor," *Rehabilitation Manpower in the West,* G. Hensley and D. Buck (eds.), Western Interstate Commission for Higher Education, 1968.
35. Mackie, R. P., "Spotlighting Advances in Special Education," *Except. Children,* 32:77, 1965.
36. Mackie, R. P., and L. M. Dunn, "College and University Programs for the Preparation of Teachers of Exceptional Children," *U.S. Office of Education Bulletin,* 1954, No. 13.
37. Mackie, R. P., L. M. Dunn, and L. Cain, "Professional Preparation for Teachers of Exceptional Children: An Overview," *U.S. Department of Health, Education, and Welfare Bulletin,* 1959, No. 6.
38. Mackie, R., P. P. Hunter, and M. A. Nauber, *College and University Programs for the Preparation of Teachers of Exceptional Children,* Washington, D.C.: Office of Education, 1968.
39. Mackie, R. P., and P. P. Robbins, "Exceptional Children in Local Public Schools," *School Life,* 43:15, 1960.
40. Miller, L. M., J. F. Garrett, and N. Stewart, "Opportunity: Rehabilitation Counseling," *Pers. Guid. J.,* Vol. 33, 1955.
41. Montessori, M., *Montessori Method,* trans. by Anne E. George, New York: Frederick A. Stokes Company, 1912.
42. Neuhaus, E. C., "Training the Mentally Retarded for Competitive Employment," *Except. Child.,* 33:625, 1967.
43. Patterson, C. H., "Counselor or Coordinator," *J. of Rehab.,* 23:13, 1957.
44. President's Committee on Mental Retardation, *A Proposed Program for National Action to Combat Mental Retardation,* Washington, D.C.: Government Printing Office, October, 1962.
45. Rhodes, W. C., "Preface," *Educational Therapy,* Bernie Straub and Jerome Hellmuth, (Eds.), Seattle: Special Child Publications, 1966.

46. Robinson, H. B., and N. M. Robinson, *The Mentally Retarded Child,* New York: McGraw-Hill, 1965.
47. Rusalem, H., "The Special Teacher on the Interdisciplinary Team," *Except. Child.,* 26:180, 1959.
48. Seguin, E., *Idiocy: and Its Treatment by the Physiological Method,* Albany, New York: Brandow Printing Company, 1866. Reprinted, New York: Teachers College, Columbia University, 1907.
49. Shane, D. G., "The Role of Special Education in the Habilitation of the Mentally Retarded," *Education and Training of the Mentally Retarded,* 2:17, 1967.
50. Switzer, M. E., "The Coordination of Vocational Rehabilitation and Special Education Services for the Mentally Retarded," *Education and Training of the Mentally Retarded,* 1:155, 1966.
51. Tizard, J., "Longitudinal and Follow-Up Studies," In A. Clarke and A. D. B. Clarke, (Eds.), *Mental Deficiency: The Changing Outlook,* New York: 1958:442.
52. Wolfensberger, W., "Vocational Preparation and Occupation," Alfred A. Baumeister, (Ed.), *Mental Retardation Appraisal, Education, Rehabilitation,* Chicago: Aldine Publishing Company, 1967.

CHAPTER 21

The Contribution of the Nursery School

by EDWARD L. LaCROSSE, Ed.D.

Historically, mental retardation has been viewed as a static, unchanging, incurable condition. Although there were a few brilliant thinkers and gifted practitioners who envisioned the potential benefit to be derived from training and treatment for the retarded, the idea "once retarded always retarded" led over the years to the general practice of providing humane treatment with little hope that the afflicted individuals could ever participate in the competitive world of employment and civic responsibility. During the past several years, however, an increasing amount of evidence has been accrued which indicates that most retarded individuals not only can but do participate in the competitive world of employment and civic responsibility; still there are many who have been deprived of this opportunity because of our failure to institute necessary programs early in the child's life.

The young child typically passes through several developmental stages which more or less spontaneously precipitate certain behaviors and activities. The norms concerning these developmental stages have been catalogued by Gesell and his associates (8). The earliest of these programmed behaviors often appear "on schedule" even when one would expect them to be missing in a particular child. For example, the deaf child will babble at the designated time, despite his handicap. These responses are thought to be precursors of later behavior, which provide the raw material on which the desired responses to particular stimuli can be based. If for any reason these behaviors are not "fixed" or established when presented, they tend to disappear. A child who is deprived of the experiences necessary to retain the important and necessary responses (for whatever reason), will usually not learn what is expected of him. The child who cannot hear the pre-speech sounds he makes will

331

soon stop making those noises. The child whose parent does not reward or reinforce his important utterances will not learn to attach meaning to his sounds. Because of the critical nature of those early, vulnerable years, it is important that the educational process begin soon enough that the desired behaviors can be rewarded as they are evoked. Despite the limited potential of retarded children, they also need this early educational stimulation.

This paper will not concern itself with the types of general education services needed for children before school, but will focus on the four major areas in which the nursery school can contribute to the development of the retarded child. These are: 1) diagnosis, 2) development of skills needed in school, 3) parent-child relationships, and 4) prevention.

DIAGNOSIS

The use of a number (IQ) to describe the intellectual functioning of an individual fails to explain *how* that individual earned his score. A child with a low IQ may have very little "scatter" among the subtest scores. Another child may obtain the same IQ, yet the subtests may reflect wide variation in patterning. It is always important to look at more than the IQ score from a test; sometimes the weak areas can be remediated, and the strengths can provide the basis for greater emphasis. What is of importance to us is that the factors causing weaknesses might be strengthened if they are identified. The identification cannot be based on the IQ alone.

A young retarded child might have several specific disabilities, resulting in inappropriate behavior. Despite the peculiarity of his behavior, he might not be observed to have these disabilities if he remains at home. There may be no opportunity for comparison with other children of the same age. The parents might not be aware of what is normal at various ages. The child's limitations might not be apparent in the familiar surroundings of his home. When the young child comes to the nursery school, however, he is observed in a different light. He is subjected to comparisons with other children his own age. He is also asked to conform to a new set of standards. His abilities and disabilities now come into much sharper focus.

The role of the nursery teacher is one of a trained observer. Often a differential diagnosis and appropriate referral is made possible because of her observations. Dybwad and LaCrosse (5) report the case of a girl attending a pre-school class for mentally retarded children:

She was referred as being mentally retarded, emotionally disturbed, with organic brain damage. The teacher observed that her apparent disorganized behavior seemed to follow a definite pattern. In the classroom she constantly ran to the opposite side of the room with apparent eagerness, but always seemed to bump into things there, and, after a moment, rapidly repeated the process in the opposite direction.

It seemed to the teacher that the child behaved as if she could see clearly at a distance, but was confused by what was close to her. Referral to an ophthalmologist was suggested and a visual distortion was discovered. Once this was alleviated, the child's "obnoxious" behavior ceased. She could fully participate in the regular nursery school activities and moved on to elementary school where she is doing satisfactory work.

Another child attending a college demonstration class was sent home ill on several occasions. When he arrived at home the mother reported he seemed "perfectly all right." The neurologist under whose care this child was placed saw him several times and could see no change. Yet at school he would become ill each afternoon. He tilted his head to one side and let his tongue hang from his mouth. Often he would vomit, complain of headaches, and would curl up on the floor and whine. The teacher carefully recorded his behavior for a week and he was returned to the hospital where the teacher's observations had been sent. On the basis of these observations the neurologist was able to determine that the child was having sub-clinical seizures and with proper adjustment of his medication, the "illness" disappeared within two days.

DEVELOPMENT OF SKILLS NEEDED IN SCHOOL

The retarded individual is handicapped in two ways. First, he is limited by his lack of experience which has resulted from retardation and his being protected from activities that normal children ordinarily enjoy. Secondly, he is handicapped by his inability to take advantage of the everyday experiences that normal children utilize in their development. Unless we develop special programs designed to provide compensatory opportunities for the retarded, they will be doubly handicapped. The nursery school can provide some of these enriching opportunities.

A nursery school can also encourage the child to enter into group activities at an age when his differences are not so accentuated and also at a time when society is more willing to accept his differences. This group experience provides him with the opportunity to acclimate himself gradually to the group situation; under these circumstances, he does not have to perform all the social graces that are ordinarily demanded of school-age children. Providing this type of activity for the individual can often break the chain of events which might otherwise lead him to function at a lower intellectual level. Early group activities can also help the child think of himself as a success rather than a failure.

The most favorable type of nursery-school setting occurs when a few retarded children attend a regular nursery for non-retarded children. It may be necessary for some children to attend a special nursery school. In both circumstances, the nursery school can provide the opportunity for the child to develop self-respect, independence and faith and respect for authority. It can also offer an opportunity for him to enjoy affection and friendship, to be challenged and yet secure, to learn about nature, to experiment with creative materials, to gain values and appreciation, to have fun, and, if possible, to prepare him for further special education.

PARENT-CHILD RELATIONSHIPS

The nursery school should provide assistance to the retarded child in relationships with his parents. If he is taken out of the home for part of the day, his relationship with his mother will probably be improved because she has been relieved for a few hours. Also in the nursery school, the teacher has the opportunity to allow the child the time he needs to put on his own coat, to tie his own shoe, etc., whereas in the home situation, the mother may be performing these tasks for the child because it is easier to do so than to teach the child to perform. Each task the child learns to perform improves the parent-child relationship. If the retarded child becomes less dependent, less fearful, and less burdensome, his parents will be more able to enjoy him as a person.

Furthermore, the nursery school can bring the parents of retarded children together. Learning that other people have the same problems helps to "lighten the load" for parents. As they visit the nursery school and have a chance to share problems with other parents, events seem to come into better focus.

In an unpublished Master's Thesis, Drexler and Grosshandler (4) reported that mothers participating in a program for pre-school deaf children learned two things: 1) that they were not alone, and 2) that their children could learn. This change in attitude had a profound effect on the way they handled their children, and possibly will prove to be the most important factor in the future education of these children.

PREVENTION

With proper treatment some potential cases of mental retardation can be prevented. The medical advances in the prevention of retardation have been widely publicized, such as the dietetic treatment for phenylketonuric children; nevertheless, the medical breakthroughs relate to only a few clinical causes of intellectual deficits. The hope for more general prevention lies in other areas. Thirty years ago, for example, Skeels and his associates conducted two important experiments which suggested that early interaction could affect the lives of retarded or deprived youngsters. The first, "The Study of the Effect of Differential Stimulation on Mentally Retarded Children" (11), included 25 children, 13 experimental and 12 control. The experimental group ranged in IQ from 35 to 89. These children spent from 6 to 52 months as house guests at the State School for the Mentally Retarded. The control had IQ's within the normal range and they remained at the orphanage. The experimental group showed an increase of from 7 to 58 IQ points, with a mean gain of 28 points. The control group showed a loss of from 8 to 45 IQ points, with a mean loss of 26 points. With the exception of one child who scored two IQ points higher on the second test, none of the control group children increased in IQ. Ten of the 12 control group children lost 15 or more IQ points. The difference was attributed to the individualized care received by the "house guests." Eleven of the 13 children in the experimental group were subsequently placed in adoptive homes, one remained in the school for feeble-minded and one was returned to the orphanage, although continued retardation made adoptive placement inadvisable. The 11 children placed in adoptive homes were re-examined approximately two and one-half years following the close of the experimental period. Their mean IQ was 101, with no child scoring an IQ below 90. Changes in IQ following the end of the experimental period ranged from plus 16 points to minus five points. With the exception of one child, the changes were in the direction of increases in IQ. The greatest gain (16 points) was made by a child placed in a superior adoptive home, whereas the child showing a loss was in a home considered far below the average of the group. Of the 12 control children, only one child was placed in an adoptive home, and that a marginal one. Six, at later stages, were stransferred to the school for feebleminded, not as "house guests" but as residents. Deterioration was so marked that it seemed improbable that placement outside an institution could be attained.

A thirty-year follow-up of the 25 youngsters showed that the 13 children in the experimental group were self-supporting, and none were wards of any institutions—public or private. Two of the children in the experimental group, one boy and one girl, earlier spent some time in a state correctional school.

At the time of the interviews, five of the twelve control group children had continued to be wards of state institutions, four at a state institution for the retarded and one in a state hospital for the mentally ill. A sixth child was committed in infancy to the state orphanage and was later transferred to a state institution for the mentally retarded where she resided until her death at 15 years of age. Of the four who were wards of the state institution for the mentally retarded, two were in residence at the institution, and one was out on a trial visit with his grandmother; another was on a protected vocational training placement.

Skeels conducted another study which related to the effects of a pre-school educational program on children living in a large orphanage (11). As in the prior investigation, an experimental group and a control group were established. The children were matched for age, IQ, MA, sex, nutritional status, physical condition and length of residence in the orphanage. Except for the experiences of the experimental group in the nursery school, both groups of children were treated the same. Following a three-year research period, the experimental group showed an average increase of about five IQ points; the control group declined about five points.

The studies of Kirk (9) and Fouracre (7) indicate quite clearly that young children identified as retarded can benefit from preschool experience. In both studies, children were discovered who appeared to be retarded, but later developed normal potential. The difficulty in identifying young children for these studies suggests that some of the children later identified as retarded (using the IQ as a criterion) in the public schools may not test at this level during their preschool years.

Preliminary reports of the Institute of Developmental Studies at the New York Medical College (2) suggest that not only can we *increase* the IQ's of deprived children through linguistic stimulation in nursery school, but also the IQ's of these children begin to drop during this period if they are not given this experience. It is evident that the influences which retard intellectual development can often be inhibited at the early, critical stage of development. Furthermore, the youngsters from the most deprived backgrounds tend to make the greatest progress although the efforts to correct retardation after age seven do not appear promising.

During recent years, a great deal of interest has developed regarding early childhood education for the handicapped. In 1968, the Handicapped Children's Early Education Assistance Act (PL 90538) was passed, which authorized the establishment and operation of model preschool and early education programs designed to develop and demonstrate effective approaches in assisting handicapped children during the early years. A number of model projects have been carried on under the provisions of this act, including home-based, public school, private agency, hospital, multi-agency, combination designs, and coordinated programs with regular nursery schools. Significant among the latter provisions is the inclusion of handicapped children in Head Start programs, and in 1972 the Congress amended the Economic Opportunity Act (PL 92424) to require that at least 10% of the enrollment in Head Start consist of children who were handicapped and required special services.

In the flurry of activities relating to legislation on special education, an increasing number of states are incorporating early childhood education as a part of the mandate for the handicapped. Included in these programs is the lowering of the age for eligibility for special education programs to birth, and many of the projects initiated under the Handicapped Children's Early Education Assistance Act are involved in the development of educational programs designed specifically for infancy.

SUMMARY

The concept that children should not participate in group activities until three years of age should be restudied, particularly with reference to the mentally retarded. Not only does the intellectually handicapped child profit educationally and emotionally from early activities, but the parent-child relationship is likely to be improved as well.

In addition to the ancillary services required by the young retarded child, it is important for formalized instruction to begin at an earlier age for the mentally retarded and high risk children, if they are to develop to their fullest potential.

Although there is an abundance of evidence of the positive contribution that the nursery school can make to the overall development of the retarded child, the organized study of the results of early intervention with retarded children and with their parents has indicated that not all programs are beneficial. A great deal of additional study is needed to determine what type of intervention at what age is most essential for the optimal development of the individual.

BIBLIOGRAPHY

1. Bacon, H., "Pre-School Nursery Classes," Paper presented at the First Annual Convention of the Mass. Assoc. for Retarded Children, Inc., 1956.
2. Deutsch, M., "Facilitating Development in the Pre-School Child: Social and Psychological Perspectives," *Merrill-Palmer Quarterly*, July, 1964.
3. DeValck, I., "The Pre-School Child Goes to School—A Special Kindergarten Program in the Netherlands," *International Child Welfare Review*, 19:4, 1964.
4. Drexler, G. and J. Grosshandler, *An Evaluation of the Newark State College Preschool Program for the Deaf: Its Effects on the Lipreading Comprehension and Vocalization of the Children and on Mental Attitudes,* unpublished masters thesis, Newark State College, 1968.
5. Dybwad, G. and E. LaCrosse, "Early Childhood Education Is Essential to Handicapped Children," *The Journal of Nursery Education,* 18:2, January, 1963.
6. Dybwad, G., H. Holadnak, E. LaCrosse, and A. Menefee, *A Report on Mental Retardation in Montreal,* Montreal: The Miriam Home for Exceptional Children, 1963.
7. Fouracre, M., F. Connor and I. I. Goldberg, *The Effects of a Pre-School Program Upon Young Educable Mentally Retarded Children,* Vol. I: The Experimental Pre-School Curriculum, New York: Columbia University Press, 1963.
8. Gesell, A., H. M. Halverson, H. Thompson, F. L. Ilg, B. M. Castner, L. B. Ames and C. S. Amatruda, *The First Five Years of Life, A Guide to the Study of the Preschool Child,* New York: Harper, 1940
9. Kirk, S. A., *Early Education of the Mentally Retarded: An Experimental Study,* Urbana: University of Illinois Press, 1958.
10. LaCrosse, E., "Schooling for the Mentally Retarded Child," *International Child Welfare Review,* 19:4, 1965.
11. Skeels, H. M., "Headstart on Headstart: A Thirty Year Evaluation," *Fifth Annual Distinguished Lectures in Special Education,* School of Education, University of Southern California, 1966.

CHAPTER 22

Utilization of Learning Principles in Retardation

by C. EDWARD MEYERS, Ph.D.
and DONALD L. MacMILLAN, Ed.D.

While the preceding chapters have been addressed to general problems of planning and operating educational programs for the retarded, the present identifies several specific learning principles which seem to be useful in attacking learning problems. Unlike the gifted learner, who to a considerable extent is self-educable, the retarded requires a wide range of sophisticated teaching strategies. These are not easy to prescribe for the individual, for the "mentally retarded" vary widely in learning abilities and deficits. Furthermore, the demands made on the individual by formal education and informal societal expectations will vary significantly with geographical location, age, and ethnic or economic status of the family. To complicate the matter, the theories of learning and instruction which might underlie practice are in disagreement with one another, particularly as applied to the retarded. It is nevertheless possible to extract many clearly useful applications of worthy principles from these theories for use in the guidance of learning.

DEFINITION OF LEARNING

Learning can be defined as a more or less *permanent behavior change due to experience.* Two features of this definition must be emphasized. *First,* the definition excludes behavior changes due to growth of tissues, to fatigue, aging, or drugs. While it is not always possible in children to distinguish the behavioral effects of growth from those of experience, we must make this distinction whenever possible because it affects practice. Waiting for a child to "outgrow" a disturbing or maladaptive behavior pattern will multiply the difficulty if the behavior can be modified easily by appropriate remedial training. Contrariwise, vigorous attempts to educate a child beyond his present biological limits will probably meet with failure.

Second, while the simplest definition of learning attributes the change to formal practice, it is necessary to point out that much learning occurs outside of formal educational settings, and a great deal of what is learned is incidental, whether the setting is formal or casual. Even in a carefully designed learning situation, the amount of incidental experience may outweigh that of carefully controlled teaching, either at home or in school. This daily and repetitious set of experiences can frequently bring about learning of unintended and unwanted behavior patterns. In many cases, careful examination of the home or school situation may indicate that the parent or teacher is unintentionally reinforcing a behavior which he or she deplores. This is particularly true in cases of retarded children where there is a tendency to excuse a variety of childish, undesirable behavior traits as part of the retardation syndrome; in fact, they may be maintained by the tolerant sympathy with which each new occurrence is greeted. Furthermore, teachers and attendants may perceive their role in working with the retarded as one which is supportive and will put up with inappropriate behavior, thereby strengthening this behavior in the belief that it is to be expected.

A sufficient definition of learning must also include more than the competencies of the traditional academic variety. The child also acquires hopes, attitudes, anxieties, skills, ideals, and prejudices through experience, with or without the purposive instruction of his elders. Some of these acquisitions may be made through very subtle experiences and at any early age.

Incidental learning, by definition, requires no formal planning. Since all formal education builds on the fund of experiences assimilated by the child, some assumptions are implied in any formal teaching plan. We cannot take for granted the same degree of incidental learning in the mentally retarded as in a normal child. Not only do many retarded children show marked deficiencies in making generalizations from their casual experiences, but they also demonstrate a lower propensity to attend to relevant stimuli. This deficiency can frequently be seen in such things as understanding simple comparisons of size, texture and weight, or in more subtle types of social behaviors such as the appropriate knowledge and observation of rules, regulations and customs expected in his cultural surroundings and for his specific age-period.

An important distinction is to be made between learning and performance. One must rely on actual behavior changes which can be observed and measured in order to infer that learning has occurred. However, if a child does not emit the behavior (i.e., he does not perform) one cannot necessarily conclude that the child has not learned. A number of factors (e.g., motivation) may account for his unwillingness to demonstrate what he has learned. Several authors (9, 12) have made this distinction and note that performance levels for the retarded are only partial indicators of the child's capacity. By manipulating certain variables (e.g., incentive), the performance level can be shown to improve immediately (27), indicating the discrepancy between learning and performance under original incentive conditions.

Finally, a useful definition of learning must acknowledge that much of child-rearing in our culture involves "negative" learning, the avoiding of certain actions. From the time the infant first learns to arrest his ongoing movement when mother says "NO," through learning not to speak out without being recognized, not to run in front of cars, or not to play with matches, he is faced with a confusing variety of negations. The perplexing character of these negations arises from the lack of clarity regarding the limits of accepted activity. From the view of the retarded child, this absence of clear distinctions may be overwhelming. He may be treated with what amounts to an unintentional inconsistency in guidance.

FUNDAMENTAL GROUPS OF LEARNING THEORIES

This chapter could not possibly review all the serious positions on the nature of learning, but rather is devoted to a few with apparent applications to the rearing and education of the retarded. In the United States, the theories group themselves into two fundamental positions, the *SR*, or stimulus-response, and the *cognitive*. The former are also labeled behaviorist, association or bond theories; the cognitive include various movements such as gestalt, organismic, self, field, and the like. SR theories are almost exclusively concerned with learning, for the fundamental SR postulate is that most significant behavior change is due to the organism's reaction to environmental cues. Such a position logically implies that behavior development should not be abandoned to incidental experiences but should from early life be purposefully guided by control of stimulus and response contingencies. The SR position also is marked by having little place for concepts of mind, insight, understanding and the like, trusting to advance the science of learning and the art of teaching by orderly observation of response changes together with the stimuli controlling them.

The cognitive theories reject none of the above except the emphasis. First, they metaphysically infer an understanding, a storehouse and reoganizer of experience capable of transforming the old experience into new competencies for meeting present tasks. This they call "mind" or "intelligence." Secondly, the cognitive position infers a growth process in the functioning capabilities of this organizer or mind. These changes come through experiences-in-time, but are not much affected by specialized training.

Current theories differ in the emphasis they put on each factor or upon one or another facet of the learning process itself. Thus, a theory seemingly appropriate to the training of self-care functions in the severely retarded might seem inappropriate to the learning of social studies in the mildly retarded. The expectation that some theorists and practitioners will blend and modify the basic positions of the SR and cognitive is, of course, well justified, as will be seen later.

OPERANT BEHAVIORISM

Over the past two decades there has been a vigorous surge of activity in the field of mental retardation by those using an approach called operant conditioning, applied behavior analysis, descriptive behaviorism, or other similar names. The most extensive attempt of explaining mental retardation in terms of "functional analysis" can be found in a chapter by Bijou (8). Initiated by Skinner (50), this position was first developed with the manipulation and shaping of behavior in laboratory animals and later was extended to school learning. One of its earliest applications in the field of education was in the development of auto-instructional techniques and teaching machines (28); however its more current applications to the training of the retarded have shown considerable success heretofore thought impossible.

It is first necessary to understand the chief article of faith. Operant theory is satisfied with a straightforward descriptive relationship between responses (i.e., behavior of the retarded individual) and the stimuli (i.e., environmental events) which exert control over them. It is not concerned with nervous system constructs or vital need states linking stimuli to responses, nor with any form of intervening variable, certainly not "mind." It attempts to describe in behavioral terms what behavior was emitted and what happened as a consequence rather than making reference to the internal state of the subject. For example, rather than inferring that a subject is "hungry" the behaviorist would objectively describe that the subject had been "deprived of food for 12 hours." Thus, this theory limits itself to what is objectively known about the learner. Concepts of need, purpose, interest, etc. are similar variables which the behaviorist does not purport to measure.

Description of Behavior Modification

A learner's response is or is not strengthened depending on its consequences. A response produces a consequence, that is, a condition tending to increase or decrease the probability that the response will occur again. Any consequence of a response which increases its likelihood is said to be reinforcing. Thus, if one wishes to strengthen a particular response, one must structure the situation to provide a consequence that is reinforcing to that individual. In other words, the presentation of a stimulus that is desired by the subject will increase the probability of that same response—it is *positively reinforced*. By the same logic, a consequence may be that an individual can terminate a noxious state (e.g., hunger) by responding in a way which leads to the *withdrawal* of the aversive state or stimulus—it is *negatively reinforcing*. Note that in the above cases, both the presentation of a desired consequence and the withdrawal of an aversive stimulus serve to strengthen the behavior on which they are made contingent—they are both reinforcing.

Consequences can also serve to weaken (or make less probable) behaviors that they follow. These kinds of consequences exist when the behavior one wishes to weaken is followed with: (a) a neutral stimulus—one that is neither desired by the subject nor aversive to the subject; (b) an aversive stimulus—one the subject attempts to avoid; or (c) the withdrawal of a desired stimulus—as when one is deprived of his driver's license for speeding. This last form of control is known as "time-out" in laboratory and clinical settings in which behavior modification is practiced with children, depriving the child of the opportunity to earn his positive reinforcers by removing him from the reward situation until his behavior improves. The last two types of consequences (b and c) are forms of punishment, which by definition weaken the behavior with which they are associated.

The operant theorist points to two critical features of such response modification. First, the situation must be such as to provide that the responses to be modified will occur; second, the situation must provide consequences for the responses made. The first are the situation cues. They exert control over the responses in the sense that they set the occasion: time of day, fatigue, introduction of competition, or preholiday excitement. These affect the likelihood that certain behaviors will occur or that certain others which one does not want to reinforce will occur instead. The second are the consequences—the reinforcers, punishments, or neutral consequences. The key to the effective application of behavior modification is the skill with which the teacher or parent controls the contingencies between responses and stimuli. By contingencies we mean the conditions under which certain responses are reinforced or punished and others are not selected for reinforcement. The parent or teacher wants to be certain to "consequate" behaviors to be either strengthened or weakened, and to avoid inadvertently strengthening behaviors they want to weaken. ("Consequate" has become the general word in behavior modification for any planned consequence, whether reinforcement, non-reinforcement, or punishment, made contingent upon target behavior.) For example, a study by Madsen et al. (33) revealed that when teachers told children to "sit down" they increased (reinforced) out-of-seat behavior in spite of intending to punish the same behavior with the sit down command.

Therefore, the contingency management approach dictates that one consider three elements in modifying the behavior of the child. First, the cues can be analyzed in terms of whether the target behavior occurs more frequently when certain cues are present, which thereby exert control over the behavior. Second, the contingency manager has to be careful to specify the precise nature of the target behavior to be reinforced or punished. Third, the contingency manager must identify stimuli that are effective as reinforcers or punishments for the particular child. Finally, these three elements must be used in a *systematic* manner—being careful to consequate the target behavior consistently.

Operant Conception of the Nature of the Retarded

Applied to mental retardation, operant theory has clear implications both for a theory of the nature of retardation and for treatment and instruction. First, there is only minimal interest in etiology—heredity, injury, disadvantage and the like—for consideration of these tends to distract from the present behavioral characteristics which are the utilitarian interests of teachers and psychologists. Rarely do etiological considerations contribute to procedures of instruction; similarly, behaviorists tend to minimize the importance of categories or classification schemes (e.g., EMR, TMR, emotionally disturbed) and traditional psychometric data. Second, and for the same reason, there is minimal interest in ongoing biological processes; the limit of interest is the extent to which these processes can be observed and measured as situational stimuli to assist in predicting or controlling behavior. Third, operant theory describes how limited motor skills, inadequate language skills, and the like deprive the child of the desired behaviors, thus more directly "explaining" handicapping function and giving prescriptions for training activities. Rather than assuming that poor performance in these areas is explained by the condition (mental retardation), the operant approach assumes that low performance is due to inappropriate learning or a failure to learn these skills. The behaviorists, however, do not assume that this is so because the child is retarded, but instead they look to designing a program based on learning principles to insure that the child does learn these skills. The now well-known effects of early stimulation on institutionalized children (49) have been exactly what the operant theorists would have predicted. Fourth, and perhaps the most important, the operant theorist secures desirable responses by (a) providing the right situational cues, thereby increasing the likelihood of correct responses, and (b) controlling the consequences or contingencies of response. Provision for the control of response contingencies would, in fact, be the essence of a properly engineered educational program for any child.

The literature is replete with examples of the power of operant techniques with children heretofore considered hopeless as candidates for many kinds of learning. Furthermore, the use of contingency management procedures by teachers is a well-established practice today in most school districts. The work of Hewett (18) and of Lovaas and his associates (30) is most impressive as these researchers generated speech in autistic children through the use of operant procedures. The application of operant procedures to toilet training of the retarded has become highly refined in more recent attempts (1, 2, 34, 56) where prosthetic devices have been employed. Self-help skills (feeding and grooming) have similarly been developed with retarded populations through the systematic use of operant conditioning procedures (6, 19, 37, 44). Some of the most dramatic work by applied behaviorists has been done in the reduction and elimination of self destructive behavior (15, 51), much of which has involved the use of contingent shock.

In the context of education, several excellent reviews of token economies in the classroom exist (26, 38) and more recently one finds discussions about the systematic use of punishment to eliminate maladaptive and potentially dangerous behavior. From the foregoing, it seems safe to conclude that the majority of studies conducted in classrooms have been conducted on young children (e.g., preschool or primary grades) or with target behaviors that readily lend themselves to sequential programming (e.g., in-seat behavior, attending). O'Leary and Drabman (38) concluded that behavior modification has to date failed to demonstrate appreciable control over achievement behaviors; in fact, while Hewett (17) increased attending behavior in the classroom there was no concomitant increase in reading or mathematics achievement.

Some Teaching-Learning Principles Derived from Operant Theory

Operant theory, heretofore discussed, yields some obvious principles. A few of these follow, together with suggested applications:

1. Fruitful instruction comes best when the situational cues are favorable for the desired response classes, i.e., attention to teacher. Teaching would *not* be attempted when there is no readiness for the desired responses. The time might be otherwise utilized for rest or relatively free play, or for constructive improvement by teaching of the response classes more likely to occur; e.g., game skills, gross motor coordination, and interpersonal cooperation.

2. Of the responses occurring, only those which meet the desired standard are followed by reinforcement; that is, the teacher provides for response-events likely to produce the desired effect. By starting at the individual's ability level through building upon previous accomplishments, the teacher provides for more appropriate responses. This suggestion gets at the heart of the problem of beginning instruction where the child is functioning. Instead of waiting for the child to mature, the teacher must take the child where he is and through the manipulation of cues and consequences move the child to higher levels of performance.

3. When the response of the child to a situation does not meet the desired criteria, the variations of that response which are closest to being acceptable are reinforced. This variation will be repeated; variations around it which are still closer to that desired continue to be reinforced, until the desired behavior is achieved. As the sculptor shapes a finished form from a crude piece of clay, the teacher *shapes* polished behaviors from very gross approximations before the reinforcer is delivered.

This is an extremely significant principle. The oft-repeated counsel to the new teacher or insecure parent, to be satisfied even with a little progress, becomes meaningful when it is seen that, by reinforcement, the behavior is progressively shaped to the desired form. This applies not only to skills and understandings, but also to the improvement of habitual conduct problems toward more acceptable behavior. Possibly the most difficult point to get across is that the approximation is worthy of reinforcement. As teachers, we seem to believe that until the target behavior is emitted in a polished form the reinforcement should be withheld. The operant paradigm, however, has shown that the reinforcement of closer and closer approximations is a more efficient means of promoting more complex behavior than simply waiting for it to occur. Perhaps the most obvious applications are in the improvement of psychomotor responses which by nature can be learned only progressively. Poor handwriting can frequently be improved through practice. By encouraging the student's progress, the teacher promotes more legible penmanship.

4. A wide selection and variation of reinforcing conditions are provided. Reinforcement is in whatever legitimate and utilitarian form that produces effective results. A reinforcer is by definition any response event which increases the future likelihood of the response. This may come in the form of a kind word of approval, a gold star, a material reward. One of the minor tragedies of teaching in home or school is that what the adult uses as a presumed incentive does *not* always work. If it does not improve behavior, it is obviously not a reinforcer and its use is futile. The tragedy is enlarged when one says about a school learner, "he is unmotivated," for the fault may lie not in the child but in the failure to provide adequate incentives. Since every child is affected by incentives of some kind or another, the strategy is to identify and employ them. All too often, the variable reinforcement schedules used within the schools are not nearly so effective as educators presume them to be. This is apparent in the fact that schools usually use teacher marks as incentives. In the case of the mildly retarded child, marks tend to be reminders of failure rather than of success, and thus prove to be inadequate incentives.

A teacher who complains that all a student cares about is to get back to the playground equipment should take this as a motivational clue. That desire can be exploited by providing scheduled turns at the playground for the necessary academic drill or improved deportment.

The point made is that *something* can always be found to work.

Some children are not yet ready for the non-material incentives of verbal approval from the teacher or parents (41). If this is the case, they are probably responsive to some type of material reinforcement. Experimental programs have demonstrated that money, candy, an opportunity to see a cartoon film strip, or to work on the parallel bars will induce learning. To some teachers, the employment of such material incentives is reprehensible. But three advantages can be given against this opposition: (1) The incentives do work—and something must be found which works initially. (2) The child is then progressively weaned from dependence on these to the more acceptable relationships of teacher and peer approval. (3) Social approval by teacher, parent or peers is just as "extrinsic" as material reward, even if symbolic. The only true intrinsic reward is the desire for the learning activity itself. An eventual outcome of good teaching is this desire. However, educators cannot assume its *a priori* presence.

As the teachers begin with child behavior at the level they find it, so must they begin with incentives. If it takes a tangible or even edible reinforcer, use it to reach the child. Carefully pair it with a higher level incentive (e.g., praise) so that the praise will acquire the reinforcing power it originally lacked. In this manner, the instructor not only teaches a specific behavior but also teaches the child to respond to incentives that are used more frequently in less contrived environments.

5. Punishment has been subjected to much bad publicity over the years and generally has been thought to be unnecessary because of the effectiveness of (a) positive reinforcement, (b) withholding of positive reinforcement, and (c) differential reinforcement of incompatible behavior. However, recently the negative aspects of punishment have been challenged (24, 32) and its use defended in *certain* instances. Nevertheless, one finding that consistently emerges from the research is that teachers inadvertently reinforce inappropriate behavior when they assume that they are in fact punishing it. For example, Johnnie runs into the school playground; the teacher runs after, pulling him back into the room scolding him on the way. The teacher is surprised to find that Johnnie persists in this behavior. What is happening is that Johnnie's behavior is positively reinforced by the attention of the teacher. The returning and scolding are seen by the teacher as aversive, but they are perceived by the child as attention, and for some children even this kind of attention is better than being ignored. As in the study by Madsen *et al.* (33), the teacher's saying "sit down" actually increased the out-of-seat behavior. The recommendation to the teacher is to ignore inap-

propriate behavior that is not dangerous and reinforce (with an effective reinforcer) a behavior that is incompatible (e.g., being in his seat).

6. Related to the above is the challenge to the assumption that certain consequences are universal reinforcers. Not all children find grades of A, compliments, smiles from the teacher, etc. to be desirable. Clearly, a majority of children find an A grade to be reinforcing, but not all. So when a behavior problem occurs, be it of an academic or deportment nature, three elements can be studied: (a) the *cues*—are the materials too difficult; are there situational cues (e.g., time of day, subject matter, competition) associated with the misbehavior? (b) the *behavior*—specify the precise nature of the behavior that is inappropriate and the *goal* toward which that behavior should be changed—be descriptive and precise; and (c) the *consequences* that may be supporting the misbehavior and that are effective for that child and might be used to alter the behavior in the desired direction.

7. Ordinarily, the reinforcement should be rather promptly given, if given at all. While it has always been a good teaching principle to give early and frequent encouragement to the learner, this is especially true in forming early habits of class routine, study techniques, and group participation. The child's success will make the teacher's overt and repetitive acts of reinforcement less necessary, especially once the learner becomes so involved in learning as to require no further outside incentive. It is obvious that most retarded learners do not often reach this level.

The above rather extensive description of operant principles has illustrated some general features of stimulus-response (SR) theory, and may be contrasted with cognitive positions to be more fully discussed later. A teacher preparing material for instruction of multiplication in arithmetic would *not* be guided, in SR theory, by inferring how the child would "understand" the correlation of multiplication and addition of equal quantities, i.e., how 3×3 is the same as $3 + 3 + 3$. Rather the teacher would present problems expecting correct or near-correct responses, reinforcing selectively those changes of response approaching the correct one. The teacher would move the child by painless variation in problems to develop response classes to the new problems (in this case, multiplication). If possible, the teacher would employ self-instructional automated processes, starting the child at the margin of his present grasp of arithmetic.

The neutral observer with doubts about behavior modification as described above would be concerned with whether the teacher would be building only a set of mechanical SR connections. That is all the teacher seems to accomplish, under operant theory in its simplest form. Whether the teacher does more depends on the frame of reference.

As a matter of record, research performed by operant behavior investigators themselves has pointed to some validation of the fears made on an armchair basis by some. One such fear is that one resorts to bribes when using reinforcers. But a bribe is made before the desired behavior; it is opposte in many respects. It has nevertheless been demonstrated that a reinforced behavior may terminate when the reinforcement terminates, and that a behavior for which the child already has intrinsic motivation risks the loss of the intrinsic quality if reinforced. These and several other telling doubts about the rampant spread of operant use have been reviewed by Levine and Faschacht (29). It should be pointed out (a) that these risks can be minimized, and (b) that use of incentives has always been with us, whether that use is conscious or not. The child, initially uninterested in, say, arithmetic, works with it on faith because he models his peers and because he responds to the expectancies of his parents and teachers, but soon is found doing arithmetic on his own. We want to emphasize that the transition to intrinsic motivation (interest) almost surely goes on all the time in initially uninterested learners.

Other objections to operant behavior score more meaningful points. There is admitted to be considerable difficulty in demonstrating not only permanence but also useful generalization of a just-formed behavior to other situations. Recently, Kazdin (25) has suggested several approaches, consistent with operant principles, which would be useful in programming for generalization, and which look to be promising. Another is that the refusal to theorize about what occurs between S and R is a debasing concept of human nature and deprives psychological theory of its opportunity to make progress through inferences about potential connections of S and R, such as other SR and all the cognitive theories do make. It was obvious from the examples that the operant theory provided no inference regarding concept development in the child and did not speculate on transfer of learning to new situations as a change within the person.

Still further, two principal cornerstones of SR theory generally, but of operant theory in particular, have been empirically destroyed for most kinds of organized, meaningful learning (35). One is prompt feedback, and the other is a degree of gradualness in shaping to provide for a very high percent of correct responding. Both may help animal learning and the learning of fully arbitrary associations in humans, but can be shown to impair typical school learning.

CLASSIC BEHAVIORIST STIMULI-ORGANISM-RESPONSE (SOR)

Two varieties of mediational SR theories may be identified. The classic one in the U.S. (under various labels of behaviorism, bond, neobehaviorism, and including such names as Thorndike, Hull, and Spence) postulates intermediating physiological states such as need, incentive, arousal state, and storage of habit tendencies from prior practice. Derived principles of learning would include reference to state of physiological needs, incentive arousal, and other conditions likely to be known only under laboratory conditions. For that reason this classic type of theory (with a physiological Organism in the SOR) does not yield many useful cues to the teacher. Although a laboratory technician may control the food and water input of the animal which is to be trained, the schools may not use hunger as a motivator by having children come to school unfed. Furthermore, it is now shown that the tissue need for food and water are at times not as strong as certain activity drives. One current SR theorist posits a basic exploratory-curiosity drive as a more significant fundamental initiator of action (7). Such a theory would exploit the desire to explore, to watch and participate in activity as motivators; i.e., turns at a toy slot machine as a reward for a neat paper in spelling.

SOR THEORY UTILIZING LANGUAGE AND IMAGERY MEDIATION

This theory of SR employs a different mediator for theorizing what happens when responses are linked to stimuli; the 0 between S and R is not physiological but a form of psychological process. Verbal mediation refers to any verbalized means (spoken or silent) which facilitates learning, retention, and understanding. Thus one assists a child to discriminate and sort out his experiences with edible and inedible apples by making up a formula, red ones are good, green ones are sour.

Imagery has recently been explored also as a way people use to help learning; the learner is instructed to imagine the various elements within the context of their relationship—for example, where the doctor's office is with reference to the grocery and the school. Each has been systematically investigated recently with both normal and handicapped learners in an attempt to identify ways by which these "strategies" can be brought earlier and more efficiently into use. (55). Investigators have found that nonretarded preschool age children are not helped much by imposed mediators; that those of about first grade age can be considerably assisted if taught various strategies; and that nonretarded children above age fourteen will spontaneously use various mediating strategies on their own without being told, and may be hindered if the teacher imposes one they are not used to. Retarded children go through this development more slowly.

General lay opinion regards the retarded as deficient either in learning ability or in retention of what has been learned, or both. Such assumptions are open to question, especially in regard to moderately or mildly retarded individuals. When compared with straightforward learning or retention of completely new material, the retarded have frequently been found to be as efficient as normals, or results have at least been ambiguous on the point. For example, if both retarded and normal children of about equal age learn something meaningful to the same degree (which may take the retarded longer), the retarded tend to retain the learning over time just as well.

How then are retarded to be explained as poor learners? Current research suggests that the deficit consists in part in the initial poverty of verbal mediators available to the retarded. The retarded do not efficiently produce or use *word mediators* or other types of mediation in attacking new material. They do not attach *class names* to new observations. and thereby cannot apply generalized conceptual properties to them as well as normal children. If, however, the retarded are pretrained on the language used in sorting and classifying or remembering, to the degree of equality with normals, then they may learn and retain as well. One needs to note that extra time has to be taken in order to get the necessary verbal readiness; but once that level has been reached, their inferiority tends to diminish.

Similarly, the work of Jensen and Rohwer (23), MacMillan (31) and Milgram (36) indicates that when specific mediators are provided for the mentally retarded they can make use of them efficiently, but they tend, as a group, to be inefficient in spontaneously generating their own mediators. The teacher and parent can be of most help by assisting where the retarded child is weak, i.e., his language. One may not take for granted the same incidental learning of critical word-concepts. This is especially true of words which depict number, size, color, forms and classes of animals, vehicles and the like. The teacher must test out preliminary grasps of the key word-concepts before employing them in new learning. The teacher must also provide time for strategic repetitions and rehearsals, for distribution of effort, and of course, for maintenance of motivation. An important point about language acquisition is that words are arbitrary symbols for the read substance; the sound or printed symbol for "dog" bears no suggestive resemblance to the visual substance of a dog. For this reason, repetitions are necessary until the assimilation of word-substance becomes automatic.

Thus, mediational SOR theory would go a step beyond operant theory. It would start by assuming that, since the retarded is less prone to have attended to the critical cues and is less able to bridge time gaps from example to example, he makes fewer generalizations. This theory would add careful training to provide what is not accomplished in everyday life experience: for example, intensive use of nursery school. Children would compare sticks and repeatedly verbalize their observations. They would order items by specific dimensions. They would weigh on simple balances and utilize words like *heavier,* not so *heavy, a little more weight.* They would train in comparative use of words like men, women, people, adults, children, always with perception of the referents.

A technique which has been found to be appropriate with young retarded children is the use of binary questioning rather than multiple questioning (52). By phrasing a question to get a direct answer (where the correct response is contained within the question itself) rather than an open-ended answer, the questioner allows the child to respond with less likelihood of failure. For example, asking the child a direct question such as "Is your name John or Joe" rather than "What is your name," eliminates the need for the child to hesitate on the question. Similarly, by first building up a simple vocabulary, a child becomes able to answer more difficult questions such as pairing two pictures, one of a cow and one of a horse, and responding to "Which animal is a cow?" As the child has less difficulty in making the correct response, the same two pictures may be used to elicit the functions, uses, and actions appropriate for the animals depicted.

As the child progresses, the number of choices may be increased, building upon the already present repertoire. Thus, a set of animals containing a horse, a cow, and two additional animals, such as a pig and a lamb which have already been similarly paired, might be added. The teacher is then allowed to test the actual performance of the learning task as to the amount of transfer taking place. Mediation SOR would also try to form class concepts, again by physical presentation, games, exchanges, etc., with associated words: cars, trucks, buses, *vehicles;* trains, planes, cars, buses, *transportation;* red, green, blue, white, *color,* etc. Thus, a child's ability to differentiate the meaning of the presented concept can be made through frequent assessment.

This brief presentation does not adequately describe the richness of research and ideas in mediation SR theory today. The interested reader might note the research reviews of Heatherington and McIntyre (16) and Stevenson (53). Specific application to the mentally retarded has been noted by Olson (39), Rosenberg (45), and Sitko and Semmel (48).

We are not yet able to make recommendations about utilizing imagery for the mentally retarded in assisting learning, for there has not yet been accumulated a sufficient body of information on its employment with this group. A discussion of issues may be found in Rohwer (43) and Reese (42). We believe some good and no harm can be done by encouraging the retarded child to imagine how this and that go or connect together or to imagine the consequences of this choice vs. that, as in being careful crossing the street vs. not looking all ways. We should also point out that recently the leading verbal learning theorists (e.g., 11, 22) have gravitated more toward a cognitive-developmental point of view, described later.

SOCIAL LEARNING THEORY

Several movements bear this title. In general, they all place emphasis upon the social context of learning and adaptation, accounting for behavior change through the manner in which significant people such as parents and peers evaluate one's behavior, putting the burden of psychological development upon the moment-to-moment success and failure in social relations where the criteria for success or failure are in the hands of people who set up the situations in which the child must interact. One emphasis in social learning is addressed to the learning which occurs by observing the behavior of others ("modeling"). Social learning may be considered not something different but rather an emphasis. In school classrooms, for example, the social learning theorist would stress pupil-pupil interaction and teacher-pupil attachment more than the mere technique of instruction itself, and would partly redefine instruction in terms of the way peers and teachers reinforce or discourage responses. Social learning has many advocates; a chief spokesman has been Rotter (46), with applications to the retarded by Cromwell (13) and Zigler (57), among others.

The significance of others in determining goals and criteria of success is illustrated by contrasting the definition of success when a child throws stones at a floating log all by himself and when he is in competition with others in the same activity. In the first he sets his own level of success; in the second, others impose the definition.

Non-success in a self-imposed activity does not affect the child much;

he can easily reset the criterion of success, or he can shift his interest to something he can master. The socially imposed task is an activity in which escape from non-success is not easy. The distinction between externally and internally imposed success criteria should always remind parents and teachers of the need to be careful in defining success and failure, to provide the right amount of incentive to guarantee progress by our criteria as well as by his own. Note this logic:

(1) The person reacts positively to success, negatively to failure. (2) The person becomes aware of tasks and the criteria for success as socially prescribed and transmitted by such authorities as parents, teachers, and others. (3) With a history of successes and failures, the child builds expectancies, concepts about himself relative to potential mastery of events and to achievement of long-range goals. (4) Any young child responds on a moment-to-moment basis, varying his activity with success and failure, not yet driving forward according to a personally organized goal structure. (5) Growth of organized personal goals is held back in a child whose responses to socially-imposed tasks are greeted with failure. He cannot escape failure experience because he cannot escape society. He can handle this in one of three ways: (a) by non-involvement; (b) by token observance of tasks; or (c) by reducing the sense of failure by not competing.

According to social learning theory, these methods of avoiding failure become the crux of much learning deficit. The retarded continue in an immature drift towards the momentarily successful experience. Everyone has witnessed the gentle teasing by older siblings or grandparents of a two-year-old in applauding his nonsensical antics. The young child reacts to their reinforcement and not to personally constructed standards. In the laboratory, the possibility of manipulating the behavior of a school-age, mildly retarded child has been demonstrated. Given a task to do and without independent knowledge of goodness criteria, he will continue his irrelevant activity, being reinforced by approbation or kindly interest that is mistaken for approbation. He has had few chances to receive this, so he continues the activity that will provide it. In another type of laboratory demonstration, one may experimentally arrange for success or failure and show its effect on the subsequent level of aspiration. The retarded are impeded in effort by failure, and show less determination to try again.

As a normal child grows, he acquires a set of constructs about his competencies, together with a set of goals. He becomes, to some degree, a determinant of his own fate, though never completely apart from social influence. The retarded child tends to be slow in development of personal constructs, but those that emerge are more likely to be negative, leading to avoidance and noncompetition, as though to keep failure minimal. This, of course, is detrimental to his education, for he is preoccupied not with the task as objectively defined, but with how to get by it or away from it with the least personal involvement. Effects of success and failure have led to such maxims of teaching as "reward any success," "provide each day for some tangible accomplishments." Recalling that the criteria for success and failure are so often the parent's or teacher's to set, much can be accomplished by way of reducing the tendency to avoid effort and involvement.

The maintenance of a fundamental *optimism* by the teacher or parent toward the retarded needs to be stressed. A teacher must start with the proposition that a retarded child has known much non-success if not "failure" and should initiate a chain of ongoing success experiences, to avoid even temporary failures to the degree possible: in short, to utilize all that the laboratory has demonstrated about the effects of repeated mastery of tasks. This certainly calls not only for prompt knowledge of results but instantaneous interpersonal support to guide the learner appropriately if the results were deemed to be unsuccessful. It definitely calls for a guaranteed high incidence of successful activity and, thus, for continual resetting of goals which the learner is capable of achieving.

Observational Learning (Learning from Modeled Behavior)

The significance of imitation in the development of children has only recently been appreciated. A considerable body of empirical information has now been generated, some of it out of concern for what effects the media, especially TV, produce in children. These investigations have clearly demonstrated that a considerable portion of children's learnings and choices can be attributed to such vicarious experience as the behavior observed not only in the media, but also in their parents, siblings, peers, and others. Children who have just witnessed a physical assault on TV or by older siblings will much more likely show aggression with friends or with puppets than those who have not. Children will adopt the apparently successful choices others make in getting to desired goals.

A striking phenomenon escaped earlier investigators, namely that the imitation may be long delayed, weeks or months going by before an appropriate opportunity for imitation. Another unanticipated result (though the evidence is somewhat moot) is that no reinforcement appears to be directly necessary for a model to be imitated, whether now or in the future. What these laboratory type demonstrations have taught us is that child development is probably replete with learnings and choices due to observing others react in similar situations. It is clear to teachers that peer modeling is a powerful determinant of choice at all grade levels, especially after second grade.

There is every reason to believe that the mentally retarded child is similarly affected by what he observes in behavior around him. This would be particularly so when he observes nonretarded children win praise and reward for given behavior for reasons he may not yet fully understand; he will imitate to secure similar treatment. They may take courage by seeing others bravely enter a feared situation; or, they may observe a model do something which results in punishment or pain and *avoid* similar behavior, taking care not to imitate. As a general rule, behavior *choices* among already learned alternatives are more likely to be influenced by observing another than by first acquiring a skill which is dependent upon one's own trial and effort, and behavior more frequently observed is easier to acquire vicariously (as in commonly used words and sentence structures) than those infrequently encountered.

One fact of life we can count on with any child, retarded or not, is that nearly any behavior he observes runs the risk of being modeled, and adults are wise to note that such behavior would include smoking, using bottled and pilled drugs of various kinds, gutter language forms, and emotional displays. There is little formal literature yet on the direct employment of the observational phenomenon with retarded learners (54), but some dramatic demonstrations have been made in producing speech puppet models in previously mute children (3) and the development of generalized imitative tendency by reinforcement. This kind of social learning theory is given excellent review by Baldwin (4), Bandura (5), and Stevenson (53).

CONTRIBUTIONS OF COGNITIVE-DEVELOPMENTAL THEORIES

A distinction was made earlier between the SR and cognitive theories. The features of the latter are principally two. To the learner is attributed a master process, the mind, which not only stores experiences for new use but is capable of the higher processes of making generalizations, inferences, discoveries, transformations, and the like.

This first postulate, that there is a self-activating and inventing mind, is in many respects only a different language for the assumption of intermediating processes between stimulus and response in SOR theory which infers mediation by means of language and imagery. However, a teacher who attributes to the learner a problem-solving, transforming mind will organize the teaching-learning situation differently from one who treats the learner as somebody who is to make appropriate responses to discriminated stimuli. The former emphasizes the presentations of opportunities for guided self discovery of principles and insights, the latter would provide more systematic drill.

Real differences between cognitive and SR theory occur in the conception of how psychological development occurs. The cognitive position is that mental functioning undergoes a more or less self-directed growth, given an environment of sufficient psychological variety with which to interact. Development is dependent upon experience; practice does not necessarily accelerate it but lack of an environment suited to the stage of the learner will handicap it. Growth is marked by stages which occur in an inexorable sequence, each a necessary prelude to the next and absorbed into the next. The pace of growth will vary among children for both natural and cultural reasons. In this discussion we speak of cognitive-developmental theory generally, but will feature the theory of Jean Piaget, the most celebrated spokesman and investigator. There are many sources here; we recommend Piaget and Inhelder (40).

Piaget's theory is that mental development occurs as a natural interaction process. Every experience is a matter of the child coping with some problem of adaptation; he accommodates his abilities to the needs of the situation, and assimilates the experience to increase his competence. The continuous development due to these processes is called the equilibration process—adaptation gets out of equilibrium because of new challenges continually being perceived. The child is constantly stirred by new challenges perceived within the level of his present competence. He masters these challenges, increasing his competence to a point where still higher level challenges are brought within the realm of his abilities.

Teaching Implication of the Cognitive Position

The development as above described is attained by the child on his own terms; you do not directly teach; you provide that he can interact. In theory there is no motivation problem; this kind of activity, which by definition is always self-provoked by the child's perception of a challenge, needs no external reinforcement.

Some parents and teachers avoid early teaching under the mistaken belief the child is too young for an experience. Precaution must be exercised in interpreting the child's readiness. Every child is ready for some learning. It may not be reading but it could well be the establishment of the vocabulary-building skills pre-requisite for reading. On the other hand, the parent or teacher may make things worse by pushing too fast or too early for the state of readiness for a particular skill; i.e., the mere fact that a child is 6 years of age does not necessarily imply that he has the necessary emotional, cultural, or perceptual ability to read.

Further teaching implications of cognitive theory are seen in the achievement of the conservation of physical reality in the child, during the period of about 5 to 8 years. At the earlier age, a change in the form of substance as in a ball of clay rolled into a sausage (in one of Piaget's celebrated demonstrations) causes a child literally to perceive that the amount of substance increased; when the clay is made again into a ball, the original amount is believed to be restored. The child could accept and understand only the evidence of his perception, and could not grasp the reciprocity of simultaneous change in two or more dimensions. By eight years of age the child is able to appreciate reciprocity, can understand that physical qualities have their own reality apart from what he perceives, and can do thinking operations which are not entrapped by the surface appearance of phenomena. How did he reach this state from his previous inability to conserve? Piaget's explanation is that, as life went on, the child interacted on his own terms with sand and clay, with pouring of water from one container to others of varying sizes and shapes, becoming progressively more able to acquire ways of conceptualizing and anticipating the effects of change of state, and of proving or disconfirming his ideas by his own experimenting. To Piaget and his believers one cannot hasten this growth, but one could hold it back by denying opportunities for the relevant interactions. Piaget would not advocate trying any educational plan to hurry things along.

Americans, even cognitive theorists like Gagné and Bruner, prefer to identify just how the growth processes occur and to experiment with ways of speeding them. Bruner would go along with Piaget in that you cannot teach if you must employ space, time, quantity, classification, and conservation competencies the child has not yet mastered, but differs in believing that technique can short-cut the normal equilibration process and that unguided provision for interaction is an inefficient way to utilize the equilibration process.

One implication of the stage aspect of cognitive theory is that there is to be a careful selection of instructional objectives and tasks. What Piaget calls "thinking operations" is the ability to make mental manipulations of physical and social reality, to anticipate what would happen if this or that change were made, to reverse processes so that if one grasped that $3 + 4 = 7$, then $7 - 4 = 3$ and $7 - 3 = 4$, etc. The "thinking" child can understand that objects and phenomena can be classified by multiple criteria such as color, size, use, etc. These thinking abilities come into being in the normal child in the period of about 6 to 9 years of age. Instruction for a child who cannot do these mental anticipations and manipulations, who is still entrapped by the appearance of things, must be suited to such limitations. Such a child is to be given abundant opportunities to count, to order by size, to experiment with some self direction, to practice relationships such as over and under, more than and less than, and a hundred others, and in due time thinking operations will be possible, and instruction can be altered to suit. Good reading on these points is provided by Furth (14), Schwebel and Raph (47) and other recent sources.

Cognitive Theory and the Retarded

Inasmuch as cognitive psychology implies that intellect grows in power to handle complexities, it follows that the retarded child is perceived as a more or less limited person. It is important not to overstate this conclusion. The cognitive-developmental position does not mean to imply an unbreakable limit on final development, though it certainly suggests it. The cognitive-developmental position of the mental development of the mentally retarded is most generally taken as that of Inhelder (20), that we should not control too much lest the intrinsic motivation of doing one's own activity be impaired. The reader is again reminded of the emphasis made by social learning theorists upon who determines the criteria of task success and how difficult we adults can make the achievement of success by imposing tasks beyond (above or below) the competence level of the child and by setting completion and perfection requirements which they find strange.

MEMORY SPAN

There is a general and common research finding which obtains when the learning and the memory of what is learned in nonretarded and retarded children are compared, namely that if the two learn to an equal degree, there will be no inferiority of retention in the retarded. However there is another kind of memory, that which is often called span, which refers to holding of a once-only stimulus for a short time, such as a few seconds. This is in contrast with retaining for days or weeks of a practiced skill or a memorized passage. An example of span is the so-called span test in psychological examination, in which a series of mixed digits or words is presented once and the subject is asked to say them back in the same order, omitting none. Another is an instruction for delayed performance, such as "when the bell rings, put the pencil on the desk." Some ability is taken for granted when parents or teachers instruct a child or when his lessons present two or more elements to be related in some process, as in arithmetic or language study.

Weakness in span is held to account for such phenomena as a child "forgetting" what a teacher has just told him or his inability to associate instruction with the material the instruction pertains to, or the inability to associate the printed symbol with the spoken word (as in early reading). The trace of one may fade before the stimulus of the other is effective.

Whether or not poor span of memory is a chief feature of retardation (there is some doubt), it is frequently evident in retarded children, apparently more so in those with histories of brain injury. To the extent the deficiency is present, certain principles may be useful.

1. Instructions to learners should be short, certainly not complex. The child may be unable, for example, to keep separate two or three different instructions given at one time. Should he need to be given more than one, one at least should be practiced, even overlearned, so that it will not vanish or be confused with another.

2. Action expected from an instruction should be immediate, if possible. An instruction calling for delay must be simple.

3. In teaching processes, as in arithmetic, single steps should be practiced till they are established, even automatic, before additional processes are added, even though the final educated skill must eventually combine them. For example, adding must be well-established before multiplication. Adding without carrying must precede adding with carrying.

4. Care is needed to be sure the child is attentive to an instruction. Unlike the normal child, who can be partially preoccupied and still fulfill requested tasks, the retarded is less likely to be successful in dividing his attention.

5. Where there is to be a learned association of elements, as in thing-

word or spoken-written word association, there must be minimal delay between the presented elements.

6. Both reinforcement of correct response and correction of a wrong response must come promptly. Returning marked papers the next day may be too late for the retarded; he merely sees an evaluation of himself, not a connection between the correction of his work and the work itself.

7. Connections, such as those between current and prior lessons, must be made clear to the child. Since the learner's full associative span may be employed in grasping current work, the teacher must make the connection with previous exercises, to establish the temporal relationship and the desired breadth of generalization. If it is obvious that the above would be appropriate pointers in dealing with normal children, especially the younger, it is even more so with the retarded.

Selecting the theory to suit the need. The parent or teacher should not be bewildered by the differences among theories, but should plan in terms of what is needed in the specific situation. Sometimes the teaching objective is one which requires SR type of technique more than, say, discovery. Those necessary learnings, often labeled "arbitrary associations," are a case in point. There is no "logic" or problem solving which can be used to learn that d-o-g is the arbitrary social symbol in English for the barking animal—the association of "dog" to dog is learned via repetition only. But cognitive-developmental principles would apply when the child is expected to form concepts and classes with respect to dogs, quadripeds, animals, mammals, etc. SR theory would apply more naturally to the acquisition of certain sensorimotor skills where practice and gradual improvement of the SRs is the principal way to improve a skill, though higher level insights might provide better strategies of practice. Most scholars in children's learning do not fixate upon one theory or another, but point out that the various theorists have rested their cases upon selected research demonstrations which are "explained" best by their own theories; the next theorist finds a different "explanation" suits better his different kind of data. For example, there is no question whatsoever that if one wants to train animals to perform complex sequences, Skinner's behavior modification is the way to go. If you want children speedily to acquire the associations between arbitrary noises called words and the meanings they stand for, you will go to SR theory for efficient ways to reach the objectives. When you want to increase learning and recollection of the relation of concepts, classes, and relations among ideas, SOR learning with the use of planned verbal mediators provides good strategies. If you now want children to form insights, to generalize their experience, to imagine new ways to apply learnings, then you go to the cognitive-developmental theories for ways to employ a laboratory for discovery learning, for finding a set of principles, for developing ways by which hypotheses can be tested in experimentation.

Cognitive-developmental theorists point out that there is no way to stop a learner from utilizing higher processes if he is capable of them; to put it another way, you do not often have a teaching-learning or laboratory situation in which you have a fully naive learner and a complete control of stimuli by the investigator. This is illustrated by a type of learning-memory task in which one presents a child with a long series of disconnected words, more than he can retain and recite back, words standing for different things. The younger child will use only memory, and will require repetitions to get more than a few words upon recital. But older children, especially above eight, without any instructions from the adult, will attempt to employ some manner of strategy in their attempt to reproduce the list, though the strategy may be inefficient and inferior to one the experimenter might have provided. Above age 12 or 14 the learner will always employ a strategy, and on his own has developed several which assist, perhaps, spontaneously using higher conceptual schemes to organize the task—for example, remembering names in meaning clusters such as four-legged animals, vehicles, plants, etc.

It is an instructional strategy to let the child use the higher process if he is capable of it, and to assist him with strategies provided he can truly use them, not to use them if they will only befuddle (because, say, he cannot yet employ the conceptual or classification ability which is required), but always to expect that the child himself reaches for higher levels and sometimes attains them. We mentioned age differences, in which the older the child, the more likely he can employ a mental strategy. It is time to point out that the retarded child will require the more primitive type of teaching-learning by means, say, of more repetitions and gradualism than insight, for a longer period than the non-retarded child, but the teacher should never make the mistake of over-employment of that principle.

OVERVIEW AND IMPLICATIONS

Viewing retardation within the framework of learning principles and theories does not necessarily presume a particular definitive characterization of the deficits of the retarded. A large segment of psychological workers rejects the notion that retardation is innately or theoretically permanent or "incurable." Although it is recognized that some individuals are impaired in a number of functions, applied learning practitioners usually assume that every individual has the capacity to "learn," i.e., to modify his behavior as the result of environmental stimulation, and to improve his level of functioning. If retardation is not considered a fixed and static clinical entity, improvement can be induced in an individual who previously had been functioning at a retarded level without our having recourse to retrospective diagnostic constructs such as "pseudo-retardation."

We can synthesize the principles derived from theory into one basic tenet: every child can learn; therefore, it is the duty of the educator to find the procedures best suited to the child. Too often we hear the criticism that learning theory is not practical in the classroom. The truth is that learning theory *does belong* in the classroom. William James has said that teaching "must everywhere agree with psychology" (21). This is an axiom just as obviously true as "medical practice must agree with physiology."

No, the issue is not whether theory belongs. The very manner adults choose to interreact with a child, as in overcontrol or undercontrol, represents a hypothesis about how to rear and educate a child, reflecting an implicit theoretical posture. Theory everywhere pertains to the individual's learning. When the practitioner says, "I can't use your idea in my class," what he means is that he cannot teach individually. That is the crux, for educators as a rule think only in terms of groups. What we have indicated is that the group idea needs to be modified if an honest attempt is to be made at teaching the retarded.

The educator must individualize as much of the instruction as possible, and use those means which take the individual pupil (not the class average) where he is; to apply the motivation which challenges him (not them); to teach these individuals (not this class).

This hope is not an impossible dream. There are many models already in good practice for implementing the goal of individualized instruction. No radical new buildings or expensive demonstrations are required to apply these models to the present-day classes for educables, trainables, and even lower-level retarded. The point of emphasis is that, among all pupils, the retarded are the ones *most* in need of the best teaching-learning, the principle by which this chapter started.

REFERENCES

1. Azrin, N. H., C. Bugle, and F. O'Brien, "Behavioral Engineering: Two Apparatuses for Toilet Training Retarded Children," *Journal of Applied Behavior Analysis,* 4:249-253, 1971.
2. Azrin, N. H., and R. M. Foxx, "A Rapid Method of Toilet Training the Institutionalized Retarded," *Journal of Applied Behavior Analysis,* 4:89-99, 1971.
3. Baer, D. M., R. F. Peterson, and J. A. Sherman, "The Development of Imitation by Reinforcing Behavioral Similarity to a Model," *J. of Exper. Analysis of Behav.,* 10:405, 1967.
4. Baldwin, A., "Social Learning. In Kerlinger, F. (Ed.), *Review of Research in Education.* Itasca, Ill.: Peacock, 1973.
5. Bandura, A., *Aggression: A Social Analysis,* Enlgewood Cliffs, N.J.: Prentice-Hall, 1973.
6. Barton, E. S., D. Guess, E. Garcia, and D. Baer, "Improvement of Retardates' Mealtime Behaviors by Time Out Procedures Using Multiple Baseline Techniques," *Journal of Applied Behavior Analysis,* 3, 1970.
7. Berlyne, D. E., "A Decade of Motivation Theory," *American Scientist,* 52:447-451, 1964.
8. Bijou, S. W., "A Functional Analysis of Retarded Development," in N. R. Ellis (Ed.), *International Review of Research in Mental Retardation,* Vol. 1, New York: Academic Press, 1966.
9. Bortner, M., and H. G. Birch, "Cognitive Capacity and Cognitive Competence," *Amer. J. of Ment. Defic.,* 75:735-744, 1970.
10. Bruner, J. S., *Toward a Theory of Instruction,* Cambridge, Mass.: Harvard University Press, 1966.
11. Cofer, C. N., "Constructive Process in Memory," *Amer. Scientist,* 61:537-543, 1973.
12. Cole, M., and J. S. Bruner, "Cultural Differences and Inferences About Psychological Processes," *Amer. Psychologist,* 26:867-875, 1971.
13. Cromwell, R. L., "A Social Learning Approach to Mental Retardation," in N. R. Ellis (Ed.), *Handbook of Mental Deficiency,* New York: McGraw-Hill, 1963.
14. Furth, Hans G., *Piaget for Teachers,* Englewood Cliffs, N.J.: Prentice-Hall, 1970.
15. Gardner, W. I., "Use of Punishment Procedures with the Severely Retarded, *Amer. J. Ment. Defic.,* 74:86-103, 1969.
16. Heatherington, E., Mavis, and Curtis W. McIntyre, "Developmental Psychology." In Mark R. Rosenzweig and Lyman W. Porter (Eds.), *Annual Review of Psychology,* 1975, 26, p. 97-136.
17. Hewett, F. M., *The Emotionally Disturbed Child in the Classroom,* Boston: Allyn and Bacon, 1968.
18. Hewett, F., "Teaching Reading to an Autistic Boy Through Operant Conditioning," *Read. Teach.,* 17:613, 1964.
19. Hunt, J. G., L. C. Fitzhugh, and K. B. Fitzhugh, "Teaching 'Exit Ward' Patients Apropriate Behaviors by Using Reinforcement Techniques," *Amer. J. Ment. Defic,.* 73:41-45, 1968.
20. Inhelder, B., *The Diagnosis of Reasoning in the Mentally Retarded,* New York: John Day, 1968.
21. James, W., *Talks to Teachers on Psychology: And to Students on Some of Life's Ideals,* New York: Henry Holt, 1939.
22. Jenkins, J., "Remember That Old Theory of Memory? Well, Forget It!" *Amer-Psychologist,* 29, 11:785-795, 1974.
23. Jensen, A. R., and W. D. Rohwer, "The Effect of Mediation on the Learning and Retention of Paired-Associates by Retarded Adults," *Amer. J. Ment. Defic.,* 68: 80-84, 1963.

24. Johnston, J. M., "Punishment of Human Behavior," *Amer. Psychologist,* 12:1033-1054, 1972,

25. Kazdin, A. E., "Issues in Behavior Modification with Mentally Retarded Persons," *Amer. J. Ment. Defic.,* 78:134-140, 1973.

26. Kazdin, A. E., and W. E. Craighead, "Behavior Modification in Special Education." In L. Mann and D. A. Sabatino (Eds.), *The First Review of Special Education,* Vol. 2, Philadelphia: Journal of Special Education Press, 1973, 51-102.

27. Geogh, B. K., and D. L. MacMillan, "Effects of Motivational and Presentation Conditions on Digit Recall of Children of Differing Socioeconomic, Racial and Intelligence Groups," *Amer. Educ. Research J.,* 8:27-38, 1971.

28. Leib, J. W., J. Cusock, D. Hughes, S. Pilette, J. Werther, and B. L. Kintz, "Teaching Machines and Programmed Instruction: Areas of Application," *Psychological Bulletin,* 67:12-266, 1967.

29. Levine, F. and G. Faschacht, "Token Rewards May Lead to Token Learning," *Amer. Psychologist,* 29, 11:816-820, 1974.

30. Lovaas, O. I., J. P. Berberich, B. F. Perioff, and B. Schaeffer, "Acquisition of Imitative Speech by Schizophrenic Children," *Science,* 151:705, 1966.

31. MacMillan, D. L., "Paired-Associate Learning as a Function of Explicitness of Mediational Set by EMR and Nonretarded Children," *Amer. J. Ment. Defic.,* 76: 686-691, 1972.

32. MacMillan, D. L., S. R. Forness, and B. M. Trumbull, "The Role of Punishment in the Classroom," *Exceptional Child.,* 40:85-96, 1973

33. Madsen, C. H., W. C. Becker, D. R. Thomas, L. Koser, and E. Plager, "An Analysis of the Reinforcing Function of 'Sit Down' Commands." In R. K. Parker (Ed.), *Readings in Educational Psychology,* Boston: Allyn & Bacon, 1968.

34. Mahoney, K., R. K. Van Wagenen, and L. Meyerson, "Toilet Training on Normal and Retarded Children," *Journal of Applied Behavior Analysis,* 4:173-181, 1971.

35. McKeachie, Wilbert J., "The Decline and Fall of the Laws of Learning," *Educational Researcher,* 3:7-11, 1974.

36. Milgram, N. A., "Retention of Mediation Set in Paired-Associate Learning of Normal and Retarded Children," *J. Exper. Child Psychol.,* 5:341-349, 1967.

37. O'Brien, F., and N. H. Azrin, "Developing Proper Mealtime Behaviors of the Institutionalized Retarded," *J. Applied Behav. Analysis,* 5:389-399, 1972.

38. O'Leary, K. D., and R. Drabman, "Token Reinforcement Programs in the Classroom: A Review," *Psychological Bulletin,* 75:379-398, 1971.

39. Olson, D. R., "Language Acquisition and Cognitive Development." In H. C. Haywood (Ed.), *Social-cultural Aspects of Mental Retardation,* New York: Appleton-Century-Crofts, 1970, 113-202.

40. Piaget, J., and B. Inhelder, *The Psychology of the Child.* New York: Basic Books, 1969.

41. Premack, D., "Toward Empirical Behavior Laws: I. Positive Reinforcement," *Psych. Review,* 66:219, 1959.

42. Reese, H. W., "Imagery and Contextual Meaning," *Psychol. Bull.,* 73:404-414, 1970.

43. Rohwer, William D., "Images and Pictures in Children's Learning," *Psychol. Bull.,* 73:393-403, 1970.

44. Roos, P., and M. Oliver, "Evaluation of Operant Conditioning with Institutionalized Retarded Children," *Amer. J. Mental Deficiency,* 74:325-330, 1969.

45. Rosenberg, S., "Problems of Language Development in the Retarded." In H. C. Haywood (Ed.), *Social-Cultural Aspects of Mental Retardation,* New York: Appleton-Century-Crofts, 1970, 203-216.

46. Rotter, J. B., *Social Learning and Clinical Psychology*, Englewood Cliffs, N. J.: Prentice-Hall, 1954.
47. Schwebel, M., and J. Raph, *Piaget in the Classroom*. New York: Basic Books, 1973.
48. Sitko, M. C., and M. I. Semmel, "Language and Language Behavior of the Mentally Retarded." In L. Mann and D. A. Sabatino Eds.), *The First Review of Special Education*, Vol. 1, 1973, 203-259.
49. Skeels, H. M., "Adult Status of Children with Contrasting Early Life Experience," *Monographs of the Society for Research in Child Development*, 31, 1966.
50. Skinner, B. F., *The Behavior of Organisms*, New York: D. Appleton Century, 1938.
51. Smolev, S. R., "Use of Operant Techniques for the Modification of Self-Injurious Behavior," *Amer. J. Mental Deficiency*, 76:295-305, 1971.
52. Spradlin, J. E., and S. Rosenberg, "Complexity of Adult Verbal Behavior in a Dyadic Situation with Retarded Children," Working Paper No. 18, Parsons Research Project, Bureau of Child Research, University of Kansas, Nov., 1959.
53. Stevenson, H. W., *Children's Learning*. New York: Appleton-Century-Crofts, 1972.
54. Strichart, S. S., and J. Gottlieb, "Imitation of Retarded Children by Their Nonregarded Peers," *Amer. J. Mental Deficiency*, 79:506-512, 1975.
55. Taylor, A. M., M. Josberger, and J. Q. Knowlton, "Mental Elaboration and Learning in EMR Children," *Amer. J. Mental Deficiency*, 7:69-76, 1972.
56. Van Wagenen, R. K., L. Meyerson, N. J. Kerr, and K. Mahoney, "Field Trials of a New Procedure for Toilet Training," *J. Exper. Psychol.*, 8:147-159, 1969.
57. Zigler, E., "Research on Personality Structure in the Retardate." In N. R. Ellis (Ed.), *International Review of Research in Mental Retardation*, Vol. 1, New York: Academic Press, 1966.

CHAPTER 23

Diagnosis and Remediation of Educational Deficiencies

by ROBERT HENDERSON, Ed.D.

The first major breakthrough in identification and classification of mentally retarded children occurred because of Binet's work in France in the early 1900's. Since that time, many other so-called intelligence tests have been developed and considerable effort expended in determining the relationship of one test to another. All of these tests, however, are designed to differentiate the retarded child from the non-retarded, and to ascertain the degree of retardation. Too often, the scores derived—the intelligence quotient (IQ) and the mental age (MA)—are assumed to possess powers which they do not have. The IQ scores have often been thought to be fixed for life, and indicative of some "native intelligence." Rather, it is an index of current performance and is subject to environmental factors as well as genetic or constitutional ones. The mental age (MA) score has too frequently been taken as an index of learning ability and interests, with all retarded children of a given MA being reported as having a given set of characteristics.

These instruments of evaluation have been used as tools to classify the child, but rarely have they been successful in providing a diagnosis —that is, an evaluation leading to some form of educational program. IQ test scores do not provide the teacher with the information needed to provide for a differentiated program adapted to the individual differences between the retarded children she seeks to educate—one of the essential ingredients of what is special about special education (8).

Perhaps the most devastating effect of this kind of procedure has been the labeling of children and their placement in special classes for the retarded from racially and/or economically disadvantaged homes. Criticism of the results of this practice are growing louder and louder (see especially: 5 and 12). One of the most valid complaints concerning special classes for the retarded has been that the teacher accepts the IQ and MA scores as being reliable indicators of *potential* as well as current (test) performance. Thus, a prophecy of mental retardation in the labeling and placing of the child becomes self-fulfilling since the teacher acts toward the child as if he were retarded, i.e., she offers him educational challenges consistent with the predicted ability level.

A research study by Goldstein, Jordan and Moss (6) demonstrated that many children labeled retarded, especially in the higher ranges of the educable classification, improved their scores on IQ tests after a year or two in school (whether in regular or special classes). This confirms the earlier work of Kirk (9) who provided a special preschool program for children from low socio-economic homes who at three or four years of age obtained scores on IQ tests in the educable mentally retarded range. Almost all of these children received higher scores on subsequent examinations after experiencing the more stimulating environment of either the preschool classes or regular first grade. Of course, higher scores are expected on a retest following low scores, as a result of the statistical phenomenon known as regression to the mean. The IQ increase in the cases mentioned above, however, were greater than would be anticipated by regression alone.

The evidence available at this time would suggest:

1. Diagnostic study of retarded children is needed (in addition to classification of retarded children) to provide a basis for an individualized program of instruction. It is not sufficient to merely classify them.

2. Clinical teaching methods can and should be employed with children labeled as "mentally retarded." The diagnostic teacher will be able to ameliorate the child's learning disabilities, at least in some cases.

3. Emphasis should be placed on preventive educational programs for preschool children from high-risk socio-economic areas of our communities. Such preventive programs, when based on an adequate diagnostic-teaching model, serve to reduce the incidence of early school failure and subsequent labeling of the child as "mentally retarded."

CLINICAL EDUCATIONAL DIAGNOSIS

One of the most fruitful alternatives to the use of current. IQ instruments has been the development of hypothetical constructs which lend themselves to development of clinical models and testable hypotheses. While all of this may sound very scientific and esoteric, it is actually very pragmatic, in that it seeks answers to educationally relevant questions: Can the child sound-blend? Can he remember what he hears? Can he remember what he sees? Can he associate something that he sees (such as a picture of a cat) and something he hears (the word "cat")? The answers to these questions and the analysis of the pattern of strengths and weaknesses are the central core of an educational diagnosis which will lead to a program of individualized instruction.

It is of extreme importance to recognize that the diagnostic process is a continuous evaluation, as opposed to a discreet one. Thus, the teacher of the mentally retarded needs to be more than just a teacher; she should become a *diagnostic-teacher*. While it would be uneconomical and educationally unfeasible to have every teacher take such additional preparation so as to become a school psychologist, each teacher can and should become skilled in the interpretation of the results supplied by the psychologist, and more, then should be able to supplement the psychologist's work by performing meaningful educational testing.

One of the most useful devices for beginning the diagnostic process has been the development of a profile of abilities and disabilities in the communication process. Kirk, McCarthy and Kirk (11) developed an instrument to assess the related factors, based on a theoretical model developed by Charles Osgood (13). Considerable research has been generated which seems to show that the instrument is useful in diagnosing specific deficits and in providing profiles which lead to programs to ameliorate the specific learning disabilities found.

Kirk (10) reviewed the findings of various studies and concluded that some children diagnosed as mentally retarded could better be classified as children with specific learning disabilities.

CLINICAL TEACHING METHODS

Diagnosis by itself is meaningless; it must become a part of a diagnostic-teaching process if it is to be anything more than another form of classification. Newer instructional methods, including programmed instruction, seem to offer hope that, given the proper educational procedure, almost any child can be taught almost anything (3). The key to development of clinical teaching methods is a determination of the areas in which the child is weakest, analysis of these to determine possible effect of one on the other, and then the development of an individual program of sequenced instruction. Quite often, the older child needs to learn that he can learn, as his first step. Deficits are usually attacked singly, with varying instructional techniques utilized to maintain interest and motivation. Individual tutoring sessions may last from ten minutes to over an hour, depending on the child's age, ability to maintain complete attention to the tasks being presented and the type of instruction being presented. Whenever the child becomes restless, distracted, annoyed or otherwise unable to proceed with a lesson, either the method of presentation should be shifted, or the lesson terminated. For children with persistent inability to attend to learning tasks, the teachers needs to employ some behavior modification techniques. Recent experience with those derived from operant conditioning has been most successful.

Several articles are available in the professional literature which describe the implications of a learning disabilities approach for teaching mentally retarded children (1, 2, 4, 7, 14).

PRESCHOOL EDUCATIONAL PROGRAMS

Public schools in the United States have traditionally started children in school at about the age of six. The preschool movement has, to a large extent, been limited to the kindergarten program which usually provided for a "readiness" program for six months to a year prior to entering the first grade. The development of full-scale programs for children from high-risk low socio-economic homes has been slow to emerge despite a rather lengthy body of literature indicating: (1) that social and sensory deprivation during a child's early years (from birth to three years of age) can be extremely devastating in terms of language development, intellectual potential as measured by IQ tests, and early academic performance; (2) that the earlier intervention takes place, the more likely will be the achievement of maximum gains; and (3) that many children from low socio-economic homes show considerable gains in IQ scores when provided with an intellectually stimulating environment. In addition, too many programs have been started with less than adequately trained personnel, and as a result, they have been criticized as being little more than baby-sitting programs. To be truly effective, such preschool programs must recognize the educational implications of the environment in which the children from culturally disadvantaged homes have been provided from birth. The reports of several newly-developed programs are available.*

---

* Appel, M. J., C. M. Williams and K. N. Fishell, "A Day Care Center Training Program for Preschool Retarded Children: A Description and Analysis of Results," *Mental Retardation*, IV:17, 1966.

In stressing the need for preschool programs for children from high-risk areas, we will be most effective in preventing stigmatization of the child by hasty labeling, and we will probably be most effective in applying remedial techniques. This can be accomplished by providing the special help needed to the child to become an adequate learner and thus be able to acquire knowledge as other children do, rather than be subjected to remedial procedures which prevent him from participating fully in the regular educational program enjoyed by his peers.

SUMMARY AND CONCLUSIONS

Children who are labeled by physicians and psychologists as "mentally retarded" deserve more than a watered-down educational curriculum. The educator should reject the assumption that an IQ or MA score prescribes absolute limits regarding how a particular child can learn or what educational techniques are best suited to his pattern of abilities and disabilities. We need to develop more and better differential diagnostic instruments that will lead to specific prescriptions of educational techniques designed to ameliorate each child's unique profile. Furthermore, we must never be satisfied with the diagnostic work-up as an end in itself since diagnosis is a continuing process which must be related to the educational activities in which the child is engaged. Teachers, therefore, must become "diagnostic-teachers" who continually re-assess each child's progress in terms of *how* he is learning as well as *how much* he has retained. Such assessment needs to be fed back into the materials and activities designed for that child's education.

In this manner, the instructional program itself becomes a part of the diagnostic process and is thus self-correcting rather than an immutable program to which the child must either adapt or fail.

Blatt, B. and F. Garfunkel, "Educating Intelligence: Determinants of School Behavior of Disadvantaged Children," *Exceptional Children,* 33:601, 1967.

Kaplan, F., and J. J. Colombatto, "Headstart Program for Siblings of Mentally Retarded Children," *Mental Retardation,* IV:30, 1966.

Karnes, M. B., A. Hodgins, and J. A. Teska, "An Evaluation of Two Preschool Programs for Disadvantaged Children: A Traditional and a Highly-Structured Experimental Preschool," *Exceptional Children,* 34:667, 1968.

Spicker, H. H., W. L. Hodges, and B. R. McCandless, "A Diagnostic Curriculum for Psychosocially Deprived Preschool, Mentally Retarded Children: Interim Report," *Exceptional Children,* 33:215, 1966.

BIBLIOGRAPHY

1. Allen, R. M., and I. Dickman, "A Pilot Study of the Immediate Effectiveness of the Frostig-Horne Training Program with Educable Retardates," *Except. Child.,* 33:41, 1966.
2. Bateman, B., "Implications of a Learning Disability Approach for Teaching Educable Retardates," *Mental Retardation,* 5:23, 1967.
3. Bruner, J. S., R. R. Oliver, and P. M. Greenfield, *Studies in Cognitive Growth,* New York: Wiley, 1967.
4. Corder, W. O., "Effects of Physical Education on the Intellectual, Physical, and Social Development of Educable Mentally Retarded Boys," *Except. Child.,* 32: 357, 1966.
5. Dunn, L. M., "Special Education for the Mildly Retarded—Is Much of It Justifiable?" *Except. Child.,* 35:5, 1968.
6. Goldstein, H., L. Jordan and J. Moss, *The Efficacy of Special Class Training on the Development of Mentally Retarded Children,* Cooperative Research Project, No. 619, Urbana, Illinois: The Institute for Research on Exceptional Children, University of Illinois, 1965.
7. Hollis, J. H., and C. E. Gorton, "Training Severely and Profoundly Developmentally Retarded Children," *Mental Retardation,* V:20, 1967.
8. Kirk, S. A., "What's Special About Special Education?" *Except. Child.,* 19:138, 1958.
9. Kirk, S. A., *Early Education of Retarded Children—An Experimental Study,* Urbana: University of Illinois Press, 1958.
10. Kirk, S. A., "Amelioration of Mental Disability through Psychodiagnostic and Remedial Procedures," in *Mental Retardation,* Ed. by G. A. Jervis, Springfield, Illinois: Charles C Thomas, 1967.
11. Kirk, S. A., J. J. McCarthy, and W. D. Kirk, *The Illinois Test of Psycholinguistic Abilities* (Rev. Ed.), Urbana: University of Illinois Press, 1968.
12. Johnson, G. O., "Special Education for Mentally Handicapped—A Paradox," *Except. Child.,* 19:62, 1962.
13. Osgood, C. E., and M. S. Miron, *Approaches to the Study of Aphasia,* Urbana: University of Illinois Press, 1963.
14. Shields, O. L., "Remediation of Learning Disabilities in a Public School System," *Mental Retardation,* III:27, 1965.

Section V.

PSYCHO-SOCIAL ASPECTS OF MENTAL
RETARDATION

CHAPTER 24

Motivational Aspects of Mental Retardation

by EDWARD ZIGLER, Ph.D.
and DAVID BALLA, Ph.D.

INTRODUCTION

Most workers will agree that the essential defining feature of mental retardation is lower intelligence than that displayed by the modal member or majority of the population. However, the behavior of the retarded is not the immutable product of low intelligence alone. In fact, a striking feature encountered among retarded individuals is the variety of behavior patterns they display. Clearly, we are not dealing with a homogeneous group of persons with low intelligence, but rather with individuals who differ widely in regard to their motives, attitudes, and experimental backgrounds. It is unfortunate that so little work directed toward understanding the behavior of the retarded has emanated from a personality point of view.

Recently progress has been made which supports the view that it is not necessary to employ constructs other than those used to account for the behavior of intellectually-average individuals in explaining the behavior of the familial retarded. Research strongly suggests that many of the reported differences between retarded and intellectually-average children of the same mental age are a result of motivational and emotional differences which reflect differences in environmental histories, and are not a function of intrinsic differences (92). This is not to say that the cause of familial retardation is motivational; the cognitive functioning of the retarded unquestionably has a profound and per-

Preparation of this paper was supported by Research Grant HD 03008 from the National Institute of Child Health and Human Development, and by the Gunnar Dybwad Award from the National Association for Retarded Citizens. The authors extend thanks to Sally J. Styfco for critically reading an earlier draft of this paper.

377

vasive influence on their behavior. The crucial questions are just how great is this influence and how does it vary across tasks with which the retarded are confronted? What must be grasped is that the behavior of the retarded, as for all human beings, reflects more than formal cognitive processes.

That personality factors are as important in the adjustment of the retarded as intellective factors has been noted by many workers (68, 71, 80, 86, 93). Even some of the earlier workers in this country, such as Fernald and Potter, felt that the difference between social adequacy and inadequacy in that large group of borderline retarded individuals was a matter of personality rather than intelligence. A number of studies have confirmed this view (61, 86). Perhaps the most notable of these is the comprehensive study by T. Weaver (84) of the adjustment of 8,000 retarded persons inducted into the United States Army, most of whom had IQs below 75. Of the total group, 56 percent of the males and 62 percent of the females made a satisfactory adjustment to military life. The median IQs of the successful and unsuccessful groups were 72 and 68, respectively. Weaver concluded that "personality factors far overshadowed the factor of intelligence in the adjustment of the retarded to military service."

The tendency to overemphasize the importance of the intellect in adjustment has been documented by Windle (86). On the basis of a survey he found that most institutions presume that intelligence is the critical factor in adjustment after release. However, as Windle, as well as McCarver and Craig (61), pointed out, the majority of studies have reported no meaningful relation between intellectual level and adjustment after release from institutions. Rather, in this literature the factors suggested as associated with poor social adjustment include anxiety, jealousy, overdependency, poor self-evaluation, hostility, hyperactivity, and failure to follow orders even when requests were well within the range of intellectual competence. (See McCarver and Craig (61) for an especially comprehensive review of the importance of nonintellective factors in the prognosis of mental retardation.)

It is hardly surprising that many of the retarded evidence such difficulties in light of their often atypical social histories. The specific atypical features of their socialization histories, and the extent to which they are atypical, may vary from child to child. Two sets of parents who are themselves familially retarded may provide quite different socialization histories for their children. At one extreme a familial retarded child may ultimately be institutionalized, not because of lack of intelligence, but because his own home represents an especially debilitating environment. At the other extreme, a familially retarded set of parents may provide their children with a relatively good home environment even though it might differ in certain important respects—values, goals, and attitudes—from the typical home in which the parents are of average or superior intelligence. In the first example, the child not only experiences a quite different socialization history while living with his parents, but also differs from the child in the second situation to the extent that institutionalization affects his behavior and development. To add even more complexity, the socialization histories of both the institutionalized and noninstitutionalized familially retarded differ markedly from the histories of the organically retarded, who do not differ from the general population in the frequency of good versus poor home environments.

In the face of such complexity, we need not consider the problem of understanding mental retardation as unassailable, nor assert that each retarded child is so unique that it is impossible for us to isolate the ontogenesis of those factors which may influence the retarded child's level of functioning. Once we conceptualize the retarded, person as occupying a position on a continuum of normalcy, we can allow our knowledge of normal development to give direction to our efforts. This does not mean that we can ignore the importance of lower intelligence per se, since personality traits and behavior patterns do not develop in a vacuum. However, in some instances the personality characteristics of the retarded will reflect environmental factors that have little or nothing to do with intellectual endowment. For example, many of the effects of institutionalization may be constant regardless of the person's intelligence level. In other instances we must think in terms of an interaction; that is, given a lower intellectual ability, a person will have certain experiences and develop certain behavior patterns differing from those of a person with higher intelligence. An obvious example is the greater amount of failure which the retarded child typically experiences. But, again, what must be emphasized is that the behavior pattern developed by the retarded person as a result of such a history of failure may not differ in ontogenesis from that of an individual of average intellect who, by some environmental circumstance, also experiences an inordinate amount of failure. By the same token, if the retarded person could be guaranteed a more typical history of success, we would expect his behavior to resemble more nearly that of the intellectually-average individual, independent of intellectual level. Within this framework, we will discuss the personality factors which have been found to influence the performance of the retarded.

In interpreting the research findings presented below, we must emphasize that caution is necessary in evaluating the role of motivational and emotional factors in the performance of the retarded. Performance on any task is most appropriately conceptualized as a function of two types of factors: intellective (cognitive) and nonintellective (e.g., motivational). The contribution of each factor will vary with the nature of the task. Motivational factors will more readily influence a perseveration task, for example, how long a retarded child will play a boring game, than they will a discrimination-learning or concept-formation task, although it has been demonstrated that performance on tasks of this type is also influenced by motivational factors (16, 34, 97). Furthermore, improved performance following a manipulation of the child's motivation should not be interpreted as evidence that basic intellectual capacity has been changed. Rather, these demonstrations suggests ways in which one may help the mentally retarded to utilize their intellectual capacity optimally.

FACTORS INFLUENCING MOTIVATION IN THE RETARDED

Social Deprivation

It has become increasingly clear that our understanding of the performance of the institutionalized retarded will be enhanced if we consider the amount of preinstitutional social deprivation they have experienced (21, 41, 90). Social deprivation has been found to affect a variety of behaviors. For example, it has been reported that increased social deprivation is associated with increased proficiency in concept-switching (15). Highly deprived retarded children have also been found to be more verbally dependent, more wary, and to show less behavior variability than less deprived children (7). Perhaps the largest and most important body of research has shown that social deprivation can result in a heightened motivation to interact with a supportive adult (an increased responsiveness to social reinforcement). While the majority of evidence to date has indicated that increased social deprivation is associated with increased responsiveness to social reinforcement (7, 50, 90, 94, 95), it has also been reported that in certain circumstances increased social deprivation may lead to an attenuation of social reinforcer effectiveness (38, 50). The heightened motivation to interact with an adult, stemming from a history of social deprivation, is consistent with frequently observed behavior in the retarded of actively seeking attention, affection, etc.

It should be noted that heightened motivation for social reinforcement has been used as an indicator of an important phenomenon discussed in the general child development literature, namely dependency. Thus, with an almost imperceptibly slight shift in terminology, we might conclude that the findings concerning responsiveness to social reinforcement indicate that a general consequence of social deprivation is overdependency. We cannot place enough emphasis on the role of such overdependency in the behavior of the retarded and on the socialization histories that give rise to overdependency. In a review of factors in the socialization of the mentally retarded, Zigler and Harter (98) concluded that given some minimal intellectual level, the shift from dependency to independence is perhaps the single most important factor which enables the retarded to become self-sustaining members of society.

Some indication of the pervasiveness of the atypical dependency of the institutionalized familially retarded may be found in a study by Zigler and Balla (94). Intellectually-average and retarded children of three mental age (MA) levels—approximately 7, 9, and 12—were compared in terms of their responsiveness to social reinforcement. In keeping with the general developmental progression from helplessness and dependence to autonomy and independence, both retarded and intellectually-average children of higher MAs were found to be less motivated for social reinforcement than those of lower MAs. However, at every MA level, the retarded children were more motivated for social reinforcement than were the nonretarded children. The disparity in motivation between groups was just as great at the upper as at the lower developmental levels. Indeed, the oldest retarded group was almost twice as dependent (as measured by responsiveness to social reinforcement) as the youngest nonretarded group.

It thus appears that the institutionalized retarded must satisfy certain affectional needs before they can cope with problems in a manner similar to individuals whose affectional needs have been relatively satisfied. Such unmet affectional needs can often interfere with certain problem-solving activities. Evidence on this point was provided by Harter (34), who found that institutionalized retarded children took significantly longer to solve a concept-formation problem in a social condition, where they were face-to-face with a warm supportive experimenter who praised their performance, than in a standard condition, where the experimenter was silent and out of view. The retarded subjects in the social condition appeared highly motivated to interact with the supportive adult, so much so that it seemed to compete with their attention to the learning task. A further illustration of this point may be found in a study by Balla (6), who observed institutionalized retarded children in a schoolroom setting. He reported that these children seemed to employ the school as a place to interact with adults in an effort to compensate for the lack of such interactions in the other segments of their lives. It thus appears that, just as in Harter's experimental situation, institutionalized retarded children utilize the school setting to satisfy their motivation for social interaction more than for learning. Some evidence that such attenuating effects of social deprivation can be overcome has been presented by McKinney and Keele (64), who found improvement in a variety of behaviors in even the severely mentally retarded following an experience of increased mothering.

Positive- and Negative-Reaction Tendencies

A phenomenon which appears to be at considerable variance with the retarded individual's increased desire for social reinforcement has been noted—namely, the retarded child's reluctance and wariness to interact with adults. This apparent inconsistency has been part of a controversy over whether social deprivation leads to an increase in the desire for interaction or to apathy and withdrawal (24, 26, 27, 39, 76, 87). Clarification of this issue has been aided by the experimental work of Zigler and his associates, which has indicated that social deprivation results both in a heightened motivation to interact with supportive adults (positive-reaction tendency) and in a reluctance and wariness to do so (negative-reaction tendency).

The construct of a negative-reaction tendency has been employed to explain certain differences between retarded and nonretarded individuals reported by Kounin (51, 52), differences that were attributed to the greater cognitive rigidity of the retarded. As one measure of rigidity, Kounin employed a simple task which the subject is allowed to perform until he wishes to stop; he is then instructed to perform a highly similar response until again satiated. A recurring finding in studies employing such a two-part task (51, 89, 90) is that the retarded have a much greater tendency than intellectually-average individuals to spend more time on task two than on task one. Zigler (89) suggested that this difference was due to the greater negative-reaction tendency of the retarded subjects, a consequence of the more negative encounters that institutionalized retarded individuals experience at the hands of adults. The reasoning was that the high negative-reaction tendency of the retarded person was reduced as a result of the pleasant experiences encountered on the first task, thus resulting in a longer playing time on the second task. Nonretarded children tend not to show such a pattern since they do not approach task one with such a strong negative-reaction tendency.

This view was tested in a study (73) in which intellectually-average and retarded children, matched on MA, were compared on a two-part experimental task similar to that used in the earlier studies. In addition to the basic procedure employed in the previous studies, three experimental games, given under two conditions of reinforcement, preceded the two-part criterion task. In a positive reinforcement condition, all of the child's responses met with success, and were further rewarded with verbal and nonverbal support by the experimenter. In a negative reinforcement condition, all of the child's responses met with failure, and the experimenter further commented on his lack of success. It was assumed that the negative-reaction tendency would be reduced in the positive reinforcement condition and increased in the negative condition. The findings of this study confirmed the prediction that both the nonretarded and retarded groups who played the experimental games under the negative condition would play part two of the criterion task longer than part one, while the two groups receiving the positive condition would play part one longer than part two.

These findings indicate that co-satiation effects are not the product of inherent rigidity, but rather of the relative strength of certain motivational varieties, i.e., positive- and negative-reaction tendencies. These tendencies and their relative strengths seem to be the product of particular environmental experiences and apparently are open to manipulation and modification. Thus the Shallenberger and Zigler study presents further evidence that on certain tasks, differences in the performance of retarded and nonretarded individuals of the same MA can be attributed most parsimoniously to different environmental histories and resulting motivations.

Evidence that the genesis of the negative-reaction tendency is to be found in socially depriving experiences, rather than in mental retardation per se, is contained in several experimental investigations. For example, S. J. Weaver (82) examined the negative-reaction tendencies of a group of noninstitutionalized retarded children who had extremely poor records of academic, social, and health adjustment. Among the tasks employed by Weaver was one which required the child to place a series of cut-out shapes on a long felt board, at one end of which sat an adult. In one experimental condition, the adult positively reinforced the behavior of the child, while in the other condition he made negative comments concerning the child's performance. Unlike the time measures used in earlier studies, Weaver employed a more direct measure of the child's approach and avoidance tendencies, namely, how far from the adult experimenter the child placed the shapes. Consistent with our thinking concerning the negative-reaction tendency, Weaver found that, over the series of trials, children in the positive reinforcement condition moved toward the experimenter, whereas children in the negative condition moved away from him. In a second study (83), experimental condition effects like those discovered by Weaver were found for institutionalized retarded children. Weaver et al. also found that institutionalized retarded children were more motivated to approach the adult experimenter but were more wary of doing so than either noninstitutionalized retarded or nonretarded children. Some evidence also exists that institutionalized retarded individuals suffer from a generalized wariness of strangers, regardless of whether the strangers are adults or peers (35).

Since positive- and negative-reaction tendencies are hardly unique to children of limited intellect, this line of investigation was pursued in a series of studies with intellectually-average children (13, 14, 38, 60, 65). These studies were directed at further validation of what has come to be known as the "valence position." Stated most simply, this position asserts that the effectiveness of an adult as a social reinforcing agent for a particular child depends upon the valence which that adult has for the child. This valence is determined by the relative amount of positive and negative experiences the child has encountered at the hands of the adult and/or other adults in the child's past from whom he has generalized. The five studies noted above employed length of playing time on a boring satiation-type task as the measure of the adult's social reinforcer effectiveness. These studies have produced considerable evidence indicating that prior positive contacts between the child and the adult increase the adult's effectiveness as a reinforcer while negative contacts decrease it. If the experimentally-manipulated negative encounters in these experiments are conceptualized as the experimental analogue of what the institutionalized retarded actually have experienced in their lives, then the often reported reluctance and wariness with which such children interact with adults becomes understandable.

It should be noted that the investigation of such positive- and negative-reaction tendencies, their interactions, and the specific events which give rise to them may clarify issues much more global in nature than the finding that, under certain conditions, retarded individuals will play a second part of a two-part co-satiation task longer than the first part. Most importantly, the wariness of adults and of the tasks that adults present can lead to a general attenuation in the retarded child's social effectiveness. Poor performance by the institutionalized retarded on tasks presented by adults, therefore, cannot be attributed entirely to intellectual factors but must be interpreted in light of the atypically high negative-reaction tendency of many retarded individuals. This tendency motivates them toward behaviors, for example, withdrawal, which reduce the quality of their performance to a level lower than that which one would expect on the basis of their intellectual capacity alone.

Failure and the Performance of the Retarded

Another factor frequently mentioned as a determinant in the performance of the retarded is their high expectancy of failure. This failure expectancy has been viewed as a consequence of a lifetime of failure experiences resulting from frequent confrontation with tasks with which the retarded are intellectually ill-equipped to deal. It has been amply documented that these failure experiences and failure expectancies affect a wide variety of behavior in the intellectually average (3, 4, 31, 42, 45, 69, 72). Of special interest to workers in the area of mental retardation is Lantz's finding (53) that a relatively simple failure experience prevented children from profiting by practice which ordinarily leads to improvement on intelligence test scores.

The experimental work employing the success-failure dimensions with retarded individuals has proceeded in two directions. The first has been an attempt to document the pervasiveness of feelings of failure in retarded individuals. The work of Cromwell (25) and his colleagues has lent support to the general proposition that retarded individuals have a higher expectancy of failure than individuals of average intellect. In a series of studies MacMillan and his colleagues (57, 58, 59) employed an interrupted task paradigm to determine whether noninstitutionalized retarded children tended to blame themselves for apparent failure to a greater extent than nonretarded children. Children were prevented from finishing several tasks which they had begun, and were subsequently asked why the tasks were not completed. In all these studies, the retarded children consistently placed blame on themselves for the tasks not being completed while nonretarded children did not place blame on themselves.

The second line of research has focused upon the effect of success and failure expectancies on problem-solving behavior. The task typically employed in these studies is a three-choice discrimination problem in which one stimulus is partially reinforced and the other two stimuli are never reinforced. It has been found that children with low expectancies of success, as gauged by aspiration level or need-achievement measures, are more likely to display a maximizing strategy (persistent choice of the partially-reinforced stimulus) on this task than children with high expectancies of success (31, 45, 67).

The prediction that retarded children would display more maximizing behavior than nonretarded children of the same MA was originally advanced by Stevenson and Zigler (79), who argued that retarded children have come to expect and settle for lower degrees of success than have children of average intellect. This rationale is consistent with Goodnow's (28) analysis of the determinants of choice behavior. Goodnow suggested that greater maximizing behavior would be found when a subject accepted less than 100 percent success as an acceptable outcome, while less maximizing behavior would be found when a subject expected 100 percent success, or a level of success greater than that allowed in the situation. Thus, on the three-choice probability task, children with higher expectancies of success would be expected to engage in strategies other than maximizing, in the hope of achieving 100 percent reinforcement. A strategy which has frequently been found in children having a high expectancy of success is that of patterning (some variant of left-middle-right, or right-middle-left responding).

Consistent with the expectancy of success formulation, retarded children have been found to exhibit more maximizing behavior than children of average intelligence (32, 79). However, the tendency of retarded individuals to employ a maximizing strategy could also be interpreted within the cognitive rigidity position rather than in terms of expectancies of failure, i.e., the rigidity of the retarded leads them to select only one of the three stmuli. Gruen and Zigler (32) attempted to resolve this issue by administering short-term success or failure experiences to a group of retarded children immediately prior to the probability-learning task. No evidence was found that these success or failure conditions differentially affected the performance of the retarded children. Since the short-term setting conditions may simply have been too weak, Ollendick, Balla, and Zigler (66) employed more intense and long-term success and failure setting conditions. They found that failure experiences resulted in a low expectancy of success, reflected by more maximizing behavior, while success experiences resulted in a higher expectancy of success. Gruen, Ottinger, and Ollendick (30) attempted to determine whether the success-failure findings could be replicated in a more life-like school setting. As predicted, retarded children in regular classes (presumably being exposed to repeated failure) were found to have higher expectancies of failure than retarded children in special classes (being exposed to relatively higher levels of success).

The Reinforcer Hierarchy

Due to a variety of experiential factors, the retarded individual's motivation for various types of incentives may be quite different from that of intellectually-average individuals of the same mental age. Stated somewhat differently, the position of various reinforcers in the reinforcer hierarchies may differ in retarded and nonretarded children. Much of the experimental work on the reinforcer hierarchy has focused on tangible and intangible reinforcement (37). It has been argued that certain factors in the histories of retarded children cause them to be less responsive to intangible reinforcement than are nonretarded children of equivalent MA (91, 97, 103). This work is of special importance, since intangible reinforcement (information that a response is correct) is the most immediate and frequently dispensed reinforcement in real-life tasks, particularly in the typical test situation. When such a reinforcer is employed in experimental studies comparing retarded and nonretarded children, one questions how many of the differences found are attributable to differences in intellectual capacity but rather to the different values that such reinforcers might have for the two types of children.

The importance of the specific reinforcer dispensed in studies with the retarded was highlighted in a study by Stevenson and Zigler (78). These investigators found that when tangible reinforcers were given, the institutionalized familially retarded were no more rigid than nonretarded subjects of the same MA on a discrimination reversal-learning task. Interestingly, on a concept-switching task both retarded and upper socio-economic status children were found to switch more readily in a tangible than in an intangible reinforcement condition (103).

Clearest support for the view that the retarded child is much less motivated to be correct for the sake of correctness than is the middle socioeconomic status (SES) child (so typically employed in comparisons with the retarded) is contained in a study by Zigler and deLabry (97). These investigators tested MA-matched middle SES, lower SES, and retarded children on a concept-switching task (51) under two conditions of reinforcement. In the first condition, the only reinforcement dispensed was the information that the child was correct. In the second condition, the child was rewarded with a toy of his choice if he switched from one concept to another. In the "correct" condition, both the retarded and lower SES groups were poorer in their concept-switching than the middle SES children. However, no differences were found among the three groups who received tangible reinforcers. Furthermore, no differences in the ability to switch concepts were found among the three groups receiving what was assumed to be their optimal reinforcer (retarded tangible, lower SES tangible, and middle SES intangible).

These studies highlight an assumption that has been noted as erroneous by many educators—namely, that the lower SES child and the retarded child are responsive to the same type of reinforcers as the typical middle SES child. However, it must be noted that although retarded children as a group may value being correct less than do middle SES children as a group, this may not hold true for any particular child. The crucial factor is not membership in a particular social class or being retarded in intellect, but rather the particular social learning experienced by the child.

This point is aptly underlined in a study by Byck (17), who examined the performance of institutionalized Down's syndrome and familially retarded subjects (matched on MA, CA, IQ, and length of institutionalization) on a concept-switching task. Half of the children in each group were reinforced for their performance with a tangible reward (a small toy), and the other half with social reinforcers, including the information that they were correct. A highly significant interaction was found indicating superior concept-switching for the Down's syndrome children in the intangible as compared to the tangible condition, whereas the reverse pattern was found for the familial groups. This finding is consistent with the social class and reinforcer effectiveness literature noted above, if one remembers that the institutionalized familial retarded almost invariably come from a lower SES background, whereas children with Down's syndrome are much more likely to come from middle SES homes. It would appear that the social learning experiences acquired fairly early in the child's life and prior to institutionalization are particularly influential in determining the potency of various reinforcers.

In more recent work on the reinforcer hierarchy, attention has shifted to the more general phenomenon of the intrinsic reinforcement that inheres in being correct, regardless of whether or not an external agent dispenses a reinforcer for such correctness. This shift in orientation owes much to White's (85) formulation concerning the pervasive influence of the effectance motive. Whether or not one accepts the view that the individual's need for effectance or mastery is a basic need that parallels certain other primary drives, there can be little question that White's effectance concept provides a rubric for a variety of behaviors that appear very central in the individual's behavioral repertoire from infancy through senility, e.g., the desire for optimal levels of sensory stimulation, manipulation, exploration, and curiosity. A series of studies (75, 100, 101, 102) have given some support to this view that using one's cognitive resources to their fullest is intrinsically gratifying and thus motivating.

As with the case of intangible reinforcers, the strength of the effectance motive may be different for retarded and nonretarded children. Evidence on this point is provided by Harter and Zigler (36), who constructed several measures of effectance motivation, including variation seeking, curiosity, mastery for the sake of competence, and preference for challenging tasks. On these measures, intellectually-average children demonstrated more effectance motivation than retarded children. The measures also proved sensitive to differences between noninstitutionalized and institutionalized retarded children. In summary, retarded children seem to be both less responsive to intangible reinforcers and less motivated by intrinsic effectance motives than children of average intellect.

Outerdirectedness

Findings (29, 99) that retarded children are more sensitive to cues provided by an adult than are intellectually-average children of the same MA have led Zigler and his co-workers to the study of a general style of problem solving referred to as outerdirected (1, 9, 70, 81, 88). This style has been defined as the degree to which the individual uses external cues to solve problems rather than relying on his own cognitive resources. The outerdirectedness dimension has been reformulated by Achenbach and Zigler (2) in terms of reliance on concrete situational cues in a problem-solving situation versus a strategy characterized by active attempts to extract abstract relations among problem elements in order to proceed from these relations to the solution of the problem.

Two factors have been advanced as important in determining the child's development and the relative incidence of success the individual has experienced when employing his cognitive resources in problem-solving situations. In general, children of lower cognitive levels have been found to be more outerdirected (9, 88). Independent of cognitive level, a child's readiness to employ his cognitive abilities is thought to be positively related to how often the use of these abilities has resulted in success.

The success-failure aspect of the outerdirectedness formulation has generated the prediction that retarded children, because of their histories of failure, are more outerdirected in their problem-solving behavior than are intellectually-average children of the same MA, a prediction that has been confirmed in several studies (2, 9, 70, 81, 88). These studies have also indicated that both nonretarded and retarded children become more outerdirected following failure experiences than success experiences, and that the noninstitutionalized retarded are more outerdirected than are the institutionalized retarded. This last finding is consistent with the outerdirectedness formulation inasmuch as the institutionalized retarded have proportionately fewer failure experiences than the noninstitutionalized retarded as a result of living in a protected environment more nearly geared to their intellectual level.

In one study, Yando and Zigler (88) focused on the effects of etiology of retardation and institutionalization on the degree of outerdirectedness. They found that organically retarded children living at home were significantly more outerdirected than those living in institutions, while institutionalization had the reverse effect for familially retarded children. (This finding with the familially retarded was at odds with the findings presented above, a discrepancy which Yando and Zigler attributed to differences across studies in age of the subject samples.) These findings are consistent with the suggestion of Sanders et al. (70) that the noninstitutionalized organically retarded child who remains in the home faces greater expectations and consequently more failure (often exacerbated by the achievement of siblings), resulting in more outerdirectedness, than he would face if he lived in an institutional environment adjusted to his intellectual shortcomings. This work on outerdirectedness suggests that the distractibility often seen in retarded individuals reflects an outerdirected style of problem solving rather than being due to a neurological defect, to which distractibility is so often attributed.

General Effects of Institutionalization

No discussion of motivational factors in the performance of the retarded would be complete without a consideration of the effects of institutionalization. The institutionalization variable has probably contaminated more research in the area of mental retardation than any other single variable. Given the penchant of many investigators for comparing the institutionalized retarded with children of average intelligence who live at home, one cannot help wondering how many differences discovered in such comparisons reflect some cognitive aspect of mental retardation as opposed to the effects of institutionalization, the factors that led to the child's institutionalization, or some complex interaction between these factors. Furthermore, many of the currently popular views concerning the retarded are based on investigations of institutionalized individuals, and investigators are now finding themselves in the position of determining to what extent these theories reflect the defining features of intellectual inadequacy and to what extent they reflect the effects of institutionalization (12, 33, 43). In view of the general consensus concerning the significance of institutionalization, it is surprising that more work has not been done to investigate its effects on retarded children.

There is little question that prior to the advent of the small community-based institution, the prevalent position was that institutions had extremely negative and monolithic effects. Support for this view comes from studies indicating that the institutionalized retarded were less intelligent or less developmentally advanced than supposedly comparable groups of noninstitutionalized retarded individuals (18, 19, 54, 55, 56, 74, 77). Kaufman (44) also found a significant advantage for home-reared retarded children as compared with a matched sample of institutionalized retarded persons. In other studies, it has been reported that the institutionalized retarded suffer from a decrement in performance on such measures as level of abstraction on a vocabulary test (5), ability to conceptualize an emotional continuum (40), and ability to form a learning set (34).

Other reports have shown that institutionalization may also have beneficial effects. Several longitudinal studies have shown an overall increase in IQ for institutionalized retarded children (11, 20, 21, 22, 95). Institutionalization has also been found to be related to an increase in the retarded child's autonomy in problem solving (88). Mueller and Weaver (65) found a consistent language advantage in an institutionalized group as compared with a matched sample of home-reared day school children. Balla, Butterfield, and Zigler (7) found that groups of retarded children became less verbally dependent, less outerdirected, and more variable in their behavior after 2.5 years of institutionaliza- tion. While these authors found no change in IQ, MA level was found to increase.

In many of the studies on institutionalization, even a simplistic char- acterization of the institution or some measure of the institutional en- vironment was missing. Thus it is impossible to reconcile inconsistent findings. In this context, it is surprising that so few cross-institutional studies have been conducted. The work that has been done in comparing institutions for their effects on the actual behavior of the retarded (47, 48, 49) has sometimes indicated that institutional differences can be striking. Findings (16, 95, 96) of differences even across large institutions in the residents' responsiveness to social reinforcement and changes in IQ following institutionalization lend credence to Cleland's (23) argu- ment that we must go beyond such gross characteristics as institution size and begin delineating the particular social-psychological characteristics and practices of institutions which may affect the behavior and develop- ment of the residents.

In an initial effort in this direction, Balla, Butterfield, and Zigler (7) examined residents in four widely geographically separated institu- tions for the retarded. Measures of MA, IQ, responsiveness to social reinforcement, verbal dependency, wariness of adults, outerdirectedness, and behavior variability were obtained. In an effort to provide a more fine-grained characterization of the institutions than in previous studies, a number of demographic measures of the institution were also gath- ered: size, number of residents per living unit, cost per resident per day, percent employee turnover rate, number of attendants per resident, pro- fessional staff per resident, and the number of volunteer hours per resident year. It was felt that an examination of these factors, com- bined with subjective impressions of the institution milieus, would provide a reasonable framework in which to evaluate behavioral changes of the residents. Surprisingly, neither subjective impressions of the insti- tutions nor the objective demographic characteristics were found to be related to residents' behavioral development. It seemed clear that a much more fine-grained analysis of institutional characteristics was needed.

McCormick, Balla, and Zigler (62) investigated institution-oriented and resident-oriented care practices for the institutionalized retarded in living units of institutions in the United States and in a Scandinavian country. In addition to the institutional demographic varables employed by Balla et al. (7), information for each living unit studied was obtained: the number of residents in each living unit investigated, the level of mental retardation in each unit (mild, moderate, severe-profound), and the age level of the residents in each unit (child, adolescent, adult). Living units in the Scandinavian country were found to be more resident-oriented than in the United States. In both countries, large central institutions were characterized by the most institution-oriented care practices, group homes by the most resident-oriented practices, with regional centers falling between these two extremes. Level of mental retardation and large living unit size were found to be predictive of institution-oriented practices, while cost per resident per day, number of aides per resident, and number of professional staff per resident did not predict care practices.

Other studies have employed different approaches to characterize the nature of institutional experience. Klaber (46) reported striking differences between institutions in terms of the number of times during the year when parents visited their resident children. Children in an institution characterized as highly depriving received fewer visits from parents than those in a more favorable setting. Other studies have consistently shown that residents who were frequently visited displayed more responsiveness to social reinforcement than less frequently visited residents (8, 10, 94).

The findings to date underline the importance of considering not only the particular institution but also the particular living unit in which a child resides in order to understand the effects of institutionalization. Complicating the matter still futrher are the findings that the same institution can have different effects on the residents depending upon their preinstitutional social deprivation (7, 11, 20, 21; 22, 88, 94, 95, 96). Clarke and Clarke (21) found that the greatest increase in IQ scores following institutionalization occurred in those retarded children who came from the worst homes. A related finding is that children whose parents were highly desirous of institutionalizing them showed an immediate increase in IQ upon institutionalization, whereas for children whose parents were not so motivated, IQs increased only after three years of institutionalization (11). Findings of several longitudinal studies (11, 95, 96, 104) indicated that institutionalization was more socially depriving for individuals from relatively supportive home environments than for those from environments characterized by a high degree of social deprivation.

Balla, Butterfield, and Zigler (7) reported a number of findings indicating that the child's preinstitutional social deprivation played an important part in determining his behavior while institutionalized: children with a history of low preinstitutional social deprivation became more variable in their behavior, while children with a preinstitutional history of high deprivation did not change. Other findings of this longitudinal cross-institutional study indicated that the particular course of development displayed by a child was a function of both that child's history of preinstitutional deprivation and the particular institution in which he resided.

Finally, the effects of institutionalization are undoubtedly related to how long the child has been institutionalized, at what age the child was institutionalized, and his sex and diagnosis. For example, Balla, McCarthy, and Zigler (18) found that children institutionalized when they were younger were less wary than children institutionalized when they were older. Ollendick et al. (66) found that institutionalized retarded males had higher expectancies of failure than females. The institutionalized girls employed by Balla, Butterfield, and Zigler (7) had higher IQs than the boys, both after six months and 2.5 years of institutionalization. In this study, both sex and diagnosis proved to be mediator variables in many of the findings involving the effects of individual institutions on children with different histories of preinstitutional social deprivation.

SUMMARY

The research conducted on several of the motivational and emotional factors in the performance of the retarded is more suggestive than definitive. It is clear, however, that these factors are extremely important in determining the retarded person's level of functioning. Furthermore, these factors seem much more open to environmental manipulation than do the cognitive processes. An increase in knowledge concerning motivational and emotional factors and their ontogenesis holds considerable promise for alleviating much of the social ineffectiveness displayed by that rather sizeable group of persons who function at a relatively low intellectual level.

BIBLIOGRAPHY

1. Achenbach, T. M., and J. R. Weisz, "The Effect of Outerdirectedness on Cognitive Development: A Longitudinal Study of IQ Changes." Unpublished manuscript, Yale University, 1975.
2. Achenbach, T., and E. Zigler, "Cue-Learning and Problem-Learning Strategies in Normal and Retarded Children," *Child Development*, 39:821-848, 1968.
3. Atkinson, J. W., "Motivational Determinants of Risk Taking Behavior." In J. W. Atkinson (Ed.), *Motives in Fantasy, Action, and Society*. Princeton: Van Nostrand, 1958, 322-340 (a).
4. Atkinson, J. W., "Towards Experimental Analysis of Human Motives in Terms of Motives, Expectancies, and Incentives." In J. W. Atkinson (Ed.), *Motives in Fantasy, Action, and Society*, Princeton: Van Nostrand, 1958, 288-305 (b).
5. Badt, M. I., "Levels of Abstraction in Vocabulary Definitions of Mentally Retarded School Children," *Amer. J. Mental Defic.*, 63:241-246, 1958.
6. Balla, D., "The Verbal Action of the Environment in Institutionalized and Noninstitutionalized Retardates and Normal Children of Two Social Classes." Unpublished doctoral dissertation, Yale University, 1966.
7. Balla, D., E. C. Butterfield, and E. Ziegler, "Effects of Institutionalization on Retarded Children: A Longitudinal Cross-Institutional Investigation." *Amer. J. Mental Defic.*, 78:530-549, 1974.
8. Balla, D., E. McCarthy, and E. Zigler, "Some Correlates of Negative Reaction Tendencies in Institutionalized Retarded Children," *J. Psychol.*, 79:77-84, 1971.
9. Balla, D., S. J. Styfco, and E. Zigler, "Use of the Opposition Concept and Outerdirectedness in Intellectually-Average, Familial Retarded, and Organically Retarded Children," *Amer. J. Mental Defic.*, 75:663-680, 1971.
10. Balla, D., and E. Zigler, "The Therapeutic Role of Visits and Vacations for Institutionalized Retarded Children," *Mental Retardation*, 9:7-9, 1971.
11. Balla, D., and E. Zigler, "Preinstitutional Social Deprivation, Responsiveness to Social Reinforcement, and IQ Change in Institutionalized Retarded Individuals: A Six-year Follow-up Study." *Amer. J. Mental Defic.*, in press.
12. Maumeister, A. A., "Problems in Comparative Studies of Mental Retardates and Normals," *Amer. J. Mental Defic.*, 71:869-875, 1967.
13. Berkowitz, H., E. C. Butterfield, and E. Zigler, "The Effectiveness of Social Reinforcers on Persistence and Learning Tasks Following Positive and Negative Social Interactions," *J. Personality and Soc. Psychol.*, 2:706-714, 1965.
14. Berkowitz, H., and E. Zigler, "Effects of Preliminary Positive and Negative Interactions and Delay Conditions on Children's Responsiveness to Social Reinforcement," *J. Personality and Soc. Psychol.*, 2:500-505, 1965.
15. Butterfield, E. C., and A. McIntyre, "Cognitive and Motivational Factors in Concept Switching Among the Retarded," *Amer. J. Mental Defic.*, 74:235-241, 1969.
16. Butterfield, E. C., and E. Zigler, "The Influence of Differing Institutional Social Climates on the Effectiveness of Social Reinforcement in the Mentally Retarded," *Amer. J. Mental Defic.*, 70:48-56, 1965.
17. Byck, M., "Cognitive Differences Among Diagnostic Groups of Retardates," *Amer. J. Mental Defic.*, 73:97-101, 1968.
18. Carr, J., "Mental and Motor Development in Young Mongol Children," *J. Mental Defic. Research*, 14:205-220, 1970.
19. Centerwall, S. A., and W. R. Centerwall, "A Study of Children with Mongolism Reared in the Home Compared to Those Reared Away from Home," *Pediatrics*, 25:678-685, 1969.
20. Clarke, A. D. B., and A. M. Clarke, "How Constant is the IQ," *Lancet*, 265:877-880, 1953.

21. Clarke, A. D. B., and A. M. Clarke, "Cognitive Changes in the Feebleminded," *Brit. J. Psychol.,* 45:173-179, 1954.
22. Clarke, A. D. B., A. M. Clarke, and S. Reiman, "Cognitive and Social Changes in the Feebleminded—Three Further Studies," *Brit. J. Psychol.,* 49:144-157, 1958.
23. Cleland, C., "Evidence on the Relationship Between Size and Institutional Effectiveness: A Review and an Analysis," *Amer. J. Mental Defic.,* 70:423-431, 1965.
24. Cox, F., "The Origins of the Dependency Drive," *Australian J. Psychol.,* 5:64-73, 1953.
25. Cromwell, R. L., "A Social Learning Approach to Mental Retardation." In N. R. Ellis (Ed.), *"Handbook of Mental Deficiency.* New York: McGraw-Hill, 1963. 41-91.
26. Freud, A., and D. Burlingham, *Infants without Families,* New York: International Universities Press, 1948.
27. Goldfarb, W., "The Effects of Early Institutional Care on Adolescent Personality," *J. Experim. Education,* 12:106-129, 1953.
28. Goodnow, J. J., "Determinants of Choice Distribution in Two-Choice Situations," *Amer. J. Psychol.,* 68:106-116, 1955.
29. Green, C., and E. Zigler, "Social Deprivation and the Performance of Retarded and Normal Children on a Satiation Type Task," *Child Development,* 33:449-508, 1962.
30. Gruen, G., D. Ottinger, and T. Ollendick, "Probability Learning in Retarded Children with Differing Histories of Success and Failure in School," *Amer. J. Mental Defic.,* 79:417-423, 1974.
31. Gruen, G., D. Ottinger, and E. Zigler, "Level of Aspiration and the Probability Learning of Middle- and Lower-Class Children," *Developmental Psychol.,* 3:133-142, 1970.
32. Gruen, G., and E. Zigler, "Expectancy of Success and the Probability Learning or Middle-Class, Lower-Class, and Retarded Children," *J. Abn. Psychol.,* 73:343-352, 1968.
33. Hagen, J. W., and N. J. Huntsman, "Selective Attention in Mental Retardates," *Developmental Psychol.,* 5:151-160, 1971.
34. Harter, S., "Mental Age, IQ, and Motivational Factors in the Discrimination Learning Set Performance of Normal and Retarded Children," *J. Experim. Child Psychol.,* 5:123-141, 1967.
35. Harter, S., and E. Zigler, "Effectiveness of Adult and Peer Reinforcement on the Performance of Institutionalized and Noninstituitonalized Retardates," *J. Abnormal Psychol.,* 73:144-149, 1968.
36. Harter, S., and E. Zigler, "The Assessment of Effectance Motivation in Normal and Retarded Children," *Developmental Psychology,* 10:169-180, 1974.
37. Havighurst, R. J., "Minority Subcultures and the Law of Effect," *Amer. Psychol.,* 25:313-322, 1970.
38. Irons, N. M., and E. Zigler, "Children's Responsiveness to Social Reinforcement as a Function of Short-Term Preliminary Social Interactions and Long-term Social Deprivation. *Developmental Psychol.,* 1:402-409, 1969.
39. Irvine, E., "Observations on the Aims and Methods of Child Rearing in Communal Settlements in Israel," *Human Relations,* 5:247-275, 1952.
40. Iscoe, I., and B. McCann, "The Perception of an Emotional Continuum by Older and Younger Mental Retardates," *J. Personality and Soc. Psychol.,* 1:383-385, 1965.
41. Kaplun, D., "The High-grade Moron: A Study of Institutional Admissions Over a Ten-Year Period," *Proceedings of the American Association of Mental Deficiency,"* 40:68-89, 1935.

42. Katz, I., "Review of Evidence Relating to Effects of Desegregation on the Intellectual Performance of Negroes," *Amer. Psychologist*, 19:381-399, 1964.
43. Katz, P. A., and S. Rosenberg, "Effects of Labels on the Perception and Discrimination Learning of Retardates," *Journal of Abnormal Psychology*, 74:95-99, 1969.
44. Kaufman, M., "The Formation of a Learning Set in Institutionalized and Non-institutionalized Mental Defectives," *Amer. J. Mental Defic.*, 67:601-605, 1963.
45. Kier, R. J., and E. Zigler, "Success Expectancies and the Probability Learning of Children of Low and Middle Socioeconomic Status." Unpublished manuscript, Yale University, 1975.
46. Klaber, M. M., "Parental Visits to Institutionalized Children," *Mental Retard.* 6:39-41, 1968.
47. Klaber, M. M., "Institutional Programming and Research: A Vital Partnership in Action." In A. A. Baumeister, and E. C. Butterfield (Eds.), *Residential Facilities for the Mentally Retarded*, Chicago: Aldine, 1970, 163-200.
48. Klaber, M. M., and E. C. Butterfield, Stereotyped Rocking—A Measure of Institution and Ward Effectiveness," *Amer. J. Mental Defic.*, 73:13-20, 1968.
49. Klaber, M. M., E. C. Butterfield, and L. J. Gould., "Responsiveness to Social Reinforcement Among Institutionalized Retarded Children," *Amer. J. Mental Defic.*, 73:890-895, 1969.
50. Kossan, N., D. Balla, and E. Zigler, "Effects of Institutionalization on the Behavior of Retarded Individuals: A Multivariate Approach." Unpublished manuscript, Yale University, 1975.
51. Kounin, J., "Experimental Studies of Rigidity: I. The Measurement of Rigidity in Normal and Feebleminded Persons," *Character and Personality*, 9:251-273, 1941 (a).
52. Kounin, J., "Experimental Studies of Rigidity: II. The Exploratory Power of the Concept of Rigidity as Applied to Feeblemindedness," *Character and Personality*," 9:273-282, 1941.
53. Lantz, B., "Some Dynamic Aspects of Success and Failure," *Psychol. Monographs*, 59 (No. 271), 1945.
54. Lyle, J. G., The Effect of an Institution Environment Upon the Verbal Development of Imbecile Children: I. Verbal Intelligence," *J. Mental Defic. Research*, 3:122-128, 1959.
55. Lyle, J. G., "The Effect of an Institution Environment Upon the Verbal Development of Imbecile Children: II. Speech and Language," *J. Mental Defic. Research*, 4:1-13, 1960 (a).
56. Lyle, J. G., "The Effect of an Institution Environment Upon the Verbal Development of Imbecile Children: III. The Brooklands Residential Family Unit," *J. Mental Defic. Research*, 4:14-23, 1960 (b).
57. MacMillan, D. L., "Motivational Differences: Cultural-familial Retardates vs. Normal Subjects on Expectancy for Failure," *Amer. J. Mental Defic.*, 74:254-258, 1969.
58. MacMillan, D. L., and B. K. Keogh, "Normal and Retarded Children's Expectancy for Failure," *Developmental Psychology*, 4:343-348, 1971.
59. MacMillan, D. L., and E. D. Knopf, "Effects of Instructional Set on Perceptions of Event Outcomes by EMR and Nonretarded Children," *Amer. J. Mental Defic.*, 76:185-189, 1971.
60. McArthur, L. A., and E. Zigler, "Level of Satiation on Social Reinforcers and Valence of the Reinforcing Agent as Determinants of Social Reinforcer Effectiveness," *Developmental Psychology*, 1:739-746, 1969.
61. McCarver, R. B., and E. M. Craig, "Placement of the Retarded in the Community: Prognosis and Outcome." In N. R. Ellis (Ed.), *International Review of*

Research in Mental Retardation, Vol. 7. New York: Academic Press, 1974, 146-199.

62. McCormick, M., D. Balla, and E. Zigler, "Child Care Practices in Institutions for the Retarded: A Cross-Institutional, Cross-Cultural Study," *Amer. J. Mental Defic.,* 1975, in press.

63. McCoy, N. and E. Zigler, "Social Reinforcer Effectiveness as a Function of the Relationship Between Child and Adult," *J. Personality and Soc. Psychol.,* 1:604-612, 1965.

64. McKinney, J. P., and T. Keele, "Effects of Increased Mothering on the Behavior of Severely Retarded Boys," *Amer. J. Ment. Defic.,* 67:556-562, 1963.

65. Mueller, M. W., and S. J. Weaver, "Psycholinugistic Abilities of Institutionalized and Noninstitutionalized Trainable Mental Retardates," *Amer. J. Ment. Defic.,* 68:775-783, 1964.

66. Ollendick, T., D. Balla, and E. Zigler, "Expectancy of Success and the Probability Learning of Retarded Children," *J. Abnormal Psychol.,* 77:275-281, 1971.

67. Ollendick, T., and G. Gruen, "Level of Need for Achievement and Probability Learning in Children," *Developmental Psychol.,* 4:486, 1971.

68. Penrose, L. S., *The Biology of Mental Defect,* London: Sidgwick & Jackson, 1963.

69. Rotter, J. B., *Social Learning and Clinical Psychology,* Englewood Cliffs, N.J.: Prentice-Hall, 1954.

70. Sanders, B., E. Zigler, and E. C. Butterfield, "Outerdirectedness in the Discrimination Learning of Normal and Mentally Retarded Children," *J. Abnormal Psychol.,* 73:368-375, 1968.

71. Sarason, S. B., *Psychological Problems in Mental Deficiency.* New York: Harper, 1953.

72. Sarason, S. B., K. S. Davidson, F. F. Lighthall, R. R. Waite, and B. K. Ruebush, *Anxiety in Elementary School Children,* New York: Wiley, 1960.

73. Shallenberger, P., and E. Zigler, "Rigidity, Negative Reaction Tendencies, and Cosatiation Effects in Normal and Feebleminded Children," *J. Abnormal and Social Psychology,* 63:20-26, 1961.

74. Shipe, E., and A. M. Shotwell, "Effect of Out-of-home Care of Mongoloid Children: A Continuation Study," *Amer. J. Mental Defic.,* 69:649-652, 1965.

75. Shultz, T., and E. Zigler, "Emotional Concomitants of Visual Mastery in Infants: The Effects of Stimulus Movement on Smiling and Vocalizing," *J. Experimental Child Psychol.,* 10:390-402, 1970.

76. Spitz, R., and K. M. Wolf, "Analytic Depression," *Psychoanalytic Study of the Child.,* 2, 1946.

77. Stedman, D. J., D. H. Eichorn, J. Griffin, and B. Gooch, "A Comparative Study of Growth and Developmental Trends of Institutionalized and Noninstitutionalized Retarded Children: A Summary Report." Paper read at the American Association on Mental Deficiency National Convention, New York, 1962.

78. Stevenson, H. W., and E. Zigler, "Discrimination Learning and Rigidity in Normal and Feebleminded Individuals," *J. Personality,* 25:699-711, 1957.

79. Stevenson, H. W., and E. Zigler, "Probability Learning in Children," *J. Experimental Psychol.,* 56:185-192, 1958.

80. Tizard, J., "The Prevalence of Mental Subnormality," *Bull. of the World Health Organizat.,* 9:423-440, 1953.

81. Turnure, J. E., and E. Zigler, "Outer-Directedness in the Problem-Solving of Normal and Retarded Children," *J. Abnormal and Soc. Psychol.,* 69:427-436, 1964.

82. Weaver, S. J., "The Effects of Motivation-hygiene Orientation and Interpersonal Reaction Tendencies in Intellectually Subnormal Children." Unpublished doctoral dissertation, George Peabody College for Teachers, 1966.

83. Weaver, S. J., D. Balla, and E. Zigler, "Social Approach and Avoidance Tendencies of Institutionalized and Noninstitutionalized Retarded and Normal Children," *J. Experim. Research in Personality*, 5:98-110, 1971.
84. Weaver, T. R., "The Incidence of Maladjustment Among Mental Defectives in Military Environment," *Amer. J. Mental Defic.*, 51:238-246, 1946.
85. White, R. W., "Motivation Reconsidered: The Concept of Competence," *Psychological Review*, 66:297-333, 1959.
86. Windle, C., "Prognosis of Mental Subnormals," *Amer. J. Mental Defic.*, 66 (Monograph Supplement 5), 1962.
87. Wittenborn, J., and B. Myers, *The Placement of Adoptive Children*, Springfield, Ill.: Charles C Thomas, 1957.
88. Yando, R., and E. Zigler, "Outer-directedness in the Problem-solving of Institutionalized and Noninstitutionalized Normal and Retarded Children," *Developmental Psychol.*, 4:277-288, 1971.
89. Zigler, E., "The Effect of Preinstitutional Social Deprivation on the Performance of Feebleminded Children." Unpublished doctoral dissertation University of Texas, 1958.
90. Zigler, E., "Social Deprivation and Rigidity in the Performance of Feebleminded Children," *J. Abnorm. and Soc. Psychol.*, 62:412-421, 1961.
91. Zigler, E., "Rigidity in the Feebleminded." In E. Trapp and P. Himelstein (Eds.), *Readings on the Exceptional Child*, New York: Appleton-Century-Crofts, 1962, 141-162.
92. Zigler, E., "Developmental vs. Difference Theories of Mental Retardation and the Problem of Motivation," *Amer. J. Mental Defic.*, 73:536-556, 1969.
93. Zigler, E., "The Retarded Child as a Whole Person." In H. E. Adams and W. K. Boardman, II (Eds.), *Advances in Experimental Clinical Psychology*, Vol. 1, New York: Pergamon Press, 1971, 47-121.
94. Zigler, E., and D. Balla, "Developmental Course of Responsiveness to Social Reinforcement in Normal Children and Institutionalized Retarded Children," *Develop. Psychol.*, 6:66-73, 1972.
95. Zigler, E., D. Balla, and E. C. Butterfield, "A Longitudinal Investigation of the Relationship Between Preinstitutional Social Deprivation and Social Motivation in Institutionalized Retardates," *J. Pers. Soc. Psychol.*, 10:437-445, 1968.
96. Zigler, E., E. C. Butterfield, and F. Capobianco, "Institutionalization and the Effectiveness of Social Reinforcement: A Five- and Eight-Year Follow-Up Study," *Develop. Psychol.*, 3:255-263, 1970.
97. Zigler, E., and J. deLabry, "Concept-Switching in Middle-Class, Lower-Class, and Retarded Children," *J. Abn. Soc. Psychol.*, 65:267-273, 1962.
98. Zigler, E., and S. Harter, "Socialization of the Mentally Retarded." In D. A. Goslin and D. C. Glass (Eds.), *Handbook of Socialization Theory and Research*. New York: Rand McNally, 1969, 1065-1102.
99. Zigler, E., L. Hodgden, and H. Stevenson, "The Effect of Support on the Performance of Normal and Feebleminded Children," *J. Personality*, 26:106-122, 1968.
100. Zigler, E., J. Levine, and L. Gould, "Cognitive Processes in the Development of Children's Appreciation of Humor," *Child Development*, 37:507-518, 1966 (a).
101. Zigler, E., J. Levine, and L. Gould, "The Humor Response of Normal, Institutionalized, and Noninstitutionalized Retarded Children," *Amer. J. Mental Defic.*, 71:572-480, 1966 (b).
102. Zigler, E., J. Levine, and L. Gould, "Cognitive Challenge as a Factor in Children's Humor Appreciation," *J. Personal. and Soc. Psychol.*, 6:332-336, 1967.
103. Zigler, E., and E. Unell, "Concept-switching in Normal and Feebleminded Children as a Function of Reinforcement," *Amer. J. Ment. Defic.*, 66:651-657, 1962.
104. Zigler, E., and J. Williams, "Institutionalization and the Effectiveness of Social Reinforcement: A Three-year Follow-up Study," *J. Abnorm. and Soc. Psychol.*, 66:197-205, 1963.

CHAPTER 25

Psychiatric Aspects of Retardation in Young Children

by FRANK J. MENOLASCINO, M.D.

In a recent report on the psychiatric aspects of mental retardation, Lott noted, "The retarded are just as human as normal people. They have the same varied emotional quirks, similar inhibitions, frustrations, guilt feelings, complexes and erroneous self-concepts as do other humans. Their intellects, however, are feebler, and their abilities are less adequate to correlate experiences and to initiate original ideas. Their sublimations are probably more in need of defense mechanisms to smooth or complicate their paths through life. When we add the frequently less effective powers of inhibition and less tolerance to frustration, it may be seen that the defective may often need the type of conflict-resolving measures which may be obtained from wise treatment" (33:139). Lott's comments are most applicable to the current concern for appropriate and complete services for the mentally retarded child. In this section we shall review the diagnostic and therapeutic aspects of the emotional disturbances that frequently complicate the mentally retarded child's adjustment in life. The overall approach will be clinical, and most of the general and specific viewpoints presented are based on the writer's clinical experience in this area.

GENERAL CONSIDERATIONS

There are a number of major problems and issues relevant to the psychiatric aspects of mental retardation. The definition of mental retardation, and the associated nomenclatural system of the American Association of Mental Deficiency (25) underscore the presence of subaverage intellectual functioning, and the associated deficits in adaptive behavior. However, the majority of the disorders listed as capable of producing the symptom of mental retardation are more descriptive of syndromes, rather than specific etiological-diagnostic entities (especially in AAMD categories VII and VIII). Add to this uncertainty of primary causes the problems of clinical description, and we have a major area of clinical confusion: symptomatic behavior which can be produced by a variety of causes. For example, the origins of a given child's hyperactivity may range from motoric expressions of anxiety to manifestations of cerebral dysfunction. Similarly, a short attention span may be the product of an inadequate mother relationship in infancy (suggesting that the mother was unable to operate as a selective stimulation barrier for the child), or secondary to defective midbrain screening of incoming stimuli. The nature of mental retardation, in association with possible multi-factorial causes for any given behavioral manifestation, increases the possibilities for more specific treatment intervention.

For the purposes of this section, the general definitions of "normal" and "abnormal" behavior in childhood have been utilized, as proposed by Chess (11). Since we shall define and discuss abnormal behavioral reactions at some length later in this section, it may be timely to review Chess' definition of normal behavior as a baseline: "He gets along reasonably well with his parents, siblings, and friends, has few overt manifestations of behavioral disturbance, is using his apparent intellectual potential close to its estimate, and is contented for a reasonable proportion of the time" (11:87). There are a number of other definitions which similarly stress the child's problems and malfunctioning in terms of a wide range of experiential factors. The recent nomenclatural system of the emotional disturbances in childhood suggested by the Group for the Advancement of Psychiatry (GAP) (26) embraces the symptomatic and developmental parameters that are important. The GAP report reviews the spectrum of emotional disturbances from the minor (e.g., Adjustment Reactions in Childhood) to the major personality disturbances (e.g., Psychoses of Childhood). These considerations suggest that a description of emotional disturbance in the mentally retarded must include minor adjustment patterns as well as serious conflicts within retarded individuals and their families. Further, the presence of a disturbing influence such as excessive anxiety may reduce their effectiveness so that they have greater difficulty in dealing with emotional and stress situations, and thus *further* hamper their adaptive behavior. This commonly leads to much unhappiness for themselves, and with the world around them.

A valuable concept in the emotional disturbances of mentally re-

CHART 1

DEVELOPMENTAL CONTINGENCIES OF PERSONALITY FUNCTIONING
IN EARLY CHILDHOOD

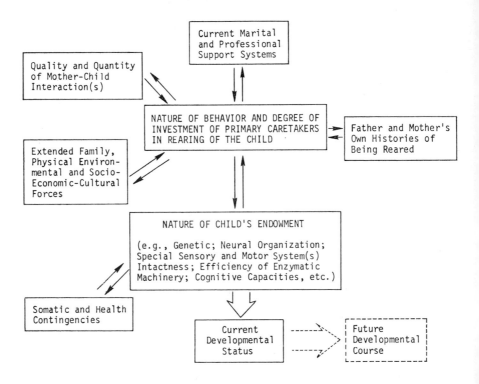

tarded children is that of "developmental contingencies." This implies that the timing of (and the interaction to) intrinsic and/or extrinsic factors may be the major determining factor in symptom production. The concept of developmental contingencies demands that a careful review of the personal and clinical histories be accomplished for any given child, with an overriding concern for capturing the dynamic flow of developmental events that produced the present set of behavioral symptoms in the child. Chart 1 reviews some of the factors that can be assessed in such a developmental-interactional approach to seeking the possible significant determinants of symptomatic behavioral manifestations in young children.

The evaluation and current status of such concepts have resulted in the delineation of what has been termed "crisis" as to psychosocial factors which produce and/or precipitate behavioral symptom formation, and suggest both treatment intervention tactics and possible preventative guidelines. More recently, Call (8) has applied similar principles to therapeutic intervention in early behavioral disorders in a Well Baby Clinic, where Cohen (13) suggests their applicability to the mother's feelings during pregnancy, and the crucial establishment of the mother-child interactional units in the neonatal and early childhood periods.

BRIEF HISTORICAL OVERVIEW

A number of excellent reviews of the literature concerning the relationships between disturbance and mental retardation are available (4, 23).

Beir succinctly reviewed some of the recurrent methodological problems in this area:

> It is generally agreed that mental retardates as a group have a higher incidence of behavior disorder than is found in the general population. This association between retardation and behavioral disorders has been of continuing and increasing interest and their co-existence in the same individuals raises several basic questions regarding this relationship. The major hypotheses regarding this association are as follows: (1) Behavioral disturbance occurs among the mentally retarded for the same reasons that they occur in persons of normal intelligence. (2) Both behavioral disturbance and mental retardation are the results of basic pathological states or dysfunctions of an anatomical, neurological, endocrinological, or biochemical nature. (3) The mentally retarded, because of their deficiencies and their inadequacies, are subject to more stresses, frustrations, and conflicts, and are consequently more liable to develop behavioral disorders. (4) Many cases are labeled "mentally retarded" though they are primarily emotionally disturbed, and the intellectual deficiencies are essentially the result of such disturbances. (5) the mentally retarded, because of their maturational lag, are slower to incorporate notions of right and wrong into personal value systems and are deficient in internal control; they are consequently apt to exhibit peculiar, inappropriate, or antisocial patterns of behavior such as delinquency or sociopathy (4:454).

Beir also notes that little has been reported concerning the relationship of emotional disturbance and mental retardation from outpatient diagnostic clinics. Accordingly, we shall focus here on experiences of the writer (35-38) at a multidisciplinary outpatient clinic for the evaluation of young children suspected of being mentally retarded. Many of the emotional disturbances noted in mentally retarded children at our clinic were secondary reactions to their general problems of adaptation to their environment. Combinations of these secondary emotional disorders demand attention to the co-existence of interacting disturbances. Ignoring these interactions is the most common error noted by the writer in current diagnostic and treatment approaches to emotionally disturbed retarded children. This particular consideration has major implications for both treatment modalities and prognosis. For example, one frequently hears the myopic viewpoint that "Once the emotional block is removed—intelligence will surge forth!" Granted that this may occur in the relatively infrequent instances of primary "pseudo-mental retardation," it tends to confuse the need for multiple treatment approaches. For example, in our reports, we noted 151 children who were both mentally retarded *and* emotionally disturbed and we referred to this group as "mixed" cases. Diagnostically, one runs the risk of focusing on the emotional aspects that are prominent in these "mixed cases" to the exclusion of the role of the accompanying mental retardation. Or the mental retardation may be viewed as the single operative factor, without consideration for the child's emotional plight. Consideration of the "mixed case" can lead to diagnostic clarity and produce specific treatment plans that can be formulated for the child and his parents. Such considerations underscore the dynamic interplay between constitutional factors, validated cerebral trauma, the quality and quantity of mothering, and determining factors such as family crisis. We shall attempt to emphasize some of these factors in a later section.

CHARACTERISTICS OF PERSONALITY GROWTH IN RETARDED CHILDREN

These characteristics will be reviewed from both the intrinsic and extrinsic environmental dimensions.

Pertinent to the *intrinsic* factors, as to psychological growth, is the emerging realization that there are unique and primary personality features in mentally retarded children. Webster (53) has listed these factors as follow: (A) the intellectual impairment and/or specific learning difficulty which is present; (B) the slow rate of overall development (e.g., physical) and (C) disturbances in the quality of emotional development itself, with distinct developmental impairments in the differentiation of the ego functions. This last factor results in a slow and rather incomplete unfolding of the personality with associated distinct personality features such as: (1) A non-psychotic autism which may be displayed as marked passivity; there is a "take it or leave it" aspect of their interactions with people (though they do have a capacity for social relatedness, if left unstimulated—they tend to settle down to contented isolated activity). (2) Repetitiousness is another distinct personality feature and is noted in the retarded child's tendency to repeat the familiar, with an associated element of contentment noted at these times. The young mentally retarded child does *not* exclude the unfamiliar—he is just not too interested in it! (3) There is also much inflexibility as to overall personality functioning and this appears to be related to both the repetitiousness and their seeming lack of interest in seeking out new external stimulation (except to a rather immediate or direct reward system). Lastly, (4) there is noted a simplicity of the emotional life wherein simple and direct expressions of needs and drives are in the foreground.

These considerations suggest that the young retarded child tends to approach reality differently than the normal child. This is seen very clearly in his early school adjustments in which he has less humor, less creativity and less interest in language jokes or abstractions; this alters his play patterns since he is relatively unable to abstract "black—like night," or to readily employ wood squares to mimic actual toasts in the play toaster, etc. Retarded children also seem less able to hold off direct actions, and this may be associated with their concretistic set and poor abstraction abilities. The high frequency of special sensory and integrative disturbances (such as visual motor problems) leads one to ask: Just how do they view reality? For example, on some of the visual motor tests they tend to see an arrow in totally opposite spatial dimensions than as presented; this factor is also noted in some of their very distorted human figure drawings. We might also ask: How do these factors alter their body image problems?

The above comments have focused on possible factors *in the child* in regard to specific problems of personality unfolding in the young mentally retarded child. Now we would like to review some pertinent *extrinsic factors* (or what have been termed the experiential factors). It has been well-documented that the effects of deprivation in all forms, from maternal to sensory, can have devastating effect on personality development. Here we would stress: (1) the significance of early mother-child interactional unit to early personality development and the construction of reality in the child; and (2) this same early mother-child interactional unit as the earliest proto-relationship for instilling the "learning to learn" attitudes in the child. In these two aspects of the primary mother-child interaction unit, one notes the raw ingredients for both future psychiatric and learning disabilities (e.g., lack of an identification model for early learning and environmetnal exploration).

Essential to the external factors for psychological growth of the mentally retarded child is the dimension of his family, and here we must focus on a wide spectrum of factors. How much does the family individualize the child as a part of the total family support system? The relationship between the mother and her own mother is most crucial, since a number of studies have shown that the maternal grandmother must support the mother emotionally in her methods of child care—or a series of events may occur which become the "reason" for institutionalization of the young mentally retarded child (18). Many young mentally retarded children tend to need "extra" parenting, and this parenting must be focused on the child's specific needs and developmental levels (both intellectually and emotionally), or emotional disaster may follow. Accordingly, the young mentally retarded child needs family and social reinforcements to promote and allow personality development to unfold and also to facilitate the evolution of important functions of intelligence, such as language. Since language is a symbolic system which, by definition, is a learned phenomenon, it does not "automatically" unfold or develop but needs continual interaction and positive reinforcement from a meaningful adult. The child thus needs a human model for language learning, and this model must be provided within the context of a passive dependent relationship with a significant authority figure (preferably one who has both a positive philosophy and attitude towards child care).

We must also approach the emotional disturbances in the mentally retarded in a preventive sense. Since we know some of their developmental personality characteristics and its related problems, we must continually seek to provide an environment that is conducive to emotional growth and prepare the child for predictable crisis situations in a positive and preventative fashion. Attention to these factors can provide the child with optimal emotional maturation for living, and also prevent developmental crises later in life.

These considerations are pertinent to a discussion of the characteristics of the retarded which place them "at risk" for psychiatric disorders. It must be remembered that the more than 350 causes of mental retardation embrace a wide spectrum which ranges from disorders where mental illness is an expected symptom (e.g., in the untreated PKU) to instances in which the incidence of mental illness approximates the level of the general population (e.g., cultural-familial retardation and the "invisible" mildly retarded young adult). Although it is hazardous to generalize across these many etiological determinants of retardation, the author will review (by level of retardation) some of the major personality characteristics which place the retarded individual "at risk" of psychiatric disorders.

The Severely Retarded

This group of individuals is characterized by gross central nervous system impairment and multiple physical signs and symptoms. They have a high frequency of multiple handicaps—especially special sensory and seizure disorders—which directly impair their ability to assess and actively participate in interpersonal-social transactions. Clinically, they manifest primitive behaviors and gross delays in their developmental progress. Primitive behaviors include rudimentary utilization of special sensory modalities with particular reference to touch, position sense, oral explorative activity, and minimal externally directed verbalizations. In the diagnostic interview, one may note mouthing and licking of toys, excessive tactile stimulation, such as "autistic" hand movements which are executed near the eyes, as well as skin-picking and body-rocking.

From a diagnostic viewpoint, the very primitiveness of the individual's overall behavior, in conjunction with much stereotyping and negativism, may be misleading (i.e., when pushed in an interpersonal setting, individuals frequently exhibit negativism and out-of-contact behavior). This primitive behavior may initially suggest a psychotic disorder of childhood. However, these children *do* make eye contact and will interact with the examiner quite readily, despite their very minimal behavioral repertoire. Similarly, one might form the initial impression that both the level of observed primitive behavior and its persistence is secondary to deprivation factors; however, these children display multiple indices of developmental biological arrest of primary or congenital origin. It should be noted that these children never seem to possess a functional ego at the appropriate chronological age, and there is an amorphic (or minimal) personality structure. The previously noted "at risk" characteristics tend to appear against this backdrop.

Recent studies by Chess, Korn, and Fernandez (12) on severely retarded children with the rubella syndrome and by Grunewald (27) on the multiply handicapped severely retarded clearly document the high vulnerability of these children to psychiatric disorders. It has been noted that without active and persistent interpersonal, special sensory, and educational stimulation (including active support of the parents) these youngsters fail to develop any meaningful contact with reality (i.e., "organic autism").

The author has been impressed by the extent of personality development which the severely retarded can attain if an appropriate milieu is initiated and maintained (39). True, they remain severely handicapped as to their cognitive and social-adaptive skills; however, there is a world of difference between the severely retarded child who graduates from a standing table to a wheelchair with a wide number of self-help skills, and the untrained severely retarded who responds with minimal effect toward any interpersonal contacts. Even in trained individuals, their paucity of language evolution remains a high vulnerability factor in blocking growth toward more complex personality development. Interestingly, these youngsters tend to be accepted by their parental support systems and peer groups (if adequate evaluations and anticipatory counseling are accomplished), perhaps reflecting empathy for the obvious handicaps which these youngsters display.

The Moderately Retarded

This level of retardation encompasses some of the same etiological dimensions noted above, accompanied by a wide variety and high frequency of associated handicaps. Their slow rate of development and their specific problems with language elaboration and concrete approaches to problem-solving situations present both unique and marked vulnerability for inadequate personality development. Here again, the high frequency of special sensory and integrative disorders seriously hamper their approach to problem-solving, which makes them more likely to develop atypical or abnormal behaviors in a variety of educational or social settings. The limited repertoire of personality defenses, coupled with their concrete approaches to problem-solving, tends to be fertile ground for overreaction to minimal stresses in the external world. Proneness to hyperactivity and impulsivity activities are characteristic of their fragile personality structures. Limitations in language further hamper their ability to fully communicate their inter/intrapersonal distress.

Lastly, unlike the severely retarded, this group of youngsters may be rejected by their parents and peers. Their significant attempts to approximate developmental expectations, coupled with the above-noted behavioral traits, may alienate them from those very interpersonal contacts which they so desperately need.

The Mildly Retarded

The author is hesitant to discuss the "at risk" personality contingencies of this level of the mentally retarded population because this group has been so harshly treated by professionals in the *remote* past (i.e., the eugenic alarm period) and in the recent past through indiscriminate labeling and the negative self-fulfilling prophesies of track system approaches in education. In addition, there is confusion over whether to view the mildly retarded as the statistical expression of the polygenic basis of retardation or as the untutored have-nots of a society which tolerates only minor deviations from the norm (39, 16). In the author's experience, the mildly retarded present the well known "at risk" vulnerabilities of a handicapped person caught in the dynamic interplay of family transactions. The typical delay in establishing that these youngsters have a distinct learning disability (usually not confirmed until 6-9 years of age) presents the mildly retarded individual with a constant source of anxiety in his inability to integrate the major societal repercussions of being labelled as a "deviant" at a crucial chronological-developmental time in his life. Usually, during this quiescent period of psychosexual personality integration, the non-retarded person is firming up his self-concept. Yet, for the mildly retarded person, this period usually brings difficulty in understanding the symbolic abstractions of school work and the complexities of social-adaptive expectations. These stresses tend to establish excessive personality defenses against potential dangers to the self-concept. The vulnerabilities of the mildly retarded are often not buffered or redirected by loved ones into new interpersonal coping styles to help correct earlier misconceptions about the self-in-the-world (42, 50).

Clinically, the entire range of mental illness symptoms has been noted in the mildly retarded. Most frequently, one notes neurotic depression, character disorders, and the symptom clusters which flow from the reaction-formation type of defense. It has been frequently noted that the mildly retarded experience repeated negative motivational and social reinforcement from their peers and teachers and that they have had many experiences at failure or unfavorable comparisons.

In conclusion, these reflections on the intrinsic and extrinsic environmental requirements of psychological growth in the young mentally retarded child strongly suggest that there is a close relationship between "failure to thrive" and "failure to learn" syndromes in childhood. There are essential ingredients needed both "inside" and "outside" of the organism—and, perhaps more importantly, in the interactional interface between these two dimensions of existence and human functioning. We must continue to focus on innovative concepts and approaches in both our therapeutic and preventative approaches to these handicapped children. These considerations may open new vistas for both treatment and management approaches ranging from (1) a more enriched environment for the mentally retarded child, which he seems to need to (2) continual research attempts to alter some of the intrinsic factors. Recent theoretical concepts and clinical trials with agents such as magnesium pemoline underscore the practical hope of possible alterations in the underlying processes of memory and learning, and possible eventual amelioration of the intellectual impairment and/or specific learning deficit itself.

THE CLINICAL EXAMINATION

Since other sections in this handbook have reviewed examination approaches from their own viewpoints of the multi-disciplinary team approach to mental retardation, I shall focus on some of the basic ingredients of the psychiatric examination of the young child who is suspected of being mentally retarded. In the clinical diagnostic approach there are many models. However, one of the main ingredients is the play interview. There are a number of techniques for accomplishing such a clinical examination* of the child, ranging from semi-structured playroom approaches to highly structured playroom and other extended observational settings. The choice of an examination technique (or setting) is important since the clinician is often required to make difficult differential diagnostic decisions (e.g., between childhood psychoses and "brain damage") in some young nonverbal children who are essentially untestable by the usual formal procedures. A structured observational assessment of the child's play can furnish helpful differential diagnostic clues (32, 34).

A structured play interview (separately scheduled as a psychiatric interview, or as part of the pediatric or psychological examinations) can be a helpful segment of the total multi-disciplinary evaluation of any young child suspected of being mentally retarded. This interview should have

---

* The writer strongly feels that any professional in the field of mental retardation should have a wide spectrum of diagnostic tools in his possession. Hence, behavioral evaluations are not the province of any particular specialty group. It follows that the method of clinical examination to be presented here is not the "only" model for this. Equally important contributing facets to a thorough understanding of a child's adaptive-behavioral problems are reviewed in other sections of this handbook.

a specific and standardized sequence of activities which are appropriate to the age level under consideration and have the potential for discrimination between frequently occurring diagnostic categories.

Following extended clinical experimentation with different interview-examination approaches, the writer and a colleague (Dr. Mary Haworth) devised a highly structured play interview technique which attempts to: (1) provide information from multiple areas of the child's ongoing behavioral repertoire; (2) take into account developmental dimensions (e.g., by the range of toy equipment available); and (3) be accomplished with a minimum of equipment and professional time. The initial standardizations as to rater reliability and comparative diagnostic impressions from observed behavior have been reported (28).

Briefly, the interview sequence allows for specific behavioral reactions, such as free choice and use of toys, persistence, imitation, and reactions to frustration and gratification, as well as increasing amounts of interaction with the examiner. Toys were selected for interest appeals to both sexes and represented four categories: animal, human (dolls, soldiers), transportation, and miscellaneous (poker chips, light switch, squeaker toys, block cubes, etc.). Play materials are arranged on low tables in front of the child and those items which are to be presented to the child at pre-determined time intervals throughout the diagnostic session are placed on a table behind the examiner. The flow of this particular diagnostic interview can be outlined as follows: The child is first asked his name, age and sex, then is invited to play with anything he likes and is permitted to do so for five minutes. The examiner then attempts to interrupt the play by suggesting another toy (to assess frustration and ability to shift behavior). The child is asked to imitate the examiner operation of a sparkler toy. Distance interaction is instigated through ball play. Verbal behavior is assessed by interaction with two toy telephones. Closer physical contact is required for the next step of hand-to-hand games (e.g., patty cake). The examiner then attempts to take the child into his lap (to assess reaction of physical closeness, eye contact, etc.). A locked box of small toys is then presented, opened, and the child is allowed to select one toy. He is then asked to watch as the examiner locks the box and leaves the key behind it. The child's approach to problem-solving (and other dimensions) is assessed as he is urged to get another toy from the locked box. The reaction to a new situation is assessed by the introduction of a mechanical rabbit at the close of the interview. The interview takes approximately twelve to fifteen minutes;

it has to be varied somewhat, depending on the extent of verbalization on the part of the child, his speed of reactions, delaying tactics, etc.

As previously mentioned, standardized psychiatric interview approaches to the young child are necessary in order to obtain an adequate sample of behavior on the day of the examination. Our play interview technique attempts to assess at least a variety of areas of the child's ongoing behavior at the time of the interview. Preliminary study suggests that the three activity sequences of ball play, toy telephones, and the locked box appear to be most effective in eliciting indications of the presence or absence of psychotic reactions in young children. Needless to say, the observed sample of behavior of any given child on the day of evaluation may be spurious (e.g., physical illness, fear of the examiner, etc.) and further information may be needed (from the observation and findings of other team members—possibly including a home-visit report by the public health nurse).

COMMON BEHAVIORAL DISORDERS IN YOUNG MENTALLY RETARDED CHILDREN

As previously noted, there has been very little information reported which describes young emotionally disturbed and mentally retarded children at outpatient clinics. The range of symptomatic behavioral patterns in retarded and non-retarded children is literally endless! Indeed, this fact illustrates one of the basic postulates of child psychiatry: Similar symptomatic manifestations have been observed from a variety of etiologic causes. As noted in an earlier section, hyperactivity can emanate from a variety of intrinsic, extrinsic or combined etiologies. Likewise, so can obstinacy, temper tantrums and "acting out" behavior be caused by a wide variety of etiologies.

It may be timely to share our experiences with a relatively large group of young children who had been thoroughly studied as part of our outpatient mental retardation program. Since 1958, a Mental Retardation Clinical Evaluation Unit has been in operation at the Nebraska Psychiatric Institute. This unit was designed as a pilot screening project with focus on children less than eight years of age. Patients were referred by a variety of sources, but all children had one feature in common—a clinical suspicion of mental retardation.

During the five-year period from 1958 to 1963, a total of 616 children from the ages of seven days to eight years were evaluated by a full clinical team consisting of a social worker, pediatrician, neurologist, psychiatrist, psychologist, and speech therapist. A routine radiographic survey included skull, chest, and wrist films. An electroencephalogram with awake, hyperventilation and sleep records was obtained regularly. Laboratory examinations included routine blood and urine studies, metabolic screening and special tests when clinical suspicion suggested their need (e.g., urinary amino acid analysis, cytogenetic survey, etc.). Psychiatric examination of each child focused on the quantity and quality of emotional interaction in the child and the parent-child unit. The family psychopathology noted in the parents of these children represented an interesting aspect of our study. The terms "normal," "reactive psychopathology," and "structured psychopathology" were operationally defined and employed to descriptively categorize the quality and quantity of family functioning. The term "normal" refers to family interactional units which are flexible, realistic, and empathic with the child's adaptational needs. "Reactive" family psychopathology referred to families who were viewed as both perplexed and unable to adjust to their child's behavior and needs. "Structured" family psychopathology denoted family units in which one or both of the parents had prominent and severe personality problems to a degree that significantly hampered both their reactions to the child and their own ability to make successful autonomous interpersonal adjustment in areas outside of their interactions with their child (e.g., social and vocational adjustments).

The findings and impressions of the examiners were fully reviewed at a case conference with all members of the clinical team. Diagnostic and possible treatment recommendations were the focal points of the case conference on each child. Whenever a problem of diagnosis or treatment could not be resolved, a re-evaluation was recommended. Thus, the psychiatric problems presented by these children were seen as part of the total clinical picture that emerged from the multi-disciplinary team evaluation. The etiologic classification of mental retardation employed was that of the American Association on Mental Deficiency (25); the psychiatric diagnoses were consistent with the nomenclature of the American Psychiatric Association (2).

Since we did not have a randomly derived sample, generalizations to the population of mentally retarded individuals are not legitimate. In fact, there were certain known biases affecting the sample we were analyzing. When the education and occupation of the parents of these children were interrelated in the Hollingshead Two-Factor Index of Social Position, 70 percent fell into the two lowest status categories. Another example of bias stems from the consideration that only 2.6 percent

TABLE 1

EMOTIONALLY DISTURBED CHILDREN

Age	MALE		FEMALE	
	Number	Percent	Number	Percent
0-1.9	2	1.0	4	2.0
2-3.9	26	13.6	11	11.5
4-5.9	61	32.0	22	11.5
6-7.9	38	19.0	27	14.1
TOTALS (N=191)	127	65.6%	64	39.1%

of the Nebraska population is non-white, and thus we would expect that, compared to the nation, there was underrepresentation in this category. Furthermore, the type of retarded child seen in our outpatient clinic is probably not representative of the retarded in general since the community takes care of many borderline or mildly retarded children, and this excluded a large number of the less seriously retarded from our sample. Further shortcomings of our sample are in the areas of the reliability and validity of our diagnostic methods and results. The relative "crudeness" of our current nomenclatural systems in both mental retardation and psychiatry tends to further complicate the analysis of this sample.

Diagnostic Aspects

It was the consensus of our clinical staff that 191 of the 616 children studied in this project displayed prominent psychiatric problems with and without an associated finding of mental retardation. Table 1 presents the age and sex of the children deemed to be emotionally disturbed. Thus, the frequency of observed emotional disturbances tended to increase sharply in children four years of age and older. The boys displayed almost a twofold increase in the number of psychiatric problems noted, both as a group and as compared to the girls at different age levels. Analysis of this group of 191 children revealed two distinct sub-groups: (1) 151 were considered to be both emotionally disturbed and mentally retarded, and (2) 40 children were considered to have primary emotional disturbances without mental retardation. For clarity, the diagnostic findings of these two distinct groups will be discussed separately.

TABLE 2

ETIOLOGIC DIAGNOSIS AND LEVEL OF INTELLIGENCE: EMOTIONALLY DISTURBED AND MENTALLY RETARDED GROUP

			Presence and Degree of Mental Retardation			
A.A.M.D. Category	Total	Border-line	Mild	Mod.	Sev.	Indefi-nite
I. Infection	8	1	2	4	1	0
II. Intoxication	2	1	1	0	0	0
III. Trauma or Physical Agents	17	6	6	3	2	0
IV. Disorder of Metabolism, Growth, or Nutrition	0	0	0	0	0	0
V. New Growth	2	2	1	1		
VI. Unknown Prenatal Inflfluence	20	1	4	7	8	0
VII. Unknown or Uncertain Cause with Structural Reaction Manifest	68	10	25	17	13	3
VIII. Unknown or Uncertain Cause with Functional Reaction Manifest	34	10	12	6	3	3
TOTAL	151	31	51	38	27	6

Emotionally Disturbed and Mentally Retarded Group

These 157 children presented a perplexing number of types of clinical findings. This group of children tested both the diagnostic acumen of our clinical team and the ability of team members to communicate freely and interweave their respective clinical impressions and treatment recommendations. Tables 2 and 3 review the etiologic diagnoses, levels of intelligence and psychiatric diagnoses of this group of children.

Our team has come to refer to this group of children as "mixed cases," since they do present signs and symptoms of multiple disorders. For example, in the chronic brain syndromes with behavioral reactions we frequently noted combined underlying cerebral dysfunction with associated physical, neurological, intellectual, and emotional symptoms. These complex disturbances represent a chronic brain syndrome with associated adaptive emotional problems. This particular group of children has forcibly focused our attention on such problems as: reformulation of the behavioral aspects of a chronic brain syndrome in early childhood; the ever-widening spectrum of causative factors noted in the autistic reactions of childhood; and relative interpretations of the interactive role played by the family psychopathology in both the evolution and maintenance of a given child's emotional problems.

TABLE 3

PSYCHIATRIC ASPECTS: EMOTIONALLY DISTURBED AND MENTALLY RETARDED GROUP

A.A.M.D. Category	C.B.S. with Behavioral Reactions	C.B.S. with Psychot. Reactions	Functional Psychoses	Personality Disorders	Adjustment Reaction	Psychiatric Disorder NFS
I. Infection	6	0	0	0	1	1
II. Intoxication	2	0	0	0	0	0
III. Trauma or Physical Agents	14	1	0	0	3	1
IV. Disorder of Metabolism, Growth or Nutrition	0	0	0	0	0	0
V. New Growth	2	0	0	0	0	0
VI. Unknown Prenatal Influence	17	1	0	0	4	2
VII. Unknown or Uncertain Cause with Structural Reaction Manifest	42	11	3	0	13	6
VIII. Unknown or Uncertain Cause with Functional Reaction Manifest	1	14	2	1	18	1
SUB-TOTALS	84	27	5	1	39	11

TOTAL: 167*

(N=151)

* The "mixed" clinical pictures (e.g., a child with a Chronic Brain Syndrome, with associated behavioral reaction and an adjustment reaction) resulted in more final diagnoses (167) than the number of children (151).

Data in Tables 2 and 3 show that the AAMD diagnostic groupings I to IV contain fewer than 25 percent of the total number of mentally retarded and emotionally disturbed children in this sample, though these six diagnostic groupings contained 51.6 percent of the total children examined in our project. The remaining two AAMD diagnostic groupings accounted for slightly more than 50 percent of the entire group of children whom we deemed to be emotionally disturbed, and these two diagnostic groupings contained 29.8 percent of the total population studied by our project. Thus, it would appear that the more indistinct the etiologic-diagnostic factors noted (a common clinical characteristic of the last two AAMD diagnostic groupings), the more psychiatrically disturbed children were tabulated. Another trend noted in the comparison of these two clusters is that the frequency of the more strictly functional disorders increased sharply in AAMD diagnostic categories VII and VIII, as contrasted to the first six diagnostic groupings (e.g., 31 adjustment reactions were noted in the last two categories, as compared to only eight adjustment reactions in the first six categories). Thus, the majority of the emotional disturbances noted in the mentally retarded children in our sample clustered in categories VII and VIII.

A Reflection

Parenthetically, the author has noted neurotic reactions in the mildly retarded, but rarely in any other levels of the mentally retarded. Although a quick answer may be gleaned through reference to the previously noted personality traits and vulnerabilities of the moderate and severely retarded, the following is another point of view. Perhaps psychiatrists have attempted to fit the current nomenclature onto their expectations of the behavioral repertoires of the moderately and severely retarded and have attributed mental illness to these stereotypes.

For example, in the past the author studied a group of community-based Down's syndrome youngsters and noted significant mental illness (37); during a later study of an institutionalized sample of Down's syndrome youngsters (40) he noted that many of them "appeared" happy, overly friendly, and would literally swarm around a visitor on the ward. On reflection, the bulk of stereotyped "Prince Charming" behavior in this particular sub-group of the mentally retarded appeared to be secondary to *affect hunger* and a far different set of diagnostic considerations and treatment challenges emerged.

It is sobering to note how the past psychiatric stereotype of moderately and severely retarded as the "happy and carefree retardate" may have blinded psychiatrists from serving a lost generation of highly vulnerable retarded youngsters grouped together in institutions. Now their task is one of providing psychiatric services in conjunction with family/home/community opportunities for educational, vocational, and personal-social accomplishments within the mainstreams of society. From this perspective, the goal in approaching the "at risk" personality contingencies of the mentally retarded must focus on helping them to develop more specific psychosocial skills for attaining *interdependence* in society. Previously, there was overattention to the goal of personality *independence*. Assisting retarded citizens to understand and manage their needs for *dependent* relationships while simultaneously fostering *interdependent* experiences with counselors, peers, citizen advocates, and employers will buffer and modify their personality vulnerabilities, and thus permit individuals to more fully develop their social-adaptive

TABLE 4

PRIMARY EMOTIONAL DISTURBANCES
WITHOUT MENTAL RETARDATION

Functional Psychosis	3
Psychoneurosis	1
Personality Disorder	2
Special Symptom Reaction	8
Adjustment Reaction	25
Psychiatric Disorder (Not Further Specified)	1
	—
TOTAL	40

potentials. Utilization of this approach can bring about the projection that nine out of ten mentally retarded citizens can be trained to live effectively in the outside world (44).

Primary Emotional Disturbance Group

Now we will focus on the remaining 40 children of the total sample of 191 children: those who manifested primary emotional problems *without* an associated finding of mental retardation. The types of primary emotional disturbances noted are presented in Table 4. These children were not mentally retarded, yet they did come through a mental retardation project for evaluation. Here the concept of pseudo-mental retardation as a misdiagnosis becomes a clinical reality.* The scarcity of psychoneurotic reactions noted may be a reflection of the age range studied in our sample. The children with functional psychoses noted in this group initially presented multiple signs of personality regression and thus could well have passed as "atypical" mental retardates. Further observations, treatment, and serial follow-up evaluations have clarified these diagnostic problems for us quite consistently (15).

The largest sub-group of the primary emotional disturbance group

---

* Though "pseudo-mental retardation" is only tangentially reviewed within the context of this chapter, the reader is referred to the following articles for more extensive review: 1) Bialer, I., "Emotional Disturbance and Conceptual Relationships." In Menolascino, F. J. (Ed.), *Psychiatric Approaches in Mental Retardation,* New York: Basic Books, 1970). 2) Clarke, A. D. B., and A. M. Clarke, "Pseudo-Feeblemindedness— Some Implications," *Amer. J. Ment. Defic.,* 59:505-509, 1955. 3) Menolascino, F. J., "The Facade of Mental Retardation: Its Challenge to Child Psychiatry," *Amer. J. Psychiat.,* 122:1227-1235, 1966.

was the Adjustment Reaction of Childhood (25 children). The most frequent "chief complaints" of both referral source and the parents of this particular group of children were behavioral and speech disturbances. Impulsivity, obstinacy and atypical language development were commonly viewed as indices of possible mental retardation in these children. Family evaluation revealed a rather uniform willingness on the part of the parents of these children to view their child as mentally retarded. We were impressed by the fact that the psychopathology noted in these child-family units was similar to that of their counterparts who are referred to our child psychiatry section. The parents frequently had (or were seeking) unitary hypotheses as explanatory rationalizations for their child's adaptational problems (e.g., "We feel that there must be something wrong with his brain," or "We think he's slow, so we don't expect too much out of him").

TREATMENT CONSIDERATIONS

In the previous section we reviewed the frequency and types of psychiatric disturbances in a sample of young retarded children evaluated at our clinic, and noted that of the sample of 616 young children who had been referred as suspected mental retarded, 191 of them displayed prominent emotional problems. They formed two distinct sub-groups: A) 40 children who had *primary* emotional disorders (without mental retardation); and B) 151 children who displayed *both* emotional disturbance and mental retardation. The forty children with primary emotional problems were managed quite successfully with traditional "triangular" treatment (i.e., child-parents approaches) and will not be reviewed at this time (46).

We shall focus on each of the diagnostic sub-groupings of the 151 children who were noted to be both emotionally disturbed and mentally retarded, and stress treatment and management considerations therein.

CHRONIC BRAIN SYNDROMES WITH BEHAVIORAL AND/OR PSYCHOTIC REACTIONS AND MENTAL RETARDATION

Descriptive Aspects

The 111 children in these two categories (chronic brain syndrome with behavioral reaction; chronic brain syndrome with psychotic reaction) displayed *similar* types of emotional disturbances which were differentiated primarily on the basis of the *degree* of the emotional disturbance noted and the associated family interactional dynamics. Here we have noted descriptive behavioral symptom clusters ranging from hyperkinesis, impulsiveness and other signs of labile emotional control, to stereotyped hand movements, frequent panic reactions (to minimal environmental stimuli), autism and withdrawal. Frequently occurring personality features in both of these groups were: inability to respond adequately and smoothly to changing environmental influences (reflecting both inadequate personality organization and limited adaptability); relative inability to delay gratification in concrete situations with resultant proneness to diffuse anxiety manifestations; and frequent instances wherein the limited intellectual abilities had apparently hampered the children's ability to learn from the psychomotor experience (perhaps because of the associated decreased capacity for conceptualization and transmission of intra- and inter-personal needs). Such personality features seemingly limited their effective ability to form close and constant interpersonal relationships which could help buffer and augment their developmental needs.

A wide range of associated handicaps, such as motor dysfunction, convulsive disorders and delayed speech development have been noted in these two groups of children (83% of these two groups of children had one or more of these associated handicaps). The majority of these children had displayed delayed borderline developmental milestones which had been of concern to the parents; however, this developmental delay apparently did not seem cause for further evaluation until the onset and persistence of the behavioral manifestations. We would like to stress this point because we have often noted that there had been an escalation of the child's behavioral disturbance during a time of family perplexity about his rate of development. Considerations such as these have made us more cautious as to viewing the behavioral components of the two groups of children as being "just due to brain damage." These interpersonal aspects were consistently intermingled with behavioral and developmental delays which became clinically more understandable if the child was viewed as being adaptively at a much younger developmental age than his current chronological age.

Management Considerations

These children initially demanded a treatment ledger sheet of their specific assets and deficits. This ledger was shared with the child's parents at the time of interpretation of our findings. Clarification of the parents' understanding of the child's multiple needs and their level of past expectations from him consistently led to mutual augmentation of treatment recommendations. It is my opinion that the most important aspect of a successful treatment approach to these children and their parents is the use of multiple treatment modalities including 1) supportive play therapy, 2) psychotropic medications, 3) family counseling, 4) correction or amelioration of any associated somatic handicaps, 5) aid in seeking community resources, and 6) sequential follow-through visits to assure continuity of services and recommendations. The family interpretation considerations are particularly helpful for the parents of the preschooler with mild mental retardation, since these parents had been frequently told "He is just slow—he will catch up." The associated emotional problems had been doubly interpreted as an "emotional block to his learning," and as being secondary to "toxic" child care practices. Though some of these family constellations were in need of individual psychotherapy for themselves (approximately 30% of these two groups), we have been impressed by the therapeutic effect of a series of structured interpretation interviews which focus on a tactful review of our findings. This approach focused on the mutual engagement of both parents in the augmentation and follow-through of recommendations for their child.

Needless to say, this management approach is not new. However, we are continually impressed by the negative results of the frequent singular diagnostic-treatment approaches to these children in the past. It appears to us that these children with chronic multiple handicaps and a propensity to emotional disorganization are too commonly treated in a symptom-to-symptom temporal time sequence, rather than with a total approach which flexibly focuses on the multi-level physical, emotional, educational, social and family needs on a long-range basis.

In contrast to the group of children with chronic brain syndromes and associated *behavioral* reactions, *all* of the children with associated *psychotic* reactions necessitated periods of brief hospitalization. The clinical features of marked personality disorganization with associated depleted family resources (emotional and physical) precluded treatment and management attempts on an outpatient basis. Therapeutic focus was placed on increased interpersonal stimulation, play therapy aimed at the child's current developmental level, psychotropic medication, and collateral family counseling. In this regard, we have been impressed by the rapid diminution of the acute aspects of these psychotic pictures shortly after admission to an inpatient setting, without residuals suggestive of personality scarring. Since many workers list childhood schizophrenia as the only psychoses noted in mentally retarded children, we would stress again the need for diagnostic clarity in this clinical area. As we have discussed elsewhere (35-37), our experience suggests that there are distinct and major differences in the historical, clinical examination, and family dimensions of this particular group of psychotic children.

The degree of emotional disorganization and the physical pathology noted should not detract from treatment considerations or prognoses in these two groups of children. From a treatment standpoint, the presence of organic pathology simply means that we are talking about the problems of learning or re-learning certain ego functions never acquired, or lost due to afflictions of the organic substratum. The collaborative employment of a psychiatrically oriented nursery school program for these children with retarded functioning (utilizing the structure of an educational setting and its behavior shaping attributes) can facilitate both the emotional and educational needs here (55).

FUNCTIONAL PSYCHOSES AND MENTAL RETARDATION

Descriptive Aspects

The presence of a functional psychosis in a child who is functioning at a subnormal intellectual level has long been problematical as to etiologic, diagnostic, and associated treatment considerations (14-15, 47, 49).

The eight children* noted in this group presented very challenging differential diagnostic problems. Three of these children were noted to have clinical signs (on pediatric and neurological examinations) of diffuse neurological impairments; the other two did not display such findings but were moderately retarded and had seizure disturbances with EEG findings of generalized brain dysrhythmia. The early developmental histories on all five of these children revealed distinct developmental delays with fairly intact psychosocial development except for personality immaturity. Betweeen two-and-a-half and four years of age the quality of the early personality adjustment in each of these children was noted to insidiously undergo change towards withdrawal, bizarre motor posturing (or ritualistic mannerisms), marked preoccupa-

---

* Though only five mentally retarded children with functional psychoses were noted in our initial sample of 616 children, we have since had the opportunity to examine and treat 11 more children. Our experiences with this total group are incorporated in this current discussion.

tion with certain inanimate objects, echolalic speech, and regression of previously acquired social-adaptive skills. When initially examined they displayed many of the features just noted, and severe signs of autism, averted eye contact, perverse and highly personalized hand movements, and brief periods of apparent loss of contact with the environment without any known precipitating environmental reasons or associated convulsive phenomena. Further, on initial examination the levels of adaptive functioning noted in these children were far below their previously described levels of delayed functioning. Thus, we felt that they represented instances of a schizophrenic adaptation with associated regressive phenomena occurring against the backdrop of delayed early developmental milestones. The family aspects revealed frequent instances of sudden family disruption (e.g., the death of a father in two instances was closely related with the onset of the child's disturbance). Major and chronic psychopathology was noted in the other three family constellations. We are aware that other workers may list these children as primary psychiatric disturbances, or as "atypical children" (45). A crucial point to differentiate here is whether we are dealing with a "primary" case of childhood schizophrenia or a schizophrenic reaction in a mentally defective child. Since we noted in the personal and clinical histories a coexistence of specific factors from both the intrinsic and extrinsic parameters and well-validated periods of personality regression and disintegration, we viewed them as Propf-schizophrenia (31, 36, 49).

Management Aspects

Our management approach to this group of children with functional psychoses and primary mental retardation was accomplished in an inpatient setting. The global quality of the child's multiple deficits in ego functioning was studied, and an attempt was made to conceptualize the ego functions which were particularly disturbed in each patient, and the possible etiologic reasons for these impairments (with due respect for the mixed etiologic factors present in this group of children). Once the pattern of ego disturbances had been delineated, it was time to plan specific treatment strategies and tactics (e.g., support of intact ego functions, personal incorporation of therapist, testing of reality determinants in sequential fashion, etc.) for improving the child's overall pattern of personality functioning. Since similar treatment approaches have been described in the literature (2), we shall only stress the corollary need for special educational dimensions in such treatment approaches.

Descriptive Aspects

The 39 children noted in this group were very complex from a diagnostic-descriptive viewpoint since all of them presented multi-dimensional problems of adaptation. The symptomatic clusters of obstinacy, neurosis, temper tantrums, disobedience, stealing, and masturbation were commonly noted against a background of much free-flowing anxiety, cognitive developmental delays, mild language retardation and frequently associated physical or special sensory handicaps. Further, the impact of each parent's emotional health status on their child, the effects of the interactional family factors, and possible situational crisis features tended to round out these complex reaction patterns. In many instances the child had seemingly sensed the parental dissatisfaction with his slow developmental abilities, and had entered into an interpersonal vendetta, with their mixed feelings being his target. Unfortunately these very parental mixed feelings became the vehicle for further confusion and acting out on the child's part.

A frequent form of adverse child-parent interactional problems noted in this group occurred when chronic parental dissension, especially with rejection overtures, had produced anxiety and confusion in the child with subsequent feelings of massive insecurity. Thus, the parental psychopathology seemed most frequently to be based on two major factors: their reaction to the child's atypical or abnormal developmental attainments, and the communications patterns and personality characteristics of the parents themselves.

Interestingly, other children in our total sample had been noted to have similar historical information of such interpersonal impasses in their past history, but they apparently had been helped by therapeutic interventions earlier (e.g., family doctors, ministers, etc.).

Management Aspects

Management considerations in this group of children necessitated a modified psychotherapeutic relationship between the child and his parents. These modifications were necessary because of the child's intellectual handicap, the frequent accompaniment of concretistic thinking, and associated limitations in how he actually perceived his environment as to perceptual-psychological considerations. The psychotherapeutic approach to these children also differs from traditional approaches since the total picture is not self-limiting after treatment. The child remains with a chronic adaptive handicap (lower adaptive-intellectual ability) and parental treatment considerations have to include guidance as to available educational and social placements, and realistic future developmental expectations from the child. In this particular group of children, work with the family was extremely important. Alterations in family attitudes with encouragement toward more healthy, constructive and consistent expectations, along with decreases in the anxiety levels in mother and father, tended to provide sufficient support to allow the child to improve in his adjustment. The clinician must be fully appreciative of the mixed etiologies that are frequently present since mixed prognoses are also in order in these instances. We would like to underscore this point since in the past we commonly had had the treatment experience (and expectations) that psychotherapeutic procedures would eventuate in the "evaporation" of the associated finding of mental retardation in these children. Reevaluation of our former viewpoint has made us more appreciative, for example, of some of the parental problems in relation to the child's normal strivings for growth toward independence. Many of these parents, especially those with other children, had sensed the child's actual need for extra supervision, although many of them had overreacted in this area. Where there was major family psychopathology and poor motivation to involve themselves in collateral treatment, we have noted that nursery school placement can provide the child at least with a partial corrective emotional-educational experience.

PSYCHIATRIC DISTURBANCE NOT FURTHER SPECIFIED

Descriptive Aspects

This group of eleven children commonly displayed frequent periods of general irritability against a personality backdrop of passivity, inflexibility, and personality immaturity. In many ways this was our "unspecified" category, since the behavioral repertoire of these children was only mildly atypical for their given mental age, and negative family interactional factors were only questionably operative when closely examined. Here we noted the behavioral ingredients of possibly more structured emotional disturbances in the future. Thus, these particular behavioral referents seemed most closely associated with the child's delayed intellectual development. All of this group of children were in the moderate range of mental retardation. They represent behavioral characteristics from which a future possible adjustment reaction of childhood might possible arise if the family interactional pattern became less cognizant and empathic about the child's innate handicaps.

Management Aspects

Management considerations in the last group of children tended to hinge on adequate transmission of diagnostic findings to the parents and subsequent help in altering their previous expectations from the child. Since realignment of parental expectations from their child tended to lead to more realistic parental demands from the child (in keeping with his developmental level), treatment considerations have embodied principles of secondary prevention (10).

PARENTAL COUNSELING

Since we have mentioned parental counseling as a frequent ingredient of a total treatment approach for these children, we would like to share some of our views on counseling for parents of the retarded.

First, a few general remarks on this entire subject. The field of counseling the parents of the retarded has many unusual features. Though there are over 150 publications dealing with or very relevant to the problem, mostly appearing since 1950, only a small number of experimental studies have been conducted (54). Further, it is questionable whether the parents described in the literature are representative of parents of the retarded in general, since two obvious areas have been misrepresented. Some authors have apparently focused too strongly on mothers of young and moderately to severely retarded children from the middle and upper socioeconomic groups only, thus distorting the picture of the problem as a whole. Also, failure to assess the father's role in such studies, and overreliance on maternal information, with the asso-sociated assumption that such maternal information, particularly regarding the father, is valid, has prompted Ross to state: "Reading the scientific literature in this field (counseling of parents of the retarded) a student unfamiliar with our culture might easily get the impression that fathers play no part in the rearing of our children" (48:64).

The stages of parental reaction and acceptance of the diagnosis of mental retardation have been delineated in the clinical literature (26). As to the parents' initial reaction to learning that their child is retarded, our formal diagnosis most frequently only confirmed the parent's apprehensions, since the parental suspicion or knowledge of mental retardation had been present for varying periods of time.

As previously noted, family treatment considerations in the parents of these emotionally disturbed and mentally retarded children frequently underscored the need for general supportive measures and guidelines as to future management. The most common parental reactions we noted were situational depressive features about their responsibility and their mixed feelings. The problem of guilt presents a further unique dimension in counseling approaches to the parents of these children. In the primary emotional disorders of childhood, the parents can usually project a good portion of their "blame" or guilt onto the child and scapegoat situations are frequently noted. In the retarded child, there is usually no direct manner whereby this guilt can be externalized and its continual lack of alleviation may present formidable resistance problems to any counseling attempts. Thus, we see that the parents of children with both mental retardation and emotional disturbance have multiple levels and types of inner turmoil which can be productive of some of their child's behavioral problems. Such considerations present treatment challenges as to the fuller appreciation of the family dynamics.

We would also urge closer professional attention to the commonly recurring parental reaction patterns subsequent to chronic sorrow stemming from the destruction of their overdetermined expectations of the child, and the reality crisis stemming from external factors which are only partially modifiable by the parents (e.g., the physical demands made by a hyperactive child in a family with several young children may not be able to be met by the mother, and these situational demands may overwhelm her). Thus, we would propose that better conceptualization of the type of crisis a family is experiencing will make it easier to identify family treatment approaches that will be most likely to succeed. Elsewhere (41), I have described a scheme in which treatment is derived from considerations of family crisis (Chart 2). For example, parents with the shock of initial diagnosis need primarily information and support; those in personal value crises need more prolonged counseling or individual psychotherapy; and those parents in reality crises require practical, down-to-earth help such as training in home management, baby-sitting arrangements, day care, and perhaps some forms of residential placement.

We have discussed parental counseling at some length because we feel that increased clinical awareness of its unique issues and problems

CHART 2

A THEORETICAL FRAMEWORK FOR THE MANAGEMENT OF PARENTS OF THE RETARDED

Nature of Responses	Novelty Shock		Value Conflict	Reality Stress
Formative initial parental responses	Confusion Disorganization Helplessness	Dependency Anguish Anger	Profound existential pain and insult to ego Ambivalence about acceptance of facts	Stress symptoms Deterioration of health Family tension
Management needs	Immediate supportive counseling to realign expectancies Medical-diagnostic interpretations that are realistic yet focus on positive developmental expectancies Preparation of parents for planning and utilization of services Provision of societal and peer support, as by referral to parent groups		Existential type of therapy or counseling (for example, pastoral counseling) Resocialization, as with group counseling, congregational support Finding a niche for the child in the parental value system Exposure of parents to models of positive conflict resolution, as in the parent movement	Correct assessment of reality-based family needs Knowledge of and rapid provision of concrete services that relieve situational demands
Adaptive parental adjustments	Acceptance of reality factors Seeking or acceptance of guidance Realignment of expectations and plans		Resolution of existential parental quandary Value change Investment of value in the child Empathy for the child	Search for resources Utilization of resources Participation in the creation of needed resources and services Placement of child outside the home where appropriate
Maladaptive parental adjustments	Rejection of the child Inappropriate discarding of child Precipitous institutionalization Denial of reality Surrender to irrational guilt Conflicted management of child Withdrawal Irrational affixing of blame		Rejection of the child Inappropriate institutionalization Denial of child or his condition Severe and continued ambivalence Shopping for invalid diagnoses and cures Reaction formation Conflicted management of child Sense of unfulfillment Chronic sorrow Prolonged emotional disorder	Rejection of the child Premature separation from child Unnecessary institutionalization Family dissolution Passive surrender to situational demands

is essential for total and effective management considerations for the majority of the child-parent units we have reviewed. Also, as previously noted, we feel that this important areas has too frequently been dominated by generalities such as "If you only knew his mother." The traditional psychiatric approach to parents of emotionally disturbed children is seemingly not too effective in the groups of children that we are discussing (43). Fully 20% of the parents of the children in our sample had experienced this approach (a brief interpretation of clinical findings, a prescription for a tranquilizer and the closing statement: "He needs schooling"). This approach has apparently led to further parental confusion, and a continuation of the shopping pattern which brought the applicants to our clinic.

An appreciation of these problems which are unique to parents of the retarded may help the professional worker in this field to be more empathic of the presenting family problems and cognizant of the need for specific treatment needs and approaches.

USEFUL PSYCHOPHARMACOLOGICAL ADJUNCTS IN TREATMENT OF EMOTIONALLY DISTURBED AND MENTALLY RETARDED CHILDREN

Psychopharmacological agents have been employed as treatment adjuncts for emotionally disturbed mentally retarded children. However, most reported studies have been in inpatient settings, and there is an apparent reluctance to combine such agents with outpatient psychotherapeutic programs (30). Fish has succinctly reviewed some of the past and recent concerns in this area as follows:

> Fears have been raised that drugs will dull perception, stifle learning, and disrupt the therapeutic relationship. Such fears have essentially proved to be groundless. Drugs tend to increase the effectiveness of the treatment program—in selected cases—and the supposed deleterious effects have failed to materialize. Recent years have witnessed a tremendous growth in the prescription of a variety of tranquilizer drugs in adult psychiatry. Actually, drug therapy was more popular and widespread in child psychiatry than in adult psychiatry even before the relatively recent interest in the tranquilizers. This is probably related to the fact that hyperactivity is common in childhood disorders and also reluctance to resort to methods utilized in the control of hyperactive, aggressive adults, such as lobotomy and electric shock treatment. Thus, since 1937, benzedrine and, subsequently, dexedrine have been widely used in the treatment of disturbed emotional states in children. Specific therapeutic aspects of new drugs must be emphasized because for

many years a variety of sedative agents, most recently the barbiturates, have been utilized in mental disease to achieve control through heavy sedation. With more recently developed drugs, the aim is to ameliorate the symptoms and restore function and, in the child, to aid maturation and enable him to participate in educational programs. These goals cannot be achieved by heavy sedation (19:55).

In attempting to provide a brief review of the use of pharmacological agents in this area, one is overwhelmed by the number of agents

CHART 3

USEFUL PSYCHOPHARMACOLOGICAL AGENTS FOR EMOTIONALLY DISTURBED AND MENTALLY RETARDED CHILDREN

Agent	Dosage	Available Forms
Phenothiazines		
chlorpromazine (Thorazine)	1-2 mg/kg/day	Tabs: 10, 25, 50 mg
thioridazine (Mellaril)	1-5 mg/kg/day	Tabs: 10 and 25 mg Conc: 30 mg/cc
trifluoperazine (Stelazine)	0.02-0.2 mg/kg/day	Tabs: 2 and 5 mg No elixir

Toxicity: Incidence of various side effects varies widely (from 0 to 50%), depending on drug used, size of dose, and individual sensitivity of the patient. Hypotension, convulsive seizures, and blood dyscrasias (agranulo-cytosis) are more common with the diethylamine phenothiazines (e.g., Thorazine). The piperazinyl phenothiazines (Mellaril, Stelazine, and so forth) can produce the above and dystonic reactions (e.g., parkinsonism, akathasia, and so forth). With all of these agents, be alert for the following: jaundice, contact dermatitis, photosensitivity, gastrointestinal syndrome, blurry vision, drowsiness, and fatigue. These drugs also potentiate central nervous system depressions (e.g., barbiturates).

Butyrophenones haloperidol (Haldol)	1.5 to 3.0 mg/day (over age 12 yr.)	

Toxicity: Drowsiness, parkinsonism, other side effects that are similar to the phenothiazines.

Reserpine reserpine (Serpasil)	0.3-2.0 mg/day	Tabs: 0.1, 0.25, 1-2 mg

Toxicity: Adverse behavioral effects (fatigue, weakness, somnolence, and so forth). Also, parkinsonism, dystonic syndrome, seizures, hypotension, edema, mental depression, and activation of peptic ulcer. Less severe side effects: nasal congestion, excess salivation, vomiting, and diarrhea.

Agent	Dosage	Available Forms
diphenylmethane (Benadryl)	1 mg/kg/day	Elixir: 10 mg/4 cc Tabs: 10-25 mg
Hydroxyzine hydroxyzine (Atarax)	6 yr: 50-100 mg/day	Syrup: 2 mg/cc

Toxicity: Drowsiness, dryness of mouth occasionally at high dosages. These groups of drugs are relatively "safe" as to paucity of serious side effects.

Propanediols meprobamate (Equanil or Miltown)	6 yr: 200-800 mg/day	Susp: 200 mg/5 cc

Toxicity: Relatively infrequent side effects. Allergic skin reactions, diarrhea, and the question of addiction (adults) have been noted. This is a relatively "safe" drug from the viewpoint of toxicity.

Miscellaneous chlordiazepoxide (Librium)	5-10 mg bid-qid	Tabs: 5 and 10 mg No syrup

Toxicity: Drowsiness, ataxia, and syncope. Paradoxical reactions (e.g., excitement): caution should be taken in patients with renal or hepatic insufficiency.

diazepam (Valium)	8.0 to 40 mg/day	

Toxicity: Drowsiness, ataxia, fatigue, and hyper-excited states; rare blood dyscrasia. Has a useful role as an anticonvulsant adjunct.

amphetamine sulfate (Benzedrine)	5-40 mg/day	Tabs: 5, 10, 15 mg
dextroamphetamine (Dexedrine)	0.2-1.0 mg/kg/day (empirical)	Tabs: 5 mg Spans: 5, 10, 15 mg Elixir: 5 mg/5 cc

Toxicity: Caution in hypertensive individuals, though this side effect has only rarely been reported with children. Weight loss, insomnia, pallor of the face, constriction of the superficial veins, and cold extremities. Many of these reported side effects tend to diminish with continuation of treatment.

methylphenidate (Ritalin)	20-40 mg daily	Tabs: 5, 10 mg

Toxicity: Caution as to rapid blood pressure (elevation) changes tend to potentiate epinephrine.

Anticonvulsants (e.g., diphenylhydantoin sodium): Empirical basis of treatment; its role is similar to reserpine in these disorders—frequently held "in reserve" for when other agents (e.g., phenothiazines) are not beneficial. Certain associated tests (14 and 6 per second positive spike abnormality in the EEG) may suggest an initial empirical trial with these agents in highly selective patients. {

As in the case of management of convulsive disorders, highly individualized dosage and close attention must be given to the administration schedule of these drugs. The therapeutic response and toxicity reactions (e.g., ataxia, blood dyscrasia, and so forth) also dictate the clinical approach with these agents.

recommended and the conflicting claims as to their efficacy (17, 29). Chart 3 delineates the psychopharmacological agents useful in the treatment of emotionally disturbed and mentally retarded children. Further complicating the picture is the placebo effect, since recent reports indicate that beneficial response is not only engendered by the patient's enthusiasm for the medication, but is also induced by the attitude of the physician.

Psychopharmacological agents are frequently employed as treatment adjuncts in the following emotional problems in this area: (1) chronic brain syndromes with behavioral reactions; (2) chronic brain syndrome with psychotic reactions; (3) functional psychoses in the mentally retarded (Propf-schizophrenia). We shall review some of the pharmacological agents that can be utilized in each of these disorders.

Chronic Brain Syndromes with Behavioral Reactions

The diphenhydramine (e.g., Benadryl), hydroxyzine (e.g., Atarax), amphetamine (e.g., Dexedrine) groups of psychopharmacological agents appear to be useful adjuncts in these disorders. Benadryl has been widely studied over a prolonged period of time, and the majority of studies document the high rate of effectiveness of this drug in this particular behavioral disorder (18, 20). It should be noted that the drug: 1) is remarkably free of side effects; 2) is useful in modifying hyperactivity, especially when the hyperactivity is associated with poorly organized behavior and immaturity; and 3) the drug is rarely useful (in this role) after age 12 years, except as a mild but effective bedtime sedative and/or antihistamine. Atarax and Suavatil are hydroxyzines that have also been widely employed (with quite similar results) and they have some effectiveness in this role after twelve years (e.g., Suavatil has been noted to be effective in the early adolescent mental retardate who displays emotional instability). The Benzodiazepines are another mainstay for these particular behavioral disorders (22). In particular, Valium is widely utilized and has been noted to be highly effective (24). Another group of drugs employed in these disorders are the amphetamine-caffeine agents (e.g., Benzedrine, Dexedrine, and Ritalin). Benzedrine has been studied extensively by Bradley (5, 6). It is important to note that Benzedrine was employed initially on a highly empirical basis for a variety of childhood behavioral difficulties, ranging from depression to hyperactivity. The reported results in retarded children (with associated emotional disturbances) have been conflicting (29). The recent studies and results with a particular type of "brain-damaged" child should be sharply delineated from the clinical indication noted above. The amphetamine agents have had a relatively high degree of success with brain-damaged children of normal (or near normal) intelligence who present a clinical picture of hyperactivity, short attention span, perseveration, and impulsivity (20). This description probably pertains to only selected numbers of brain-damaged children. Ritalin (methylphenidate) has been reported to be equally efficacious in this particular syndrome.

Chronic Brain Syndrome with Psychotic Reactions

The phenothiazine family of drugs has consistently offered beneficial treatment adjuncts in these disorders (1, 3, 52). The phenothiazines seem most efficacious when marked motor restlessness, symptoms of manifest anxiety, and relationship problems with peers and adults are present. In these particular disorders, the phenothiazines can produce motor and emotional quiescence, thus counteracting the marked disorganization of personality functioning that is commonly noted on initial examination. The haloperidols are as efficacious as the phenothiazines. Haldol (7) is particularly effective in obtaining behavioral quieting without excessive toxic effects. Reserpine has not been consistently useful in this group of behavioral problems. Further, this agent is slow acting and has formidable side effects. It is frequently held in reserve, for use when the phenothiazines and other agents are not beneficial.

Functional Psychoses in the Mentally Retarded (Propf-schizophrenia)

The pharmacological agents employed here are similar to those in the preceding group. The clinician tends frequently to employ larger dosages over a more prolonged period of time, and with more active types of interpersonal engagements with the child (and his parents) as to the ongoing total treatment approach. It is interesting to note that there are a number of reports that suggest that some of the phenothiazine derivatives appear to have different effects on "target" symptoms in this group of children. For example, it has been reported that Stelazine can have a highly stimulating and activational effect on certain autistic children (17, 19).

Clinicians may employ different variants of the spectrum of psychopharmacological adjuncts discussed herein. However, it is unlikely that any of these drugs will be successful if they are employed as a singular treatment approach. In contrast to the former "magic bullet" approaches, the clinician must always utilize these agents as only part of a total treatment approach that underscores the mutual engagement of the child's parents as the keystone to any therapeutic interventive efforts.

DISCUSSION

As in other areas of medicine, diagnosis and treatment of the mentally retarded must be individualized in terms of the child, his presenting symptomatology, and the psychosocial family milieu. Concerning the psychiatric aspects of mental retardation, this medical maxim becomes clinically more difficult to apply because of the wide etiologic umbrella of mental retardations, the frequently associated multiple handicaps, the rapidly changing psychosocial needs of the developing child, and the complexity of family interactional patterns. The experiential factor may also mask, modify or exaggerate the underlying pathophysiological processes in some of these children. For example, the quality and quantity of early mothering, the parental handling of developmental crisis situations, social-cultural factors, the family's initial and long-range reaction and adjustment to the child's chronic disabilities, the effect of overt distortions of bodily appearance on the child's self-image, and the timing of the etiologic insult in relation to the state of physical growth and psychosexual adjustment—any or all of these factors may determine the child's future quality of adjustment *more* than the intrinsic factors that are present. These considerations again caution one against singular hypotheses as to etiology or treatment.

In the previously presented descriptive and treatment overview of the four most common behavioral reactions which we have noted in a relatively large sample of young mentally retarded children, we have attempted to delineate some of the behavioral reaction patterns secondary to cerebral insults, the role of superimposed interpersonal conflicts and their residuals, and those instances where all of these factors were noted to be operative. We have stressed that treatment approaches must address themselves first to the global nature of the childs' interactional problems, and only secondarily focus on specific handicaps such as a seizure disorder, motor dysfunction, or speech and language delay.

Many of these behavioral disorders can be helped by widely differing treatment methods and approaches. This is not surprising when we consider that they are the outcome of a multifactorial complex of forces, which suggests that the equilibrium is likely to be positively altered by modifying any of a number of factors. Selective inattention to the multiple diagnostic-treatment challenges that these children commonly present can lead to faulty diagnosis and incomplete treatment. These considerations were particularly pertinent to our previously reviewed group of mentally retarded children with concomitant adjustment reactions, since this particular emotional disturbance is, by definition, a transitory disorder. Delineation of the child's multiple assets and deficits (emotional, physical, social, sensory, etc.) and close attention to realignment of the family support system can lead to a secondary prevention approach to these child-parent units (9). Helping these individuals to deal effectively with the conflicts that led to the presenting clinical symptoms, and then to develop new ways of mutual problem-solving, so that similar conflicts in the future would not have to be dealt with by past psychopathological mechanisms, provided effective treatment intervention.

No treatment approach is successful unless a long-range working relationship with the family can be established. Initial tactful interpretation interviews can provide the "foothold" for the establishment of such a relationship with the family. Within the context of such a mutual contract of help with the family, these multidimensional treatment needs can be delineated, augmented, and followed through. Here the psychiatrist must be aware of the special contributions of the allied professions in his efforts to arrange a life plan for the child which will be therapeutically positive and bring about the child's self-realization. In such treatment planning we have noted that it is helpful to focus not on what the child presently *is* but on what he can become.

Sex Education

One of the more anxiety-producing duties of parenthood is the sex education of children. Beyond the inability or unwillingness to talk about sex is a genuine concern for conveying attitudes, behaviors, and practices which are (to parents) moral and practical. The parents of the mentally retarded face the dilemma of all parents—what to say, how to say it, and when. In the past, few of them had to say anything: The mentally retarded were segregated away in large institutions on sex-segregated wards and subject to mandatory sterilization laws. Now these same parents must face the age-old problem with a more perplexing set of circumstances: 1) The mentally retarded individual, with his lowered intellectual abilities and delayed social-adaptive behaviors, requires concrete explanations about human sexuality using "street language" and more socially acceptable terminology for the various bodily functions, yet he has the same need to understand; 2) with the recent increase in community-based services, more retarded children remain in the homes and thus their parents must directly cope with explanations of the facts from birth, through puberty, dating, intercourse, venereal disease, and birth control; 3) the increasing recognition of the civil rights of retarded individuals to marry and have children, if they are able, and the abolition of the mandatory sterilization laws in many states.

In dealing with sex education for the mentally retarded, parents have some very informative resources, including "Puberty in the Girl Who Is Retarded" (1969) distributed by the National Association for Retarded Citizens. These resources not only provide factual information about bodily functions, but also stress that parents must begin early in life if they want to firmly convey positive attitudes toward human affection, warm feelings, sexual desires and tastes, and responsibility for appropriate behavior within the context of their personal beliefs and sexual needs.

The retarded have the same need for understanding sex and for healthy, guilt-free attitudes as normal children. Extra attention is needed in teaching appropriate sexual behavior in appropriate settings, since the retarded youngster's lowered understanding and discrimination of social cues and expectations tend to produce behaviors which are inappropriate for their chronological age. Friendliness to strangers, open affection for children, or genital exploration in public are inappropriate behaviors which must be discouraged. Yet these same behaviors, when properly self-monitored (after explicit instructions from their parents and teachers), can be socially acceptable in the right place, at the right time, etc. We have done a great disservice to the retarded by not teaching them about socially acceptable outlets for positive personal relationships, including sexual transactions. Lack of sex information among the mentally retarded can have the same negative effects (unwanted pregnancy, venereal disease, needless guilt feelings) as among all children, but with more devastating emotional consequences when the individual has a lessened level of comprehension.

SUMMARY

In summary, the foregoing considerations imply that behavioral disorders in young mentally retarded children are relatively frequent occurrences and differ qualitatively from what is noted in non-mentally retarded children. We would underscore the urgent need to evolve more specific methods of treatment for this large group of handicapped young children.

Future clinical research in the evaluation and treatment of emotionally disturbed and mentally retarded young children must attempt to elucidate further guidelines as to the types and modifications of personality development in these young children with multiple handicaps. We also need more basic information on possible impairments in their usual mechanisms for handling conflicts (e.g., are they able to fantasize adequately? Are the psychosexual stages of personality also atypical because of the associated cognitive defects? Do their chronic brain syndrome aspects impair their ability to delay gratification with resultant proneness to diffuse anxiety, etc.?). Thus, mental retardation may provide a limitation for emotional maturation above and beyond the emotional consequences of social non-acceptance or decreased adaptive abilities because of the cognitive functions.

Some of the challenges for wider utilization of psychiatric principles concerning child care and personality functioning in the field of mental retardation have been reviewed. The larger community issue of the need for training the future psychiatrist to provide comprehensive services for the mentally retarded may be the supreme challenge to the attitudinal changes that must continue to evolve if we are to truly embrace the potential for change in the field of mental retardation.

The psychiatric treatment and management aspects of emotional disturbances in mentally retarded children have been largely neglected. Yet it is apparent that the need for these services does not vanish as the IQ drops below 70. The increasing realization that the mentally retarded child can benefit from appropriate treatment programs is likely to be accompanied by further positive developments in this clinical area.

BIBLIOGRAPHY

1. Allen, M., G. Shannon, and D. Rose, "Thioridazine Hydrochloride in the Behavior Disturbance of Retarded Children," *Amer. J. Ment. Defic.*, 68:63, 1963.
2. American Psychiatric Association, *Diagnostic and Statistical Manual-Mental Disorders.* (Rev. Ed.), Washington, D.C., APA, 1969.

3. Beaudry, P., and D. Gibson, "Effect of Trifluoperazine in Mental Deficiency," *Brit. J. of Psychiat.,* 109:403, 1963.
4. Beir, D. C., "Behavioral Disturbances in the Mentally Retarded," in H. A. Stevens and R. Heber (Eds.), *Mental Retardation: A Review of Research,* Chicago: University of Chicago Press, 1964.
5. Bradley, C., "Behavior of Children Receiving Benzedrine," *Amer. J. Psychiat.,* 94:577, 1937.
6. Bradley, C., "Benzedrine and Dexedrine in the Treatment of Children's Behavior Disorders," *Pediatrics,* 5:24, 1950.
7. Burk, H. W., and F. J. Menolascino, "Halperidol in Emotionally Disturbed Mentally Retarded Individuals," *Amer. J. Psychiat.,* 1968, 123 (11), 1581-1591.
8. Call, J., "Prevention of Autism in a Young Infant in a Well-Child Clinic," *J. Amer. Acad. Child Psychiat.,* 2:451, 1963.
9. Caplan, G., "Patterns of Parental Response to the Crisis of Premature Birth," *Psychiatry,* 23:365, 1960.
10. Caplan, G., *Principles of Preventative Psychiatry,* New York: Basic Books, 1964.
11. Chess, S., *An Introduction to Child Psychiatry,* New York: Grune & Stratton, 1959.
12. Chess, S., S. Korn, and P. B. Fernandez, *Psychiatric Disorders of Children with Congenital Rubella.* New York: Brunner/Mazel, 1971.
13. Cohen, R. L., "Some Maladaptive Syndromes of Pregnancy and the Puerperium," *J. of Obstet. and Gynecol.,* 27:562, 1966.
14. Despert, J. L., and A. C. Sherwin, "Further Examination of Diagnostic Criteria in Schizophrenic Illness Psychoses of Infancy and Early Childhood," *Amer. J. Psychiat.,* 114:784, 1958.
15. Eaton, L., and F. J. Menolascino, "Psychotic Reactions in Childhood: Experiences of a Mental Retardation Clinic: A Follow-Up Study," *Amer. J. Orthopsychiat.,* 37 (3): 521, 1967.
16. Eisenberg, L., "Caste, Class and Intelligence." In Murray, R. F. ,and Rosser, P. L. (Eds.), *The Genetic, Metabolic, and Developmental Aspects of Mental Retardation.* Springfield, Ill., Charles C Thomas, 1972.
17. Eveloff, H. H., "Psychopharmacological Agents in Child Psychiatry: A Survey of the Literature Since 1960," *Arch. Gen. Psychiat.,* 14:472, 1966.
18. Farber, B., "Family Organization in Crisis: Maintenance of Integration in Families with a Severely Mentally Retarded Child," Monograph, *Soc. Res. Child Dev.,* 25, No. 1, 1960.
19. Fish, B., "Drug Therapy in Child Psychiatry: Pathological Aspects," *Compr. Psychiat.,* 1:55, 1960.
20. Fish, B., "Drug Therapy in Child Psychiatry: Pharmacological Aspects," *Compr. Psychiat.,* 1:212, 1960.
21. Freedman, A. M., A. Effron, and L. Bender, "Pharmacotherapy in Children with Psychiatric Illness," *J. Nerv. and Ment. Dis.,* 122:479, 1955.
22. Freeman, R. D., "Psychopharmacology and the Retarded Child." In Menolascino, F. J. (Ed.), *Psychiatric Approaches to Mental Retardation.* New York: Basic Books, 1970.
23. Garfield, S. L., "Abnormal Behavior in Mental Deficiency." In N. R. Ellis (Ed.), *Handbook of Mental Deficiency: Psychological Theory and Research,* New York: McGraw-Hill, 1963.
24. Greenblatt, D. J., and R. I. Shader, "Drug Therapy. Benzodiazepines," *New Engl. J. Medic.,* 291:1239, 1974.
25. Grossman, H. J. (Ed.), *Manual for Terminology and Classification in Mental Retardation.* (Rev. Ed.), Washington, D. C.: Amer. Assoc. of Mental Deficiency, 1973.

26. Group for the Advancement of Psychiatry, *Basic Considerations in Mental Retardation: A Preliminary Report,* New York, G.A.P., 1959.

27. Grunewald, K., "International Trends in the Care of the Severely and Profoundly Retarded and Multiple Handicapped." In Menolascino, F. J., and Pearson, P. II. (Eds.), *Beyond the Limits: Innovations in Services for the Severely and Profoundly Retarded.* Seattle: Special Child Publications, 1974.

28. Haworth, M. R., and F. J. Menolascino, "Video-Tape Observations of Disturbed Young Children," *J. Clin. Psychol.,* 23:135, 1967.

29. Himwich, H. C., "The Place of Psychoactive Drugs in Eclectic Therapy of Disturbed Children." In C. C. Carter (Ed.), *Medical Aspects of Mental Retardation,* Springfield, Ill.: Charles C. Thomas, 1965.

30. Kurlander, L. F., and D. Colodny, "Panacea, Palliation, or Poison: The Dynamics of a Controversy," *Amer. J. Psychiat.,* 12:1168, 1965.

31. Lanzkron, J., "The Concept of Propf-Schizophrenia and Its Prognosis," *Amer. J. Ment. Defic.,* 61:544, 1957.

32. Loomis, E. A., L. M. Hilgeman, and L. R. Meyer, "Play Patterns of Non-Verbal Indices of Ego Functions: A Preliminary Report," *Amer. J. Orothopsychiat.,* 27:691, 1957.

33. Lott, G. M., "Psychotherapy of the Mentally Retarded: Values and Cautions," *J.A.M.A.,* 196:139, 1966.

34. Lovaas, O. I., G. Freitag, V. J. Gold, and I. C. Kassorla, "Recording Apparatus and Procedures for Observation of Behaviors of Children in Free Play Settings," *J. Exper. Child Psychol.,* 2:108, 1965.

35. Menolascino, F. J., "Emotional Disturbance and Mental Retardation," *Amer. J. Ment. Defic.,* 70:248, 1965.

36. Menolascino, F. J., "Psychotic Reactions of Childhood: Experiences of a Mental Retardation Project," *Amer. J. Ment. Defic.,* 70:83, 1965.

37. Menolascino, F. J., "Psychiatric Aspects of Mongolism," *Amer. J. Ment. Defic.,* 69:653, 1965.

38. Menolascino, F. J., "Mental Retardation and Comprehensive Training in Psychiatry," *Amer. J. Psychiat.,* 124:459, 1967.

39. Menolascino, F. J., "Emotional Disturbance in Institutionalized Retardates: Primitive, Atypical, and Abnormal Behaviors," *Mental Retardation,* 10:8, 1972.

40. Menolascino, F. J., "Changing Developmental Perspectives in Down's Syndrome," *Child Psychiatry and Human Development,* 4:205, 1974.

41. Menolascino, F. J., "Understanding Parents of the Retarded—A Crisis Model for Helping Them Cope More Effectively." In Author and Pearson, P. H. (Eds.), *Beyond the Limits: Innovations in Services for the Severely and Profoundly Retarded.* Seattle: Special Child Publications, 1974.

42. Mowatt, M. H., "Emotional Conflicts of Handicapped Young Adults and Their Mothers." In Menolascino, F. J. (Ed.), *Psychiatric Approaches to Mental Retardation,* New York: Basic Books, 1970.

43. Oshansky, S., "Parents Response to a Mentally Defective Child," *Mental Retardation,* 4:21, 1966.

44. President's Committee on Mental Retardation, *MR '72: Islands of Excellence.* Washington, D.C.: Government Printing Office, 1973.

45. Rank, F., "Adaptation of the Psychoanalytic Technique for the Treatment of Young Children with Atypical Development," *Amer. J. Orthopsychiat.,* 19:130, 1949.

46. Rimland, B., *Infantile Autism,* New York: Appleton-Century-Crofts, 1964.

47. Robinson, J. F., "The Psychoses of Early Childhood," *Amer. J. Orthopsychiat.,* 3:536, 1961.

48. Ross, A. O., *The Exceptional Child in the Family—Helping Parents of Exceptional Children,* New York: Grune & Stratton, 1964.
49. Rutter, M., "The Influence of Organic and Emotional Factors on the Origins, Nature and Outcome of Childhood Psychosis," *Dev. Med. and Child Neurol.,* 7:518, 1965.
50. Schechter, M. D., "Learning Problems of Handicapped Children." *Lancet,* 1965, 510-515.
51. Starr, P. H., "The Triangular Treatment Approach in Child Therapy: Complementary Psychotherapy of Mother and Child," *Amer. J. Psychother.,* 10:40, 1956.
52. Tarjan, G., J. E. Lowery, and S. W. Wright, "Use of Chlorpromazine in Two Hundred Seventy Eight Mentally Deficient Patients," *Amer. J. Dis. Child.,* 94:294, 1957.
53. Webster, T. G., "Problems of Emotional Development in Young Retarded Children," *Amer. J. Psychiat.,* 120:37, 1963.
54. Wolfensberger, W., "Counseling Parents of the Retarded," In A. Baumeister (Ed.), *Mental Retardation: Selected Problems in Appraisal and Treatment,* Chicago: Aldine Press, 1967.
55. Woodward, K. F., N. Jaffe, and D. Brown, "Psychiatric Program for Very Young Retarded Children," *Amer. J. Dis. Child.,* 108:221, 1964.

CHAPTER 26

Societal Attitudes Toward the Mentally Retarded

by BETTY V. GRALIKER, M.S.W.

The way in which a society discharges its responsibility to the mentally retarded is directly influenced by the attitudes of its members toward the retarded. Every society has been faced with the problem of what to do with the less fortunate members who are unable to meet the demands and expectations of its culture. "The fortunes and misfortunes of the retarded . . . guided initially by superstition, ignorance and fear . . . date back many centuries. Most often these individuals were shunned, exploited, or persecuted. Sometimes their strange behavior caused them to be regarded as having supernatural powers. At other times, due to the compassion of religious leaders, they received kindly treatment. Seldom, however, were they looked upon as individuals with rights and responsibilities. Rarely were they thought of as persons deserving of help and capable of assuming a productive role in the community" (5).

It was not until the 19th century that concern for the care and treatment of the retarded resulted in organized programs and in the development of services for this segment of the population. Prior to the 19th century, the mentally defective individual was usually found in the almshouse, lunatic asylum or poor farm, if he was not sheltered or protected in his small community or hidden in his home. The growth of services may be roughly described in three periods: 1) the development of institutions from about 1850 to 1900; 2) the development of intelligence tests and the organization of special classes in public schools from about 1900 to the present day; and, 3) the development of community resources from about 1950.

441

1. *Institutions*

The first institution for the retarded was founded in 1848 in South Boston by Dr. Samuel G. Howe. It was later moved to Waverly, Massachusetts, and is well known today as the Walter E. Fernald State School. The early emphasis was educational. One of the first leaders in the United States in planning instruction was Dr. Edward Seguin, a physician. Dr. Seguin had developed a system of sensory and motor training in a private school for the retarded which he had established in Paris in 1837. The present Syracuse State School in New York State was the first building expressly planned for educating the retarded and was built in 1854. Other states also followed the pattern of planning state schools for the retarded so that there were 26 by 1910, with many more being founded steadily as the years went by.

The state schools, however, rather quickly became custodial in nature. This was a logical consequence of the ignorance on the subject of mental deficiency. Usually severely defective children with obvious impairments and anti-social behaviors were easily identified and thus institutionalized. Consequently, it was believed that those afflicted with mental retardation required lifelong custody for their protection and that of society. The state schools thus became depositories for all sorts of children who presented difficulties in the community. Children ranging from mild to severe mental handicaps and those with mental illness and emotional disorders formed the undifferentiated population in many of the institutions for the mentally retarded.

Over the years, institutional programs have changed their concept of care as knowledge about mental retardation was gained. Today, in a more enlightened atmosphere, institutions are regarded as residential facilities, with the therapeutic goal of rehabilitating and returning as many patients as possible to the community in a useful capacity. Adequate medical care, social services, educational and rehabilitation services require the help of many disciplines to attain the desired goals for patients. For some patients, twenty-four hour nursing care will always be required because of the severity of the handicap, or the limited treatment success possible with our present tools and knowledge. In some cases, residential care outside the home should be viewed as a therapeutic measure needed in the best interests of the child, parents or community. The decision to place a child out of his home must most often be the responsibility of the parents to make; there are exceptions, such as when parents are not living, or where there is danger to the child, family or community which requires protective intervention, if parents fail to act responsibly on the problem. The decision to institutionalize a child is a painful, sorrowful step and produces considerable conflict for the parents. Residential facilities, community clinics and social agencies often provide casework services to assist parents with this problem. The decision to remove a child from his home may be contingent on reasons basic to the specific condition of the child or to problems inherent in the individual family situation. However, most authorities today recommend that professionals concerned with children (be they retarded or not) should strongly uphold and support the basic, inherent right of children to live with their parents.

Attempts have been made in some communities and facilities to help parents maintain emotional contact with their children even after placement has occurred. This can be done by involving parents actively and meaningfully in the training and rehabilitation process. Realistically, much work needs yet to be done in respect to this area of the parent-child-residential facility relationships and problems.

Since 1920, institutions in a number of states have been conducting traveling clinics staffed by teams which periodically visit central areas. In general, they are held in semi-rural or rural areas to evaluate problem children, leaving recommendations with local welfare agencies, courts and schools. Usually, the traveling hospital team holds clinics to evaluate children for whom state hospitalization is being considered. As a rule, this has not been a successful procedure because of the shortage of hospital staff, lack of services in the local community to provide care and carry out recommendations, and because of large sparsely populated geographical areas which make the service impracticable.

Family care, which was also first developed in Massachusetts early in the 19th century, is modeled on the plan of Gheel, Belgium, which has provided family care for the mentally ill for more than 100 years. According to this plan, patients are placed in selected private homes. This is often called a foster-home program, and is suitable for both children and adults. Usually the state pays for the care and the family supervises the patient with the help of a social worker. Children have the advantage of being able to attend local schools and learn to adjust to home and community life. This program has been most effective in the State of California. As of June 30, 1968, a total of 2,145 patients had been placed in family care homes from the four institutions serving the mentally retarded (1). This represents about one-fifth of a total patient population for the same four institutions of 10,809.

Although institutions and their out-patient services are essential, it must be remembered that only about four to five percent of all retarded individuals are placed there. The remainder live in their own homes and their care is definitely a community responsibility.

## 2.	*Intelligence Tests and Special Classes*

Until the advent of the intelligence tests developed by Binet and others in 1905, there had been no method of rating the retardate or evaluating the extent of his handicap. Physicians had not come to much agreement as to diagnosis or classification of retardation. The significance of the new measurements of intelligence (later modified by Terman and others), lay in the fact that this paved the way for a different social attitude towards mental retardation. It was learned that many children living in the community had mild to moderate handicaps and needed special training. In addition, the development of performance tests (without the use of language) added a new understanding that the human intellect is represented by many factors which must be assessed in determining the level of mental abilities and functioning. Psychological tests designed to measure these factors are important in establishing criteria for planning training programs. Later, the use of personality tests, the increased medical knowledge of organic aspects, the social functioning and behavior, and newer scientific discoveries of genetic and biochemical factors, all added to the appreciation that many factors need to be measured in order to evaluate the retardate and plan a training or rehabilitation program for him.

Organization of special classes for retardates began as early as 1895 in Providence, Rhode Island. Springfield, Boston and Chicago provided special classes before 1900, and Philadelphia and Los Angeles soon after. However, the number of classes provided has always lagged far behind the need for the service in the large school systems, with smaller school districts and rural districts being even more poorly served. These special classes have traditionally been for the educable mentally retarded child (IQ 50-75), although there has been a rapid growth since 1950. Special classes for the severely retarded were started in St. Louis in 1914, in New York City in 1929, and in St. Paul in 1934, illustrating the early recognition of need for providing this special experience for children at the trainable level.

Educational services are now being extended to the more severely retarded child with an IQ of less than 30 to 35, and with multiple handicapping conditions. This broadens the concept of education and calls for the inclusion of other disciplines on the educational team. The social planning for these children must go hand in hand with that of the educator. It is incumbent on the social worker/counselor in this field to have a broad understanding of the roles of other disciplines, but it is even more important that they understand the contribution made to the retarded by the agencies these disciplines represent. With the development of the specialty of school social work in the world of social welfare, there is increasing reason to believe that these workers will be dealing more and more with the parents of children in special classes. Casework skills can aptly be applied here in counseling parents about their child's problems in school adjustment, in interpreting learning goals and other problems. The school social worker has an appropriate place on the educational team, helping in the evaluation process and in enabling the child to benefit from his education program.

3. *Development of Community Resources*

Since 1950 there has been a very rapid growth of services for the retarded, which are beginning to fill the vacuum-like gaps which existed prior to this time. This rapid growth can largely be attributed to the activities of the National Association for Retarded Citizens. This association, whose membership consists primarily of parents of retarded children, is mobilized to help children wherever they are—in home, school, or institution. It has been responsible for the improvement, expansion and development of services. The N.A.R.C., which was organized in 1950, has brought the needs of the retarded child and his family to the attention of the public at large. It now has over 1000 branches functioning in every state. The membership has expanded rapidly and the organization operates activities on national, state and local levels. The program includes parent education, training of personnel, research, public information and attempts to influence legislation.

Parent groups have established many training school facilities to serve those children for whom there was no place in the public schools. They have pioneered projects in sheltered workshops, recreational facilities and summer camp programs. It has largely been through the activities of parent groups that families of retarded children have begun to lose their sense of isolation. Some parent groups have also established their own counseling, diagnostic and evaluation centers, employing social workers as part of the staff to provide counseling and casework services. Perhaps more importantly, parent groups have provided the stimulus to public agencies to initiate and expand services to the retarded.

The action of Congress in 1954 allotting funds to the Children's Bureau to initiate programs for the mentally retarded child was largely attributable to the work and influence exerted by parents through their association. The Children's Bureau has focused its mental retardation programs on the preventive aspects, the pediatric concomitants of the problem in the very young retardate, and on the public health approach to the problem of mental retardation. Since 1954, when the first Children's Bureau grant in mental retardation was awarded for a longitudinal study of preschool children, projects have been established in every state of the union and in Puerto Rico. In most of the projects, demonstration of services to the community in the evaluation, treatment and counseling of the retarded child has been accompanied by clinical and applied research studies, training and teaching activities. Some projects have been attached to university teaching centers, some to hospitals, others in health departments. Almost all have had multidisciplinary team approaches, involving pediatricians, psychologists, social workers and public health nurses. Other disciplines have been variously involved. Much emphasis has been placed on expanding services, assessing the needs of the families in the communities and developing the services to the retarded by existing agencies.

Certain professional groups have also been instrumental in assisting retarded children and their families. The American Association on Mental Deficiency, established in 1876, is one of the oldest professional organizations in the field that has offered leadership and professional direction to expanding programs. In October, 1972, the President's Committee on Mental Retardation presented "A Proposed Program for National Action to Combat Mental Retardation" (6). President Kennedy in his message to the 88th Congress, February 5, 1963, called for a "bold new approach" to the problems of mental illness and mental retardation which he defined as "among our most critical health problems." The blueprint proposed by the Panel's report included over 100 recommendations, embracing research, prevention, clinical and social services, education, vocational rehabilitation and training, residential care, legal aspects, planning and coordination of services and public awareness. The concept of the continuum of care emphasizing the chronicity of the problem of mental retardation has provided a guideline for comprehensive community planning.

Another program which has increased services to the retarded since 1950 resulted from the 1954 Amendments to the Federal Vocational Rehabilitation Act. This service is planned to train the retarded for employment and to give adequate supervision until they can function independently. The 1954 Amendments permitted expansion of these services by making grants available for studies of suitable occupational fields for the retarded to both public and private agencies. The development of the sheltered workshop has been slow, however, and there is a need for more and better training facilities to enable more retarded persons to find and keep jobs.

As one example of the use of Children's Bureau funds, in 1959 the Child Development Clinic at the Childrens Hospital, Los Angeles, began a demonstration project of Traveling Clinics to Southern California. The threefold purpose was: 1) to demonstrate the multidisciplinary approach to mental retardation; 2) to stimulate and train professionals in the problems associated with mental retardation; and 3) to help the community develop its own diagnostic, counseling service. The project is described in a later chapter by Baerwald and Rock.

During the period between the beginning of the 88th Congress, First Session (1963), and the ending of the 90th Congress, First Session (1967), there were 26 major laws enacted which affect the handicapped (3). There were four major laws covering many aspects of the handicapped person's life:

1. *Social Security Amendments of 1963 (P.L. 88-156).*

Between 1935 and 1963 the Social Security Act has been developed by successive amendments to provide: 1) a general base of support for the aged and disabled on the insurance principle (social security); 2) cash assistance through the state welfare systems to those in dire need because of age, disability or blindness or dependence of children deprived of their fathers; and 3) an extension program of project grants and formula grants to the states to support such programs as Maternal and Child Health Services, Crippled Children's Services and Child Welfare Services.

The Amendments of 1963 authorized federal expenditures of $265 million over a five-year period beginning with fiscal year 1964. They expanded maternal and child health and crippled children's services, authorized project grants to provide health care services for expectant mothers from low income disadvantaged areas, approved grants for research projects in maternal and child health and crippled children's services which might provide for breakthroughs in these programs, and provided grants to the states to assist in a comprehensive planning action to combat mental retardation at the state and community level.

2. *Mental Retardation Facilities and Community Mental Health Centers Construction Act of 1963 (P.L. 88-164).*

This law provided for construction of research centers and training facilities relating to mental retardation, construction and establishment of community mental health centers, research and demonstration in the education of handicapped children, and amended P.L. 85-926 to provide training of personnel in all areas of education for the handicapped at all levels of preparation—for teacher training to the training of college instructors, research personnel, and the administrators and supervisors of teachers of the handicapped.

3. *The Elementary and Secondary Education Act of 1965 (P.L. 89-10)*

This law authorized a total expenditure of $1.33 billion during fiscal year 1966 for the improvement of elementary and secondary education. The law authorized $1 billion of assistance to local school agencies, to be provided through the states for use in programs to meet the special needs of educationally deprived children. It also authorized major programs to assist the states in the acquisition of library resources and textbooks; to create supplemental educational centers providing special scientific, cultural, and other educational resources; to increase educational research and to establish a series of national and regional educational research laboratories; and to strengthen state educational agencies.

4. *Vocational Rehabilitation Act Amendments of 1965 (P.L. 89-333)*

The 1965 Amendments improved and expanded the existing vocational rehabilitation legislation by making possible more flexible financing and administration of state vocational rehabilitation programs. The 1967 and 1968 amendments further expanded services to the physically or mentally disabled person. In fiscal year 1968, over 200,000 disabled persons were restored to more productive lives. More than 18,000 of those rehabilitated were mentally retarded, which has been reported to be 16 times more than the number of retarded helped 10 years ago.

The following summarizes legislation passed between 1972 and 1974 that has significant implications for the mentally retarded (9, 10):

1. *Social Security Amendments of 1972 (P.L. 92-603)*

The 1972 Amendments supplant existing state administered programs for Old Age Assistance (Title I), Aid to the Blind (Title X), and Aid to the Permanently and Totally Disabled (Title XIV). Legislative provisions combined these programs into a single, federally financed and administered program of cash assistance to those target populations effective January 1, 1972.

2. *Social Security Amendments 1973 (P.L. 93-66 and P.L. 93-233)*

The main thrust of both sets of 1973 Amendments was to assure elderly and disabled individuals an adequate income and protect certain recipients against loss of benefits.

3. *Rehabilitation Amendments of 1973 (P.L. 93-112)*

General Scope: The Rehabilitation Amendments of 1973 extend one of the nation's oldest and most effective grant-in-aid programs. Originally enacted in 1920 as the Smith-Fess Act, the scope of the initial legislative authority was subsequently enlarged in 1943, 1954, 1965, 1968. The 1973 Amendments completely recodify the old Vocational Rehabilitation Act and place emphasis on expanding services to more severely handicapped clients.

4. *Education Amendments of 1974 (P.L. 93-380)*

General Scope: The Education Amendments of 1974 extend and amend the Elementary and Secondary Act of 1965, the Education of the Handicapped Act and a variety of other federal education statuses. In total, $25.2 billion in federal aid to education is authorized under the 1974 Amendments, including expanded assistance to schools serving handicapped children.

5. *Housing and Community Development Act of 1974*
   (P.L. 93-383)

Among the major features of P.L. 93-383 are: (1) the adoption of a new system of block grants for community development to replace ten existing urban renewal programs; and (2) the initiation of an expanded leasing program to provide direct housing subsidies to low income families. In addition to these and other significant provisions, the omnibus bill contains several important amendments which should expand federal housing assistance on behalf of handicapped persons. The overall thrust of the new legislation is toward decentralization of decision-making authority in the federal housing program. Increased responsibility is delegated to state and local public housing agencies and the 38 Housing and Urban Development area offices.

6. *Social Services Amendments of 1974 (P.L. 93-647)*

The new law establishes statutory goals, spells out new eligibility criteria and specifies operating procdures for a completely revamped federal-state social services program. *Overall organization:* A new Title XX is added to the Social Security Act authorizing grants to the states for social services. This new title is designed to consolidate under a single authority present authorizations for social service grants under Titles IV A and VI. Existing provisions in Tittles IV A and VI are repealed.

Goals of the Program: The new legislation provides that social service funds must be directed toward the achievement of the following goals:

Achieving or maintaining economic self-support to prevent, reduce or eliminate dependency.

Achieving or maintaining self-sufficiency, including reduction or prevention of dependency; preventing or remedying neglect, abuse or exploitation of children and adults unable to protect their own interests, or preserving, rehabilitating or reuniting families.

Preventing or reducing inappropriate institutional care by providing for community-based care, home-based care, or other forms of less intensive care.

Securing referral or admission for institutional care when other forms of care are not appropriate, or providing services to individuals in institutions.

The past twenty years has also brought an increase in diagnostic and counseling services to the young mentally retarded child and his family. Services have been offered through very specific agencies with specific functions. Primarily, these programs have been reaching the white, middle-class families; unfortunately, large numbers of retardates rarely receive these comprehensive care programs. The more knowledgeable and sophisticated individual is more likely to seek professional services when they are needed.

Three-fourths of the nation's mentally retarded are to be found in the isolated and impoverished urban and rural slums. Conservative estimates of the incidence of mental retardation in inner city neighborhoods begin at 7 percent. A child in a low-income rural or urban family is 15 times more likely to be diagnosed as retarded than is a child from a high-income family (4). Having identified one of the major causes of mental retardation, what are the approaches to use in ameliorating the problem?

In 1957, a project was undertaken at the State University of Iowa by the Child Development Clinic in the Department of Pediatrics in association with the College of Education. Its purpose was twofold: 1) to learn as much as possible about a group of children with familial mental retardation and their families from medical, psychological, social, and educational points of view and 2) to determine whether the sources of depressed intellectual development could be modified in these children (who would be between the ages of three and six when admitted to the project), through a program of intensive environmental enrichment (7). Sixteen lower-class families were studied and it was found that almost half of the members of these families were mentally retarded, as defined by current definitions. The conclusions from the data suggest that many of the children who were regarded as mentally retarded were so in part because of mild encephalopathy, in part because of psychosocial factors, and frequently as a result of a combination of the two influences. The data suggested that it might be possible to ameliorate some of the pernicious factors so that these persons need not be condemned to lifelong crippling mental subnormality; however, organized assistance must be given to children less than three or four years of age. Any effort to change the environmentally deprived person must include intensive work with the total family, providing better housing, securing stable employment, improving the health of the total family, and upgrading the educational experiences of the individual. A total approach, perhaps with efforts to reach the child and his family soon after birth, should be considered. This could more readily be accomplished by a revamping of agency structure and function in an effort to get services to families in a coordinated comprehensive fashion. These services should also be provided to the adult mental retardate. The vocational, recreational, medical and social needs of these older individuals need serious consideration as a result of the expected increase in life span and the focus on community care of the retarded. As Stedman (8) has warned:

> It is a mistake to understate a consideration of changing concepts in an area as complex as that of mental retardation without first dealing with underlying issues affecting program development and operations. We have had an unusual opportunity over the past few years to view both stimulation on the national level of a variety of programs and state and local reactions to and attempts at implementation of federal plans. The federal stimulation of programs has met alternately with roadblocks and beds of roses. Some of the roadblocks are inherent in local structures; others are necessary perversions of federal notions to suit local needs. Some of the rosebeds represent readiness to fill gaps with federal support; others are naive and grandiose receptivity to federal support without planning and preparation for long-term commitment or follow-through. For this reason it is dangerous to try to identify new concepts of lasting value.

We are making a beginning in meeting needs and perhaps "we are still too near to the great revolution that has occurred in mental retardation and in all the areas affected by the increased social consciousness now characteristic of the professional and lay person alike in America" (8). However, the very presence of new programs is certainly indicative of a change in attitudes toward the mentally retarded. Hopefully, these signs indicate that society is increasingly more dedicated to the right of every member to cultivate and utilize his maximum potential.

BIBLIOGRAPHY

1. Department of Mental Hygiene, State of California, Bureau of Biostatics, August 26, 1968.
2. "Progrgams for the Handicapped," U.S. Department of Health, Education, and Welfare, Washington, D. C., August 9, 1968.
3. "Summary of Selected Legislation Relating to the Handicapped, 1963-1967," U.S. Department of Health, Education, and Welfare, Washington, D. C., May, 1968.
4. "M.R. 68, The Edge of Change," The President's Committee on Mental Retardation, Washington, D. C., Pg. 19.
5. Begab, M. J., "The Mentally Retarded Child, A Guide to Services of Social Agencies," U.S. Department of Health, Education, and Welfare, Welfare Administration, Children's Bureau, Washington, D. C., 1963.
6. President's Committee on Mental Retardation, *A Proposed Progrgam for National Action to Combit Mental Retardation,* Superintendent of Documents, Washington, D. C., U.S. Government Printing Office, 1962.

7. Kugel, R., and M. H. Parsons, "Children of Deprivation," U. S. Department of Health, Education, and Welfare, Welfare Administration, Children's Bureau, Washington, D. C., 1967.
8. Stedman, D., "Changing Concepts for Programs for the Retarded," *Prevention and Treatment of Mental Retardation,* New York: Basic Books, Inc., 1966.
9. A Summary of Selected Legislation Relating to the Handicapped, 1972. Washington, D. C., U.S. Department of Health, Education, and Welfare.
10. A Summary of Selected Legislation Relating to the Handicapped, 1974. Washington, D. C., U.S. Department of Health, Education and Welfare.

CHAPTER 27

The Family of the Retarded Child

by SYLVIA SCHILD, D.S.W.

INTRODUCTION

Recent years have brought about a shift of public attitudes toward the problem of mental retardation, resulting in a more enlightened concern and understanding of the retarded and their families. Increasingly, the retardate is recognized as having the same needs and rights as any other member of society. The young child, retarded or not, requires the loving care, protection, and guidance from his parents to foster his growth and development in a positive direction. The child needs the stimulus of social interaction and the presence of environmental opportunities for learning how to cope with life problems and for developing his innate potentials to the fullest degree. Each retardate, whenever possible, is deserving of the chance to find his place in society where he can become a useful, productive member of his community. Just as with the normal child, the retardate's major arena of socialization in the early years of life is his family.

Adams (2) has said that the rationale for providing adequate social services to the retarded is based not only on the retardate's needs (justified as this may be), but of more importance, on the needs of the total family unit containing retarded members. Modern social welfare has been moving steadily away from gearing services around persons with specific disabilities (such as the mentally ill, the alcoholic, the cerebral-palsied) towards thinking of *the handicapped person in his family* and *the family in a social setting*. This means that services should be related to the relevant forces of the social structure impinging on the family and which shape the context in which the family performs its socializing functions. Services, while focused on the needs of the retarded child, should primarily be family-centered and community-concerned.

454

Generally, mental retardation presents a problem of life-long disability for the affected individual. Treatment or rehabilitation goals for the retarded necessarily focus on helping these individuals to utilize all the abilities with which they are endowed, to capitalize on their positive attributes, and to compensate wherever possible for their handicaps. It is generally the parents who can best provide the maximum opportunities in the early childhood years to achieve these goals. The home is usually the prime training ground for the development of socially desirable behavior and the emotional security of the child.

Families struggling to cope with the problem of mental retardation need equally appropriate and available services, as do families wrestling with other social problems, such as economic difficulties, mental illness, and delinquency. Whenever the stresses of a difficult life situation threaten the intactness and mental health of the family, interventive services may often strategically assist families to attain healthier resolutions to the social problem. The President's Committee on Mental Retardation stressed that:

> The families of today are subject to many stresses and the rate of family breakup is alarming. This is, of course, one of the conditions in which mental retardation and other social ills thrive (12:89).

In addition to socio-economic stresses, ethnicity, cultural backgrounds, religious aspects, and parental adequacies may have pervasive and far-reaching effects on the intellectual and social development of family members. Begab points out:

> An important concept in child development is that the rate of intellectual growth can be changed—up or down—by altering the child's life experience. Among these life circumstances none are more crucial than those encountered within the family circle. . . . Indeed, the impact of intra-family relationships on the mental growth and behavior of the retarded child is particularly vital, for it may not only raise or lower performance but may determine in some instances whether the child is not to be classed as retarded (4:19).

Families with retarded children face very complex problems which are often complicated by still prevalent negative and stigmatic societal attitudes about mental retardation. This occurs in spite of the fact that the problem of mental retardation is shared by a broad cross-section of the population. For example, families in the middle and upper strata of our society are being increasingly afflicted as medical advances help babies with congenital defects survive. The condition of mental retardation cannot be solely, and conveniently, ascribed to being the particular evil of the less fortunate socio-economic group at the lower level of the societal scale. Because of this, many families who have been functioning independently find themselves suddenly confronted with unusual difficulties related to their retarded child with which they cannot cope by themselves. The established family equilibrium is often upset and families who under normal circumstances would not be clients of social agencies find they are in need of helping services from community resources.

On the other hand, because they are less articulate and less powerful, the disadvantaged poor often neglect to seek special help with their retarded members. Also, these families are plagued with more urgent problems of survival and have little energy to devote to dealing singularly with intellectual deficits of their retarded members. The problems stemming from poverty are, as Begab (4) says, "hostile to growth." Intellectual impairment due to economic and social deprivation needs to be dealt with concomitantly with the global attack for eradication of poverty. However, the assumption can be made that these families are subject to many of the same emotions and stresses related to having a retarded member, particularly if the degree of retardation or nature of the disorder is highly deviant and not a result merely of socio-economic deprivation.

Above all, it is important to keep in mind that families, like people, vary one from the other. Each family needs to be treated individually. And yet, families in many respects are more alike than different. It is this which makes possible some generalized understanding of the needs and problems of families of the retarded regardless of the etiology of the mental defect.

This chapter is divided into the following sections: The first examines the reactions of parents to the identification of mental retardation in their families. The second discusses some strains placed on the roles of family members and the impact of retardation on the family relationships. The third part deals with a brief overview of problems confronting families having a retarded member.

PARENTAL REACTIONS TO MENTAL RETARDATION

There is general agreement in the literature that parental reactions to the diagnosis of retardation in their child are highly individualistic.

The intensity of responses and manifestations of reactions vary widely among and between parents, depending upon a variety of dynamic factors: individual personality, nature of the marital interactions, parental aspirations, feelings about deviancy, social class, etc. Despite the wide range of reactions described in the literature, some are noted to be more prevalent than others: guilt, ambivalence, disappointment, frustration, anger, shame, and sorrow.

Guilt is perhaps the most commonly reported response to the impact of the diagnosis. Parents frequently feel rejecting, hostile, and destructive towards the defective child; unable to tolerate their negative feelings, they become guilt-stricken. In seeking reasons for why they were afflicted, parents often resort to self-shame in reviewing events and their behavior prior to the birth of the child. It is not uncommon for parents to blame each other. For certain religious parents, the child may be viewed as a punishment for past sins. One study (10) found that twelve percent of parents with Down's Syndrome children believed that a direct act of God caused the condition.

Guilt may or may not have a reality basis. For example, if a mother attempts but fails to abort a pregnancy by crude methods the fetus may well be damaged in the process. Wolfensberger (15) cautions that if guilt is reality-based, then it belongs to the parents and may be a constructive force in stimulating them in caring for the retarded child. However, most guilt expressed by parents is without a reality basis but appears rather to be a normal response for dealing with unanswerable questions as to the occurrence of the retardation. It is not rare for parents to be caught in the web of guilt feelings very soon following the ascertainment of the diagnosis—a situation which is compounded in intensity because of the discomfort produced by self-blame and damaged self-esteem. It is for this reason that parents need to be helped early in their contacts with professional people to "work through their guilt." Given the known facts with proper support and empathy, most parents can resolve their guilt feelings and then can more realistically adapt to the presence of the retardation.

Ambivalence is another reaction to diagnosis generally aroused in parents. In such a stressful situation, both positive and negative feelings come into play. Parents show mixed emotions about their adequacies to cope with the problem, about the affected child, and about their contacts with professional personnel. Anger, disappointment, grief, and frustration are often evoked. On the positive side, parents have normal impulses to love and nurture their child and to cope independently with their life problems. Ambivalence is stirred up by each recurrent crisis and may never be a completely resolved conflict for the parent (13). The ambivalence is often sustained by the fact that no rational way can be found to project blame on the child and the ever-present confrontation with the defective family member.

Parents who vacillate in feelings are prone to vacillate in their responses to their child. It is not surprising to see parents, conflicted emotionally, resorting to a pattern of over-indulgence, over-protection, authoritarianism, and/or rigid child-rearing practices, or swinging between these patterns. The recognition of the dynamics of ambivalence is important in the counseling of parents. Much of the problem-solving work in counseling can be focused on helping parents to resolve their ambivalences so they can make more effective use of their energies in developing adequate adaptive strategies to cope with the problems of retardation. Resolution of as much of the ambivalence as possible paves the way for parents to live more comfortably with their retarded child.

Other parental reactions frequently seen are those of disappointment, frustration, anger, shame, and sorrow. This was not the looked-forward-to-child, the heir, the carrier of the family line. "Why did this happen to us" is a bitter cry often heard. Concepts of self are undermined by the knowledge of having produced a defective child; the results are often intense feelings of shame and stigma. The concept that the intense and often chronic emotionality of parents is related to grief and sorrow is widely accepted and well described in the literature (3, 5, 11, 14). A common thread in the views presented is the concept of grief work around an object loss.

Beddie and Osmond (3) viewed the institutionalization of a retarded child as similar to the death of a child, but a death without proper rites. Hence, mourning may be delayed and prolonged. Solnit and Stark (14) found two extreme parental reactions occurring as defenses to the traumatic feelings about the defective child who is perceived as an "object-loss"—that is, either extreme involvement and martyrdom or extreme denial or rejection. Olshansky (11) believes that parents find it culturally unacceptable to express their pervasive grief which is a normal response to a tragic reality situation.

Parents have a right to sadness and to be able to grieve over the diagnosis. Why, after all, should they *like* what in fact has happened to them? Counselors must be aware that any pathology in and of itself evokes responses and problems which are normal consequences of the deviant situation (13). If these normal complements of pathology are not adequately dealt with by the parents, maladaptive coping may result. The real danger lies in the perpetuation and rigidity of maladaptive coping to other life difficulties as well as to the problems of their retarded child.

The intensity of parental reactions to the diagnosis has often been construed to characterize the parents of the retarded as psychologically disturbed individuals. When parents are viewed, instead, as actors in a reality crisis situation their behavior takes on rationality. The disorganized behavior which occurs frequently reflects the upset in the equilibrium of the families involved. Understood in this context, one can readily appreciate why professional counseling can be so essential at the point of diagnosis. Sensitivity to the off-balance behavior of parents, empathetic response to the deepness of their hurt, ego-support, and a reality orientation can strategically help parents to regain equilibrium and cope with their emotional reactions to the diagnosis.

IMPACT ON THE FAMILY

Families of the retarded, in general, tend to have more problems in individual and marital adjustment, child-rearing practices, and sibling relationships. They are significantly affected—socially, economically, and emotionally—by mental retardation. This is not to state that the effects are necessarily always negative. Holt (8) concluded from a study of British families that they often gained better spiritual and ethical values. Farber's study (7) on the impact of a retarded child on family life, despite some research short-comings, lends support to clinical impressions that the nature of family adjustment to retardation is related to the nature of the marital integration of the parents, sex of the retarded child, social class status, and family interactional patterns.

The stressful impact of retardation is felt by all members of the family unit. Having a retarded sibling causes difficulties for the normal children—a fact which is beginning to take on new emphasis and to receive more attention. Adams (2) stresses several reasons for clinical concern with the adjustment problems of the normal children: 1) From a preventive perspective, the family with the burden of mental retardation is *ipso facto* a family at social and psychological risk and there is real danger that the normal child's development may suffer from emotional neglect, distorted family relationships and roles, and curtailed opportunity for social contacts due to the pressures of caring for the handicapped child; 2) the development of healthy children and gratifying child-rearing can neutralize parental disappointment about having a retarded offspring; and 3) the normal siblings can do a great deal to help the social and emotional development of the retarded child if they have a realistic and positive attitude about the handicap. Adams summarizes: "The combination of high vulnerability and a good potential for adjustment makes the normal sibling group a very appropriate target for professional concern" (2:4).

And what are some of the problems experienced by normal siblings? One is the danger of becoming the targets for excessively high parental aspirations to compensate for parental disappointments and frustrations about the retarded child. Another is that of having needs unmet by parents overwhelmed or overinvolved with the care of the handicapped child. At an early age, normal siblings need to deal with peer reactions to their retarded sibling—sometimes at an age when they are unusually vulnerable to teasing and taunting and when they lack the life experience and intellectual maturity to fully comprehend the nature of the sibling's problem. Sometimes guilt develops about being the "normal" child and the glad feelings about not being the afflicted one. Role problems develop—how much responsibility should the normal child share for the retarded one? The list can be considerably extended—however, what is important to recognize is that having a retarded sibling is stressful and traumatic for the average child. In dealing with his dilemmas and difficulties about the retarded sibling, the normal child struggles to develop defensive and adaptive behaviors which often only thrust him into further conflict when his coping efforts are not readily understood by his parents.

And parents are beset by their own difficulties—aside from adapting to the strains and stresses of the daily care of the retarded child, there are tensions related to their own roles. This problem has been aggravated by the current approach to mental retardation characterized by a philosophy supporting community care for the retarded. Wherever possible, the family is expected to manage and rear the retardate in his own home. This had evolved from a reconsideration of the inherent rights of the retardates to the nurture and protection of his parents and to the services and support of his community. In the early phases of the community-centered approach, there was much emphasis placed upon helping parents with their intra-psychic problems related to retardation. A stereotyped picture of the parents as a pathological group emerged and was supported, in part, by the aggressive actions of parents desperately seeking help for their burdensome problems. The parent associations developed norms of behavior and a kind of subculture peculiar to their needs which led to the aspect of pseudo-professionality being incorporated as a part of the parental role. Though this activity was performed primarily by middle and upper-class parents of severely retarded children, this perception of a parent-of-a-retarded-child was generalized to cover all parents of the retarded.

There has been increasing cognizance, however, that central to the problem of family dysfunction related to mental retardation are the role strains and conflicts placed on the family members. The norms and expectations of a parent-of-a-retarded-child have not been clearly delineated or understood; nor for that matter, have the roles of the siblings of the retarded or of the retardates themselves.

Some assumptive generalizations may be ventured concerning the kind of role tensions besetting the parents of the retarded. It may well be that the psychological reactions parents have to the impact of retardation in their child results in a priority accommodation of the marital partners to the specific role requirements of "parent-of-a-retarded-child." The parental functions of the marital role may become subordinate to other marital functions and bind the marital ties around the affected child. This may occur despite other strains and conflicts in the marital relationship. This may also partially explain why many parents often assert they are "drawn close" following diagnosis. On the other hand, one explanation for the higher incidence of marital disruption following institutionalization of the retardate may be related to the emergence of other problems or marital conflicts which were not dealt with when the parents jointly strove to care for the retarded member in the home. It can be speculated that in many families where marital problems exist the retardate welds the parents to the joint responsibility for his care and that temporizing solutions are found to cope with the marital conflicts.

The division of role tasks may also be shaped by the presence of the pathology. Contingent upon the degree of retardation and/or the extension of time of the child's dependency, the parents may be constrained to adhere more closely to instrumental and expressive role tasks (the former assigned usually to father and the latter to the mother) over time than do families without deviant members. Normal families can be more flexible in the sharing and distribution of responsibilities based on individual or family needs and desires. To illustrate, mothers of retarded children have greater restrictions on their ability to move out in social activities or work away from the home than mothers of normal children.

The problem for the parents of the retarded is further complicated by the need to learn a new role which they have to integrate as a piece within an existing and defined parental role. An almost schizoid-like character attaches itself to a parent who is to behave one way to normal children and another way to the retarded offspring. Granted, parental behavior and child-management are perceptibly differentiated with the individualism of each child. The uniqueness which exists is that so often the goal aspirations and role demands which are relevant for the normal siblings are not applicable to the retarded one. The parents must walk an invisible tight-rope if they are to avoid arousing sibling rivalries, and yet at the same time meet the special needs of the handicapped child. The expectations flow from the normal parental role uncontrollably into the deviant parent role, and vice versa. The situation becomes ambiguously confusing. How often, too, professional advice is given to "go home and treat him like a normal child" (so easy to say, so difficult to do). Professional counselors have an express challenge in working with parents. They can help parents to integrate the conflicting role demands, to understand them, and to organize their role functioning in tune with reality so as to enhance their parental behavior.

The retardate's role as a member of the total family system is no less important. He has similar needs to establish satisfying interactions and relationships with his family members. Obviously this presumes the retardate has at least minimal capacity for intellectual and affective behavior. Retardates generally need assistance in forming interpersonal relationships and in learning appropriate role behavior. They frequently suffer from limited social experiences and are further handicapped by the social rejection or negative attitudes expressed to them by other people. The stresses emanating from their mental handicaps make them a more vulnerable group to behavioral and personality disorders. Given a warm, accepting family, the retardate can learn to fill a useful and compatible role. If respected and perceived as an individual with emotional capacity and some ability for learning (though at a slow pace and on a lower level of abstraction), the retardate can be given his own responsibilities which contribute to family functioning. Behaviorally, the retardate can be expected to take on accountability for his actions within the limits of his mental ability. His needs and potentials as a growing, developing, and maturing individual provide guidelines for his parents and siblings for assessing and assigning tasks to the retarded member.

For some families, it is a moot question as to whether or not the nature of their stability and functioning enables them to tolerate the retarded member. One should not pass value judgments—some persons are unable psychologically to cope with the problem. Others may derive subsidiary gratifications out of meeting the needs of the retarded individual. Institutional care should be determined after long and careful consideration of the needs and interests of all the family members, including those of the retardate.

PROBLEMS FACING FAMILIES

Mental retardation, viewed appropriately as a chronic disability, poses a problem for the family of long-time burden of care and management of the retarded individual. This means that families may be, and usually are, confronted with many crises in the areas of their psychological and emotional lives as well as in their daily living experiences. Families may be faced with the unique and cruel torment of social isolation as they frequently feel ostracized and indeed in reality are often shunned by the community in which they reside. This is partly a reflection of the lack of understanding of retardation as well as the stigma attached to it; partly due to the realistic living problems stemming from mental limitations; and, in part, a result of the lack of adequate resources available to serve the needs of retardates and their families.

Foremost for parents of severely retarded children are the problems presented by the excessive and prolonged dependency. Some retardates require twenty-four-hour nursing care. Others, able to manage simple functions such as feeding, eating, and dressing, present behavioral difficulties requiring vigilant and constant supervision. Many families are burdened by the extra care, time, and money needed to obtain specialized medical care and other social services.

As the retardate matures, families are hard-pressed to meet special needs of schooling, recreation, vocational training and employment. Problems of parental supervision are aggravated as the retardate develops sexually and physically at a rate disproportionate to his mental and emotional growth.

Most parents are strained, covertly or overtly, with diffuse anxieties related to the future care and adjustments of retardates. Who is to care for them after parents are elderly or have passed on? Can the retardate achieve self-sufficiency? Will he work and stay out of trouble? Guardianship and legal protection of his human rights are serious concerns. The Parent Associations for Retarded Children have been an influential force in focusing attention on these issues. They have also encouraged and counseled families on financial planning to provide economic security for the retarded member. Under the Social Security Program, some income protection is offered to adult retardates, as well as to those in out-of-home care, affording a measure of relief to families.

There is much which needs to be done yet to provide adequate social provisions to retardates and their families. In the effort to meet the needs of the handicapped individual, it is ever essential to meet concomitantly the needs of his family. One such family need which has been afforded too little attention concerns the rights of parents to be relieved of extended child-rearing functions and to be able to progress developmentally to other phases of family life when the retardate is chronologically an adult. One way of meeting this need is through institutionalization in a state facility. For a relatively few families, private residential care can be provided if the family has the financial means. For some families, normal gratifications are thwarted in order to provide care for the retardate. Much more planning and development of community-living facilities for adult retardates need to be accomplished so that the normal processes of parent-child emancipation can be possible.

SUMMARY

Viewing the family as a system in which the common needs and purposes are met through role interactions of its members, the need for a family approach to mental retardation seems self-evident. The impact of retardation on the family is generally stressful and traumatic and adds to the family's vulnerability in coping with life problems. Much elaboration is needed to delineate and understand the nature of the role responsibilities and expectations of the family members: parents, siblings, and retardates. Family members have a difficult responsibility for reconciling normal role performance with the new tasks required of them to cope with and meet the needs of their retarded member. Retardates, too, have a role in life to fulfill and need the milieu and life experiences offered to them by their family.

Kelman has described the significance of the family of the retarded in writing:

> The retarded child must be viewed as an integral part of his family's group and as having distinct relationships to its members. The child, the parents, and the siblings mutually influence one another's functioning and contribute their respective influence to the dynamics of the family's unit functioning as well (9:37).

BIBLIOGRAPHY

1. Adams, M., (Ed.), *The Mentally Subnormal—The Social Casework Approach*, London: Heineman Medical Books, Ltd., 1960.
2. Adams, M., (Ed.), "Siblings of the Retarded and Their Problems and Treatment," Paper presented at the 90th Annual Conference, American Association of Mental Deficiency, Chicago: May, 1966.
3. Beddie, A. and H. Osmond, "Mothers, Mongols, and Mores," *Canad. Med. Assoc. J.*, 73:167-170, 1955.
4. Begab, M. J., *The Mentally Retarded Child: A Guide to Services of Social Agencies*, Washington, D.C.: Government Printing Office, 1963.
5. Cohen, P. C., "The Impact of the Handicapped Child on the Family," *Social Casework*, 42:137-142, 1962.
6. Eliot, T. S., *The Cocktail Party*, New York: Harcourt, Brace, 1950.
7. Farber, B., W. Jenne, and R. Toigo, "Family Crisis and the Decision to Institutionalize the Retarded Child," *C.E.C. Res. Monog.*, No. 1, 1960.
8. Holt, K. S., "Home Care of Severely Retarded Children," *Pediatrics*, 22:744-775, 1958.
9. Kelman, H. R., "Social Work and Mental Retardation: Challenge or Failure?" *Social Work*, 2:35-39, 1958.
10. Kramm, E. R., *Families of Mongoloid Children*. Washington, D.C.: Government Printing Office, 1963.
11. Olshansky, S., "Chronic Sorrow: A Response to Having a Mentally Defective Child," *Social Casework*, 43:191-194, 1962.
12. President's Panel on Mental Retardation, *National Action to Combat Mental Retardation: A Report to the President*, Washington, D.C., 1962.
13. Schild, S., "Counseling with Parents of Mentally Retarded Children Living at Home," *Social Work*, 9:86-91, 1964.
14. Solnit, A. J., and M. H. Stark, "Mourning and the Birth of a Defective Child," *Psychoanalytic Study of the Child*, 16:523-537, 1961.
15. Wolfensberger, W., "Counseling the Parents of the Retarded," in A. A. Baumeister, ed., *Mental Retardation*, Chicago: Aldine Publishing Co., 1967.

Section VI.

COMMUNITY SERVICES FOR THE MENTALLY RETARDED

CHAPTER 28

A Teaching and Community Organization Demonstration

by ANN BAERWALD, A.C.S.W. and HERBERT L. ROCK, M.S.W.

Previous authors in this book have described the comprehensive life-long network of services required to meet the complex social problem posed by mental retardation. One might assume that such a pattern of programs can only be provided in a megalopolis, but (as described by Dr. Mooring), fortunately, this pessimistic view is unfounded. This chapter will describe a model for development of comprehensive services through a demonstration project reaching out from a medical center which has applicability both in smaller urban centers and in rural communities. In addition, the California system of Regional Center services will be covered briefly.

THE PROJECT

This chapter is based upon the authors' experiences working with the Traveling Clinic Project* operated from the Division of Child Development, Childrens Hospital of Los Angeles, and with the Regional Center program. The Project was in existence from 1959 to 1970 and its goals were: 1) to demonstrate the multidisciplinary approach to the problem of the young mentally retarded child; 2) to interest and inform professional personnel in the field of mental retardation; and 3) to stimulate communities to develop resources and facilities for the care of retarded persons and their families. The Project utilized an interdisciplinary core team, consisting of a pediatrician, a psychologist, a public

---

* This project was supported by a grant from the Children's Bureau, Department of Health, Education, and Welfare, Washington, D.C., through the Bureau of Maternal and Child Health of the California Department of Public Health.

health nurse, and a social worker, in working with communities to achieve these goals.

The Project proposal originally developed from the expressed need for interdisciplinary diagnostic services for young retarded children and their families near their homes. Local service facilities were to follow up care with a community-based center. Prior experience made us aware of the lack of services available in areas removed from primary centers of care and of local ignorance of those in existence. Also, there was recognition that one or two large centers could not provide services for a population as large as that in Southern California. Further, it was clearly evident that professionals who were knowledgeable about mental retardation were available in insufficient numbers. Thus, the Project team as a whole, and most particularly the coordinator of the team, became engaged in the process of community organization.

The role of coordinator became the responsibility of the social worker, since he was the only member of the team whose formal professional training included community organization content. In addition, the coordination role was assigned to the social worker because social workers are, by professional education and commitment, social-action oriented in terms of developing and mobilizing professional services on behalf of disadvantaged persons.

Let us look briefly at the approach of the Project team in relation to a "community" (a community in most instances being a county). The Project had two aspects. One involved utilization of a time-limited demonstration with the objective of leaving an independently functioning local clinic upon termination of the Project; for this, the communities selected had a minimum population of 100,000, which was thought to be a sufficient size to maintain professional resources to staff a local clinic. The other aspect was the use of the Project staff in sparsely populated rural communities which could not mantain independent clinics; here the Project team continued to provide services in consultation to the sponsoring agency.

Request for services was initiated by the local communities, either from one agency or a group representing a wide spectrum of those serving retarded persons. The request for the demonstration usually came from the local county Public Health Department, since in almost all communities they assumed local administrative responsibility for the program. In California the Health Departments are highly visible, community-wide agencies with clearly defined responsibilities for the provision of services to young children regarding general health management,

case-finding, and prevention. Pressure for establishment of a mental retardation program may have been placed on these agencies from various
sources within the community, such as the schools, parent associations,
and private physicians. In one community, those most directly involved
in working with retarded persons organized a committee whose goal
became one of documenting the need for the services of the Project
team; it then utilized its broad representation of community desire to
encourage the Health Department to administer the program. The Project coordinator met with this committee on a number of occasions to
interpret the Project's program and to discuss what it could offer to the
local community. The coordinator was also instrumental in helping the
committee obtain sanction of its activities by the community planning
body. As part of the preplanning stage in all communities, a number of
meetings between local community personnel and the Project's director
and coordinator took place prior to the decision to proceed with the
demonstration in order to clarify mutual expectations and roles during
the demonstration and to establish long-range plans for the clinic from
the outset.

The administrating agency assumed the local coordinating role in the
organization of the clinic, provision of the physical facilities for the
clinic, maintenance of records, etc. A local coordinator was appointed
by the administrative personnel of the sponsoring agency. The person
chosen may or may not have had previous experience in community
planning or coordination of services and frequently had had little or no
contact with the mentally retarded. The local coordinator was thrust
into a new role which he may not have sought or desired and which altered relationships to co-workers. Coordinators came from various disciplines, but most often were public health nurses because the clinics
were usually conducted by the Health Department. The Project coordinator provided extensive consultation to his local counterpart in community organization and involvement of other agencies, as well as in
teaching the various steps involved in diagnostic evaluation and counseling. As soon as possible, a local multidisciplinary case selection committee was developed.

The Project team, in conjunction with the local administrating
agency, initiated in-service training programs for local professionals.
Included were a number of sessions with local professional counterparts,
providing materials regarding mental retardation and orientation to the
interdisciplinary approach. These sessions were usually climaxed by a
day-long workshop presenting the program to representatives of the

larger community; both didactic presentations by Project team members and a clinic staffing of a retarded child were utilized as a basis for a general discussion. Over a period of twelve to twenty-four months following these initial functions, monthly clinics were held. Three children were evaluated to provide the basis for training, both through the Project team's professional performance and by utilizing actual case material to convey specific knowledge and principles related to mental retardation. The children were evaluated by the individual team members and then staffed in the presence of community professionals, sometimes numbering 30 to 40 persons. Local counterparts to the Project team gradually participated directly as team members with consultation being provided by the Project team until the local team was established and ready to function independently. Local participants came from various sources: the physician from the Health Department or pediatric society; the public health nurse from the Health Department; the psychologist from the schools or private practice; and the social worker from a family or welfare agency. At times, it was difficult to interest certain professionals in becoming so involved.

While these demonstrations were occurring, the Project coordinator continued to meet with representatives of community agencies in planning sessions focusing on the organization of the permanent local clinic. In several communities, steering committees became established. They served many functions, including the provision of liaison between the community and the Project, giving direction and long-range planning to the local clinic. The committees also encompassed such ongoing concerns as staffing and funding of local clinics and their relationship to other community services and the Project team. From the outset, the Project belonged to the local community—a philosophy which is basic to the principles of good community organization. It was neither imposed upon the community from an outside authority nor established by a power within the community. This was insured by the preplanning which took place between the Project staff, state consultants and local professionals, by the involvement of any existing planning body in the community, and by the felt need of the community for such a service. The variations in the clinics from one community to another reflected the widely differing resources supporting the clinics. Strong effort was made to integrate with preexisting programs, such as local migrant projects. As was indicated, the Project coordinator worked closely with the local leadership to gain commitments for participation during the demonstration and beyond. Possible sources of ongoing funding (local, state, federal, or private) were explored. Funding could entail direct monies made available to the administrating agency and/or a contribution of in-kind services through participation of professionals from other agencies to the local clinic team.

There has been much discussion at all professional levels as to whether retarded persons should be served through specialized programs or as part of the general services offered to all persons. The community clinic developed as a specialized diagnostic and counseling service to the young retarded child, and his family served as a focal point for the community regarding mental retardation. However, by being placed within a generic agency such as the Health Department and involving a number of other generic agencies in obtaining professionals for the local team, the Project rendered services to retarded persons in a broader way and could serve as a model for comprehensive planning to meet the needs of any disadvantaged group. Such a model is in concert with the principles of normalization.

The in-service training in mental retardation permitted many professionals to become more knowledgeable about retarded persons and their families, enabling them to recognize and serve the retarded population in their regular work. The imparting of basic knowledge was only one way in which the Project team influenced services. It also performed an enabling role to assist the community in modifying its attitudes and perceptions about mental retardation; such changes must occur for both agencies and individuals in order for them to be free to serve retarded persons. Thus, agencies which formerly did not offer services to retarded persons were assisted in altering their policies to include retarded persons and their families, through the support of a specialized diagnostic clinic to provide consultation and demonstrate this extension of function.

The effect of more positive attitudes resulting from new information, altered philosophy of care, and destruction of stereotypes can lead to extension of services within existing agencies. For example, a kindergarten that formerly excluded all children with Down's Syndrome became willing to accept a child with this diagnosis during the clinic staffing, based on a more realistic understanding of his potential and needs. Another example involved a welfare agency which was reluctant to participate because it did not see an acceptable role for itself in service to non-aided families. With encouragement by the Project coordinator and knowledge that other social work agencies were to provide active participation, the director agreed that during the period of the actual demonstration his agency's participation could be justified as in-service training. The supervisory staff who worked with the Project team became so emotionally involved that they continued to serve on the local team after the demonstration and caused the agency to reconsider some of its policies.

The Project served as a catalyst to enhance communication among agencies by providing a focal point around which various agencies and professionals came together to discuss specific cases. From this, at times, there grew a new appreciation of the special expertise available from other organizations and the mutual contributions each could make to the solution of various problems. The Project team represented an additional "neutral" dimension which could help to refocus thinking and assist in removing barriers to effective coordinated service.

Any diagnostic evaluation carries with it the need for treatment in the broadest sense. Unfortunately, it is a common error for professionals to equate diagnostic evaluation with solution of a problem; diagnosis, counseling, and recommendations are generally wasted if a comprehensive network of services is unavailable to implement these recommendations. Teaching from case material can aid in mobilization of the community in spite of the absence of services. Evaluation of a number of children in a community in the presence of professionals involved with the problem of retardation can begin to identify gaps in services and can promote community planning to meet them; the Project team was able to bring knowledge of services not known to the local community. In addition, such an emphasis can provide an incentive for systematic study of persons who are retarded, what services exist for them, and what their needs are. This type of study must precede any meaningful planning to solve a social problem. In one rural community, a number of children in need of a special education program for trainable mentally retarded children were identified; the names were submitted to the board of education and a class was developed for them. For many years, the state education consultant and local school personnel had attempted to gain authorization for such a program, but had been unsuccessful. In another community, the welfare planning body had begun to consider the needs of retarded persons just prior to the initiation of the demonstration. They had obtained a grant to hire a person to study the problem of retardation in the county and to develop task force groups to work on various areas related to mental retardation. Considerable impetus was given to the study by the Project, and the team coordinator collaborated closely with the person working under the grant. Among the permanent results, a Coordination Center was created which served as a fixed point of information and referral in the county.

The focus so far has been on the community organization factors of the Project as they relate to didactic training, program planning, and agency involvement. Another important aspect is that of the actual development of the local diagnostic team. The functioning of a full-time interdisciplinary team is fraught with problems even under the most ideal of circumstances. A well functioning team which includes representatives from different agencies as well as different disciplines is even more difficult to achieve. Success within the local team was, first of all, dependent upon the ability of the Project team members, as consultants, to convey mutual respect for and understanding of what each member of the team could contribute. Since the goal is individualization of need in each situation, it is essential, as elements in each case are identified, to maintain flexibility of role and shared leadership among team members. Within an ongoing, full-time team, professional identification (referred to as "professional preciousness") can be manifested by such concern over roles that client care can become fragmented as each member of the team proceeds in his own direction. On the other hand, working together in a team can lead to increased appreciation of one another's specialized areas of competency, as well as provide an opportunity to learn from one another and help create an understanding of overlapping areas of expertise. Members of the team can become somewhat divorced from their rigid identification with their own disciplines and, by consideration of the case, mobilize their individual strengths to solve the problem at hand.

As indicated above, coordinated cooperation is made much more difficult in a situation where team members meet only occasionally, coming from various agencies and thus differing not only in regard to identification with their own disciplines, but also with the agencies they represent. Thus, we saw a physician appear fearful of disagreeing openly with a social worker from one of the family agencies, lest he threaten his subsequent position with her outside the clinic. At another time, the psychologist assigned to the clinic by the school district was reluctant to support a recommendation which was counter to his district's policy regarding class placement of students. The fact that the Project was carried out in a medical setting often added to the problem of the physician who may, for the first time, have found himself dealing on an equal level with other disciplines.

A mechanism to foster the more adequate functioning of the local team developed out of the recognition of these problems. At the end of each clinic day, a post-clinic conference was held which included the Project team, the local coordinator, all local personnel who participated indirectly in the evaluation of the clients seen, and any local persons assuming follow-up responsibility for a client. Each case was reviewed in terms of findings, recommendations, and counseling with the family; the summary as written by the physician was used as the focal point.

During the early part of the demonstration phase, the conference was often concerned with concrete matters regarding follow-up, procedures, diagnosis, and so forth. Gradually, the focus changed and the local team members became able to question one another and discover what occurred within the clinic in relation to the needs of the client. The Project team, in its consultant role, could facilitate this movement, initially by free communication among its own members and later by aiding the local personnel to question the Project team and subsequently each other. Usually the individual disciplines were more comfortable with their own colleagues and tended to talk with them rather than with other team members; the conference provided a time when the Project team members could intervene and assist in altering this pattern. Matters of professional status, such as who spoke for the team, came to the fore and, once expressed, could be dealt with, freeing the local team's energies to cope with the problems of the client and his family.

Likewise, agency differences came to light. One could begin to see a movement toward increased concern over how to coordinate existing services and consideration of how to plan for non-existing ones. The communication thus opened could extend beyond the clinic itself to create an atmosphere in which case contact between agencies increased for persons never actually seen in the clinic. Generally, relationships between agencies were enhanced.

The post-clinic conference, by its focus on the organizational aspects and gaps in services, helped to alleviate the danger of permitting too great an absorption in the fascinating problem area of mental retardation. The difficulty in this situation was that the community professionals could become so interested in the subject area, particularly when new and/or unusual scientific and medical findings were brought out, that the broader goals of the demonstration could become lost. The Project coordinator, as leader of the post-clinic conference, had to redirect discussions to a more general view of the problem at such times. As the local team coalesced, a pride of ownership and a desire for independence emerged, signalling a beginning readiness to be free of the Project team. With the advent of increased experience and security in the local team, the Project team's role changed from teacher to consultant. The local team was helped to make the modifications required in the demonstration model in view of the characteristics of the particular community. Obviously, this transition was difficult for the Project staff in light of its own emotional investment in the program.

SUMMARY AND FINAL CONSIDERATIONS

Thus far, a model has been described which utilizes an interdisciplinary diagnostic team on a demonstration basis for extension of services to mentally retarded persons in a number of communities surrounding large metropolitan areas. Methods and techniques utilized, as well as problems encountered, have been discussed. Implicit in some of the problems was the question of the long-term viability of a local team based on the contribution of professional services by a number of agencies.

Support to parent groups, data collection, and cooperative community activity provided political leverage which influenced program planning and legislation on a state level. This is seen most clearly in the passage of the Lanterman Mental Retardation Services Act of 1969 (8), subsequently amended to include other developmental disabilities, which established a network of Regional Centers throughout the State of California ". . . to meet the needs of each retarded person, regardless of age or degree of handicap, at each stage of his life's development." The State Department of Health contracts with local non-profit agencies to administer the Centers, thus allowing maximal individualization of services to meet the needs of the local communities. The Centers provide diagnosis, counseling, long-term planning, and funds to purchase needed services for clients; in addition, they are charged with documenting gaps in services and, in conjunction with Area Planning Boards, encouraging development of services to meet client needs. In a number of the communities involved with the demonstration project, the local clinic and its advisory board became a focal point for the application for Regional Centers. In some areas, the functions of the local clinic were absorbed totally by the Regional Centers with full-time, comprehensive, interdisciplinary services; in others, the clinic served as one community resource utilized by the Regional Center.

In retrospect, the Project provided one vehicle for raising the level of community awareness to the problems of retarded persons and their families, training local professionals to provide services to this group of clients, expanding services to retarded persons, and developing local community planning/advisory bodies which were valuable supports to newly developing Regional Centers. The community organization and manpower development activities which were an integral part of the Project are included in the responsibilities of the Regional Centers.

BIBLIOGRAPHY

1. Begab, M. J., *The Mentally Retarded Child. A Guide to Services of Social Agencies,* Washington, D.C.: U.S. Children's Bureau, 1963.
2. Begab, M. J., "Some Basic Principles as a Guide to More Effective Social Services," *Source Book on Mental Retardation for Schools of Social Work,* M. Schreiber and S. Barnhardt (Eds.), New York: Selected Readings, 1967.
3. Butler, G., and D. M. Bramwell, "From Trial and Error—How We Developed a Traveling Clinic Program," *Mental Retardation,* 2:286, 1964.
4. Child Development Clinic, Childrens Hospital, *Annual Reports,* 1959-1969.
5. Child Development Clinic and California Bureau of Maternal and Child Health, *Extending Clinic Services for Mentally Retarded at the Community Level,* Washington, D.C.: U.S. Children's Bureau, 1965.
6. Dybwad, G., "Community Organization for the Mentally Retarded," *Source Book on Mental Retardation for Schools of Social Work,* M. Schreiber and S. Barnhardt (Eds.), New York: Selected Readings, 1967.
7. Koch, R., A. Baerwald, J. McDonald, K. Fishler, and D. Boyle, "The Child Development Traveling Clinic Project in Southern California, a Report on the First Seven Years (1959-1965)," *J. of Ped.,* 3:505, 1968.
8. Lanterman Mental Retardation Services Act of 1969 (A.B. 225).
9. Philips, I., "Children, Mental Retardation and Planning, *Amer. J. Orthopsych.,* 35:899, 1965.
10. Philips, I., (Ed.), *Prevention and Treatment of Mental Retardation,* New York: Basic Books, Inc., 1966.
11. Wolfensberger, W., et al., *The Principle of Normalization in Human Services,* Toronto: National Institute on Mental Retardation, 1972.

CHAPTER 29

Community Planning for the Mentally Retarded

by IVY MOORING, Ph.D.

Recent enactment of federal legislation requires local planning in health, education, welfare and recreation which must then be integrated into a comprehensive state plan. This legislation makes the need for a rational basis for planning urgent.

While each community may have specific planning problems which vary, the basic planning premises and the factors with which the planner must deal remain the same. There is perhaps no area in the United States which has greater problems of size and complexity than Los Angeles County. In Los Angeles, a uniquely organized planning group was established to cope with the foregoing problems of planning and coordinating services to the retarded. The purpose of the present article is to describe the planning experiences of this group, identify the principles and elements of planning, and to examine complexities of the planning process in order to aid other professionals in the development of their framework for planning.

Effective planning for services and facilities for the retarded requires the understanding and utilization of basic concepts which provide the framework for the system of care to be developed. Mental retardation is not a disease entity, but an aggregation of symptoms resulting from many different causes, biological, psychological, educational, cultural and economic, which are manifested in impaired intellectual development or adaptation. Once incurred, mental retardation is chronic, causing persons who are so afflicted to be dependent or semi-dependent throughout their lifetime, requiring that planning of services be systematic and comprehensive with some provision for life-long supervision.

There is no single measure of mental retardation. How it is defined generally depends on the prevailing educational and cultural standards.

Services must be specifically designed to meet the needs of the retarded and their families in a designated community, taking into account the organization of its social and political structures. The term mental retardation designates a group having significant variance from the mildest degree which cannot be differentiated from normalcy, to the most profound, which is often associated with multiple physical handicaps and limited ability for adjustment. However, approximately 89 percent of the retarded have an impairment of mild degree, 6 percent are only moderately impaired, and it is only the remaining 5 percent who are severely or profoundly impaired. Services must be planned then to meet the full spectrum of needs presented by such a diverse group.

In many instances, mental retardation can be perceived as a treatable condition, provided that there is a broad range of services available and those services are delivered in a way that the patient is assured continuity of care. When these components are present, the majority of those who are labeled mentally retarded can remain in the community, and also function productively. The development of comprehensive services at the community level then becomes central in any planning efforts.

The mentally retarded are like all other human beings, differing only in degree but not in kind. Once we perceive the retarded as human beings whose needs for security, shelter, health, education, employment and recreation are the same as for all others, we can plan to meet these needs through the normal channels of the existing generic agencies in the community, and services for the retarded can be dispersed throughout the community. When the special needs of the retarded require specialized services, these too should be distributed in appropriate settings throughout the community, and placed in relationship to other and supportive services. However, when the mentally retarded are perceived as a special group without normal human needs, their isolation is reinforced and services remain fragmented.

When the necessary range of services is provided in sufficient supply so that each retarded individual has an opportunity to attain his fullest potential, absorption within the mainstream of society can be better realized. To provide the necessary range of services in sufficient supply and to have them accessible through a delivery system which assures continuity of care requires foresighted planning and painstaking coordination. The alternative is to treat the retarded as we have treated the mentally ill for so many years, that is as hopelessly disabled persons who have no place to go except state hospitals where they are maintained at tremendous loss of individual dignity and horrendous financial burden to the taxpayer.

How can a community organize itself in order to provide the required spectrum of services and the necessary continuity of care? The Mental Retardation Services Board of Los Angeles County is one community's response to this question. The Board was formed under a section of the California Government Code which permits the joint exercise of powers of governmental agencies. The public agencies which are represented on the Board are: The California Departments of Employment, Mental Hygiene, Public Health, Rehabilitation, Social Welfare, and Education; the County Departments of Health, Mental Health, Public Social Services, and Hospitals; the Los Angeles County School system, and the Los Angeles City School system. In addition, the Joint Powers Agreement also created the Welfare Planning Council's Mental Retardation Commission, which is composed of the private and voluntary agencies and also has a representative on the Board. Thus, the total power and expertise of all the public and private agencies involved in serving the mentally retarded are joined together in one planning and coordinating mechanism. Each Board member has voting powers to commit the resources and energies of his official agency to the implementation of the master plan of services.

This is admittedly a complicated structure, but it is doubtful that anything less complex would have given the underpinning needed to implement our philosophy of planning. Central to this philosophy is the concept that the mentally retarded should have access to all the services provided by the generic agencies. The alternative is to permit the retarded to receive services from highly specialized agencies, which tends to remove them from the mainstream of community life. Sophisticated planning and coordination are required, obviously, if we are to gear services for the mentally retarded to the existing operating pattern of generic agencies. Without such safeguards, the retarded individual, instead of getting all needed services, may get none; in short, he may get lost "between the cracks." The involvement of so many agencies leads to the necessity for agency role definition, and the acceptance by agencies of agreed-upon responsibilities. If generic agencies are to have repeated and sustained encounters with the mentally retarded, the workers in those agencies must receive in-service training to orient them to this population group. In turn, each generic agency must have specialists in retardation on their staffs to carry out this in-service training and to form a network of specialists throughout the community. Lastly, standards must be set within and among agencies to determine referral criteria, rate structures, etc.

To develop a service system consistent with the foregoing principles lies beyond the competence of any single agency (1). What is needed is an organized mechanism for planning and coordination. The Mental Retardation Services Board is one such mechanism. How did such combined effort come about? Obviously the kind of official support embodied in a Joint Powers Agreement was not forthcoming without a considerable amount of careful advance planning. The planning stage for the Los Angeles program extended over two years. It took place under a grant from the Department of Mental Hygiene and the planning staff was housed by a neutral agency, the Welfare Planning Council. Both these factors, the length of time allowed and the independence of the planning staff, were essential elements to the successful establishment of the Board.

To assure that the Joint Powers Agreement would ultimately be signed, the power structure in the community was identified and constituted as a Steering Committee to provide direction to the planning project. To be sure that the recommendations of the plan could be implemented, those persons who might be called upon for the implementation were banded together in a Project Committee. The Steering Committee and the Project Committee combined to form what was called the Mental Retardation Joint Agencies Project. Under the sponsorship of this Joint Agencies Project, a complete survey was carried out of the 335 public and private agencies in Los Angeles County which claimed to serve the mentally retarded. A model of services was developed, and existing services, as identified through the survey, were compared with this ideal model. In this way, duplications and gaps in services could readily be identified. Survey findings were then taken to the Project Committee which functioned as four task forces: social services, clinical services, educational services, and rehabilitation services. The task forces developed recommendations based on the survey findings, and these became the basis for the master plan.

This involvement of the community in the development of the master plan was a key element in the subsequent successful implementation of the plan. The Steering Committee of the Joint Agencies Project became the nucleus of the Board membership; the Project Committee provided the core of the Welfare Planning Council's Mental Retardation Commission, which also has a seat on the Board and which represents the private and voluntary agencies that must, in many instances, deliver the services specified in the master plan. Thus emerged from two years of preparation a community committed to a master plan it had developed, and a coordinating body back-stopped with the power and expertise to put that plan into action.

The Board provides planning and coordinating services to the community by contract with the County Department of Mental Health, a contract made possible by the Short-Doyle program through which the State provides 90 percent of the funds and the County the remaining 10 percent. The Board also had a three-year grand from the Vocational Rehabilitation Administration. Through these sources of funding, it has obtained a professional staff. Additional staff is provided in the form of personnel loaned by signators to the Joint Powers Agreement. This availability of loaned staff is, incidentally, one of the many flexibilities and advantages enjoyed by virtue of operating through a Joint Powers Agreement. Once it was established, the Board delineated the following major planning units:

A. Geography—the territory to be served.
B. Population—the characteristics and size of the group within that territory needing services.
C. Services—the quantity and quality of services needed and who should provide them.
D. Delivery System—the mechanism through which services and population could be brought together within the defined territory.

Geography

Los Angeles County was defined under the terms of the Short-Doyle Retardation Services Board. The County extends over 4,083 square miles, and as of January 1, 1968, had an estimated population of 7,087,677, totaling approximately 40 percent of the state population. To convey the size and complexity of the area served, it might be helpful to keep in mind that seven of the largest cities in the United States could be fitted within the boundaries of Los Angeles County. The characteristics and density of the population vary considerably from one part of the county to another, as do the adequacy of transportation and degree of urbanization. Given the size and complexity of the territory, encompassing both heavily populated urban areas and scarcely populated desert regions, it was necessary to divide it into small components in order to plan services realistically. Each of the units had to be large enough to support a spectrum of services but small enough to make it possible to coordinate those services and organize them into a delivery system. Five service areas were delineated within the County. Each service area has approximately the same size population, although the central area is smaller in geography than the others, which represents the population congestion in the center of the city and the transportation difficulties which are present there. The service areas were established to be as consistent as possible with some of the other planning boundaries already in existence in the County. For example, the boundaries of the areas served by the State hospitals for the retarded were not violated. The district boundaries of the County Health Department, a basic planning unit, remain intact. Nor do our service areas conflict with the regional units already established for the delivery of mental health services.

Population

The population to receive services within the territory could have been estimated by accepted prevalence rates with respect to mental retardation. However, across-the-board estimates do not take into account such factors as the relative invisibility of the retarded population, particularly the adult retarded; these gross estimates also ignore the early mortality of the profoundly retarded and the correlation between retardation and relevant population characteristics, such as poverty, ethnic origin, etc. Consequently, in the fall of 1966, the Mental Retardation Services Board conducted, with limited funds, a patient identification study. Data were collected concerning the profoundly, severely and moderately retarded. We know not only how many such persons there are in the County, but where they live and whether they are receiving services from public or private agencies or are on the waiting list for such services. Persons who have never requested services were not included in this identification project.

In addition to the population thus identified, we could readily locate the 23,000 persons in public school classes for the educable mentally retarded; persons in State hospitals could similarly be located. Had these two groups been added to the ones we identified through our data collection, we would have identified and mapped the location of approximately 1 percent of the retarded population in the County which, according to Dr. George Tarjan, is the proportion of the retarded population which is visible (2). The data also indicate the existence of a correlation between poverty and severe, profound, and moderate retardation— a correlation which the literature indicates exists only with respect to mild retardation. Additional mapping has indicated that although patients who are gravely impaired by retardation tend to cluster in poverty areas, admissions to State hospitals are lower from these areas than from middle class areas. In other words, there is a sizable portion of retarded persons badly in need of a range of services whose needs are *not* being met, either in the State hospitals or by community resources. These findings served to define our planning task.

SERVICES

Identification of Services

In order to estimate the number of and types of services within each geographic area, and fulfill one of its major functions as a central point of information about services to the retarded, the Board updated its inventory of available services and facilities for the retarded. Data compiled from a number of reliable State and County sources were transferred to Public Health District maps, to show the location and distribution of services.

The maps highlighted a number of problems. Among them:

a. There is faulty distribution of services and facilities for the retarded. Services are often inaccessible to the mentally retarded because no attempt has been made to locate facilities in proximity to that population.
b. Sources of services are not placed in rational relationship to each other. For example, classes for the trainable mentally retarded should be (but are not) adjacent to sheltered workshops. Residential facilities should be (but are not) near medical facilities and schools which offer special education classes.
c. In terms of priorities assigned by State planners, facilities are perceived as interchangeable brick-and-mortar units, rather than as mechanisms in which services are delivered. Thus, a day care facility licensed for the care of two children may be given the same priority as a sheltered workshop, licensed to serve 50 retarded persons.
d. Specialized diagnostic facilities for the retarded have been established without reference to a master plan. They tend to be located in medical facilities which are concentrated in the central, more populous areas, where there is a dearth of additional supportive services. The reverse situation exists in the outlying areas.
c. There are not enough residential facilities to meet the needs of a community the size of Los Angeles, and the existing ones tend to cluster in poverty areas, where there is also a dearth of supportive services.

It is not feasible, within the limits of this paper, to present a comprehensive account of how the necessary services are being developed and made available to the retarded. For purposes of illustrating the strategies employed to mobilize the community, this paper is limited to one of our four service categories—that of education, with a few examples of what has been done with respect to educational services for the mentally retarded. These examples illustrate how basic planning principles are applied. Among the strategies by which the Board has strengthened the capacity of the school systems (a generic agency) to serve the mentally retarded: 1) filling gaps, 2) increasing services, 3) maximizing coordination, and 4) minimizing duplication.

(1) *Filling Gaps.* One of the major gaps in services identified in the survey conducted in our pre-planning stage related to the opportunity for preschool education for the retarded child. These preschool opportunities were not provided for in the Head Start program, but the Board recognized that they *could* be provided for through existing State legislation (the Compensatory Education Act), provided proper persuasion was applied. Using this legislative leverage, the Board negotiated with the State Department of Social Welfare and the State Department of Education and the County Department of Public Social Services (signator agencies to the Joint Powers Agreement) for the purpose of developing a network of nursery schools through the County, located for the most part in poverty areas and serving disadvantaged retarded youngsters from ages three to five. Many of these children, having been given the benefit of preschool experience, are now enrolled in regular public school classes.

A second identified gap involved educational programs for the multiple-handicapped, severely retarded child who could not qualify for the mandated classes for the trainable mentally retarded. A pilot program of Development Centers for such young persons, administered by the State Department of Education, was in existence in Northern California. Mobilizing the broad and politically powerful base contained in the private and voluntary agencies which make up the Mental Retardation Commission, the Board assisted in obtaining the passage of legislation which substantially expanded the Development Center program, and supported the efforts of local school districts to establish such centers. Because of the legislation alluded to, this program has substantially increased in the past two years. There are currently eight such centers in the County, one-half the total number in the State.

Professional staff loaned by the Los Angeles City and County School

Systems have effected coordination between the Development Centers and classes for the trainable mentally retarded when their functional level permitted this advancement. To date, 25 percent of the students have qualified for this advancement as a result of their Development Center experience.

(2) *Increasing Services Through Signator Agencies.* Using the data obtained from its patient identification study, the Board demonstrated that there was a heavy concentration of retarded children within the boundaries of the Los Angeles City School System who were not the beneficiaries of *any sort* of education, despite the fact that all school systems throughout the State are mandated to provide educational services to all children who can benefit from them. The Mental Retardation Services Board made an appeal to the Los Angeles Board of Education to expand its classes for the trainable mentally retarded immediately and to make long-range plans to absorb the waiting list for such classes, a list of names for which the Mental Retardation Services Board could explicitly identify and establish the places of residence. Within a year after this action, classes for the trainable mentally retarded had increased by 50 percent, and a master plan had been developed by the Board of Education, which assured the Mental Retardation Services Board that the waiting list of children eligible for TMR classes would be absorbed.

(3) *Maximizing Coordination.* The Division of Protective Services of the State Department of Social Welfare has thousands of children in home placement throughout the County, many of them on leave from State hospitals. While these children were in the hospitals, they were recipients of a broad array of services, including educational services for those who could benefit from them. Yet once they left the hospital, no plan was made to provide those services; frequently they were cared for in homes where the most stimulating activity available to them was hour-after-hour of watching television. Through Board intervention, lines of communications were opened between the School Systems and the Department of Social Welfare to make educational services available to post-hospital youngsters. As a consequence, children are now being placed in homes located within the boundaries of school districts which offer special education classes scaled to their ability, instead of being placed without any reference to the availability of necessary services. Schools, on their part, are cooperating with social workers to facilitate the entry of these youngsters into their special education classes.

(4) *Minimizing Duplication.* Many children who have already un-

dergone elaborate diagnostic procedures in institutional settings or in out-patient diagnostic treatment facilities are subjected to additional psychometric tests by school psychologists when they apply for admission to public school special education classes. A contractual agreement spearheaded by the Board has resulted in an arrangement whereby psychometric data obtained by certified psychologists housed in other agencies are to be accepted by school personnel in processing applications for special education classes, thus eliminating lengthy waiting periods and costly duplication of professional time.

Delivery System

To provide a full spectrum of services, quantitatively and qualitatively, does not complete the task of planning and coordination for the mentally retarded. It is also required that these persons be assured continuity of care and life-long supervision. This can best be accomplished by a delivery system which provides a fixed point of entry for each patient seeking services and a fixed point of return when those services break down or when new or additional services are needed. The delivery system should also perform the function of opening doors to generic agencies for the mentally retarded and their families, rather than leaving burdened and bewildered families to find their way through the bureaucratic red tape which still binds many agencies.

In Los Angeles County, the fixed point of entry and return is the Regional Center, one of two such facilities in the State. The Center is funded to provide free diagnostic services to families of mentally retarded children and to either refer them to other public agencies for needed services or to purchase those services for them from private agencies. The Childrens Hospital of Los Angeles is the prime contractor for Regional Center services in Los Angeles; it achieves a measure of geographic coverage affiliation with four co-contractors.

The delivery system, as conceptualized by the Mental Retardation Services Board, is still in its developmental stage, and is being tested as a pilot operation in a portion of the County. The system assumes that the Regional Center should assign the responsibility for one of the five mental retardation service areas to each of its facilities. The Center conducts the initial diagnosis and continues to provide or procure whatever medical services are needed. After the diagnostic work-up, a prescription is written to fill the needs of the patient. A Regional Center counselor is then assigned to see that the patient is referred to and accepted by the public agencies performing those services; or, if that is not possible, the counselor arranges for payment to a private agency to provide the services. If there is no existing agency in the community capable of providing the patient with the needed services, the Regional Center itself provides it. If the service needed by the patient is hospitalization, the Regional Center refers him to the appropriate State hospital where, by contractual agreement, the diagnostic procedures which have already been done are accepted. If the patient is discharged from the hospital, he returns to the Regional Center for referral to schools, rehabilitation programs, or whatever services he may need. Similarly, if he is receiving services from any source in the community and those services are discontinued or are no longer suitable to his needs, he returns to the Regional Center.

It is envisioned that ultimately a Regional Center counselor will be stationed in each of the public health districts throughout the County. When that is realized, all the mentally retarded patient and his family needs to know is where his health district office is located or what its phone number is; when services break down or when there is a family crisis, he knows exactly where to turn.

SUMMARY

The Los Angeles community spent two years developing a master plan of services for the mentally retarded. Through a Joint Powers Agreement, the Mental Retardation Services Board was established. Through the efforts of the Board, there is being developed a spectrum of services required to fulfill the life-long needs of the mentally retarded and to make it possible for most of them to remain in the community. Recently, the Board's activities have been devoted to designing and putting into effect a delivery system conceptualized to provide a fixed point of entry and return into the continuum of services.

It is well recognized that there is a long road ahead to complete the spectrum of services and the continuity of care, but at least one community has made a start down that road.

BIBLIOGRAPHY

1. Jaslow, R. I., "A Modern Plea for Modern Services to the Mentally Retarded," Division of Mental Retardation, Department of Health, Education and Welfare (in-house publication), 1967.
2. Tarjan, G., "The Next Decade: Expectations from the Biological Sciences," *JAMA*, 191, January, 1965.

CHAPTER 30

Concepts and Theory of Normalization

by WILLIAM G. BRONSTON, M.D.

PHILOSOPHY AND BACKGROUND

The Essence of Dehumanization

> *To respond*
> *To a significant degree . . .*
> *To a human being*
> *As if he were not what he is . . .*
> *Or could never be . . .*
> *What he might be*

I am very deeply honored and feel privileged to be here to share this historic occasion with you. When the Down's Syndrome Congress was born last year, I had the very special sense, having attended that meeting, that you really represented the rebirth of something that happened in the 50's when the then National Association for Retarded Children was established. Then, people arose out of common need to defend their rights and the rights of their sons and daughters who had special needs. There was an inspiration, an enthusiasm, a militance in the 50's as a new social force came into being in this country—a force to oppose dehumanization, to oppose human abuse, to oppose second-class citizenship. As the years have rolled on, two decades and a half since the founding of the National Association, there has been a quieting, a placidity, a loss of some of the inspiration in that movement at a time when we need that inspiration and militance more than ever. I believe that you represent a resurgence of that conviction and devotion and sacrifice

---

This chapter was presented to the Down's Syndrome Congress, Milwaukee, Wisconsin, September 30, 1974. It presents a valuable philosophical base for all services.

to the common good based on very moral, deeply felt beliefs in the interests of your sons and daughters who have Down's Syndrome.

You are not alone. Naturally, the question of the rights of preschool age children is a burning issue. The preschool community represents a minority group in this country, demanding special and decent quality services for their special needs. The Black, Chicano, and native American communities are asserting their needs. The same is true of the elderly, a national minority that is beginning to realize, little by little, that on a strategic level, they are destined to be institutionalized, and die in loneliness, abandonment, misery, and dehumanization in the vast institutional program that is being erected for all citizens in their advanced years. Ladies and gentlemen, one out of three of you sitting in this room will die in an institution for the elderly if the present rate of construction of nursing homes continues and the ideology persists. Women, the largest national minority, have also raised their concerns for a different kind of society. You, as representatives of another national minority, citizens with Down's Syndrome, will and must take your place alongside the other great national and historical movements whose objectives include no less than survival in our culture, a better quality of life, and social justice.

If one group is devalued, all are devalued. If one group is attacked, all groups will be attacked. I would like to bring to your attention a piece of legislation that was passed in Florida last year by the lower house of the State Legislature, entitled "Death with Dignity." This rider was attached to legislation entitled the "Sunshine Bill," a benefit package for the elderly in Florida. The essence of "Death with Dignity" related to a large number of people residing in the state's institutions for the mentally retarded who were not considered citizens because they were labeled severely and profoundly impaired. The bill proposed that all life-supports be cut off from this labeled population. Fifteen hundred people would have been threatened in Florida had that bill passed the State Senate. That bill may pass the Senate within the next few years. After a bill is passed to exterminate those whom the bureaucracy labels profoundly retarded, who will be the next group that will be selected to be exterminated because they are a burden, not worth the expense, or lack advocates? In "Death with Dignity" regulations, the priorities for extermination fell upon those people who did not have a parent, guardian, or advocate, and were in the institution.

Therefore, it is not elective that you are here concerned with your rights, though you may feel that you have freely chosen to come. It is imperative that you are here! For as one group struggles for what is just and human, all groups who live at high risk outside the mainstream will gain.

It is in this context that normalization has to be studied and shared. Normalization has four basic thrusts today:

1. The first is for *consciousness-raising*. Normalization will help us dislodge some of the prejudices and biases that both we and the general society at large hold against people who are different. Unless we surface these massive, deeply held, often unconscious beliefs about differentness, as they are directed towards those labeled retarded in our society, we will make very slow headway in transforming social institutions.

2. Normalization is one of the most powerful *organizing tools* that has developed in the human services scene for consumers and advocates to marshall their strength and have a clear vision of where they are going and where human services ought to be going.

3. Normalization is a fundamental tool to *initially indoctrinate and train* all potential human service workers . . . physicians, nurses, therapists, teachers, administrators, anybody in the human services embarking on their educational course. Technology must derive from the normalization concerns, and not vice versa. Sadly, technology today, as we know it, is so entrenched in attitudes and practices which dehumanize and devalue people served that normalization, taught apart from the core curriculum, becomes rhetoric to cloak business as usual.

4. Finally, normalization, or the socio-developmental model of growth, *provides one of the most coherent and systematic ideologies to light the road for all human services*: a guide, a direction in an era of turmoil, arbitrary scientific innovation, grass roots disenfranchisement and moral bankruptcy of so many of our professions.

Normalization is a value-based set of principles. Whether or not we can say scientifically or empirically that normalization works better than other service approaches is a consequence of how we look at things through what we hold to be important, not, as some try to hold, objective "value-free" evidence or data. What are the values that underlie normalization? All human beings are special and precious. All human beings, like all living things, change constantly and grow. Everyone has the right and need to be loved, have a family, have intimates; each person has the right to be productive, have an education, to have a comfortable dwelling and quality life-supports. These are values. We cannot prove that these work better than pitching people into institutions. That is a matter of value-based attitudes in ourselves and our culture. Normalization is therefore deeply rooted in culture and values.

Three basic rationales for normalizing services are that devalued people will be perceived and treated as: human beings, citizens, and developing, adaptive and responsive organisms.

I would like to share with you some of the historical background of normalization. Some key dates and highlights should suffice for our overview. In 1959, Denmark was the first nation which passed legislation that established a unified agency concerned with the health, education, and welfare of people with special needs, specifically based on helping them experience life as normally as possible. This attitude was explicit in the legislation which confronted basic approaches. Where there had been a permissiveness toward institutions, there would now be a policy of providing home-like living arrangements for all persons needing residential services. Where there had been a domination of the "medical model" based on seeing people as sick or diseased, dependent on health technicians for assistance, the "educational-developmental model" became the dominant approach. Where people had been perceived as subhuman they would be emulated as citizens with rights. Where segregation pervaded the public educational scene discriminating against and separating children with special needs from the mainstream, integration would be a guiding principle and objective goal of the school system in Denmark.

Nearly a decade went by before Sweden passed a similar law in 1967-68, creating an agency to unite service resources for retarded persons based on the normalization principle. Then things began to move. Wolf Wolfensberger, Frank Menolascino and a small circle of co-workers mobilized a campaign in Nebraska, spreading over 2 or 3 years to focus efforts of the movement upon establishing a sweeping law that would bring all the elements of normalization into a service system for persons labelled retarded. The upshot was the creation of an agency in 1969 called the Eastern Nebraska Community Office of Retardation (ENCOR), the first model system of regional proportions to completely embrace ideology and goals to enhance people who need help and totally reject the institution as a legitimate way to serve people with developmental handicaps in the United States. In 1972, Dr. Wolfensberger summarized the historical experience and formulated, in depth, the philosophical and practical aspects of normalization in his now renowned book (1). It is to him that we all owe a profound debt. The same year, monumental Federal law suits, class actions, were filed against human abuse in the institutions for retarded persons in Alabama (the Partlow State School) and in the Commonwealth of Massachusetts (Belchertown State School), both for violating human and constitutional rights of residents in the institutions. The Pennsylvania ARC then filed its landmark Federal suit against the Commonwealth of Pennsylvania for excluding children from their rightful place in public education.

In 1972, the parent-created National Institute on Mental Retardation in Toronto, the research, development and manpower training center of the Canadian Association for Mental Retardation, made a commitment to establishing a demonstration region-wide comprehensive normalizing service system in each of the provinces of Canada. The project has come to be known as ComServ. That same year, class action law suits were filed in New York State against Willowbrook State School, and in Tennessee against the use of peonage in all institutions for mental retardation. Ten other such human rights federal-level challenges were filed. In 1973, the demand for preparing more and more people to take leadership in community-based systems brought large scale training in normalization and comprehensive services to California and Pennsylvania as a new popular hope for change evolved. Now, in 1974, you are the first massive public organization that has stepped forward to do more than pay simple lip service to the principles of human dignity and growth and to devote major time and policy to understanding the developmental growth model as the cornerstone for your parent training and public service role.

At the heart of these events is a philosophy, an ideology which provides a clearer vision of the future. Individual growth is the first benefactor of normalization. The natural strengthening of the parent and voluntary advocacy organizations flows from our personal transformation. The impact of the voluntary associations must affect societal attitudes and values which in turn must precede the movement for more progressive laws by which our relations and services are governed. Value-based services with human rights safeguards against abuses can flourish given the social and legal nourishment and will lead to the enhancement of all generic human services upon which everyone relies. Ignoring the central role of ideology, a minority such as those affected by Down's Syndrome is placed in great danger and at the mercy of the present community of professionals and their traditional ways of "helping." Clearly, we have a great challenge to take up over the next four or five years if we are to even begin to set a new direction.

I would like to share with you the normalization principle in simplified form. The essence of that principle requires the use of *culturally normative means and methods . . . to offer a person life conditions at least as good as the average citizen . . . and to as much as possible enhance or support his/her behavior experiences, status and reputation.* By *culturally normative means,* we speak about using those techniques, tools, media and methods that are most familiar and valued in our culture. *Life conditions* refer to global considerations including housing, income, health care, and all social resources which we have come to link with quality of life. *Behavior* means skills and competencies; *appearance* relates to clothing, grooming, demeanor, and mannerisms; *experiences* are those feelings of well-being and social adjustment of the growing person. Status and reputation, which flow from the labels, images, interpretations and attitudes of others toward the person with special needs, are by far the most powerful and decisive factors in determining the fate of any individual in our society. How many human services take these considerations as the starting point for planning? How many professionals use the expectations and characteristics of their own values and respected lives as a starting point in establishing programs and services for others, especially when the people they are supposed to serve are held in such little esteem by tradition and culture?

Does this mean that we treat everyone the same? What of those persons whose special needs are so significant?

The guiding principle, one that requires the greatest good faith and openness, is to employ normalization *to the greatest possible degree . . . at any given time . . . for each individual according to his/her developmental needs.* We cannot make the crude generalization: Everyone who has been segregated must be thrown into open society to fend for himself. That is not normalization! Normalization is profoundly anchored in individualization. Each and every person must be treated and served as special. All services and all relations for people who are devalued must be aimed at upgrading that person's status in the society. This consideration, universally ignored in deference to clinical considerations, is the single most important basis for the provision of caregiving, beyond any benefit of a clinical nature.

The retort—"Who wants to be normal?"—reflects how easily normalization can be misconstrued today. *Normalization does not mean being normal! It does not mean good or bad, moral or immoral. It does not mean being or doing like everybody else. It does not mean being deprived of all choices!* If you examine each of these distortions of the normalization principle you will readily see how widespread the misinterpretation of normalization really is for each of us. It is common for us to bring one or more of these misinterpretations unconsciously to the philosophy, and, based on this distortion, correctly reject the logic. Therefore, we must be impeccable in clarifying not only the affirmative definition, but in exposing the misinterpretation. When it is said that to "normalize," a person is to make that person "average," we must explain that normalization as a methodology says *"at least as good* as the average citizen."* This means that we have a reasonably common statistically occurring *floor* below which no human being can be allowed to slip. Furthermore, we have a range of options in relation to any given situation that falls within a normative spectrum from which to choose an appropriate course. Though normalization has its roots in moral considerations and rationales, its application is empirical and statistical. Is it more normative to use a classroom setting with teachers and precision teaching to educate children with special needs or to use a cattle prod in an institutional ward? Is the correlation of physical stigmata —crossed eyes, obesity, and other deformities—more culturally normative among persons of value?

Normalization is not a concept or an approach that will be evident in all its complex manifestations, especially in the face of the tradition of rejection of differentness that grips our culture. I hope to but open the door to you where further thought and study will inevitably be needed for each of you to internalize the principles. The implications and subtleties do not allow for simplification. Ultimately, to grasp normalization, you will need to feel and live the principles, or you will be an outsider to the personal revelations that will come from the surfacing of the deeply held prejudices we each harbor—parent or not. Until we can reflexively and instinctively startle when we see breaches of normalization, we will be unable to overcome our own underdevelopment. I have been struggling with normalization for almost two years now. The more I understand the ideas and their implications, the more self-conscious I become about my own life and relations, and how profoundly crippled I am inside in my instinctive responses to people who are different and devalued.

Let us look at the roots of such response to deviancy. "Deviancy" is a social science term. Deviancy does not mean "deviateness." (Deviate relates to a person's essence, their being.) Deviancy is a concept that relates to how a person is *perceived by others.* The social science definition of deviancy is that a person becomes deviant by being different from others in one or more dimensions which are perceived as significant by others who value this difference negatively. In our American society, many groups are considered or preceived as deviant. The mentally retarded, visually limited, physically handicapped, mentally disordered, aurally limited, sexually unorthodox, epileptics, addicts, alcoholics, the aged, the unemployed, dissidents, criminals, the delinquent and unassimilated racial, religious, or ethnic groups are among the prominent categories. Lots and lots of people in our society are negatively valued because of some significant aspect that is different from the mainstream's.

Dr. Wolfensberger (2) has put forward 10 role perceptions that come from our social history in relation to deviant individuals, especially common to the community labelled mentally retarded. Be aware of these roles, for you will see how they are mediated in our society and reflected in our service system. First and foremost, the retarded are perceived as subhuman, as animals, objects, or vegetables. Second, as unspeakable objects of "dread." Third, the retarded are seen as menaces; fourth, they are seen as objects of ridicule; fifth, as objects of pity; sixth, burdens of charity. The seventh historical role is that of eternal children. The eighth as diseased organisms, sick things, or sick persons. The ninth perception is that of the holy innocent, the opposite extreme of the "subhuman" role—the suprahuman role—nevertheless dehumanizing. What we can expect from "angels" in the factories and schools? Finally, the tenth and least common role perception is that of human being, developing person and citizen. Historically, I suggest that if we trace the advent of democracy and its progressive exercise to include not just the privileged few, but all peoples, we will find the growing expression of the last role perception at the forefront, only recently.

Three themes have been voiced by those who have traditionally been the arbiters of morality in relation to the devalued person. These entrepreneurs have touted deviants as injuring themselves in this life or the next. Deviancy is described as "catchy." If you sit close to someone that is different, you may get it. Sexual contact, a sneeze, and the like make deviancy contagious. Thirdly, deviancy is described as predatory. Deviancy will eat us up; it will eat our society up. Thus, in the service system, when a person is identified as deviant, he is put into a group of other people who are perceived as deviant. That person will imitate others who are different and will then be expected to act deviantly. This role expectation from those about us is the single most powerful determiner of behavior that we know. To break out of the role of father, brother, wife, sister, boss, joker, and the like is almost impossible when it is reinforced by those around us. Thus, the person complies with the expectations to act deviantly and is kept in the devalued group. All social ties and relationships are confined to devalued ones which entrench more and more the differentness and, naturally, how that person is perceived. The vicious cycle is in motion. It is no wonder that among the community that has been so ruthlessly segregated, those persons labelled and perceived as retarded have been locked into roles which could lead nowhere but down. Whether the segregation was warranted is not here at issue. What I want to underscore is the insight that for good or evil such role models and consequent practices result in predictable social attitudes which happen. If we are not sensitive to this phenomenon, if we do not respect this occurrence, then we are doomed to repeat service approaches that in the short and long run destroy the very people we aspire to help.

Another phenomenon has occurred because of our blindness to the dynamics of devaluing people. We have taken service workers who have tended to drift into those places where devalued people are served, who themselves may be perceived deviantly. They have often identified with devalued professional models, learned to act differently with the people they serve, have been kept in image-degrading jobs and service settings, established all their social ties with others in similar status and the result has been the creation of a massive subculture of differentness and dehumanization.

Institutions have been the most classic example of these subcultures of deviancy that have been perpetuated over the centuries. Virtually, to the present day, we have had but one solution. Due to mysticism, prejudices, underdevelopment, the lack of resources, we have incurred a heritage of systemic human abuse that is unparalleled. Children who have been perceived as different in our society have been offered *no care* or total care. The form of total care in our culture has been the large, overcrowded, dehumanizing, isolated institution. These have been separated from modern science and technology, separated from our populous communities. Within these institutions, all seven major functions in our society have been clustered: domicile, school or place of employment, recreation, place of worship, hospital, and place of detention. These spheres, if you examine your own lives, are normally highly differentiated and physically dispersed in everyday life. You do not work where you sleep. You do not receive an education where you worship, you do not recreate where you eat. Yet the institution has created a culture that has congregated all these activities under one roof, in one place. More than the cultural aspects that determine expectations of persons traditionally served in this way, there is another group of reasons why institutions are so prevalent. These reasons may upset you. They are certainly presented much too superficially in this overview. There are very concrete and material reasons why institutions thrive.

Institutions cost from $30,000 to $100,000 per bed to construct and range in size from 100 to 3,000 beds, thus providing an enormous building contract and benefits derived to the contractor therefrom. In those states where construction is financed by bonds, the large financial houses own the mortgages until they are paid off with debt service which, at a minimum, doubles the cost in every instance. Because of the natural concern for "fiscal responsibility" enforced by these banks and their representatives in government, questions of public policy regarding the abuses inherent in institutions are not central considerations as the public is locked into decades of dehumanization in keeping with the 20 to 30 years mortgages for construction. Over and above the profits and patronage within the construction contracts go the massive maintenance contracts to supply food, drugs, bedding, furniture, and the like to the institutions. The use of low paid and undertrained staff which is virtually universal in institutions results in high turnover which keeps salaries low, but more importantly, enforces an impersonality on the part of the workers who resist identification with their dependent clients who are everywhere victimized. Finally, the institutions employ highly paid bureaucrats who are usually only loyal to the bureaucracy and see community-based services as competitive to their empires. In short, the political and economic realities of institutions have had as much to do with their longevity as has the cultural heritage of dehumanization which encumbers us all. These realities make public hostages of persons who become institutionalized and the payment of public ransom for their release axiomatic, philosophy notwithstanding. Once built, if we cannot turn the institutions' mortgage-encumbered physical plants into something else to pay off the banks, as we provide enhancing, developmentally-based and normalizing service forms, then we will be exhorted to surrender a better future so the state will not lose its low-risk credit status and low-interest, tax-exempt borrowing capacity in the private money market.

Those who have instinctively understood the risks of institutionalizing their sons and daughters, those who have rejected this public "solution," have generally sought a private answer, a parallel answer for services in the community which coexisted with the institutional system. Thus, the Associations for Retarded Children opted for this coexistence. They lacked the power and the ideology of normalization to demand that the staggering public resources poured into institutions be rerouted *in toto*, and failed to call for the end to institutions. A tragic example in my own state of New York shows how parallel services were mounted by the state ARC over the years, building to a budget just under $10 million. Meanwhile, the state's mental retardation budget soared to $351 million. Simultaneously with the growth of the ARC, the state built 25 warehouses for the retarded where 25,000 persons languish. In fact, the entire department's budget for mental hygiene, for the most part used in institutional settings, has reached the billion dollar mark, while the voluntary associations are preoccupied with their less than token pay-off from the state. They have cashed in their independence and morality and foresaken organizing people in meaningful ways or even demanding accountability from the monolithic public bureaucracy.

The institutional system has therefore become the single most important contradiction in forestalling the change in public attitudes and practices in providing developmental services to people. The institutions are grave obstacles materially and ideologically, incompatible with everything we have learned scientifically, educationally, socially, economically, and morally.

Another example should suffice to make the point indelible. In Nebraska, there is a single state institution for persons labelled retarded, Beatrice State Home. Beatrice serves 1,200 citizens. The budget for Beatrice is $15 million dollars. In addition, a satellite building program is slated over the next seven years to erect bungalows around the remote institution to "normalize" living there. The cost: $7 million. The total: $22 million. ENCOR, the community-based, comprehensive service system has an annual budget of $4 million serving 2,700 people, including persons of all ages, whose disabilities are as complex and significant as any person's left in the institution. If we look at the rate of growth of the institutional budget as compared to the community services budget, we can predict a public backlash against such expenditures, as the institution gobbles up, like a wild cancer, the vital, limited resources of the state.

New York and Nebraska, poles apart in size, poles apart in coming to grips with normalization, are both usurped by institutions. For institutions, like every other approach to human service, owe their existence to ideology, social values, and beliefs. Their origins lie among the beliefs that the retarded needed to be put away, far away. They could not be "cured." They could not learn. They menaced society. And science obliged by producing the necessary evidence to corroborate the prevailing social values and beliefs. All this by virtue of a label.

We know that this institutional system violates families, clients, and workers alike. It undermines all other human services and diminishes society. As long as we have a place for the child or adult whose special needs challenge the school system, or the paucity of dignified jobs for people who are dependent in some area of their functioning, institutions will be an easy out.

Therefore, unless we are able to combat the old myths, we will be stuck with out-moded models of the past. We need a modern, intelligible, publicly acceptable and moral ideology. *No clinical solutions will work, no new technology, no new method will do the job for us!* It will require an approach to human services that people on the street will be able to understand, identify with and internalize to make our clinical advances workable.

By clinical solutions, I would pose such questions as: Will an operation or particular medicine change the situation for a devalued person? Will either segregated or integrated schools as such alter how people are seen? Will group homes or foster homes or community-based services, behavior modification, special education alter society's treatment of differentness? No, these are all tactical questions. Yet, they are posed for us time and time again as the "answer" to our search. I am saying emphatically that if *the ideology behind the technology is unworkable, the technology will not work!*

The best teachers fail. The best doctors and health workers fail. The best therapists fail. The best administrators fail. The best plans and programs fail. Many of you have seen that. One of the best opthalmologists in Montreal was presented with an 18-month-old youngster with Down's Syndrome because the child had crossed eyes. The surgeon refused to operate! One of my dearest friends in Staten Island where I have recently been living had a three-year-old boy with Down's Syndrome who since birth had been unable to defecate independently. During the week, the infant would become more and more distended, and remained nutritionally underdeveloped. The outstanding pediatrician whom the family relied upon and who had been caring for the family's three other children told the mother "You will just have to evacuate this child every week with your finger." After two years of this regular, painful and demoralizing procedure, the mother again confronted the doctor who all this time had never looked at the child, but always at the mother. The doctor said to the mother "You are just complaining too much," and implied that Marie was not a good mother. This man was a fine physician, highly respected in the medical community.

When I first saw this boy, I recognized the classical manifestations of a condition that a second-year medical student would have identified as easily—Hirshsprungs Disease, a condition where the lower bowel lacks nerve endings in the muscle wall of the colon and cannot squeeze the digested waste along and out. The solution was simply to surgically remove the short part of the bowel that was defective and the child was as good as new. Yet, for three years, both the mother and child had lived in misery because of this physician's ideology, not his technology!

These are questions of method or technology:

> What program do we develop for kids with low IQs?
> Can we help children with Down's Syndrome?
> Are community-based services better than institutions?
> How do we train teachers to work with the disabled?
> What curriculum is best?

These are questions of value:

> What quality of life can we build?
> How can we enhance a person in every way?
> What is full citizenship?
> How can we insure each person democratic power?
> How can human services normalize and enrich life?
> How can we integrate and nourish all citizens with special needs in our society?

We have to be able to tell the difference. We must make the value-based questions the foundation of our organizations. For if we do not have the values and goals, then we will become the slaves of technology and of the technicians, who are for the most part paid by the old way, through the institutional system and the bureaucracy.

Only you, as an organization and as individuals, in this entire nation stand between the abuses and insensitivities heaped upon citizens with Down's Syndrome and the advent of social progress.

In closing this first part of the presentation, let me say that normalization, though I am fervent about the concept, is not a panacea to solve all of our problems. I'm sure all of you sense that. But it does carry a profound power to bring about change. We have but to look carefully at those persons who scoff at normalization, who distort it, who are all too ready to oversimplify, to deny its practicality, to deny its applications.

If we look at those persons who resist to the end, we either will find persons who have endured and suffered too long and can no longer adapt to change, or persons with material conflict of interest. It is from the detractors that we best can sense the power of normalization. True change never comes without true sacrifice and often great pain.

THEORY INTO PRACTICE

In the first part of this presentation of normalization, we took a look at its theoretical or philosophical underpinnings. The emphasis was on appreciating how profoundly important ideology and values are in determining the implementation of human services. Traditional human service models have invariably interpreted the people served as less than human. This image has both grown from expectations of citizens labelled retarded and other devalued people who have had to "fit in" to dehumanizing services.

In this second part of the presentation, let us review how services and society see, interpret, and care for devalued citizens and how the application of normalization can affect this. Unfortunately, we must cover much too much in too short a time. I urge you all to take responsibility for continuing to study on your own. Understanding normalization is a continuous process, and like ridding oneself of intolerance, it must be refreshed continuously to prevent old attitudes and unconscious prejudices from creeping back in to obscure our aspirations for the present and the future. Certainly the most elegant and thorough analysis of the application of normalization to practice is to be found in Program Analysis of Service Systems by Wolfensberger and Glenn (3), which is a systematic evaluation scheme that breaks services down into 48 areas that relate to quality of care.

If we were to boil down the highlights of implementing a developmental social model of services—a normalizing model—it would have at least seven major areas:

A. Aspects of the physical settings or place
B. Image, interpretations, labels (devaluing vs. enhancing)
C. Age appropriate continuum
D. Integration
E. Dignity of risk and program intensity
F. Future systems—comprehensive, continuous, normalizing services
G. Voluntary associations and their role

A. Aspects of Physical Setting

Where have we located our human services for people who by society's standards have little or negative value? Far away. Away from our community, away from family, away from resources, away from sight and mind. Institution after institution has been built in a former corn field. Where we place a service tells a lot about how we value the people served.

What considerations have been made for ease of access to and from our services? Have we considered bus routes, freeways, auto convenience, parking, in relation to speed and comfort? All too often access is a barrier to client, family, workers and/or ordinary citizens coming and going.

How large is a service, how many people are congregated in one place? We have traditionally piled up our devalued citizens in numbers, a system which in and of itself stigmatizes in our culture. Our state residential and treatment institutions have ranged between 100 and 6000 people. People have been lumped together because they shared a common label: the retarded, aged, mentally ill. Even now, we congregate 12-30 people in group homes, knowing full well there is no normative models in our culture where that many *valued* people share a dwelling. Over and above just the image barrier of putting a lot of people in one place, a strain is usually put on local resources called on to absorb unnaturally congregated children or adults. Can the restaurants, movies, stores, recreation settings absorb a large population of people who may look or act different? Thus, normalization mandates bringing the size of services down and dispersing services—especially residences— to reduce and eliminate the stigma that excess congregation brings.

How harmonious is a service setting with its surroundings? Is the service—whether it is residential, school, work, play, coordinative— placed where such settings are usually found? Are homes where people live, work places in industrial or business areas where people work and the like? By ignoring the inappropriateness of placing a dwelling or school in an industrial park, or a workshop in a school building or church, one denies the dissonance that people experience faced with such incongruities. Expectations differ from type of setting to type of setting. Human relations and functional community resources vary in residential, or business, or industrial areas. All too often, experience, a donation, cheapness, community rejection, conflict of interest have been decisive in determining where we have established our services for devalued citizens. It is time that we recognize how such short-sightedness has cruelly undone our service efforts.

What range of resources exists immediately about a service? Are there banks, libraries, parks, theaters, stores, restaurants, laundries, barber or beauty shops, markets, bars, post offices in the vicinity? Are these not basic "media" for a program of social integration and habilitation? Traditionally, in keeping with our heritage of segregation, normative resources have been absent. Today, though plans are made to relocate service projects back into society, human service managers are still not locating services in the center of things—undoubtedly an unconscious carry-over from our dark past.

Are settings comfortable by everyday-everybody basic standards? Is there good light, sunshine, temperature and noise level control, space, definition in the setting to accommodate different kinds of grouping and activity, furniture which is inviting, food which is nourishing and appetizing in appearance? Are we thoroughly apt to overlook comfort or provide a low common denominator, considerations based upon the attitude that, "comfort is not important nor appreciated by *them*"? Or, "they" get along quite well with a lot less than we do and don't mind a bit.

What attention has been paid to beauty, environmental decor and aesthetic sensibilities? How do you make a living or working place beautiful? What place do plants, art, arrangement, color, architecture have in the lives of people who are negatively labelled and expected to be impervious to or unaware of their surroundings. It is shameful that questions such as comfort and beauty must be raised, but across the entire human service system, the devalued have been deprived of such elementary conditions and then blamed for tolerating barrenness and monotony.

These aspects of the place are important as ways of communicating how we value people. More than words or plans, the structures we use clearly sum up our expectations toward those who rely on us for help. These are physical *preconditions* that must be scrupulously designed in our movement to reinterpret the rejected and pitied, the eternal child, and return the victimized to society and real citizenship.

B. *Images, Interpretations, Labels*

More complex is the second large area of practical concern to normalization. The most abstract, the most elusive, the most entangled of our prejudices focus on image and interpretation of people with special needs. Let one slogan be repeated over and over until it completely guides all our thought and actions. Johnny Mercer said it loud and clear in his old song *Accentuate the Positive—Eliminate the Negative.* Were we to have the power to measure every service by this guideline, we would demand a total about-face and launch into a new area of care-giving.

How do we employ "accentuate the positive" in our language? Ladies and gentlemen, here is such a transparent window to our own feelings and convictions. For ourselves, for the valued, words are: we, us, our, I, normal, whole, good, majority, parents, professionals, smart, adjusted, peers, friends. Listen to each other carefully, for when we speak of persons who lack value, we say: they, them, their, those, retarded, different, minority, client, patient, bad one, handicapped, my mongoloid, our brain-injured, C.P., L.P., E.D., . . . son or daughter.

Ridding ourselves of these tainted, apologetic, dehumanizing, stigmatizing words and the innuendo that goes with them is rough even when you are aware and try. It takes extra words to positively describe a child with special needs. It is awkward and slows down talk, but it is worth every drop of discomfort and conflict to really *identify with* the strengths of people who are different, and whom society has robbed of humanity.

Look at the labels we put on our services: hope workshop, where there is no hope; New Opportunities Center, where people are one step away from the institution; Garden of Optimism; Home of the Angels; Guiding Hands Home; Rescue Mission; Convalescent Hospital— on and on in keeping with historical role perceptions of holy innocents, diseased objects and the like. Spastic Children's Foundations where *adults* are served in equal numbers imposes the eternal child interpretation. Workshop or Occupational Training Center, Goodwill Industry—such titles never applied in a typical industry.

What should be the purpose of names and labels if it is not to enhance, to dignify, to normalize people's images and expectations? How paralyzed are we by pity, charity, apology, defeatism, that we inadvertently advertise *our* attitudes when we name our traditional programs? Even the label *group home* is a signal of deviancy here. How do we label or refer to our own homes?

The elderly suffer grievously by such settings labelled Sunshine Haven, Placid Lakes Home, Golden Hopes, Tranquil Acres, euphemisms soaked with the imminence of death, disability, inactivity—in short, stigma.

An image, whether it be good or bad, transfers. This phenomenon, though readily understood, is remarkably denied in actual practice. If a highly valued person associates with one who is devalued, a positive gradient occurs and an aura of the valued person transfers to the less valued. This is the rationale of traditionally associating glamorous people with less than glamorous causes. Likewise, negative images transfer as readily. Placing a symbol, person, or thing that has a strong negative image near a devalued person compounds the image injury. We do this everyday in our human services: funeral flowers donated daily to a senior citizens' residence, children in the institution playing on a coffin box or in a sewer pipe at a segregated playground, street signs by institutions—"Dead End," "Sewerage Process Area," and "Animal Control Center"—are common scenes. Barbed wire or chain link fences around human service settings, garbage and refuse juxtaposed to a facility, all say these low-valued or ominous things and people all naturally belong together.

By far the most damaging deviant image comes from charity. Charity says people do not have rights like everybody else. They do not deserve or cannot get social benefits and privileges of first-class citizenship. It says the dependent must survive on a second tax. Charity has undermined the establishment of a single high quality, rightfully based, human service system. It has divided volunteer associations by competition for monies and cast an image on those who rely on charity as pitiable, helpless, and submissive. Though eliminating charity and pity-image fund raising is a terribly difficult step forward, it must ultimately be taken and be placed on our agenda of critical normalization goals. We can start now to educate ourselves and the public to a different way of thinking once we believe people with mental retardation and all others with devaluating labels are real people, like us!

The history of our service settings often brings indelible insult to the image of those served. When tuberculosis was finally treated and cured, citizens with mental retardation inherited the evacuated sanatoriums. When the drug addiction centers moved from detention to community maintenance, the retarded were again the beneficiaries of the image-tainted buildings. Bankrupt, overbuilt nursing homes and institutions for the mentally disordered have become depositories for the least powerful and most heavily stigmatized social minority. This thoughtless trend to use the cast-off, the evacuated places soaked with a previous misery and dehumanizing history, is to be universally found and represents a public betrayal in human services.

There are other major ways in which we have ignored how people are interpreted and perceived by others. We simply have relied on "clinical" solutions and closed our eyes to social considerations that have determined the clinical outcomes to a large extent. We have consistently clustered devalued groups with different labels in one place or area— erecting pockets of deviancy, ghettos of the disabled, in our communities that degrade everyone within. For example, building settings for the mentally disordered, retarded, delinquent, ill, aged are clustered all in one place. Zoning has been a real factor in this phenomenon, but then our notions of devalued people have been coupled with congregating people in such unnaturally large groups that no typical community in its right mind would want these "institutions" in their midst. *Normalization demands smallness, dispersal, and high degree of relevance of a service to the special needs for growth and development of persons served in each setting.*

We have consistently placed our services next to cemeteries, mortuaries, places for the sick, dying, and hopeless. The elderly are invariably within eyeshot of where they are destined to die. The expectations are fixed in everyone's mind and services are molded, virtually becoming self-fulfilling prophecies of doom.

The most common breach of our concern for enhancing the image of people with special needs has been the labelling associated with sources of administration, coordination or regulation. When a person receives aid to the totally disabled funds, rather than unemployment compensation, what image and interpretation are raised?

C. Age Appropriate Continuum

If there is a single basis upon which people are identified across culture, it is on their age. Every culture, every society has evolved a whole range of age-specific, age-identifying relations and settings. Almost everything we do considers how old we are. One of the eeriest cultural experiences that we all have is when we encounter a situation where there is a disregard for a person's age that usually denies growth. Horror movies often use this device to heighten ominousness and discomfort. There are at least 6 major areas upon which age continua can be identified. Normalization demands ruthless respect for age appropriateness in each and all of these areas.

1. Is the *decor and appointment* of a setting age-appropriate? Are toys and mural cartoons about where adults reside and work that create a dissonance? Is an adult service placed in a setting usually reserved for children, propagating the image of "eternal child?"

2. Are *possessions* of a person age-appropriate and age-enhancing?

3. Are the *daily activities* age-appropriate? Are midday naps confined to the below four-year-old age group? Are full school-day or work-day schedules operating for the proper age group? Are the *rhythms of the day week, month, and year* age-appropriate: vacations, holidays, seasonal considerations experienced along an age continuum? Are the *daily and weekly routines,* lunch breaks, learning or working, or recreation operations and the like organized with respect to age?

4. Are the *rights of each person* based on an age-appropriate continuum: the right to privacy; the right to movement; the right to privileged communication; the right to socializing, drink, smoking; the right to health care; the right to property and possessions which increase with age; the right to education, work, leisure; the right to choose with whom one lives; legal rights—equal protection, due process, etc.; political rights which include more than just voting, but the right to dissent?

We have entered an era of incredible expansion of consciousness of what is rightful, human, dignifying, democratic. This is a new experience for many of us who have never really thought about these things. This new awareness, these discoveries are startling and often painful to come to grips with for ourselves, let alone for those who have been seen as less than citizens, less than human, without rights. Many of our rights exist on an age continuum in our culture.

5. *Sexuality* is probably the most controversial area that has been a stumbling point for all of us who fancy ourselves to know what is right for our children and society. We have feared the myth that the retarded are more promiscuous than everyone else—not true. We have feared *our* own sexuality more than anything. We cannot unravel these very complicated questions here, but the point that must be made is that, in our culture, sexuality exists on a very clear continuum based on a person's age. If we are to be true to defending the image and enhancing the status of our sons and daughters with special needs, we must struggle to keep the relations between the sexes on the continuum from childhood through the mature years. Normalization is not a call for abandonment to carelessness or a trip to a bordello. Normalization requires the same delicate and loving considerations we expect in our

own lives to be extended to the lives of people who may be more interdependent than is typical. Moreover, we must be on the lookout for dehumanizing sex-tracking for our constituency. Are girls tracked into limited roles in schools, work, recreation? Are we continuing traditional sex-role differences among those people whose lives we powerfully dominate and control?

6. Possibly the most obvious area that is *a powerful interpreter of age is appearance.* Clothing, accessories, mannerisms, demeanor are sensitively perceived along age lines. Hairdos, jewelry, cosmetics, colors and complexities of dress are highly associated with age. Nothing is more uncomfortable to our sense of appropriateness than to see an adult decked out as a child. When any of these six considerations is violated, a dehumanizing cycle evolves: A handicapped adult is seen and treated as a child. He/she responds as a child. He/she sees self as a child, and is seen and treated by others as a child which continues the cycle.

Concretely, some examples of the most common violations of normalization principles with regard to respecting a person's age include:*

—the use of the "poster child" to symbolize mental retardation or other disability;

—the use of child-related names of action groups where adults are involved;

—referring to handicapped adults as "boys," "girls," "kids";

—neglecting to call handicapped persons by their full names when appropriate, such as "Mary," when "Mrs. Smith" says a lot about our perception or interpretation;

—taking adults to workshops in vehicles marked "school bus";

—teaching or conducting child-like forms of recreation;

—claiming that handicapped adults prefer to associate with children because they have more in common with them;

—dressing handicapped adults in styles appropriate to a younger age.

These are but a few of the practices that dominate our present service system. Further, in this area of age considerations, there are four

---

* Many of these lists were developed from training aids by Dr. Wolf Wolfensberger at the Training Institute for Human Service Planning, Leadership and Change Agentry, Syracuse University.

major drawbacks in grouping people with special needs of widely differing ages.

1. Handicapped children imitate older handicapped models rather than non-handicapped peers.
2. The image of child or adolescent is transferred to the older handicapped person.
3. Staff, which is oriented to one age group that dominates programming, will never be able to adjust with quality in other age group needs.
4. The public's image of the "helplessness" of the aged is transferred to younger handicapped people.

Thus, unlike any other ideology, normalization concretizes the issue of how important respecting and enhancing a person's age must be in all of our social and service relations and interpretations. This is all the more critical in dealings with people who already experience such status injuries due to their differentness.

D. *Integration*

Like the issue of age respect, the issue of integration stands at the heart of normalizing our service and community relations.

What is integration? Being a part of things, rather than being excluded. Having the same privileges and rights as others. Being close to non-handicapped age peers and learning from them . . . receiving special services without being segregated . . . working near non-handicapped persons . . . living in ordinary housing near or with non-handicapped persons and not in large groups . . . being treated with respect . . . not being labelled unnecessarily and *never* in a devaluing fashion.

Our culture has traditionally elevated a few, and strung the large majority along a descending ladder of "less than" statuses. At a point along the descending ladder of social value, people have been segregated and treated as less than *human!* No one suffers a greater social cost of segregation than those people with handicaps, and especially those labelled retarded who traditionally have been powerless and required others to advocate for their rights. The consequences of this isolation—a removal of people with disabilities from the mainstream—are too cruel to list. They disgrace all of us and constitute crimes against humanity which will one day require a public confrontation with those who have personally and socially benefited from this strategy. Instead, let us crystalize the empirical rationales for integrating our dependent citizens.

1. Real integration is invariably associated with a much greater variety of experiences, access to valued peer models, and a greater likelihood of expectations of a normalizing kind. These add up to *more learning experiences.* This has been documented over and over again in our everyday experience.

2. Integration is linked with a greater likelihood that services will be truly based on human and civil rights and be of good quality.

3. The opportunity to exercise more autonomy, choices, citizenship benefits, and freedoms exists in integrated situations.

4. There are more opportunities to meet a wide variety of people and form mutually satisfying relationships.

5. There is a clear transfer of image from valued to devalued persons in integrated settings.

6. People respond positively to normative behavior, and this behavior is more likely to occur in integrated settings of a normative kind.

7. One's self-image is greatly strengthened.

8. The likelihood of contributing to society is greater.

These are compelling rationales that no segregationist can compete with. They are founded not only in the values of social justice, but in fact. They apply both to the workers in the field who are victims of segregation and to the handicapped.

Nevertheless, the resistance is deep and old. It must be made clear that integration *does not* mean:

—being forced into impossible competition;

—being denied special services;

—mixing persons with different types of handicaps;

—merely using services already in existence;

—combining agencies.

Why should we go backward in our approach to providing a decent life for people with special needs? Why should we tolerate the practices of those who would strip us of all the benefit and advances, the support system, and the individualized attention, by equating integration with "dumping" and denying the specialness of every person? Integration is a call to insure each and every person a special, valued place in life and society, not mediocrity and conformity to the present level of bureaucratized schooling, health care and work, known as the mainstream. Yet, as advocates of individualization in all human services, we have been too ready to surrender our progressive role in upgrading all society and accepted an outsider's status, used outside solutions and felt like outsiders. By retiring from alliances with the mainstream families, not asserting *every* child is special, we have remained a special interest minority. The mainstream has suffered by our withdrawal to separate services for our sons and daughters. *Integration must come to grips with quality and safeguards against abuse for everyone or it is not integration!*

E. Dignity of Risk and Program Intensity

The dignity of risk is a concept that comes directly from grasping the fact that human beings constantly grow and constantly change. This implies being continuously at the forefront of new and unknown experiences. The risk of failure is always present, yet if this risk is denied, the reality of how we grow and learn is also denied.

When we arrange a service or program to exclude physical and social risk, it tells how we see a person. We make a compelling judgment about people's humanity and future. It tells others what we expect. It over-emphasizes the traditional concerns to protect, comfort, keep safe, take care of, and watch over people seen as being less than you and I.

Normative protection is one thing—protection that occurs for most of society. *Over-protection* is another matter. We have built walls, fences, doors, used restraints, drugs and rules where they would not be tolerated in open society. We have diminished educational programs, jobs, social and sexual relations to remove most or all of the risk and in so doing, we deny a person's dignity by saying this person cannot be allowed to err or, for that matter, strive. Normalization requires that *risk be programmed in* to insure humanity is preserved and people will be raised to be part of this real world with all its dangers, cruelty, and discovery.

Above and beyond eliminating overprotection, normalization demands *maximal intensity* in human services—maximal challenge in our developmental programs. This is vital for the young age group, such that the consequences of idleness and low expectations which have prevailed in our services do not result in more generations of truly injured people, retarded by our training and service inadequacy. How many people have we inadvertently crippled by setting limits on what we thought they could do? Life is adaptive; it responds to challenges. If these are limited, the outcomes will be limited.

Growth occurs in a rational developmental sequence. Do we destroy our one-year-olds because they are midgets? Yet we will surrender hope of walking or speech or productivity in people when they are just delayed and need more time and support. All too often, I have heard my professional colleagues say a parent "is not facing reality," "is expecting too much," "must accept his or her child's limitations." Well, why not expect everything and work toward that? Let the child set limits—not us! Our job is to throw in everything that we know and constantly dream up new ways to open the doors and windows of development to every child and adult.

F. Future Systems

There remains the issue of the future to touch upon in our swift overview of how the theory and principles of normalization are applied in practice. We live whole lives, complexly textured in a way that has yet not been matched by our human services. We have slowly come to face the awful fragmentation that characterizes these health, education, and welfare services. There is bureaucracy, duplication, with gaps everywhere. We cannot convey a *feeling* of "living unity" and well-being to a person whose life depends on supports and nourishment from outside his/her family, given the nature of our human services. We have anarchy and chaos now. Normalization cannot work as an island refuge where an ocean of dehumanization stretches in every direction. Thus, we must come to grips with the system in its entirety—first on a regional basis, for here there is the building block for the establishment of comprehensive continuous normalizing systems of services. Beginning at the regional level, serving a population between 200,000 and one million, we can truly meet a wide variety of human needs—prevent the experience of fragmentation by people served, respond to needs in ways that enhance human dignity and status, and maximize economy and effective use of resources.

Such systems are only to be found in a scant few places. Nebraska is the only place in the United States that has constructed such a system based on normalization. The people to run them are yet to be trained. The people to monitor them, people like yourselves, self-conscious citizens, have yet to be organized and educated. I am talking about our movement, which will need to carve out a different future.

Normalization demands comprehensiveness in practice and dimensions—not a residential component, but a system of residences beginning with the family home, foster, adoptive, boarding homes, group homes, apartments—in short, an entire spectrum of community living arrangements to serve all ages and age-appropriate behavior levels, to address progress, integration and independence appropriate to a person's age and competencies. The components are limited by our imaginations.

We must provide not just a "sheltered" workshop, but the entire spectrum of training settings from segregated, supervised work to independent work to insure *movement* through the system as growth and skills inevitably occur.

Normalization requires not a segregated preschool or regular school setting, but a continuum of highly demanding, progressively integrated developmental settings to individualize each child's needs and emphasize the most powerful teaching-learning relation—peer modeling. I never could understand the logic of working to get a child to talk in a setting where other children didn't talk and relying on a speech technician as opposed to having the child with delayed speech among other children who talk!

These, what I call *hard services*, services that build and maintain life skills, are needed first; then we should include the "soft services" and support systems: administration, fiscal services, staff development, research, public relations and education, transportation, family guidance and support, counseling, recreation, and citizen advocacy.

We have suffered with a domination of soft services and "soft" professionals that would drive anyone crazy—counseling and referral—until a circular grove, 10 miles deep, has been trudged by most families. Where are the hard services? Where has our emphasis been? The consequence is underdevelopment and defeatism.

If we want normalization, we had better roll up our sleeves and put our heaviest boots on and collectively flex our muscles because we must reach higher than society has ever reached before. We are in a new place in history, science, and technology. With these new conditions, we must have an equally powerful action ideology at the forefront of our movement.

I am convinced, if we are clear about our goals and stick to them, that we will certainly overcome the difficulties ahead. What are the service outcomes toward which we aspire?

1. Prevent institutionalization.
2. Return people from institutions.
3. Prevent emotional breakdowns.
4. Avert family destruction.
5. Dispel loneliness.
6. Preserve health.
7. Insure social participation.

8. Provide proper treatment and helps.
9. Habilitate people.
10. Save money.
11. Save and enhance workers in human services.
12. Render justice.

Is this not what our service systems must achieve? This is the direction in which normalization moves.

G. *Voluntary Associations*

I know many of you harbor great fears and apprehensions. I do. There is good reason, for our historical experience, our political and social experience, has been one of underdevelopment and injury related to people with Down's Syndrome. Yet there are grave dangers in just defending one's self and not taking the offensive toward social change. We live in a dynamic society. The forces for euthanasia, segregation, institutionalization have had great traditional influence. We are still kicked about by the expert who knows best, where bureaucracy is king. If we do not become active, if we just defend what little there is that we hold onto, we will never rise to meet the challenge of social progress and innovation, or know the unlimited potential for solving problems inherent among us as people.

As a voluntary association, beginning on your struggle, learn from the errors of other efforts of the past that have bogged down or sold out.

Our role is not to compete with the public sector but to secure the proper quality of life which is rightfully ours as citizens. Our role is to *organize:* to change public attitudes, monitor human services, take legislative action, litigate against abuse, build liaison with generic services, obtain unmet needs and services, trailblaze, volunteer within services, promote development of workers in human services, engender applied research and those special jobs for task force groups that are always needed! In short, we must become a force for social change in harmony with our status as a national minority at high risk.

Normalization provides a fine beginning point. Let us get on with it! Together!

BIBLIOGRAPHY

1. Wolfensberger, W., *The Principles of Normalization in Human Services,* National Institute on Mental Retardation. Toronto, Canada, 1972.
2. Wolfensberger, W., *The Origin and Nature of Our Institutional Models.* Syracuse, N. Y.: Policy Press, 1974.
3. Wolfensberger, W. and L. Glenn, *Program Analysis of Service Systems* (PASS 3), National Institute on Mental Retardation, Kinsmen NIMH Building, York University Campus, Downsview (Toronto), Ontario, Canada.

Glossary

Adjustment
> The effectiveness of a person's efforts to meet his own needs and to change or modify his behavior in response to requirements of other people or situations. Children who suffer from brain injury usually have difficulty doing this, so we need to modify environmental requirements where possible to protect the child from too much stress or stimulation.

Alpha Rhythm
> Normal rhythm seen in adult electroencephalogram varying 8-12 cycles per second in frequency.

Amaurotic Family Idiocy
> (a) A familial disease occurring almost exclusively in Jewish children, usually manifesting symptoms during the fourth month of life; characterized by flaccid muscles, convulsions, decerebrate rigidity, and progressive blindness marked by the appearance of a cherry-red spot in the maculae associated with optic atrophy. Also called Tay-Sachs disease.
>
> (b) A late infantile type in which the symptoms first appear at the age of three or four years. The patient may live about four years.
>
> (c) A juvenile type beginning between seven and twelve years; running a longer course; not associated with macular changes; occurring in Gentiles.

Amino Acids
> Any one of a large group of organic compounds with the basic formula NH_2-R-COOH, R representing any aliphatic radical. These compounds represent the end products of protein hydrolysis. From amino acids, the body resynthesizes its proteins. Aminoaciduria refers to amino acids in urine.

Anabolic
> To build up.

Anomaly
> Abnormality.

517

Anoxia

Inadequate supply of oxygen, or the disturbance of bodily functions resulting from a deficiency of oxygen.

Antibody

A substance produced in the blood as a reaction against foreign substances introduced into the bloodstream.

Anticonvulsant

Drug used to control seizures. Supervision by a physician is essential if this is prescribed for a person.

Aphasia

Inability to comprehend and/or to use language meaningfully. This condition is often associated with brain damage.

Apneic

A transient suspension of respiration because of a decrease of carbon dioxide tension of the blood with the resultant absence of stimulation of the respiratory center.

Articulation

In speech the forming of the individual sounds of speech in a connected pattern—the movements of the muscles used in speech which result in the formation of speech sounds.

Aspiration, level of

Level of performance or achievement which a person tries or hopes to reach. A child who gives up easily or does not put forth effort when he is challenged to do something new is considered to have a low level of aspiration and needs stimulation along the lines of his natural interests.

Astereognosis

Inability to recognize objects by touching them. It is a defect of sensation.

Asymptomatic

Showing no symptoms.

Ataxia

Impairment of muscular coordination which is manifested by difficulty walking or maintaining balance.

Athetosis

Involuntary, worm-like movements caused by injury to the brain.

Audiologist

A professional person who is engaged in the study of the hearing function. He is responsible for the evaluation of persons with hearing problems, planning education programs for people with hearing impairments, and conducting research on causes and treatment of hearing problems.

Audiometry

The measurement of the ability to hear sound, usually by the use of standard tests.

Audiometry, pure tone

A common technique for testing thresholds of hearing. The individual's ability to hear tones at various frequencies (125-8000) is determined. Two kinds of pure tone threshold measurements can be made:

(1) Air conduction testing where the sound enters the ear canal and passes through the eardrum to the inner ear; the stimulus then goes up the auditory nerve to the brain.

(2) In bone conduction hearing tests, pure tone is directed through the bone behind the ear to the inner ear fluid, which stimulates the nerve of hearing.

Autism

A disorder in which the person does not respond normally to external stimulation and seems to act in response to internal demands and is often said to "live in a world of his own." Often associated with brain damage, convulsions, or prematurity.

Autosome

An ordinary chromosome as distinguished from a sex-determining chromosome.

Beta-Amino Isobutyric Acid

Amino acid found in the urine normally in some people.

Bilateral Colobomata

An absence of part of the eyelid.

Bilirubin

A bile pigment. Excessive amounts in the blood can cause brain damage due to decreased oxygen uptake.

Brachycephaly

Shortness of the head, the cephalic index being 81.0 to 85.4.

Brain Injury

A term used to define a condition in which brain cells have been damaged either before birth by disease or accident, during birth or after birth. It may be detected by a number of medical and psychological techniques. In general, though, the brain injured child is hyperactive, has a short attention span, poor impulse control, and may be perseverative in his responses.

Buccal Smear

Preparation of cells from the mucous membranes of the cheek for microscopic study, made by spreading them on a glass slide. This technique is used for sex determination.

Cataract

Condition in which the lens of the eye is clouded.

C.A.—Chronological Age

Age of a person in terms of years and months. It is written, for example: 4-6—four years and six months.

Cattell Scale

A graded series of tasks designed to measure the ability of infants and young children from the 2nd month through four years. It yields a score which is transmuted to a Mental Age or I.Q. equivalent. The reliability of measurement in this age bracket is not impressively high. It is somewhat similar to the Gesell scale.

Centromere
    The constriction of the chromosome located where the arms of the
    chromosome meet.
Cephalic Delivery
    Baby delivered head first.
Cerebral Angiogram
    A radiograph of the brain made visible by injection of dye into the
    cerebral arteries.
Cerebral Palsy
    Neuromuscular disfunction due to brain damage.
Chiasma
    A cross.
Chorea (Sydenham's)
    A nervous disease with involuntary and irregular movements; pop-
    ularly called St. Vitus' Dance.
Chromosome
    Any one of the separate, deeply staining bodies, commonly rod
    or V-shaped, which arise from the nuclear network during mito-
    sis, and which split longitudinally in the course of that process.
    They carry the hereditary factors (genes), and are present in con-
    stant number in each species. In man, there are 46 in each cell,
    except in the mature ovum and sperm where the number is halved.
    A complete set of 23 is inherited from each parent.
Cleft Palate
    A congenital failure in development of the roof of the mouth.
Clonic Block
    Repetition of speech sounds or parts of words produced by in-
    voluntary, jerky movements of the speech muscles.
Communication
    The use of speech, sounds, writing, or gestures, usually in the
    presence of another (or with the expectation that another person
    will receive the message), for the purpose of making one's needs,
    feelings, intentions or ideas understood.
Conductive Hearing Loss
    A failure of the air vibrations to be transmitted to the inner ear.
    The failure may be caused by an obstruction or blocking in the
    outer or middle ear, or a defective mechanical conducting system.
Congenital
    Present at birth.
Congenital Acromicria
    Abnormal smallness of the extremities existing at birth, as a result
    either of heredity or of some nonhereditary factor operative during
    intrauterine development. Synonym for Down's Syndrome.
Congenital Neurocutaneous Syndrome
    Disease of the nerves and skin as a result either of heredity or of
    some nonhereditary factor operative during intrauterine develop-
    ment. Tuberous sclerosis, etc.

Convulsive Disorder—Convulsions—Epilepsy—Seizures—Fits
A condition caused by damage to the brain and resulting in abnormal involuntary movements of the body. The person is not usually aware of his movements.

Coxsackie
Virus infection—usually respiratory.

Craniopharyngioma
A tumor arising from the remnants of the craniopharyngeal duct in the area of the pituitary gland.

Cranio-Stenosis
Narrowing or shortening of the cranium due to premature closure of the cranial sutures. Synonym—craniosynostosis.

Craniosynostosis
Premature closure of the cranial sutures.

Craniotomy
Incision of the skull.

Cretinism
Congenital lack of thyroid secretion, with arrested physical and mental development.

Crouzon's Disease
Ocular hyperterlorism. Hereditary disease sometimes associated with mental retardation.

Cyanosis
Blueness of the skin due to insufficient oxygen in the blood.

Cytomegalic Disease
Virus infection of mother causing anomalies in fetus if mother is pregnant.

Dart and Dome Wave
Typical electroencephalographic pattern of petit mal epilepsy.

Deaf
The individual who has little or no hearing. Hearing is non-functional for life's purposes.

Decibel
Units which express amounts of increase of intensity of one sound compared with another—a slightly perceptible change in volume. Hearing loss is measured in decibels.

Deprivation
Reduction or lack of normal environmental experiences or opportunities for learning.

Dull-Normal—same as slow learner
A term sometimes used to describe the intellectual level of persons who have I.Q. scores between 75-90. They are accepted in regular classes in the public schools, but they generally have difficulty keeping up with the normal requirements.

Dyslalia
Any of the disorders in the articulation of speech not due to central nervous system damage.

Ectoderm
> The outermost of the three primitive germ layers of the embryo. From it are derived the epidermis and epidermic tissues, such as the nails, hair, and glands of the skin, the nervous system, external sense organs (eye, ear, etc.), and mucous membrane of the mouth and anus.

Educable-Retarded
> A range of retardation including those persons who are able to learn elementary school skills such as reading, writing and arithmetic to about the fourth grade level. The I.Q. range of this group is roughly between 50 and 75.

Electroencephalogram
> The record produced by an electroencephalograph, an instrument used to record changes in electric potential between different areas of the brain.

Encephalitis
> A viral infection of the brain.

Encopresis
> Involuntary discharge of stool.

Entoderm
> The innermost of the three primitive germ layers of the embryo. From it are derived the epithelium of the pharynx, respiratory tract (except nose), digestive tract, bladder and urethra.

Enuresis
> Involuntary discharge of the urine.

Epicanthal Folds
> Vertical folds of skin at the inner canthus of the eyes.

Epilepsy
> A name for a condition in which the person has seizures. May be congenital or developed after illness or injury.

Erythroblastosis
> A condition caused by incompatibility of the baby's and mother's blood. It causes jaundice and anemia and may cause kernicterus.

Etiology
> The cause of a disease

Febrile
> Having a fever.

Fetus (foetus)
> The child in the womb after the end of the second month until birth.

Focal Motor Seizures
> A seizure caused by damage in one location in the brain. The convulsive movements occur only in the part of the body controlled by the damaged area of the brain.

Functional Speech Problem
> A speech disorder which is traced to faulty learning of the correct form, and not due to an existing physical condition.

Galactosemia
An inborn error of metabolism, due to inability to convert galactose to glucose.

Gamete
An egg or a sperm.

Gargoylism
Lipochondrodystrophy. A lipoid disturbance involving many body tissues, characterized by dwarf stature, shortness of neck and trunk, kyphosis of spine, depression of bridge of nose, clouding of cornea, shortness of fingers, and mental deficiency.

Genetic
Pertaining to or transmitted by the genes.

Gestation
Pregnancy.

Gonadal Dysgenesis
Underdevelopment of the reproductive organs.

Grand Mal Seizure
A major seizure attended by loss of consciousness.

Hard of Hearing
Those persons with reduced hearing acuity, either since birth or acquired at any time during life. Hearing, though defective, is functional.

Hemiparesis
Paresis is weakness of the muscles. Hemiparesis is weakness of the muscles of one side of the body.

Heterozygote
An individual possessing different alleles (one of two or more contrasting genes) in regard to a given character.

High Frequency Sounds
Consonants which are composed of pitch at above 2400 cycles per second. These are most difficult for the hard of hearing person to produce correctly.

Homologous
Arising from common primordia and similar in basic plan and development, but having a different function.

Homozygote
An individual possessing identical alleles (one of two or more contrasting genes) in regard to a given character.

Hurler's Disease
Lipochondrodystrophy (See *Gargoylism*).

Hydrocephalus
Abnormal enlargement of the head caused by interference with the drainage of cerebral fluid.

Hydrophthalmia
Distention of eyeball from watery effusion. (Glaucoma)

Hyperactivity
Excessive and uncontrollable movement, such as is found in persons with central nervous system damage.

Hyperbilirubinemia
Excess of bilirubin in the blood.
Hypercalcemia
Excess of calcium in the blood.
Hypersynchrony
Mass synchronous discharge of electrical energy as seen on electro-encephalogram.
Hyperthyroidism
Disease state produced by excessive secretion of the thyroid.
Hyperventilation
Abnormally prolonged and deep breathing.
Hypoglycemia
Deficiency of sugar in the blood.
Hypoplasia
Failure of an organ or tissue to achieve full adult size because of incomplete development.
Hypsarrhythmia
Unusual electroencephalographic pattern characteristic of myoclonic seizures.
Idiopathic Hypercalcemia
Self-originated; occurring without known cause, excess of calcium in the blood.
Idiopathic Seizure
True or typical epilepsy.
Inhibition
Control of impulses or feelings. It is accomplished by central processes in the brain so that in some cases of brain damage the inhibitory function is impaired and a child is not able to control his impulses or emotions.
Intelligence
Problem-solving behavior; ability to adapt appropriately to environmental demands, and ability to deal with abstract relationships. It is measured by means of standardized intelligence tests administered by qualified psychometrists or psychologists.
Intelligence Test
A standardized measuring instrument consisting of a graded series of tasks which are designed to test performance in a variety of areas, e.g., memory, reasoning, recall, abstract or symbolic thinking, visuomotor, verbal, etc. The most commonly used tests for use with children are the Stanford-Binet Intelligence Scale and the Wechsler Intelligence Scale for Children (WISC).
I.Q.—Intelligence Quotient
Ratio between M.A. (mental age) and C.A. (chronological age); M.A. is divided by C.A. times $100 = $ I.Q. A number which tells how a person's performance on a standardized test compares with the performance of an average person of his same C.A. Average I.Q. is 100; Average Range 90-110.
Example: M.A. $= 3$-0
    C.A. $= 4$-0
    I.Q. $= 3.4 \times 100 = 75$ I.Q.

Jaundice

A disease or disorder of the liver resulting in a yellowish appearance of the skin.

Karyotype

The chromosomal constitution of the nucleus of a cell, being characteristic of an individual, species, genus, or larger grouping.

Kernicterus

Damage caused to a certain part of the brain by the pigments causing jaundice.

Ketogenic

Forming ketones. (A compound containing a bivalent radical = C:O.)

Kinesthetic Sense

The sense of movement of the various muscular and skeletal tissues of the body. The receptors which carry this information to the brain are called "proprioceptors."

Larynx

The voice box. That portion of the respiratory mechanism located between the upper ring of the trachea and the tip of the epiglottis.

Lethargic

Slow, sluggish in response to stimulation.

Leucine-Sensitive Hypoglycemia

Unusual form of low blood sugar syndrome induced by amino acid leucine.

Lowe's Syndrome

See Oculo-Cerebral-Renal Syndrome.

Maple Syrup Disease

Rare disorder of amino acid metabolism involving valine, isoleucine and leucine.

Meiosis

A process occurring in the formation of gametes, involving a pair of cell divisions in which the number of chromosomes is reduced to half.

M.A. (Mental Age)

An expression of the level of performance obtained on a standardized test, such as the Stanford-Binet, compared with the performance of the average person of a given chronological age. For example: a child with a C.A. of 6-0 who passes all tests at the six-year-level would have a M.A. of 6-0, etc.

Mental Defective, Mental Deficiency

This condition is one in which there is impairment of the central nervous system which affects mental functioning and limits mental growth. Environmental change or training may sometimes alleviate pressures or reduce hazards.

Mental Retardation

Educational and social performance which is markedly lower than would be expected. Retardation means suboptimal functioning.

Mental Subnormality

A general term to describe the mentally retarded and also the mentally defective, as well as those whose mental endowment is so poor that they are remarkable for their dullness, even if functioning to the best of their abilities. It is defined by a set of psychological findings which may in different individuals reflect any of a number of conditions, ranging all the way from hereditary inadequacy, through environmental deprivation, to personality disturbance.

Mesoderm

An intermediate layer of cells developing between the ectoderm and entoderm; from it are formed all types of muscle, connective tissue, bone marrow, blood, lymphoid tissue, and the epithelium of body and joint cavities, blood vessels, etc.

Metabolism

Use of energy by the body.

Mental disorders may be associated with metabolic disorders.

Examples: Cretinism, Phenylketonuria.

Metaphase

The second stage of mitosis in which the chromosomes split.

Microcephaly

Abnormally small cranium.

Micro-Ophthalmus

Abnormal smallness of the eyes.

Mongolism— (Down's Syndrome)

A condition in which the child has certain physical characteristics and is almost always mentally retarded.

Moro Reflex

On sudden removal of support or a loud noise, an infant throws his arms outward and then brings them together in a jerky manner; the fingers are extended at first and then the hands are closed.

Myoclonus

Sudden spasm of a muscle.

Myopia

Ametropia in which parallel rays come to a focus in front of the retina, vision being better for near objects than for far.

Nasopharyngeal

Pertains to the part of pharynx which lies above the level of the soft palate.

Neonatal, Perinatal

Occurring around the time of birth.

Neonatal Anoxia

Reduction of oxygen in body tissues below physiologic levels in the newborn.

Neonatal Atelectasis

Nonexpansion of the lungs in the newborn.

Neonatal Asphyxia

A morbid condition caused by failure of the tissues to receive or utilize oxygen, the fault occurring in the lungs in the newborn.

Neonatal Death

Death of an infant within 28 days after birth.

Neurologist

A physician who has special training in the diagnosis and treatment of diseases involving the nervous system (brain, spinal cord, and nerves). He limits his practice to treatment of patients who have such conditions.

Neuromuscular
Pertaining to the nerves and muscles.

Neurosis
An emotional conflict which reduces the effectiveness of a person's social, intellectual, or other functioning, but in which contact with reality is maintained.

Nystagmus
Involuntary rapid movement of the eyeball.

Ocular
Pertaining to the eye.

Oculo-Cerebral-Renal (Lowe's Disease)
Rare disorder of amino acid metabolism characterized by cataracts, mental retardation, hypotonia and amino-aciduria.

Ophthalmologist
A physician who specializes in the eye and its diseases.

Organic Involvement
Any condition which affects mental, motor, or communication functions which is due to such central nervous system impairment as results from cerebral palsy, epilepsy, or brain damage, etc.

Orthodontia, Orthodontist
The practice of straightening the dental structures, aligning the teeth and shaping the jaw by braces so as to bring the two sets of teeth into proper relationship to each other. The person who does this work is called an orthodontist.

Ossicles
Three small bones located in the cavity of the middle ear known as the malleus, incus, and stapes. Important in conducting sound to the inner ear.

Palate
The roof of the mouth; the front portion is the hard palate, the back portion is the soft palate or velum.

Pallor
Paleness.

Paroxysmal Headache
A sudden uncontrollable occurrence, recurrence or intensified headache.

Pediatrician
A physician who has special training in diagnosing and treating diseases of children. He limits his practice to the treatment of children.

Perception
Ability of a person to organize what he sees, feels, hears, etc., into recognizable patterns. This ability is needed in all learning, so that if a child is found to have a disorder of perception he needs special methods of teaching just as much as if he had a defect of the senses.

Perinatal
Relating to the period between the end of the 20th week of fetal life and the end of the first month after birth.

Peristatic Amentia
>Synonym for Down's' Syndrome suggested by Benda.

Perseveration
>Tendency to continue a response, verbal, motor, emotional, etc., after the need for it has passed. This is one of the characteristics of brain-injured persons, whose ability to shift their attention or activity in response to the environment is impaired.

Personality Disorder
>Disturbance in social behavior which may or may not be treatable by psychotherapy. Some disorders may be related to conditions which are not subject to change, such as biological inadequacies or early environmental emotional deprivation, etc.

Petit Mal Epilepsy
>A mild attack of epilepsy characterized by a transient loss of consciousness.

Phenylalanine
>A naturally occurring amino acid, discovered in 1879, one of those essential for human metabolism, which is converted to tyrosine. Failure of this conversion, as a result of an inborn error of metabolism, is associated with mental deficiency in phenylketonuria.

Phenylketonuria—PKU
>Defect of metabolism which sometimes causes mental retardation. The treatment consists of a special diet started during infancy.

Physiatrist
>A physician specializing in physical medicine or physical means of therapy.

Physical Therapist
>One who has graduated from one of the schools of physical therapy approved by the Council on Medical Education and Hospitals of the American Medical Association.

Placenta
>The afterbirth.

Pneumoencephalogram
>Roentgenography of the brain after injection of the ventricles with air or gas via the spinal canal.

Post-Natal
>After birth.

Premature
>A baby born before the expected date and requiring special attention because of the immaturity of his body functions, weighing less than 5 lb. 8 oz.

Prenatal
>Before birth.

Primordium
>The first beginnings of an organ or part in the developing embryo.

Prognosis
>Forecast of the course and outcome of a disease.

Projective Test
>A psychological tool for studying personality characteristics of peo-

ple. It is designed to elicit responses at a subconscious level (as opposed to an objective test. For example: Rorschach, TAT, etc.)

Prophylaxis

Preventive treatment—the prevention of disease.

Protozoa

A phylum of the animal kingdom, made up of organisms consisting of a single cell.

Protozoan

Any species or organism of the Protozoa.

Pseudo-Hypoparathyroidism

False insufficient activity of the parathyroid glands.

Psychiatry

A branch of medicine concerned with diagnosis and treatment of mental and/or emotional illness. A psychiatrist is an M.D. who has specialized in mental diseases.

Psychogenic (disorder)

Caused by emotional rather than organic factors.

Psychology

The scientific study of human or animal behavior and its measurement in relation to a standard or norm. There are many different branches in the field of psychology, such as clinical, experimental, educational, abnormal, etc. The person who evaluates children for Day Care Centers is generally a clinical or educational psychologist.

Psychometric

Measurement of psychological functioning, usually done by means of standard objective tests. Must be performed by a certified psychologist or psychometrist.

Psychomotor Seizures

A seizure during which the person carries on some form of behavior such as running, repetitive speech, or smacking the lips. It is caused by damage in an area of the brain.

Psychosis

An emotional disturbance in which contact with reality, i.e., orientation in time, space, relationship, is tenuous or lost.

Psychotherapy

Treatment of emotional disorders by various techniques. Should be administered only by a qualified professional therapist.

Ptosis (means falling)

Abnormal depression or falling down of an organ.
Example: drooping of the upper eyelid.

Purulent

Consisting of or containing pus.

Reading Disability (*Dyslexia*)

Inadequate reading skill which is measured to be two grades or more below grade of placement.

Retrolental Fibroplasia

Fibroplastic overgrowth of vascular tissue in the eye, occurring in premature infants of low weight due to excess administration of oxygen.

Rubella
   German Measles or three-day measles.
Satellitosis
   A gathering of free cell nuclei around the ganglion cells of the
   brain cortex in general paresis.
Schema
   1. A simple design to illustrate a complex mechanism.
   2. An outline of a subject.
Sequela
   Lesion or affection following and resulting from an attack of
   disease.
Slow Learner (See dull-normal)
   A designation for a person whose intellectual functioning is meas-
   ured to be in the sub-average range, roughly between 75 and 90.
   The slow learner is able to profit from public school education,
   but needs special help and a longer time to achieve normal progress.
   He generally does not achieve beyond high school and may not
   be able to benefit from the regular high school curriculum, but is
   better trained in some vocational skill after the 8th grade.
Social Work, Medical
   Social work techniques focused on the purpose of discovering and
   helping with problems which affect health, grow out of illness, or
   interfere with attaining maximum benefits from health services
   and medical care.
Spasticity
   Tightness of the muscles, making it difficult for the person to
   control them.
Speech Clinician (Synonymous with Speech Correctionist and Speech
   Therapist)
   The professional person who is engaged in treating persons with
   speech and language disorders. Usually, he works under supervision
   of a senior clinician or consultant (or another person with advanced
   training in speech pathology). He may, himself, be the senior staff
   member, however.
Speech and Hearing Evaluation
   A series of tests which are designed to discover the nature and
   underlying reasons for a disorder in communication.
Speech Pathologist
   A professional person who is engaged in the study of the disorders
   of speech and language. He may be responsible for conducting
   research programs for the purpose of finding out more about causes
   of speech problems, better means of helping persons with speech
   problems, etc. He is usually the person who is responsible for
   diagnosing a child with a speech problem, and frequently supervises
   therapy. He frequently has a doctorate level of training in Speech
   Pathology, and always has Advanced Clinical Certification from
   the American Speech and Hearing Association.
Speech Reading (lip reading)
   The art of comprehending speech by watching the movements of

the face and the movements of the articulatory organs (lips, jaw, tongue, etc.).

Speech Stimulation
The use of spoken language in an effort to call forth a specific language response in a person.

Speech Reception Threshold
An individual's threshold of speech is the level at which he can repeat 50% of the words presented to him.

Stigmata
Bodily abnormalities found in considerable number of degenerate persons.

Strabismus
Deviation of the eye which the patient cannot overcome. This is an effect of imbalance of eye muscle control or spasm.

Subdural Hematoma
A massive blood clot beneath the dura mater of the brain. Usually due to trauma.

Sutures
As usually used in discussing mental retardation, this means spaces between the bones of the head.

Synapsis
The pairing off and union of homologous chromosomes from male and female pronuclei at start of mitosis.

Synchronous
Occurring at the same time.

Syncope
Fainting.

Syndrome
A specific collection of symptoms.

Tay-Sachs Disease
See Amaurotic Family Idiocy.

Testicular Fibrosis
Formation of fibrous tissue; fibroid degeneration of the genital gland of the male, in which the spermatozoa are produced; the male gonad corresponding with the ovary in the female.

Threshold (as applied to hearing)
The level of loudness at which a person is able to hear 50% of the sounds presented to him.

Tonic Movement
Steady sustained msucular contraction.

Toxoplasmosis
Infection with a genus of protozoan organisms which is transmitted to the baby before birth from the mother.

Trainable Retarded
A range of mental retardation including those persons who are not able to learn elementary school subjects, but are able to learn how to take care of daily life activities, such as feeding and clothing himself, mobility, communication, and a few of the more practical social conventions. The I.Q. range of this group is roughly between 30 and 50.

Tranquilizers
>Drugs which are intended to keep a person calm. Supervision by a physician is essential if these are prescribed for a person.

Transillumination
>A test in which a light is placed against the head of an infant to see if the light shines through. If it does there is no brain in that area.

Trauma
>Any injury, physical or psychological.

Trimester
>Three-month period during pregnancy, viz., first trimester refers to first three months.

Triploidy
>Three chromosomes instead of two.

Tuberous Sclerosis
>A familial disease with tumors on the surfaces of the lateral ventricles of the brain and sclerotic patches on its surface, and marked by mental deterioration and seizures.

Tyrosine
>A naturally occurring amino acid discovered in 1846; metabolism in the body leads to production of epinephrine and melanin, as well as thyroxine.

Urine Polysaccharide Test
>A urine test for mucopolysaccharides characteristic of Hurler's Syndrome.

Uvula
>The very back-most part of the soft palate. It has little function in the speech of English-speaking persons.

Validity
>As used in psychological testing, the extent to which an instrument measures the attribute or function which it purports to measure. The validity of an intelligence test, therefore, would be measured against some other measure or test of intelligence, the reliability and validity of which have already been established.

Ventriculogram
>Roentgenogram of brain after injection of air into the cerebral ventricles directly through the brain by needle.

Vineland Scale of Social Maturity (a psychological test)
>A graded series of accomplishments to measure social development of children from infancy to five years. The scale is scored from responses by an informant, usually the parent. Its reliability naturally depends upon the reliability of the informant. The score on this test is reported as S.A. (Social Age) and S.Q. (Social Quotient).

WBC
>Abbreviation for white blood count.

Wilson's Disease
>Progressive lenticular degeneration due to defect in copper metabolism.

Index